TREATIES AND OTHER INTERNATIONAL ACTS OF THE UNITED STATES OF AMERICA

TREATIES

AND OTHER

INTERNATIONAL ACTS OF THE UNITED STATES OF AMERICA

EDITED BY

HUNTER MILLER

VOLUME 2

DOCUMENTS 1–40 : 1776–1818

UNITED STATES
GOVERNMENT PRINTING OFFICE
WASHINGTON : 1931

For sale by the Superintendent of Documents, Washington. D. C. Price $4 (cloth)

PUBLICATIONS OF THE DEPARTMENT OF STATE

No. 175

PREFACE

The scheme of this work as a whole is fully described in Volume 1. It is sufficient to say here that the arrangement of the documents is chronological according to date of signature; each document has a serial number, 1, 2, and so on; but the numbers are merely for convenience and have no other significance. All international acts of the United States which have gone into force are, in general, included, whether now in force or not; but postal conventions and treaties with Indian tribes are not included. Extrinsic and related documents which are referred to in the documents proper are also printed, so far as possible. The headnote to each document gives the relevant dates; the notes which follow each document are textual and procedural only. Other notes dealing with the diplomatic and juridical history of the documents will appear subsequently and in separate volumes.

The print of the documents and of the quotations in the notes is literal and thus includes any peculiarities and even any errors of the original.

This is the first volume of document texts. There are no documents in Volume 1; that volume is limited to descriptive matter and to various tables and lists covering this and subsequent volumes up to a date not yet fixed. Accordingly Volume 1 will not appear in final form until all document volumes to which it refers have been published. As the document volumes are to be globally indexed, there is no separate index for this volume.

This volume contains the first forty documents of the treaty edition. The period covered begins with July 4, 1776, the textual date of the Declaration of Independence. As the earlier part of that period was prior to the Constitution, there are included a table of the Presidents of the Continental Congress and a note regarding the two Secretaries for Foreign Affairs who served from 1781 to 1789; there is also a tabulation of the dates pertaining to the adoption of the Articles of Confederation; and the courtesy of Dr. Edmund C. Burnett, of Washington, has permitted the use of an unpublished paper of his in order to give some account (page xv) of the Papers of the Continental Congress, to which frequent reference is made in the notes to the documents of that time.

Among the documents of this volume are most of the treaties with the Barbary States; the editorial treatment of them is described at page xx; acknowledgment is due in this regard to the learning of Professor C. Snouck Hurgronje and of Dr. J. H. Kramers, of Leiden.

H. M.

December 31, 1930.

CONTENTS OF VOLUME 2

LIST OF DOCUMENTS IN VOLUME 2

LIST OF DOCUMENTS IN VOLUME 2—*Continued*

PRESIDENTS OF THE CONTINENTAL CONGRESS

Name	State	Date elected
Peyton Randolph	Virginia	September 5, 1774.
Henry Middleton	South Carolina	October 22, 1774.
Peyton Randolph	Virginia	May 10, 1775.
John Hancock	Massachusetts	May 24, 1775.
Henry Laurens	South Carolina	November 1, 1777.
John Jay	New York	December 10, 1778.
Samuel Huntington	Connecticut	September 28, 1779.
Thomas McKean	Delaware [1]	July 10, 1781.
John Hanson	Maryland	November 5, 1781.
Elias Boudinot	New Jersey	November 4, 1782.
Thomas Mifflin	Pennsylvania	November 3, 1783.
Richard Henry Lee	Virginia	November 30, 1784.
John Hancock	Massachusetts	November 23, 1785.
Nathaniel Gorham	Massachusetts	June 6, 1786.
Arthur St. Clair	Pennsylvania	February 2, 1787.
Cyrus Griffin	Virginia	January 22, 1788.

[1] Thomas McKean was a representative from Delaware, although at the same time that he was President of Congress he was Chief Justice of Pennsylvania, the State in which he was born (Journals, XXI, 1054, 1060, 1069, 1090).

SECRETARIES FOR FOREIGN AFFAIRS, 1781–1789

Before the adoption of the Constitution, the control of the foreign relations of the United States was exercised by the Congress which sat at first under no written agreement and later under the Articles of Confederation. Subject to that control and prior to October 20, 1781, the management of foreign affairs was in the hands of committees of Congress. The committee first appointed, on November 29, 1775, "for the sole purpose of corresponding with our friends in Great Britain, Ireland, and other parts of the world," consisted of Benjamin Harrison, Benjamin Franklin, Thomas Johnson, John Dickinson, and John Jay (Journals, III, 392). The name of the committee was altered on April 17, 1777, to the Committee for Foreign Affairs (Journals, VII, 274); its membership was frequently changed; and Congress often acted on foreign affairs either without reference to any committee or after report of a special committee.

On January 10, 1781, Congress created the Department of Foreign Affairs and the office of Secretary for Foreign Affairs (Journals, XIX, 43).

On August 10, 1781, Robert R. Livingston was elected Secretary for Foreign Affairs (Journals, XXI, 851–52) and took the oath of office on October 20, 1781 (Wharton, Diplomatic Correspondence, IV, 795).

New regulations for the Department of Foreign Affairs were adopted by Congress on February 22, 1782 (Journals, XXII, 87–92); in these the Secretary was styled "Secretary to the United States of America, for the department of foreign affairs."

The resignation of Secretary Livingston was accepted by Congress June 4, 1783 (Journals, XXIV, 382).

Pending the appointment and qualification of a successor, the President of Congress acted as Secretary for Foreign Affairs *ad interim*.

John Jay was elected Secretary for Foreign Affairs on May 7, 1784 (Journals, XXVI, 355), but did not take office until the following December 21 (Pellew, John Jay, 230; Diplomatic Correspondence, 1783–1789, I, 105).

Jay held the office of Secretary for Foreign Affairs during the remaining period of the Continental Congress and continued to act in

a similar capacity, though without further appointment, under the Constitution. The Journal of the Senate refers to him as "Secretary of Foreign Affairs" on July 21, 1789. The Department of Foreign Affairs was created by the act of July 27, 1789 (1 Statutes at Large, 28–29) and became the Department of State on September 15, 1789 (*ibid.*, 68). Although the nomination of Jay as Chief Justice was confirmed by the Senate on September 26, 1789 (Executive Journal, I, 29), he continued to act as Secretary of State until Thomas Jefferson (commissioned Secretary of State on September 26, 1789) took office on March 22, 1790.

THE ARTICLES OF CONFEDERATION

On November 15, 1777, Congress adopted the Articles of Confederation (Journals, IX, 907) and on November 17 ordered copies transmitted to the several States "for the consideration of the respective legislatures" (*ibid.*, 932, 935).

The legislatures of the States took favorable action on the dates shown in the table below; the references are to the texts of the respective acts or resolves:

State	Date	Reference
Virginia	December 15, 1777	Journals, XI, 669.
South Carolina	February 4, 1778	*Ibid.*, 670.
New York	February 6, 1778	*Ibid.*, 665–67.
Connecticut	February 12, 1778	*Ibid.*, 665.
Rhode Island	February 18, 1778	*Ibid.*, 663–65.
Georgia	February 26, 1778	*Ibid.*, 671.
New Hampshire	March 4, 1778	*Ibid.*, 662.
Pennsylvania	March 5, 1778	*Ibid.*, 668.
Massachusetts	March 10, 1778	*Ibid.*, 663.
North Carolina	April 25, 1778	*Ibid.*, 669.
New Jersey	November 20, 1778	*Ibid.*, XII, 1162–63.
Delaware	February 1, 1779	*Ibid.*, XIII, 187.
Maryland	February 2, 1781	*Ibid.*, XIX, 138–40.

A formal ratification of the Articles of Confederation for signature on behalf of the several States was approved by Congress on June 26, 1778 (Journals, XI, 657). That ratification was signed at Philadelphia July 9, 1778, on behalf of eight States (*ibid.*, 677); for North Carolina on July 21, for Georgia on July 24, and for New Jersey on November 26, 1778; for Delaware on February 22, 1779; and finally for Maryland on March 1, 1781 (see *ibid.*, XIX, 208–23).

THE PAPERS OF THE CONTINENTAL CONGRESS[1]

In the present volume the Papers of the Continental Congress are frequently cited in the notes to the earlier documents (*e. g.*, 81 C. C. Papers, I, folio 445).

All of the Continental Congress Papers, except a few volumes in the archives of the Department of State, are now in the Division of Manuscripts of the Library of Congress. They are numbered serially from 1 to 196, each number comprising one or several volumes. (The original Journal, for instance, which is No. 1 of the series, is in thirty-nine volumes; No. 78 is in twenty-four volumes.)

A calendar of the series from No. 1 to No. 194 was issued by the Department of State in 1893 as Bulletin of the Bureau of Rolls and Library, No. 1. This book may be helpfully consulted, although it should be borne in mind that the brief descriptions attached to the respective numbers do not by any means characterize the whole of the contents of the volume or group of volumes.

Not included in that calendar are No. 195 (Oaths of Allegiance) and No. 196 (Letters of Marque); and there is also an unnumbered volume, the Marine Committee Letter Book, 1776–1780. There has also been at least one addition to the list, the correspondence of John Hancock, which is in six volumes and is now known as No. 12A.

A bound volume of the Papers of the Continental Congress as it stands on the shelf is not necessarily the same as a volume which constitutes an element in the series. The bound volume may be identical with a volume of the series, but oftener than otherwise it is not. A bound volume may contain only part of a series volume, or it may contain parts of two or more series volumes. In other words, the papers of a given series were merely bound up in convenient sizes, in a serial order, to be sure, but without regard to the serial designation of its parts. Furthermore, record books such as journals and letter books have the pages numbered, and the individual documents are numbered by folios for each volume of the series. Accordingly, references are customarily made to number, volume, and folio or page.

[1] This note is in large part adapted from an unpublished paper by Dr. Edmund C. Burnett which is on file in the Division of Manuscripts of the Library of Congress.

It needs also to be said that the arrangement of the papers as they have come down to us is to a considerable extent haphazard and without logic. Groups of closely related papers are found widely separated in the numbered series; even parts of essentially the same body of documents are, in a number of instances, so separated; while, on the other hand, groups of wholly unrelated papers are frequently found constituting a volume of the series, the documents being numbered consecutively and thus bound together. It should never be assumed that all papers of a given sort are to be found in the group so designated; nor, on the other hand, can it be taken for granted that the label on a volume always gives a clue to its principal contents.

That number of the Continental Congress Papers which is most frequently cited in the present volume is No. 135, which is in two volumes; they are among the few volumes of the Papers of the Continental Congress which remain in the archives of the Department of State. No. 135 is entitled "Foreign Treaties and Contracts." It is a record book of the treaties of the United States. Volume I contains the texts of treaties of the United States made prior to the Consular Convention with France of 1788. In most cases the document which was transcribed was the United States instrument of ratification; accordingly, the original language of each treaty is reproduced (except in the case of the treaty with Morocco of 1786), and where necessary a translation is added. The record could not have been commenced until 1783, as the first document recorded is the contract with France of 1782, which was ratified in 1783. The arrangement of the record is thus not wholly chronological, as treaties of earlier date come later in the same volume. Various documents which are not treaties with foreign countries are included; Volume I of No. 135 contains the text of the Tobacco Contract of 1781 with the Farmers General of France, three loan contracts with Dutch bankers, two Indian treaties of 1784 and 1785, and the decree of the French Council of State of December 29, 1787, with an accompanying letter. Volume II contains only one document, namely, a loan agreement of March 13, 1788, with merchants of Amsterdam.

No. 135 of the Papers of the Continental Congress is of high value as authority supplemental to the original and other documents of the time; but for the period prior to 1782 it cannot be regarded as a strictly contemporaneous record; the documents of earlier years which it contains were certainly transcribed from other copies; and most of the documents contained in No. 135, though not all, appear, at least in English, in the Journals.

THE JOURNALS

The edition of the Journals of the Continental Congress which is usually cited in this volume when possible, is the Library of Congress edition, which has been in process of publication since 1904 and now includes the years 1774–1784, with volumes for 1785 and 1786 in edited manuscript. That edition contains not only the complete text of the Journals from all the original sources, but also the texts of the committee reports with their erasures and amendments, constituting a work of enormous value for the period.

The student of the congressional proceedings will, however, find it often desirable to go behind the Journals to other documents. While the same individual, Charles Thomson, was Secretary of the Continental Congress throughout the whole period of its existence (1774–1789), the Journals of Congress were not continuously written according to one logical and uniform system. At times the record is much briefer than at others; in particular, the use of what Thomson called despatch books and committee books, from 1779 on, brought about the omission from the Journal record proper of proceedings similar to those which at times were included therein.

The very earliest prints of the Journals appeared during the life of Congress at varying intervals, but always with many omissions of matters which it was thought either undesirable or unnecessary to publish. The Secret Journals, Foreign Affairs, were not published at all until 1820–1821. The edition of the Journals most widely used prior to the Library of Congress edition is that of 1823; that reprint, however, was from the earlier printed documents and not from the original records and accordingly is incomplete.

The Journals as they are at the present time among the Papers of the Continental Congress in the Manuscript Division of the Library of Congress, will now be generally characterized.[1]

First, there is the original or "Rough" Journal, No. 1 of the Continental Congress Papers, in thirty-nine volumes, covering the whole period of the Congress. It should be noted, however, that Volume 15 of the series (March 19 to May 2, 1778) has been missing for a great many years.

With the same series is a small volume (now 6a of No. 1) which contains records of proceedings upon foreign affairs from September

[1] See Dr. Worthington C. Ford's prefatory note in the Library of Congress edition of the Journals, II, 5–8, and also a paper by Dr. Herbert Friedenwald in the Annual Report of the American Historical Association for the Year 1896, I, 85–135.

17, 1776, to January 1, 1779, together with a copy and continuation of the signatures to the Agreement of Secrecy of November 9, 1775. This volume had remained unknown until it was brought to light at the time of the transfer of papers from the Department of State to the Library of Congress in 1922. A description of the volume by Dr. John C. Fitzpatrick is in The American Historical Review, XXVII, 489–91 (April, 1922).

Secondly, there is what is sometimes called the "Corrected" Journal, No. 2, which is in the main a transcript of the original, though with occasional differences. It covers, however, only the period from September 5, 1775, to January 20, 1779, and occupies ten volumes.

No. 3 is the Secret Domestic Journal, May 10, 1775, to October 26, 1787, in one volume.

No. 4 is the Secret Journal, Foreign and Domestic, October 18, 1780, to March 29, 1786, in one volume. The reason for the existence of this volume is not altogether clear, for it contains nothing not to be found in No. 3 or No. 5.

No. 5 is the Secret Journal of Foreign Affairs, November 29, 1775, to September 16, 1788, in three volumes. These volumes contain many entries not to be found elsewhere, and it was from them that the Secret Journals, Foreign Affairs, were printed in 1820–1821.

No. 6, usually called the "Imperfect" Secret Journal, in three volumes, contains extracts of proceedings from September 17, 1776, to September 16, 1788, but there is nothing in it not to be found elsewhere.

No. 7, in one volume, is called the "More Secret Journal," and principally records proceedings bearing upon the peace settlement, from June 6, 1781, to August 8, 1782.

No. 8, in one volume, is called "Secret Journal A" and contains various entries from 1776 to 1783 which were subsequently entered in the public Journal.

No. 9, which is called "History of the Confederation," may in a sense be regarded as a part of the Journals, although it is not so called. It merely segregates in one volume matters pertaining to the formation of the Confederation, from July 21, 1775, the date of Franklin's proposed articles, to March 1, 1781, the date when the Confederation was finally ratified. There may be coupled with that volume No. 47, also in one volume, which contains much of the same sorts of materials (including Franklin's and Dickinson's drafts of articles of confederation); but No. 47 contains also some of the pro-

ceedings upon plans of treaties from 1775 to 1784. For instance, in No. 47 is found the original of the unratified Consular Convention between France and the United States which was signed by Vergennes and Franklin July 29, 1784, and also a printed text of that convention.

No. 10 is a volume of the Journal of the Committee of the States, June 4 to August 19, 1784. This Committee of the States, to sit during the adjournment of Congress, was provided for in the Articles of Confederation but was never called into existence until June, 1784. It broke up in a short time and was never tried again.

The essential record of the proceedings of Congress is to be found, therefore, in No. 1 (with some modifications from No. 2), in No. 3, and in No. 5, with No. 10 covering a sort of interregnum.

THE BARBARY TREATIES

In the half century from 1786 to 1836 the United States made nine treaties with the Barbary States, as they were then called: Morocco, Algiers, Tunis, and Tripoli. Seven of those treaties appear in the present volume (Documents 14, 17, 20, 21, 31, 34, and 37).

In three of the Barbary treaties Arabic is the language of the original: Morocco, 1786 and 1836, and Tripoli, 1796–1797. In the treaty with Tripoli of 1805 both English and Arabic seem to have been used. Turkish is the language of two treaties: Algiers, 1795, and Tunis, 1797–1799. While it is not entirely certain, the remaining three treaties appear to have been in English only: Algiers, 1815 and 1816, and Tunis, 1824; however, in the original treaty with Algiers of 1816 there is written, on the respective pages opposite the English, a Turkish summary of the English text. The texts in Arabic or Turkish are, so far as they are available, reproduced.

Reproduction of such texts presents a question as to the order or arrangement of the pages or articles. Pursuant to advice from eminent orientalists, in this edition, which is essentially one of American volumes, the ordinary order of pagination from left to right is maintained throughout, even in the case of pages or articles of Arabic or of Turkish text; and accordingly such pages or articles have, when necessary, been rearranged and are reproduced in the order usual and customary here.

An English translation is written in the originals of the treaties with Algiers of 1795 and with Tripoli of 1796–1797; similarly, a French translation is written in the original of the treaty with Tunis of 1797–1799. The English translation of the treaty with Morocco of 1786 is a separate document (91 C. C. Papers, I, folio 213) signed and sealed by Jefferson and Adams. A copy of the treaty with Morocco of 1836 has an English translation on pages opposite the Arabic; that copy bears the signature of James R. Leib, the American Commissioner. All of the above-mentioned translations are printed literally, that is, with no revision of capitalization, punctuation, or spelling. (The treatment of translations in the ordinary case is to make the style conform to modern usage.)

The original treaties with Tripoli of 1805, Algiers of 1815, and Tunis of 1824, are missing; copies of the two latter in English and a copy of the first in English and Arabic and bearing the signature of Tobias Lear, are in the respective files. It is of record that the Dey of Algiers possessed a Turkish translation of the treaty with Algiers of 1815, but there is no such translation in the Department of State archives.

The early English translations of the Barbary treaties in all cases but one, that made from the French translation of the treaty with Tunis of 1797–1799, are printed literally; in the notes the transliteration of the months of the Mohammedan calendar conforms to that in Webster's Dictionary.

Something should also be said as to dates stated in terms of the Mohammedan calendar, or, in other words, in the years of the Hegira. Whenever the equivalent of a date given by that calendar is found, in a document of the period, stated in the new style of the Christian era, that equivalent is accepted as the then current calendar usage, even though a calculation by the ordinary tables would not, to the day, agree; and preference for then current practice over calculation is extended even to cases where there is a nearly contemporaneous record of an equivalent date written by the two calendars; usage of the past is preferred to mathematics of the present; though it should be added that no instance of a difference greater than one or two days has been noticed.

The years of the Mohammedan calendar are purely lunar, consisting of twelve lunar months, each beginning with the approximate new moon. The length of the year is 354 days except in intercalary years, when it is 355.

The divergences between the astronomical Mohammedan calendar and the usage locally current are thus to be explained. Nearly all Mohammedan countries, since the spread of Islam, have had their calendars calculated astronomically beforehand and have used them for all secular purposes. There is also a regular calendar for religious purposes; their Sacred Law obliges all Mohammedans to fix the dates of their religious feasts (in the first place, the beginning and the end of the ninth month, Ramadan, and the beginning of the twelfth month, Zu'lhijjah) not by means of calculation, but by the observation of the appearance of the new moon, taking, however, as their point of departure that a month can have only twenty-nine or thirty days. In order to get the required dates for the religious feasts, not only the beginning of the months in which those feasts occur, but

the beginning of all the months, is fixed by the observation of the appearance of the new moon, as a deviation from that method in any month might have the consequence of error (from the point of view of the religious law) in the fixation of the dates of the feasts; thus, if the new moon is not visible on the eve of the thirtieth day of a certain month, that month is counted full and the next one commences after the thirtieth day of its predecessor. So, by the religious calendar, the beginning and the end of any month may always differ by one or two days in different countries, and even in two places a few miles distant from each other; and while the Mohammedan law authorities do not prohibit the dating of letters, contracts, events, etc., in accordance with the astronomical calendar, still the writers of letters, documents, and chronicles often deviate in their datings from the astronomical calendar in the same degree as does the actual feast-calendar of their dwelling place.[1]

An elaborate discussion of the calendar, with valuable tables, is in Osmanische Zeitrechnungen, by Joachim Mayr, which is printed as a supplement to Die Geschichtsschreiber der Osmanen und ihre Werke, by Franz Babinger. One statement there made as to the calendar day is to be noted (page 418, translation):

> As divisions of the day the Turks use twenty-four hours of equal length, twelve of the day and twelve of the night, but begin the enumeration with sunset, so that there is a notable shifting of the hours during the course of the year.

The era of the Hegira, or the Mohammedan era, is dated from July 19, A. D. 622, according to the Gregorian calendar.

The names of the Mohammedan months, according to Webster's Dictionary, and the number of days in each, are as follows: Muharram, 30; Safar, 29; Rabia I, 30; Rabia II, 29; Jumada I, 30; Jumada II, 29; Rajab, 30; Shaban, 29; Ramadan, 30; Shawwal, 29; Zu'lkadah, 30; Zu'lhijjah, 29 (30 in intercalary years).

---

[1] The statements in this paragraph are adapted from letters to the editor from Dr. C. Snouck Hurgronje, of Leiden.

WRITINGS CITED IN VOLUME 2

(Citations abbreviated in the text are included, with cross references where necessary.)

Adams, Charles Francis. The Works of John Adams. Boston, Little, Brown & Co., 1850–1856. 10 vols.

Allen, Gardner W. Our Navy and the Barbary Corsairs. Boston, Houghton, Mifflin & Co., 1905. xiv+354 pp.

American Historical Review, The. Vol. XXVII, October, 1921–July, 1922. New York, The Macmillan Co.

American State Papers. Foreign Relations. Washington, Gales & Seaton, 1832–1859. 6 vols.

——— Indian Affairs. Washington, Gales & Seaton, 1832–1834. 2 vols.

A New English Dictionary on Historical Principles; Founded Mainly on the Materials Collected by the Philological Society. Edited by James A. H. Murray, etc. Oxford, Clarendon Press, 1888–1928. 10 vols. in 13.

Annual Report of the American Historical Association for the Year 1896. Washington, Government Printing Office, 1897–.

Aurora General Advertiser, Philadelphia, December 2, 1800.

Babinger, Franz. Die Geschichtsschreiber der Osmanen und ihre Werke, mit einen Anhang: Osmanische Zeitrechnungen von Joachim Mayr. Leipzig, Otto Harrassowitz, 1927. viii+477 pp.

Bancroft's Transcripts. *See* Manuscript, New York Public Library.

Bemis, Samuel Flagg. Pinckney's Treaty. Baltimore, The Johns Hopkins Press, 1926. xii+421 pp.

Boston Gazette, March 23, 1795.

British and Foreign State Papers, 1812–. London, 1825 [?]–.

Bulletin of the Bureau of Rolls and Library of the Department of State, No. 1. Catalogue of the Papers of the Continental Congress. Washington, Department of State, 1893. 104+46 pp.

Bulletin of the Bureau of Rolls and Library of the Department of State, No. 8, pt. 2. Calendar of the Correspondence of Thomas Jefferson; Letters to Jefferson. Washington, Department of State, 1895. ii+593 pp.

Burnett, Edmund Cody. Letters of Members of the Continental Congress. Washington, The Carnegie Institution of Washington, 1921–1928. 4 vols.

Callahan, James Morton. *See* Johns Hopkins University Studies.

Cathcart, James Leander. The Captives. Compiled by J. B. Cathcart Newkirk. La Porte, Ind.. Herald Print, 1895 [?]. xvi+312 pp.

C. C. Papers. (Continental Congress Papers.) *See* Manuscript, Library of Congress.

Chalmers, George. A Collection of Treaties between Great Britain and Other Powers. London, John Stockdale, 1790. 2 vols.

Claypoole's American Daily Advertiser, Philadelphia, March 10, 1796; June 10, 1796; August 3, 1798.

Coleccion de los tratados de paz, alianza, comercio &c., ajustados por la corona de España con las potencias extrangeras. "De orden del Rey." Madrid, La Imprenta Real, 1796–1801. 3 vols.

Compilation of Reports of the Committee on Foreign Relations, United States Senate, 1789–1901. Washington, Government Printing Office, 1901. 8 vols.

Conway, Moncure Daniel. Omitted Chapters of History Disclosed in the Life and Papers of Edmund Randolph. New York and London, G. P. Putnam's Sons, 1888. vi+401 [406] pp.

Correspondence and Public Papers of John Jay, 1794–1826, The. Edited by Henry P. Johnston. New York and London, G. P. Putnam's Sons, 1890–1893. 4 vols.

Crandall, Samuel Benjamin. Treaties, Their Making and Enforcement. 2d ed. Washington, John Byrne & Co., 1916. xxxii+663 pp.

Daily Advertiser, New York, June 6, 1786; July 21, 1787; April 12, 1790.

Daily National Intelligencer, Washington, February 15 and 16, 1815; April 30, 1818; December 24, 1818; February 14, 1822.

Davis, J. C. Bancroft. Treaties and Conventions Concluded between the United States of America and Other Powers since July 4, 1776. Rev. ed. Washington, Government Printing Office, 1873. 1167 pp.

De Onis, Luis. Memoria sobre las negociaciones entre España y los Estados-Unidos de America, que dieron motivo al tratado de 1819. Madrid, D. M. de Burgos, 1820. vi+108+70 pp.

——— Memoir upon the Negotiations between Spain and the United States of America Which Led to the Treaty of 1819. Translated by Tobias Watkins. Washington, E. de Krafft, 1821. 152 pp.

Diplomatic Correspondence of the United States of America from 1783 to 1789, The. Washington, Blair & Rives, 1837. 3 vols.

Documentos históricos de la Florida y la Luisiana, siglos XVI al XVIII. Edited by Manuel Serrano y Sanz. Madrid, Victoriano Suárez, 1912. viii+467 pp.

Doniol, Henri. Histoire de la participation de la France à l'établissement des États-Unis d'Amérique. Edited by Alphonse Picard. Paris, Imprimerie Nationale, 1886–1892. 5 vols.

D. S. (Archives of the Department of State.) *See* Manuscript, Department of State, for a list of the volumes cited.

D. S., Manuscript. Unbound manuscript in the archives of the Department of State.

Ellicott, Andrew. Astronomical and Thermometrical Observations Made in the Years 1796, 1797, 1798, 1799, and 1800. Philadelphia, Thomas Dobson, 1801. 151 pp.

——— The Journal of Andrew Ellicott for Determining the Boundary between the United States and the Possessions of His Catholic Majesty in America. Philadelphia, Thomas Dobson, 1803. vii+299+151 pp.

Evening Mail, London, December 3–5 and 15–17, 1794; April 20–22, 1795.

Executive Journal. *See* Journal of the Executive Proceedings of the Senate of the United States of America.

Federal Gazette and Baltimore Daily Advertiser, Baltimore, October 22, 1803; November 4, 1803.

Godoy, Don Manuel. Memorias de Don Manuel Godoy, Príncipe de la Paz, ó sea cuenta dada de su vida política. Madrid, I. Sancha and Alegría y Charlain, 1836–1842. 6 vols.

——— Memoirs of Don Manuel de Godoy, Prince of the Peace. London, Richard Bentley, 1836. 2 vols.

Haswell, John H. Treaties and Conventions Concluded between the United States of America and Other Powers since July 4, 1776. Washington, Government Printing Office, 1889. xiii+1434 pp.

Hobson-Jobson. *See* Yule.

Johns Hopkins University Studies in Historical and Political Science. Vol. XVI, Nos. 1–4. "The Neutrality of the American Lakes and Anglo-American Relations," by James Morton Callahan. Baltimore, The Johns Hopkins Press, January–April, 1898.

Journal of the Executive Proceedings of the Senate of the United States of America. Washington, Duff Green, 1828. 3 vols.

Journals. *See* Journals of the Continental Congress, 1774–1789.

Journals of the American Congress from 1774 to 1788. Washington, Way & Gideon, 1823. 4 vols.

Journals of the Continental Congress, 1774–1789. Edited by Worthington Chauncey Ford and Gaillard Hunt. Washington, Government Printing Office, 1904–.

Kappler, Charles J. Indian Affairs; Laws and Treaties. Vol. II. (Treaties.) 2d ed. Washington, Government Printing Office, 1904.

Laws of the United States of America. Philadelphia, John Bioren & W. John Duane; Washington, R. C. Weightman, etc., 1815–1845. 10 vols. in 11.

Laws of the United States of America, The. Philadelphia and Washington, Richard Folwell, etc., 1796–1815. 12 vols.

Lossing, Benson J. The Pictorial Field-Book of the War of 1812; or, Illustrations, by Pen and Pencil, of the History, Biography, Scenery, Relics, and Traditions of the Last War for American Independence. New York, Harper & Bros., 1869. 1084 pp.

Malloy, William M. Treaties, Conventions, International Acts, Protocols, and Agreements between the United States of America and Other Powers, 1776–1909. Washington, Government Printing Office, 1910. 2 vols.

Manuscript, Department of State. Archives, Tunis, 1793–1801. Vol. 1. (A volume from the consular archives at Tunis.)

——— Consular Despatches, Algiers. Vols. 1, 2, 3, 7, 8, 9.

——— Consular Despatches, Tangier. Vol. 5.

——— Consular Despatches, Tripoli. Vols. 2, 3.

——— Consular Despatches, Tunis. Vols. 1, 5.

——— 121 Continental Congress Papers, Foreign Letters.

——— 122 Continental Congress Papers, Resolve Book.

——— 130 Continental Congress Papers, Passports.

——— 135 Continental Congress Papers, Foreign Treaties and Contracts, I, II.

——— Credences. Vol. 1.

——— Despatches, France. Vols. 1, 8, 99.

——— Despatches, Great Britain. Vols. 1, 2, 3, 4, 7, 26.

——— Despatches, Netherlands. Vols. 1, 4.

——— Despatches, Spain. Vols. 3, 4, 6.

——— Despatches, Sweden and Norway. Vol. 2.

——— Domestic Letters. Vols. 5, 9, 14.

——— Ghent, etc. American Commissioners, 1813–1816.

——— Instructions, France. Vol. 21.

——— Instructions to Consuls. Vol. 1.

——— Instructions, United States Ministers. Vols. 2, 3, 4, 5, 6, 7, 8.

——— Journal [of the Commissioners under Article 5 of the Jay Treaty].

——— Manuscript. Unbound manuscript in the archives of the Department of State.

——— Miscellaneous Letters, January–April, 1796; August–December, 1796; October–December, 1814.

——— Negotiations Mediterranean [1815–1817].

——— Notes from the British Legation. Vols. 1, 8, 9.

——— Notes from the Spanish Legation. Vol. 1A

——— Notes to Foreign Legations. Vol. 2.

Manuscript, Library of Congress. 1 Continental Congress Papers, XVI.

——— 47 Continental Congress Papers.

——— 81 Continental Congress Papers, I.

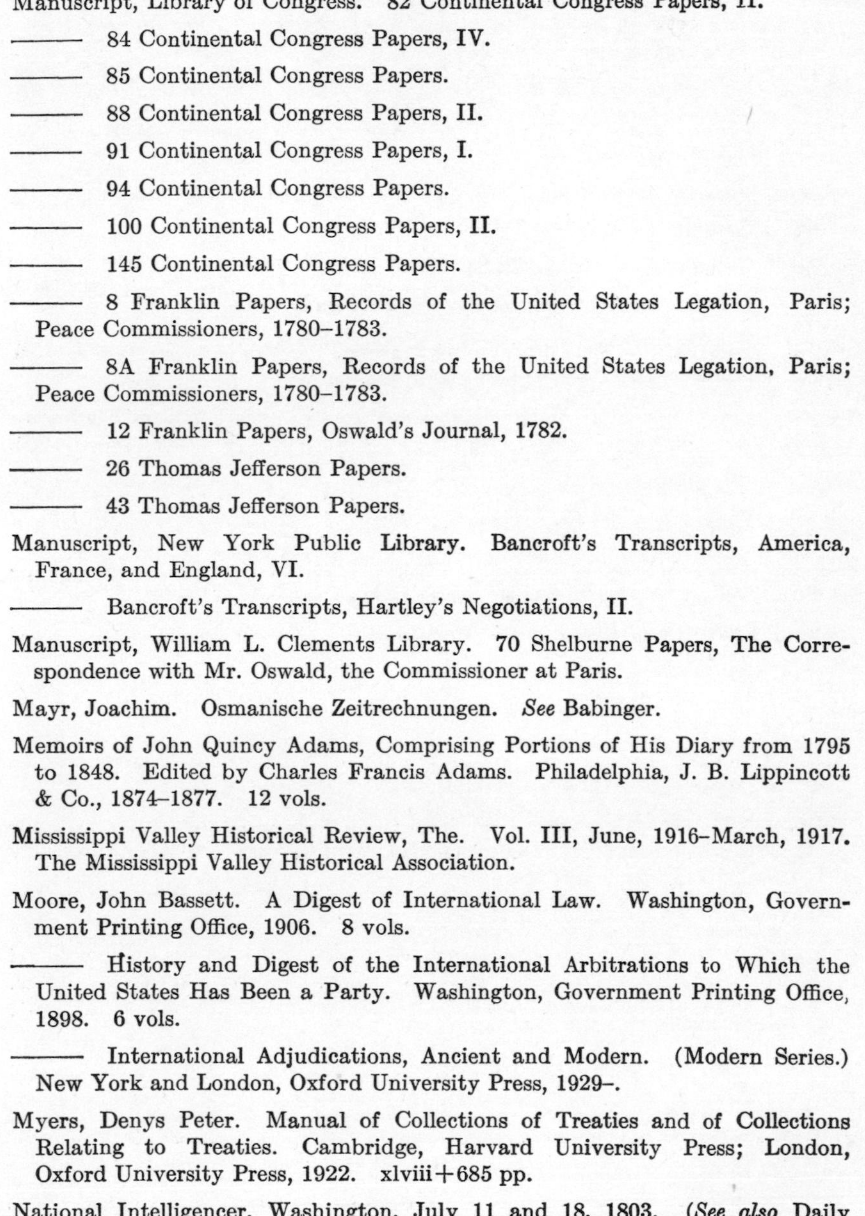

Manuscript, Library of Congress. 82 Continental Congress Papers, II.

——— 84 Continental Congress Papers, IV.

——— 85 Continental Congress Papers.

——— 88 Continental Congress Papers, II.

——— 91 Continental Congress Papers, I.

——— 94 Continental Congress Papers.

——— 100 Continental Congress Papers, II.

——— 145 Continental Congress Papers.

——— 8 Franklin Papers, Records of the United States Legation, Paris; Peace Commissioners, 1780–1783.

——— 8A Franklin Papers, Records of the United States Legation, Paris; Peace Commissioners, 1780–1783.

——— 12 Franklin Papers, Oswald's Journal, 1782.

——— 26 Thomas Jefferson Papers.

——— 43 Thomas Jefferson Papers.

Manuscript, New York Public Library. Bancroft's Transcripts, America, France, and England, VI.

——— Bancroft's Transcripts, Hartley's Negotiations, II.

Manuscript, William L. Clements Library. 70 Shelburne Papers, The Correspondence with Mr. Oswald, the Commissioner at Paris.

Mayr, Joachim. Osmanische Zeitrechnungen. *See* Babinger.

Memoirs of John Quincy Adams, Comprising Portions of His Diary from 1795 to 1848. Edited by Charles Francis Adams. Philadelphia, J. B. Lippincott & Co., 1874–1877. 12 vols.

Mississippi Valley Historical Review, The. Vol. III, June, 1916–March, 1917. The Mississippi Valley Historical Association.

Moore, John Bassett. A Digest of International Law. Washington, Government Printing Office, 1906. 8 vols.

——— History and Digest of the International Arbitrations to Which the United States Has Been a Party. Washington, Government Printing Office, 1898. 6 vols.

——— International Adjudications, Ancient and Modern. (Modern Series.) New York and London, Oxford University Press, 1929–.

Myers, Denys Peter. Manual of Collections of Treaties and of Collections Relating to Treaties. Cambridge, Harvard University Press; London, Oxford University Press, 1922. xlviii+685 pp.

National Intelligencer, Washington, July 11 and 18, 1803. (*See also* Daily National Intelligencer.)

Niles' Weekly Register. Vol. IV, March–September, 1813; Vol. VII, September, 1814–March, 1815; Vol. IX, September, 1815–March, 1816; Vol. XV, September, 1818–March, 1819. Baltimore, Franklin Press.

NYPL. *See* Manuscript, New York Public Library.

Parliamentary History of England from the Earliest Period to the Year 1803, The. London, Longman, Hurst, Rees, Orme & Brown, etc., 1806–1820. 36 vols.

Pellew, George. John Jay. Boston and New York, Houghton, Mifflin & Co., 1890. viii+374 pp.

Prentiss, Charles. The Life of the Late Gen. William Eaton. Brookfield, E. Merriam & Co., 1813. 448 pp.

Richardson, James D. A Compilation of the Messages and Papers of the Presidents, 1789–1897. Washington, Government Printing Office, 1896–1899. 10 vols.

Satow, Ernest Mason. A Guide to Diplomatic Practice. 2d ed. New York and Toronto, Longmans, Green & Co., 1922. 2 vols.

Scott, James Brown. Sovereign States and Suits before Arbitral Tribunals and Courts of Justice. New York, The New York University Press, 1925. x+360 pp.

Secret Journals of the Acts and Proceedings of Congress. Boston, Thomas B. Wait, 1820–1821. 4 vols.

Serrano y Sanz, Manuel. España y los Indios Cherokis y Chactas en la segunda mitad del siglo XVIII. Seville, "Guia Oficial," 1916. 93 pp.

[Session Laws.] Acts Passed at the . . . Session of the . . . Congress of the United States. 1789–.

Shaler, William. Sketches of Algiers. Boston, Cummings, Hilliard & Co., 1826. viii+310 pp.

Statutes at Large of the United States of America, The. Boston, Little, Brown & Co.; Washington, Government Printing Office, 1846–.

Tratados, convenios, y declaraciones de paz y de comercio desde el año de 1700 hasta el dia. Edited by Don Alejandro del Cantillo. Madrid, Alegria y Charlain, 1843. xli+908 pp.

Treaty Series. Washington, Government Printing Office, 1908–.

Tripoli. First War with the United States. Inner History. Letter Book of James Leander Cathcart, First Consul to Tripoli, and Last Letters from Tunis. Compiled by J. B. Cathcart Newkirk. La Porte, Ind., Herald Print, 1901. viii+355 pp.

United States Reports: Cases Adjudged in the Supreme Court. Vol. 19 (*cited* 6 Wheaton).

Von Martens, Georg Friedrich. Recueil des principaux traités. 1st ed. Gottingue, Jean Chretien Dieterich, 1791–1801. 7 vols.

——— Recueil de traités. 2d ed. Gottingue, Dieterich, 1817–1835. 8 vols.

——— Supplément au recueil des principaux traités. Gottingue, Henri Dieterich, 1802–1808. 4 vols.

Webster's New International Dictionary of the English Language. Edited by W. T. Harris and F. Sturges Allen. Springfield, Mass., G. & C. Merriam Co., 1923. lcii+2620 [2624] pp.

Wharton, Francis. The Revolutionary Diplomatic Correspondence of the United States. Washington, Government Printing Office, 1889. 6 vols.

Wheaton, Henry. Reports of Cases Argued and Adjudged in the Supreme Court of the United States. New York, R. Donaldson, 1816[?]–1827. 12 vols. *See* United States Reports.

Whitaker, Arthur Preston. The Spanish-American Frontier: 1783–1795. Boston and New York, Houghton Mifflin Co., 1927. xiv+255 pp.

Wilson, James Grant. John Pintard, Founder of the New York Historical Society. New York, printed for the New York Historical Society, 1902.

Works of Thomas Jefferson, The. Federal ed. Edited by Paul Leicester Ford. New York, G. P. Putnam's Sons, 1905. 12 vols.

Yule, Henry, and A. C. Burnell. Hobson-Jobson—A Glossary of Colloquial Anglo-Indian Words and Phrases, and of Kindred Terms, Etymological, Historical, Geographical, and Discursive. Edited by William Crooke. London, John Murray, 1903.

DOCUMENTS 1–40 : 1776–1818

Treaty Series, No. 83
8 Statutes at Large, 12–31

1

FRANCE : FEBRUARY 6, 1778

Treaty of Amity and Commerce, signed at Paris February 6, 1778. Original in English and French; but "originally composed and concluded in the French Language" (see the attestation clause). Ratified by the United States May 4, 1778. Ratified by France July 16, 1778. Ratifications exchanged at Paris (or Versailles) July 17, 1778. Not proclaimed; but on May 6, 1778, Congress (see Journals, XI, 468–69) approved a "draught for publication" containing Articles 6, 7, 14–17, 20, 21, 25–27, and 29 and the form of the passports, mentioning also the Treaty of Alliance with France of the same date. That publication appeared generally in American newspapers during May, 1778. On November 4, 1778, Congress ordered printed 300 copies of this treaty and of the Treaty of Alliance (see Journals, XII, 1101).

Treaty of Amity and Commerce.

The most Christian King, and the thirteen United States of North America, to wit, New-Hampshire, Massachusetts Bay, Rhodeisland, Connecticut, New York, New-Jersey, Pennsylvania, Delaware, Maryland, Virginia, North-Carolina, South Carolina, & Georgia, willing to fix in an equitable and permanent manner the Rules which ought to be followed relative to the Correspondence & Commerce which the two Parties desire to establish between their respective Countries, States, and Subjects, his most Christian Majesty and the said United States have judged that the said End could not be better obtained than by taking

Traité d'Amitié et de Commerce

Le Roi Très chretien et les treize Etats-unis de l'Amérique septentrionale, savoir, Newhampshire la Baye de Massachusset, Rhode-Island, Connecticut, New York, New Jersey, Pensylvanie, Les Comtés de Newcastle de Kent et de Sussex sur la Delaware, Maryland, Virginie, Caroline septentrionale, Caroline Méridionale et Georgie voulant établir d'une maniere équitable et permanente les règles qui devront être suivies relativement à la Correspondance et au Commerce que les deux parties désirent d'établir entre leurs Païs, Etats et Sujets respectifs, Sa Majesté Très chretienne et les dits Etats unis ont jugé ne pouvoir mieux atteindre à ce but

for the Basis of their Agreement the most perfect Equality and Reciprocity, and by carefully avoiding all those burthensome Preferences, which are usually Sources of Debate, Embarrasment and Discontent; by leaving also each Party at Liberty to make, respecting Commerce and Navigation, those interior Regulations which it shall find most convenient to itself; and by founding the Advantage of Commerce solely upon reciprocal Utility, and the just Rules of free Intercourse; reserving withal to each Party the Liberty of admitting at its pleasure other Nations to a Participation of the same Advantages. It is in the Spirit of this Intention, and to fulfil these Views, that his said Majesty having named and appointed for his Plenipotentiary Conrad Alexander Gerard, Royal *Sindic* of the City of Strasbourg, Secretary of his Majesty's Council of State, and the United States on their Part, having fully impower'd Benjamin Franklin Deputy from the State of Pennsylvania to the general Congress, and President of the Convention of said State, Silas Deane late Deputy from the State of Connecticut to the said Congress, and Arthur Lee Councellor at Law; The said respective Plenipotentiaries after exchanging their Powers, and after mature Deliberation, have concluded and agreed upon the following Articles.

qu'en prenant pour base de leur arrangement l'égalité et la réciprocité la plus parfaite, et en observant d'éviter toutes les préférences onéreuses, source de discussions, d'embarras et de mecontentemens, de laisser à chaque partie la liberté de faire relativement au Commerce et à la Navigation les réglemens intérieurs qui seront à sa convenance, de ne fonder les avantages du Commerce que sur son utilité reciproque et sur les loix d'une juste concurrence, et de conserver ainsi de part et d'autre la liberté de faire participer, chacun selon son gré, les autres Nations aux mêmes avantages. C'est dans cet esprit et pour remplir ces vues que Sa d^e Majesté ayant nommé et constitué pour son Plénipotentiaire le S. Conrad-Alexandre Gerard, Sindic Roïal de la Ville de Strasbourg, Secretaire du Conseil d'Etat de Sa Majesté, et les Etats unis aïant, de leur coté, munis de leurs pleinspouvoirs les Srs Benjamin Franklin Député au Congrès général de la part de l'Etat de Pensylvanie et Président de la Convention dud^e Etat, Silas Deane ci-devant Député de l'Etat de Connecticut et Arthur Lée *Conseiller ès loix.* Les d^s Plénipotentiaires respectifs après l'échange de leurs pouvoirs et après mure déliberation ont conclu et arrêté les points et articles suivans.

ARTICLE. 1.st.

There shall be a firm, inviolable and universal Peace, and a true and sincere Friendship between the most Christian King, his Heirs and Successors, and the United States of America; and the Subjects of the most Christian King and of the said States; and between the Countries, Islands, Cities, and Towns, situate under the Jurisdiction of the most Christian King, and of the said United States, and the People and Inhabitants of every Degree, without exception of Persons or Places; & the Terms herein after mentioned shall be perpetual between the most Christian King his Heirs and Successors and the said United States.

ART. 1.er

Il y aura une paix ferme, inviolable et universelle et une amitié vraie et sincère entre le Roi Très chrétien, ses héritiers et successeurs, et entre les Etats unis de l'Amérique ainsi qu'entre les sujets de Sa Majesté Très chretienne et ceux des dits Etats, comme aussi entre les peuples Isles, Villes et places situés sous la Jurisdiction du Roi Très chretien et des dits Etats unis, et entre leurs peuples et habitans de toutes les classes, sans aucune exception de personnes et de lieux; Les conditions mentionnées au present Traité seront perpetuelles et permanentes entre le Roi très Chretien, ses héritiers et successeurs et les dits Etats unis.

ART. 2.nd.

The most Christian King, and the United States engage mutually not to grant any particular Favour to other Nations in respect of Commerce and Navigation, which shall not immediately become common to the other Party, who shall enjoy the same Favour, freely, if the Concession was freely made, or on allowing the same Compensation, if the Concession was Conditional.

ART. 2.

Le Roi Très chretien et les Etats unis s'engagent mutuellement à n'accorder aucune faveur particulière à d'autres Nations en fait de Commerce et de Navigation qui ne devienne aussitôt commune à l'autre partie, et celle ci jouira de cette faveur gratuitement, si la concession est gratuite, ou en accordant la même compensation si la concession est conditionnelle.

ART. 3d

The Subjects of the most Christian King shall pay in the Ports, Havens, Roads, Countries Islands, Cities or Towns, of the

ART. 3.

Les Sujets du Roi Très chretien ne païeront dans les Ports, havres, rades, Contrées, Isles, Cités et lieux des Etats unis ou d'aucun

United States or any of them, no other or greater Duties or Imposts of what Nature soever they may be, or by what Name soever called, than those which the Nations most favoured are or shall be obliged to pay; and they shall enjoy all the Rights, Liberties, Privileges, Immunities and Exemptions in Trade, Navigation and Commerce, whether in passing from one Port in the said States to another, or in going to and from the same, from and to any Part of the World, which the said Nations do or shall enjoy.

d'entr'eux d'autres ni plus grands droits ou impôts, de quelque nature qu'ils puissent être, et quelque nom qu'ils puissent avoir, que ceux que les Nations les plus favorisées sont, ou seront tenües de païer; Et ils jouiront de tous les droits, libertés, privilèges immunités et exemtions en fait de négoce, navigation et commerce, soit en passant d'un Port des dits Etats à un autre, soit en y allant ou en revenant de quelque partie ou pour quelque partie du Monde que ce soit, dont les d.es Nations jouissent ou jouiront.

Art. 4.

The Subjects, People and Inhabitants of the said United States, and each of them, shall not pay in the Ports, Havens Roads, Isles, Cities & Places under the Domination of his most Christian Majesty in Europe, any other or greater Duties or Imposts, of what Nature soever, they may be, or by what Name soever called, than those which the most favour'd Nations are or shall be obliged to pay; & they shall enjoy all the Rights, Liberties, Privileges, Immunities & Exemptions, in Trade, Navigation and Commerce, whether in passing from one Port in the said Dominions in Europe to another, or in going to and from the same, from and to any Part of the World, which the said Nations do or shall enjoy.

Art. 4.

Les Sujets peuples et habitans des d. Etats-unis et de chacun d'iceux ne païeront dans les Ports, havres, rades, Isles, Villes et places de la Domination de Sa Majesté Très chretienne en Europe d'autres ni plus grands droits ou impots de quelque nature qu'ils puissent être et quelque nom qu'ils puissent avoir que les Nations les plus favorisées sont ou seront tenües de païer, et ils jouiront de tous les droits, libertés privilèges immunités et exemtions en fait de négoce, navigation et commerce soit en passant d'un port à un autre des d.s Etats du Roi Très chretien en Europe, soit en y allant ou en revenant de quelque partie ou pour quelque partie du monde que ce soit dont les nations susd.es jouissent ou jouiront.

ART. 5.

In the above Exemption is particularly comprised the Imposition of 100 Sols pr Ton, established in France on foreign Ships; unless when the Ships of the United States shall load with the Merchandize of France for another Port of the same Dominion, in which Case the said Ships shall pay the Duty abovementioned so long as other Nations the most favour'd shall be obliged to pay it. But it is understood that the said United States or any of them are at Liberty when they shall judge it proper, to establish a Duty equivalent in the same Case.

ART. 5.

Dans l'exemtion ci dessus est nommément compris l'imposition de cent sous par Tonneau établie en France sur les Navires étrangers, si ce n'est lorsque les Navires des Etats-unis chargeront des marchandises de France dans un port de France pour un autre port de la même Domination auquel cas les ds navires des ds Etats-unis acquiteront le droit dont il s'agit aussi longtems que les autres nations les plus favorisées seront obligées de l'acquiter. Bien entendu qu'il sera libre aux dits Etats unis ou à aucun d'iceux d'établir, quand ils le jugeront àpropos, un droit equivalent à celui dont il est question pour le même cas pour lequel il est etabli dans les Ports de Sa Majesté Très chretienne.

ART. 6.

The most Christian King shall endeavour by all the means in his Power to protect and defend all Vessels and the Effects belonging to the Subjects, People or Inhabitants of the said United States, or any of them, being in his Ports, Havens or Roads or on the Seas near to his Countries, Islands, Cities or Towns and to recover and restore to the right owners, their agents or Attornies all such Vessels & Effects, which shall be taken within his Jurisdiction; and the Ships of War of his most Christian Majesty or any Convoys sailing

ART. 6.

Le Roi Très Chretien fera usage de tous les moïens qui sont en son pouvoir pour protéger et defendre tous les Vaisseaux et effets apartenants aux sujets, peuples et habitans des dits Etats-unis et de chacun d'iceux qui seront dans ses ports, havres ou rades ou dans les Mers près de ses Pays, Contrées, Isles, Villes et places et fera tous ses efforts pour recouvrer et faire restituer aux propriétaires légitimes, leurs Agens ou Mandataires, tous les vaisseaux et effets qui leur seront pris dans l'étenduë de sa jurisdic-

under his authority shall upon all Occasions take under their Protection all Vessels belonging to the Subjects, People or Inhabitants of the said United States, or any of them & holding the same Course or going the same Way, and shall defend such Vessels, as long as they hold the same Course or go the same way, against all Attacks, Force and Violence in the same manner, as they ought to protect and defend the Vessels belonging to the Subjects of the most Christian King.

tion; Et les Vaisseaux de guerre de Sa Majesté Très chretienne ou les convois quelconques faisant voile sous son autorité, prendront, en toute occasion, sous leur protection tous les Vaisseaux apartenants aux sujets peuples et habitans des ds Etats unis ou d'aucun d'iceux, les quels tiendront le meme cours et feront la même route, et ils défendront les dits Vaisseaux aussi longtems qu'ils tiendront le même cours et suivront la meme route, contre toute attaque force ou violence de la même manière qu'ils sont tenus de défendre et de protéger les Vaisseaux appartenans aux sujets de Sa Majesté Très chretienne.

Art. 7.

In like manner the said United States and their Ships of War sailing under their Authority shall protect and defend, conformable to the Tenor of the preceeding Article, all the Vessels and Effects belonging to the Subjects of the most Christian King; and use all their Endeavours to recover & cause to be restored the said Vessels and Effects, that shall have been taken within the Jurisdiction of the said United States or any of them.

Art. 7.

Pareillement les dits Etats unis et leurs Vaisseaux de guerre faisant voile sous leur autorité protégeront et défendront conformement au contenu de l'arte précédent, tous les Vaisseaux et effets apartenants aux sujets du Roi Très Chretien et feront tous leurs efforts pour recouvrer et faire restitüer les dits vaisseaux et effets qui auront été pris dans l'étendüe de la Jurisdiction des dits Etats et de chacun d'iceux.

Art. 8.

The most Christian King will employ his good Offices and Interposition with the King or Emperor of Morocco or Fez, the

Art. 8.

Le Roi Très chretien emploïera ses bons offices et son entremise auprès des Roi ou Empereur de Maroc ou Fez, des Regences

Regencies of Algier, Tunis and Tripoli, or with any of them, and also with every other Prince, State or Power of the Coast of Barbary in Africa, and the Subjects of the said King Emperor, States and Powers, and each of them; in order to provide as fully and efficaciously as possible for the Benefit, Conveniency and Safety of the said United States, and each of them, their Subjects, People, and Inhabitants, and their Vessels and Effects, against all Violence, Insult, Attacks, or Depredations on the Part of the said Princes and States of Barbary, or their Subjects.

d'Alger, Tunis et Tripoli ou auprès aucune d'entr Elles, ainsi qu'auprès de tout autre Prince Etat ou Puissance des côtes de Barbarie en Affrique et des sujets des ds Roi Empereur, Etats et Puissance et de chacun d'iceux à l'effet de pourvoir aussi pleinement et aussi efficacement qu'il sera possible, à l'avantage, commodité et sûreté des dits Etats-unis et de chacun d'iceux, ainsi que de leurs sujets, peuples et habitans, leurs Vaisseaux et effets contre toute violence, insulte, attaque ou déprédations de la part des ds Princes et Etats Barbaresques ou de leurs sujets.

Art. 9.

The Subjects, Inhabitants, Merchants, Commanders of Ships Masters and Mariners of the States, Provinces, and Dominions of each Party respectively shall abstain and forbear to fish in all Places possessed or which shall be possessed by the other Party: The most Christian Kings Subjects shall not fish in the Havens, Bays, Creeks, Roads Coasts or Places, which the said united States hold or shall hereafter hold; and in like manner the Subjects, People and Inhabitants of the said United States shall not fish in the Havens Bays, Creeks, Roads, Coasts or Places, which the most Christian King possesses or shall hereafter possess; and if any and if any Ship

Art. 9.

Les sujets habitans, marchands, Commandans des Navires, Maitres et gens de Mer des Etats, Provinces et Domaines des deux parties s'abstiendront et éviteront reciproquement, de pêcher dans toutes les places possédées ou qui seront possedées par l'autre partie. Les sujets de Sa Majesté Très Chretienne ne pêcheront pas dans les havres, Bayes, Criques, rades, côtes et places que les dits Etats-unis possédent ou possèderont à l'avenir, et de la même manière les sujets, peuples et habitans des ds Etats unis ne pêcheront pas dans les havres, Bayes, Criques, rades, Côtes et places que Sa Majesté Très chretienne posséde actuellement ou possèdera à l'avenir, et si quelque

or Vessel shall be found fishing contrary to the Tenor of this Treaty, the said Ship or Vessel with its lading, proof being made thereof, shall be confiscated. It is however understood, that the Exclusion stipulated in the present Article shall take place only so long, and so far as the most Christian King or the United States shall not in this respect have granted an Exemption to some other Nation.

navire ou Batiment étoit surpris pêchant en violation du present Traité, le dit navire ou Batiment et sa Cargaison seront confisqués, après que la preuve en aura été faite düement. Bien entendu que l'exclusion stipulée dans le present article n'aura lieu qu'autant et si longtems que le Roi et les Etats-unis n'auront point accordé à cet egard d'exception à quelque Nation que ce puisse être.

ART. 10

The United States their Citizens and Inhabitants shall never disturb the Subjects, of the most Christian King in the Enjoyment and Exercise of the Right of Fishing on the Banks of Newfoundland; nor in the indefinite and exclusive Right which belongs to them on that Part of the Coast of that Island which is designed by the Treaty of Utrecht; nor in the Rights relative to all and each of the Isles which belong to his most Christian Majesty; the whole conformable to the true Sense of the Treaties of Utrecht and Paris.

ART. 10.

Les Etats unis, leurs citoïens et habitans ne troubleront jamais les sujets du Roi Très chretien dans la jouissance et exercice du droit de pêche sur les bancs de Terreneuve, non plus que dans la jouissance indéfinie et exclusive qui leur apartient sur la partie des Côtes de cette Isle designée dans le Traite d'Utrecht ni dans les droits relatifs à toutes et chacune des Isles qui appartiennent à Sa Majesté très Chretienne. Le tout conformement au véritable sens des Traités d'Utrecht et de Paris.

ART. 11.[1]

It is agreed and concluded that there shall never be any Duty imposed on the Exportation of the Mellasses that may be taken by the Subjects of any of the United

ART. 11.[1]

Il est convenu et arrêté qu'il ne sera jamais imposé aucun droit sur l'exportation des Melasses qui pourront être tirées par les Sujets d'aucun des Etats-unis des Isles

[1] Articles 11 and 12 were suppressed. See the notes following the text of this treaty.

States from the Islands of America which belong or may hereafter appertain to his most Christian Majesty.

d'Amérique qui appartiennent ou pourront apartenir à Sa Majesté très Chretienne.

ART. 12.[1]

In compensation of the Exemption stipulated by the preceeding Article, it is agreed and concluded that there shall never be any Duties imposed on the Exportation of any kind of Merchandize which the Subjects of his most Christian Majesty may take from the Countries and Possessions present or future of any of the thirteen United States, for the Use of the Islands which shall furnish Mellasses.

ART. 12.[1]

En compensation de l'exemtion stipulée par l'article précédent, il est convenu et arrêté qu'il ne sera jamais imposé aucun droit sur l'exportation d'aucune espèce de denrées et marchandises que les sujets de Sa Majesté Très Chretienne pourront tirer des Pays ou possessions actuelles ou futures d'aucun des Treize Etats-unis pour l'usage des Isles qui fournissent les melasses.

ART 13 [11].

The Subjects and Inhabitants of the said United States, or any one of them, shall not be reputed Aubains in France, & consequently shall be exempted from the *Droit d'Aubaine* or other similar Duty under what name soever. They may by Testament, Donation, or otherwise dispose of their Goods moveable and immoveable in favour of such Persons as to them shall seem good; and their Heirs, Subjects of the Said United States, residing whether in France or elsewhere, may succeed them *ab intestat,* without being obliged to obtain Letters of Naturalization, and

ART. 13 [11].

Les sujets et habitans des dits Etats-unis ou de l'un d'eux ne seront point reputés Aubains en France et conséquemment seront exemts du droit d'Aubaine ou autre droit semblable quelque nom qu'il puisse avoir; pourront disposer par Testament, Donation ou autrement de leurs biens meubles et immeubles en faveur de telles personnes que bon leur semblera; Et leurs héritiers sujets des dits Etats-unis, residans soit en France soit ailleurs pourront leur succéder *ab intestat,* sans qu'ils aïent besoin d'obtenir des lettres de naturalité, et sans que l'effet de cette concession leur puisse être

[1] Articles 11 and 12 were suppressed. See the notes following the text of this treaty.

without having the Effect of this Concession contested or impeded under Pretext of any Rights or Prerogatives of Provinces, Cities, or Private Persons. And the said Heirs, whether such by particular Title, or *ab intestat*, shall be exempt from all Duty called *Droit de Detraction*, or other Duty of the same kind; saving nevertheless, the local Rights or Duties as much and as long as similar ones are not established by the United States or any of them. The Subjects of the most Christian King shall enjoy on their Part, in all the Dominions of the s[d] States, an entire and perfect Reciprocity relative to the Stipulations contained in the present Article.

contesté ou empêché sous pretexte de quelques droits ou prérogatives des Provinces, Villes, ou personnes privées. Et seront les dits héritiers, soit à titre particulier, soit *ab intestat* exemts de tout droit de détraction ou autre droit de ce genre, sauf néanmoins les droits locaux, tant et si longtems qu'il n'en sera point etabli de pareils par les dits Etats-unis ou aucun d'iceux. Les sujets du Roi Très chretien jouiront de leur côté, dans tous les Domaines des dits Etats d'une entière et parfaite reciprocité relativement aux stipulations renfermées dans le present Article.

But it is at the same Time agreed that its Contents shall not affect the Laws made or that may be made hereafter in France against Emigrations, which shall remain in all their Force and Vigour; and the United States on their Part, or any of them, shall be at Liberty to enact such Laws relative to that Matter, as to them shall seem proper.

Mais il est convenu en même tems que son contenu ne portera aucune atteinte aux loix promulguées en France contre les émigrations, ou qui pourront être promulguées dans la suite, les quelles demeureront dans toute leur force et vigueur. Les Etats-unis de leur côté ou aucun d'entr'eux, seront libres de statüer sur cette matière telle loi qu'ils jugeront àpropos.

Art. 14 [12].

The merchant Ships of either of the Parties, which shall be making into a Port belonging to the Enemy of the other Ally and concerning whose Voyage & the Species of Goods on board her

Art. 14 [12].

Les Navires Marchands des deux parties qui seront destinés pour des Ports appartenants à une Puissance ennemie de l'autre Allié, et dont le voïage ou la nature des marchandises dont ils seront

there shall be just Grounds of Suspicion shall be obliged to exhibit as well upon the high Seas as in the Ports and Havens not only her Passports, but likewise Certificates expressly shewing that her Goods are not of the Number of those, which have been prohibited as contraband.

ART. 15 [13].

If by the exhibiting of the above said Certificates, the other Party discover there are any of those Sorts of Goods, which are prohibited and declared contraband and consigned for a Port under the Obedience of his Enemies, it shall not be lawful to break up the Hatches of such Ship, or to open any Chest, Coffers, Packs, Casks, or any other Vessels found therein, or to remove the smallest Parcels of her Goods, whether such Ship belongs to the Subjects of France or the Inhabitants of the said United States, unless the lading be brought on Shore in the presence of the Officers of the Court of Admiralty and an Inventory thereof made; but there shall be no allowance to sell, exchange, or alienate the same in any manner, untill after that due and lawful Process shall have been had against such prohibited Goods, and the Court of Admiralty shall, by a Sentence pronounced, have confiscated the same: saving always as well the Ship itself as

chargés donneroit de justes soupçons, seront tenus d'exhiber, soit en haute Mer, soit dans les Ports et Havres non seulement leurs passeports, mais encore les Certificats qui constateront expressement que leur chargement n'est pas de la qualité de ceux qui sont prohibés comme contrebande.

ART. 15 [13].

Si l'exhibition des dits Certificats conduit à découvrir que le Navire porte des marchandises prohibées et reputées contrebande consignées pour un Port ennemi, il ne sera pas permis de briser les écoutilles des dits Navires, ni d'ouvrir aucune Caisse, Coffre, Malle, Ballots, Tonneaux, et autres Caisses qui s'y trouveront, ou d'en déplacer et détourner la moindre partie des marchandises, soit que le Navire apartienne aux sujets du Roi Très Chretien ou aux habitans des Etats unis jusqu'a ce que la Cargaison ait été mise à terre en presence des Officiers des Cours d'Amirauté, et que l'Inventaire en ait ete fait, mais on ne permettra pas de vendre, échanger ou aliéner les Navires ou leur Cargaison en manière quelconque avant que le procès ait été fait et parfait legalement pour déclarer la contrebande, et que les Cours d'Amirauté auront prononcé leur confiscation par Jugement sans préjudice néanmoins des Navires ainsi que des marchandises, qui,

any other Goods found therein, which by this Treaty are to be esteemed free: neither may they be detained on pretence of their being as it were infected by the prohibited Goods, much less shall they be confiscated as lawful Prize: But if not the whole Cargo, but only part thereof shall consist of prohibited or contraband Goods and the Commander of the Ship shall be ready and willing to deliver them to the Captor, who has discovered them, in such Case the Captor having received those Goods shall forthwith discharge the Ship and not hinder her by any means freely to prosecute the Voyage, on which she was bound. But in Case the Contraband Merchandises, cannot be all receiv'd on board the Vessel of the Captor, then the Captor may, notwithstanding the Offer of delivering him the Contraband Goods, carry the Vessel into the nearest Port agreable to what is above directed.

en vertu du Traité doivent étre censées libres. Il ne sera pas permis de retenir ces marchandises sous pretexte qu'elles ont été entachées par les marchandises de Contrebande, et bien moins encore de les confisquer comme des prises légales. Dans le cas où une partie seulement et non la totalité du chargement consisteroit en marchandises de Contrebande, et que le Commandant du vaisseau consente à les délivrer au Corsaire qui les aura découverts, àlors le Capitaine qui aura fait la prise après avoir reçu ces marchandises doit incontinent relâcher le Navire et ne doit l'empêcher, en aucune manière, de continuer son voïage. Mais dans le cas où les marchandises de contrebande ne pourroient pas être toutes chargées sur le Vaisseau capteur, àlors le Capitaine dud: Vaisseau sera le Maitre, malgré l'offre de remettre la contrebande, de conduire le patron dans le plus prochain port, conformement à ce qui est préscrit plus haut.

ART. 16 [14].

On the contrary it is agreed, that whatever shall be found to be laden by the Subjects and Inhabitants of either Party on any Ship belonging to the Enemys of the other or to their Subjects, the whole although it be not of the Sort of prohibited Goods may be confiscated in the same

ART. 16 [14].

On est convenu au contraire que tout ce qui se trouvera chargé par les sujets respectifs sur des Navires apartenants aux ennemis de l'autre partie, ou à leurs sujets sera confisqué sans distinction des marchandises prohibées ou non prohibées, ainsi et de même que si elles apparte-

manner, as if it belonged to the Enemy, except such Goods and Merchandizes as were put on board such Ship before the Declaration of War, or even after such Declaration, if so be it were done without knowledge of such Declaration. So that the Goods of the Subjects and People of either Party, whether they be of the Nature of such as are prohibited or otherwise, which, as is aforesaid were put on board any Ship belonging to an Enemy before the War, or after the Declaration of the same, without the Knowledge of it, shall no ways be liable to confiscation, but shall well and truely be restored without Delay to the proprietors demanding the same; but so as that, if the said Merchandizes be contraband, it shall not be any Ways lawful to carry them afterwards to any Ports belonging to the Enemy. The two contracting Parties agree, that the Term of two Months being passed after the Declaration of War, their respective Subjects, from whatever Part of the World they come, shall not plead the Ignorance mentioned in this Article.

ART. 17 [15].

And that more effectual Care may be taken for the Security of the Subjects and Inhabitants of both Parties, that they suffer no injury by the men of War or Privateers of the other Party, all

noient à l'ennemi, à l'exception toute fois des effets et marchandises qui auront été mis à bord des dits navires avant la déclaration de guerre, ou même après la d^{e} déclaration, si au moment du chargement on a pu l'ignorer, de manière que les marchandises des sujets des deux parties, soit qu'elles se trouvent du nombre de celles de contrebande ou autrement, les quelles comme il vient d'être dit auront été mises à bord, d'un Vaisseau apartenant à l'ennemi avant la guerre ou même après la d^{e} déclaration, lorsqu'on l'ignoroit ne seront, en aucune manière, sujetes à confiscation, mais seront fidèlement et de bonne foi rendües sans delai à leurs propriétaires qui les reclameront; bien entendu néanmoins qu'il ne soit pas permis de portee dans les Ports ennemis les marchandises qui seront de contrebande. Les deux parties contractantes conviennent que le terme de deux mois passés depuis la déclaration de guerre, leurs sujets respectifs, de quelque partie du monde qu'ils viennent ne pourront plus alléguer l'ignorance dont il est question dans le présent article.

ART. 17 [15].

Et afin de pourvoir plus efficacement à la sûreté des sujets des deux parties contractantes, pour qu'il ne leur soit fait aucun prejudice par les Vaisseaux de guerre de l'autre partie ou par des Arma-

the Commanders of the Ships of his most Christian Majesty & of the said United States and all their Subjects and Inhabitants shall be forbid doing any Injury or Damage to the other Side; and if they act to the contrary, they shall be punished and shall moreover be bound to make Satisfaction for all Matter of Damage, and the Interest thereof, by reparation, under the Pain and obligation of their Person and Goods.

teurs particuliers, il sera fait défense à tous Capitaines des Vaisseaux de Sa Majesté très Chretienne et des dits Etats-unis, et à tous leurs sujets de faire aucun dommage ou insulte à ceux de l'autre partie, et au cas où ils y contreviendroient, ils en seront punis et de plus ils seront tenus et obligés en leurs personnes et en leurs biens de reparer tous les dommages et intérêts.

Art. 18 [16].

All Ships and Merchandizes of what Nature soever which shall be rescued out of the Hands of any Pirates or Robbers on the high Seas, shall be brought into some Port of either State and shall be delivered to the Custody of the Officers of that Port, in order to be restored entire to the true Proprietor as soon as due and sufficient Proof shall be made concerning the Property thereof.

Art. 18 [16].

Tous Vaisseaux et marchandises de quelque nature que ce puisse être, lorsqu'ils auront été enlevés des mains de quelques Pirates en pleine Mer, seront amenés dans quelque Port de l'un des deux Etats, et seront remis à la garde des Officiers dud.t Port, âfin d'être rendus, en entier, a leur veritable propriétaire, aussitôt qu'il aura düement et sufisament fait conster de sa propriété.

Art. 19 [17].

It shall be lawful for the Ships of War of either Party & Privateers freely to carry whithersoever they please the Ships and Goods taken from their Enemies, without being obliged to pay any Duty to the Officers of the Admiralty or any other Judges; nor shall such Prizes be arrested or seized, when they come to and enter the Ports of either Party; nor shall the Searchers or other Officers of those Places search the same or

Art. 19 [17].

Les Vaisseaux de guerre de Sa Majesté Trés Chretienne et ceux des Etats-unis, de même que ceux que leurs sujets auront armés en guerre, pourront, en toute liberté, conduire oú bon leur semblera les prises qu'ils auront faites sur leurs ennemis, sans être obligés à aucuns droits, soit des Sieurs Amiraux ou de l'Amirauté, ou d'aucuns autres, sans qu'aussi les dits Vaisseaux ou les d.es prises, entrant dans les havres ou Ports

make examination concerning the Lawfulness of such Prizes, but they may hoist Sail at any time and depart and carry their Prizes to the Places express'd in their Commissions, which the Commanders of such Ships of War shall be obliged to shew: On the contrary no Shelter or Refuge shall be given in their Ports to such as shall have made Prize of the Subjects, People or Property of either of the Parties; but if such shall come in, being forced by Stress of Weather or the Danger of the Sea, all proper means shall be vigorously used that they go out and retire from thence as soon as possible.

de Sa Majesté Très Chretienne ou des dits Etats-unis puissent être arrêtés ou saisis, ni que les officiers des lieux puissent prendre connoissance de la validité des d^{es} prises, les quelles pourront sortir et être conduites franchement et en toute liberté aux lieux portés par les Commissions dont les Capitaines des dits Vaisseaux seront obligés de faire aparoir. Et au contraire ne sera donné asile ni retraite dans leurs ports ou havres à ceux qui auront fait des prises sur les sujets de Sa Majesté ou des dits Etats unis; Et s'ils sont forcés d'y entrer par tempête ou peril de la Mer, on les fera sortir le plustôt qu'il sera possible.

ART. 20 [18].

If any Ship belonging to either of the Parties their People or Subjects, shall, within the Coasts or Dominions of the other, stick upon the Sands or be wrecked or suffer any other Damage, all friendly Assistance and Relief shall be given to the Persons shipwrecked or such as shall be in danger thereof; and Letters of safe Conduct shall likewise be given to them for their free and quiet Passage from thence, and the return of every one to his own Country.

ART. 20 [18].

Dans le cas où un vaisseau apartenant à l'un des deux Etats ou à leurs sujets, aura échoué, fait naufrage ou souffert quelqu'autre dommage sur les Côtes ou sous la Domination de l'une des deux parties, il sera donné toute aide et assistance amiable aux personnes naufragées ou qui se trouvent en danger, et il leur sera accordé des conduits pour assûrer leur passage et leur retour dans leur patrie.

ART. 21 [19].

In Case the Subjects and Inhabitants of either Party with their shipping whether publick and of War or private and of Mer-

ART. 21 [19].

Lorsque les sujets et habitans de l'une des deux parties avec leurs vaisseaux soit publics et de guerre, soit particuliers et mar-

chants, be forced, through Stress of Weather, pursuit of Pirates or Enemies, or any other urgent necessity for seeking of Shelter and Harbour, to retreat and enter into any of the Rivers, Bays, Roads or Ports belonging to the other Party, they shall be received and treated with all humanity and Kindness and enjoy all friendly Protection & Help; and they shall be permitted to refresh and provide themselves at reasonable Rates with victuals and all things needful for the sustenence of their Persons or reparation of their Ships and conveniency of their Voyage; and they shall no Ways be detained or hindred from returning out of the said Ports or Roads but may remove and depart when and whither they please without any let or hindrance.

chands, seront forcés par une tempête, par la poursuite des Pirates et des ennemis, ou par quelqu'autre nécessité urgente de chercher refuge et un abri, de se retirer et entrer dans quelqu'une des Rivières, Bayes, rades ou Ports de l'une des deux parties, ils seront reçus et traités avec humanité,[1] et jouiront de toute amitié protection et assistance, et il leur sera permis de se pourvoir de rafraichissemens, de vivres et de toutes choses nécessaires pour leur subsistance, pour la reparation de leurs Vaisseaux, et pour continüer leur voïage, le tout moïennant un prix raisonable, et ils ne seront retenus, en aucune manière ni empêchés de sortir des dits ports ou rades, mais pourront se retirer et partir quand, et comme il leur plaira sans aucun obstacle ni empêchement.

Art. 22 [20].

For the better promoting of Commerce on both Sides, it is agreed that if a War shall break out between the said two Nations, six Months after the Proclamation of War shall be allowed to the Merchants in the Cities and Towns, where they live, for selling and transporting their Goods and Merchandizes; and if any thing be taken from them, or

Art. 22 [20].

Âfin de promouvoir d'autant mieux le Commerce de deux Côtés, il est convenu que dans le cas où la guerre surviendroit entre les deux nations susdites, il sera accordé, six mois après la déclaration de guerre, aux marchands dans les Villes et Cités qu'ils habitent, pour rassembler et transporter les marchandises, et s'il en est enlevé quelque chose,

[1] There is a variance here between the instruments of ratification and the original of the treaty which is in the Department of State file. In the United States instrument of ratification, after "humanité" appear the words "et honêteté," and in the French instrument, "et honnêteté." The English text shows that the omission of the two words was an error of the scrivener.

any Injury be done them within that Term by either Party or the People or Subjects of either, full Satisfaction shall be made for the same.

ou s'il leur a été fait quelqu' injure durant le terme préscrit ci-dessus, par l'une des deux parties, leurs peuples ou sujets, il leur sera donné à cet égard pleine et entière satisfaction.

ART. 23 [21].

No Subjects of the most Christian King shall apply for or take any Commission or Letters of marque for arming any Ship or Ships to act as Privateers against the said United States or any of them or against the Subjects People or Inhabitants of the said United States or any of them or against the Property of any of the Inhabitants of any of them from any Prince or State with which the said United States shall be at War. Nor shall any Citizen Subject or Inhabitant of the said United States or any of them apply for or take any Commission or letters of marque for arming any Ship or Ships to act as Privateers against the Subjects of the most Christian King or any of them or the Property of any of them from any Prince or State with which the said King shall be at War: And if any Person of either Nation shall take such Commissions or Letters of Marque he shall be punished as a Pirate.

ART. 23 [21].

Aucun sujet du Roi Très Chretien ne prendra de commission ou de lettres de marque pour armer quelque Vaisseau ou Vaisseaux à l'effet d'agir comme Corsaires contre les dits Etats-unis ou quelques uns d'entr'eux, ou contre les sujets, peuples ou habitans d'iceux, ou contre leur propriété ou celle des habitans d'aucun d'entr'eux, de quelque Prince que ce soit avec lequel les dits Etats-unis seront en guerre. De même aucun Citoïen, sujet ou habitant des susdits Etats-unis et de quelqu'un d'entr'eux ne demandera ni n'acceptera aucune commission ou lettres de marque pour armer quelque vaisseau, ou vaisseaux pour courre sus aux sujets de Sa Majesté Très chretienne ou quelques uns d'entre eux ou leur propriété de quelque Prince ou Etat que ce soit avec qui Sa d[e] Majesté se trouvera en guerre, et si quelqu'un de l'une ou de l'autre Nation prenoit de pareilles commissions ou lettres de marque il sera puni comme Pirate.

ART. 24 [22].

It shall not be lawful for any foreign Privateers, not belonging

ART. 24 [22].

Il ne sera permis à aucun Corsaire étranger non apartenant

to Subjects of the most Christian King nor Citizens of the said United States, who have Commissions from any other Prince or State in enmity with either Nation to fit their Ships in the Ports of either the one or the other of the aforesaid Parties, to sell what they have taken or in any other manner whatsoever to exchange their Ships, Merchandizes or any other lading; neither shall they be allowed even to purchase victuals except such as shall be necessary for their going to the next Port of that Prince or State from which they have Commissions.

à quelque sujet de Sa Majesté Très chretienne ou à un Citoïen des dits Etats-unis, lequel aura une commission de la part d'un Prince ou d'une Puissance en guerre avec l'une des deux Nations, d'armer leurs Vaisseaux dans les Ports de l'une des deux parties, ni d'y vendre les prises qu'il aura faites, ni décharger en autre manière quelconque les Vaisseaux, Marchandises ou aucune partie de leur Cargaison; Il ne sera même pas permis d'acheter d'autres vivres que ceux qui lui seront nécessaires pour se rendre dans le Port le plus voisin du Prince ou de l'Etat dont il tient sa commission.

ART. 25 [23].

It shall be lawful for all and singular the Subjects of the most Christian King and the Citizens People and Inhabitants of the said United States to sail with their Ships with all manner of Liberty and Security; no distinction being made, who are the Proprietors of the Merchandizes laden thereon, from any Port to the places of those who now are or hereafter shall be at Enmity with the most Christian King or the United States. It shall likewise be Lawful for the Subjects and Inhabitants aforesaid to sail with the Ships and Merchandizes aforementioned and to trade with the same Liberty and security from the Places, Ports and Havens

ART. 25 [23].

Il sera permis à tous et un chacun des sujets du Roi Très chretien et aux Citoïens, peuple et habitans des susdits Etats-unis de naviguer avec leurs Batimens avec toute liberté et sûreté, sans qu'il puisse être fait d'exception à cet égard, à raison des propriétaires des marchandises chargées sur les dits Batimens venant de quelque Port que ce soit, et destinés pour quelque place d'une Puissance actuellement ennemie ou qui pourra l'être dans la suite de Sa Majesté Très Chretienne ou des Etats-unis. Il sera permis également aux sujets et habitans susmentionnés de naviguer avec leurs Vaisseaux et marchandises, et

of those who are Enemies of both or either Party without any Opposition or disturbance whatsoever, not only directly from the Places of the Enemy afore mentioned to neutral Places; but also from one Place belonging to an Enemy to another place belonging to an Enemy, whether they be under the Jurisdiction of the same Prince or under several; And it is hereby stipulated that free Ships shall also give a freedom to Goods, and that every thing shall be deemed to be free and exempt, which shall be found on board the Ships belonging to the Subjects of either of the Confederates, although the whole lading or any Part thereof should appertain to the Enemies of either, contraband Goods being always excepted. It is also agreed in like manner that the same Liberty be extended to Persons, who are on board a free Ship, with this Effect, that although they be Enemies to both or either Party, they are not to be taken out of that free Ship, unless they are Soldiers and in actual Service of the Enemies.

de fréquenter avec la même liberté et sûreté les Places, Ports, et havres des Puissances ennemies des deux parties contractantes ou d'une d'entre Elles, sans opposition ni trouble et de faire le Commerce non seulement directement des Ports de l'ennemi susdit à un port neutre, mais aussi d'un Port ennemi à un autre Port ennemi, soit qu'il se trouve sous sa jurisdiction ou sous celle de plusieurs; Et il est stipulé par le present Traité que les Batimens libres assûreront également la liberté des marchandises, et qu'on jugera libres toutes les choses qui se trouveront àbord des Navires apartenants aux sujets d'une des parties contractantes, quand même le chargement ou partie d'icelui apartiendroit aux ennemis de l'une des deux, bien entendu néanmoins que la contrebande sera toujours exceptée. Il est également convenu que cette même liberté s'étendroit aux personnes qui pourroient se trouver àbord du Batiment libre, quand même Elles seroient ennemies de l'une des deux parties contractantes, et Elles ne pourront être enlevées des dits Navires, à moins qu'Elles ne soient militaires, et actuellement au Service de l'Ennemi.

Art. 26 [24].

This Liberty of Navigation and Commerce shall extend to all kinds of Merchandizes, excepting those

Art. 26 [24]

Cette liberté de navigation et de commerce doit s'étendre sur toutes sortes de marchandises, à

only which are distinguished by the name of contraband; And under this Name of Contraband or prohibited Goods shall be comprehended, Arms, great Guns, Bombs with the fuzes, and other things belonging to them, Cannon Ball, Gun powder, Match, Pikes, Swords, Lances, Spears, halberds, Mortars, Petards, Granades Salt Petre, Muskets, Musket Ball, Bucklers, Helmets, breast Plates, Coats of Mail and the like kinds of Arms proper for arming Soldiers, Musket rests, belts, Horses with their Furniture, and all other Warlike Instruments whatever. These Merchandizes which follow shall not be reckoned among Contraband or prohibited Goods, that is to say, all sorts of Cloths, and all other Manufactures woven of any wool, Flax, Silk, Cotton or any other Materials whatever; all kinds of wearing Apparel together with the Species, whereof they are used to be made; gold & Silver as well coined as uncoin'd, Tin, Iron, Latten, Copper, Brass Coals, as also Wheat and Barley and any other kind of Corn and pulse; Tobacco and likewise all manner of Spices; salted and smoked Flesh, salted Fish, Cheese and Butter, Beer, Oils, Wines, Sugars and all sorts of Salts; & in general all Provisions, which serve for the nourishment of Mankind and the sustenence of Life; furthermore all kinds of

l'exception seulement de celles qui sont designées sous le nom de contrebande. Sous ce nom de contrebande ou de marchandises prohibeés doivent être compris les armes, Canons, bombes avec leurs fusées et autres choses y relatives, boulets, poudre à tirer, méches, piques, epées, lances, dards, hallebardes, mortiers, petards, grenades, salpêtre, fusils, Balles, Boucliers Casques, Cuirasses, Cote de mailles et autres armes de cette espèce propres à armer les Soldats, porte-mousqueton, baudriers, chevaux avec leurs Equipages, et tous autres instrumens de guerre quelconques. Les marchandises dénommées ci-après ne seront pas comprises parmi la contrebande ou choses prohibées, savoir toutes sortes de draps et toutes autres étoffes de laine, lin, soye, coton ou d'autres matieres quelconques; Toutes sortes de vétemens avec les étoffes dont on a coutume de les faire, l'or et l'argent monnoïé ou non, l'étain, le fer, laiton cuivre, airain, charbons, de même que le froment et l'orge et toute autre sorte de bleds et légumes; Le tabac et toutes les sortes d'épiceries, la viande salée et fumée, poisson sallé fromage et beurre, bierre, huiles, vins, sucres et toute espece de sel, et en général toutes provisions servant pour la nourriture de l'homme et pour le soutien de la vie; De plus toutes sortes de coton, de chanvre, lin, goudron, poix, cordes, cables,

Cotton, hemp, Flax, Tar, Pitch, Ropes, Cables, Sails, Sail Cloths, Anchors and any Parts of Anchors; also Ships Masts, Planks, Boards and Beams of what Trees soever; and all other Things proper either for building or repairing Ships, and all other Goods whatever, which have not been worked into the form of any Instrument or thing prepared for War by Land or by Sea, shall not be reputed Contraband, much less such as have been already wrought and made up for any other Use; all which shall be wholly reckoned among free Goods: as likewise all other Merchandizes and things, which are not comprehended and particularly mentioned in the foregoing enumeration of contraband Goods: so that they may be transported and carried in the freest manner by the Subjects of both Confederates even to Places belonging to an Enemy such Towns or Places being only excepted as are at that time beseiged, blocked up or invested.

voiles, toiles à voiles, ancres, parties d'ancres, mats, planches, madriers, et bois de toute espèce et toutes autres choses propres à la construction et reparation des Vaisseaux et autres matieres quelconques qui n'ont pas la forme d'un instrument préparé pour la guerre par terre comme par Mer, ne seront pas reputées contrebande, et encore moins celles qui sont déja preparées pour quelqu'autre usage: Toutes les choses dénommées ci-dessus doivent être comprises parmi les marchandises libres de même que toutes les autres marchandises et effets qui ne sont pas compris et particulièrement nommés dans l'énumeration des marchandises de Contrebande; De manière qu'elles pourront être transportées et conduites de la manière la plus libre par les sujets des deux parties contractantes dans des places ennemies, à l'exception néanmoins de celles qui se trouveroient actuellement assiégées bloquées ou investies.

Art. 27 [25].

To the End that all manner of Dissentions and Quarrels may be avoided and prevented on one Side and the other, it is agreed, that in case either of the Parties hereto should be engaged in War, the Ships and Vessels belonging

Art. 27 [25]

Afin d'écarter et de prévenir de part et d'autre toutes discussions[1] et querelles, il a été convenu que dans le cas où l'une des deux parties se trouveroit engagée dans une guerre, les Vaisseaux et Batimens apartenans aux Sujets

[1] In the French instrument of ratification this word is *dissensions*.

to the Subjects or People of the other Ally must be furnished with Sea Letters or Passports expressing the name, Property and Bulk of the Ship as also the name and Place of habitation of the Master or Commander of the said Ship, that it may appear thereby, that the Ship really & truely belongs to the Subjects of one of the Parties, which Passport shall be made out and granted according to the Form annexed to this Treaty; they shall likewise be recalled every Year, that is if the Ship happens to return home within the Space of a Year. It is likewise agreed, that such Ships being laden are to be provided not only with Passports as above mentioned, but also with Certificates containing the several Particulars of the Cargo, the Place whence the Ship sailed and whither she is bound, that so it may be known, whether any forbidden or contraband Goods be on board the same: which Certificates shall be made out by the Officers of the Place, whence the Ship set sail, in the accustomed Form. And if any one shall think it fit or adviseable to express in the said Certificates the Person to whom the Goods on board belong, he may freely do so.

ou Peuple de l'autre Allié devront être pourvus de lettres de Mer, ou passeports, les quels exprimeront le nom, la propriété et le port du Navire, ainsi que le nom et la demeure du maitre ou Commandant dud: Vaisseau, âfin qu'il aparoisse par là que le même vaisseau apartient réellement et véritablement aux sujets de l'une des deux parties contractantes, le quel passeport devra être expédié selon le modèle annexé au present Traité. Ces passeports devront également être renouvellés chaque année dans le cas ou le Vaisseau retourne chez lui dans l'espace d'une année. Il a été convenu également que les Vaisseaux susmentionnés, dans le cas où ils seroient chargés devront être pourvus non seulement de passeports, mais aussi de Certificats contenant le détail de la Cargaison, le lieu d'où le vaisseau est parti et la déclaration des marchandises de Contrebande qui pourroient se trouver àbord; Les quels Certificats devront être expédiés dans la forme accoutumée par les officiers du lieu d'où le vaisseau aura fait voile, Et s'il étoit jugé utile ou prudent d'exprimer dans les dits passeports la personne à la quelle les marchandises apartiennent, on pourra le faire librement.

ART. 28 [26].

The Ships of the Subjects and Inhabitants of either of the Par-

ART. 28 [26].

Dans le cas ou les Vaisseaux des sujets et habitans de l'une des

ties, coming upon any Coasts belonging to either of the said Allies, but not willing to enter into Port, or being entred into Port and not willing to unload their Cargoes or break Bulk, they shall be treated according to the general Rules prescribed or to be prescribed relative to the Object in Question.

ART. 29 [27].

If the Ships of the said Subjects, People or Inhabitants of either of the Parties shall be met with either sailing along the Coasts or on the high Seas by any Ship of War of the other or by any Privateers, the said Ships of War or Privateers, for the avoiding of any Disorder shall remain out of Cannon Shot, and may send their Boats aboard the Merchant Ship, which they shall so meet with, and may enter her to number of two or three Men only to whom the Master or Commander of such Ship or Vessel shall exhibit his passport concerning the Property of the Ship made out according to the Form inserted in this present Treaty, and the Ship, when she shall have shewed such Passport shall be free and at Liberty to pursue her Voyage, so as it shall not be law ful to molest or search her in any manner or to give her chase, or force her to quit her intended Course.

deux parties contractantes aprocheroient des côtes de l'autre, sans cependant avoir le dessein d'entrer dans le port, ou, après être entré, sans avoir le dessein de décharger la Cargaison ou rompre leur charge, on se conduira à leur égard suivant les réglemens généraux préscrits ou à prescrire relativement à l'objet dont il est question.

ART. 29 [27].

Lorsqu'un Batiment apartenant aux dits sujets, peuple et habitans de l'une des deux parties, sera rencontré navigant le long des Côtes ou en pleine Mer par un vaisseau de guerre de l'autre, ou par un Armateur, le dit Vaisseau de guerre ou Armateur, àfin d'éviter tout désordre, se tiendra hors de la portée du Canon, et pourra envoïer sa Chaloupe àbord du Batiment marchand et y faire entrer deux ou trois hommes aux quels le Maitre ou Commandant du Batiment montrera son passeport, le quel devra être conforme à la formule annexée au present Traité, et constatera la propriéte du Batiment, et après que le dit Batiment aura exhibé un pareil passeport, il lui sera libre de continüer son voïage, et il ne sera pas permis de le molester ni de chercher, en aucune manière, de lui donner la chasse ou de le forcer de quiter la Course qu'il s'étoit proposée.

ART. 30 [28].

It is also agreed that all Goods, when once put on board the Ships or Vessels of either of the two contracting Parties shall be subject to no farther Visitation; but all Visitation or Search shall be made before hand, and all prohibibited Goods shall be stopped on the Spot, before the same be put on board, unless there are manifest Tokens or Proofs of fraudulent Practice; nor shall either the Persons or goods of the Subjects of his most Christian Majesty or the United States be put under any arrest or molested by any other kind of Embargo for that Cause; and only the Subject of that State, to whom the said Goods have been or shall be prohibited and who shall presume to sell or alienate such sort of Goods shall be duly punished for the Offence

ART. 30 [28].

Il est convenu que lorsque les marchandises auront été chargées sur les Vaisseaux ou Batimens de l'une des deux parties contractantes, elles ne pourront plus être assujeties à aucune visite; Toute visite et recherche devant être faite avant le chargement, et les marchandises prohibées devant être arrêtées et saisies sur la plage avant de pouvoir être embarquées, à moins qu'on n'ait des indices manifestes ou des preuves de versements frauduleux. De même aucun des Sujets de Sa Majesté Très Chretienne ou des Etats-unis, ni leurs marchandises ne pourront être arrêtés ni molestés pour cette cause par aucune espèce d'embargo; Et les seuls sujets de l'Etat, auxquels les d.[es] marchandises auront été prohibées, et qui se seront emancipés à vendre et aliéner de pareilles marchandises, seront düement punis pour cette contravention.

ART. 31 [29].

The two contracting Parties grant mutually the Liberty of having each in the Ports of the other, Consuls, Vice Consuls, Agents and Commissaries, whose Functions shall be regulated by a particular Agreement.

ART 31 [29].

Les deux parties contractantes se sont accordées mutuellement la faculté de tenir dans leurs ports respectifs des Consuls, Vice-Consuls, Agents et Commissaires, dont les fonctions seront reglées par une Convention particulière.

ART. 32 [30].

And the more to favour and facilitate the Commerce which the

ART. 32 [30].

Pour d'autant plus favoriser et faciliter le Commerce que les

Subjects of the United States may have with France, the most Christian King will grant them in Europe one or more free Ports, where they may bring and dispose of all the Produce and Merchandize of the thirteen United States; and his Majesty will also continue to the Subjects of the said States, the free Ports which have been and are open in the french Islands of America. Of all which free Ports, the said Subjects of the United States shall enjoy the Use, agreable to the Regulations which relate to them.

sujets des Etats-unis feront avec la france, le Roi Très Chretien leur accordera en Europe un ou plusieurs ports francs dans les quels ils pourront amener et débiter toutes les denrées et marchandises provenant des treize Etats-unis; Sa Majesté conservera d'un autre côté aux sujets des dits Etats les ports francs qui ont été et sont ouverts dans les Isles françoises de l'Amerique. De tous les quels Ports francs les dits sujets des Etats-unis jouiront conformement aux règlemens qui en déterminent l'usage.

ART. 33 [31].

The present Treaty shall be ratified on both Sides and the Ratifications shall be exchanged in the Space of Six Months, or sooner if possible.

In Faith whereof the respective Plenipotentiaries have signed the above Articles, both in the French and English Languages, declaring nevertheless that the present Treaty was originally composed and concluded in the French Language, and they have thereto affixed their Seals.

Done at Paris, this Sixth Day of February, one thousand seven hundred & seventy eight

C. A. GERARD [Seal] B FRANKLIN [Seal]

ART. 33 [31].

Le present Traité sera ratifié de part et d'autre et les ratifications seront echangées dans l'espace de six mois ou plustôt si faire se peut.

En foi de quoi les Plenipotentiaires respectifs ont signé les articles ci-dessus tant en langue Françoise qu'en langue Angloise; Déclarant néanmoins que le present Traité a eté originairement redigé et arrêté en langue françoise; Et Ils y ont apposé le cachet de leurs armes.

Fait à Paris le sixieme jour du mois de fevrier mil sept cent soixante dix huit./.

SILAS DEANE [Seal] ARTHUR LEE [Seal]

Form of the Passports and Letters, which are to be given to the Ships and Barks, according to the twenty seventh Article of this Treaty.

To all who shall see these Presents greeting: It is hereby made known that leave and Permission has been given to .... Master and Commander of the Ship called .... of the town of .... burthen .... Tons or thereabouts lying at present in the Port and Haven of .... and bound for .... & laden with .... after that his Ship has been visited and before sailing he shall make Oath before the Officers, who have the Jurisdiction of Maritime Affairs, that the said Ship belongs to one or more of the Subjects of .... the Act whereof shall be put at the End of these presents, as likewise that he will keep and cause to be kept by his Crew on board, the Marine Ordinances and regulations and enter in the proper Office a List signed and witnessed containing the Names and Sirnames, the Places of Birth and abode of the Crew of his Ship and of all who shall embark on board her, whom he shall not take on board without the Knowledge and permission of the Officers of the Marine; and in every Port or Haven where he shall enter with his Ship he shall shew this present Leave to the Officers & Judges of the Marine, and shall give a faith-

Forme des passeports et lettres qui doivent être donnés aux Vaisseaux et Barques conformement à l'article vingt sept du Traité cidessus.

À tous ceux qui les presentes verront, soit notoire que faculté et permission a été accordée à .... Maitre ou Commandant du Navire appellé .... de la ville de .... de la capacite de .... Tonneaux ou environ, se trouvant presentement dans le Port et Havre de .... est destiné pour .... chargé de .... qu'après que son Navire a été visité, et avant son départ, il prêtera serment entre les mains des Officiers de Marine, que le d. Navire apartient à un ou plusieurs sujets de .... dont l'acte sera mis à la fin des présentes; de même qu'il gardera et fera garder par son Equipage les ordonnances et réglements maritimes, et remettra une liste signée et confirmée par Temoins, contenant les noms et surnoms, les lieux de naissance et la demeure des personnes composant l'équipage de son Navire et de tous ceux qui s'y embarqueront, lesquels il ne recevra pas àbord sans la connoissance et la permission des Officiers de Marine; Et dans chaque Port ou Havre où il entrera avec son Navire, il montrera la presente permission aux Officiers et Juges de Marine et leur fera un raport fidèle de ce qui s'est passé durant

ful Account to them of what passed and was done during his Voyage, and he shall carry the Colours, Arms and Ensigns of the (King, or United-States) during his Voyage. In witness whereof we have signed these Presents and put the Seal of our Arms thereunto, and caused the same to be counter signed by .... at .... the .... Day of .... A D ....

son voïage, et il portera les couleurs, armes et enseignes du (Roi ou des Etats unis) durant son dit voïage. En temoin de quoi nous avons signé les presentes, les avons fait contresigner par .... et y avons fait apposer le sceau de nos armes. Donné .... le .... de l'an de grace le ....

NOTES

Notwithstanding the statement in the attestation clause of this treaty that it was "originally composed and concluded in the French Language," much of the language of the English text is that of the "plan of a treaty" voted by Congress on September 17, 1776 (Journals, V, 768–79).

As stated elsewhere generally, pencil notes on an original document are disregarded in the printed text. Thus in the "Form of the Passports" the word "Subjects" (sujets de) is in the original of this treaty crossed out in pencil and in its place is written "citizens," and in the blank following, "the U. S. of A." (citoyens des etats unis d'Amerique); but these and other pencil notations obviously postdate the signature of the treaty and were made after the original was received in this country.

Prior to the Constitution, ratification of treaties by the United States was effected by resolution of Congress; and either as part of the resolution or by separate vote Congress also passed on the form of the instrument of ratification, which in this case is copied in 135 C. C. Papers, I; also in Journals, XI, 462–63. A facsimile of the instrument, received from the French archives, is now in the Department of State file. Like the corresponding French ratification, it recites both the French and the English texts at length, with the English in the left of the two columns. The signature of Henry Laurens (President of Congress) and the attest of Charles Thomson, as Secretary, are at the end; the seal is that of Laurens, as there was then no Great Seal of the United States.

This treaty, with the Treaty of Alliance and the Act Separate and Secret of the same date, was received by Congress on May 2, 1778 (Journals, XI, 418). The three agreements were ratified on May 4, 1778, and the ratifications were concurrently exchanged.

The ratification of the three agreements was prior to the entering into force of the Articles of Confederation (March 1, 1781) and was voted unanimously, although there is no record of the States represented or voting.

Perhaps only nine States were fully represented at that session of Congress on May 4, 1778. It seems clear that New Hampshire and North Carolina were not then represented at all (Journals, X, 399–401; XI, 519, 555); there is doubt as to Delaware, which is recorded as voting on April 26 and again on May 11 (Journals, X, 396; XI, 489), but not in the interval; there is also uncertainty as to Massachusetts, the presence of three delegates being then necessary from that State (Journals, X, 27). Gerry, Lovell, and Dana voted for Massachusetts on April 29 and again on May 8 (Journals, X, 409; XI, 483); but on May 5, when the vote on Articles 11 and 12 of the treaty was recorded, Gerry was absent (Journals, XI, 460). There is no record of any vote in Congress on April 30, May 1, 2, or 4; but there is no reason to doubt that on May 4 all of the remaining nine States were represented (see Burnett, Letters of Members of the Continental Congress, III, li–lxii). So the unanimous vote then taken was that of not more than eleven States and probably of only nine or ten.

The urgency of the occasion overrode any technical necessity of a ratification voted by thirteen States; at least the requirements of the Articles of Confederation for a vote of nine States were satisfied; and while not in force, those Articles had been adopted by Congress on November 15, 1777, and by May 4, 1778, had been ratified by the legislatures of ten States (all but Delaware, New Jersey, and Maryland); and the record of Congress was clear, for it merely recorded unanimity without any listing of the States assenting. Similarly the United States instrument of ratification states that Congress had "unanimously ratified & confirmed."

In June, 1779, there was a separate ratification of this treaty and of the Treaty of Alliance of the same date (Document 2) by Virginia (for an account of this, see Scott, Sovereign States and Suits, 55–56); but whatever political significance this act of Virginia may have had in the circumstances of the time (a point which is interestingly discussed in Doniol, IV, Ch. III), it cannot be considered as adding to the legal effect of the ratifications of the United States and of France, which had been exchanged on July 17, 1778. Each of the two treaties in terms speaks of "the two contracting Parties" (*e. g.*, Treaty of Amity and Commerce, Article 31; Treaty of Alliance, Article 3); and it seems that Congress considered the ratification by Virginia to be *ultra vires* (Doniol, IV, 167, "Le Congrès est un peu affecté d'une démarche qu'il croit contraire à sa prérogative").

The Department of State file contains no protocol or other record of the exchange of ratifications, and no such record has been found in the archives of France. The date is reported in the letter of Benjamin Franklin, Arthur Lee, and John Adams of July 20, 1778 (see Wharton, Diplomatic Correspondence, II, 650–52).

The French Minister (Gérard) seems not to have been consulted regarding the printing, ordered by Congress November 4, 1778, of this treaty and of the Treaty of Alliance. At that time Gérard had been only a few months in the United States; he had received his

first audience of Congress on August 6, 1778; it was he who had signed the treaties of February 6, 1778, on behalf of France. Gérard, whose full style of name was Conrad Alexandre Gérard de Rayneval, had a younger brother, also in the French diplomatic service, Joseph Matthias Gérard de Rayneval; while Doniol, I, ix, speaks of the notes "des deux Gérard de Rayneval," the older brother is almost invariably mentioned as Gérard and the younger as De Rayneval; the two are not always properly distinguished (see Wharton, Diplomatic Correspondence, I, 124, 209, 335).

Gérard submitted a memorial to Congress on November 20, 1778 (see Wharton, Diplomatic Correspondence, II, 843; Journals, XII, 1149); the original thereof and a translation, which follows, are in 94 C. C. Papers, folios 38, 42:

The Minister of France thinks himself called to the honor of communicating to the President of Congress the Suggestion that usually Treaties are not published till the respective Ratifications are exchanged; and, so far as I am acquainted, that of the King is not yet arrived.

If, however, Congress had motives for proceeding immediately in that publication, the Minister begs them not to desist upon his Suggestion, the Wisdom of its Views meriting all Preference above what we should regard only as a simple Formality.

Gerard

Philad[a], *20th Novr, 1778.*

Later on the French comments were much more severe in tone: "such a proceeding is but little consistent with reason, and with the general practice of courts and nations" (see Journals, XIV, 830, 832, July 14, 1779).

Note Regarding Article 10

As to the Treaty of Paris, see the note regarding Article 6 of the Treaty of Alliance (Document 2).

The Treaty of Utrecht mentioned in Article 10 is the Treaty of Peace and Friendship between Great Britain and France, one of the various acts of April 11, 1713. For references to the text, which was in Latin and French, see Myers, Manual of Collections of Treaties, 58–61. The relevant clauses of the Treaty of Utrecht regarding fishing are Articles 12 and 13, which follow in translation (from British and Foreign State Papers, XXXV, 842–43):

XII. The most Christian King shall take care to have delivered to the Queen of Great Britain, on the same day that the ratifications of this Treaty shall be exchanged, solemn and authentic letter, or instruments, by virtue whereof it shall appear that the Island of St. Christophers is to be possessed alone hereafter by British subjects, likewise all Nova Scotia or Accadie, with its ancient boundaries, as also the city of Port Royal, now called Annapolis Royal, and all other things in those parts, which depend on the said lands and islands, together with the dominion, propriety, and possession of the said islands, lands, and places, and all rights whatsoever, by Treaties, or by any other way obtained, which the most Christian King, the crown of France, or any the subjects thereof, have hitherto had to the said islands, lands, and places, and the inhabitants of the same, are yielded and made over to the Queen of Great Britain, and to her crown for ever, as the most Christian King doth at present yield and make over all the

particulars abovesaid; and that in such ample manner and form, that the subjects of the most Christian King shall hereafter be excluded from all kind of fishing in the said seas, bays, and other places, on the coasts of Nova Scotia, that is to say, on those which lie towards the east, within 30 leagues, beginning from the island commonly called Sable, inclusively, and thence stretching along towards the south-west.

XIII. The island called Newfoundland, with the adjacent islands, shall from this time forward belong of right wholly to Britain; and to that end the town and fortress of Placentia and whatever other places in the said island are in the possession of the French, shall be yielded and given up, within 7 months from the exchange of the ratifications of this Treaty, or sooner if possible, by the most Christian King, to those who have a commission from the Queen of Great Britain for that purpose. Nor shall the most Christian King, his heirs and successors, or any of their subjects, at any time hereafter lay claim to any right to the said island and islands, or to any part of it or them. Moreover it shall not be lawful for the subjects of France to fortify any place in the said Island of Newfoundland, or to erect any buildings there, besides stages made of boards and huts necessary and usual for drying of fish; or to resort to the said island, beyond the time necessary for fishing and drying of fish. But it shall be allowed to the subjects of France to catch fish, and to dry them on land, in that part only, and in no other besides that of the said Island of Newfoundland, which stretches from the place called Cape Bonavista to the northern point of the said island, and from thence running down by the western side, reaches as far as the place called Point Riche. But the island called Cape Breton, as also all others, both in the mouth of the River St. Lawrence and in the gulf of the same name, shall hereafter belong of right to the French; and the most Christian King shall have all manner of liberty to fortify any place or places there.

Note Regarding Articles 11 and 12

The treaty is here printed as it was originally signed, with the numbering of the articles unchanged. The very early records and prints in the United States were in this form; and on June 7, 1779, original Article 31 was referred to in Congress by its original number (Journals, XIV, 696). Very soon thereafter, however, and certainly from 1781 on, the prints of the treaty omit Articles 11 and 12 from the text and renumber the articles following so that original Article 13 becomes 11, and so on; indeed the signed treaty has, in pencil, a marginal note to Articles 11 and 12, reading, "to be omitted, & the subsequent numbers changed accordingly." See the reference to various articles of this treaty in Article 22 of the Treaty of Amity and Commerce with the Netherlands of October 8, 1782 (Document 5). In France, however, the very earliest prints, of October, 1778, had no reference to original Articles 11 and 12 (Doniol, III, 521; and see a facsimile of the French print following page 554). Accordingly the article numbers bracketed in the text, from 11 to 31, inclusive, are those of usual reference.

The congressional ratification of May 4, 1778, was complete and unconditional. The next day, however, Congress (by a vote of seven States to two, with one State partially represented but not counted) expressed the desire that Articles 11 and 12 "be revoked and utterly expunged" (Journals, XI, 460; there can be no doubt that this was the vote taken, although the original record in 1 C. C. Papers, XVI, is crossed with three strokes of the pen). While the American Commissioners were instructed accordingly, their formal authority was

not at hand on July 17, 1778, and the ratifications then exchanged recited the entire treaty; although at that time the omission of the two articles received the verbal assent of Count de Vergennes (Wharton, Diplomatic Correspondence, II, 651). It had been discussed even before the signature of the treaty (*ibid.*, 481–82, 485).

Under date of September 1, 1778, Articles 11 and 12 were formally suppressed pursuant to the declarations given below. The original French declaration, which is in French only, and a copy of the American declaration (which is said to be in part in the handwriting of Franklin) are in the Department of State file; but the copy is neither correct nor complete. There is now also in the file a facsimile of the original American declaration, obtained from the French archives; and from this, which is in both languages, the text here is printed. No reference to these declarations has been found in the Journals of Congress, although they are printed in the Library of Congress edition (XI, 461); it is there stated that they are not mentioned in the correspondence of the time; but it appears that the actual exchange of the declarations took place on November 2, 1778, and a copy of the French declaration was transmitted to Congress on November 7 (Wharton, Diplomatic Correspondence, II, 817, 819, 829, 830). With his letter of August 10, 1780, Franklin sent "copies of the instruments" to James Lovell, of the Committee of Foreign Affairs, referring to the numbering of the articles (*ibid.*, IV, 27); and Luzerne made a formal communication to Congress on September 15, 1780, stating that "some American merchants" did not know that Articles 11 and 12 had been suppressed (*ibid.*, IV, 57).

The translation of the French declaration here printed is from that made by John Pintard, which is in the Department of State file; it is substantially the same as that in the Statutes at Large and in various treaty collections.

Numerous translations from the French signed by John Pintard are among the Continental Congress papers. He was born May 18, 1759, was nephew to Elias Boudinot of New Jersey (President of the Continental Congress from 1782 to 1783), was a prominent citizen of New York, and founded the New York Historical Society in 1804. He died June 21, 1844 (James Grant Wilson, John Pintard, Founder of the New York Historical Society).

Le Congrès général des Etats unis de l'Amérique Septentrionale ayant represente au Roi que l'éxécution de l'Article onze du Traité d'amitié et de commerce signé le six du mois de fevrier dernier pourroit entrainer des inconvenients après soi, et ayant desiré en conséquence que cet article demeurât suprimé, consentant en échange que l'Article douze soit également regardé comme non avenu, Sa Majesté, pour donner aux Etats unis de l'Amérique Septentrionale une nouvelle preuve de

[Translation]

The General Congress of the United States of North America having represented to the King that the execution of the eleventh article of the Treaty of Amity and Commerce, signed the sixth of February last, might be productive of inconveniences, and having therefore desired the suppression of this article, consenting in return that the twelfth article shall likewise be considered of no effect, His Majesty, in order to give a new proof of his affection, as also of his desire to consolidate the union and

son affection, ainsi que de son desir de consolider l'union et la bonne correspondance etablies entre les deux Etats, a bien voulu avoir égard à leurs représentations; En consequence Sa M^{té} a déclaré et déclare par les présentes qu'Elle consent à la Suppression des articles onze et douze susmentionnés, et que son intention est, qu'ils soient regardés comme n'ayant jamais été compris dans le Traité signé le six fevrier dernier.

Fait à Versailles le premier jour du mois de Septembre mil sept cent soixante et dixhuit.

GRAVIER DE VERGENNES

good correspondence established between the two States, has been pleased to consider their representations. His Majesty has consequently declared, and does declare by these presents, that he consents to the suppression of the eleventh and twelfth articles aforementioned, and that his intention is that they be considered as having never been comprehended in the treaty signed the sixth of February last.

Done at Versailles the first day of the month of September, one thousand seven hundred and seventy-eight.

GRAVIER DE VERGENNES

DÉCLARATION.

Le Roi trés Chretien ayant voulu avoir égard aux Representations que lui a faites le Congrés-général de l'Amerique Septentrionale, relativement a l'Article onziéme du Traité de Commerce, signé le six Février de la presente Année, et sa Majesté ayant consenti en consequence que le dit Article demeurat suprimé à Condition que l'Article douzieme du même Traité fut également regardé comme nonavenu; le Congrés-général a déclaré de son Coté, et déclare qu'il consent à la suppression des Articles onze & douze susmentionnés et son Intention est qu'ils soient régardée comme n'ayant jamais été compris dans le Traité signé le six Fevrier.

Fait à Versailles le premier Septembre mil Sept cens Soixante dix huit./.

B FRANKLIN
ARTHUR LEE
JOHN ADAMS.

DECLARATION.

The most Christian King having been pleased to regard the Representation made to him by the general Congress of North America, relating to the eleventh Article of the Treaty of Commerce signed the sixth of February in the present Year, and his Majesty having therefore consented that the said Article should be suppressed on Condition that the twelfth Article of the same Treaty be equally regarded as of none Effect; the general Congress hath declar'd on their Part, and do declare, that they consent to the suppression of the eleventh and twelfth Articles of the abovementioned Treaty, and that their Intention is, that these Articles be regarded as having never been comprised in the Treaty sign'd the Sixth of February.

Done at Versailles this first of September One thousand seven hundred and seventy eight.

Treaty Series, No. 82
8 Statutes at Large, 6–11

2

FRANCE : FEBRUARY 6, 1778

Treaty of Alliance, signed at Paris February 6, 1778. Original in English and French; but "originally composed and concluded in the French Language" (see the attestation clause).
Ratified by the United States May 4, 1778. Ratified by France July 16, 1778. Ratifications exchanged at Paris (or Versailles) July 17, 1778. Not proclaimed; but see observations as to publication of the Treaty of Amity and Commerce of the same date (Document 1).

Treaty of Alliance	Traité d'Alliance éventuelle et déffensive
The most Christian King and the United States of North America, to wit, Newhampshire, Massachusetts Bay, Rhodesisland, Connecticut, Newyork, New Jersey, Pennsylvania, Delaware, Maryland, Virginia, North Carolina, South Carolina, and Georgia, having this Day concluded a Treaty of amity and Commerce,[1] for the réciprocal advantage of their Subjects and Citizens have thought it necessary to take into consideration the means of strongthening those engagements and of rondring them useful to the safety and tranquility of the two parties, particularly in case Great Britain in Resentment of that connection and of the good correspondence which is the object of the said Treaty, should	Le Roi Très Chrétien et les Etats-unis de l'Amerique Septentrionale, savoir New-hampshire, la Baye de Massachusset, Rhode-Island Connecticut, New-york, New-Jersey, Pensylvanie, Delaware, Maryland, Virginie, Caroline Septentrionale, Caroline Meridionale et Georgie; ayant conclu ce jourd'huy un Traité d'Amitié, de bonne intelligence et de commerce,[1] pour l'avantage réciproque de leurs Sujets et Citoyens, ils ont cru devoir prendre en considération les moyens de resserrer leurs liaisons, et de les rendre utiles à la Sureté et à la tranquilité des deux Parties, notament dans le cas où la Grande Bretagne, en haine de ces mêmes liaisons et de la bonne correspondance qui for-

[1] Document 1.

115605°—31—vol. 2——5

break the Peace with france, either by direct hostilities, or by hindring her commerce and navigation, in a manner contrary to the Rights of Nations, and the Peace subsisting between the two Crowns; and his Majesty and the said united States having resolved in that Case to join their Councils and efforts against the Enterprises of their common Enemy, the respective Plenipotentiaries, impower'd to concert the Clauses & conditions proper to fulfil the said Intentions, have, after the most mature Deliberation, concluded and determined on the following Articles.

ment l'objet du dit Traité, se porteroit à rompre la paix avec la france, soit en l'attaquant hostilement, soit en troublant son commerce et sa navigation, d'une maniere contraire au droit des gens et à la paix subsistante entre les deux Couronnes; Et Sa Majesté et les dits Etats-unis ayant résolu éventuellement d'unir, dans le cas prévû, leurs conseils et leurs efforts contre les entreprises de leur ennemi commun, les Plenipotentiaires respectifs, chargés de concerter les clauses et conditions propres à remplir leurs intentions, ont, après la plus mure délibération, conclu et arresté les points et articles qui s'ensuivent.

Art. 1.

If War should break out betwan france and Great Britain, during the continuence of the present War betwan the United States and England, his Majesty and the said united States, shall make it a common cause, and aid each other mutually with their good Offices, their Counsels, and their forces, according to the exigence of Conjunctures as becomes good & faithful Allies.

Article premier.

Si la guerre éclate entre la france et la Grande Brétagne, pendant la durée de la guerre actuelle entre les Etats-unis et l'Angleterre, Sa Majesté et les dits Etats-unis feront cause commune et s'entr'aideront mutuellement de leurs bons offices, de leurs conseils et de leurs forces, selon l'exigence des conjonctures, ainsy qu'il convient à de bons et fideles Alliés.

Art. 2.

The essential and direct End of the present defensive alliance is to maintain effectually the liberty, Sovereignty, and independance absolute and unlimited

Article Second.

Le but essentiel et direct de la présente alliance deffensive, est de maintenir efficacement la liberte, la souveraineté, et l'indépendance absolue et illimitée

of the said united States, as well in Matters of Gouvernement as of commerce.

des dits Etats unis, tant en matiére politique que de commerce.

ART. 3.

The two contracting Parties shall each on its own Part, and in the manner it may judge most proper, make all the efforts in its Power, against their common Ennemy, in order to attain the end proposed.

ARTICLE TROIS.

Les deux Parties contractantes feront chacune de leur côté, et de la maniére qu'elles jugeront plus convenable, tous les efforts, qui seront en leur pouvoir, contre leur ennemi commun, afin d'atteindre au but qu'elles se proposent.

ART. 4.

The contracting Parties agree that in case either of them should form any particular Enterprise in which the concurrence of the other may be desired, the Party whose concurrence is desired shall readily, and with good faith, join to act in concert for that Purpose, as far as circumstances and its own particular Situation will permit; and in that case, they shall regulate by a particular Convention the quantity and kind of Succour to be furnished, and the Time and manner of its being brought into action, as well as the advantages which are to be its Compensation.

ARTICLE QUATRE.

Les Parties contractantes sont convenues que dans le cas où l'une d'entre Elles formeroit quelqu'entreprise particuliére, pour laquelle elle désireroit le concours de l'autre, celle ci, se prêteroit de bonne foi à un concert sur cet objet, autant que les circonstances et sa propre Situation pourront le lui permettre, et dans ce cas, on reglera par une Convention particuliére la portée des Secours à fournir, et le tems et la maniére de le faire agir, ainsy que les avantages destinés à en former la compensation.

ART. 5.

If the united States should think fit to attempt the Reduction of the British Power remaining in the Northern Parts of America, or the Islands of Bermudas, those Contries or Islands in case of Success, shall be

ARTICLE CINQ.

Si les Etats-unis jugent à propos de tenter la reduction des Isles Bermudes et des parties septentrionales de l'Amérique qui sont encore au pouvoir de la Grande Bretagne, les dites Isles et Contrées, en cas de Succès,

confederated with or dependant upon the said united States.

entreront dans la confedération ou seront dépendantes des dits Etats-unis.

ART. 6.

The Most Christian King renounces for ever the possession of the Islands of Bermudas as well as of any part of the continent of North america which before the treaty of Paris in 1763. or in virtue of that Treaty, were acknowledged to belong to the Crown of Great Britain, or to the united States heretofore called British Colonies, or which are at this Time or have lately been under the Power of The King and Crown of Great Britain.

ARTICLE SIX.

Le Roi très Chrétien renonce à posseder jamais les Bermudes ni aucune des parties du Continent de l'Amerique Septentrionalle qui, avant le Traité de Paris de mil sept cent soixante trois, ou en vertu de ce Traité, ont été reconnuës appartenir à la Couronne de la Grande Bretagne ou aux Etats-unis, qu'on appelloit ci devant Colonies Britanniques, ou qui sont maintenant ou ont été récemment sous la Jurisdiction et sous le pouvoir de la Couronne de la Grande Bretagne.

ART. 7.

If his Most Christian Majesty shall think proper to attack any of the Islands situated in the Gulph of Mexico, or near that Gulph, which are at present under the Power of Great Britain, all the said Isles, in case of success, shall appertain to the Crown of france.

ARTICLE SEPT.

Si Sa Majesté Très Chrétienne juge à propos d'attaquer aucune des Isles situées dans le Golphe de Méxique ou près du dit Golphe, qui sont actuellement au pouvoir de la Grande Bretagne, toutes les dites Isles, en cas de succès, appartiendront à la Couronne de France.

ART. 8.

Neither of the two Parties shall conclude either Truce or Peace with Great Britain, without the formal consent of the other first obtain'd; and they mutually engage not to lay down their arms, until the Independence of the united states shall have been for-

ARTICLE HUIT.

Aucune des deux Parties ne pourra conclure ni treve ni paix avec la Grande Brétagne, sans le consentement préalable et formel del'autre Partie, et Elles s'engagent mutuellement à ne mettre bas les armes, que lorsque l'indépendance des dits Etats-unis aura été

mally or tacitly assured by the Treaty or Treaties that shall terminate the War.

ART. 9.

The contracting Parties declare, that being resolved to fulfil each on its own Part the clauses and conditions of the present Treaty of alliance, according to its own power and circumstances, there shall be no after claim of compensation on one side or the other whatever may be the event of the War.

ART. 10.

The Most Christian King and the United states, agree to invite or admit other Powers who may have received injuries from England to make common cause with them, and to accede to the present alliance, under such conditions as shall be freely agreed to and settled between all the Parties.

ART. 11.

The two Parties guarantee mutually from the present time and forever, against all other powers, to wit, the united states to his most Christian Majesty the present Possessions of the Crown of france in America as well as those which it may acquire by the future Treaty of peace: and his most Christian Majesty guarantees on his part to the united states, their liberty, Sovereignty, and Independence absolute, and unlimited,

assurée formellement ou tacitement par le Traité ou les Traités qui termineront la guerre.

ARTICLE NEUF.

Les Parties contractantes déclarent, qu'etant resolues de remplir chacune de son côté les clauses et conditions du présent Traité d'alliance selon son pouvoir et les circonstances, Elles n'auront aucune repetition, ni aucun dedommagement à se demander réciproquement, quelque puisse etre l'evenement de la guerre.

ARTICLE DIX.

Le Roi Très Chretien et les Etats-unis sont convenus d'inviter de concert ou d'admettre les Puissances, qui auront des griefs contre l'Angleterre, à faire cause commune avec Eux, et à accéder à la présente alliance, sous les conditions qui seront librement agrées et convenuës entre toutes les Parties.

ARTICLE ONZE

Les deux Parties se garantissent mutuellement dès à present et pour toujours envers et contre tous, savoir les Etats-unis à Sa Majesté très Chrétienne les possessions actuelles de la Couronne de France en Amérique, ainsy que celles qu'Elle pourra acquérir par le futur Traité de paix; Et Sa Majesté Très Chretienne garantit de son côté aux Etats-unis leur liberté, leur souveraineté et leur indépendance absolue et illimitée,

as well in Matters of Government as commerce and also thair Possessions, and the additions or conquests that their Confedération may obtain during the war, from any of the Dominions now or heretofore possessed by Great Britain in North America, conformable to the 5th & 6th articles above written, the whole as their Possessions shall be fixed and assured to the said States at the moment of the cessation of their present War with England.

Art. 12.

In order to fix more precisely the sense and application of the preceding article, the Contracting Parties declare, that in case of a rupture between france and England, the reciprocal Guarantee, declared in the said article shall have its full force and effect the moment such War shall break out; and if such rupture shall not take place, the mutual obligations of the said guarantee shall not commence, until the moment of the cessation of the present War between the united states and England shall have ascertained their Possessions.

Art. 13.

The present Treaty shall be ratified on both sides and the Ratifications shall be exchanged in the space of six months, or sooner if possible.

tant en matiére de politique que de commerce, ainsy que leurs possessions et les accroissements ou conquêtes que leur confédération pourra se procurer pendant la guerre, d'aucun des Domaines maintenant ou ci devant possedés par la Grande Bretagne dans l'Amérique Septentrionale, conformément aux articles cinq et six ci dessus, et tout ainsy que leurs possessions seront fixées et assurées aux dits Etats, au moment de la cessation de leur guerre actuelle contre l'Angleterre.

Article douze.

Affin de fixer plus précisément le sens et l'application de l'article précédent, les Parties contractantes déclarent qu'en cas de rupture entre la france et l'Angleterre, la garantie réciproque enoncée dans le sus dit article, aura toute sa force et valeur du moment où la guerre éclatera, et si la rupture n'avoit pas lieu, les obligations mutuelles de la ditte garantie, ne commenceroient, que du moment sus dit, où la cessation de la guerre actuelle entre les Etats unis et l'Angleterre, aura fixé leurs possessions.

Article treize.

Le present Traité sera ratiffié de part et d'autre et les ratiffications seront échangées dans l'espace de six mois ou plustôt, si faire se peut.

In faith where of the respective Plenipotentiaries, to wit on the part of the most Christian King Conrad Alexander Gerard royal syndic of the City of Strasbourgh & Secretary of his majestys Council of State and on the part of the United States Benjamin Franklin Deputy to the General Congress from the State of Pensylvania and President of the Convention of the same state, Silas Deane heretofore Deputy from the State of Connecticut & Arthur Lee Councellor at Law have signed the above Articles both in the French and English Languages declaring Nevertheless that the present Treaty was originally composed and concluded in the French Language, and they have hereunto affixed their Seals

Done at Paris, this sixth Day of February, one thousand seven hundred and seventy eight.

En foi de quoi les Plenipotentiares respectifs savoir de la part du Roi Très Chretien le Sr Conrad, Alexandre Gerard Sindic royal de la ville de Strasbourg et Sécrétaire du Conseil d'Etat de Sa Majesté, et de la part des Etats-unis les Srs Benjamin franklin Deputé au Congrès général de la part de l'Etat de Pensylvanie et President de la Convention du meme Etat, Siles Deane Cy devant Député de l'Etat de Connecticut et Arthur Leé *Conseiller ès loix* ont signé les articles ci dessus, tant en langue françoise qu'en langue Angloise, déclarant néanmoins que le present Traité a été originairement redigé et arrêté en langue françoise, et ils les ont munis du cachet de leurs armes.

Fait à Paris le sixieme jour du mois de fevrier mil sept cent soixante dixhuit./.

C. A. Gerard [Seal] B Franklin [Seal] Silas Deane [Seal] Arthur Lee [Seal]

NOTES

As to the ratifications and exchange of ratifications of this treaty, and also as to the publication thereof, see the notes to the Treaty of Amity and Commerce (Document 1).

The United States instrument of ratification is copied in 135 C. C. Papers, I; also in Journals, XI, 462–63. A facsimile of the instrument, received from the French archives, is now in the Department of State file. It is similar in form to the United States instrument of ratification of the Treaty of Amity and Commerce; unlike the corresponding French instrument of ratification, however, it does not include the Act Separate and Secret (Document 3); as copied in 135 C. C. Papers, I, the instrument includes both agreements.

The opening words of this treaty and of the Treaty of Amity and Commerce are similar; in this treaty they are "The most Christian King and the United States of North America."

The principle of the *alternat* would now require that in the text of that one of the two signed originals of a bilateral treaty which was intended for this country, the United States should be named first and the other party to the treaty second. In the eighteenth century this was not the case; there was then a relative precedence in this and other respects, as among certain monarchs (see Satow, Diplomatic Practice, I, Ch. IV; Crandall, Treaties, Their Making and Enforcement, 5, 32); and a monarch was named in a treaty before a republic (Diplomatic Correspondence, 1783–1789, I, 380–81).

The comment in Moore's Digest, V, 181, refers to the fact of such rank in various early treaties with Great Britain; but the practice prevailed in most of the European treaties made by the United States prior to 1815, including those with France of 1778, 1782, 1783, and 1788, the Netherlands of 1782, Sweden of 1783, Prussia of 1785 and 1799, and Spain of 1795 and 1802.

So far as concerns precedence between texts when there were two, the practice varied during the period in question. In the three treaties with France of February 6, 1778, and in the treaty with Spain of 1795, the English text is in the left column of the originals in the Department of State archives; but in the treaties with the Netherlands of 1782, with Prussia of 1785 and 1799, and with Spain of 1802, the foreign text is to the left (column or page) of the English.

Note Regarding Article 6

The Treaty of Paris was signed, in French, on February 10, 1763. The parties were France, Great Britain, and Spain, and Portugal acceded. For the text see Von Martens, Recueil de traités, 2d ed., I, 104–21.

Various articles, perhaps even the whole treaty, are relevant either here or in respect of Article 10 of the Treaty of Amity and Commerce (Document 1).

Those which follow in translation (from Chalmers, A Collection of Treaties between Great Britain and Other Powers, I, 471–75, 479–80) are Articles 4–9 and Article 20:

IV. His most Christian Majesty renounces all pretensions, which he has heretofore formed, or might form, to Nova Scotia or Acadia, in all its parts, and guaranties the whole of it, and with all its dependencies, to the King of Great Britain: moreover, his most Christian Majesty cedes and guaranties to his said Britannic Majesty, in full right, Canada, with all its dependencies, as well as the Island of Cape Breton, and all the other islands and coasts in the gulph and river St. Laurence, and, in general, every thing that depends on the said countries, lands, islands, and coasts, with the sovereignty, property, possession, and all rights, acquired by treaty or otherwise, which the most Christian King, and the crown of France, have had till now over the said countries, islands, lands, places, coasts, and their inhabitants, so that the most Christian King cedes and makes over the whole to the said King, and to the crown of Great Britain, and that in the most ample manner and form, without restriction, and without any liberty to depart from the said cession and guaranty, under any pretence, or to disturb Great Britain in the possessions above-mentioned. His Britannic Majesty, on his side, agrees to grant the liberty of the Catholic religon to the inhabitants of Canada: he will consequently give the most precise and most effectual orders,

that his new Roman Catholic subjects may profess the worship of their religion, according to the rites of the Romish church, as far as the laws of Great Britain permit. His Britannic Majesty further agrees, that the French inhabitants, or others who had been subjects of the most Christian King in Canada, may retire, with all safety and freedom, wherever they shall think proper, and may sell their estates, provided it be to subjects of his Britannic Majesty, and bring away their effects, as well as their persons, without being restrained in their emigration, under any pretence whatsoever, except that of debts, or of criminal prosecutions: the term limited for this emigration shall be fixed to the space of eighteen months, to be computed from the day of the exchange of the ratifications of the present treaty.

V. The subjects of France shall have the liberty of fishing and drying, on a part of the coasts of the Island of Newfoundland, such as it is specified in the XIIIth article of the treaty of Utrecht; which article is renewed and confirmed by the present treaty (except what relates to the island of Cape Breton, as well as to the other islands and coasts in the mouth and in the gulph of St. Laurence:) and his Britannic Majesty consents to leave to the subjects of the most Christian King the liberty of fishing in the gulph St. Laurence, on condition that the subjects of France do not exercise the said fishery but at the distance of three leagues from all the coasts belonging to Great Britain, as well those of the continent, as those of the islands situated in the said gulph St. Laurence. And as to what relates to the fishery on the coasts of the island of Cape Breton out of the said gulph, the subjects of the most Christian King shall not be permitted to exercise the said fishery but at the distance of fifteen leagues from the coasts of the island of Cape Breton; and the fishery on the coasts of Nova Scotia or Acadia, and every where else out of the said gulph, shall remain on the foot of former treaties.

VI. The King of Great Britain cedes the islands of St. Pierre and Miquelon, in full right, to his most Christian Majesty, to serve as a shelter to the French fishermen: and his said most Christian Majesty engages not to fortify the said islands; to erect no buildings upon them, but merely for the convenience of the fishery; and to keep upon them a guard of fifty men only for the police.

VII. In order to re-establish peace on solid and durable foundations, and to remove for ever all subject of dispute with regard to the limits of the British and French territories on the continent of America; it is agreed, that, for the future, the confines between the dominions of his Britannic Majesty, and those of his most Christian Majesty, in that part of the world, shall be fixed irrevocably by a line drawn along the middle of the river Mississippi, from its source to the river Iberville, and from thence, by a line drawn along the middle of this river, and the lakes Maurepas and Pontchartrain, to the sea; and for this purpose, the most Christian King cedes in full right, and guaranties to his Britannic Majesty, the river and port of the Mobile, and every thing which he possesses, or ought to possess, on the left side of the river Mississippi, except the town of New Orleans, and the island in which it is situated, which shall remain to France; provided that the navigation of the river Mississippi shall be equally free, as well to the subjects of Great Britain as to those of France, in its whole breadth and length, from its source to the sea, and expresly that part which is between the said island of New Orleans and the right bank of that river, as well as the passage both in and out of its mouth. It is further stipulated, that the vessels belonging to the subjects of either nation shall not be stopped, visited, or subjected to the payment of any duty whatsoever. The stipulations, inserted in the IVth article, in favour of the inhabitants of Canada, shall also take place with regard to the inhabitants of the countries ceded by this article.

VIII. The King of Great Britain shall restore to France the islands of Guadeloupe, of Marie Galante, of Desirade, of Martinico, and of Belleisle; and the fortresses of these islands shall be restored in the same condition they were in when they were conquered by the British arms; provided that his Britannic Majesty's subjects, who shall have settled in the said islands, or those who shall have any commercial affairs to settle there, or in the other places restored to France by the present treaty, shall have liberty to sell their lands and their estates, to settle their affairs, to recover their debts, and to bring away their effects, as well as their persons, on board vessels, which they shall be permitted to send

to the said islands, and other places restored as above, and which shall serve for this use only, without being restrained on account of their religion, or under any other pretence whatsoever, except that of debts or of criminal prosecutions: and for this purpose, the term of eighteen months is allowed to his Britannic Majesty's subjects, to be computed from the day of the exchange of the ratifications of the present treaty; but, as the liberty, granted to his Britannic Majesty's subjects, to bring away their persons and their effects, in vessels of their nation, may be liable to abuses, if precautions were not taken to prevent them; it has been expressly agreed between his Britannic Majesty and his most Christian Majesty, that the number of English vessels, which shall have leave to go to the said islands and places restored to France, shall be limited, as well as the number of tons of each one; that they shall go in ballast; shall set sail at a fixed time; and shall make one voyage only, all the effects, belonging to the English, being to be embarked at the same time. It has been further agreed, that his most Christian Majesty shall cause the necessary passports to be given to the said vessels; that, for the greater security, it shall be allowed to place two French clerks, or guards, in each of the said vessels, which shall be visited in the landing places and ports of the said islands, and places, restored to France, and that the merchandise, which shall be found therein, shall be confiscated.

IX. The most Christian King cedes and guaranties to his Britannic Majesty, in full right, the islands of Grenada, and of the Grenadines, with the same stipulations in favour of the inhabitants of this colony, inserted in the IVth article for those of Canada: and the partition of the islands, called Neutral, is agreed and fixed, so that those of St. Vincent, Dominica, and Tobago, shall remain in full right to Great Britain, and that of St. Lucia shall be delivered to France, to enjoy the same likewise in full right; and the high contracting parties guaranty the partition so stipulated.

XX. In consequence of the restitution stipulated in the preceding article, his Catholic Majesty cedes and guaranties, in full right, to his Britannic Majesty, Florida, with Fort St. Augustin, and the Bay of Pensacola, as well as all that Spain possesses on the continent of North America, to the east, or to the southeast, of the river Mississippi; and, in general, every thing that depends on the said countries, and lands, with the sovereignty, property, possession, and all rights, acquired by treaties or otherwise, which the Catholic King, and the crown of Spain, have had, till now, over the said countries, lands, places, and their inhabitants; so that the Catholic King cedes and makes over the whole to the said King, and to the crown of Great Britain, and that in the most ample manner and form. His Britannic Majesty agrees, on his side, to grant to the inhabitants of the countries, above ceded, the liberty of the Catholic religion: he will consequently give the most express and the most effectual orders, that his new Roman Catholic subjects may profess the worship of their religion, according to the rites of the Romish church, as far as the laws of Great Britain permit: his Britannic Majesty further agrees, that the Spanish inhabitants, or others, who had been subjects of the Catholic King in the said countries, may retire, with all safety and freedom, wherever they think proper; and may sell their estates, provided it be to his Britannic Majesty's subjects, and bring away their effects, as well as their persons, without being restrained in their emigration, under any pretence whatsoever, except that of debts, or of criminal prosecutions: the term limited for this emigration being fixed to the space of eighteen months, to be computed from the day of the exchange of the ratifications of the present treaty. It is moreover stipulated, that his Catholic Majesty shall have power to cause all the effects, that may belong to him, to be brought away, whether it be artillery or other things.

Treaty Series, No. 83
17 Statutes at Large, 795-96

3

FRANCE : FEBRUARY 6, 1778

Act Separate and Secret, signed at Paris February 6, 1778. Original in English and French.
Ratified by the United States May 4, 1778. Ratified by France July 16, 1778. Ratifications exchanged at Paris (or Versailles) July 17, 1778. Not proclaimed.

Act separate and secret.

The most Christian King declares in consequence of the intimate union which subsists between him and the King of spain, that in concluding with the united states of America this Treaty of amity and commerce,[1] and that of eventual and defensive alliance,[2] his Majesty hath intended and intends to reserve expressly, as he reserves by this present separate and secret act, to his said Catholick Majesty, the Power of acceding to the said Treatys, and to participate in their stipulations at such time as he shall judge proper. It being well understood nevertheless, that if any of the Stipulations of the said Treatys are not agreable to the King of Spain, his Catholick Majesty may propose other conditions analogous to the principal aim of the alliance and conformable to the Rules of equality, reciprocity & friendship.

Acte Séparé et Secret.

Le Roi très Chrétien déclare en conséquence de l'union intime qui subsiste entre lui et le Roi d'Espagne, qu'en concluant avec les Etats-unis de l'Amérique Septentrionale le traité d'amitié et de commerce [1] et celui d'alliance eventuelle et deffensive,[2] Sa Majesté a entendu et entend reserver expressement, comme elle reserve par le présent acte Séparé et Secret à Sa dite Majesté Catholique la faculté d'acceder aux dits Traités, et de participer à Leurs Stipulations, dans quelque tems qu'Elle le juge à propos, bien entendu néanmoins que si quelques unes des Stipulations des dits Traités ne convenoient point au Roi d'Espagne, Sa Majesté Catholique seroit Maitresse de proposer d'autres conditions analogues au but principal de l'Alliance, et conformes aux loix de l'égalité, de la réciprocité et de l'amitié.

[1] Document 1.

[2] Document 2.

The Deputies of the united states in the name of their constituents, accept the present Declaration in its full extent and the Deputy of the said states who is fully impowerd to treat with Spain, promises to sign on the first Requisition of his Catholic Majesty, the act or acts necessary to communicate to him the Stipulations of the Treaties above written; and the said Deputy shall endeavour in good faith the adjustment of the points in which the King of spain may propose any alteration, conformable to the principles of equality, reciprocity and the most sincere and perfect amity; he the said Deputy not doubting but that the Person or Persons impower'd by his Catholic Majesty to treat with the United States will do the same with regard to any Alterations of the same kind that may be thought necessary by the said Plenipotentiary of the United States. In Faith whereof the respective Plenipotentiaries have signed the present separate and secret Article, and affixed to the same their Seals.

Done at Paris, this sixth Day of February, one thousand seven hundred and seventy-eight.

C. A. Gerard [Seal] B Franklin [Seal]

Les Députés des Etats-unis au nom de leurs commettans acceptent la présente Déclaration dans toute son étendue, et le Député des dits Etats spécialement chargé des pleinpouvoirs, pour traiter avec la Couronne d'Espagne, promet de signer à la premiére réquisition de Sa Majesté Catholique l'acte ou les actes nécéssaires, pour lui rendre communes les Stipulations des Traités ci dessus relatés, et le dit Député se prêtera de bonne foi à l'ajustement des points auxquels le Roi d'Espagne voudroit apporter quelques changemens, conformément aux principes de l'égalité, de la réciprocité et de l'amitié la plus parfaite et la plus sincére, ne doutant pas le dit Député que la personne ou les personnes qui seront autorisées par le Roi Catholique à traiter avec les Etats unis, n'en usent de même, relativement aux changemens de la même nature que le dit Plenipotentiaire des Etats unis pourra juger nécéssaires

En foi de quoi les Plénipotentiaires respectifs ont signé le présent article Separé et Secret, et y ont apposé le cachet de leurs armes.

Fait à Paris le sixieme jour du mois de fevrier mil sept cent soixante dixhuit./.

Silas Deane [Seal]

Arthur Lee

Deputé plenipotentiaire pour la France et l'Espagne [Seal]

NOTES

As to the ratifications and exchange of ratifications of this act, see generally the notes to the two preceding documents. The instrument of ratification of the Treaty of Alliance on the part of France includes this act also. The United States instrument of ratification of this act is a separate document. A facsimile thereof, received from the French archives, is now in the Department of State file; in form it is similar to the ratifications of the Treaty of Amity and Commerce and the Treaty of Alliance. In 135 C. C. Papers, I, the United States instrument is set forth as including both the Treaty of Alliance and the Act Separate and Secret; in this regard the copy in Journals, XI, 462–63, is more correct.

Treaty Series, No. 83¼
8 Statutes at Large, 614-17

4

FRANCE : JULY 16, 1782

Contract between the King and the Thirteen United States of North America, signed at Versailles July 16, 1782. Original in French. Ratified by the United States January 22, 1783. Ratified by France December 21, 1783. Ratifications exchanged at Paris (or Versailles) about January 1, 1784. Not proclaimed; but on April 26, 1783 (April 24 erroneously in Journals, 1823 ed., IV, 194), Congress voted an "Address to the States," which, as published, contained as "Paper No. V" a copy of the ratification of this contract by Congress on January 22, 1783, but reciting the contract in English as if that were the language of the original (see Journals, XXIV, 285-90). That address was widely published, and at least seven prints of it are extant.

Contrat entre le Roi et les Treize Etats-Unis de l'Amérique Septentrionale.

Le Roi ayant bien voulu avoir égard aux demandes qui lui ont été faites au nom et de la part des Provinces-Unies de l'Amérique Septentrionale, de les assister dans l'état de guerre et d'invasion où elles gémissent depuis plusieurs années, et Sa Majesté après avoir fait avec lesdites Provinces Confédérées un Traité d'amitié et de Commerce[1] en datte de 6 Fevrier 1778. ayant eû la bonté de les soutenir non seulement par ses forces de terre et de mer, Mais encore par des avances de secours pécuniaires aussi abondans qu'efficaces, dans la crise et le besoin où elles étoient réduites, il a été

[Translation]

Contract between the King and the Thirteen United States of North America.

The King having been pleased to attend to the requests made to him in the name and on behalf of the united provinces of North America for assistance in the war and invasion under which they had for several years groaned; and His Majesty, after entering into a Treaty of Amity and Commerce[1] with the said confederated provinces on the 6th of February, 1778, having had the goodness to support them, not only with his forces by land and sea, but also with advances of money, as abundant as they were effectual in the critical situation to which their affairs were re-

[1] Document 1.

jugé convenable et nécessaire de constater d'une maniere positive le montant desdites avances, les conditions sous lesquelles le Roi s'est porté à les faire, les époques auxquelles le Congrès desdits Etats-Unis s'est engagé de les rembourser au Trésor Royal de Sa Majesté, et d'éclaircir enfin cet objet de maniere à prévenir dans l'avenir toutes difficultés capables d'altérer la bonne harmonie que Sa Majesté est résolüe de maintenir et conserver entre Elle et lesdits Etats-Unis; Pour remplir un dessein aussi louable et dans la vüe d'affermir les liens de Commerce et d'amitié qui subsistent entre Sa Majesté et lesdits Etats-Unis; Nous Charles Gravier Comte de Vergennes &c^a Conseiller du Roi en tous ses Conseils, Commandeur de ses Ordres, Ministre et Secretaire d'Etat et de ses Commandemens et finances, muni des pleins pouvoirs de Sa Majesté à Nous donnés à l'effet des présentes.

Et Nous Benjamin Franklin Ministre plénipotentiaire des Etats-Unis de l'Amérique Septentrionale pareillement muni des pouvoirs du Congrès desdits Etats au même effet des présentes, après nous être düement communiqué nos pouvoirs respectifs, avons arrêté les articles qui suivent.

duced; it has been judged proper and necessary to state exactly the amount of those advances, the conditions on which the King made them, the periods at which the Congress of the United States have engaged to repay them to His Majesty's royal treasury, and, in fine, to state this matter in such a way as for the future to prevent all difficulties capable of interrupting the good harmony which His Majesty is resolved to maintain and preserve between him and the said United States. For executing so laudable a purpose, and with a view to strengthen the bands of amity and commerce which subsist between His Majesty and the said United States, we, Charles Gravier de Vergennes, etc., Counselor of the King in all his Councils, Commander of his Orders, Minister and Secretary of State, and of his Commands and Finances, vested with full powers of His Majesty to us given for this purpose—

And we, Benjamin Franklin, Minister Plenipotentiary of the United States of North America, in like manner vested with full powers of the Congress of the said States for the present purpose, after duly communicating our respective powers, have agreed to the following articles:

Article Ier

Il a été calculé et vérifié que les Sommes avancées à titre de prêt par Sa Majesté au Congrès desdits Etats-Unis pendant les années 1778. 1779. 1780. 1781. et la présente 1782. montent á la somme de Dix huit millions de livres argent de france suivant Vingt-une reconnoissances ci-dessous mentionnées que le Ministre soussigné du Congrès en a fournies en vertu de ses pouvoirs, Savoir:

La 1re du 28 Fevrier.. 1778. de..		750,000.	
La 2e du 19 May......	id.....	750,000.	
La 3e du 3. Août......	id.....	750,000.	3,000,000.
La 4e du 1er Novembre................	id.....	750,000.	
La 5me du 10 Juin.... 1779. de..		250,000.	
La 6e du 16 Septembre................	id.....	250,000.	
La 7e du 4. Octobre...	id.....	250,000.	1,000,000.
La 8e du 21. Décembre................	id.....	250,000.	
La 9me du 29 Fevrier.. 1780. de..		750,000.	
La 10e du 23 May.....	id.....	750,000.	
La 11e du 21 Juin.....	id.....	750,000.	4,000,000.
La 12e du 5. Octobre..	id.....	750,000.	
La 13e du 27 Novembre................	id.....	1,000,000.	
La 14me du 15 Fevrier. 1781. de..		750,000.	
La 15e du 15 May.....	id.....	750,000.	
La 16e du 15 Août.....	id.....	750,000.	
La 17e du 1er Octobre................	id.....	1,000,000.	4,000,000.
La 18e du 15 Novembre................	id.....	750,000.	
La 19me du 10. Avril.. 1782. de..		1,500,000.	
La 20 du 1er Juillet....	id.....	1,500,000.	6,000,000.
La 21 du 5 dudt mois..........		3,000,000.	
Somme égale à celle ci-dessus de Dix huit millions, Cy................			18,000,000.

Par lesquelles reconnoissances le Ministre susdit a promis au nom du Congrès et solidairement

Article 1

It is agreed and certified that the sums advanced by His Majesty to the Congress of the United States under the title of a loan, in the years 1778, 1779, 1780, 1781, and the present 1782, amount to the sum of eighteen million of livres, money of France, according to the following twenty-one receipts of the above-mentioned underwritten Minister of Congress, given in virtue of his full powers, to wit:

1.	28 February... 1778.......	750, 000	
2.	19 May .... do	750, 000	3, 000, 000
3.	3 August ..... do	750, 000	
4.	1 November.. do	750, 000	
5.	10 June .... 1779.......	250, 000	
6.	16 September.. do	250, 000	1, 000, 000
7.	4 October .... do	250, 000	
8.	21 December .. do	250, 000	
9.	29 February... 1780.......	750, 000	
10.	23 May .... do	750, 000	
11.	21 June .... do	750, 000	4, 000, 000
12.	5 October .... do	750, 000	
13.	27 November.. do	1, 000, 000	
14.	15 February ... 1781.	750, 000	
15.	15 May .... do	750, 000	
16.	15 August ..... do	750, 000	4, 000, 000
17.	1 August ..... do.........	1, 000, 000	
18.	15 November.. do	750, 000	
19.	10 April.... 1782..........	1, 500, 000	
20.	1 July.... do.............	1, 500, 000	6, 000, 000
21.	5 of the same month......	3, 000, 000	
Amounting in the whole to eighteen millions, viz..........			18, 000, 000

By which receipts the said Minister has promised, in the name of Congress and in behalf

pour les Treize Etats-Unis, faire payer et rembourser au Trésor Royal de Sa Majesté le premier Janvier 1788. au domicile du S. Grand Banquier [1] à Paris, ladite somme de Dix huit millions argent de france avec les intérêts à Cinq pour cent l'an.

Article 2.

Considérant que le remboursement d'un Capital aussi considérable en un seul terme stipulé au premier Janvier 1788. géneroit infiniment les opérations de la finance du Congrès desdits Etats-Unis et seroit même peut-être impracticable sur ce pied, Sa Majesté a bien voulu par ce motif déroger à cet égard à la teneur des reconnoissances que le Ministre du Congrès a fournies des Dix huit millions de livres Tournois énoncés en l'article cy dessus, et consentir que le remboursement de ce Capital soit fait en argent comptant à son Trésor Royal à Paris, en Douze parties égales de 1,500 M. chacune et en douze années seulement, à commencer de la troisieme après l'époque de la paix.

Article 3.

Quoique les reconnoissances du Ministre du Congrès desdits Etats-Unis portent, que les Dix huit millions de livres dont il s'agit seront payés et remboursés

of the thirteen United States, to cause to be paid and reimbursed to the royal treasury of His Majesty, on the 1st of January, 1788, at the house of his Grand Banker [1] at Paris, the said sum of eighteen millions, money of France, with interest at five per cent per annum.

Article 2.

Considering that the payment of so large a capital at the one stipulated period, the 1st of January, 1788, may greatly injure the finances of the Congress of the United States, and it may perhaps be even impracticable on that footing, His Majesty has been pleased for that reason to recede in that respect from the tenor of the receipts which the Minister of Congress has given for the eighteen million livres tournois mentioned in the foregoing article, and has consented that the payment of the capital in ready money at the royal treasury be in twelve equal payments of 1,500,000 livres each, and in twelve years only, to commence from the third year after a peace.

Article 3.

Although the receipts of the Minister of the Congress of the United States specify that the eighteen million of livres above mentioned are to be paid at the

[1] See the note regarding Article 1.

au Trésor Royal avec les intérêts à Cinq pour cent l'an, Sa Majesté voulant donner auxdits Etats-Unis une nouvelle preuve de son affection et de son amitié, Elle a bien voulu leur faire don et remise de la totalité des arrérages des intérêts échus jusqu'à ce jour et de ceux à écheoir jusqu'à l'èpoque du Traité de Paix; Faveur que le Ministre du Congrès reconnoit émaner de la pure munificence du Roi et la recevoir au nom desdits Etats-Unis, avec une profonde et vive reconnoissance.

Article 4.

Le remboursement des Dix huit millions de livres tournois dont il s'agit, sera fait en argent comptant au Trésor Royal de Sa Majesté à Paris, en douze parties égales et aux termes stipulés en l'article deux ci-dessus; Les intérêts de ladite somme à Cinq pour cent l'an, commenceront seulement à courir de l'époque du Traité de paix, seront acquittés à chaque terme de remboursement partiel du Capital, et diminueront à mesure et en proportion des payemens; Le Congrès et lesdits Etats-Unis restant au surplus libre de devancer le terme de leur libération, par des remboursemens anticipés, au cas que la situation de leur finances leur en donnât la facilité.

royal treasury, with interest at five per cent per annum, His Majesty, being willing to give the said United States a new proof of his affection and friendship, has been pleased to make a present of, and to forgive the whole arrears of interest to this day, and from thence to the date of the treaty of peace; a favor which the Minister of the Congress of the United States acknowledges to flow from the pure bounty of the King, and which he accepts in the name of the said United States with profound and lively acknowledgments.

Article 4.

The payment of the said eighteen millions of livres tournois shall be in ready money at the royal treasury of His Majesty at Paris, in twelve equal parts and at the terms stipulated in the above second article. The interest of the said sum, at five per cent per annum, shall commence with the date of the treaty of peace, and shall be paid at every period of the partial payments of the capital, and shall diminish in proportion with the payments; the Congress of the said United States being left, however, at liberty to free themselves sooner from this obligation by anticipated payments in case the state of their finances will admit.

ARTICLE 5.

Quoique l'emprunt de Cinq millions de florins de Hollande consenti par les Etats généraux des Provinces Unies des Pays bas, aux termes de l'obligation[1] passée le 5 Novembre 1781. entre Sa Majesté et lesdits Etats généraux, ait été stipulé sous le nom de Sa Majesté et garanti par Elle, Il est néanmoins reconnu par ces présentes que ledit emprunt a été fait réelement pour le compte et le service des Etats-Unis de l'Amérique septentrionale, et que le Capital, montant par évaluation modérée à la somme de Dix Millions de livres Tournois, en a été payé auxdits Etats-Unis suivant la reconnoissance du solde de ladite somme que le Ministre soussigné du Congrès en a fournie le sept Juin dernier.

ARTICLE 5.

Although the loan of five millions of florins of Holland, agreed to by the States General of the United Provinces of the Netherlands on the terms of the obligation[1] passed on the 5th of November, 1781, between His Majesty and the said States General, has been made in His Majesty's name and guaranteed by him; it is nevertheless acknowledged by these presents that the said loan was made in reality on account and for the service of the United States of North America, and that the capital, amounting at a moderate valuation to the sum of ten millions livres tournois, has been paid to the said United States, agreeably to a receipt for the payment of the said sum, given by the undersigned Minister of Congress the seventh day of June last.

ARTICLE 6.

Par la convention dudit jour 5 Novembre 1781. le Roi a bien voulu promettre et s'engager de fournir et restituer au Comptoir Général des Etats Généraux des Pays bas, le Capital dudit emprunt avec les intérêts à quatre pour cent par an, sans aucuns frais ou déduction quelconques pour les prêteurs, de maniere que ledit Capital soit entierement remboursé après l'espace de quinze années, les remboursemens

ARTICLE 6.

By the convention of the said 5th of November, 1781, the King has been pleased to promise and engage to furnish and pay at the general counter of the States General of the Netherlands, the capital of the said loan, with the interest at four per cent per annum, without any charge or deduction whatever to the lenders; so that the said capital shall be wholly repaid after the space of five[2] years, the payments to be

[1] See the note regarding Article 5.

[2] Error for *fifteen*

devant se faire en dix termes égaux, dont le premier écherra dans la sixieme année à compter de la date dudit emprunt et ainsi de suite d'année en année jusqu'au remboursement final de la susdite somme; Mais il a été pareillement reconnu par le présent Acte, que cet engagement n'a été pris par le Roi à la priere du Ministre soussigné desdits Etats-Unis, que sous la promesse par lui faite au nom du Congrès et solidairement pour les Treize Etats Unis, de faire rembourser et restituer au Trésor Royal de Sa Majesté à Paris, le Capital, les intérêts et frais dudit emprunt, suivant les conditions et aux époques fixées par la convention susdite du 5 Novembre 1781.

Article 7.

Il a été arrêté en conséquence et convenu, que la Somme de Dix millions de livres Tournois formant par modération le principal de l'emprunt de Cinq millions de florins de Hollande cidessus mentionné, sera remboursée et restituée en argent comptant au Trésor Royal de Sa Majesté à Paris, avec les intérêts à quatre pour cent par an, en Dix parties égales d'un Million chacune et en dix termes dont le premier écherra le 5. Novembre de l'année 1787. Le second au 5. Novembre 1788. et ainsi de suite d'année en année jusqu'au remboursement final de la susdite

made in ten equal periods, the first of which to commence the sixth year from the date of the loan, and afterwards from year to year to the final payment of the said sum; but it is in like manner acknowledged by this act that this engagement was entered into by the King at the request of the undersigned Minister of the United States, and on the promise by him made in the name of Congress and on behalf of the thirteen United States, to cause to be reimbursed and paid at the royal treasury of His Majesty at Paris, the capital, interest, and cost of the said loan, according to the conditions and terms fixed by the said convention of the 5th of November, 1781.

Article 7.

It is accordingly agreed and settled that the sum of ten million livres tournois, being by a moderate computation the principal of the loan of five millions of Holland florins above mentioned, shall be reimbursed and paid in ready money at the royal treasury of His Majesty at Paris, with the interest at four per cent per annum, in ten equal payments of one million each, and in ten terms, the first of which shall be on the 5th of November, 1787, the second the 5th of November, 1788, and so from year to year till the final payment of the said sum of ten millions, the interest lessen-

somme de Dix millions, les intérêts diminuant à mesure et en proportion des remboursemens partiels du Capital. Mais par une suite des sentimens d'affection du Roi pour les Etats-Unis de l'Amérique, Sa Majesté a bien voulu prendre à sa charge les frais de Commission et de Banque dudit emprunt, desquels frais Sa Majesté a fait don et remise auxdits Etats, ce que leur Ministre soussigné a accepté avec reconnoissance au nom du Congrès, comme une nouvelle marque de la générosité et de l'amitié de Sa Majesté pour lesdits Etats-Unis.

ing in proportion with the partial payments of the capital. But in consequence of the King's affection for the United States, His Majesty has been pleased to charge himself with the expense of commissions and bank for the said loan, of which expenses His Majesty has made a present to the United States, and this their undersigned Minister accepts, with thanks, in the name of Congress, as a new proof of His Majesty's generosity and friendship for the said United States.

Article 8.

A l'égard des intérêts dudit emprunt pendant les cinq années qui précéderont celle du premier terme de remboursement du Capital, Comme le Roi s'est engagé à les payer au Comptoir Général des Etats Généraux des Pays bas, sur le pied de quatre pour cent par an et d'année en année, à compter du 5 Novembre 1781. suivant la convention du même jour, le Ministre du Congrés reconnoit que la restitution en est due à Sa Majesté par les Etats-Unis et s'engage au nom desdits Etats à les faire payer et rembourser aux mêmes époques et sur le même pied au Trésor Royal de Sa Majesté la premiere année d'arrérages d'intérêts devant être

Article 8.

With regard to the interest of the said loan during the five years preceding the first term of payment of the capital, as the King has engaged to pay it at the general counter of the States General of the Netherlands, at the rate of four per cent yearly, and every year, counting from the 5th of November, 1781, according to the convention of that day, the Minister of Congress acknowledges that the repayment of that is due to His Majesty by the United States, and he engages in the name of the said United States to cause payment thereof to be made, at the same time and at the same rate, at the royal treasury of His Majesty; the first year's interest to be paid the

acquittée le 5. Novembre prochain et ainsi de suite pendant chacune des cinq années qui précéderont celle du premier terme de remboursement du Capital fixé cy dessus au 5 Novembre 1787.

Les hautes parties contractantes se garantissent réciproquement l'observation fidéle du présent Contrat, dont les Ratifications seront échangées dans l'espace de neuf mois à compter de ce jour ou plutôt s'il est possible. En foi de quoi Nous Plénipotentiaires susdits de Sa Majesté Trés Chretienne et des Treize Etats-Unis de l'Amérique Septentrionale, en vertu de nos pouvoirs respectifs, avons signé ces présentes et y avons fait apposer le Cachet de nos Armes.

Fait à Versailles le Seizieme jour du mois de Juillet Mil sept cent quatre vingt deux.

Gravier De Vergennes
[Seal]
B Franklin
[Seal]

5th of November next, and so yearly during the five years preceding the first term for the payment of the capital, fixed as above on the 5th of November, 1787.

The high contracting parties reciprocally bind themselves to the faithful observance of this contract, the ratifications of which shall be exchanged in the space of nine months from this day, or sooner if possible. In testimony whereof we, the said Plenipotentiaries of His Most Christian Majesty and of the thirteen United States of North America, in virtue of our respective powers, have signed these presents and thereunto fixed the seal of our arms.

Done at Versailles the sixteenth day of July, one thousand seven hundred and eighty-two.

Gravier De Vergennes
[Seal]
B Franklin
[Seal]

NOTES

The original of this contract is in the Library of Congress, 145 C. C. Papers, folios 311–19; a facsimile thereof is in the Department of State file, which contains also a facsimile of the other original—that is, the one in the archives of France; the latter was brought from Paris in 1925 by Ambassador Herrick. With it is an imperfect typewritten translation.

The United States instrument of ratification is copied in 135 C. C. Papers, I; also in Journals, XXIV, 51–64. A facsimile of the original instrument, received from the French archives, is now in the Department of State file. The Great Seal of the United States, which was adopted by Congress June 20, 1782, was affixed to this

instrument of ratification, beginning a practice which has since continued; it is at the upper left of the first page, with the signature of Elias Boudinot under it, and the attest of Charles Thomson as Secretary at the end of the document.

The exchange of ratifications of this contract and of the subsequent contract of February 25, 1783 (Document 9), were concurrent; and, so far as this contract was concerned, took place after the period of nine months prescribed in its text.

Neither in the archives of France nor in those of the Department of State has been found any protocol or other similar record of the exchange of ratifications. The fact of ratification by Congress was known by Franklin and communicated to Count de Vergennes before July 22, 1783 (Wharton, Diplomatic Correspondence, VI, 585). The date of exchange was after December 25, 1783 (*ibid.*, 742), but cannot be stated with precision.

The translation printed is from that set forth in 135 C. C. Papers, I. The text in the "Address to the States" of April 26, 1783, in Journals, 1823 ed., IV, 203–5, is an almost literal copy thereof. That translation was probably prepared by Charles Thomson, Secretary of Congress; for in 145 C. C. Papers, folios 333–45, in his handwriting, is a draft of the United States instrument of ratification, followed by this translation of the French text of the contract, interlined and corrected. It is the same translation, with perhaps trifling variations, as that in 8 Statutes at Large (although not there noted as a translation), and the one which has generally been used. In various respects, and quite aside from the errors specifically noted, the translation is erroneous or imperfect.

Note Regarding Article 1

The translation of the words "au domicile du S. Grand Banquier à Paris" gave rise from early days to doubt and divergence of opinion on the part of various officials and others. Precisely the same French wording is found also in Article 1 of the contract of February 25, 1783 (Document 9).

The translation here printed, which may be called the Thomson translation, renders the expression "at the house of his Grand Banker at Paris," and this is followed in the Statutes at Large except as to capitalization. Other editions give various renderings of the French in either one contract or the other. While they need not be mentioned in detail, the early doubts are best illustrated by the print of the Secret Journals of Congress, III, 283, which, with its brackets, reads "at the house of his grand [of the sieur grand] banker at Paris."

When John Pintard came to translate this expression in the contract of February 25, 1783, he wrote "at the house of the Sieur Grand, banker at Paris." And this is the correct translation. The reference in each of the two contracts is to Ferdinand Grand, whom Franklin, in his letter to Count de Vergennes of January 25, 1783, called "our banker" (see Wharton Diplomatic Correspondence, VI, 230).

Some account of Mr. Grand, who was a Swiss, is found in the diary of John Adams (see *ibid.*, II, 784, note). Appointment of Grand as "a banker in the affairs of the United States" was made by Robert Morris on December 3, 1781 (*ibid.*, V, 35); but Grand had been designated "our banker" (although not named) by Franklin and the other Commissioners on January 17, 1777 (*ibid.*, II, 250; see also the letters of Grand to Franklin, September 9, 1786, and Durival to Grand, September 10, 1786, in Diplomatic Correspondence, 1783–1789, I, 403–4).

Note Regarding Article 5

The texts of the French obligation for the loan of five millions of florins under date of November 5, 1781, and of the act of the States General of the Netherlands in respect thereof, are (in Dutch) in Von Martens, Supplément au recueil des principaux traités, II, 162–64.

Treaty Series, No. 249
8 Statutes at Large, 32–51

5

THE NETHERLANDS : OCTOBER 8, 1782

Treaty of Amity and Commerce, signed at The Hague October 8, 1782. Original in Dutch and English.

Ratified by the United States January 23, 1783. Ratified by the Netherlands December 27, 1782. Ratifications exchanged at The Hague June 23, 1783. Proclaimed January 23, 1783.

Tractaat van Vriendschap en Commercie tusschen Haar Hoog Mogende, de Staten Generaal der Vereenigde Nederlanden, en de Vereenigde Staten van America, te weeten New-Hampshire, Massachusetts, Rhode Island, en Providence Plantations, Connecticutt, New-York, New-Jersey, Pensylvania, Delaware, Maryland, Virginia, Noord Carolina, Zuyd-Carolina en Georgia.

Haar Hoog Mogende de Staten Generaal der Vereenigde Nederlanden, en de Vereenigde Staten van America, te weeten New-Hampshire, Massachusetts, Rhode Island en Providence Plantations, Connecticutt, New-York, New-Jersey, Pensylvanien, Delaware, Maryland, Virginien, Noord-Carolina, Zuyd-Carolina en Georgien, geneegen zynde, op een bestendige en billyke wyze te bepalen de regelen, die in acht genomen moeten worden, ten opzigte van de Correspondentie en Commercie welke zy verlangen vast te stellen tusschen haare res-

A Treaty of Amity and Commerce between Their High Mightinesses the States-General of the United Netherlands, and the United States of America, to wit New-Hampshire, Massachusetts, Rhode Island, and Providence Plantations, Connecticutt, New-York, New-Jersey, Pensylvania, Delaware, Maryland, Virginia, North-Carolina, South-Carolina and Georgia.

Their High Mightinesses the States General of the United Netherlands, and the United-States of America, to wit New-Hampshire, Massachusetts, Rhode Island, and Providence Plantations, Connecticutt, New-York, New-Jersey, Pensylvania, Delaware, Maryland, Virginia, North-Carolina, South-Carolina and Georgia, desiring to ascertain, in a permanent and equitable manner, the Rules to be observed, relative to the Commerce, and Correspondence, which They intend to establish, between Their respective States, Countries and

pective Landen, Staten, Onderdanen en Ingezeetenen, hebben geoordeelt, dat het gezegde einde niet beeter kan worden bereikt, dan door te stellen tot een bazis van haar Verdrag, de volmaekste egaliteit en reciprociteit, en met vermyding van alle die lastige præferentien, dewelke doorgaans de bronäders zyn van twist, verwarring en misnoegen; door aan iedere Party de Vryheid te laten, om weegins de Commercie en Navigatie verder zulke Reglementen te maken, als die voor zig zelven het gevoeglykst zal oordeelen; en door de voordeelen van Commercie eeniglyk te gronden op weederzyds nut, en de juiste regels van vrye handel over en weer; reserveerende by dat alles aan iedere Parthy de vryheid, om, na deszelfs goedvinden, andere Natien te admitteeren tot het participeeren aan dezelfde voordeelen.

Inhabitants, have judged, that the said End cannot be better obtained, than by establishing the most perfect Equality and Reciprocity, for the Basis of Their Agreement, and by avoiding all those burthensome preferences, which are usually, the sources of debate, Embarrassment and discontent; by leaving also each party at liberty, to make respecting Commerce and Navigation such ulterior Regulations, as it shall find most convenient to itself; and by founding the Advantages of Commerce solely upon reciprocal utility, and the just Rules, of free Intercourse: reserving, with all, to each Party, the liberty of admitting, at its pleasure, other Nations to a participation of the same Advantages.

Op deeze grondbeginzelen, hebben voorgemelde haar Hoog Mogende de Staten Generaal der Vereenigde Nederlanden, tot hunne Plenipotentiarissen, uit het midden hunner Vergadering benoemd, de Heeren derselver Gedeputeerden tot de buitenlandsche Saaken, En de gemelde Vereenigde Staten van America, van hunne zyde met volmagt voorsien, den Heer John Adams, laatst Commissaris van de Vereenigde Staten van America aan het Hof van Versailles, geweezen Afgevaardigde op het Congres weegens

On these principles, Their said High Mightinesses, the States General of the United Netherlands, have named, for Their Plenipotentiaries, from the midst of their Assembly, Messieurs their Deputies for the foreign affairs; And the said United States of America, on their part, have furnished with full powers, M[r] John Adams, late Commissioner of the United-States of America at the Court of Versailles, heretofore Delegate in Congress from the State of Massachusetts-Bay, and chief Justice of the said State,

de Staten van Massachusetts Baay, en Opper-Regter van den gemelden Staat dewelke zyn overeengekomen, en geaccordeert.

who have agreed and concluded, as follows, to witt.

Art! 1.

Daar zal een vaste, onverbreekelyke, en Universeele Vreede, en opregte Vriendschap zyn, tusschen Haar Hoog Mogende de Heeren Staten Generaal der Vereenigde Nederlanden, en de Vereenigde Staten van America, en de Onderdanen en Ingezeetenen van de voornoemde Parthyen, en tusschen de Landen, Eilanden, Steeden en Plaatsen, geleegen onder de Jurisdictie van de gemelde Vereenigde Nederlanden, en de gemelde Vereenigde Staten van America, en derselver Onderdanen en Ingezeetenen, van allerley Staat, sonder onderscheid van Persoonen en plaatsen.

Article 1.

There shall be a firm, inviolable and universal peace, and sincere friendship, between Their High Mightinesses, the Lords the States-General of the United-Netherlands, and the United-States of America; and between the Subjects and Inhabitants of the said Parties, and between the Countries, Islands, Cities and Places, situated under the Jurisdiction of the said United Netherlands, and the said United States of America, their Subjects and Inhabitants, of every degree, without exception of Persons or Places.

Art! 2.

De Onderdanen van de gemelde Staten Generaal der Vereenigde Nederlanden, zullen in de Havens, Rheeden, Landen, Eilanden, Steeden of plaatsen van de Vereenigde Staten van America, of eenige van dezelve, geen andere of grootere Regten of Impositien, van wat natuur die ook mogen zyn, of hoedanig dezelve ook genoemt mogen werden, betaalen, dan die welke de meest gefavoriseerde Natien zyn, of zullen worden verpligt aldaar te betaalen. En zy zullen genieten alle de Regten, Vryheeden, Privilegien,

Article 2.

The Subjects of the said States-General of the United Netherlands, shall pay in the Ports, Havens, Roads, Countries, Islands, Cities or Places, of the United States of America, or any of them, no other nor greater Duties, or Imposts, of what ever nature or denomination they may be, than those which the Nations the most favoured, are or shall be obliged to pay: And they shall enjoy all the Rights, Liberties, Priviledges, Immunities, and Exemptions in Trade, Navigation and Commerce, which the

Immuniteiten en Exemptien in Handel, Navigatie, en Commercie, het zy in het gaan van eene Haven in de gemelde Staaten na eene andere, of gaande van eenige van deeze Havens na eenige vreemde Haven van de Wereld, of van eenige vreemde Haven van de Wereld na eenige van deeze Havens, welke de gemelde Natien reeds genieten of zullen genieten.

ART! 3.

Insgelyks zullen de Onderdanen en Ingezeetenen van de gemelde Vereenigde Staten van America, in de Havens, Rheeden, Landen, Eilanden, Steeden of plaatsen van de gemelde Vereenigde Nederlanden, of eenige van dezelve, geen andere, of grootere Regten of Impositien, van wat natuur die ook mogen zyn, of hoedanig dezelve ook genoemt mogen worden, betaalen, dan die, welke de meest gefavoriseerde Natien zyn, of zullen worden verpligt aldaar te betalen. En zy zullen genieten alle de Regten, Vryheeden, Privilegien, Immuniteiten en Exemptien in Handel, Navigatie en Commercie, het zy in het gaan van eene haven in de gemelde Staaten na eene andere, of gaande na en van dezelve, van en na eenige vreemde Haven van de Wereld, welke de meest gefavoriseerde Natien reeds genieten of sullen genieten. En zullen de Vereenigde Staten van America, beneevens haare Onderdanen, en

said Nations do or shall enjoy, whether in passing from One Port to another, in the said States, or, in going from any of those Ports, to any foreign Port of the World, or from any foreign Port of the World, to any of those Ports.

ARTICLE 3.

The Subjects and Inhabitants of the said United States of America, shall pay in the Ports, Havens, Roads, Countries, Islands, Cities or Places, of the said United-Netherlands, or any of them, no other nor greater Duties, or Imposts, of what ever nature or denomination they may be, than those, which the Nations, the most favoured, are or shall be obliged to pay: And they shall enjoy all the Rights, Liberties, Priviledges, Immunities and Excemptions in Trade, Navigation and Commerce, which the said Nations do or shall enjoy, whether in passing from One Port to another, in the said States, or, from any one towards any one of those Ports, from or to any foreign Port of the World. And the United-States of America, with their Subjects and Inhabitants, shall leave to those of Their High Mightinesses the peacable enjoyment of their Rights, in the Countries, Islands and Seas, in

Ingezeetenen aan die van Haar Hoog Mogende laten het gerust genot van haare regten, omtrent de Landen, Eilanden en Zeeën in Oost en West Indien, sonder haar daar in eenig belet, of hindernis te doen.

the East- and West-Indies, without any hindrance or molestation.

ART[!] 4.

Er zal eene volle, volkomene en geheele vryheid van Conscientie worden toegestaen aan de Onderdanen en Ingezeetenen van iedere Parthy, en aan derselver Familien, en zal niemand ter zake van den Godtsdienst, worden gemolesteert, mits hem omtrent publique demonstratie onderwerpende aan de Wetten van het Land. Daar en boven zal vryheid worden gegeeven aan de Onderdanen en Ingezeetenen van iedere Parthye, die in des anderen's Territoir overlyden, om begraven te worden in de gewoone begraafplaatsen of gevoeglyke en decente plaatsen, daar toe te bepaalen, zoo als de geleegendheid zal vereisschen; nogte zullen de doode Lighaamen van die geene die begraven zyn, eenigzints werden gemolesteert. En zullen de beide Contracteerende Mogendheeden ieder onder hun gebied, de nodige voorsieninge doen, ten einde de respective Onderdanen en Ingezeetenen van behoorlyke bewyzen van Sterfgevallen, waar by dezelve zyn geinteresseert, voortaan zullen kunnen worden gedient.

ARTICLE 4.

There shall be an entire and perfect liberty of Conscience allowed to the Subjects and Inhabitants of each Party, and to their Families: and no one shall be molested in regard to his worship, provided he submits, as to the public demonstration of it, to the Laws of the Country: There shall be given more over, liberty, when any Subjects or Inhabitants of either Party shall die in the Territory of the other, to bury them in the usual Burrying-places or in decent and convenient Grounds to be appointed for that purpose, as occasion shall require: and the dead Bodies of those who are burried, shall not in any wise be molested—. And the Two Contracting Parties shall provide, each one in His Jurisdiction, that Their respective Subjects and Inhabitants may hence forward obtain the requisite Certificates, in cases of Deaths, in which they shall be interested.

ART^l 5.

Haar Hoog Mogende de Staten Generaal der Vereenigde Nederlanden, en de Vereenigde Staten van America, zullen tragten, zoo veel eenigzints in haar vermogen is, te beschermen en defendeeren alle Scheepen en andere effecten, toebehoorende aan wederzydsche Onderdanen en Ingezeetenen, of eenige van dezelve, zynde in haare Havens of Rheën, binnenlandsche Zeeën, Stroomen, Rivieren, en zoo verre haare Jurisdictie zeewaards strekt, en wederom te bekomen en te doen restitueeren aan de regte Eigenaers, húnne Agenten of Gevolmagtigden, alle zodanige Scheepen en Effecten, die onder haare Jurisdictie zullen genomen worden: en haare convoyeerende Oorlog Scheepen zullen, voor zoo verre zy eenen gemeenen Vyand mogen hebben, onder haare protectie neemen alle Scheepen, toebehoorende aan elkanders Onderdanen en Ingezeetenen, dewelke geene Contrabande goederen, volgens de beschryving hier na daar van te doen, zullen hebben ingelaaden naar plaatsen, waar meede de eene parthy in Vreede, en de andere in Oorlog is, en na geen geblocqueerde plaats gedestineert zyn, en zullen houden dezelve Cours, of gaan dezelve weg, en zullen zodanige Scheepen defendeeren, zoo lang als zy dezelve Cours houden, of deselve weg gaan, teegens alle aanvallen, magt

ARTICLE 5.

Their High-Mightinesses, the States-General of the United Netherlands, and the United-States of America, shall endeavor, by all the means in their power, to defend and protect all Vessells and other Effects, belonging to their Subjects and Inhabitants respectively, or to any of them, in their Ports, Roads, Havens, internal Seas, Passes, Rivers, and as far as their Jurisdiction extends at Sea, and to recover, and cause to be restored to the true Proprietors, their Agents or Attornies, all such Vessells and Effects, which shall be taken under their Jurisdiction: And their Vessells of War and Convoys, in cases, when they may have a common Enemy, shall take under their Protection, all the Vessells, belonging to the Subjects and Inhabitants of either Party, which shall not be laden with Contraband-Goods, according to the description, which shall be made of them here after, for Places, with which one of the Parties is in Peace, and the other at War, nor destined for any Place blocked, and which shall hold the same Course or follow the same Rout; and they shall defend such Vessells as long as they shall hold the same Course, or follow the same Rout, against all attacks, Force and Violence of the common Enemy, in the same manner, as they ought to protect and defend

en geweld van den gemeenen Vyand, op dezelve wys als zy zouden moeten beschermen en defendeeren de Scheepen toebehoorende aan weedersyds eigen Onderdanen.

the Vessells, belonging to their own respective Subjects.

ART! 6.

De Onderdanen der Contracteerende Parthyen zullen over en weeder, in weedersydsche Landen en Staten, van hunne goederen by Testamenten, Donatien, of andersints mogen disponeeren; en hunne Erfgenamen, zynde Onderdanen van een der Parthyen, in de Landen van de andere, of wel elders woonagtig, zullen dezelve Nalatenschappen ontfangen, selfs *ab intestato*, het zy in persoon, het zy by hun Procureur of gemagtigde, schoon zy geen brieven van naturalisatie zouden mogen hebben geobtineert, zonder dat het effect van die Commissie hun zal kunnen worden betwist, onder prætext van eenige regten, of voorregten van eenige Provincie, Stad of particulier Perzoon: en soo de Erfgenamen, aan welke de Erffenissen mogten vervallen zyn, minderjarig waren, zullen de Voogden of Curateurs by den Domiciliairen Regter der genoemde minderjarigen aangestelt, kunnen regeeren, bestieren, Administreeren, verkoopen en veralieneeren de goederen, welke de gemelde minderjarigen by erffenissen zullen zyn te beurt gevallen; en generalyk met op-

ARTICLE 6.

The Subjects of the contracting Parties may, on one side and on the other, in the respective Countries and States, dispose of their Effects, by Testament, Donation, or otherwise; and their Heirs, subjects of one of the Parties, and residing in the Country of the other, or elsewhere, shall receive such successions, even ab intestato, whether in person or by their Attorney or Substitute, even although they shall not have obtained Letters of Naturalization, without having the effect of *Such Commission* contested under pretext of any Rights or Prerogatives of any Province, City or private Person: And if the Heirs, to whom such successions may have fallen, shall be Minors, the Tutors or Curators, established by the Judge Domiciliary, of the said Minors, may govern, direct, administer, sell, and alienate the Effects fallen to the said Minors, by Inheritance, and, in general, in relation to the said Successions and Effects, use all the Rights, and fullfill all the functions, which belong, by the disposition of the Laws, to Guardians, Tutors and Curators: Provided, never the less, that this

sigt tot de voorscž: successien en goederen waarneemen alle regten, en functien, die aan Voogden en Curateurs, na dispositie der Wetten competeeren, behoudens nogtans, dat deeze dispositie geen plaats zal kunnen hebben, dan in gevalle als wanneer de Testateur by Testament, Codicille, of ander wettig Instrument, geene Voogden, of Curateurs sal hebben genomineert.

disposition cannot take place, but in cases where the Testator shall not have named Guardians, Tutors, Curators, by Testament, Codicil, or other legal Instrument.

ART[l] 7.

Het zal wettig en vry zyn aan de Onderdanen van iedere Parthye, zodanige Advocaten, Procureurs, Notarissen, Solliciteurs of Factoors te employeeren, als zy zullen goedvinden.

ARTICLE 7.

It shall be lawfull and free for the Subjects of each Party, to employ such Advocates, Attorneys, Notaries, Solicitors, or Factors, as they shall judge proper.

ART[l] 8.

Kooplieden, Schippers, Eigenaers, Bootsgezellen, Lieden van alderhande soort, Scheepen en Vaartuigen, en alle Koopmanschappen en goederen in 't generaal, en Effecten van een der Bondgenooten, of van derselver Onderdanen, zullen niet mogen worden in beslag genomen of aangehouden in eenige der Landen, Gronden, Eilanden, Steeden, Plaatsen, havens, Stranden of Dominien, hoe genaamt van den anderen Bondgenoot, tot eenige Militaire Expeditie, publicq of privaat gebruik van iemand, door arrest, geweld, of eenigsints daar na gelykende: veel minder zal het gepermitteert zyn aan de onder-

ARTICLE 8.

Merchants, Masters and Owners of Ships, Mariners, Men of all kinds, ships and Vessells, and all Merchandizes, and Goods, in general, and Effects, of one of the Confederates, or of the Subjects thereof, shall not be seized, or detained in any of the Countries, Lands, Islands, Cities, Places, Ports, Shores, or Dominions, what so ever of the other Confederate, for any Military Expedition, publick or private use of any one, by Arrests, Violence, or any Colour thereof: much less shall it be permitted to the Subjects of either Party, to take or extort by force, any thing from the Subjects of the other Party,

danen van iedere Parthy iets te neemen, of door geweld te ontvreemden van de Onderdanen van de andere Parthy, sonder bewilliging van den Persoon die het toebehoord: het geen egter niet te verstaan is van die aanhalingen detentien en Arresten, welke zullen worden gedaan op bevel en authoriteit van de Justitie, en volgens de Ordinaire weegen, ten opzigte van Schulden of misdaden, waar omtrent de procedures moeten geschieden by wege van Regten, ingevolge de form van Justitie.

without the consent of the Owner: which, however, is not to be understood of Seizures, Detentions and Arrests, which shall be made by the command and authority of Justice, and by the ordinary methods, on account of debts or Crimes, in respect whereof, the Proceedings must be, by way of Law, according to the forms of Justice.

Art! 9.

Verders is overeengekomen en besclooten, dat het volkomen vry zal staan aan alle Kooplieden, Bevelhebbers van Scheepen, en andere Onderdanen of Ingezeetenen der beide contracteerende Mogendheeden in alle plaatsen respectivelyk gehoorende onder het gebied en de Jurisdictie der weederzydsche Mogendheeden húnne eige saaken, zelfs te verrigten; zullende deselve wyders, omtrent het gebruik van Tolken, of Makelaars, mitsgaders met opzigt tot het laaden, of ontladen, hunner Scheepen, en al het geen daar toe betrekkelyk is, over en weeder, op den Voet van eige Onderdanen, of ten minsten, in gelykheid met de meest gefavoriseerde Natie geconsidereert, en gehandelt worden.

Article 9.

It is further agreed and concluded, that it shall be wholly free for all Merchants, Commanders of Ships, and other Subjects and Inhabitants, of the contracting Parties, in every Place, subjected to the Jurisdiction of the Two Powers respectively, to manage, themselves, their Own Business: And more over, as to the use of Interpreters or Brokers, as also, in relation to the loading, or unloading of their Vessells, and every thing which has relation there to, they shall be, on one side and on the other, considered and treated upon the footing of natural Subjects, or, at least, upon an equality with the most favored Nation.

ARTl 10.

De Koopvaardy Scheepen van een ieder der Parthyen, komende, soo wel van een Vyandelyke, als eige of Neutrale haven, zullen vry mogen vaaren naa eenige Haven van een Vyand van den anderen Bondgenoot; dog verpligt zyn, soo dikwils het gevordert word, haare Zeebrieven, en verdere Bescheiden, in het 25ste Artl beschreeven, zoo wel op de open Zee, als in de havens te exhibeeren, expresselyk aantonende, dat haare goederen niet zyn van het getal dier geene, dewelke als Contrabande verbooden zyn, en geene Contrabande goederen voor een Vyandelyke Haven gelaaden hebbende, na de Haven van een Vyand, haare reize vryelyk, en onverhindert mogen vervolgen; dog sal geen visitatie van papieren gevergt worden van Scheepen onder Convoy der Oorlog Scheepen, maar geloof worden gegeeven aan het woord van den Officier, het Convoy leidende.

ARTICLE 10.

The Merchant Ships, of either of the Parties, coming from the Port of an Enemy, or from their Own, or a Neutral Port, may navigate freely towards any Port of an Enemy of the other Ally: They shall be, never the less, held, when ever it shall be required, to exhibit, as well upon the high-Seas, as in the Ports, their Sea-Letters, and other Documents, described in the Twenty Fifth Article, stating expressly that their Effects are not of the Number of those, which are prohibited, as Contraband: And, not having any Contraband Goods, for an Enemy's Port, they may freely, and without hindrance, pursue their Voyage towards the Port of an Enemy. Nevertheless, it shall not be required to examine the Papers of Vessells, convoyed by Vessells of War, but Credence shall be given to the word of the Officer, who shall conduct the Convoy.

ARTl 11.

Indien by het vertoonen der zee-brieven, en andere bescheiden, by het 25ste Artl van dit Tractaat nader beschreeven, de andere Parthy ontdekt, dat er eenige van die soort van goederen zyn, dewelke verbooden en Contrabande gedeclareert zyn, en geconsigneert naar een haven, onder de Gehoorsaemheid van den Vyand, zal het niet geoorloft zyn

ARTICLE 11.

If by exhibiting the Sea-Letters, and other Documents, described more particularly in the Twenty Fifth Article of this Treaty, the other Party shall discover there are any of those sorts of Goods, which are declared prohibited, and Contraband, and that they are consigned for a Port under the obedience of his Enemy, it shall not be lawfull to break up

de Luyken van zodanig Schip op te breeken, of eenige Kist, Koffers, Pakken, Kassen of ander Vaatwerk, daar in gevonden wordende, te openen, of het geringste gedeelte van haare goederen te verplaatsen, het sy sodanige Scheepen toebehooren aan de Onderdanen van Haar Hoog Mogende de Staten Generaal der Vereenigde Nederlanden, of aan Onderdanen, en Ingezeetenen van de gemelde Vereenigde Staaten van America, ten zy de lading aan Land gebragt worde in presentie van de Officieren van het Admiraliteits hoff, en een Inventaris van deselve gemaakt, dog sal niet worden toegelaten om deselve op eenigerhande wyse te verkoopen, verruilen of veralieneeren, dan, na dat behoorlyke en wettige Procedures tegens zodanige verbodene Contrabande goederen zullen zyn gehouden, en het Admiraliteits hof by een gepronuntieerde Sententie dezelve zal hebben geconfisqueert, daar van altoos vry latende, zoo wel het Schip zelve, als eenige andere goederen daar in gevonden wordende, welke voor vry werden gehouden, nogte mogen dezelve worden opgehouden, onder voorgeeven dat die, als't ware, door de geprohibeerde goederen zouden zyn geinfecteert, veel min zullen deselve als wettige Prys worden geconfisqueert: Maar in teegendeel, wanneer by de Visitatie aan Land word bevonden, dat er geen Con-

the Hatches of such Ship, nor to open any Chest, Coffer, Packs, Casks, or other Vessells found therein, or to remove the smallest Parcell of her Goods, whether the said Vessell belongs to the Subjects of Their High-Mightinesses, the States General of the United-Netherlands, or to the Subjects or Inhabitants of the said United States of America, unless the Lading be brought on Shore, in presence of the Officers of the Court of Admiralty, and an Inventary thereof made, but there shall be no allowance to sell, exchange, or alienate the same, untill, after that, due and lawfull Process, shall have been had against such prohibited Goods of Contraband, and the Court of Admiralty, by a Sentence pronounced, shall have confiscated the same, saving always as well the Ship itselff, as any other Goods found therein, which are to be esteemed free, and may not be detained, on pretence of their being infected by the prohibited Goods, much less shall they be confiscated as lawfull Prize: But, on the contrary, when, by the visitation at Land, it shall be found that there are no Contraband Goods in the Vessell, and, it shall not appear by the Papers, that he, who has taken and carried in the Vessell, has been able to discover any there, he ought to be condemned in all the Charges, Damages and Interests of them,

trabande waaren in de Scheepen zyn, en uit de Papieren niet bleek, dat de neemer en opbrenger het daar uit niet had konnen ontdekken, zal deselve moeten worden gecondemneert, in alle de kosten en Schaden, die hy zoo aan de Eigenaaren der Scheepen als aan de Eigenaars, en Inlaaders der goederen, waar meede de Scheepen belaaden zullen zyn, door zyne rukelooze aanhouding, en opbrenging der Scheepen zal hebben veroorsaakt, met de Interessen van dien, wordende wel expresselyk verklaart, dat een Vry Schip zal vry maaken de waaren daar in gelaaden, en dat die vryheid zig ook zal uitstrekken over de persoonen, die haar zullen bevinden in een Vry-Schip, dewelke daar uit niet geligt zullen mogen worden, ten zy het waren Oorlogsluiden, in effectiven dienst van den Vyand.

which he shall have caused, both to the Owners of Vessells, and to the Owners and Freighters of Cargoes, with which they shall be loaded, by his temerity in taking and carrying them in; declaring most expressly the free Vessells shall assure the liberty of the Effects, with which they shall be loaded, and that this liberty shall extend it selff equally to the Persons who shall be found in a free Vessell, who may not be taken out of her, unless they are Military Men, actually in the service of an Enemy.

ART[l] 12.

In tegendeel is overeengekomen, dat al het geen bevonden zal worden gelaaden te zyn door de Onderdanen en Ingezeetenen van een der beide Parthyen in eenig Schip de Vyanden van den anderen, of aan deszelfs Onderdanen toebehoorende, geheel, of schoon niet zynde van de soort van verbodene goederen, mag worden geconfisqueert, op dezelve wys als of het den Vyand toequam, uitgesondert zodanige goederen en Koopmanschappen, als aan Boord van

ARTICLE 12.

On the contrary, it is agreed, that whatever shall be found to be laden by the Subjects and Inhabitants of either Party, on any Ship, belonging to the Enemies of the other, or to their Subjects, although it be not comprehended under the sort of prohibited Goods, the whole may be confiscated, in the same manner, as if it belonged to the Enemy; except, never the less, such Effects and Merchandizes, as were put on board such Vessell, before the

zodanig Schip gedaan waren voor de Oorlogs-Declaratie, of binnen Ses Maanden na deselve, welke goederen in geenen deele confiscatie zullen onderheevig zyn, maar wel en getrouwelyk, sonder uitstel, aan de Eigenaers, die deselve voor de confiscatie, en verkoop zullen te rug vragen of doen vragen, in natura zullen worden gerestitueert, gelyk meede het provenu daar van indien de reclame binnen agt Maanden na de Verkoping, dewelke publicq zal moeten worden gedaen, eerst konde geschieden, dog zoo, dat, indien de gemelde Koopmanschappen contrabande zyn, het geenzints geoorloft zal zyn, deselve naderhand te vervoeren na eenige Havens, de Vyanden toebehoorende.

Declaration of War, or in the space of Six Months after it, which effects shall not be, in any manner, subject to confiscation, but shall be faithfully and without delay, restored in nature to the Owners, who shall claim them, or cause them to be claimed, before the Confiscation and sale, as also their Proceeds, if the Claim could not be made, but in the space of Eight Months, after the sale, which ought to be publick: provided nevertheless, that if the said Merchandizes are contraband, it shall, by no means, be lawfull to transport them afterwards to any Port, belonging to Enemies.

ART! 13.

En ten einde de best mogelyke zorg mag worden gedragen voor de Securiteit van de Onderdanen, en het Volk van een der beide Parthyen, dat dezelve geen overlast komen te lyden van weegens de Oorlog Scheepen of Kapers van de andere Parthy, zullen alle de Bevelhebbers van Oorlog Scheepen en Gewapende Vaartuigen van de voorsz: Staten Generaal der Vereenigde Nederlanden, en van de gemelde Vereenigde Staten van America, mitsgaders alle derselver Officieren, Onderdanen en Volk, verbooden worden eenige beleediging of schade, aan die van de andere zyde, toe te brengen, en

ARTICLE 13.

And, that more effectual care may be taken for the Security of Subjects, and People of either Party, that they do not suffer molestation from the Vessells of War or Privateers of the other Party, it shall be forbidden to all Commanders of Vessells of War, and other armed Vessells of the said States-General of the United-Netherlands, and the said United-States of America, as well as to all their Officers, Subjects and People, to give any offence or do any damage to those of the other Party: And, if they act to the contrary, they shall be, upon the first complaint, which shall be

zoo zy dien contrarie handelen, zullen zy op de eerste klagten, daar over te doen, na behoorlyk ondersoek schuldig bevonden wordende, door haar eige Regters gestraft worden, en daar en boven verpligt worden satisfactie te geeven voor alle schade, en den Interest daar van, door vergoeding onder pœne en verbintenis van hunne personen en goederen.

made of it, being found guilty, after a just examination, punished by their proper Judges, and, moreover, obliged to make satisfaction for all damages and Interests thereof, by reparation, under pain and obligation of their Persons and Goods.

ART! 14.

Tot meerder verklaring van het geen voorsez̃: is, zullen alle kaper Capiteinen, of Rheeders van Scheepen op particuliere bestelling en Commissie ten Oorlog uitgerust, voor dezelve gehouden zyn, voor derselver vertrek, goede en suffisante Cautie te stellen voor de competente Regters, of in't geheel te verantwoorden de malversatien, die ze in haare Courssen, of op haare reizen zouden mogen begaan, en voor de contraventien van haare Capiteinen en Officieren, teegen het teegenwoordig Tractaat en de Ordonnantien, en Edicten, die gepubliceert zullen worden, in kragte, en conform de dispositie van dien, op pœne van verval, en nulliteit der voorscz̃: Commissien.

ARTICLE 14.

For further determining of what has been said, all Captains of Privateers, or Fitters-out of Vessells, armed for War, under Commission and on account of private Persons, shall be held, before their departure, to give sufficient Caution, before competent Judges, either, to be entirely responsible for the Malversations, which they may commit in their Cruizes or Voyages, as well as, for the Contraventions of their Captains and Officers against the present Treaty and against the Ordinances and Edicts, which shall be published in consequence of, and conformity to it, under pain of forfeiture and nullity of the said Commissions.

ART! 15.

Alle Scheepen en Koopmanschappen van wat natuur dezelve ook zyn, die hernomen zullen worden uit handen van Piratten en Zeerovers, sonder behoorlyke

ARTICLE 15.

All Vessells and Merchandizes, of whatsoever nature, which shall be rescued out of the Hands of any Pirates or Robbers, navigating the High-Seas, without

Commissie op de open Zee varende, zullen gebragt worden in eenige Haven van eene der beide Staten, en zullen aan de bewaring der Officieren van die Haven worden overgeleevert, ten einde geheel gerestitueert te worden aan den regten Eigenaer, zoo dra als behoorlyk en genoegsaam bewys, weegens den Eigendom der zelve, zal gedaan zyn.

requisite Com̄issions, shall be brought into some Port of one of the Two States, and deposited in the hands of the Officers of that Port, in order to be restored entire to the true Proprietor, as soon as due and sufficient proofs shall be made, concerning the Property thereof.

Art^t. 16.

Indien eenige Scheepen of Vaartuigen toebehooreende aan een van beide de Parthyen, hunne Onderdanen of Ingezeetenen, op de Kusten of Dominien van den anderen zullen komen te stranden vergaan, of eenige andere Zee-Schade te lyden, zal alle vriendelyke assistentie en hulp worden gegeeven aan de Persoonen Schipbreuk geleeden hebbende, of die zig in gevaar daar van zullen bevinden; En de Scheepen, Goederen en Koopmanschappen, en het geen daar van geborgen zal zyn, of het provenu van dien, by aldien die goederen verderffelyk zynde, zullen weezen verkogt, alle door de Schippers of door de Eiganaars, of van haare gelaste; of volmagt hebbende, binnen Jaar en dag gereclameert wordende, worden gerestitueert; mits betaelende alleen de reedelyke onkosten, en het geen voor bergloon door de eige Onderdanen, in het zelve geval, betaalt moet worden; zullende insgelyks Brieven van Vry-

Article 16.

If any Ships or Vessells, belonging to either of the Parties; their Subjects or People, shall, within the Coasts or Dominions of the other, stick upon the Sands, or be wrecked or suffer any other Sea-Damage, all friendly assistance and relief shall be given to the Persons shipwrecked, or such as shall be in danger thereof; and the Vessells, Effects and Merchandizes, or the part of them which shall have been saved, or the proceeds of them, if, being perishable, they shall have been sold, being claimed within a Year and a day, by the Masters or Owners, or their Agents or Attornies, shall be restored, paying only the reasonable Charges, and that which must be paid, in the same case, for the salvage, by the proper Subjects of the Country: There shall also be delivered them safe Conducts or Passports, for their free and safe passage from thence, and to returne, each one, to his own Country.

geley aan hun worden gegeeven, voor hunne vrye en geruste passage van daar, en retour van een ieder na syn eigen Land.

ART! 17.

In gevalle de Onderdanen of Ingezeetenen van een der beide Parthyen, met húnne Scheepen, het zy publique en ten Oorlog varende, of bysondere en ter Koopvaardy uitgerust, door onstuimig weer, najaaging van Zeerovers of Vyanden, of eenige andere dringende nood, gedwongen zullen worden, ter bekoming van een schuilplaats en Haaven, zig te retireeren en binnen te loopen in eenige der Rivieren, Creeken Baayen, Havens, Rheeden of Stranden, toebehoorende aan de andere Parthye, zullen dezelve met alle menschlievendheid en goedwilligheid werden ontfangen, en alle vriendelyke protectie en hulp genieten, en zal hun worden toegestaan zig te ververschen en proviandeeren teegens reedelyke prysen, met Victuaille, en alle dingen benoodigt tot onderhoud van haare persoonen, of reparatie van húnne Scheepen, en zy zullen op geenerley wys worden opgehouden, of verhindert uit de gemelde Havens of Rheeden te vertrekken, maar mogen verzylen en gaan wanneer en waar het hun behaagt, zonder eenig belet of verhindering.

ARTICLE 17.

In case the Subjects or People of either Party, with their shipping, whether public and of War, or private and of Merchants, be forced, through stress of Weather, pursuit of Pirates or Enemies, or any other urgent necessity for seeking of shelter and Harbour, to retract and enter in to any of the Rivers, Creeks, Bays, Ports, Roads, or Shores, belonging to the other Party, they shall be received with all humanity and kindness, and enjoy all friendly Protection and help, and they shall be permitted to refresh and provide them selves, at reasonable Rates, with Victualls, and all things needfull for the sustenance of their Persons, or reparation of their Ships, and they shall no ways be detained or hindred from returning out of the said Ports, or Roads, but may remove and depart, when and whither they please, without any let or hindrance.

ART! 18.

Tot des te beeter voortzetting der weedersydsche Commercie, is overeengekomen, dat indien een Oorlog mogt komen te ontstaan tusschen Haar Hoog Mogende de Staten Generaal der Vereenigde Nederlanden, en de Vereenigde Staten van America, altyd aan de Onderdanen van de een of andere zyde zal worden gegeeven den tyd van neegen Maanden, na dato van de rupture of proclamatie van Oorlog, om haar te mogen retireeren met haare effecten, en dezelve te vervoeren, waar het haar believen zal, het welk haar geoorloft zal zyn te mogen doen; als meede te mogen verkoopen of transporteeren haare goederen en meubilien in alle vryheid, sonder dat men haar daar in eenig belet zal doen; ook zonder geduurende den tyd van de voorscz̄: Neegen Maanden te mogen procedeeren tot eenig arrest van haare effecten, veel min van haare persoonen, maar zullen inteegendeel voor haare Scheepen, en effecten, die zy zullen willen meede voeren, worden gegeeven Pasporten van Vry geleide tot de naeste Havenen, in elkanders Landen voor den tyd, tot de reizen nodig. Ook zullen geen Pryzen op Zee genomen, voor wettig genomen gehouden mogen worden, ten minsten indien de Oorlogs-Declaratie niet bekent was geweest, of had kunnen zyn, in de Haven, die het genoome Schip

ARTICLE 18.

For the better promoting of Commerce, on both sides, it is agreed, that if a War should break out, between Their High Mightinesses, the States General of the United Netherlands, and the United States of America, there shall always be granted, to the Subjects on each side, the Term of Nine Months, after the date of the Rupture, or the proclamation of War, to the end that they may retire, with their Effects, and transport them, where they please, which it shall be lawfull for them to do, as well as to sell or transport their Effects and Goods, in all freedom, and without any hindrance, and without being able to proceed, during the said Term of Nine Months, to any Arrest of their Effects, much less of their Persons; on the contrary, there shall be given them, for their Vessells and their Effects, which they would carry away, Passports and safe Conducts, for the nearest Ports of their respective Countries, and for the time necessary for the Voyage. And no Prize, made at Sea, shall be adjudged lawfull, at least, if the Declaration of War was not or could not be known, in the last Port, which, the Vessell taken, has quitted. But, for what ever may have been taken from the Subjects and Inhabitants of either Party, and, for the Offences, which may have been given them, in the Interval of the

het laast heeft verlaten, maar zal voor al, het geen aan de Onderdanen en Ingezeetenen van weederzyden binnen de voorscž: termynen ontnomen mogt zyn, en de beleedigingen die hun aangedaan zouden mogen zyn, volkomen satisfactie gegeeven worden.

Art! 19.

Geen Oonderdaan van Haar Hoog Mogende de Staten Generaal der Vereenigde Nederlanden, zullen mogen versoeken of aanneemen eenige Commissien, of Lettres de Marque, tot het wapenen van eenig Schip of Scheepen, ten einde als Kapers te ageeren teegens de gemelde Vereenigde Staten van America, of eenige der zelve, of tegens de Onderdanen of Ingezeetenen der gemelde Vereenigde Staten, of eenige der zelve, of teegens den Eigendom der Ingezeetenen van eenige der zelve, van eenige Prins of Staat, met wien de voorscž: Vereenigde Staten van America in Oorlog mogten zyn; nochte zal eenige Onderdaen of Ingezeeten van degemelde Vereenigde Staten van America, of eenige derselve eenige Commissie off Lettres de Marque versoeken of aanneemen, tot het Wapenen van eenig Schip of Scheepen, om ter Kaap te vaaren tegens de Hoog Mogende Heeren Staten Generaal der Vereenigde Nederlanden, of teegens de Onderdanen of Ingezeetenen van gem̃: Haar Hoog Mogende, of eenige van deselve, of den Eigendom van eenige der zelve, van eenige Prins

said Terms, a compleat satisfaction shall be given them.

Article 19.

No Subject of Their High-Mightinesses the States General of the United-Netherlands, shall apply for, or take any Commission or Letters of Marque, for arming any Ship or Ships, to act as Privateers, against the said United-States of America, or any of them, or the Subjects and Inhabitants of the said United-States, or any of them, or against the Property of the Inhabitants of any of them, from any Prince or State, with which the said United-States of America may happen to be at War: Nor shall any subject or Inhabitant of the said United States of America, or any of them, apply for or take any Commission or Letters of Marque, for arming any Ship or Ships, to act as Privateers against the High and Mighty Lords, the States-General of the United Netherlands, or against the subjects of Their High-Mightinesses, or any of them, or against the Property of any one of them, from any Prince or State, with which Their High Mightinesses may be at war: And if any person, of either Nation, shall take such

of Staat, met wien Haar Hoog Mogende in Oorlog zullen zyn; en indien eenig persoon van een van beide Natien zodanige Commissie of Lettres de Marque zal aanneemen, zal deselve als een Zeerover worden gestraft.

Commission, or Letters of Marque, he shall be punished as a Pirate.

ART! 20.

De Scheepen der Onderdanen of Ingezeetenen van een van beide de parthyen, komende aan eenige Kust, toebehoorende aan de een of andere der gemelde Bondgenooten, doch niet voorneemens zynde in een Haven binnen te loopen, of binnen geloopen zynde, en niet begeerende hunne Ladingen te lossen, of Last te breeken, of by te laden, zullen niet gehouden zyn voor haare Scheepen of Laadingen eenige inkomende, of uitgaende regten te betalen, nog eenige reekenschap van haare Laadingen te geeven, ten minsten indien er geen wettig vermoeden is dat zy aan een Vyand toevoeren Koopmanschappen van Contrabande.

ARTICLE 20.

If the Vessells of the Subjects or Inhabitants, of one of the Parties, come upon any Coast, belonging to either of the said Allies, but not willing to enter in to Port, or, being entered in to Port and not willing to unload their Cargoes or break Bulk, or take in any Cargoe, they shall not be obliged to pay, neither for the Vessells, nor the Cargoes, any Duties of Entry in, or out, nor to render any Account of their Cargoes, at least, if there is not just cause to presume, that they carry, to an Enemy, Merchandizes of Contraband.

ART! 21.

De twee Contracteerende Parthyen vergúnnen over en weeder aan elkanderen de vryheid, om ieder in de Havens van den anderen, Consuls, Vice-Consuls, Agenten en Commissarissen van húnne eigen aanstelling te hebben, welkers functien gereguleert zullen worden by particuliere overeenkomst, wanneer ooit eene der beide Parthyen goedvind zodanige aanstelling te doen.

ARTICLE 21.

The Two contracting Parties grant to each other, mutually, the liberty of having, each in the Ports of the other, Consuls, Vice-Consuls, Agents and Commissaries of their own appointing, whose Functions shall be regulated by particular Agreement, when ever either Party chuses to make such Appointments.

ARTl 22.

Dit Tractaat zal in geenerhande opsigten verstaan worden te derogeeren aan de 9e 10e 19e en 24ste Articulen van het Tractaat met Vrankryk, soo als die genummert zyn geweest in het zelve Tractaat den 6 February 1778 geslooten, zynde de 9e 10e 17e en 22ste Articulen van het Tractaat van Commercie,[1] soo als het nu in kragt is tusschen de Vereenigde Staten van America, en de Kroon van Vrankryk: en zal meede niet beletten, dat syne Catholicque Majesteit aan t'selve zoude accedeeren, en van het beneficie der gemelde Vier Articulen jouisseeren.

ARTICLE 22.

This Treaty shall not be understood, in any manner, to derogate from the Ninth, Tenth, Nineteenth, and Twenty Fourth Articles of The Treaty with France, as they were numbered in the same Treaty, concluded the sixth of February 1778, and which make the Articles Ninth, Tenth, Seventeenth, and Twenty second of the Treaty of Commerce,[1] now subsisting, between the United-States of America and the Crown of France: Nor shall it hinder his Catholic Majesty, from acceeding to that Treaty, and enjoying the Advantages of the said Four Articles.

ARTl 23.

By aldien de Vereenigde Staten van America, t'eeniger tyd, nodig mogten vinden, om by den Koning of Keizer van Marocco of Fez, mitsgaders by de Regeeringen van Algiers, Tunis of Tripoli, of by eenige van dezelve, Negotiatien te entameeren tot het verkrygen van Pasporten ter beveiliging van hunne Navigatie op de Middelandsche Zee, zoo beloven Haar Hoog Mogende, op het aanzoek van Hoogstgedagte Vereenigde Staten, die Negotiatien, door middel van hunne by den voorsž: Koning of Keizer en Regeeringen resideerende Consuls op de favorabelste wyze te zullen Secondeeren.

ARTICLE 23.

If at any time, the United-States of America, shall judge necessary, to commence Negotiations, with the King or Emperor of Marocco and Fez, and with the Regencies of Algiers, Tunis or Tripoli, or with any of them to obtain Passports for the security of their Navigation in the Mediteranean Sea, Their High-Mightenesses promise, that, upon the Requisition, which the United States of America shall make of it, they will second such Negotiations, in the most favourable manner, by means of Their Consuls, residing near the said King, Emperor, and Regencies.

[1] Document 1.

Contrabande.

ART! 24.

De Vryheid van Navigatie en Commercie zal zig uitstrekken tot alle soorten van Koopmanschappen, uitgesondert alleen deeze, welke onderscheiden zyn onder den Naam van Contrabande of Verbodene goederen: en onder deeze benoeming van Contrabande of Verbodene goederen zullen alleen begreepen zyn de Oorlogs Ammunitien, of Wapenen, als Mortieren, Geschut, met zyne Vuurwerken, en het geen daar toe behoort; Geweeren, Pistoolen, Bomben, Granaden, Buspulver, Salpeeter, Zwavel, Lonten, Koogels, Pieken, Zwaarden, Lancien, Helbaarden, Casquetten, Cuirassen, en diergelyk soort van Wapen tuig, ook Soldaten, Paarden, Zadels, en toerusting van Paarden.

Alle andere goederen, en Koopmanschappen, hier boven niet uitdrukkelyk gespecificeert, jaa selfs alle soorten van Scheepsmaterialen, hoe zeer dezelve ook zouden mogen zyn geschikt, tot het bouwen of Equipeeren van Oorlogscheepen of tot het maken van het een of ander Oorlogstuig te Water of te Lande, zullen mitsdien, nog volgens den Letter, nog volgens eenige voor te wende interpretatie van dezelve, hoe ook genaamt, onder Verboodene, of Contrabande goederen begreepen kunnen of mogen worden: zoo dat alle dezelve goederen,

Contraband.

ARTICLE 24.

The liberty of Navigation and Commerce shall extend to all sorts of Merchandizes, excepting only those, which are distinguished under the name of Contraband or Merchandizes prohibited: And, under this Denomination of Contraband and Merchandizes-prohibited, shall be comprehended only Warlike Stores and Arms, as Mortars, Artillery, with their Artifices and Appurtenances, Fusils, Pistols, Bombs, Grenades, Gun-Powder, Salt-Petre, Sulphur, Match, Bullets and Balls, Pikes, Sabres, Lances, Halberts, Casques, Cuirasses, and other sorts of Arms; as also, Soldiers, Horses, Saddles and Furniture for Horses. All other Effects and Merchandizes, not before specified expressly, and even all sorts of Naval Matters, however proper they may be, for the Construction and Equipment of Vessells of War, or for the Manufacture of one or another sort of Machines of War, by Land or sea, shall not be judged Contraband, neither by the Letter, nor, according to any pretended Interpretation whatever, ought they, or can they be comprehended, under the Notion of Effects prohibited or Contraband: so that all Effects and Merchandizes, which are not expressly before named, may, without any exception, and in per-

waaren en Koopmanschappen, hier boven niet uitdrukkelyk genoemt, sonder eenig onderscheid, zullen mogen worden getransporteert, en vervoert in alle Vryheid door de Onderdanen en Ingezeetenen van beide Bondgenooten, van en na Plaatsen aan den Vyand toebehoorende, zodanige Steeden of plaatsen alleen uitgesondert, welke op die tyt beleegert, geblocqueert of geinvesteert zyn, waar voor alleenlyk worden gehouden de zulke, die door een der Oorlog voerende Mogendheeden van na by ingeslooten worden gehouden

fect liberty, be transported, by the Subjects and Inhabitants of both Allies, from and to Places, belonging to the Enemy; excepting only the Places, which, at the same time, shall be beseiged, blocked or invested; and those Places only shall be held for such, which are surrounded nearly, by some of the belligerent Powers.

ART! 25.

Ten einde alle dissentie en twist mag werden vermyd en voorgekomen, is over een gekomen, dat ingeval een van beide de Parthyen in Oorlog mogt komen te geraken, de Scheepen en Vaartuigen, toebehoorende aan de Onderdanen of Ingezeetenen van de andere Geallieerde, met Zeebrieven of Pasporten moeten werden voorsien, expresseerende den naam, eigendom en de groote van het Schip of Vaartuig, als meede den Naam, plaats of woninge van den Schipper of Bevelhebber van het gemelde Schip of Vaartuig, ten einde daar by mag blyken, dat het Schip reëel en in waarheid aan de Onderdanen of Ingezeetenen van eene der Parthyen toebehoord, welk pasport zal worden opgemaakt en uitgegeeven volgens het

ARTICLE 25.

To the end that all dissention and Quarrel may be avoided, and prevented, it has been agreed, that in case that one of the Two Parties happens to be at War, the Vessells belonging to the Subjects or Inhabitants of the other Ally, shall be provided with Sea-Letters or Passports, expressing the Name, the property and the Burthen of the Vessell, as also the Name and the Place of Abode of the Master, or Commander of the said Vessell; to the end that, thereby, it may appear, that the Vessell, really and truly, belongs to Subjects or Inhabitants of one of the Parties; which Passports shall be drawn and distributed, according to the Form, annexed to this Treaty, each time that the Vessell shall return, she should have such her Passport renewed,

Formulier agter dit Tractaat gevoegt. Deselve zullen ieder reize, dat het Schip thuys is geweest, op nieuw verleent moeten zyn, of ten minsten niet ouder mogen zyn, als twee Jaar, voor de tyd, dat het Schip laast is thuys geweest. Het is insgelyks vastgestelt, dat zodanige Scheepen of Vaartuigen gelaaden zynde, moeten weezen voorsien niet alleen met Pasporten of Zeebrieven bovengemeld; maar ook met een Generaal Pasport, of particuliere Pasporten, of Manifesten, of andere publicque Documenten, die in de Havenen, van waar de Scheepen laast gekomen zyn, gewoonlyk gegeeven worden aan de Uitgaende Scheepen, inhoudende een Specificatie van de Lading, de plaats van waar het Schip gezeild is, en waar heenen het gedestineert is, of by gebreeke van alle deselve met Certificaten van de Magistraten of Gouverneurs der Steeden, plaatsen, en Colonien, van waar het Schip vertrokken is, in de gewoone form gegeeven, op dat geweeten kan worden, of eenige verboode of Contrabande goederen aan boord van de Scheepen zyn, en of zy daar meede na's Vyands Landen gedestineert zyn, of niet. En by aldien iemand goetdunkt, of raadsaem vind, om in de gemelde bescheiden uit te drukken de persoonen, aan wien de aan boord zynde goederen toekomen, vermag hy zulks vryelyk te doen, sonder

or, at least, they ought not to be of more antient Date than Two Years, before the Vessell has been returned to her Own Country. It has been also agreed, that such Vessells, being loaded, ought to be provided not only with the said Passports or Sea-Letters; but also, with a general Pasport, or with particular Passports, or Manifests, or other publick Documents, which are ordinarily given to Vessells outward bound, in the Ports from whence the Vessells have set sail in the last place, containing a specification of the Cargo, of the Place from whence the Vessell departed; and of that of her destination, or, instead of all these, with Certificates from the Magistrates or Governors of Cities, Places and Colonies from whence the Vessell came, given in the usual Form, to the end that it may be known, whether there are any Effects prohibited or Contraband, on board the Vessells, and whether they are destined to be carried to an Enemy's Country or not. And in case any one judges proper, to express, in the said documents, the Persons, to whom the effects, on board, belong, he may do it freely, without, however, being bound to do it; and the Omission of such expression cannot and ought not to cause a Confiscation.

egter daar toe gehouden te syn of dat gebrek van die uitdrukking geleegenheid tot confiscatie kan of mag geeven.

ART! 26.

Indien de Scheepen of Vaartuigen van de gemelde Onderdanen of Ingezeetenen van een van beide de Parthyen, zeilende langs de kusten off in de open Zee, ontmoet zullen worden door eenig Schip van Oorlog, Kaper of Gewapend Vaartuig van de andere Parthy, zullen de gemelde Oorlog-Scheepen, Kapers of Gewapende Vaartuigen, tot vermyding van alle disordre, buiten bereik van het geschut blyven, dog hunne Booten mogen zenden aan boord van het Koopvaardy Schip, welke zy op die wys zullen ontmoeten, en op het zelve mogen overgaan ten getalle alleen van twee a drie Man, aan wien de Schipper of Bevelhebber van zodanig Schip of Vaartuig zyn Pasport zal vertoonen, inhoudende den Eigendom van het Schip of Vaartuig, ingevolge het Formulier agter dit Tractaat gevoegt, en zal het Schip of Vaartuig na de vertooning van dusdanig Pasport, Zee-brief en verdere bescheiden, vry en liber zyn om deszelfs reis te vervolgen, zoo dat niet geoorloft zal zyn het zelve op eenigerhande wyze te molesteeren of doorzoeken, nog jagt op haar te maken, of het selve te forceeren haare voorgenomen Cours te verlaten.

ARTICLE 26.

If the Vessells of the said subjects or Inhabitants of either of the parties, sailing along the Coasts, or on the High-Seas, are met by a Vessell of War, or Privateer, or other Armed Vessell of the other Party, the said Vessells of War, Privateers, or armed Vessells, for avoiding all disorder, shall remain, without the reach of Cannon, but may send their Boats on board the Merchant Vessell, which they shall meet in this manner, upon which, they may not pass more than two or three men, to whom the Master or Commander shall exhibit his Passport, containing the Property of the Vessell, according to the Form annexed to this Treaty: And the Vessell, after having exhibited such a Passport, Sea-Letter, and other Documents, shall be free to continue her Voyage, so that it shall not be lawfull to molest her, or search her, in any manner, nor to give her Chase, nor to force her to alter her Course.

Art! 27.

Het zal geoorloft zyn aan Koopliedent, Capiteins en Bevelhebbers van Scheepen, het zy publicque en ten Oorlog, of particuliere en ter Koopvaardy vaarende, toebehoorende aan de gemelde Vereenigde Staten van America, of eenige van dezelve, of aan de Onderdanen en Ingezeetenen van eenige derzelve, vryelyk in hunne dienst aan te neemen, en aan Boord van haare gemelde Scheepen te ontfangen, in iedere der havens of plaatsen onder de Jurisdictie van voornoemde Haar Hoog Mogende, eenige Bootsgezellen of anderen, zynde Inboorlingen of Ingezeetenen van eenige der gemelde Staten, op zulke voorwaarden als zal werden over een gekomen, zonder daar voor aan eenige boete, pœne, straffe, Proces of berisping hoe genaamt, onderheevig te zyn.

En zullen reciproquelyk alle Kooplieden, Capiteinen en Bevelhebbers van Scheepen, behoorende tot de voorschreeven Vereenigde Nederlanden, in alle de Havens en plaatsen, onder het gebied van de gemelde Vereenigde Staten van America, het zelve voorregt genieten tot aanneeming en ontfangen van Bootsgezellen of anderen, zynde Inboorlingen of Ingezeetenen van eenige der domeinen van de gemelde Staten Generaal, met dien verstande, dat men nog aan de eene, nog aan de andere zyde zig zal mogen bedie-

Article 27.

It shall be lawfull, for Merchants, Captains and Commanders of Vessells, whether public and of War, or private and of Merchants, belonging to the said United-States of America, or any of them, or to their Subjects and Inhabitants, to take freely into their service, and receive on board of their Vessells, in any Port or Place, in the Jurisdiction of Their High-Mightinesses, aforesaid, Seamen or others, Natives or Inhabitants of any of the said States, upon such conditions, as they shall agree on, with out being subject, for this, to any Fine, Penalty, Punishment, Process, or Reprehension, whatsoever.

And reciprocally, all Merchants, Captains and Commanders, belonging to the said United Netherlands, shall enjoy, in all the Ports and Places under the obedience of the said United States of America, the same Priviledge of engaging and receiving, Seamen or others, Natives or Inhabitants of any Country of the Domination of the said States-General; provided, that neither on One side nor the other, they may not takein to their service such of their Countrymen, who have already engaged in the service of the other Party con-

115605°—31—vol. 2——8

nen van zodanige zyner Landsgenooten, die zig reeds in dienst van de andere contracteerende Parthye, het zy ten Oorlog, het zy op Koopvaardy Scheepen heeft geengageert, het zy men deselve aan de vaste wal, dan wel in Zee zoude mogen ontmoeten, ten minsten indien de Capiteinen of Schippers, onder wiens bevel zodanige persoonen zig mogten bevinden, deselve niet vrywillig uit húnnen dienst wilde ontslaan, op pœne, dat dezelve andersints op den Voet van Weglopers zullen worden behandelt en gestraft.

tracting, whether in War or Trade, and whether they meet them by Land or Sea; at least, if the Captains or Masters, under the command of whom such Persons may be found, will not, of his own consent, discharge them from their Service; upon pain of being otherwise treated and punished as Deserters.

ART! 28.

De toeleg voor refractie,[1] Sal in alle reedelykheid en billykheid worden gereguleert, by de Magistraten der respective Steeden, alwaar men oordeelt, dat eenige bezwaaren desweegens plaets hebben.

ARTICLE 28.

The affair of the Refraction[1] shall be regulated, in all equity and Justice, by the Magistrates of Cities respectively, where it shall be judged, that there is any room to complain, in this respect.

ART! 29.

Het tegenwoordig Tractaat zal werden Geratificeert en geapprobeert by Hoogstgemelde Staten Generaal der Vereenigde Nederlanden, en Hooggemelde Vereenigde Staten van America, en zullen de Acten van Ratificatien aan de eene en de andere zyde in goede ende behoorlyke forme werde overgeleeverd binnen den tyd van Zes Maanden, ofte eerder zo het zelve kan geschieden, te reekenen van den dag van de onderteekening.

ARTICLE 29.

The present Treaty shall be ratified and approved, by Their High Mightinesses, the States General of the United-Netherlands, and by the United-States of America; and, the Acts of Ratification, shall be delivered, in good and due form, on one side and on the other, in the space of Six Months, or sooner, if possible, to be computed from the Day of the signature.

[1] See the note regarding Article 28.

Ten oirkonde deezes hebben Wy Gedeputeerden en Plenipotentiarissen van de Heeren Staten Generaal der Vereenigde Neederlanden en Minister Plenipotentiaris der Vereenigde Staten van America, uit kragte van Onze respective Authorisatie en Pleinpouvoir deeze onderteekent, en met Onze gewoone Cachetten bekragtigt. In den Hage den Agtsten October, Een duysent Seeven hondert twee en tagtig.

[Seal] George van Randwyck
[Seal] B: V: D: Santheuvel
[Seal] P: V: Bleiswyk
[Seal] W C H Van Lynden.
[Seal] D I Van Heeckeren
[Seal] Joan van Kuffeler.
[Seal] F: G: Van Dedem.
tot den Gelder.
[Seal] H: Tjassens

In Faith of which, We the Deputies and Plenipotentiaries of the Lords the States General of the United Netherlands, and the Minister Plenipotentiary of the United-States of America, in virtue of our respective Authorities and full Powers, have signed the present Treaty and apposed thereto the Seals of our Arms.

Done at the Hague the Eight of October, One Thousand Seven Hundred Eighty Two.

[Seal] John Adams.

Formulier van het Pasport dat gegeeven sal worden aan de Scheepen of Vaartuigen ingevolge het 25ste Articul van dit Tractaat.

Aan alle de geenen die deeze teegenwoordige sullen sien Salut: doen te weeten, dat by deezen vryheid en permissie gegeeven werd aen Schipper en Bevelhebber van het Schip /: of Vaartuig:/ genaamt van de van groot Tonnen of daar omtrent, leggende teegenswoordig in de Haaven van gedestineert naar en beladen met om te vertrekken, en met zyn

The Form of the Passport which shall be given to Ships and Vessells, in consequence of the 25th Article of this Treaty.

To all who shall see these presents, Greeting: Be it known, that leave and permission, are, hereby, given to Master or Commander of the Ship or Vessell, called of the Burthen of Tons, or there abouts, lying at present in the Port or Haven of bound for and laden with to depart and proceed with his said Ship or Vessell on his said

Schip of Vaartuig deszelfs gemelde reize voort te zetten, zodanig Schip of Vaartuig gevisiteert zynde, en de voornoemde Schipper of Bevelhebber onder Eede, voor den daar toe gestelden Officier, verklaart hebbende, dat het gemelde Schip of Vaartuig aan een of meerder Onderdanen Volk of Ingezeetenen van toebehoort, en aan hem (: of hun:) alleen.

Voyage, such Ship or Vessell having been visited, and the said Master and Commander having made Oath before the proper Officer, that the said Ship or Vessell belongs to one or more of the Subjects, People, or Inhabitants of and to him or them only.

In getuigenis waarvan wy deeze teegenswoordige met Onze Naemen hebben Onderteekent, en het Zeegel van Ons Waepen daar aan gehegt, en het zelve doen contrasigneeren door tot deezen dag van in het Jaer Onzes Heeren Christi

In wittness whereof, We have subscribed our Names to these presents, and affixed the Seal of our Arms thereto, and caused the same to be countersigned by at this day of in the Year of our Lord Christ

Formulier van het Certificaat het welk aan de Scheepen of Vaartuigen zal werden gegeeven ingevolge het 25ste. Articul van dit Tractaat.

Form of the Certificate, which shall be given to Ships or Vessells, in consequence of the 25th. Article of this Treaty.

Wy de Magistraat (: of Officieren der Convoyen:) van de Stad of Haven van Certificeeren en attesteeren dat op den dag van in het Jaer onzes Heeren C D van in Persoon voor Ons is gecompareerd, en onder Solemneelen Eede heeft verklaard, dat het Schip of Vaartuig genaamt van Tonnen of daar omtrent, waar van van teegenswoordig Schipper of Bevelhebber is, gereg-

We Magistrates or Officers of the Customs, of the City or Port of do Certify and attest, that on the day of in the Year of our Lord C D of personally appeared, before us, and declared by solemn Oath, that the Ship or Vessell, called of Tons or there abouts, whereof of is at present Master or Commander, does, rightfully and proper belong to him or them only:

telyk en behoorlyk aan hem (: of hun :) alleen is toebehoorende:

Dat het zelve thans gedestineert is van de Stad of Haaven van na de Haaven van gelaaden met goederen en Koopmanschappen hier onder particulier gespecificeert en opgenoemt als volgt.

In getuigenis waar van wy dit Certificaat hebben Onderteekent, en met Zeegel van Ons Officie bekragtigt deezen dag van in het Jaar onzes Heeren Christi.

That she is now bound, from the City or Port of to the Port of laden with goods and Merchandizes hereunder particularly described and enumerated, as follows.

In Witness whereof, we have signed this Certificate, and sealed it with the Seal of our Office, this day of in the Year of our Lord Christ

Formulier van Zee-Brief.

Alder Doorluchtigste, Doorluchtigste, Doorluchtige, Grootmachtigste, Grootmachtige, Hoogh ende Wel Geboorne, Wel Edele, Erentfeste, Achtbaare, Wyze, Voorsienige Heeren, Keizeren, Koningen, Republiquen, Princen, Fursten, Hertogen, Graeven, Baronnen, Heeren, Burgemeesteren Scheepenen, Raden, mitsgaders Rechteren, Officieren, Justicieren ende Regenten aller goede Steeden en Plaatsen, het zy Geestelyke of Waereldlyke die deeze opene Letteren zullen sien ofte hooren leezen: Doen Wy Burgemeesteren en Regeerders der Stad to weeten dat Schipper van (:voor Ons Compareerende:) by solemneelen Eede verklaert heeft, dat het Schip genoemd groot omtrent Lasten, t'welk hy althans voert in

Form of the Sea-Letter

Most Serene, Serene, Most Puissant, Puissant, High, Illustrious, Noble, Honourable, Venerable, Wise and Prudent, Lords, Emperors, Kings, Republicks, Princes, Dukes, Earls, Barons, Lords, Burgomasters, Schepens, Councillors, as also Judges, Officers, Justiciaries and Regents of all the good Cities and Places, whether Ecclesiastical or Secular, who shall see these patents, or hear them read: We Burgomasters and Regents of the City of make known that the Master of appearing before us, has declared upon Oath, that the Vessell, called of the Burthen of about Lasts, which he at present navigates, is of the United Provinces, and that no Subjects of the Enemy, have any Part or Portion therein, directly

de Geunieerde Provincien 't huis behoord, en dat geen Onderdanen van den Vyand daar in direct of indirect eenige portie of deel hebben, Soo waarlyk moest hem God Almagtig helpen; Ende want Wy den voorsez̃: Schipper gaarne gevordert zagen in syne rechtvaardige Zaaken, Zoo is Ons versoek allen voornoemd ende yder in het bysonder, daar den voornoemden Schipper met zyn Schip ende ingelaeden goederen komen sal, dat dezelve gelieven den voornoemden Schipper goedelyken te ontfangen, en behoorlyk te tracteeren, gedoogende hem op syne gewoonelyke Tollen ende Ongelden in het door ende voor by vaaren, Havenen, Stroomen en Gebied te passeeren, vaaren en frequenteeren omme syne Negotie te doen, daar en soo hy te raede vinden zal, het welk wy gaerne willen verschuldigen.

Des t'Oirconde deezer Steede Zeegel ter oorzake hier aan hangende den

(:in margine stont:)

Ter Ordonnantie van de Hoog ende Mogende Heeren Staten Generaal der Vereenigde Nederlanden.

nor indirectly, So may God Almighty help him. And as we wish to see the said Master prosper in his lawfull Affairs, our prayer is, to all the before mentioned, and to each of them separately, where the said Master shall arrive, with his Vessell and Cargo, that they may please to receive the said Master, with goodness, and to treat him in a becoming manner, permitting him, upon the usual Tolls and Expences, in passing and repassing, to pass, navigate and frequent the Ports, Passes and Territories, to the End to transact his Business, where, and in what manner he shall judge proper: whereof We shall be willingly indebted.

In Witness and for cause where of, we affix hereto the Seal of this Citty.

(:in the Margin:)

By Ordinance of the High and Mighty Lords, the States-General of the United-Netherlands.

NOTES

It appears that this treaty and the accompanying convention (Document 6) were drawn up in quintuplicate; the eight signatures for the Netherlands were according to the usage that two deputies signed on the part of Holland and one on the part of each other province (Wharton, Diplomatic Correspondence, V, 732, 733, 786, 803). The Department of State files contain one original of each document and two copies of each, in the same form and in part in the same hand, attested by a Dutch official and by John Adams. Similar attested copies were embodied in the respective United States instruments of ratification of the two agreements; so it is probable that two only of the "five fair copies" mentioned by Adams, were signed as originals of the treaty and of the convention.

The United States instrument of ratification is copied in 135 C. C. Papers, I; also in Journals, XXIV, 66. A facsimile of the first and last pages of the original instrument in the Netherland archives is now in the Department of State file. It has the signature of Robert R. Livingston at the end and that of Elias Boudinot, with the Great Seal, in the upper left margin of the first page. Like the corresponding instrument of the Netherland Government, it recites both texts, the Dutch at the left.

The Department of State archives contain no protocol or other similar record of the exchange of ratifications. The ratifications of this treaty and of the convention with the Netherlands of the same date (Document 6) were concurrently exchanged. The date of exchange is given as June 23, 1783, in the registers of the Netherland archives (see Diplomatic Correspondence, 1783–1789, III, 622–23); it is also reported in a letter from The Hague of the same date (Wharton, Diplomatic Correspondence, VI, 502).

The proclamation of this treaty was the first instance of a formal proclamation of a treaty of the United States. For the form see Journals, XXIV, 67–82. It is to be observed that the proclamation was ordered on the very day of ratification by Congress and thus five months prior to the exchange of ratifications. The original proclamation has not been found. There are two identic prints of it in the Library of Congress. In the Department of State file is a facsimile of a print in the New York Public Library. The proclamation included the English text of this and the following convention of the same date. As the form in the Journals shows, it bore no seal; the printed copies have at the foot the names of Elias Boudinot, President (at the right), and Charles Thomson, Secretary (at the lower left).

Note Regarding Article 28

In his report regarding this treaty, dated October 8, 1782 (Wharton, Diplomatic Correspondence, V, 804; original in 84 C. C. Papers, IV, folio 194) John Adams wrote:

> The Refraction, as they call it, upon Tobacco in the Weigh-houses, is a thing that enters so deeply into their commercial Policy, that I could not obtain any thing, more particular or more explicit, than what is found in the Treaty.

The "refraction" appears to have been an allowance or deduction from the weight of tobacco. The word is still used in a somewhat analogous sense (see A New English Dictionary). It seems that in the Dutch text "refractie" should be "refactie," a commercial term for "deduction," now more commonly written "rafactie"; the French "réfaction" has about the same meaning.

Note Regarding the Sea Letter

A note from the Minister of the Netherlands dated December 8, 1784, gave notice that the Netherland Government had made a change in the form of the sea letter by striking out the words "and that no Subjects of the Enemy have any Part or Portion therein directly or indirectly."

A report on the note by Secretary Jay, to whom it had been referred, was made on November 1, 1785, and was read in Congress the same day (Journals for the year 1785, not yet in print; Diplomatic Correspondence, 1783–1789, III, 423–26; 81 C. C. Papers, I, folios 485–89).

This report pointed out that the consent of the United States had not "been obtained or asked." It contained an "Opinion that no Article, Paragraph or Sentence in any Treaty or Contract or in any Paper directed and settled thereby can of Right be altered by one of the Parties without the Consent of the other." It then mentioned the fact that the sea letters were to be issued only in time of war, so that "prudential Considerations should . . . induce Congress to observe Silence on this subject for the present"; but suggested certain inconclusive instructions to the Minister at The Hague, if and when such a minister was appointed.

So far as appears, Congress took no action on this report of Jay, and no further steps of any kind were taken in the matter.

Treaty Series, No. 250
8 Statutes at Large, 50–53

6

THE NETHERLANDS : OCTOBER 8, 1782

Convention Concerning Vessels Recaptured, signed at The Hague October 8, 1782. Original in Dutch and English.
Ratified by the United States January 23, 1783. Ratified by the Netherlands December 27, 1782. Ratifications exchanged at The Hague June 23, 1783. Proclaimed January 23, 1783.

Conventie tusschen de Heeren Staten Generaal der Vereenigde Nederlanden, en Vereenigde Staten van America, rakende de hernomen Scheepen.

De Heeren Staten Generaal der Vereenigde Nederlanden, en Vereenigde Staten van America, geneegen synde, eenige gelykvormige grondbeginzelen vast te stellen, omtrent het opbrengen van Prysen, door de Oorlog-Scheepen eñ Commissie-vaarders van wedersÿds Contracteerende Parthyen, op derselver gemeene Vyanden genomen, en omtrent de Scheepen van elkanders Onderdanen, door den Vyand genomen, en by de Oorlog Scheepen eñ Commissie-vaarders van weederzyden hernomen, zyn met den anderen over eengekomen, omtrent de navolgende Articulen

ART! 1.

De Scheepen van eene der beide Natien door Kapers van den andere hernomen, zullen aan den eersten Eigenaer wedergegeeven

Convention between the Lords, the States-General of the United Netherlands, and the United States of America, concerning Vessells recaptured.

The Lords, the States-General of the United Netherlands, and the United States of America, being inclined to establish some uniform Principles, with relation to Prizes, made by Vessells of War, and Commissioned by the Two contracting Powers, upon their common Enemies, and to Vessells of the Subjects of either Party, captured by the Enemy, and recaptured by Vessells of War, commissioned by either Party, have agreed upon the following Articles.

ARTICLE 1.

The Vessells of either of the Two Nations, recaptured by the Privateers of the other, shall be restored to the first Pro-

worden, indien die Scheepen nog geen Vier en twintig Uuren in de magt van den Vyand geweest zyn, mits door den Eigenaer van het hernoome Schip daar voor betaald worde een derde van de waarde van het Schip, mitsgaders van de Laading, Canons, en Scheepstoerustingen, welk derde in der minne begroot zal worden door de geinteresseerde Parthyen; of andersints, en zoo zy desweegens niet over een konden komen, zullen zÿ zich adresseeren aan de Bedienden der Admiraliteit van de plaats alwaar de Kaper die het Schip hernomen heeft, het zelve zal hebben opgebracht.

prietor, if such Vessells have not been Four and Twenty Hours in the Power of the Enemy; provided the Owner of the Vessell recaptured pay therefor, one Third of the Value of the Vessell, as also, of that of the Cargo, the Cannons and Apparel, which Third shall be valued, by agreement, between the parties interested; or, if they cannot agree, thereon, among themselves they shall address themselves to the Officers of the Admiralty, of the Place, where the Privateer, who has retaken the Vessell, shall have conducted her.

ART! 2.

Indien het hernomen Schip langer dan Vier en twintig Uuren in's Vyands magt geweest is, zal het in't geheel aan den Kaper, die het zelve hernomen heeft, toebehooren.

ARTICLE 2.

If the Vessell recaptured, has been, more than Twenty Four Hours, in the power of the Enemy, she shall belong, entirely, to the Privateer who has retaken her.

ART! 3.

In gevalle een Schip zal hernomen geweest zyn door een Oorlog-Schip of Vaartuig, toebehoorende aan de Staten Generaal der Vereenigde Nederlanden, of aan de Vereenigde Staten van America, zal het zelve aan den eersten Eigenaer wedergegeeven worden, mits betalende een dertigste gedeelte van de waarde van het Schip en deszelfs Laading, Canons, en Scheepstoerustingen, by aldien het binnen de Vier en twintig Uuren hernomen is, en het

ARTICLE 3.

In case a Vessell shall have been recaptured, by a Vessell of War, belonging to the States General of the United-Netherlands, or to the United-States of America, she shall be restored to the first Owner, he paying a Thirtieth Part of the Value of the Ship, her Cargo, Cannons and Apparel, if she has been recaptured, in the Interval of Twenty Four Hours, and the Tenth Part, if she has been recaptured, after the Twenty Four

tiende gedeelte zoo het naa de Vier en twintig Uuren hernomen is: welke Sommen als een Gratificatie verdeeld zullen worden onder de Equipagien van de Scheepen die het zelve hernomen zullen hebben.

De begroting der bovengemelde dertigste, en tiende gedeeltens zal gereguleerd worden naar luid van het eerste Articul der jegenswoordige Conventie.

ART[l] 4.

De restitutie der Pryzen, het zy door Oorlog Scheepen of Kapers hernomen, zal ondertusschen en tot dat behoorlyk en voldoende bewys van den eigendom der hernomen Scheepen gegeeven kan werden, onder suffisante Cautie wegens het nakomen der bovenstaande Articulen, binnen een reedelyken tyt geadmittert werden.

ART[l] 5.

De Oorlog- en Kaper Scheepen van de eene en de andere der beide Natien zullen wederzyds, zoo in Europa als in de andere Weerelds-deelen in elkanders respective havens toegelaten worden met hunne pryzen, welke aldaar zullen mogen ontlāden en verkocht worden, naar de formaliteiten gebruikelyk in den Staat, alwaar de prys zal weezen opgebragt, soo ver het bestaanbaar is met het 22[ste] Articul van het Tractaat van Commercie;[1] met dien verstande,

Hours: which Sums shall be distributed, in form of Gratifications, to the Crews of the Vessells, which shall have retaken her.

The valuation of the said Thirtieth Parts and Tenth Parts, shall be regulated, according to the Tenour of the first Article of the present Convention.

ARTICLE 4.

The restitution of Prizes, whether they may have been retaken by Vessells of War, or by Privateers, in the meantime and untill requisite and sufficient Proofs can be given of the Property of Vessells recaptured, shall be admitted in a reasonable time, under sufficient sureties, for the observation of the aforesaid Articles.

ARTICLE 5.

The Vessells of War and Privateers, of One and of the other of the Two Nations, shall be reciprocally, both in Europe, and in the other Parts of the World, admitted in the respective Ports of each, with their Prizes, which may be unloaded and sold, according to the formalities used in the State where the Prize shall have been conducted, as far as may be consistent with the 22[d] Article of the Treaty of Commerce:[1] Provided always, that

[1] Document 5.

dat de wettigheid der Prysen door Nederlandsche Scheepen gemaakt zal beslist worden, naar luid der Wetten en Reglementen, te deezer zake in de Vereenigde Nederlanden vast gesteld, gelyk ook die der Pryzen door Americaansche Scheepen gemaakt, zal beoordeelt worden volgens de Wetten en Reglementen by de Vereenigde Staten van America bepaald.

ART! 6.

Voor het overige zal het aan de Staten Generaal der Vereenigde Nederlanden, als meede aan de Vereenigde Staten van America, vry staan, zodanige Reglementen te maken als zy zullen oordeelen te behooren; met betrekking tot het gedrag't geen hunne Scheepen en Kapers weedersyds verpligt zullen weezen te houden, ten opzigt der Scheepen die zy genomen, en opgebragt zullen hebben in de Havens der beide Mogendheeden.

Ten Oirkonde deezes hebben Wy Gedeputeerden en Plenipotentiarissen van de Heeren Staten Generaal der Vereenigde Nederlanden, en Minister Plenipotentiaris der Vereenigde Staten van America, uyt kragt van Onze respective Authorisatie, en pleinpouvoir, deeze Onderteekent, en met Onze gewoone Cachetten bekragtigt.

the Legality of Prizes, by the Vessells of the Low-Countries, shall be decided conformably to the Laws and Regulations, established in the United-Netherlands; as likewise, that, of Prizes, made by American Vessells, shall be judged, according to the Laws and Regulations determined by the United-States of America.

ARTICLE 6.

More over, it shall be free, for the States-General of the United-Netherlands, as well as for the United States of America, to make such Regulations, as they shall judge necessary, relative to the Conduct, which their respective Vessells and Privateers ought to hold, in relation to the Vessells, which they shall have taken and conducted in to the Ports of the Two Powers.

In Faith of which, We, the Deputies and Plenipotentiaries of the Lords, the States-General of the United-Netherlands, and Minister Plenipotentiary of the United-States of America, have, in virtue of our respective Authorities and Full-Powers, signed these presents and confirmed the Same, with the Seal of our Arms.

Gedaan in's Hage den Agtsten October, Een duysent Seeven hondert twee en tagtig.

[Seal] George van Randwyck
[Seal] B: V: D: Santheuvel
[Seal] P: V: Bleiswyk
[Seal] W C H Van Lynden.
[Seal] D I Van Heeckeren
[Seal] Joan van Kuffeler.
[Seal] F: G: Van Dedem *tot den Gelder*.
[Seal] H: Tjassens

Done at the Hague, the Eight of October, One Thousand Seven Hundred Eighty Two.

[Seal] John Adams.

NOTES

The United States instrument of ratification is copied in 135 C. C. Papers, I; also in Journals, XXIV, 67. A facsimile of the first and last pages of the original instrument in the Netherland archives is now in the Department of State file. Like the corresponding instrument of the Netherland Government, it recites both texts and is the same in form as that described in the notes to Document 5.

As to the signature of this convention, the exchange of ratifications, and the proclamation thereof, see generally the notes to the preceding document, the Treaty of Amity and Commerce with the Netherlands of the same date.

Treaty Series, No. 102
8 Statutes at Large, 54–57

7

GREAT BRITAIN : NOVEMBER 30, 1782

Preliminary Articles of Peace. Articles to be inserted in and to constitute the Treaty of Peace (with separate article which was not ratified), signed at Paris November 30, 1782. Original in English.

Ratified by the United States April 15, 1783. Ratified by Great Britain August 6, 1783. Ratifications exchanged at Paris August 13, 1783. Proclaimed April 15, 1783; see the note regarding the proclamation.

Articles agreed upon, by and between Richard Oswald Esquire, the Commissioner of his Britannic Majesty, for treating of Peace with the Commissioners of the United States of America, in behalf of his said Majesty, on the one part; and John Adams, Benjamin Franklin, John Jay, and Henry Laurens, four of the Commissioners of the said States, for treating of Peace with the Commissioner of his said Majesty, on their Behalf, on the other part. To be inserted in, and to constitute the Treaty of Peace proposed to be concluded, between the Crown of Great Britain, and the said United States; but which Treaty is not to be concluded, untill Terms of a Peace shall be agreed upon, between Great Britain and France; and his Britannic Majesty shall be ready to conclude such Treaty accordingly.

Whereas reciprocal Advantages, and mutual Convenience are found by Experience, to form the only permanent foundation of Peace and Friendship between States; It is agreed to form the Articles of the proposed Treaty, on such Principles of liberal Equity, and Reciprocity, as that partial Advantages, (those Seeds of Discord!) being excluded, such a beneficial and satisfactory Intercourse between the two Countries, may be establish'd, as to promise and secure to both perpetual Peace and Harmony.

ARTICLE 1st

His Britannic Majesty acknowledges the said United States, Vizt New Hampshire, Massachusetts Bay, Rhode Island and Providence Plantations, Connecticut, New York, New Jersey, Pennsylvania, Delaware, Maryland, Virginia, North Carolina, South Carolina and Georgia, to be free Sovereign and independent States; That he treats

with them as such; And for himself, his Heirs and Successors, relinquishes all Claims to the Government, Propriety, and territorial Rights of the same, and every part thereof; and that all Disputes which might arise in future, on the Subject of the Boundaries of the said United States, may be prevented, It is hereby agreed and declared that the following are, and shall be their Boundaries Viz^t

Article 2^d

From the north west Angle of Nova Scotia, Viz^t that Angle which is form'd by a Line drawn due north, from the Source of St Croix River to the Highlands, along the said Highlands which divide those Rivers that empty themselves into the River St Laurence, from those which fall into the Atlantic Ocean, to the northwesternmost Head of Connecticut River; thence down along the middle of that River to the 45th Degree of North Latitude; from thence by a Line due West on said Latitude, untill it strikes the River Iroquois, or Cataraquy; thence along the middle of said River into Lake Ontario; through the middle of said Lake, untill it strikes the Communication by Water between that Lake and Lake Erie; thence along the middle of said Communication into Lake Erie, through the middle of said Lake, untill it arrives at the Water Communication between that Lake and Lake Huron; thence along the middle of said water communication into the Lake Huron; thence through the middle of said Lake to the Water Communication between that Lake and Lake Superior; thence through Lake Superior northward of the Isles Royal & Phelipeaux, to the Long Lake; thence through the middle of said Long Lake, and the water Communication between it and the Lake of the Woods, to the said Lake of the Woods, thence through the said Lake to the most Northwestern point thereof, and from thence on a due west Course to the River Missisippi; thence by a Line to be drawn along the middle of the said River Missisippi, untill it shall intersect the northernmost part of the 31st Degree of North Latitude. South, by a Line to be drawn due East, from the Determination of the Line last mentioned, in the Latitude of 31 Degrees North of the Equator, to the middle of the River Apalachicola or Catahouche; thence along the middle thereof, to its junction with the Flint River; thence strait to the Head of St Mary's River, and thence down along the middle of St Mary's River to the Atlantic Ocean. East, by a Line to be drawn along the middle of the River St Croix, from its Mouth in the Bay of Fundy to its Source; and from its Source directly North, to the aforesaid Highlands which divide the Rivers that fall into the

Atlantic Ocean, from those which fall into the River St Laurence; comprehending all Islands within twenty Leagues of any part of the Shores of the united States, and lying between Lines to be drawn due East from the points where the aforesaid Boundaries between Nova Scotia on the one part and East Florida on the other shall respectively touch the Bay of Fundy, and the Atlantic Ocean; excepting such Islands as now are, or heretofore have been within the Limits of the said Province of Nova Scotia.

Article 3d

It is agreed, that the People of the United States shall continue to enjoy unmolested the Right to take Fish of every kind on the Grand Bank, and on all the other Banks of Newfoundland; Also in the Gulph of St Laurence, and at all other Places in the Sea where the Inhabitants of both Countries used at any time heretofore to fish. And also that the Inhabitants of the united States shall have Liberty to take Fish of every kind on such part of the Coast of Newfoundland, as British Fishermen shall use, (but not to dry or cure the same on that Island,) and also on the Coasts, Bays, and Creeks of all other of his Britannic Majesty's Dominions in America, and that the American Fishermen shall have Liberty to dry and cure Fish in any of the unsettled Bays Harbours and Creeks of Nova Scotia, Magdalen Islands, and Labrador, so long as the same shall remain unsettled; but so soon as the same or either of them shall be settled, it shall not be lawful for the said Fishermen to dry or cure Fish at such Settlement, without a previous Agreement for that purpose with the Inhabitants Proprietors or Possessors of the Ground.

Article 4th

It is agreed that Creditors on either side, shall meet with no lawful Impediment to the Recovery of the full value in Sterling Money of all bonâ fide Debts heretofore contracted.

Article 5th

It is agreed that the Congress shall earnestly recommend it to the Legislatures of the respective States, to provide for the Restitution of all Estates, Rights, and Properties which have been confiscated, belonging to real British Subjects; and also of the Estates Rights and Properties of Persons resident in Districts in the Possession of his Majesty's Arms; and who have not borne Arms against the said United States: And that Persons of any other Description

shall have free Liberty to go to any part or parts of any of the thirteen United States, and therein to remain twelve months unmolested in their Endeavours to obtain the Restitution of such of their Estates, Rights and Properties as may have been confiscated; And that Congress shall also earnestly recommend to the several States a Reconsideration and Revision of all Acts or Laws regarding the premises, so as to render the said Laws or Acts perfectly consistent not only with Justice and Equity, but with that spirit of Conciliation which on the Return of the Blessings of Peace should universaly prevail. And that Congress shall also earnestly recommend to the several States, that the Estates Rights and Properties of such last mention'd Persons shall be restored to them; they refunding to any Persons who may be now in Possession the bonâ fide Price, (where any has been given,) which such Persons may have paid on purchasing any of the said Lands, Rights, or Properties since the Confiscation.

And it is agreed that all Persons who have any Interest in confiscated Lands, either by Debts, Marriage Settlements or otherwise, shall meet with no lawful Impediment in the prosecution of their just Rights.

Article 6th

That there shall be no future Confiscations made, nor any prosecutions commenced against any Person or Persons, for or by reason of the Part which he or they may have taken in the present War, and that no person shall on that account suffer any future Loss or Damage either in his Person, Liberty or Property; and that those who may be in confinement on such charges, at the time of the Ratification of the Treaty in America, shall be immediately set at Liberty, and the Prosecutions so commenced be discontinued.

Article 7th

There shall be a firm and perpetual Peace, between his Britannic Majesty and the said States, and between the Subjects of the one and the Citizens of the other, Wherefore all Hostilities both by Sea and Land shall then immediately cease: All Prisoners on both sides shall be set at Liberty, & his Britannic Majesty shall, with all convenient speed, & without causing any Destruction or carrying away any Negroes, or other Property of the American Inhabitants withdraw all his Armies Garrisons and Fleets from the said United States, and from every Port, Place, and Harbour within the same; leaving in all Fortifications the American Artillery that may be

115605°—31—vol. 2——9

therein: And shall also order and cause all Archives, Records, Deeds and Papers belonging to any of the said States, or their Citizens, which in the Course of the War may have fallen into the hands of his Officers to be forthwith restored and delivered to the proper States & Persons to whom they belong.

ARTICLE 8th

The Navigation of the River Mississippi from its Source to the Ocean, shall for ever remain free and open to the Subjects of Great Britain and the Citizens of the United States.

ARTICLE 9th

In case it should so happen that any Place or Territory belonging to Great Britain, or to the United States, should be conquered by the Arms of either, from the other, before the Arrival of these Articles in America, It is agreed that the same shall be restored, without Difficulty, and without requiring any Compensation.

Done at Paris, the thirtieth day of November, in the year One thousand Seven hundred Eighty Two

RICHARD OSWALD [Seal]
JOHN ADAMS. [Seal]
B FRANKLIN [Seal]
JOHN JAY [Seal]
HENRY LAURENS. [Seal]

[On the page of the original next after the above signatures, is the following, the brackets being in the original:]

Witness

The Words [and Henry Laurens] between the fifth and sixth Lines of the first Page; and the Words [or carrying away any Negroes, or other Property of the American Inhabitants] between the seventh and eighth Lines of the eighth Page, being first interlined

CALEB WHITEFOORD
Secretary to the British Commission.
W. T. FRANKLIN
Secy to the American Commission

[On the last written page of the original appears the separate article, which was not ratified.[1]]

NOTES

No original of this treaty is to be found in the archives of the Department of State or in the Library of Congress. The available evidence tends to support the view that no such original was ever received in the United States.

The text of the treaty here printed is from the original signed treaty which is in the British archives, a facsimile whereof is now in the Department of State file.

John Adams in his Journal for November 30, 1782, the date of signature, writes:

> We met first at Mr Jay's, then at Mr Oswald's, examined & compared the Treaties. . . . Then the Treaties were signed, sealed & delivered, & we all went out to Passy to dine with Dr Franklin. (84 C. C. Papers, IV, folio 278.)

While the language quoted does not exclude the possibility of more than duplicate originals, still it seems more appropriate for two than for a greater number. Adams's letter of December 4, 1782, to Robert R. Livingston, Secretary for Foreign Affairs, purports to transmit an original. He says, "It is with much pleasure that I transmit you the Preliminary Treaty between the K. of G. Britain & the United States of America."

However, the words regarding the treaty may not have been used with precision and perhaps meant only a copy of the treaty. The letter (84 C. C. Papers, IV, folios 301–4), while signed by Adams, is endorsed, in Thomson's hand, "Duplicate from Mr Adams," and the enclosure following (folio 305) is a copy of the treaty.

It is to be remembered that at this period letters overseas were usually written in from two to four or even more originals, all of which were signed and sent, if possible, by different ships. Complaints of tampering with the despatches were frequent. Formal documents were often prepared in various originals for this reason. Con-

---

[1] It reads as follows:

SEPARATE ARTICLE.

It is hereby understood and agreed, that in case Great Britain at the Conclusion of the present War, shall recover, or be put in possession of West Florida, the Line of North Boundary between the said Province and the United States, shall be a Line drawn from the Mouth of the River Yassous where it unites with the Mississippi due East to the River Apalachicola.

Done at Paris the thirtieth day of November, in the year One thousand Seven hundred and Eighty Two.

Attest
CALEB WHITEFOORD
Secy to the British Commission.
Attest
W. T. FRANKLIN
Secy to the American Commission

RICHARD OSWALD [Seal]
JOHN ADAMS. [Seal]
B FRANKLIN [Seal]
JOHN JAY [Seal]
HENRY LAURENS. [Seal]

gress ordered six ratifications of the treaties of February 6, 1778, to be transmitted abroad "by different conveyances" and directed the Marine Committee to "provide vessels for carrying the said despatches" (Journals, XI, 463–64).

But when there was an enclosure to a letter, it might well be that there was available only one original of the enclosure; so, while each one of the (say) four texts of the letter was in a strict sense an original, the enclosure in three of them would be a copy; and consequently one may and does find an original letter which says it encloses an original document, when the enclosure with it is a copy.

The report of December 14, 1782, addressed to the Secretary for Foreign Affairs and signed by Adams, Franklin, Jay, and Laurens, the body of which is in the writing of William Temple Franklin (85 C. C. Papers, folio 254), enclosed "a Copy of the Articles," and the enclosure (folio 262) *is* a copy. Adams's Journal for November 30 and the two letters of December 4 and 14, 1782, above cited, are printed in Wharton, Diplomatic Correspondence, VI, at pages 90, 106, and 131, respectively.

Further light is thrown on the question by certain letters of Richard Oswald (who signed the treaty on behalf of Great Britain), copies of which are in the Library of Congress (12 Franklin Papers, Oswald's Journal, 1782; but that book is not properly a "journal"; it is a transcript of volume 70 of the Shelburne Papers, now in the William L. Clements Library and entitled "The Correspondence with Mr. Oswald the Commissioner at Paris").

On November 30, 1782, Oswald wrote to his chief, the Right Honorable T. Townshend (Secretary of State for Colonial Affairs), enclosing "the Articles of Treaty, signed and sealed." On December 4, 1782, another letter of Oswald to Townshend states:

> This goes by the Messenger Coates, and accompanies Two Copies of the said Treaty, certified, as Duplicates of the abovementioned Original, by the Gentlemen who witnessed the same, when executed. The Commissioners did not incline to sign any more than the two Original that were executed on the 30th Ultimo being satisfied that Copies, so certified, will not be objected to in America, and is all that will be transmitted by them in the Packet they are to send to that Country.

Still another letter of the same date, addressed by Oswald to H. Strachey, who had been with him during the latter part of the negotiations, further discusses the procedure and refers to two copies certified by Doctor Franklin.

The conclusion from the foregoing is this. While it was a common practice at the time to sign more than duplicate originals of a treaty, that course was not followed in this instance. Only two originals were signed. It was agreed that certified copies would be sufficient for use in the United States, and accordingly various certified copies were prepared, some of them being certified by Benjamin Franklin. One of the two originals was delivered to Oswald and sent by him to London. The other original was retained by the American Commissioners in Paris; and at the time only certified copies were sent to the

United States, both in Adams's letter of December 4 and in the report of the Commissioners of December 14, 1782.

The Department of State file, so far as it goes, confirms these conclusions, because it contains two certified copies of the treaty; one of them is certified by W. T. Franklin, without date, with the words "A true Copy from the Original in my Possession." The other has on its final page a certification under the seal of Benjamin Franklin, which is over the original blue ribbon which still binds the sheets together; it is dated at Passy December 4, 1782, and reads, over Franklin's signature, "A true Copy, examined and compared with the Original by."

Neither of those two certified copies notes or has any interlineations; and neither is the same as the signed original in punctuation; each omits one word; and the two differ in those regards *inter se;* the text of the treaty in the Statutes at Large appears to have been taken from the copy certified by Doctor Franklin; for in that copy the word "said" is omitted in the phrase "along the said Highlands" in the opening sentence of Article 2; and in the same article "Phelipeaux" is "Phelippeaux."

However, there *was* one original in the possession of the American Commissioners at Paris, and the question remains, What became of it? The evidence on this point is negative.

After Franklin came back to the United States in the summer of 1785, he wrote a letter on September 19 to Jay, who by this time had become Secretary for Foreign Affairs, saying that he transmitted by the hands of his grandson (W. T. Franklin) all the original treaties which he had been concerned in negotiating (Diplomatic Correspondence, 1783–1789, I, 398–99).

That letter did not contain a list of the enclosed papers; but on October 11, 1785, Jay, in a report to the President of Congress, made such a list (81 C. C. Papers, I, folios 445–47). That list is very interesting. It includes instruments of ratification, as well as original treaties; indeed, it includes about every original paper that one would expect to find in it, with the single exception of this treaty of November 30, 1782; it includes even the British instrument of ratification of this treaty; and, furthermore, every original paper mentioned in the list is either in the archives of the Department of State or in the Library of Congress.

A possible inference is that the original of this treaty in some way disappeared from the Paris files of the American Commissioners. Clearly Franklin would have brought it with him if it had then been found. He said he transmitted the originals of all the treaties which he had been concerned in making, and this was one of them, and he did bring with him the British instrument of ratification of this very treaty.

There are two copies of the treaty which have some bearing on the form of the originals. One of them is in Oswald's Journal (beginning at page 646). Toward the end of that copy, after the signatures but before the separate article, there is a note of two interlineations. It

seems clear from them that that copy was written directly and literally from one of the signed originals, namely, the one delivered to Oswald and now in the archives of the British Government; and the facsimile of that original shows this to be the case.

The other copy is that written in the journal of the American Commissioners, beginning at page 62; the book is in the Library of Congress (8 Franklin Papers, Records of the U. S. Legation, Paris; Peace Commissioners, 1780–1783. There is a duplicate journal, 8A, of the same title, but it has a different pagination and lacks some pages.)

Toward the end of that copy, after the signatures but before the separate article, appears a note of four interlineations, witnessed by the two secretaries; it thus appears probable that that copy was also written directly and literally from a signed original which the American Commissioners in Paris retained. This seems the more likely in view of the fact that the notes of interlineations in the respective journals differ as to their line and page numbers; and the American record shows four interlineations, while the British record shows only two. Furthermore, one of the interlineations recorded in each list is of the words (in Article 7) "or carrying away any Negroes, or other Property of the American Inhabitants."

The insertion of those words was, as Adams's Journal shows, a change made almost at the moment of the signature of the treaty (Wharton, Diplomatic Correspondence, VI, 90).

Note Regarding Ratification

The Department of State file now contains a facsimile of the United States instrument of ratification. The cover page reads "Ratification of the Preliminary Articles of Peace between Great Britain and the United States of America. Done at Paris November 30th 1782." The instrument is dated April 15, 1783; it is signed at the end by Elias Boudinot and Robert R. Livingston and attested by Charles Thomson, Secretary. The Great Seal is impressed at the left top of the first page. So there can be no doubt that April 15, 1783, is the correct date of ratification by the United States (see Journals, XXIV, 243–51). The approval by Congress on April 11, 1783, of the proclamation printed below, was a real assent to the articles of November 30, 1782, but was not a formal ratification thereof. The letter of Livingston to John Adams of April 14, 1783 (Wharton, Diplomatic Correspondence, VI, 375), says that "Congress, the day before yesterday, agreed to ratify the Provisional Articles as such." This must refer to the vote of April 11; but the ratification was voted on April 15.

Indeed, there was much divergence of opinion in Congress as to the propriety or necessity of ratification of the "Provisional Articles." A majority of the committee which reported on the matter (James Madison and Richard Peters) opposed ratification. The minority (Alexander Hamilton) favored it. The form of the treaty was thought to be somewhat ambiguous; James Wilson called it "contingently definitive." Finally unanimous ratification was voted (see the notes of Madison, Journals, XXV, 958–60).

It is to be remembered that Congress at this time was aware of the fact that the Preliminaries of Peace between France and Great Britain, and also between Great Britain and Spain, had not only been signed on January 20, 1783, but had gone into force by the respective exchanges of ratifications on the following February 3 and 9.

There is no protocol or other similar record of the exchange of ratifications in the Department of State file; and no such record has been found in the British archives.

The date of exchange is reported in a letter of John Adams to Livingston, August 13, 1783 (Wharton, Diplomatic Correspondence, VI, 645); also in a letter of Hartley to Fox (Secretary of State for Foreign Affairs) of the same date (copied in Bancroft's Transcripts, Hartley's Negotiations, II, 41, NYPL).

Note Regarding the Separate Article

The separate article did not go into force. It is omitted from the instrument of ratification of Great Britain and also from that of the United States, although in the draft voted by Congress (Journals, XXIV, 250–51) it appears. See the letter of Livingston (Secretary for Foreign Affairs) to the Commissioners, under date of April 21, 1783 (Wharton, Diplomatic Correspondence, VI, 387), where he says:

> You will observe that the [enclosed] ratification [of the provisional articles] does not extend to the separate article. The treaty between Spain and Great Britain [the preliminaries of January 20, 1783, by the third article whereof Great Britain yielded both East and West Florida to Spain] renders it unnecessary, and *Congress not caring to express any sentiment upon that subject.* (Italics not in original.)

The separate article was supposed to be secret; but according to Livingston, it very soon became an open secret (letter to the Commissioners, March 25, 1783, Wharton, Diplomatic Correspondence, VI, 338–39).

Note Regarding the Proclamation

The United States instrument of ratification of April 15, 1783, was published at the time and served as a proclamation of the text. There is a print of it among the broadsides in the Library of Congress (see Journals, XXV, 985, item 403); a facsimile thereof is in the Department of State file; like the original instrument it omits the separate article.

It has at various times been stated that Congress ordered the proclamation of the above articles (except the separate article) on April 11, 1783. This, in the correct sense of a proclamation of the text, is erroneous. On the date mentioned, Congress agreed unanimously to a proclamation (printed below) which declared "the Cessation of Arms" and which mentioned generally the "Provisional Articles" of November 30, 1782, but more particularly the various documents signed at Versailles January 20, 1783; namely, the "Preliminaries for restoring Peace" between France and Great Britain and between

Spain and Great Britain, and the Declarations for Suspension of Arms between Great Britain and the United States (Document 8).

The date of that proclamation has been given as April 12 (Wharton, Diplomatic Correspondence, VI, 370–72). But April 11 is the date of the original. Six early prints are noted in Journals, XXV, 984–85. The Journals of Congress give April 11 as the date (Journals, XXIV, 238–40), and on that day it was transmitted to Sir Guy Carleton, Commander of the British forces in New York, although the circular letter to the governors of the States was under date of April 12 (Wharton, Diplomatic Correspondence, VI, 367–68).

The original proclamation is in the archives department of the office of the Secretary of the Commonwealth of Massachusetts; not in the Massachusetts State Library, as stated in Journals, XXV, 984, item 400. The text here printed is from a facsimile thereof which is now in the Department of State file of the Declarations for Suspension of Arms (Document 8).

By the UNITED STATES of America In Congress Assembled. A PROCLAMATION, Declaring the Cessation of Arms, as well by Sea as by Land, agreed upon between the United States of America and His Britannic Majesty; and enjoining the Observance thereof.

Whereas Provisional Articles were signed at Paris on the Thirtieth Day of November last, between the Ministers Plenipotentiary of the United States of America for treating of Peace, and the Minister Plenipotentiary of His Britannic Majesty, to be inserted in and to constitute the Treaty of Peace proposed to be concluded between the United States of America and his Britannic Majesty, when Terms of Peace should be agreed upon between their Most Christian and Britannic Majesties: And Whereas Preliminaries for restoring Peace between their Most Christian and Britannic Majesties were signed at Versailles, on the Twentieth Day of January last, by the Ministers of their Most Christian and Britannic Majesties: And Whereas Preliminaries for restoring Peace between the said King of Great Britain and the King of Spain were also signed at Versailles, on the same Twentieth Day of January last.

By which said Preliminary Articles it hath been agreed, That as soon as the same were ratified, Hostilities between the said Kings, their Kingdoms, States and Subjects, should Cease in all Parts of the World; and it was farther agreed, That all Vessels and Effects that might be taken in the Channel and in the North Seas, after the Space of Twelve Days from the Ratification of the said Preliminary Articles, should be restored; that the Term should be One Month from the Channel and North Seas as far as the Canary Islands inclusively, whether in the Ocean or the Mediterranean, Two Months from the said Canary Islands as far as the Equinoctial Line or Equator; and lastly, Five Months in all other Parts of the World, without any Exception or more particular Description of time or Place: And Whereas it was Declared by the Minister Plenipotentiary of the King of Great Britain, in the Name and by the express Order of the King his Master, on the said Twentieth day of January last, that the said United States of America, their Subjects and their Possessions shall be comprised in the above mentioned Suspension of Arms, at the same Epochs, and in the same manner, as the three Crowns above mentioned, their Subjects and Possessions respectively; upon Condition that on the Part, and in the Name of the United States of America, a similar Declaration shall be Delivered, expressly Declaring their Assent to the said Suspension of Arms, and containing an Assurance of the most perfect Reciprocity on their Part: And Whereas the Ministers Plenipotentiary of these United States, did, on the same Twentieth Day of January, in the Name and by the Authority of the said United States, accept the said Declaration, and declare, that the said States should cause all Hostilities to Cease against His Britannic Majesty, his Subjects and his Possessions, at the Terms

and Epochs agreed upon between His said Majesty the King of Great-Britain, His Majesty the King of France, and His Majesty the King of Spain, so, and in the same Manner, as had been agreed upon between those Three Crowns, and to produce the same Effects: And Whereas the Ratifications of the said Preliminary Articles between their Most Christian and Britannic Majesties were exchanged by their Ministers on the Third Day of February last, and between His Britannic Majesty and the King of Spain on the Ninth Day of February last: And Whereas it is Our Will and Pleasure that the Cessation of Hostilities between the United States of America and his Britannic Majesty, should be conformable to the Epochs fixed between their Most Christian and Britannic Majesties.

We have thought fit to make known the same to the Citizens of these States, and we hereby strictly Charge and Command all our Officers, both by Sea and Land, and others, Subjects of these United States, to Forbear all Acts of Hostility, either by Sea or by Land, against His Britannic Majesty or his Subjects, from and after the respective Times agreed upon between their Most Christian and Britannic Majesties as aforesaid.

And We do further require all Governors and others, the Executive Powers of these United States respectively, to cause this our Proclamation to be made Public, to the end that the same be duly observed within their several Jurisdictions.

Done in Congress, at Philadelphia, this Eleventh Day of April, in the Year of our Lord One Thousand Seven Hundred and Eighty-Three, and of our Sovereignty and Independence the Seventh.

Attest

CHA THOMSON *Sec*[y]

ELIAS BOUDINOT *Presid*[t]

Treaty Series, No. 103
8 Statutes at Large, 58–61

8

GREAT BRITAIN : JANUARY 20, 1783

Declarations for Suspension of Arms and Cessation of Hostilities, signed at Versailles January 20, 1783. Both original declarations in French, and American declaration also in English.

No ratification in the formal sense on either part, and consequently no exchange of ratifications; but proclamations "declaring the cessation of arms" were made by both countries; that of Great Britain is dated February 14, 1783 (text in Wharton, Diplomatic Correspondence, VI, 251–52). The American Commissioners in Paris under date of February 20, 1783, made a proclamation (styled a declaration) which follows very closely the wording of the British proclamation; and a proclamation was voted by Congress on April 11, 1783; the text thereof is with the notes to Document 7, which see generally.

Nous soussignés Ministres plénipotentiaires des Etats-unis de l'Amérique septentrionale aïant reçu de la part de M. Fitzherbert, Ministre plenipotentiaire de Sa Majesté Britannique une déclaration relative à une suspension d'armes à établir entre Sa d^e. Maj^{té}. et les dits Etats dont la teneur s'ensuit.

We the underwritten Ministers Plenipotentiary of the United States of North America, having received from Mr Fitz-Herbert, Minister Plenipotentiary of his Britannic Majesty, a Declaration relative to a Suspension of Arms to be establish'd between his said Majesty and the said States, of which the following is a Copy. Viz:

Comme les articles préliminaires arrêtés et signés aujourdhui entre Sa Majesté le Roi de la grande-Bretagne et Sa Majesté le Roi très Chretien d'une part, et aussi entre Sa d^e Majesté Britannique et Sa Majesté Catholique d'autre part, renferment la stipulation de la cessation des hostilités entre ces trois Puissances, la quelle doit commencer

"Whereas the Preliminary "Articles agreed to and signed "this Day between his Majesty "the King of Great Britain, and "his most Christian Majesty on "the one Part, and also between "his said Britannic Majesty and "his Catholic Majesty on the other "Part, stipulate a Cessation of "Hostilities between those three "Powers, which is to Commence

après l'échange des ratifications des dits articles préliminaires; Et comme par le Traité provisionel[1] signé le trente Novembre dernier entre Sa Majesté Britannique et les Etats-unis de l'Amérique Septentrionale, il a été stipulé, que ce traité sortiroit son effet aussitôt que la paix entre les dites Couronnes seroit retablie, Le soussigné Ministre plenipotentiaire de Sa Majesté Britannique déclare au nom, et par ordre exprès du Roi son Maitre, que les dits Etats-unis de l'Amérique Septentrionale, leurs sujets et leurs possessions seront compris dans la suspension d'armes susmentionné, et qu'ils jouiront en conséquence du benefice de la cessation des hostilités aux mêmes époques et de la même manière que les trois Couronnes susd^{es}, leurs sujets et leurs possessions respectives, le tout à condition que de la part, et au nom des dits Etats-unis de l'Amérique septentrionale, il soit delivré une déclaration semblable, qui constate leur assentiment à la presente suspension d'armes et renferme l'assûrance de la plus parfaite reciprocité de leur part.

En foi de quoi Nous Ministre plénipotentiaire de Sa Majesté

"upon the Exchange of the "Ratifications of the said Preliminary Articles; And whereas by "the Provisional Treaty [1] signed "the thirtieth of November last, "between his Britannic Majesty "and the United States of "North America, it was stipulated "that the said Treaty should "have its Effect as soon as Peace "between the said Crowns should "be established; The underwrit-"ten Minister Plenipotentiary of "his Britannic Majesty declares "in the Name, and by the express "Order of the King his Master, "that the said United States of "North America, their Subjects "and their Possessions, shall be "comprised in the suspension of "Arms above-mentioned, And "that they shall consequently "enjoy the Benifit of the Cessa-"tion of Hostilities, at the same "Periods and in the same Manner "as the three Crowns aforesaid "and their Subjects and Posses-"sions respectively: On Condi-"tion however, that on the Part "and in the Name of the Said "United States of North America, "there shall be deliver'd a similar "Declaration expressing the As-"sent to the present Suspension "of Arms, and containing an "Assurance of the most perfect "Reciprocity on their Part."

In faith whereof, we, the Min-"ister Plenipotentiary of his Bri-

[1] Document 7.

Britannique avons signé la présente Déclaration et y avons apposé le cachet de nos armes.

Signé Alleyne Fitz-herbert
(L S.)

Avons au nom des dits Etats-unis de l'Amérique Septentrionale, et en vertu des pouvoirs dont ils nous ont munis, accepté la déclaration ci-dessus, l'acceptons par ces presentes purement et simplement, et déclarons reciproquement que les dits Etats feront cesser toutes hostilités contre Sa Majesté Britannique, ses sujets et ses possessions aux termes et aux époques convenus entre Sa d° Majesté le Roi de la grande-Bretagne, Sa Majesté le Roi de France et Sa Majesté le Roi d'Espagne, ainsi et de la même manière qu'il a été convenu entre ces trois Couronnes, et pour produire le même effet.

En foi de quoi Nous Ministres plenipotentiaires des Etats-unis de l'Amérique Septentrionale avons signé la presente déclaration et y avons apposé les cachets de nos armes. À Versailles le vingt Janvier mil sept cent quatre vingtrois./.

John Adams. [Seal] B Franklin [Seal]

"tannic Majesty, have signed "this present Declaration, and "have thereto caused the Seal "of our Arms to be affixed, at "Versailles this twentieth Day "of January One Thousand seven "hundred & Eighty three."

(signed)
Alleyne Fitz-Herbert
(L S.)

We have in the Name of the said United States of North America & in Virtue of the Powers we are vested with, received the above Declaration and do accept the same by these Presents, and we do reciprocally declare, that the said States shall cause to cease all Hostilities against his Britannic Majesty, his Subjects and Possessions at the Terms or Periods agreed to between his said Majesty the King of Great Britain, his Majesty the King of France, and his Majesty the King of Spain, in the same manner as is stipulated between these three Crowns, and to have the same Effect.

In faith whereof, We Ministers Plenipotentiary from the United States of America, have signed the present Declaration and have hereunto affixed the Seals of our Arms. At Versailles the twentieth of January one thousand seven hundred and eighty three.

John Adams. [Seal] B Franklin [Seal]

NOTES

The declarations of January 20, 1783, have in various compilations been printed in English, and as if originally in that language only.

That the declaration on the part of the United States was in both French and English is certain; a facsimile thereof from the British archives is now in the Department of State file. The British declaration was certainly in French, and almost certainly in French only; in any case, both were first drawn up in French.

In a letter to Lord Grantham from Fitzherbert (who signed for the British Government) enclosing the American declaration and written on the date of signature (Bancroft's Transcripts, America, France, and England, VI, 109–10, NYPL), he says:

> This declaration they [the American Commissioners] gave me on receiving a similar one from me a copy of which I do not send as it is comprehended *verbatim* in theirs. These papers were drawn up by M. de Vergennes & I agreed to them readily as they appeared liable to no other objection but that of being in the French language which objection Messrs. Adams & Franklin have partly removed by agreeing to sign duplicates of it in English.

No trace has been found of the receipt in the United States of the original of the British declaration, which was delivered to Benjamin Franklin and John Adams at the office of Count de Vergennes at Versailles during the morning of Monday, January 20, 1783. The letters of both Franklin and Adams to Livingston (January 21 and 22, 1783, Wharton, Diplomatic Correspondence, VI, 225–26) purport to transmit copies, though that word, then as now, was sometimes used in a loose sense as meaning duplicate originals.

The Department of State file contains (*a*) a copy of the French text of the American declaration, which recites textually (in French) the British declaration; and (*b*) a paper, the first portion of which is headed "A Declaration" and has the word "Translation" in parentheses, and which is an English text (translation) of the British declaration; then follows a copy of an English text (not as signed, but translated from the French) of the American declaration, which last omits the textual recital of the British declaration, inserting in lieu thereof "Here follows the Declaration as above"; the two papers are both endorsed "taken from Dr. Franklin's file."

Also in the file, as above mentioned, is a facsimile of the original declaration on the part of the United States, signed by Adams and Franklin, in English and French.

The text here printed is from that facsimile; and the British declaration, being therein textually recited in each language, is not separately printed. It is to be added that the English of the British declaration which has been most frequently printed (*e. g.*, in the Statutes at Large) is the above-mentioned translation in the Department of State file; this differs in various respects from the text here. Still another variant translation of the period is that in 84 C. C. Papers, IV, folios 329–30, by John Pintard.

Furthermore, the text heretofore usually printed as the English of the American declaration (aside from its recital of the British declara-

tion) is a translation from the French, taken from that in the Department of State file; and as indicated above, it differs from the English text signed; for example:

In 8 Statutes at Large, 58: "do by these presents merely and simply accept it."

As signed: "and do accept the same by these Presents."

The French is: "l'acceptons par ces presentes purement et simplement."

Pintard wrote: "we do accept of it by these presents, without exception or reserve."

Note Regarding the Agreements of January 20, 1783

The declarations of Great Britain and the United States formed part of a general scheme of an armistice and a peace for all the belligerents; they were signed concurrently with the Preliminary Articles of Peace between Great Britain and France and between Great Britain and Spain to which they refer; the relevant terms of those agreements, as well as the respective dates of exchange of ratifications, are stated in the proclamation voted by Congress on April 11, 1783, the text of which is with the notes to Document 7, and reference is made to them also in the proclamation or declaration of the American Commissioners in Paris of February 20, 1783, the text of which follows these notes. The full text of the preliminaries between France and Great Britain and between Spain and Great Britain (in French) are in Von Martens, Recueil de traités, 2d ed., III, 503–14; English translations are in The Parliamentary History of England, XXIII, 346–54.

In particular, these declarations and the proclamations made pursuant thereto by the two countries, brought into the agreement the terms of Article 22 of the Preliminaries of Peace between Great Britain and France of January 20, 1783. As that treaty was written in French and the various proclamations in English, there was, in effect, an English version of the French text of that article; and subsequent diplomatic exchanges (*e. g.*, Adams to Carmarthen, July 14 and 27, 1785, Diplomatic Correspondence, 1783–1789, II, 401–6, and also Adams to Jay, August 25, 1785, *ibid.*, 455–62), following divergent judicial views as to the phrase regarding the Canary Islands, were based somewhat on the point of equivalence. Article 22 of the treaty between Great Britain and France reads as follows:

> Pour prévenir tous les sujets de plainte et de contestation qui pourroient naître à l'occasion des prises qui pourroient être faites en mer depuis la signature de ces Articles préliminaires, on est convenu réciproquement, que les vaisseaux et effets qui pourroient être pris dans la Manche et dans les mers du Nord, après l'espace de douze jours, à compter depuis la ratification des présens Articles préliminaires, seront de part et d'autre restitués; que le terme sera d'un mois depuis la Manche et les mers du Nord jusqu'aux isles Canaries inclusivement, soit dans l'Océan, soit dans la Méditerranée, de deux mois depuis lesdites isles Canaries, jusqu'à la ligne équinoxiale ou l'équateur; et enfin de cinq mois dans tous les autres endroits du monde sans aucune exception ni autre distinction plus particulière de temps et de lieu. (Von Martens, Recueil de traités, 2d ed., III, 508–9.)

Note Regarding the Proclamations

The British proclamation of February 14, 1783 (text in Wharton, Diplomatic Correspondence, VI, 251–52), was also issued in New York as a broadside; a print, "Re-printed by James Rivington, Printer to the King's Most Excellent Majesty," is in the New York Public Library; a facsimile thereof is in the Department of State file.

The text of the proclamation voted by Congress on April 11, 1783, is with the notes to Document 7.

The paper, called a declaration, which was signed by the American Commissioners (Adams, Franklin, and Jay) in Paris on February 20, 1783, was in substance a proclamation, following the earlier British form; it was issued at the request of the British Government (Wharton, Diplomatic Correspondence, VI, 255; the text is printed at pages 257–58). The original paper is in the British archives; the text following is from the facsimile of that original which is now in the Department of State file.

By the Ministers Plenipotentiary of the United States of America, for making Peace with Great Britain. A Declaration of the Cessation of Hostilities as well by Sea as Land, agreed upon between His Majesty, the King of Great Britain, and the United States of America.

Whereas Preliminary Articles were signed, at Paris, on the thirtieth Day of November last, between the Plenipotentiaries of his said Majesty the King of Great Britain, and of the said States, to be inserted in, and to constitute the Treaty of Peace to be concluded between his said Majesty, and the said United States when Terms of Peace should be agreed upon between his said Majesty and his most Christian Majesty: and Whereas Preliminaries for restoring Peace, between his said Majesty, the King of Great Britain, and his most Christian Majesty, were signed at Versailles, on the twentieth day of January last, by the respective Ministers of their said Majesties: and Whereas Preliminaries for restoring Peace, between his said Majesty the King of Great Britain, and his Majesty the King of Spain, were also signed at Versailles, on the twentyeth Day of January last, by their respective Ministers: and Whereas, for putting an End to the Calamity of War, as soon and as far as possible, it hath been agreed, between the King of Great Britain, his most Christian Majesty, the King of Spain, the States General of the United Provinces and the United States of America as follows, that is to say.

That such Vessells and Effects, as should be taken, in the Channell and in the North Seas, after the Space of twelve Days, to be computed from the Ratification of the said Preliminary Articles should be restored on all Sides; that the Term should be one Month from the Channell and North Seas, as far as the Canary Islands inclusively, whether in the Ocean or the Mediterranean; two Months from the said Canary Islands, as far as the Equinoctial Line, or Equator, and lastly five Months in all other Parts of the World, without any Exception or any other more particular Description of Time or Place.

And Whereas the Ratifications of the said Preliminary Articles between his said Majesty, the King of Great Britain, and his most Christian Majesty, in due Form, were exchanged by their Ministers on the third day of this instant February, from which Day the several Terms abovementioned, of Twelve Days, of one Month, of two Months, and of five Months are to be computed, relative to all British and American Vessells and Effects

Now therefore, We, the Ministers Plenipotentiary, from the United States of America, for making Peace with Great Britain do notify to the People and Citizens, of the said United States of America, that Hostilities, on their Part, against his Britannic Majesty, both by Sea and Land are to cease, at the Expiration of the Terms herein before specified therefor, and which Terms are to be

computed, from the third day of February instant. And We do, in the Name and by the Authority of the said United States, accordingly warn and enjoin all their Officers and Citizens, to forbear all Acts of Hostility, whatever, either by Land or by Sea against his said Majesty, the King of Great Britain, or his Subjects under the Penalty of incurring the highest Displeasure of the said United States.

Given at Paris the Twentieth Day of February, in the Year of our Lord, One Thousand, Seven hundred and Eighty Three, under our Hands and Seals

John Adams. [Seal]
B Franklin [Seal]
John Jay [Seal]

Treaty Series, No. 83½
17 Statutes at Large, 797-801

9

FRANCE : FEBRUARY 25, 1783

Contract between the King and the Thirteen United States of North America, signed at Versailles February 25, 1783. Original in French.
Ratified by the United States October 31, 1783. Ratified by France December 21, 1783. Ratifications exchanged at Paris (or Versailles) about January 1, 1784. Not proclaimed.

Contrat entre le Roi et les Treize Etats-Unis de l'Amérique Septentrionale.

La paix rétablie entre les Puissances belligérantes, les avantages d'un Commerce libre dans toutes les parties du Globe et l'Indépendance des Treize Etats-Unis de l'Amérique Septentrionale, reconnüe et fondée sur une base solide et honorable, promettoient de voir lesdits Etats en situation de pourvoir dès aprésent à leurs besoins par les ressources qui leurs sont propres, sans être forcés d'implorer la continuation des Secours que le Roi leur a si libéralement accordés pendant la durée de la guerre; Mais le Ministre plénipotentiaire desd[ts] Etats-Unis près Sa Majesté, lui ayant exposé l'épuisement où les a réduit une guerre longue et désastreuse, Sa Majesté a daigné prendre en considération la demande faite par le Ministre susdit

[Translation]

Contract between the King and the Thirteen United States of North America.

The reestablished peace between the belligerent powers, the advantages of a free commerce to all parts of the globe, and the independence of the thirteen United States of North America, acknowledged and founded on a solid and honorable basis, rendered it probable that the said States would be in a condition to provide hereafter for their necessities, by means of the resources within themselves, without being compelled to implore the continuation of the succors which the King has so liberally granted during the war; but the Minister Plenipotentiary of the said United States to His Majesty having represented to him the exhausted state to which they have been reduced by a long and disastrous war, His Majesty has conde-

au nom du Congrès desdits Etats, d'une nouvelle avance d'argent pour subvenir à une multitude d'objets de dépenses urgentes et indispensables dans le Cours de la présente année; Sa Majesté s'est déterminée en conséquence, malgré les besoins non moins pressants de son propre service, à accorder au Congrès une nouvelle assistance pécuniaire qu'-Elle a fixée à la somme de Six millions de livres tournois, à titre de prêt et sous la garantie solidaire des Treize Etats-Unis, ce que le Ministre du Congrès a déclaré accepter avec la plus vive reconnoissance au nom desdits Etats.

scended to take into consideration the request made by the aforesaid Minister in the name of the Congress of the said States for a new advance of money to answer numerous purposes of urgent and indispensable expenses in the course of the present year; His Majesty has, in consequence, determined, notwithstanding the no less pressing necessities of his own service, to grant to Congress a new pecuniary assistance, which he has fixed at the sum of six millions livres tournois, under the title of loan and under the guaranty of the whole thirteen United States, which the Minister of Congress has declared his acceptance of, with the liveliest acknowledgments in the name of the said States.

Et comme il est nécessaire au bon ordre des finances de Sa Majesté et même utile aux opérations de la finance des Etats-Unis, d'assigner les époques de payement des Six millions de livres dont il s'agit et de régler les conditions et les termes du remboursement qui doit en être fait au Trésor Royal de Sa Majesté à Paris, à l'exemple de ce qui a été stipulé pour les précédentes avances, par un premier Contrat[1] du 16. Juillet 1782.

And as it is necessary to the good order of His Majesty's finances, and also useful to the operations of the finances of the United States, to assign periods for payment of the six millions livres in question, and to regulate the conditions and terms of reimbursement, which should be made at His Majesty's royal treasury at Paris after the manner of what has been stipulated for the preceding advances by a former contract[1] of the 16th July, 1782—

Nous Charles Gravier Comte de Vergennes &c? Conseiller du Roi en tous ses Conseils, Com-

We, Charles Gravier, Count de Vergennes, etc., Counselor of the King in his Councils, Commander

[1] Document 4.

mandeur de ses Ordres, Chef du Conseil Royal des Finances, Conseiller d'Etat et d'Epée, Ministre et Secretaire d'Etat et de ses Commandemens et finances, muni des pleins pouvoirs de Sa Majesté à nous donnés à l'effet des présentes.

Et Nous Benjamin Franklin Ministre plénipotentiaire des Etats-Unis de l'Amérique Septentrionale, pareillement muni des pouvoirs du Congrès desdits Etats au même effet des présentes, après en avoir conféré et nous être düement communiqué nos pouvoirs respectifs, Avons arrêté les articles qui suivent.

ARTICLE P^er

Le payement des Six Millions de livres Argent de france énoncés ci-dessus, sera fait des fonds du Trésor-Royal, à raison de Cinq cens mille livres par chacun des douze mois de la présente année, sur les reconnoissances du Ministre desdits Etats-Unis, portant promesse au nom du Congrès et solidairement pour les Treize Etats-Unis, de faire rembourser et restituer en argent comptant au Trésor Royal de Sa Majesté, au domicile du S. Grand Banquier à Paris, ladite somme de Six millions de livres, avec les intérêts à Cinq pour cent l'an, aux époques stipulées par les articles Trois et quatre ci-après; Les avances que Sa Majesté a bien

of his Orders, Chief of the Royal Council of Finances, Counselor of State, etc., Minister and Secretary of State and of his Commands and Finances, invested with full powers by His Majesty, given to us for the purpose of these presents—

And we, Benjamin Franklin, Minister and Plenipotentiary of the United States of North America, likewise invested with powers by the Congress of said States for the same purpose of these presents, after having compared and duly communicated to each other our respective powers, have agreed upon the following articles:

ARTICLE 1.

The payment of the six millions livres, French money, above mentioned, shall be made from the funds of the royal treasury, in proportions of five hundred thousand livres during each of the twelve months of the present year, under the acknowledgments of the Minister of the said United States, promising, in the name of Congress and in behalf of the thirteen United States, to reimburse and refund the said six million livres in ready money at His Majesty's royal treasury, at the house of the Sieur Grand, banker at Paris, with interest at five per cent per annum, at periods hereafter stipulated in the third and fourth articles. The

voulu permettre qui soient faites à compte des Six millions dont il s'agit, seront imputées sur les payemens des premiers mois de cette année.

ARTICLE 2.

Pour l'intelligence de la fixation des termes de remboursement des Six millions au Trésor Royal, et pour prévenir toute ambiguité à ce sujet, il a été trouvé convenable de récapituler ici le montant des précédens secours accordés par le Roi aux Etats-Unis, et de les distinguer suivant leurs différentes Classes; La premiere est composée de fonds successivement prêtés par Sa Majesté montans ensemble à la Somme de Dix huit millions de livres remboursables en especes au Trésor Royal en douze parties égales de Quinze cens mille livres chacune, outre les intérêts et en douze années à commencer seulement de la troisieme après l'époque de la paix; Les intérêts commençant à courir de l'époque de la paix pour être acquittés chaque année, doivent diminuer à mesure et en proportion du remboursement des Capitaux, dont le dernier terme écherra dans l'année 1798.

La seconde Classe comprend l'emprunt de Cinq millions de florins de Hollande, montant par évaluation modérée à Dix millions de livres tournois, ledit emprunt fait en Hollande en 1781.

advances which His Majesty has been pleased to allow to be made on account of the six millions in question, shall be deducted in the payments of the first month of this year.

ARTICLE 2.

For better understanding the fixing of periods for the reimbursement of the six millions at the royal treasury, and to prevent all ambiguity on this head, it has been found proper to recapitulate here the amount of the preceding aids granted by the King to the United States, and to distinguish them according to their different classes. The first is composed of funds lent successively by His Majesty, amounting in the whole to the sum of eighteen million livres, reimbursable in specie at the royal treasury in twelve equal portions of a million five hundred thousand livres each, besides the interest, and in twelve years, to commence from the third year after the date of the peace, the interest, beginning to reckon at the date of the peace, to be discharged annually, shall diminish in proportion to the reimbursement of the capital, the last payment of which shall expire in the year 1798.

The second class comprehends the loan of five million Dutch florins, amounting, by a moderate valuation, to ten million livres tournois, the said loan made in Holland in 1781 for the service of

pour le service des Etats-Unis de l'Amerique Septentrionale, sous l'engagement du Roi d'en restituer le Capital avec les intérêts à 4 p%. l'an, au Comptoir général des Etats Généraux des Provinces-Unies des Pays Bas en dix parties égales à compter de la Sixieme année de la datte dudit emprunt; Et sous pareil engagement de la part du Ministre du Congrès et solidairement pour les Treize Etats-Unis, de faire le remboursement des Dix millions dud^t emprunt, en argent comptant au Trésor Royal avec les intérêts a 4 p%. par an, en dix parties égales d'un million chacune et en dix termes d'année en année, dont le premier écherra au mois de Novembre 1787. et le dernier dans le même mois de l'année 1796., Le tout conformément aux conditions exprimées au Contrat[1] du 16. Juillet 1782.

Dans la troisieme Classe sont compris les Secours et Subsides fournis au Congrès des Etats-Unis, à titre d'assistance gratuite de la pure générosité du Roi, dont Trois millions accordés antérieurement au Traité[2] du mois de fevrier 1778. et Six millions en 1781., desquels Secours et Subsides montans ensemble à Neuf millions de livres tournois, Sa Majesté confirme ici, en tant que de besoin, le don gratuit au Congrès desd^ts Treize Etats-Unis.

the United States of North America, under the engagement of the King to refund the capital, with interest at four per cent per annum, at the general counter of the States General of the United Provinces of the Netherlands in ten equal portions, reckoning from the sixth year of the date of said loan; and under the like engagement on the part of the Minister of Congress and in behalf of the thirteen United States, to reimburse the ten millions of said loan in ready money at the royal treasury, with interest at four per cent per annum, in ten equal portions of a million each, and in ten periods from year to year, the first of which shall take place in the month of November, 1787, and the last in the same month, 1796; the whole conformable to the conditions expressed in the contract[1] of 16th July, 1782.

In the third class are comprehended the aids and subsidies furnished to the Congress of the United States under the title of gratuitous assistance from the pure generosity of the King, three millions of which were granted before the treaty[2] of February, 1778, and six millions in 1781; which aids and subsidies amount in the whole to nine million livres tournois. His Majesty here confirms, in case of need, the gratuitous gift to the Congress of the said thirteen United States.

---

[1] Document 4.

[2] See Documents 1, 2, and 3.

ARTICLE 3.

Le nouveau prêt de Six millions de livres tournois qui fait la matiere du présent Contrat, sera restitué et remboursé en argent comptant au Trésor Royal de Sa Majesté, en six parties égales d'un Million chacune avec les intérêts à Cinq pour cent par an, et en Six termes dont le premier écherra en l'année 1797. et ainsi d'année en année jusqu'en 1,802. que le dernier remboursement sera effectué.

ARTICLE 3.

The new loan of six millions livres tournois, the subject of the present contract, shall be refunded and reimbursed in ready money at His Majesty's royal treasury in six equal portions of a million each, with interest at five per cent per annum, and in six periods, the first of which shall take place in the year 1797, and so on from year to year until 1802, when the last reimbursement shall be completed.

ARTICLE 4.

Les Intérêts à 5. pour cent l'an, du Capital de Six millions énoncé en l'article ci-dessus, commenceront à courir du Per Janvier de l'année 1784. et seront payés comptant au Trésor Royal de Sa Majesté à Paris au même jour de chacune année dont la premiere écherra le premier Janvier 1785. et ainsi d'année en année jusqu'au remboursement définitif du Capital, Sa Majesté voulant bien par un nouvel acte de générosité faire don et remise aux Treize Etats-Unis des intérêts partiels de la présente année, ce que le Ministre soussigné du Congrès a déclaré accepter avec reconnoissance, au nom desdits Etats-Unis.

ARTICLE 4.

The interest of five per cent per annum of the capital of the six millions mentioned in the preceding article shall begin to be reckoned from the 1st of January of the year 1784 and shall be paid in ready money at His Majesty's royal treasury at Paris on the same day of each year, the first of which shall take place the 1st of January, 1785, and so on from year to year until the definitive reimbursement of the capital; His Majesty being pleased, by a new act of generosity, to present and remit to the thirteen United States the partial interest of the present year, which the underwritten Minister of Congress has declared to accept with acknowledgment in the name of the said United States.

ARTICLE 5.

Les Intérêts du Capital de Six millions diminueront dans la pro-

ARTICLE 5.

The interest of the capital of the six millions shall diminish in

portion des remboursemens aux époques fixées en l'article ci-dessus; Le Congrès et les Etats-Unis se réservent néanmoins la faculté d'accélerer leur libération par des remboursemens anticipés, Si l'état de leur finance pouvoit le leur permettre.

ARTICLE 6.

Les parties contractantes se garantissent réciproquement l'observation fidéle des articles ci-dessus, dont les ratifications seront échangées dans l'espace de Neuf mois ou plutôt s'il est possible, à compter de la datte du présent contrat.

En foi de quoi Nous Ministres plénipotentiaires de Sa Majesté et du Congrès des Treize Etats-Unis de l'Amérique Septentrionale, en vertu de Nos plein-pouvoirs respectifs, avons signé le présent Contrat et y avons fait apposer le Cachet de nos armes.

Fait à Versailles le 25me jour du mois de Fevrier Mil sept cent quatre vingt trois./.

GRAVIER DE VERGENNES
[Seal]
B FRANKLIN
[Seal]

proportion to the reimbursements at the periods fixed in the preceding article, Congress and the United States reserving, however, the liberty of freeing themselves by anticipated payments, should the state of their finances admit.

ARTICLE 6.

The contracting parties will reciprocally guarantee the faithful observation of the foregoing articles, the ratifications of which shall be exchanged in the space of nine months from the date of this present contract, or sooner if possible.

In faith whereof we, the Ministers Plenipotentiary of His Majesty and the Congress of the thirteen United States of North America, in virtue of our respective full powers, have signed the present contract and thereunto affixed the seal of our arms.

Done at Versailles the twenty-fifth day of February, one thousand seven hundred and eighty-three.

GRAVIER DE VERGENNES
[Seal]
B FRANKLIN
[Seal]

NOTES

The original of this contract is in the Library of Congress (145 C. C. Papers, folios 323–27). The seals are in large part missing. When examined in 1929, the said original was *in between* various pages of another document, a certified copy of a full power to Count de Vergennes, dated February 24, 1783, which is on folios 320–21 and

329; a facsimile of that original is in the Department of State file, which contains also a facsimile of the other original—that is, the one in the archives of France; the latter was brought from Paris in 1925 by Ambassador Herrick. With it is an imperfect typewritten translation.

The United States instrument of ratification is copied in 135 C. C. Papers, I; also in Journals, XXV, 773–78. A facsimile of the original instrument, received from the French archives, is now in the Department of State file. The Great Seal of the United States and the signatures of Boudinot and of Thomson as Secretary are in the left margin of the first page.

Neither in the archives of France nor in those of the Department of State has been found any protocol or other similar record of the exchange of ratifications. The date of exchange was after December 25, 1783 (Wharton, Diplomatic Correspondence, VI, 742), but cannot be stated with precision. The exchange of ratifications of this contract and of the prior contract of July 16, 1782 (Document 4), were concurrent.

The translation here printed is that which is with the above-mentioned copy of the United States instrument of ratification in 135 C. C. Papers, I. It appears to have been made by John Pintard, for the text, over his signature, is in 145 C. C. Papers, folios 361–65. This translation has been copied in various treaty collections, although usually not noted as a translation. See generally the notes to Document 4.

No record of a proclamation of this contract has been found.

Treaty Series, No. 346
8 Statutes at Large, 60-79

10

SWEDEN : APRIL 3, 1783

Treaty of Amity and Commerce, with Separate Article and with Separate Articles 1-5, signed at Paris April 3, 1783. Original in French. Ratified (with the various separate articles) by the United States July 29, 1783. Ratified (to the same extent) by Sweden May 23, 1783. Ratifications exchanged at Paris February 6, 1784. Proclaimed September 25, 1783.

Traité d'Amitié et de Commerce Conclu entre Sa Majesté le Roi de Suede et les États Unis de l'Amerique Septentrionale.

Le Roi de Suede des Goths et des Vandales &c. &c. &c. Et les Treize États Unis de l'Amerique Septentrionale, sçavoir New-Hampshire, Massachusetts Bay, Rhode Island, Connecticut, New-York, New-Jersey, Pensylvanie, les Comtés de New-Castle, de Kent et de Sussex sur la Delaware, Maryland, Virginie, Caroline Septentrionale, Caroline Meridionale et Georgie, desirant d'établir d'une maniere stable et permanente les regles qui doivent être suivies relativement à la Correspondance et au Commerce que les deux Parties ont jugé necessaire de fixer entre leurs Pays, États et Sujets respectifs, Sa Majesté et les États Unis ont cru ne pouvoir mieux remplir ce but qu'en posant pour base de

[Translation]

A Treaty of Amity and Commerce Concluded between His Majesty the King of Sweden and the United States of North America.

The King of Sweden, of the Goths and Vandals, etc., etc., etc., and the thirteen United States of North America, to wit: New Hampshire, Massachusetts Bay, Rhode Island, Connecticut, New York, New Jersey, Pennsylvania, the counties of New Castle, Kent, and Sussex on Delaware, Maryland, Virginia, North Carolina, South Carolina, and Georgia, desiring to establish, in a stable and permanent manner, the rules which ought to be observed relative to the correspondence and commerce which the two parties have judged necessary to establish between their respective countries, states, and subjects; His Majesty and the United States have thought that they could not better accomplish that

leurs Arrangemens, l'Utilité et l'Avantage reciproques des deux Nations, en évitant toutes les Preferences onereuses qui sont ordinairement une Source de discussions, d'embarras et de mécontentements; et en laissant à chaque Partie la Liberté de faire au Sujet du Commerce et de la Navigation, les reglemens intérieurs qui seront à Sa Convenance.

Dans cette vue Sa Majesté le Roi de Suede a nommé et constitué pour son Plenipotentiaire le Comte Gustave Philippe de Creutz, son Ambassadeur Extraordinaire près sa Majesté très Chretienne et Chevalier Commandeur de ses ordres; et les Etats Unis ont de leur Côté pourvû de leurs Pleinpouvoirs le Sieur Benjamin Franklin leur Ministre Plenipotentiaire près Sa Majesté très Chretienne; Les quels Plenipotentiaires, après avoir échangé leurs Pleinpouvoirs, et en consequence d'une mure deliberation ont arrêté, conclu et signé les Articles Suivants.

ART. 1.

Il y aura une Paix ferme, inviolable et universelle, et une Amitié vraie et sincere entre le Roi de Suede, Ses Heritiers et Successeurs, et entre les États Unis de l'Amerique, ainsi qu'entre les Sujets de Sa Majesté et ceux des dits Etats, comme aussi entre les Pays, Isles, Villes et Places,

end than by taking for a basis of their arrangements the mutual interest and advantage of both nations, thereby avoiding all those burthensome preferences which are usually sources of debate, embarrassment, and discontent, and by leaving each party at liberty to make, respecting navigation and commerce, those interior regulations which shall be most convenient to itself.

With this view, His Majesty the King of Sweden has nominated and appointed for his Plenipotentiary Count Gustavus Philip de Creutz, his Ambassador Extraordinary to His Most Christian Majesty, and Knight Commander of his Orders; and the United States, on their part, have fully empowered Benjamin Franklin, their Minister Plenipotentiary to His Most Christian Majesty. The said Plenipotentiaries, after exchanging their full powers and after mature deliberation, in consequence thereof have agreed upon, concluded, and signed the following articles:

ARTICLE 1.

There shall be a firm, inviolable, and universal peace and a true and sincere friendship between the King of Sweden, his heirs and successors, and the United States of America, and the subjects of His Majesty, and those of the said States, and between the countries, islands, cities, and towns situated

situées sous la Jurisdiction du Roi et des dits États Unis, sans exception aucune de Personnes et de Lieux; les Conditions stipulées dans le present Traité devant être perpetuelles et permanentes entre le Roi, ses Heritiers et Successeurs et les dits États Unis.

ART. 2d

Le Roi et les États Unis s'engagent mutuellement à n'accorder par la Suite aucune faveur particuliere en fait de commerce et de Navigation à d'autres Nations, qui ne devienne aussitôt commune à l'autre Partie; et celle cy jouira de cette faveur gratuitement si la Concession est gratuite; ou en accordant la même Compensation si la Concession est conditionelle.

ART. 3.

Les Sujets du Roi de Suede ne payeront dans les Ports, Havres, Rades, Contrées, Isles, Villes et Places des États Unis, ou dans aucun d'iceux, d'autres ni de plus grands Droits et impôts de quelque nature qu'ils puissent être, que ceux que les Nations les plus favorisées sont ou seront tenues de payer; et ils jouiront de tous les Droits, Libertés, Privileges, Immunités et exemptions en fait de Negoce, Navigation et de Commerce dont jouissent ou jouiront les dites Nations, soit en passant d'un Port à l'autre des dits États, soit en y allant ou en

under the jurisdiction of the King and of the said United States, without any exception of persons or places; and the conditions agreed to in this present treaty shall be perpetual and permanent between the King, his heirs and successors, and the said United States.

ARTICLE 2

The King and the United States engage mutually not to grant hereafter any particular favor to other nations, in respect to commerce and navigation, which shall not immediately become common to the other party, who shall enjoy the same favor freely, if the concession was freely made, or on allowing the same compensation, if the concession was conditional.

ARTICLE 3.

The subjects of the King of Sweden shall not pay in the ports, havens, roads, countries, islands, cities, and towns of the United States, or in any of them, any other nor greater duties or imposts, of what nature soever they may be, than those which the most favored nations are or shall be obliged to pay; and they shall enjoy all the rights, liberties, privileges, immunities, and exemptions in trade, navigation, and commerce which the said nations do or shall enjoy, whether in passing from one port to another of the United States,

revenant de quelque Partie ou pour quelque partie du monde que ce soit.

Art. 4.

Les Sujets et Habitants des dits États Unis ne payeront dans les Ports, Havres, Rades, Isles, Villes et Places de la Domination du Roi de Suede, d'autres ni de plus grands Droits ou impôts, de quelque nature qu'ils puissent être, et quelque nom qu'ils puissent avoir, que ceux que les Nations les plus favorisées sont ou seront tenues de payer; et ils jouiront de tous les Droits, Libertés, Privileges, immunités et exemptions en fait de Negoce, Navigation et Commerce dont jouissent ou jouiront les dites Nations, soit en passant d'un Port à un autre de la Domination de sa dite Majesté, soit en y allant ou en revenant de quelque Partie du monde, ou pour quelque partie du monde que ce soit.

Art. 5.

Il sera accordé une pleine, parfaite et entiere Liberté de Conscience aux habitants et Sujets de chaque Partie et personne ne sera molesté à l'égard de son Culte, moyennant qu'il se soumette, quant à la Demonstration publique aux Loix du Pays. De plus on permettra aux habitans et Sujets de chaque Partie, qui decedent dans le Territoire de l'autre Partie, d'être enterrés dans les endroits convenables et

or in going to or from the same, from or to any part of the world whatever.

Article 4.

The subjects and inhabitants of the said United States shall not pay in the ports, havens, roads, islands, cities, and towns under the dominion of the King of Sweden, any other or greater duties or imposts, of what nature soever they may be, or by what name soever called, than those which the most favored nations are or shall be obliged to pay; and they shall enjoy all the rights, liberties, privileges, immunities, and exemptions in trade, navigation, and commerce which the said nations do or shall enjoy, whether in passing from one port to another of the dominion of His said Majesty, or in going to or from the same, from or to any part of the world whatever.

Article 5

There shall be granted a full, perfect, and entire liberty of conscience to the inhabitants and subjects of each party, and no person shall be molested on account of his worship, provided he submits, so far as regards the public demonstration of it, to the laws of the country. Moreover, liberty shall be granted, when any of the subjects or inhabitants of either party die in the territory of the other, to

décents qui seront assignés à cet éffet, et les deux Puissances contractantes pourvoiront chacune dans sa Jurisdiction, à ce que les Sujets et habitans respectifs puissent obtenir les Certificats de mort, en cas qu'il soit requis de les livrer.

ART. 6.

Les Sujets des Parties contractantes pourront dans les États respectifs disposer librement de leurs fonds et biens, soit par Testament, Donation ou autrement, en faveur de telles personnes que bon leur semblera, et leurs Heritiers dans quelque endroit où ils demeureront, pourront recevoir ces Successions, même *ab intestato,* soit en personne, soit par un procureur, sans qu'ils aient besoin d'obtenir des Lettres de Naturalisation. Ces heritages, aussi bien que les Capitaux et fonds que les Sujets des deux Parties, en changeant de demeure, voudront faire sortir de l'endroit de leur Domicile, seront exemts de tout droit de Detraction, de la part du Gouvernement des deux États respectifs. Mais il est convenu en même tems, que le contenu de cet article ne derogera en aucune maniere aux ordonnances promulguées en Suede contre les Emigrations, ou qui pourront par la suite être promulguées, les quelles demeureront dans toute

bury them in convenient and decent places, which shall be assigned for the purpose; and the two contracting parties will provide, each in its jurisdiction, that the subjects and inhabitants respectively may obtain certificates of the death, in case the delivery of them is required.

ARTICLE 6.

The subjects of the contracting parties in the respective states may freely dispose of their goods and effects, either by testament, donation, or otherwise, in favor of such persons as they may think proper; and their heirs, in whatever place they shall reside, shall receive the succession even *ab intestato*, either in person or by their attorney, without having occasion to take out letters of naturalization. These inheritances, as well as the capitals and effects which the subjects of the two parties, in changing their abode, shall be desirous of removing from the place of their abode, shall be exempted from all duty called *droit de détraction* on the part of the Government of the two states respectively. But it is at the same time agreed that nothing contained in this article shall in any manner derogate from the ordinances published in Sweden against emigrations, or which may hereafter be published, which shall remain in full force and vigor. The United States on their

leur force et Vigueur. Les États Unis, de leur côté, ou aucun d'entre eux seront libres de statuer sur cette matiere telle Loi qu'ils jugeront à propos.

part, or any of them, shall be at liberty to make, respecting this matter, such laws as they think proper.

ART. 7.

Il sera permis à tous et un chacun des Sujets et habitans du Royaume de Suede, ainsi qu'à ceux des États Unis de naviguer avec leurs Bâtimens en toute Sureté et Liberté et sans distinction de ceux à qui les Marchandises et leurs Chargemens appartiendront, de quelque port que ce soit. Il sera permis également aux Sujets et habitans des deux Etats de naviguer et de negocier avec leurs Vaisseaux et marchandises et de frequenter avec la même Liberté et Sureté, les Places Ports et havres des Puissances ennemies des deux Parties contractantes, ou de l'une d'elles, sans être aucunement inquietés ni troublés, et de faire le Commerce non seulement directement dès Ports de l'Ennemi à un port neutre, mais encore d'un Port ennemi à un autre Port ennemi; soit qu'il se trouve sous la Jurisdiction d'un même ou de differents Princes. Et comme il est reçu par le present Traité, par rapport aux Navires et aux Marchandises, que les Vaisseaux libres rendront les marchandises libres, et que l'on regardera comme libre tout ce qui sera à Bord des Navires appartenants aux Sujets

ARTICLE 7.

All and every the subjects inhabitants of the Kingdom of Sweden, as well as those of the United States, shall be permitted to navigate with their vessels in all safety and freedom, and without any regard to those to whom the merchandises and cargoes may belong, from any port whatever. And the subjects and inhabitants of the two states shall likewise be permitted to sail and trade with their vessels, and with the same liberty and safety to frequent the places, ports, and havens of powers enemies to both or either of the contracting parties, without being in any wise molested or troubled, and to carry on a commerce not only directly from the ports of an enemy to a neutral port, but even from one port of an enemy to another port of an enemy, whether it be under the jurisdiction of the same or of different princes. And as it is acknowledged by this treaty, with respect to ships and merchandises, that free ships shall make the merchandises free, and that everything which shall be on board of ships belonging to subjects of the one or the other of the contracting parties shall be considered as free,

d'une ou de l'autre des Parties contractantes, quand même le Chargement ou partie d'icelui appartiendroit aux ennemis de l'un des deux, bien entendu néanmoins, que les Marchandises de contrebande seront toujours exceptées; les quelles étant interceptées, il sera procedé conformement à l'esprit des articles suivants. Il est également convenu que cette même Liberté s'étendra aux Personnes qui naviguent sur un Vaisseau libre; de maniere que quoi qu'elles soient ennemies des deux Parties, ou de l'une d'elles, elles ne seront point tirées du Vaisseau libre, si ce n'est que ce fussent des gens de Guerre actuellement au Service des dits ennemis.

even though the cargo, or a part of it, should belong to the enemies of one or both; it is nevertheless provided that contraband goods shall always be excepted; which, being intercepted, shall be proceeded against according to the spirit of the following articles. It is likewise agreed that the same liberty be extended to persons who may be on board a free ship, with this effect, that although they be enemies to both or either of the parties, they shall not be taken out of the free ship unless they are soldiers in the actual service of the said enemies.

Art. 8.

Cette Liberté de Navigation et de Commerce s'étendra à toutes Sortes de Marchandises, à la reserve seulement de celles qui sont exprimées dans l'article suivant et designées sous le nom de Marchandises de Contrebande.

Article 8.

This liberty of navigation and commerce shall extend to all kinds of merchandises, except those only which are expressed in the following article and are distinguished by the name of contraband goods.

Art. 9.

On comprendra sous ce nom de marchandises de Contrebande ou defendues, les armes, Canons, Boulets, Arquebuses, Mousquets, Mortiers, Bombes, Petards, Grenades, Saucisses, Cercles poissés, Affuts, Fourchettes, Bandoulieres, poudre à canon, meches, Salpetre, Souffre, Balles, Piques, Sabres, Epées, Morions, Casques, Cuiras-

Article 9.

Under the name of contraband or prohibited goods shall be comprehended arms, great guns, cannon balls, arquebuses, muskets, mortars, bombs, petards, grenades, saucisses, pitch balls, carriages for ordnance, musket rests, bandoleers, cannon powder, matches, saltpeter, sulphur, bullets, pikes, sabers, swords, mo-

ses Halbardes, Javelines, Pistolets et leurs Fourreaux, Baudriers, Bayonettes, Chevaux avec leurs Harnois et tous autres semblables genres d'armes et d'instruments de guerre servant à l'usage des Troupes.

rions, helmets, cuirasses, halberds, javelins, pistols and their holsters, belts, bayonets, horses with their harness, and all other like kinds of arms and instruments of war for the use of troops.

ART. 10

On ne mettra point au nombre des Marchandises defendues celles qui suivent, sçavoir toutes Sortes de draps et tous autres ouvrages de Manufactures de Laine, de Lin, de Soye, de Cotton et de toute autre matiere, tout genre d'habillement, avec les choses qui servent ordinairement à les faire; Or, Argent monnoyé ou non monnoyé, Etaim, Fer, plomb, Cuivre, Laiton, Charbon à fourneau, bled, orge et toute autre Sorte de Grains et de legumes, la Nicotiane, vulgairement apellée Tabac, toutes Sortes d'aromates, Chaires Salées et fumées, Poissons salés, fromage et Beurre, Bierre, Huile, Vins, Sucres, Toutes sortes de Sels et de Provisions servant à la Nourriture et à la Subsistance des hommes; Tous genres de Coton, Chanvre, Lin, Poix, tant liquide que Seche, Cordages, Cables, voiles, Toiles propres à faire des voiles, Ancres et Parties d'Ancres quelles qu'elles puissent être, Mats de Navire, Planches, Madriers, Poutres et toute Sorte d'arbres et toutes autres choses necessaires pour construire ou pour radouber les

ARTICLE 10.

These which follow shall not be reckoned in the number of prohibited goods, that is to say: All sorts of cloths and all other manufactures of wool, flax, silk, cotton, or any other materials, all kinds of wearing apparel, together with the things of which they are commonly made; gold, silver coined or uncoined, brass, iron, lead, copper, latten, coals, wheat, barley, and all sorts of corn or pulse; tobacco, all kinds of spices, salted and smoked flesh, salted fish, cheese, butter, beer, oil, wines, sugar; all sorts of salt and provisions which serve for the nourishment and sustenance of man; all kinds of cotton, hemp, flax, tar, pitch, ropes, cables, sails, sailcloth, anchors and any parts of anchors, ship-masts, planks, boards, beams, and all sorts of trees and other things proper for building or repairing ships; nor shall any goods be considered as contraband which have not been worked into the form of any instrument or thing for the purpose of war by land or by sea, much less such as have been prepared or wrought up for any other use.

Vaisseaux. On ne regardera pas non plus comme marchandise de Contrebande, celles qui n'auront pas pris la forme de quelque instrument ou attirail, servant à l'usage de la Guerre sur Terre ou sur Mer; encore moins celles qui sont preparées ou travaillées pour tout autre usage. Toutes ces Choses seront censées Marchandises Libres de même que toutes celles qui ne sont point comprises et specialement designees dans l'article precedent, de Sorte qu'elles ne pourront sous aucune interpretation pretendue d'icelles être comprises sous les éffets prohibés ou de contrebande; au contraire elles pourront être librement transportées par les Sujets du Roiet des États Unis, même dans les lieux ennemis, excepté seulement dans les Places assiegés, bloquées ou investies; et pour telles, seront tenues uniquement les places entourées de près par quelqu'une des Puissances Belligerantes.

All which shall be reckoned free goods, as likewise all others which are not comprehended and particularly mentioned in the foregoing article; so that they shall not by any pretended interpretation be comprehended among prohibited or contraband goods. On the contrary, they may be freely transported by the subjects of the King and of the United States, even to places belonging to an enemy, such places only excepted as are besieged, blocked, or invested, and those places only shall be considered as such, which are nearly surrounded[1] by one of the belligerent powers.

ART. 11.

Afin d'écarter et de prevenir de part et d'autre toutes sortes de Discussions et de Discorde, il a été convenu que dans le cas où l'une des deux Parties se trouveroit engagée dans une Guerre, les Vaisseaux et Batimens appertenants aux Sujets ou habitans de l'autre devront être munis de Lettres de Mer ou Passeports, exprimant le nom, la Proprieté et

ARTICLE 11.

In order to avoid and prevent, on both sides, all disputes and discord, it is agreed that in case one of the parties shall be engaged in a war, the ships and vessels belonging to the subjects or inhabitants of the other shall be furnished with sea letters or passports expressing the name, property, and port of the vessel, and also the name and place of abode

[1] The French means "closely beleaguered" rather than "nearly surrounded."

le Port du Navire, ainsi que le nom et la Demeure du maitre ou Commandant du dit Vaisseau, afin qu'il apparoisse par là que le dit Vaisseau appartient réellement et veritablement aux Sujets de l'une ou de l'autre Partie. Ces Passeports qui seront dressés et expediés en due et bonne forme, devront également être renouvellés toutes les fois que le Vaisseau revient chez lui dans le Cours de l'an. Il est encore convenu que ces dits Vaisseaux chargés devront être pourvus non seulement de Lettres de Mer, mais aussi de Certificats contenant les Details de la Cargaison, le lieu d'où le Vaisseau est parti, et celui de sa Destination, afin que l'on puisse connoitre s'ils ne portent aucune des Marchandies defendues ou de Contrebande specifiées dans l'article 9. du present Traité, les quels Certificats seront également expediés par les officiers du lieu d'où le Vaisseau sortira.

of the master or commander of the said vessel, in order that it may thereby appear that the said vessel really and truly belongs to the subjects of the one or the other party. These passports, which shall be drawn up in good and due form, shall be renewed every time the vessel returns home in the course of the year. It is also agreed that the said vessels, when loaded, shall be provided not only with sea letters, but also with certificates containing a particular account of the cargo, the place from which the vessel sailed, and that of her destination, in order that it may be known whether they carry any of the prohibited or contraband merchandises mentioned in the ninth article of the present treaty; which certificates shall be made out by the officers of the place from which the vessel shall depart.

Art. 12.

Quoique les Vaisseaux de l'une et de l'autre Partie pourront naviguer librement et avec toute Sureté, comme il est expliqué à l'Art. 7. ils seront néanmoins tenus, toutes les fois qu'on l'exigera, d'exhiber tant en pleine Mer que dans les Ports, leurs passeports et Certificats cy dessus mentionnés. Et n'ayant pas chargé des Marchandises de Contrebande pour un port ennemi,

Article 12.

Although the vessels of the one and of the other party may navigate freely and with all safety, as is explained in the seventh article, they shall, nevertheless, be bound at all times when required, to exhibit, as well on the high sea as in port, their passports and certificates above mentioned. And not having contraband merchandise on board for an enemy's port, they may freely and with-

ils pourront librement et sans empechement poursuivre leur voyage vers le lieu de leur Destination. Cependant on n'aura point le Droit de demander l'exhibition des Papiers aux Navires Marchands convoyés par des Vaisseaux de Guerre; mais on ajoutera foi à la parole de l'officier commandant le Convoy.

out hindrance pursue their voyage to the place of their destination. Nevertheless, the exhibition of papers shall not be demanded of merchant ships under the convoy of vessels of war, but credit shall be given to the word of the officer commanding the convoy.

ART. 13.

Si en produisant les dits Certificats il fut decouvert que le Navire porte quelques uns de ces effets qui sont déclarés prohibés ou de Contrebande, et qui sont consignés pour un port ennemi, il ne sera cependant pas permis de rompre les Ecoutilles des dits navires, ni d'ouvrir aucune Caisse, Coffre, malle, Ballot et Tonneau, ou d'en deplacer ni d'en detourner la moindre partie des Marchandises, jusqu'à ce que la Cargaison ait été mise à Terre, en presence des officiers preposés à cet effet, et que l'inventaire en ait été fait. Encore ne sera t'il pas permis de vendre, échanger ou aliener la Cargaison, ou quelque partie d'icelle, avant qu'on aura procedé legalement au Sujet des marchandises prohibées et qu'elles auront été declarées confiscables par Sentence; à la reserve neanmoins tant des navires même que des autres marchandises qui y aurons été trouvées et qui, en vertu du present Traité, doivent être censées libres; les quelles ne

ARTICLE 13.

If, on producing the said certificates, it be discovered that the vessel carries some of the goods which are declared to be prohibited or contraband, and which are consigned to an enemy's port, it shall not, however, be lawful to break up the hatches of such ships, nor to open any chest, coffers, packs, casks, or vessels, nor to remove or displace the smallest part of the merchandises, until the cargo has been landed in the presence of officers appointed for the purpose and until an inventory thereof has been taken. Nor shall it be lawful to sell, exchange, or alienate the cargo, or any part thereof, until legal process shall have been had against the prohibited merchandises and sentence shall have passed declaring them liable to confiscation, saving, nevertheless, as well the ships themselves as the other merchandises which shall have been found therein, which by virtue of this present treaty are to be esteemed free, and which are not to be

peuvent être retenues sous pretexte qu'elles ont été chargées avec des Marchandises defendues, et encore moins être confisquées comme une prise Legitime. Et supposé que les dites Marchandises de Contrebande, ne faisant qu'une partie de la Charge, le Patron du Navire agréat, consentit et offrit de les livrer au Vaisseau qui les aura decouvertes; en ce cas celui cy, apres avoir reçu les Marchandises de bonne prise, sera tenu de laisser aller aussitôt le Batiment, et ne l'empechera en aucune maniere de poursuivre sa route vers le lieu de sa Destination. Tout Navire pris et amené dans un des Ports des Parties contractante, sous pretexte de Contrebande, qui se trouve, par la visite faite n'être chargé que de marchandises declarées libres, L'armateur ou celui qui aura fait la prise, sera tenu de payer tous les fraix et dommages au Patron du Navire retenu injustement.

detained on pretence of their having been loaded with prohibited merchandise, and much less confiscated as lawful prize. And in case the contraband merchandise be only a part of the cargo, and the master of the vessel agrees, consents, and offers to deliver them to the vessel that has discovered them, in that case the latter, after receiving the merchandises which are good prize, shall immediately let the vessel go and shall not by any means hinder her from pursuing her voyage to the place of her destination. When a vessel is taken and brought into any of the ports of the contracting parties, if, upon examination, she be found to be loaded only with merchandises declared to be free, the owner, or he who has made the prize, shall be bound to pay all costs and damages to the master of the vessel unjustly detained.

Art. 14.

On est également convenu que tout ce qui se trouvera chargé par les Sujets d'une des deux Parties dans un Vaisseau appartenant aux Ennemis de l'autre Partie, sera confisqué en entier, quoi que ces effets ne soient pas au nombre de ceux declarés de contrebande, comme si ces effets appartenoient à l'Ennemi même; à l'exception néanmoins des éffets et Marchan-

Article 14.

It is likewise agreed that whatever shall be found to be laden by the subjects of either of the two contracting parties on a ship belonging to the enemies of the other party, the whole effects, although not of the number of those declared contraband, shall be confiscated as if they belonged to the enemy, excepting, nevertheless, such goods and merchandises as

dises qui auront été chargées sur des vaisseaux ennemis avant la Declaration de Guerre et même six mois après la Declaration, après le quel Terme l'on ne sera pas censé d'avoir pu l'ignorer; les quelles marchandises ne seront en aucune maniere sujettes à Confiscation, mais seront rendues en nature fidelement aux Proprietaires qui les reclameront ou feront reclamer avant la Confiscation et vente; comme aussi leur provenu, si la reclamation ne pouvoir se faire que dans l'intervalle de huit mois après la vente, la quelle doit être publique; bien entendu néanmoins, que si les dites Marchandises sont de Contrebande, il ne sera nullement permis de les transporter ensuite à aucun Port appartenant aux ennemis.

were put on board before the declaration of war, and even six months after the declaration, after which term none shall be presumed to be ignorant of it; which merchandises shall not in any manner be subject to confiscation, but shall be faithfully and specifically delivered to the owners, who shall claim or cause them to be claimed before confiscation and sale, as also their proceeds, if the claim be made within eight months and could not be made sooner after the sale, which is to be public; provided, nevertheless, that if the said merchandises be contraband, it shall not be in any wise lawful to carry them afterward to a port belonging to the enemy.

Art. 15.

Et afin de pourvoir plus efficacement à la Sureté des deux Parties contractantes, pour qu'il ne leur soit fait aucun prejudice par les Vaisseaux de Guerre de l'autre Partie ou par des armateurs particuliers, il sera fait defense à tous les Capitaines et Commandants de Vaisseaux de Sa M.[té] Suédoise et des Etats Unis, et tous leurs Sujets, de faire aucun Dommage ou insulte à ceux de l'autre Partie; et au cas qu'ils y contreviennent, ayant été trouvés coupables, apres l'examen fait par leurs propres Juges, ils seront tenus de donner Satis-

Article 15.

And that more effectual care may be taken for the security of the two contracting parties, that they suffer no prejudice by the men-of-war of the other party or by privateers, all captains and commanders of ships of His Swedish Majesty and of the United States, and all their subjects, shall be forbidden to do any injury or damage to those of the other party, and if they act to the contrary, having been found guilty on examination by their proper judges, they shall be bound to make satisfaction for all damages and the interest thereof, and to make

faction de tout dommage et intérêt; et de les bonifier sous peine et obligation de leurs Personnes et Biens.

them good under pain and obligation of their persons and goods.

ART. 16.

Pour cette cause chaque particulier voulant armer en course, sera obligé avant que de recevoir les patentes ou ses Commissions speciales de donner par devant un Juge competent, caution de Personnes solvables, chacun solidairement, pour une Somme suffisante, afin de repondre de tous les dommages et Torts que l'armateur, ses officiers, ou autres étant à Son Service, pourroient faire en leurs Courses, contre la teneur du present Traité et contre les Edits faits de part et d'autre en vertu du même Traité par le Roi de Suede et par les États Unis, même sous peine de revocation et Cassation des dites Patentes et Commissions speciales.

ARTICLE 16.

For this cause, every individual who is desirous of fitting out a privateer shall, before he receives letters patent or special commission, be obliged to give bond with sufficient sureties, before a competent judge, for a sufficient sum to answer all damages and wrongs which the owner of the privateer, his officers, or others in his employ may commit during the cruise, contrary to the tenor of this treaty and contrary to the edicts published by either party, whether by the King of Sweden or by the United States, in virtue of this same treaty, and also under the penalty of having the said letters patent and special commission revoked and made void.

ART. 17.

Une des Parties contractantes étant en Guerre, et l'autre restant neutre, s'il arrivoit qu'un navire marchand de la Puissance neutre fut pris par l'ennemi de l'autre partie et repris ensuite par un vaisseau ou par un Armateur de la Puissance en Guerre; de même que les Navires et Marchandises de quelle Nature qu'elles puissent être lors qu'elles auront été enlevées des mains de quelque Pirate ou Ecumeur de Mer, elles seront emmenées dans

ARTICLE 17.

One of the contracting parties being at war and the other remaining neuter, if it should happen that a merchant ship of the neutral power be taken by the enemy of the other party, and be afterwards retaken by a ship of war or privateer of the power at war, also ships and merchandises of what nature soever they may be, when recovered from a pirate or sea rover, shall be brought into a port of one of the two powers and shall be committed to the cus-

quelque Port de l'un des deux États et seront remises à la Garde des officiers du dit Port, afin d'être rendus en entier à leur veritable Proprietaire, aussitôt qu'il aura produit des preuves suffisantes de la proprieté. Les Marchands, Patrons et proprietaires des Navires, Matelots, gens de toute Sorte, Vaisseaux et Batimens et en general aucunes marchandises ni aucuns effets de chacun des Alliés ou de leurs Sujets ne pourront être assujetis à aucun embargo, ni retenus dans aucun des Pays, Territoires, Isles, villes, Places, Ports Rivages ou Domaines quelconques de l'autre Allié, pour quelque expedition militaire, usage public ou particulier de qui que ce soit, par saisie, par force ou de quelque maniere semblable. D'autant moins sera t'il permis aux Sujets de chacune des Parties de prendre ou enlever par force quelque chose aux Sujets de l'autre Partie, sans le consentement du proprietaire; ce qui néanmoins ne doit pas s'entendre des Saisies, Detentions et arrets qui se feront par ordre et autorité de la Justice et selon les voyes ordinaires pour dettes ou delits, au Sujet des quels il devra être procedé par voye de droit selon les formes de Justice.

tody of the officers of the said port, that they may be restored entire to the true proprietor as soon as he shall have produced full proof of the property. Merchants, masters and owners of ships, seamen, people of all sorts, ships and vessels, and in general all merchandises and effects of one of the allies or their subjects, shall not be subject to any embargo nor detained in any of the countries, territories, islands, cities, towns, ports, rivers, or domains whatever, of the other ally, on account of any military expedition or any public or private purpose whatever, by seizure, by force, or by any such manner; much less shall it be lawful for the subjects of one of the parties to seize or take anything by force from the subjects of the other party, without the consent of the owner. This, however, is not to be understood to comprehend seizures, detentions, and arrests made by order and by the authority of justice and according to the ordinary course for debts or faults of the subject, for which process shall be had in the way of right according to the forms of justice.

Art. 18.

S'il arrivoit que les deux Parties contractantes fussent en même tems en guerre contre un ennemi

Article 18.

If it should happen that the two contracting parties should be engaged in a war at the same time

commun, on observera de part et d'autre les Points suivants.

1º Si les Batimens de l'une des deux Nations repris par les Armateurs de l'autre n'ont pas été au pouvoir de l'Ennemi au delà de 24 heures, ils seront restitués au premier proprietaire, moyennant le Payement du Tiers de la Valeur du Batiment et de celle de la Cargaison. Si au contraire le vaisseau repris a été plus de 24 heures au Pouvoir de l'ennemi, il appartiendra en entier à celui qui l'aura repris.

2º Dans le cas que dans l'intervalle de 24 heures un navire est repris par un Vaisseau de Guerre de l'une des deux Parties, il sera rendu au premier Proprietaire, moyennant qu'il paye un Trentieme de la Valeur du Navire et de sa Cargaison, et le dixieme, s'il a été repris après les 24 heures, les quelles sommes seront distribuées en guise de gratification aux Equipages des Vaisseaux qui l'auront repris.

3º Les prises faites de la maniere susdite seront restituées aux proprietaires, après les preuves faites de la Proprieté, en donnant caution pour la part qui en revient à celui qui a tiré le navire des mains de l'ennemi.

4º Les Vaisseaux de guerre et Armateurs des deux Nations seront reciproquement admis avec leurs prises, dans les Ports respectifs de chacune, mais ces Prises ne pour-

with a common enemy, the following points shall be observed on both sides:

1. If the ships of one of the two nations, retaken by the privateers of the other, have not been in the power of the enemy more than twenty-four hours, they shall be restored to the original owner on payment of one third of the value of the ship and cargo. If, on the contrary, the vessel retaken has been more than twenty-four hours in the power of the enemy, it shall belong wholly to him who has retaken it.

2. In case, during the interval of twenty-four hours, a vessel be retaken by a man-of-war of either of the two parties, it shall be restored to the original owner on payment of a thirtieth part of the value of the vessel and cargo, and a tenth part if it has been retaken after the twenty-four hours, which sums shall be distributed as a gratification among the crew of the men-of-war that shall have made the recapture.

3. The prizes made in manner above mentioned shall be restored to the owners, after proof made of the property, upon giving security for the part coming to him who has recovered the vessel from the hands of the enemy.

4. The men-of-war and privateers of the two nations shall reciprocally be admitted with their prizes into each other's ports; but the prizes shall not be un-

ront y être dechargées ni vendues qu'après que la Legitimité de la Prise faite par des Batimens Suedois aura été decidée selon les Loix et reglemens établis en Suede; tout comme celle des Prises faites par des Batimens Americains, sera jugée selon les Loix, et réglemens determinés par les États Unis de l'Amerique.

5º Au Surplus il sera libre au Roi de Suede, ainsi qu'aux États Unis de l'Amerique, de faire tels reglemens qu'ils jugeront necessaires relativement à la conduite que devront tenir leurs vaisseaux et armateurs respectifs à l'égard des Batimens qu'ils auront pris et conduits dans les Ports des deux Puissances.

ART. 19.

Les Vaisseaux de Guerre de sa Majesté Suedoise et ceux des États Unis, de même que ceux que leurs Sujets auront armés en guerre, pourront en toute Liberté conduire les Prises qu'ils auront faites sur leurs ennemis dans les Ports ouverts en tems de Guerre aux autres Nations amies, sans que ces Prises, entrant dans les dits Ports, puissent être arretées ou saisies, ni que les officiers des lieux puissent prendre connoissance de la validité de dites Prises, les quelles pourront sortir et être conduites franchement et en toute Liberté aux lieux portés par les Commissions, dont les Capitaines des dits vaisseaux seront obligés de faire montre.

loaded or sold there until the legality of a prize made by Swedish ships shall have been determined according to the laws and regulations established in Sweden, as also that of the prizes made by American vessels shall have been determined according to the laws and regulations established by the United States of America.

5. Moreover, the King of Sweden and the United States of America shall be at liberty to make such regulations as they shall judge necessary respecting the conduct which their men-of-war and privateers respectively shall be bound to observe with regard to vessels which they shall take and carry into the ports of the two powers.

ARTICLE 19.

The ships of war of His Swedish Majesty and those of the United States, and also those which their subjects shall have armed for war, may with all freedom conduct the prizes which they shall have made from their enemies into the ports which are open in time of war to other friendly nations; and the said prizes, upon entering the said ports, shall not be subject to arrest or seizure, nor shall the officers of the places take cognizance of the validity of the said prizes, which may depart and be conducted freely and with all liberty to the places pointed out in their commissions, which the captains of the said vessels shall be obliged to show.

ART. 20.

Au cas que quelque Vaisseau appartenant à l'un des deux Etats, ou à leurs Sujets, aura échoué, fait naufrage ou souffert quelque autre Dommage sur les Côtes ou sous la Domination de l'une des deux Parties, il sera donné toute aide et assistance aux Personnes naufragées ou qui se trouvent en danger, et il leur sera accordé des Passeports pour assurer leur retour dans leur Patrie. Les Navires et marchandises naufragées ou leur provenu, si ces effets eussent été vendus, étant reclamés dans l'an et Jour par les Proprietaires, ou leur ayant cause, seront restitués, en payant les fraix du Sauvement, conformement aux Loix et coutumes des deux Nations.

ARTICLE 20.

In case any vessel belonging to either of the two states, or to their subjects, shall be stranded, shipwrecked, or suffer any other damage on the coasts or under the dominion of either of the parties, all aid and assistance shall be given to the persons shipwrecked, or who may be in danger thereof, and passports shall be granted to them to secure their return to their own country. The ships and merchandises wrecked, or their proceeds, if the effects have been sold, being claimed in a year and a day by the owners or their attorney, shall be restored on their paying the costs of salvage, conformable to the laws and customs of the two nations.

ART. 21.

Lors que les Sujets et habitans de l'une des deux Parties avec leurs vaisseaux soit publics, soit équipés en guerre, soit particuliers, ou employés au Commerce, seront forcés par une Tempête, par la poursuite des Corsaires et des ennemis, ou par quelqu'autre necessité urgente de se retirer, et d'entrer dans quelqu'une des Rivieres, Bayes, rades ou Ports de l'une des deux Parties, ils seront reçus et traités avec humanité et honnêteté, et jouiront de toute amitié, protection et assistance; et il leur sera permis de se pourvoir de rafraichissemens, de vivres

ARTICLE 21.

When the subjects and inhabitants of the two parties, with their vessels, whether they be public and equipped for war, or private, or employed in commerce, shall be forced by tempest, by pursuit of privateers and of enemies, or by any other urgent necessity, to retire and enter any of the rivers, bays, roads, or ports of either of the two parties, they shall be received and treated with all humanity and politeness, and they shall enjoy all friendship, protection, and assistance, and they shall be at liberty to supply themselves with refreshments,

et de toute chose necessaires pour leur Subsistance, pour la reparation de leurs vaisseaux et pour continuer leur voyage; le tout moyennant un prix raisonable; et ils ne seront retenus en aucune maniere, ni empêchés de sortir des dits Ports ou Rades, mais pourront se retirer et partir quand et comme il leur plaira sans aucun obstacle ni empéchement.

provisions, and everything necessary for their sustenance, for the repair of their vessels, and for continuing their voyage; provided always, that they pay a reasonable price; and they shall not in any manner be detained or hindered from sailing out of the said ports or roads, but they may retire and depart when and as they please, without any obstacle or hindrance.

Art. 22.

Afin de favoriser d'autant plus le Commerce des deux côtés, il est convenu que dans le cas où la guerre surviendroit entre les deux Nations sus dites, ce qu'à Dieu ne plaise, il sera accordé un tems de neuf mois apres la Declaration de Guerre, aux marchands et Sujets respectifs de part et d'autre, pour pouvoir se retirer avec leurs effets et meubles, les quels ils pourront transporter, ou faire vendre où ils voudront, sans qu'on y mette le moindre obstacle, ni qu'on puisse arrêter les éffets et encore moins les Personnes pendant les dits neuf mois; mais qu'au contraire on leur donnera pour leurs vaisseaux et éffets qu'ils voudront prendre avec eux des Passeports valables pour le tems qui sera necessaire pour leur retour; mais s'il leur est enlevé quelque chose, ou s'il leur a été fait quelqu'injure, durant le Terme prescrit cy dessus, par l'une des

Article 22.

In order to favor commerce on both sides as much as possible, it is agreed that in case a war should break out between the said two nations, which God forbid, the term of nine months after the declaration of war shall be allowed to the merchants and subjects respectively on one side and the other, in order that they may withdraw with their effects and moveables, which they shall be at liberty to carry off or to sell where they please, without the least obstacle; nor shall any seize their effects, and much less their persons, during the said nine months; but, on the contrary, passports which shall be valid for a time necessary for their return, shall be given them for their vessels and the effects which they shall be willing to carry with them. And if anything is taken from them, or if any injury is done to them by one of the parties, their people and subjects, during the term

Parties, leurs peuples et Sujets, il leur sera donné à cet égard pleine et entiere Satisfaction. Ces Passeports susmentionnés serviront également de Saufconduits contre toutes insultes ou prises que les Armateurs pourront intenter de faire contre leurs personnes et leurs effets.

ART. 23.

Aucun Sujet du Roi de Suede ne prendra de Commission ou lettre de Marque pour armer quelque Vaisseau afin d'agir comme Corsaire contre les États Unis de l'Amerique ou quelques uns d'entre Eux, ou contre les Sujets, peuples ou habitans d'iceux, ou contre la Proprieté des Habitans de ces États, de quelque Prince ou État que ce soit, avec le quel ces dits Etats Unis seront en Guerre. De même aucun Citoyen Sujet ou habitant des dits États Unis et de quelqu'un d'entre eux ne demandera ni n'acceptera aucune Commission ou Lettre de Marque afin d'armer quelque Vaisseau pour courre sus aux Sujets de sa M.té Suedoise ou quelqu'un d'entre eux ou leur propriété, de quelque Prince ou état que ce soit avec qui sa dite Majesté se trouvera en guerre. Et si quelqu'un de l'une ou de l'autre Nation prenoit de pareilles Commissions ou Lettres de Marque il sera puni comme Pirate.

above prescribed, full and entire satisfaction shall be made to them on that account. The abovementioned passports shall also serve as a safe-conduct against all insults or prizes which privateers may attempt against their persons and effects.

ARTICLE 23.

No subject of the King of Sweden shall take a commission or letters of marque for arming any vessel to act as a privateer against the United States of America, or any of them, or against the subjects, people, or inhabitants of the said United States, or any of them, or against the property of the inhabitants of the said States, from any prince or state whatever, with whom the said United States shall be at war. Nor shall any citizen, subject, or inhabitant of the said United States, or any of them, apply for or take any commission or letters of marque for arming any vessel to cruise against the subjects of His Swedish Majesty, or any of them, or their property, from any prince or state whatever with whom His said Majesty shall be at war. And if any person of either nation shall take such commissions or letters of marque, he shall be punished as a pirate.

ART. 24.

Les Vaisseaux des Sujets on Habitants d'une des deux Parties, abordant à quelque côte de la Dependance de l'autre, mais n'ayant point dessein d'entrer au Port, ou y étant entré, ne desirant pas de decharger leur Cargaison, ou rompre leur Charge n'y seront point obligés, mais au contraire jouiront de toutes les Franchises et exemtions accordees par les Reglemens qui subsistent relativement à cet objet.

ARTICLE 24.

The vessels of the subjects of either of the parties coming upon any coast belonging to the other, but not willing to enter into port, or being entered into port and not willing to unload their cargoes or to break bulk, shall not be obliged to do it, but, on the contrary, shall enjoy all the franchises and exemptions which are granted by the rules subsisting with respect to that object.

ART. 25.

Lors qu'un Vaisseau appartenant aux Sujets et Habitans de l'une des deux Parties, naviguant en pleine Mer, sera recontré par un Vaisseau de Guerre ou Armateur de l'autre, le Dit vaisseau de Guerre ou Armateur, pour éviter tout desordre, se tiendra hors de la portée du Canon, mais pourra toutes fois envoyer sa Chaloupe à bord du Navire Marchand et y faire entrer deux ou trois hommes, aux quels le maitre ou Commandant du dit Navire, montrera son Passeport qui constate la proprieté du Navire; et après que le dit Batiment aura exhibé le Passeport, il lui sera libre de continuer son Voyage; et il ne sera pas permis de le molester, ni de chercher en aucune maniere à lui donner la Chasse ou à le forcer de quitter la Course qu'il s'étoit proposé.

ARTICLE 25.

When a vessel belonging to the subjects and inhabitants of either of the parties, sailing on the high sea, shall be met by a ship of war or privateer of the other, the said ship of war or privateer, to avoid all disorder, shall remain out of cannon shot, but may always send their boat to the merchant ship and cause two or three men to go on board of her, to whom the master or commander of the said vessel shall exhibit his passport, stating the property of the vessel; and when the said vessel shall have exhibited her passport, she shall be at liberty to continue her voyage, and it shall not be lawful to molest or search her in any manner or to give her chase or force her to quit her intended course.

ART. 26.

Les deux Parties contractantes se sont accordé mutuellement la Faculté de tenir dans leurs Ports respectifs des Consuls, Vice Consuls, Agents et Commissaires dont les fonctions seront reglées par une Convention particuliere.

ART. 27.

Le present Traité sera ratifié de part et d'autre, et les Ratifications seront échangées dans l'Espace de huit mois, ou plustôt si faire se peut; à compter de Jour de la Signature.

En foi de quoi les Plenipotentiares respectifs ont signé les Articles cy dessus, et y ont apposé le Cachet de leur Armes.

Fait à Paris le trois Avril L'an de grâce mil Sept cent, quatre-vingt trois.

GUSTAV PHILIP
COMTE DE CREUTZ
[Seal]
B FRANKLIN
[Seal]

ARTICLE SEPARÉ.

Le Roi de Suede et les États Unis de l'Amerique Septentrionale sont convenus que le present Traité aura son plein Effet pendant l'espace de quinze Ans consecutifs à compter du Jour de sa Ratification; et les deux Parties

ARTICLE 26.

The two contracting parties grant mutually the liberty of having, each in the ports of the other, consuls, vice consuls, agents, and commissaries, whose functions shall be regulated by a particular agreement.

ARTICLE 27.

The present treaty shall be ratified on both sides, and the ratifications shall be exchanged in the space of eight months, or sooner if possible, counting from the day of the signature.

In faith whereof the respective Plenipotentiaries have signed the above articles and have thereunto affixed their seals.

Done at Paris the third day of April in the year of our Lord one thousand seven hundred and eighty-three.

GUSTAV PHILIP
COMTE DE CREUTZ
[Seal]
B FRANKLIN
[Seal]

SEPARATE ARTICLE

The King of Sweden and the United States of North America agree that the present treaty shall have its full effect for the space of fifteen years, counting from the day of the ratification, and the two contracting parties reserve to

contractantes se reservent la faculté de le renouveller au bout de ce tems.

Fait à Paris le trois Avril l' an de grâce mil Sept cent quatre vingt trois.

GUSTAV PHILIP
COMTE DE CREUTZ
[Seal]
B FRANKLIN
[Seal]

ARTICLES SEPARÉS.

ART: 1.

Sa Majesté Suedoise fera usage de tous les moyens qui sont dans son pouvoir pour proteger et defendre les Vaisseaux et Effets, appartenans aux Citoyens ou Habitans des États Unis de l'Amerique Septentrionale et à chacun d'iceux, qui seront dans les Ports, Havres ou Rades ou dans les Mers près des Païs, Isles, Contrees, Villes et Places de sa dite Majesté et fera tous ses Efforts pour recouvrer et faire restituer aux Proprietaires legitimes tous les Vaisseaux et Effets qui leur seront pris dans l'Etendue de sa Jurisdiction.

ART: 2.

De même les Etats Unis de l'Amerique Septentrionale protegeront et defendront les Vaisseaux et Effets, appartenans aux Sujets de sa Majesté Suedoise qui seront dans les Ports, Havres ou Rades,

themselves the liberty of renewing it at the end of that term.

Done at Paris the third of April in the year of our Lord one thousand seven hundred and eighty-three.

GUSTAV PHILIP
COMTE DE CREUTZ
[Seal]
B FRANKLIN
[Seal]

SEPARATE ARTICLES

ARTICLE 1.

His Swedish Majesty snall use all the means in his power to protect and defend the vessels and effects belonging to citizens or inhabitants of the United States of North America, and every of them, which shall be in the ports, havens, roads, or on the seas near the countries, islands, cities, and towns of His said Majesty, and shall use his utmost endeavor to recover and restore to the right owners all such vessels and effects which shall be taken from them within his jurisdiction.

ARTICLE 2.

In like manner, the United States of North America shall protect and defend the vessels and effects, belonging to the subjects of His Swedish Majesty, which shall be in the ports,

ou dans les Mers près des Païs, Isles, Contrees, Villes et Places des dits Etats, et feront tous leurs Efforts pour recouvrer et faire restituer aux Proprietaires legitimes tous les Vaisseaux et Effets qui leur seront pris dans l'Etendue de leur Jurisdiction.

Art: 3.

Si durant une Guerre Maritime à venir les deux Puissances contractantes prennent le parti de rester neutres et d'observer comme telles, la plus exacte Neutralité, alors on est convenu que s'il arrivoit que les Vaisseaux Marchands de l'une des Puissances, se trouvassent dans un Parage où les Vaisseaux de Guerre de la même Nation ne fussent pas stationnés, ou bien s'ils se rencontrent en pleine Mer sans pouvoir avoir recours à leurs propres convois, dans ce cas le Commandant des Vaisseaux de Guerre de l'autre Puissance, s'il en est requis, doit de bonne foi et sincerement leur prêter les Secours dont ils pourront avoir besoin et en tel cas les Vaisseaux de Guerre et Fregates de l'une des Puissances serviront de Soutien et d'appui aux Vaisseaux Marchands de l'autre, bien entendu cependant que les Reclamans n'auroient fait aucun Commerce illicite ni contraires aux Principes de la Neutralité.

havens, or roads, or on the seas near to the countries, islands, cities, and towns of the said States, and shall use their utmost efforts to recover and restore to the right owners all such vessels and effects which shall be taken from them within their jurisdiction.

Article 3.

If, in any future war at sea, the contracting powers resolve to remain neuter and, as such, to observe the strictest neutrality, then it is agreed that if the merchant ships of either party should happen to be in a part of the sea where the ships of war of the same nation are not stationed, or if they are met on the high sea without being able to have recourse to their own convoys, in that case the commander of the ships of war of the other party, if required, shall in good faith and sincerity give them all necessary assistance; and in such case the ships of war and frigates of either of the powers shall protect and support the merchant ships of the other; provided, nevertheless, that the ships claiming assistance are not engaged in any illicit commerce contrary to the principles of the neutrality.

Art: 4.

Il est convenu et arrêté que tous les Marchands, Capitaines des Navires Marchands ou autres Sujets de sa Majesté Suedoise, auront l'entiere Liberté dans toutes les Places de la Domination ou Jurisdiction des Etats Unis de l'Amerique, de conduire eux mêmes leurs propres affaires, et d'employer qui il leur plaira pour les conduire, et qu'ils ne seront point obligés de se servir d'aucun Interprete ou Courtier, ni leur payer aucun honoraire à moins qu'ils ne s'en servent. En outre les Maitres des Navires ne seront point obligés, chargeant ou dechargeant leurs Navires, de se servir des Ouvriers qui peuvent être établis pour cet effet par l'autorite publique; mais ils seront entierement libres de charger ou de decharger eux mêmes leurs Vaisseaux, et d'employer pour charger ou decharger ceux qu'ils croiront propres pour cet effet, sans payer aucuns Honoraires à titre de Salaire à aucune autre Personne que ce soit, et ils ne pourront être forcés de verser aucune espece de Marchandises dans d'autres Vaisseaux ou de les recevoir à leur bord et d'attendre pour être chargés, plus long tems qu'il ne leur plaira et tous et un chacun des Citoyens, Peuples et Habitans des Etats Unis de l'Amerique, auront et jouiront reciproquement des mêmes Privi-

Article 4.

It is agreed and concluded that all merchants, captains of merchant ships, or other subjects of His Swedish Majesty, shall have full liberty, in all places under the dominion or jurisdiction of the United States of America, to manage their own affairs and to employ in the management of them whomsoever they please; and they shall not be obliged to make use of any interpreter or broker, nor to pay them any reward unless they make use of them. Moreover, the masters of ships shall not be obliged, in loading or unloading their vessels, to employ laborers appointed by public authority for that purpose; but they shall be at full liberty, themselves, to load or unload their vessels, or to employ in loading or unloading them whomsoever they think proper, without paying reward under the title of salary to any other person whatever. And they shall not be obliged to turn over any kind of merchandises to other vessels, nor to receive them on board their own, nor to wait for their lading longer than they please; and all and every of the citizens, people, and inhabitants of the United States of America shall reciprocally have and enjoy the same privileges and liberties in all places under the jurisdiction of the said realm.

115605°—31—vol. 2——12

leges et Libertés dans toutes les Places de la Jurisdiction du dit Royaume.

ART: 5.

Il est convenu que lors que les Marchandises auront été chargées sur les Vaisseaux ou Bâtimens de l'une des deux Parties contractantes, elles ne pourront plus être assujetties à aucune Visite; toute Visite et Recherche devant être faite avant le Chargement, et les Marchandises prohibées devant être arrêtées sur la Plage avant de pouvoir être embarquées, à moins qu'on ait des Indices manifestes ou des Preuves de Versement frauduleux de la part du Proprietaire du Navire ou de celui qui en a le Commandement. Dans ce cas seul il en sera responsable et soumis aux Loix du Païs où il se trouve. Dans aucun autre cas, ni les Sujets d'une des Parties contractantes se trouveront avec leurs Navires dans les Ports de l'autre, ni leurs Marchandises, ne pourront être arrêtés ou molestés pour cause de Contrebande, qu'ils auront voulu prendre à leur bord, ni aucune espece d'embargo mis sur leurs navires, les Sujets ou Citoyens de l'Etat ou ses Marchandises sont declarées de Contrebande, ou dont la Sortie est defendue, et qui néanmoins auront vendu ou voulu vendre, et aliener les dites Marchandises, devant

ARTICLE 5.

It is agreed that when merchandises shall have been put on board the ships or vessels of either of the contracting parties, they shall not be subjected to any examination, but all examination and search must be before lading, and the prohibited merchandises must be stopped on the spot before they are embarked, unless there is full evidence or proof of fraudulent practice on the part of the owner of the ship, or of him who has the command of her. In which case, only he shall be responsible and subject to the laws of the country in which he may be. In all other cases, neither the subjects of either of the contracting parties who shall be with their vessels in the ports of the other, nor their merchandises, shall be seized or molested on account of contraband goods which they shall have wanted to take on board, nor shall any kind of embargo be laid on their ships, subjects, or citizens of the state whose merchandises are declared contraband, or the exportation of which is forbidden; those only who shall have sold or intended to sell or alienate such merchandise being liable to punishment for such contravention.

être les seuls qui seront duement punis pour une pareille Contravention.

Fait à Paris le trois Avril l'an de Grâce mil Sept cent quatrevingt trois.

Gustav Philip
Comte de Creutz
[Seal]
B Franklin
[Seal]

Done at Paris the third day of April in the Year of our Lord one thousand seven hundred and eighty-three.

Gustav Philip
Comte de Creutz
[Seal]
B Franklin
[Seal]

NOTES

Despite the fact that the treaty is very clearly dated April 3, 1783, there is a question as to the actual date of its signature. Franklin's letter to Livingston of March 7, 1783 (Wharton, Diplomatic Correspondence, VI, 276), states that the treaty was signed "on Wednesday last," or March 5, 1783. There can hardly be any error in the date of that letter; it is correctly copied from the original in 82 C. C. Papers, II, folio 361; and the reference therein to the resignation of the Earl of Shelburne as recent news is internal evidence of accuracy; for that resignation took place on the previous February 24.

Certain formal amendments to the opening words of the treaty were proposed (in English) by Congress after ratification (Journals, XXIV, 477); instructions were given to Franklin accordingly by letter of August 15, 1783 (Diplomatic Correspondence, 1783–1789, I, 34–35); but it seems that as formal amendments, those proposals were not pressed. However, on the exchange of ratifications Franklin informed Baron Stael von Holstein, the Ambassador of Sweden at Paris, according to the letter of the latter of February 6, 1784, mentioned below, "that the United States in their titles will henceforth exclude *North* and call themselves only the United States of America, and that the State which has been known as New Castle, Kent, and Sussex on the Delaware from now on will be called only Delaware" (translation from the Swedish).

The United States instrument of ratification is copied in 135 C. C. Papers, I; also in Journals, XXIV, 457–77. The latter of these copies recites the text of the treaty in translation only and as if the original were in English; the former includes the French text, and the translation runs on the lower part of its pages. There is now in the Department of State file a facsimile of the original instrument in the Swedish archives; it recites the French only. The Great Seal and the signatures of Elias Boudinot and Charles Thomson, Secretary, are all in the left margin of its first page.

There has been found no protocol or other similar record of the exchange of ratifications either in the archives of the Department of State or in those of Sweden. The date stated is from an apostil to a letter of February 6, 1784, from the Swedish Ambassador at Paris to the Swedish Minister for Foreign Affairs, a facsimile of which is now in the Department of State file. The date of the exchange was more than two months after the term fixed by Article 27 of the treaty.

Congress voted the proclamation (Journals, XXV, 613–14) on a report (apparently first read July 24, 1783; see Journals, XXIV, 477, note 1) from a committee to whom had been referred the treaty with Sweden and a letter of Franklin "of the 15th of April last." There is a long letter of that date from Franklin to Livingston, and mention is made therein of the treaty with Sweden; but it seems more likely that the report on September 25, or at least the vote of the proclamation, was based on the letter of Franklin to Livingston of June 12, which said that the ratification on the part of Sweden "has come" (see Wharton, Diplomatic Correspondence, VI, 377–78, 480, 483).

The original proclamation has not been found. There is a broadside of it, "Philadelphia: Printed by David C. Claypoole" (see Journals, XXV, 989, item 415), in the Library of Congress; a facsimile thereof is in the Department of State file; it follows the form in the Journals of Congress and does not purport to have been sealed.

The translation of the treaty here printed is that which is written in 135 C. C. Papers, I, with the insertion of four or five words obviously omitted by the first scrivener and noted in pencil on the ancient record in a different hand. In substance the translation in 8 Statutes at Large, 60–79, is the same; but there the record used, it seems, was the manuscript translation in the Department of State file, which is in the handwriting of Charles Thomson, Secretary of Congress. The differences between that manuscript and the C. C. Papers text are trifling and consist of an occasional word only; but there are some errors of copying in the Statutes at Large, *e. g.*, Article 18, line 13, "a tenth part of it," should read "a tenth part if it." In 18 Statutes at Large, pt. 2, Public Treaties, 727, this becomes "a tenth part of it if it," and so elsewhere.

Note Regarding Article 6

In the English translation the expression "fonds et biens" is rendered "goods and effects," which is more limited in meaning than the French; the manuscript of the Thomson translation shows that he had doubts; the three French words are written over the English and crossed out; and later on in the article, "fonds" appears similarly over "effects"; so the translator wrote "goods" for "biens," a word which in French law has a very extensive signification. Compare "effets et meubles" in Article 22, translated "effects and moveables."

Because of subsequent agreements reviving various articles of the treaty, including Article 6, the point has been one of importance in various cases in courts of this country.

Treaty Series, No. 104
8 Statutes at Large, 80-83

11

GREAT BRITAIN : SEPTEMBER 3, 1783

Definitive Treaty of Peace, signed at Paris September 3, 1783. Original in English.
Ratified by the United States January 14, 1784. Ratified by Great Britain April 9, 1784. Ratifications exchanged at Paris May 12, 1784. Proclaimed January 14, 1784.

In the Name of the most Holy & undivided Trinity.

It having pleased the divine Providence to dispose the Hearts of the most Serene and most Potent Prince George the third, by the Grace of God, King of Great Britain, France & Ireland, Defender of the Faith, Duke of Brunswick and Lunebourg, Arch Treasurer, and Prince Elector of the Holy Roman Empire &c.ª and of the United States of America, to forget all past Misunderstandings and Differences that have unhappily interrupted the good Correspondence and Friendship which they mutually wish to restore; and to establish such a beneficial and satisfactory Intercourse between the two Countries upon the Ground of reciprocal Advantages and mutual Convenience as may promote and secure to both perpetual Peace & Harmony, and having for this desirable End already laid the Foundation of Peace & Reconciliation by the Provisional Articles signed at Paris on the 30th of Novr. 1782. by the Commissioners empower'd on each Part, which Articles were agreed to be inserted in and to constitute the Treaty of Peace proposed to be concluded between the Crown of Great Britain and the said United States, but which Treaty was not to be concluded until Terms of Peace should be agreed upon between Great Britain & France, And his Britannic Majesty should be ready to conclude such Treaty accordingly: and the Treaty between Great Britain & France having since been concluded, His Britannic Majesty & the United States of America, in Order to carry into full Effect the Provisional Articles abovementioned, according to the Tenor thereof, have constituted & appointed, that is to say His Britannic Majesty on his Part, David Hartley Esqr, Member of the Parliament of Great Britain; and the said United States on their Part, John Adams Esqr, late a Commissioner of the United States of

America at the Court of Versailles, late Delegate in Congress from the State of Massachusetts and Chief Justice of the said State, and Minister Plenipotentiary of the said United States to their High Mightinesses the States General of the United Netherlands; Benjamin Franklin Esqre late Delegate in Congress from the State of Pennsylvania, President of the Convention of the s^d State, and Minister Plenipotentiary from the United States of America at the Court of Versailles; John Jay Esqre late President of Congress, and Chief Justice of the State of New-York & Minister Plenipotentiary from the said United States at the Court of Madrid; to be the Plenipotentiaries for the concluding and signing the Present Definitive Treaty; who after having reciprocally communicated their respective full Powers have agreed upon and confirmed the following Articles.

Article 1st

His Britannic Majesty acknowledges the s^d. United States, viz. New-Hampshire Massachusetts Bay, Rhode-Island & Providence Plantations, Connecticut, New York, New Jersey, Pennsylvania, Delaware, Maryland, Virginia, North Carolina, South Carolina & Georgia, to be free sovereign & Independent States; that he treats with them as such, and for himself his Heirs & Successors, relinquishes all Claims to the Government Propriety & Territorial Rights of the same & every Part thereof.

Article 2^d.

And that all Disputes which might arise in future on the Subject of the Boundaries of the said United States, may be prevented, it is hereby agreed and declared, that the following are and shall be their Boundaries, Viz. From the North West Angle of Nova Scotia, viz. That Angle which is formed by a Line drawn due North from the Source of Saint Croix River to the Highlands along the said Highlands which divide those Rivers that empty themselves into the River S^t. Lawrence, from those which fall into the Atlantic Ocean, to the Northwestern-most Head of Connecticut River: Thence down along the middle of that River to the forty fifth Degree of North Latitude; From thence by a Line due West on said Latitude until it strikes the River Iroquois or Cataraquy; Thence along the middle of said River into Lake Ontario; through the Middle of said Lake until it strikes the Communication by Water between that Lake & Lake Erie; Thence along the middle of said Communication into Lake Erie; through the middle of said Lake, until it arrives at the Water Com-

munication between that Lake & Lake Huron; Thence along the middle of said Water-Communication into the Lake Huron, thence through the middle of said Lake to the Water Communication between that Lake and Lake Superior, thence through Lake Superior Northward of the Isles Royal & Phelipeaux to the Long Lake; Thence through the Middle of said Long-Lake, and the Water Communication between it & the Lake of the Woods, to the said Lake of the Woods; Thence through the said Lake to the most Northwestern Point thereof, and from thence on a due West Course to the River Mississippi, Thence by a Line to be drawn along the Middle of the said River Mississippi until it shall intersect the Northernmost Part of the thirty first Degree of North Latitude. South, by a Line to be drawn due East from the Determination of the Line last mentioned, in the Latitude of thirty one Degrees North of the Equator to the middle of the River Apalachicola or Catahouche. Thence along the middle thereof to its Junction with the Flint River; Thence strait to the Head of S^t^. Mary's River, and thence down along the middle of St Mary's River to the Atlantic Ocean. East, by a Line to be drawn along the Middle of the River St Croix, from its Mouth in the Bay of Fundy to its Source; and from its Source directly North to the aforesaid Highlands, which divide the Rivers that fall into the Atlantic Ocean, from those which fall into the River S^t^. Lawrence; comprehending all Islands within twenty Leagues of any Part of the Shores of the United States, & lying between Lines to be drawn due East from the Points where the aforesaid Boundaries between Nova Scotia on the one Part and East Florida on the other, shall respectively touch the Bay of Fundy and the Atlantic Ocean, excepting such Islands as now are or heretofore have been within the Limits of the said Province of Nova Scotia.

Article 3^d^.

It is agreed that the People of the United States shall continue to enjoy unmolested the Right to take Fish of every kind on the Grand Bank and on all the other Banks of New-foundland, also in the Gulph of St Lawrence, and at all other Places in the Sea where the Inhabitants of both Countries used at any time heretofore to fish. And also that the Inhabitants of the United States shall have Liberty to take Fish of every Kind on such Part of the Coast of New-foundland as British Fishermen shall use, (but not to dry or cure the same on that Island) And also on the Coasts Bays & Creeks of all other of his Britannic Majesty's Dominions in America, and that the American Fishermen

shall have Liberty to dry and cure Fish in any of the unsettled Bays Harbours and Creeks of Nova Scotia, Magdalen Islands, and Labrador, so long as the same shall remain unsettled but so soon as the same or either of them shall be settled, it shall not be lawful for the said Fishermen to dry or cure Fish at such Settlement, without a previous Agreement for that purpose with the Inhabitants, Proprietors or Possessors of the Ground.

Article 4th

It is agreed that Creditors on either Side shall meet with no lawful Impediment to the Recovery of the full Value in Sterling Money of all bona fide Debts heretofore contracted.

Article 5th

It is agreed that the Congress shall earnestly recommend it to the Legislatures of the respective States to provide for the Restitution of all Estates, Rights and Properties which have been confiscated belonging to real British Subjects; and also of the Estates Rights and Properties of Persons resident in Districts in the Possession of his Majesty's Arms, and who have not borne Arms against the said United States. And that Persons of any other Description shall have free Liberty to go to any Part or Parts of any of the thirteen United States and therein to remain twelve Months unmolested in their Endeavours to obtain the Restitution of such of their Estates Rights & Properties as may have been confiscated. And that Congress shall also earnestly recommend to the several States, a Reconsideration and Revision of all Acts or Laws regarding the Premises, so as to render the said Laws or Acts perfectly consistent, not only with Justice and Equity, but with that Spirit of Conciliation, which, on the Return of the Blessings of Peace should universally prevail. And that Congress shall also earnestly recommend to the several States, that the Estates, Rights and Properties of such last mentioned Persons shall be restored to them, they refunding to any Persons who may be now in Possession, the Bonâ fide Price (where any has been given) which such Persons may have paid on purchasing any of the said Lands, Rights or Properties, since the Confiscation.

And it is agreed that all Persons who have any Interest in confiscated Lands, either by Debts, Marriage Settlements, or otherwise, shall meet with no lawful Impediment in the Prosecution of their just Rights.

ARTICLE 6th

That there shall be no future Confiscations made nor any Prosecutions commenc'd against any Person or Persons for or by Reason of the Part, which he or they may have taken in the present War, and that no Person shall on that Account suffer any future Loss or Damage, either in his Person Liberty or Property; and that those who may be in Confinement on such Charges at the Time of the Ratification of the Treaty in America shall be immediately set at Liberty, and the Prosecutions so commenced be discontinued.

ARTICLE 7th

There shall be a firm and perpetual Peace between his Britannic Majesty and the said States and between the Subjects of the one, and the Citizens of the other, wherefore all Hostilities both by Sea and Land shall from henceforth cease: All Prisoners on both Sides shall be set at Liberty, and his Britannic Majesty shall with all convenient speed, and without causing any Destruction, or carrying away any Negroes or other Property of the American Inhabitants, withdraw all his Armies, Garrisons & Fleets from the said United States, and from every Port, Place and Harbour within the same; leaving in all Fortifications the American Artillery that may be therein: And shall also Order & cause all Archives, Records, Deeds & Papers belonging to any of the said States, or their Citizens, which in the Course of the War may have fallen into the Hands of his Officers, to be forthwith restored and deliver'd to the proper States and Persons to whom they belong.

ARTICLE 8th

The Navigation of the River Mississippi, from its source to the Ocean shall for ever remain free and open to the Subjects of Great Britain and the Citizens of the United States.

ARTICLE 9th

In Case it should so happen that any Place or Territory belonging to great Britain or to the United States should have been conquer'd by the Arms of either from the other before the Arrival of the said Provisional Articles in America it is agreed that the same shall be restored without Difficulty and without requiring any Compensation.

ARTICLE 10th

The solemn Ratifications of the present Treaty expedited in good & due Form shall be exchanged between the contracting Parties in

the Space of Six Months or sooner if possible to be computed from the Day of the Signature of the present Treaty. In Witness whereof we the undersigned their Ministers Plenipotentiary have in their Name and in Virtue of our Full Powers signed with our Hands the present Definitive Treaty, and caused the Seals of our Arms to be affix'd thereto.

Done at Paris, this third Day of September, In the Year of our Lord one thousand seven hundred & eighty three.

D HARTLEY	JOHN ADAMS.	B FRANKLIN	JOHN JAY
[Seal]	[Seal]	[Seal]	[Seal]

NOTES

There are two originals of this treaty in the Department of State file; in trifles, such as punctuation, they are not literally identical; the provisions of the one reproduced are in the handwriting of William Temple Franklin. With each original, following the signatures, are copies of the full powers of David Hartley, dated May 14, 1783, and of John Adams, Benjamin Franklin, John Jay, Henry Laurens, and Thomas Jefferson, dated June 15, 1781; these are certified "to be authentic" by George Hammond, Secretary to the British Commission, and by William Temple Franklin, Secretary to the American Commission. The certificate of the example from which the text here printed is taken is undated; the other is dated at Paris September 3, 1783.

The treaty was signed at Paris for the reason that David Hartley, the representative of Great Britain, refused to go to Versailles for the purpose (Wharton, Diplomatic Correspondence, VI, 674, 740).

No facsimile of the United States instrument of ratification is available; the original instrument has not been found in the British archives; it is copied in 135 C. C. Papers, I; also in Wharton, Diplomatic Correspondence, VI, 756. Certain objections, which Franklin called "trivial and absurd," were made to its form (see Diplomatic Correspondence, 1783–1789, I, 380–84) but were not pressed. The British instrument of ratification is copied in Wharton, Diplomatic Correspondence, VI, 757–58, note. The original is in the treaty file.

Neither in the British archives nor in those of the Department of State has been found any protocol or other similar record of the exchange of ratifications. The date is reported in the letter of Franklin of May 12, 1784 (Diplomatic Correspondence, 1783–1789, I, 379–80).

The treaty was laid before Congress on December 13, 1783. As to the non-attendance of six States, see proceedings of December 23, 1783 (Journals, XXV, 836). The period allowed by Article 10 of the treaty for the exchange of ratifications was six months from the date of signature; no objection was made by Great Britain to the necessary prolongation of the term (Wharton, Diplomatic Correspond-

ence, VI, 789–90; other letters on the point, Thomson to the American Commissioners January 5, 1784, Hartley to Carmarthen March 22, 1784, Carmarthen to Hartley March 25, 1784, are copied in Bancroft's Transcripts, Hartley's Negotiations, II, 167–75, NYPL).

The proclamation is copied in Wharton, Diplomatic Correspondence, VI, 755.

The original proclamation is in the Library of Congress. A facsimile thereof is in the Department of State file. It is a folio broadside, bearing the imprint, "Annapolis: Printed by John Dunlap, Printer for the United States in Congress assembled." The seal is affixed at the upper left corner; just below is the signature of Thomas Mifflin; and about halfway down, in the margin, is the signature of Charles Thomson, Secretary.

Note Regarding the Alternat

The form of the treaty was the subject of some correspondence between Fox, Secretary of State for Foreign Affairs, and Hartley. Copies of the letters are in Bancroft's Transcripts, Hartley's Negotiations, II, 53, 57, NYPL. On August 21, 1783, Fox wrote to Hartley:

> One thing only I must remind you of in point of form. When a treaty is signed between two Crowned Heads in order to prevent disputes about precedency, the name of the one stands first in one instrument and that of the other in the other but when the Treaty is between a crowned Head and a Republic, the name of the Monarch is mentioned first in each instrument. I believe if you will inquire upon this subject among the *Corps Diplomatique,* you will find this to have been the constant practice.

Hartley replied as follows under date of September 1:

> The treaties are drawn out for signature as you have expressed it viz: giving precedence to the Crowned Head. The American Ministers never had a thought of disputing the priority or equality of rank & therefore I have had no occasion to mention the subject.

12

FRANCE : AUGUST 27 AND SEPTEMBER 3 AND 9, 1784

Exchange of Notes Referring to Articles 2 and 3 of the Treaty of Amity and Commerce with France of February 6, 1778 (Document 1). Original French notes (Versailles, August 27 and September 9, 1784) in French. Original American note (Passy, September 3, 1784) in English. Not proclaimed and (semble) not published at the time.

À VERSAILLES,
Le 27 août 1784.

M. FRANKLIN:

Vous m'avez fait remettre, Monsieur, un extrait des instructions que le Congrès vous a addressées le 11 mai dernier. Elles portent qu'en aucun cas les États-Unis ne traiteront aucune nation, relativement au commerce, plus avantageusement que la nation françoise. Cette disposition est d'autant plus sage, qu'elle prévient les malentendus qui auroient pu résulter des termes équivoques dans lesquels est conçu l'article second du traité d'amitié et de commerce signé le 6 février 1778. Mais pour que la résolution du Congrès à cet égard soit bien constatée, il conviendroit, Monsieur, que vous me la transmissiez par le moyen d'une déclaration, ou au moins par celui d'une notte

[Translation]

VERSAILLES,
27th August, 1784.

SIR:

You have communicated to me an extract from the instructions which Congress addressed to you the 11th May last, which imports that the United States will in no case treat any other nation, with respect to commerce, more advantageously than the French. This disposition is much the wisest, as it will prevent those misunderstandings which might arise from the equivocal terms in which the second article of the Treaty of Amity and Commerce signed 6th February, 1778, is conceived. But that the resolution of Congress on this subject may be clearly stated, it would be best, Sir, that you furnish me with it in the form of a declaration, or at least in an official note signed by yourself. I have no doubt, Sir,

ministérielle que vous signeriez. Je ne doute pas, Monsieur, que vous n'adoptiez sans difficulté l'une de ces deux formes.

J'ai l'honneur d'être, etc.,
GRAVIER DE VERGENNES

but that you will adopt one of these two forms.

I have the honor to be, etc.,
GRAVIER DE VERGENNES

PASSY, *Sept. 3, 1784*

SIR,

I have the Honour to transmit to your Excellency by Order of Congress a Resolution of theirs, dated the 11th of May last, which is in the Words following, Viz,

"Resolved,

"That Doctor Franklin be instructed to express to the Court of "France the constant Desire of Congress to meet their Wishes; "That these States are about to form a general System of Commerce "by Treaties with other Nations: That at this Time they cannot "foresee what Claim might be given to those Nations by the explana-"tory Propositions[1] from the Count de Vergennes on the 2d & 3d "Articles of our Treaty of Amity & Commerce with His most Christian "Majesty; but that he may be assured it will be our constant Care to "place no People on more advantageous Ground than the Subjects "of his Majesty."

With great Respect I am. Sir, Your Excellency's, most obedient and most humble Servant.

B. FRANKLIN

His Exy the COUNT DE VERGENNES.

À VERSAILLES,
Le 9 septembre 1784.

M. FRANKLIN:

J'ai reçu, Monsieur, la lettre que vous m'avez fait l'honneur de m'écrire le trois de ce mois. Vouz y déclarez, au nom du Congrès, que les États-Unis auront soin de ne traiter aucune nation, relativement au commerce, plus avantageusement que la nation françoise. Cette décla-

[Translation]

VERSAILLES,
9th September, 1784.

SIR:

I have received the letter which you did me the honor to write me the third instant. You there declare in the name of Congress that the United States will be careful not to treat any other nation, in matters of commerce, more advantageously than the French nation. This declara-

[1] See the note regarding the proposals of Vergennes.

ration fondée sur le traité du 6 février 1778 a été très agréable au Roi, et vous pouvez, Monsieur, assurer le Congrès que les États-Unis éprouveront constamment une parfaite réciprocité en France.

J'ai l'honneur d'être, etc.,
GRAVIER DE VERGENNES

tion, founded on the treaty of the 6th February, 1778, has been very agreeable to the King; and you, Sir, can assure Congress that the United States shall constantly experience a perfect reciprocity in France.

I have the honor to be, etc.,
GRAVIER DE VERGENNES

NOTES

The texts of these notes, and translations of the French, are set forth in 100 C. C. Papers, II, folios 223–26, as enclosures A, B, and C to a letter of Franklin to Charles Thomson dated November 11, 1784, from which the following is an extract:

> To explain the Papers. I had first sent to Count Vergennes, by my Secretary, a Copy of the Instruction of May 11th He seems to have thought it should have come to him in a more formal Manner, and wrote me the Letter A. I accordingly sent it to him in B. and received his Answer in C.

The extract quoted is omitted from the text of the letter printed in Wharton, Diplomatic Correspondence, VI, 829, and in Diplomatic Correspondence, 1783–1789, I, 389–90.

The original French notes have not been found. The texts of them here printed are from drafts in the French archives, facsimiles of which are now in the archives of the Department of State. The translations thereof are from the above-mentioned enclosures to the letter of Franklin of November 11, 1784. The text of the American note is from the original, a facsimile of which is now in the Department of State archives.

The American note and translations of the French are printed in Wharton, Diplomatic Correspondence, VI, 819–20, and also in Diplomatic Correspondence, 1783–1789, I, 385–87. The resolution of Congress of May 11, 1784, which is quoted in the American note of September 3, 1784, appears in Journals, XXVII, 368–69.

The policy of Congress at the time regarding official communications from abroad was expressed by the following order of May 3, 1784, voted on motion of Jefferson seconded by Richard Dobbs Spaight of North Carolina (Journals, XXVI, 331):

> *Ordered*, That all letters from the ministers of these United States in Europe, be considered, at all times, as under an injunction of secrecy, except as to such parts of them as Congress shall, by special permission, allow to be published or communicated.

This is a very early use of the expression "injunction of secrecy," which still remains in the rules of the Senate.

Note Regarding the Proposals of Vergennes

The "explanatory propositions" from the Count de Vergennes under date of May 20, 1783, were in French, in the form of a draft convention (8 Franklin Papers, Records of the U. S. Legation, Paris, 145–47). With immaterial omissions they are printed in translation in Wharton, Diplomatic Correspondence, VI, 436–37, as follows:

The intention of his most Christian majesty and the United States of North America, in concluding between them a treaty of amity and commerce, having been that their respective subjects should enjoy all the advantages, privileges, and exemptions which the most favored nations enjoy or may enjoy, and his said majesty and the United States, wishing to prevent any misunderstandings that may arise by a false application of the 2d and 3d articles of the treaty of commerce of February 6th, 1778, have thought it proper to determine in a precise manner the principles which ought to be followed on one part and the other concerning the matter in question. In consequence it is proposed that his majesty and the Congress of the United States agree to the following articles:

Article I. To interpret, as far as is necessary, the 2d article of the treaty of amity and commerce concluded February 6th, 1778, the United States declare that all the advantages, privileges, and exemptions which are accorded, or may be accorded hereafter, in regard to navigation and commerce, to any nation, power, or state whatever, shall be common to the French nation, and that these shall be enjoyed conformably to article 3d of the treaty, in such manner that in no case, or under any pretext, shall the said United States exact any compensation from his most Christian majesty.

Article II. His most Christian majesty promises and engages on his part, to cause the subjects of the United States to enjoy, in conformity with the 3d article above mentioned, all the advantages, privileges, and exemptions which the most favored nations now enjoy, or may enjoy hereafter, and that without exacting any compensation from the said States.

Adams, Franklin, and Jay made this comment in their letter to the President of Congress of September 10, 1783 (85 C. C. Papers, 385; printed in Wharton, Diplomatic Correspondence, VI, 691):

Count de Vergennes communicated to us a Proposition (. . . herewith inclosed) for explaining the 2d & 3d Articles of our Treaty with France, in a manner different from the Sense in which we understand them. This being a Matter in which we had no Right to interfere, we have not express'd any Opinion about it to the Court.

Treaty Series, No. 292
8 Statutes at Large, 84–99

13

PRUSSIA : SEPTEMBER 10, 1785

Treaty of Amity and Commerce, signed at The Hague (on behalf of Prussia) September 10, 1785, and previously (on behalf of the United States) at Passy (Franklin) July 9, 1785, at Paris (Jefferson) July 28, 1785, and at London (Adams) August 5, 1785. Original in French and English.

Ratified by the United States May 17, 1786. Ratified by Prussia September 24, 1785. Ratifications exchanged at The Hague August 8, 1786. Proclaimed May 17, 1786.

Traité d'Amitié et de Commerce entre sa Majesté le Roi de Prusse et les États-Unis de l'Amérique.

Sa Majesté le Roi de Prusse &c. &c, et les Etats Unis de l'Amerique désirant de fixer d'une maniére permanente et équitable les regles qui doivent être observées relativement à la correspondance et au commerce á établir entre les États respectifs des deux parties Sa Majeste et les Etats Unis ont cru ne pouvoir mieux remplir ce but, qu'en posant pour base de leurs engagemens la plus parfaite égalité et reciprocité.

Dans cette vue Sa Majesté le roi de Prusse a nommé et constitué pour son Plenipotentiaire le Baron Frédéric Guillaume de Thulemeier son conseiller privé d'Ambassade et Envoyé extraordinaire auprès de L. H. P. les États Généraux des Provinces-Unies; Et les Etats-Unis ont de

A Treaty of Amity & Commerce between his Majesty the King of Prussia & the United States of America

His Majesty the King of Prussia & the United States of America desiring to fix in a permanent & equitable manner the rules to be observed in the intercourse & commerce they desire to Establish between their respective Countries his Majesty & the United States have judged that the said end can not be better obtained than by taking the most perfect equality & reciprocity for the basis of their agreement.

With this View his Majesty the King of Prussia has nominated and constituted as his Plenipotentiary the Baron Frederick William de Thulemeier his Privy Counsellor of Embassy and Envoy Extraordinary with their high Mightinesses the States General of the United Netherlands: and

leur côté pourvu de leurs Pleinpouvoirs le Sieur John Adams cidevant l'un de leurs Ministres Plenipotentiaires pour traiter de la paix, Délegué au Congrès de la part de l'Etat de Massachusetts et chef de Justice du dit État, actuellement Ministre Plenipotentiaire des États Unis près sa Majesté le Roi de la Grande-Britagne, le Docteur Benjamin Franklin en dernier lieu leur Ministre Plènipotentiaire à la Cour de S. M. T. C. et aussi l'un de leurs Ministres Plenipotentiaires pour traiter de la paix; Et le Sieur Thomas Jefferson, cidevant Délegué au Congrès de la part de l'Etat de Virginie et Gouverneur du dit Etat, actuellement Ministre Plénipotentiaire à la Cour de S. M. T. C. les quels Plénipotentiaires respectifs, après avoir échangé leurs pleinpouvoirs et en consequence d'une mure déliberation, ont conclu, arrêté et signé les Articles suivans:

ARTICLE 1.

Il y aura une Paix ferme inviolable et universelle, et une Amitié sincère entre Sa Majesté le Roi de Prusse, ses heritiers, Successeurs et Sujets, d'une part et les États Unis d'Amérique et leurs Citoyens, d'autre part, sans excéption de personnes ou de lieux.

ARTICLE 2d

Les Sujets de Sa Majesté le Roi de Prusse pourront fréquenter

the United States have on their part given full powers to John Adams Esquire late one of their Ministers Plenipotentiary for negotiating a peace heretofore a delegate in Congress from the State of Massachusetts & Chief Justice of the same, and now Minister plenipotentiary of the United States with his Britannic Majesty, Doctor Benjamin Franklin late Minister Plenipotentiary at the court of Versailles and another of their Ministers Plenipotentiary for negotiating a peace and thomas Jefferson heretofore a délegate in Congress from the State of Virginia & Governor of the said State & now Minister Plenipotentiary of the United States at the court of his most christian Majesty, which respective Plenipotentiaries after having exchanged their full powers, and on mature deliberation, have concluded settled & signed the following articles.

ARTICLE 1er There shall be a firm inviolable, and universal peace & sincere friendship between his Majesty the King of Prussia, his heirs successors & Subjects on the one part and the United States of America & their Citizens on the other, without exception of persons or places.

ARTICLE 2. The Subjects of his Majesty the King of Prussia may

toutes les Côtes et tous les pays des États-Unis de l'Amérique, y résider et trafiquer en toutes Sortes de Productions, manufactures et Marchandises, et ne payeront d'autres ni de plus forts impôts, Charges ou droits dans les dits Etats-Unis, que ceux que les Nations les plus favorisées sont ou seront obligées de payer; et ils jouiront de tous les droits, priviléges et éxemptions dans la Navigation et le commerce, dont jouit ou jouira la Nation la plus favoriseé; se soumettant néanmoins aux Loix et Usages y établis, et aux quels sont soumis les Citoyens des Etats Unis et les Citoyens et Sujets des nations les plus favorisées.

Article 3. Pareillement les Citoyens des Etats Unis de l'Amérique pourront fréquenter toutes les côtes et tous les Pays de Sa Majesté le Roi de Prusse, y resider et trafiquer en toutes Sortes de Productions Manufactures et Marchandises et ne payeront d'autres ni plus forts impots, charges ou droits dans les Domaines de sa dite Majesté, que ceux que la Nation la plus favorisée est ou sera obligée de payer; et ils jouiront des tous les droits, priviléges et exemptions dans la navigation et le commerce, dont jouit ou jouira la nation la plus favorisée; se soumettant néanmoins aux Loix et Usages y établis, et aux quels sont soumis les Sujets de Sa Majesté le Roi

frequent all the coasts & countries of the United States of America and reside & trade there in all Sorts of produce, Manufactures & Merchandize, and shall pay Within the said united States no other or greater duties, charges or fees whatsoever than the most favoured nations are or shall be obliged to pay: and they shall enjoy all the rights privileges and exemptions in navigation & Commerce which the most favoured nation does or shall enjoy: submitting themselves nevertheless to the laws & usages there established, and to which are submitted the Citizens of the united States and the Citizens & Subjects of the most favoured nations.

Article 3. In like manner the Citizens of the united States of America may frequent all the coasts & countries of his Majesty the King of Prussia and reside & trade there in all sorts of Produce, Manufactures &. merchandize, and shall pay in the dominions of his said Majesty no other or greater duties, charges or fees whatsoever than the most favoured nation is or shall be obliged to pay: and they shall enjoy all the rights privileges & Exemptions in navigation & commerce which the most favoured nation does or shall enjoy, submitting themselves nevertheless to the laws & usages there established, and to which are submitted the Subjects of his Majesty the King of Prussia

de Prusse; et les Sujets et Citoyens des Nations les plus favorisées.

ARTICLE 4. En particulier chacune des deux Nations aura le droit d'importer ses propres productions, manufactures et Marchandises, à bord de ses propres Bâtiments ou de tel autre, dans toutes les parties des Domaines de l'autre, où il sera permis à tous les Sujets et Citoyens de l'autre nation de les acheter librement; comme aussi d'y charger les productions, manufactures et marchandises de l'autre que tous les dits Sujets ou Citoyens auront la liberté de leur vendre; en payant dans l'un et l'autre cas tels impots, droits et charges seulement, que ceux qui sont ou seront payés par la nation la plus favorisée. Cependant le Roi de Prusse et les Etats Unis de l'Amérique, et chacun d'eux en particulier, se reservent le droit, au cas que quelque nation restreigne le transport des Marchandises aux Vaisseaux des pays dont elles sont la production ou la Manufacture, d'établir envers cette nation des réglemens reciproques. Se reservant de plus le Droit de prohiber dans leurs pays respectifs l'importation ou l'exportation de toute Marchandise quelconque, dès que la raison d'Etat l'exige. En ce cas les Sujets ou Citoyens d'une des Parties contractantes ne pourront importer ni exporter les marchandises prohibées par

and the Subjects &. Citizens of the most favoured nations.

ARTICLE 4. More especially each party shall have a right to carry their own produce manufactures & merchandize, in their own or any other vessels to any parts of the dominions of the other where it shall be lawful for all the Subjects or Citizens of that other freely to purchase them; and thence to take the produce, Manufactures &. merchandize of the other which all the said Citizens or Subjects shall in like manner be free to sell them paying in both cases such duties, charges & fees only as are or shall be paid by the most favoured nation. Nevertheless the King of Prussia and the United States & each of them reserve to themselves the right where any nation restrains the transportation of Merchandize to the Vessels of the country of which it is the growth or Manufacture to establish against such nation restaliating regulations; and also the right to prohibit in their respective countries the importation & exportation of all merchandize whatsoever when reasons of State shall require it. In this case the Subjects or Citizens of either of the contracting parties shall not import nor export the Merchandize prohibited by the other, but if one of the contracting parties permits

l'autre. Mais si l'une des parties contractantes permet à quel qu'autre Nation d'importer ou d'exporter ces mêmes marchandises, les Citoyens ou Sujets de l'autre partie contractante jouiront tout aussitôt d'une liberté pareille.

any other nation to import or export the same merchandize the Citizens or Subjects of the other shall immediately enjoy the same liberty.

Article 5. Les Marchands Commandans de Vaisseaux, et autres Sujets ou Citoyens de chacune des deux Nations, ne seront pas forcés dans les ports ou dans la jurisdiction de l'autre, de décharger aucune Sorte de Marchandises dans d'autres Vaisseaux, ni de les recevoir à bord de leurs propres navires, ni d'attendre leur chargement plus longtemps qu'il ne leur plaira.

Article 5. the merchants commanders of Vessels or other Subjects or Citizens of either party shall not within the ports or jurisdiction of the other be forced to unload any Sort of merchandize into any other Vessels, nor to receive them into their own, nor to wait for their being loaded Longer than they please.

Article 6. Pour eviter que les Vaisseaux de l'une des deux parties contractantes ne soyent point inutilement molestés ou detenus dans les Ports ou sous la Jurisdiction de l'autre, il a été convenu que la visite des marchandises, ordonnée par les loix, se fera avant qu'elles ne soyent chargées sur le navire, et qu'ensuite elles ne seront plus assujetties à aucune Visite. Et en général il ne se fera point de recherche à bord du Vaisseau, à moins qu'on n'y ait chargé clandestinement et illégalement des Marchandises prohibées. Dans ce cas celui par l'ordre du quel elles ont été portées à bord, ou celui qui les y a porté sans ordre, sera soumis aux loix du Pays où il se

Article 6. That the Vessels of either party Loading within the ports or jurisdiction of the other may not be uselessly harassed or detained, it is agreed that all examinations of goods required by the laws shall be made before they are laden on board the Vessel &. that there shall be no examination after; nor shall the Vessel be searched at any time unless articles shall have been laden therein clandestinely & illegaly, in which case the person by whose order they were carried on board, or who carried them without order, shall be liable to the laws of the Land in which he is, but no other person shall be molested, nor shall any other groods nor

trouve, sans que le reste de l'équipage soit molesté, ni les autres marchandises ou le Vaisseau saisis ou detenus par cette raison.

the Vessel be seized or detained for that cause.

Article 7. Chacune des deux parties contractantes tâchera, par tous les moyens qui seront en son pouvoir, de protéger et de défendre tous les Vaisseaux et autres effets appartenants aux Citoyens ou Sujets de l'autre, et se trouvant dans l'étendue de sa Jurisdiction par mer ou par terre: et elle employera tous ses efforts pour recouvrer et faire restituer aux Propriétaires légitimes les Vaisseaux et effets qui leur auront été enlevés dans l'étendue de sa dite Jurisdiction.

Article 7. Each party shall endeavour by all the means in their power to protect & desend all Vessels & other Effects belonging to the Citizens or Subjects of the other, which shall be within the extent of their jurisdiction by sea or by land; and shall use all their efforts to recover, & cause to be restored to the right owners their Vessels & effects which shall be taken from them within the extent of their said jurisdiction.

Article 8. Les Vaisseaux des Sujets ou citoyens d'une des deux parties contractantes, arrivant sur une côte appartenante à l'autre, mais n'ayant pas dessein d'entrer au port, ou, y étant entrés, ne desirant pas de decharger leurs Cargaisons, ou de rompre leur charge, auront la liberté de repartir et de poursuivre leur route sans empêchement, et sans être obligés de rendre compte de leur cargaison, ni de payer aucuns impôts, charges et droits quelconques, excepté ceux établis sur les Vaisseaux une fois entrés dans le port, et destinés à l'entretien du port même ou à d'autres établissemens qui ont pour but la Sûretê et la commodité des Navigateurs; les

Article 8. The Vessels of the Subjects or Citizens of either party coming on any coast belonging to the other, but not willing to enter into port, or being entered into port & not willing to unload their cargoes or break bulk shall have Liberty to depart & to pursue their voyage without molestation, & without being obliged to render account of their cargo, or to pay any duties charges or fees whatsoever except those established for Vessels entered into port & appropriated to the maintenance of the port itself, or of other establishments for the safety & convenience of navigators, which duties, charges & fees shall be the same, and

quels droits, charges et impôts seront les mêmes et se payeront sur le même pied qu'ils sont acquittés par las Sujets ou Citoyens de l'Etat où ils sont établis.

shall be paid on the same footing as in the case of Subjects or Citizens of the country where they are established.

ARTICLE 9. Au cas que quelque Vaisseaux appartenant à l'une des deux Parties contractantes auroit fait naufrage, échoué ou souffert quelque autre Dommage sur les côtes ou sous la domination de l'autre, les Sujets ou Citoyens respectifs recevront, tant pour eux que pour leurs Vaisseaux et effets, la même assistance qui auroit été fournie aux habitans du Pays où l'accident arrive; et ils payeront seulement les mêmes charges et droits, aux quels les dits habitants auroient été assujettis en pareil cas. Et si la réparation du Vaisseaux exigeoit que la cargaison fût dechargée en tout ou en partie, ils ne payeront aucun impôt, charge ou droit de ce qui sera rembarqué et emporté. L'ancien et barbare droit de naufrage sera entiérement aboli à l'égard des Sujets ou Citoyens des deux Parties contractantes.

ARTICLE 9. When any Vessel of either party shall be wrecked, foundered or otherwise damaged on the coasts or within the dominion of the other, their respective Subjects or Citizens shall receive, as well for themselves as for their Vessels & Effects the same assistance which would be due to the inhabitants of the country where the damage happens, and shall pay the same charges & dues only as the said inhabitants would be subject to pay in a like case: and if the opérations of repair shall require that the whole or any part of their cargo be unladed they shall pay no duties, charges or fees on the part which they shall relade & Carry away. The antient & Barbarous right to wrecks of the sea shall be entirely abolished with respect to the Subjects or Citizens of the two contracting parties.

ARTICLE 10. Les Citoyens ou Sujets de l'une des deux parties contractantes auront dans les États de l'autre la Liberté de disposer de leurs biens personels, soit par testament, donation ou autrement, et leurs héritiers étant Sujets ou Citoyens de l'autre partie contractante, succederont

ARTICLE 10. The Citizens or Subjects of each party shall have power to dispose of their personal goods within the Jurisdiction of the other by testament, donation or otherwise and their representatives, being subjects or Citizens of the other party, shall succeed to their said personal goods

à leurs biens, soit en vertu d'un Testament, ou ab-intestat, et ils pourront en prendre possession, soit en personne, soit par d'autres agissant en leur place, et en disposeront à leur Volonté, en ne payant d'autres droits que ceux aux quels les habitants du Pays où la Succession est devenue vacante, sont assujettis en pareille occurrence. Et en cas d'absence des Héritiers, on prendra aussi long-temps des biens qui leur sont échus, les mêmes soins qu'on auroit pris en pareille occasion des biens des natifs du Pays, jusqu'à ce que le Proprietaire légitime ait agrée des Arrangemens pour recuillir l'heritage. S'il s'éleve des Contestations entre différens pretendans ayant droit à la Succession, elles seront decidées en dernier ressort selon les loix et par les Juges du Pays où la Succession est Vacante. Et si par la mort de quelque personne possédant des biens-fonds sur le territoire de l'une des parties contractantes, ces biens-fonds venoient a passer, selon les loix du Pays, à un citoyen ou sujet de l'autre Partie, celui ci, si par sa qualité d'étranger, il est inhabile de les posseder, obtiendra un delai convenable pour les vendre et pour en retirer le provenu, sans obstacle, exempt de tout droit de retenue, de la part du gouvernement des Etats respectifs. Mais cet article ne derogera en aucune manière à la force

whether by testament or ab intestato, and may take possession thereof either by themselves or by others acting for them & dispose of the same at their will, paying such dues only as the inhabitants of the country wherein the said goods are shall be Subject to pay in Like cases. and in case of the absence of the represèntative, such care shall be taken of the said goods & for so long a time as would be taken of the goods of a native in like case until the lawful owner may take measures for receiving them. And if question shall arise among several claimants to which of them the said goods belong, the same shall be decided finally by the laws & Judges of the land wherein the said goods are. And where on the death of any person holding real estate within the territories of the one party such real estate would by the laws of the land descend on a Citizen or Subject of the other were he not disqualified by alienage, such Subject shall be allowed a reasonable time to sell the same & to withdraw the proceds without molestation, and exempt from all rights of détraction on the part of the government of the respective States. But this article shall not derogate in any manner from the force of the laws already published or hereafter to be published by his Majesty the

des Loix qui ont déja été publiées ou qui le seront dans la suite par sa Majesté le Roi de Prusse, pour prevenir l'emigration de ses Sujets.

King of Prussia to prevent the émigration of his Subjects.

Article 11. Il sera accordé la plus parfaite Liberté de conscience et de culte aux citoyens et Sujets de chaque partie contractante dans les États de l'autre, et personne ne sera molesté à cet égard pour quelque cause que ce soit, si ce n'est pour insulte faite à la Religion de l'autre. De plus si des Sujets et citoyens de l'une de parties contractantes venoient à mourir dans la Jurisdiction de l'autre, leurs corps seront enterrés dans les endroits où l'on a coutume de faire les enterremens, ou dans tel autre lieu decent et convenable, et ils seront protegés contre toute Violence et trouble.

Article 11 The most perfect freedom of conscience & of worship is granted to the Citizens or Subjects of either party within the jurisdiction of the other, without being liable to molestation in that respect for any cause other than an insult on the religion of others. Moreover when the Subjects or Citizens of the one party shall die within the jurisdiction of the other their bodies shall be buried in the usual burying grounds, or other decent & suitable places, and shall be protected from violation or disturbance.

Article 12. Si l'une des Parties contractantes étoit en guerre avec une autre Puissance, la libre correspondance et le Commerce des citoyens ou Sujets de la partie qui demeure neutre envers les Puissances belligerantes, ne seront point interrompus. Au contraire, et dans ce cas comme en pleine paix, les Vaisseaux de la Partie neutre pourront naviger en toute Sûreté dans les Ports et sur les côtes des Puissances belligérantes; les Vaisseaux libres rendant les marchandises libres, en tant qu'on regardera comme libre tout ce qui sera à bord d'un navire apparte-

Article 12. If one of the contracting parties should be engaged in war with any other power the free intercourse & commerce of the Subjects or Citizens of the party remaining neuter with the belligerent powers shall not be interrupted. On the contrary in that case as in full peace, the Vessels of the neutral party may navigate freely to & from the ports and on the coasts of the belligerent parties, free Vessels making free goods insomuch that all things shall be adjudged free which shall be on board any Vessel belonging to the neutral party,

nant à la partie neutre, quand même ces effets appartiendroient à l'ennemi de l'autre. La même liberté s'étendra aux Personnes qui se trouveront à bord d'un Vaisseau libre, quand mêmes elles seroient ennemis de l'autre Partie, excepté que ce fussent des gens de guerre, actuellement au Service de l'ennemi.

Article 13. Dans le cas où l'une des Parties contractantes se trouveroit en guerre avec une autre Puissance, il a été convenu que pour prevenir les difficultés et les discussions qui surviennent ordinairement par rapport aux Marchandises ci-devant appellées de contrabande, telles que armes, munitions et autres provisions de guerre de toute espéce, aucun de ces articles, chargés à bord des vaisseaux des Citoyens ou Sujets de l'une des parties, et destinés pour l'ennemi de l'autre, ne sera censé de contrebande, au point d'impliquer confiscation ou condamnation, et d'entrainer la perte de la proprieté des individus. Néanmoins il sera permis d'arrêter ces Sortes de Vaisseaux et effets, et de les retenir pendant tout le temps que le preneur croira nécessaire pour prévenir les inconveniens et le Dommage qui pourroient en resulter autrement; mais dans ce cas on accordera une compensation raisonable pour les pertes qui auront été occasionnées par la Saisie. Et il sera permis en outre aux Preneurs d'employer

although such things belong to an enemy of the other: and the same freedom shall be extended to persons who shall be on bourd a free Vessel, although they should be enemies to the other party unless they be Soldiers in actual Service of such enemy.

Article 13. And in the same case of one of the contracting parties being engaged in war with any other power, to prevent all the difficulties & misunderstandings that usually arise respecting the merchandize heretofore called contraband, such as arms ammunition & military stores of every Kind, no such articles carried in the Vessels or by the Subjects or Citizens of one of the parties to the enemies of the other shall be deemed contraband so as to induce confiscation or condemnation & a loss of property to individuals. Nevertheless it shall be lawful to stop such Vessels & articles and to detain them for such length of time as the captors may think necessary to prevent the inconvenience or damage that might ensue from their proceeding, paying however a reasonable compensation for the loss such arrest shall occasion to the proprietors: And it shall further be allowed to use in the Service of the captors the whole or any part of the military stores so detained paying the owners the full value

à leur service, en tout ou en partie les munitions militaires detenues, en en payant aux Proprietaires la pleine Valeur, à determiner sur le prix qui aura cours à l'endroit de leur destination; mais que dans le cas énoncé d'un Vaisseau arrêté pour des Articles ci-devant appellés contrebande, si le Maitre du navire consentoit à delivrer les marchandises suspectes, il aura la Liberté de le faire, et le navire ne sera plus amené dans le port, ni detenu plus long-temps, mais aura toute Liberté de poursuivre sa route.

ARTICLE 14. Dans le cas où l'une des deux Parties contractantes se trouveroit engagée dans une guerre avec une autre Puissance, et afin que les Vaisseaux de la partie neutre soyent promptement et sûrement reconnus, on est convenu qu'ils devront être munis de Lettres de mer ou Passeports, exprimant le nom le proprietaire, et le port du navire, ainsi que le nom et la demeure du maitre. Ces Passeports, qui seront expediés en bonne et due forme (à determiner par des conventions entre les Parties, lors que l'occasion le requerra) devront être renouvellés toutes les fois que le vaisseau retournera dans son port, et seront exhibés à chaque requisition tant en pleine mer que dans le port. Mais si le navire se trouve sous le convoi d'un ou plusieurs Vaisseaux de Guerre appartenants a la partie neutre, il

of the same to be ascertained by the current price at the place of its destination. But in the case supposed of a Vessel stopped for articles heretofore deemed contraband, if the master of the Vessel stopped will deliver out the goods supposed to be of contraband nature, he shall be admitted to do it & the Vessel shall not in that case be carried into any port, nor further detained but shall be allowed to proceed on her voyage.

ARTICLE 14. And in the same case where one of the parties is engaged in war with another power that the Vessels of the neutral party may be readily & certainly Known, it is agreed that they shall be provided with sea letters or passports which shall express the name the property & burthen of the Vessel, as also the name & dwelling of the master; which passports shall be made out in good & due forms (to be settled by conventions between the parties whenever occasion shall require) shall be renewed as often as the Vessel shall return into port; and shall be exhibited whensoever required as well in the open sea as in port. But if the said Vessel be under Convoy of one or more Vessels of war belonging to the neutral party, the simple déclaration of the officer commanding the Convoy that the said Ves-

suffira que l'officier commandant du convoi déclare que le navire est de son parti moyennant quoi cette simple déclaration sera censée établir le fait, et dispensera les deux Parties de toute visite ultérieure.

sel belongs to the party of which he is shall be considered as establishing the fact, and shall releive both parties from the trouble of further éxamination.

ARTICLE 15. Pour prevenir entiérement tout desordre et toute violence en pareil cas, il a été stipulé que lors que des navires de la Partie neutre, navigeans sans convoi, rencontreront quelque Vaisseau de Guerre public ou particulier de l'autre partie, le vaisseau de Guerre n'approchera le navire neutre qu'au delà de la portée du canon, et n'enverra pas plus de deux ou trois hommes dans sa chaloupe à bord, pour examiner les Lettres de Mer ou Passeports. Et toutes les personnes appartenantes à quelque Vaisseau de guerre public ou particulier, qui molesteront ou insulteront en quelque maniére que ce soit l'équipage, les Vaisseaux ou effets de l'autre Partie, seront responsables en leurs personnes et en leurs biens, de tous dommages et intérêts; pour les quels il sera donné caution suffisante par tous les commandans de Vaisseaux armés en course, avant qu'ils reçoivent leurs Commissions.

ARTICLE 15. And to prevent entirely all disorder & violence in such cases, it is stipulated that when the Vessels of the neutral party sailing without Convoy, shall be met by any Vessel of war public or private of the other party, such Vessel of war shall not approach within cannon shot of the said neutral Vessel, nor send more than two or three men in their boat on board the same to examine her sealetters or passports. And all persons belonging to any Vessel of war public or private who shall molest or injure in any manner whatever the people, Vessels or effects of the other party shall be responsible in their persons & property for damages & interest sufficient security for which shall be given by all Commanders of private armed Vessels before they are commissioned.

ARTICLE 16. Il a été convenu que les Sujets ou Citoyens de l'une des parties contractantes, leurs Vaisseaux ni effets, ne pourront être assujettis à aucun embargo,

ARTICLE 16. It is agreed that the Subjects or Citizens of each of the contracting parties, their Vessels & Effects shall not be liable to any embargo or deten-

ni retenus de la part de l'autre pour quelque expédition militaire, usage public ou particulier de qui que ce soit. Et dans les cas de saisie, de detention, ou d'arrêt, soit pour dettes contractées, ou offenses commises par quelque citoyen ou Sujet de l'une des Parties contractantes dans la Jurisdiction de l'autre, on procedera uniquement par ordre et autorité de la Justice et suivant les voyes ordinaires en pareil cas usitées

ARTICLE 17. S'il arrivoit que les Bâtimens ou effets de la puissance neutre fussent pris par l'ennemi de l'autre, ou par un Pirate, et ensuite repris par la Puissance en Guerre, ils seront conduits dans un Port de l'une des deux Parties contractantes et remis à la garde des officiers du Port, afin d'être restitués en entier au proprietaire legitime, dès qu'il aura duement constaté son droit de propriété.

ARTICLE 18. Lors que les Citoyens ou Sujets de l'une des deux Parties contractantes seront forcés par des tempêtes, par la poursuite des corsaires ou vaisseaux ennemis, ou par quelqu' autre accident, à se refugier avec leurs Vaisseaux ou effets dans les havres, ou dans la Jurisdiction de l'autre, ils seront reçus, protégés et traités avec humanité et honnêteté. Il leur sera permis de se pourvoir à un prix raisonable de rafraichissemens, de Provisions et

tion on the part of the other, for any military expedition or other public or private purpose whatsoever. And in all cases of seizure, détention, or arrest for debts contracted or offences committed by any Citizen or Subject of the one party within the jurisdiction of the other the same shall be made & prosecuted by order & authority of law only and according to the regular course of proceedings usual in such cases.

ARTICLE 17. If any Vessel or effects of the neutral power be taken by an enemy of the other or by a pirate, & retaken by that other, they shall be brought into some port of one of the parties, and delivered into the custody of the Officers of that port, in order to be restored entire to the true proprietor as soon as due proof shall be made concerning the property thereof.

ARTICLE 18. If the citizens or Subjects of either party, in danger from tempests, pirates, enemies, or other accident, shall take refuge with their Vessels or effects within the harbours or jurisdiction of the other, they shall be received, protected & treated with humanity & Kindness, and shall be permitted to furnish themselves at reasonable prices with all refreshments, provisions, & other things necessary for their sustestance, heath & accomoda-

de toutes choses nécessaires pour leur Subsistance Santé et commodité et pour la reparation de leurs Vaisseaux.

tion and for the repair of their Vessels.

Article 19. Les Vaisseaux de Guerre publics et particuliers des deux parties contractantes pourront conduire en toute Liberté, par tout où il leur plaira, les Vaisseaux et effets qu'ils auront pris sur leurs ennemis, sans être obligés de payer aucuns impôts, charges ou droits aux officiers de l'amirauté, des douanes ou autres. Ces prises ne pourront être non plus ni arrêtées, ni visitées, ni soumises à des procédures légales, en entrant dans le port de l'autre Partie, mais elles pourront en sortir librement, et être conduites en tout temps par le Vaisseau preneur aux endroits portés par les commissions, dont l'officier commandant le dit Vaisseau sera obligé de faire montre. Mais tout Vaisseau qui aura fait des Prises sur les Sujets de S. M. T. C. le Roi de France, ne sauroit obtenir un droit d'asile dans les ports ou havres des États Unis; et s'il étoit forcé d'y entrer par des tempêtes ou dangers de mer, il sera obligé d'en repartir le plutôt possible, conformement à la teneur des traités[1] subsistants entre S. M. T. C. et les Etats Unis.

Article 19. The Vessels of war public & private of both parties, shall carry freely wheresoever they please the Vessels & effects taken from their enemies without being obliged to pay any duties, charges, or fees to Officers of admiralty, of the customs, or any others, nor shall such prizes be arrested, searched, or put under legal process when they come to, and enter the ports of the other party, but may freely be carried out again at any time by their captors to the places expressed in their Commissions, which the commanding officer of such Vessel shall be obliged to shew. But no Vessel which shall have made prises on the Subjects of His most Christian Majesty the King of France shall have a right of asylum in the ports or havens of the said United States; & if any such be forced therein by tempest or dangers of the sea, they shall be obliged to depart as soon as possible according to the tenor of the treaties[1] existing between his said Most Christian Majesty & the said United States.

Article 20. Aucun Citoyen ou sujet de l'une des deux Parties contractantes n'acceptera d'une

Article 20. No Citizen or Subject of either of the contracting parties shall take from any

[1] Documents 1 and 2.

Puissance avec la quelle l'autre pourroit être en guerre, ni commission, ni lettre de marque, pour armer en course contre cette derniére, sous peine d'être puni comme pirate. Et ni l'un ni l'autre des deux Etats ne louera, prêtera ou donnera une partie de ses forces navales ou militaires à l'ennemi de l'autre, pour l'aider à agir offensivement ou défensivement contre l'état qui est en guerre.

Article 21. S'il arrivoit que les deux parties contractantes fussent en même temps en guerre contre un ennemi commun, on observera de part et d'autre les points suivants. 1º Si les Bâtimens de l'une des deux nations repris par les armateurs de l'autre, n'ont pas été au pouvoir de l'ennemi au dela de 24 heures, ils seront restitués au premier proprietaire, moyennant le payement du tiers de la Valeur du Bâtiment et de la Cargaison. si au contraire le Vaisseau repris a été plus de 24 heures au pouvoir de l'ennemi, il appartiendra en entier à celui qui l'a repris. 2º Dans le cas qu'un navire est repris par un vaisseau de Guerre de l'une des Puissances contractantes, il sera rendu au Proprietaire, moyennant qu'il paye un trentieme du navire et de la cargaison, si le Batiment n'a pas été plus de 24 heures au pouvoir de l'ennemi, et le dixieme de

power with which the other may be at war any Commission or letter of marque for arming any Vessel to act as a privateer against the other, on pain of being punished as a pirate. Nor shall either party hire, lend, or give Any part of their naval or military force to the enemy of the other to aid them offensively or defensively against that other.

Article 21. If the two contracting parties should be engaged in war against a common enemy the following points shall be observed between them. 1. if a Vessel of one of the parties retaken by a privateer of the other shall not have been in possession of the enemy more than twenty four hours, she shall be restored to the first owner for one third of the value of the Vessel & cargo: but if she shall have been more than twenty four hours in possession of the enemy she shall belong wholly to the recaptor. 2. if in the same case the recapture were by a public Vessel of war of the one party, restitution shall be made to the owner for one thirtieth part of the value of the vessel & cargo; if she shall not have been in possession of the enemy more than twenty four hours, & one tenth of the said value where she shall have been longer: which sums shall be dis-

cette valeur, s'il y a été plus longtemps; les quelles Sommes seront distribuées en guise de gratification à ceux qui l'auront repris. 3º Dans ces cas la Restitution n'aura lieu qu'après les preuves faites de la propriété, sous caution de la quote-part qui en revient à celui qui a repris le navire. 4° Les Vaisseaux de guerre publics et particuliers des deux Parties contractantes seront admis reciproquement avec leur prises dans les ports respectifs; cependant ces prises ne pourront y être dechargées ni vendues, qu'après que la légitimité de la prise aura été decidée suivant les loix et réglemens de l'Etat dont le préneur est sujet, mais par la Justice de lieu où la prise aura été conduite. 5º Il sera libre à chacune des parties contractantes de faire tels réglemens qu'elles jugeront nécessaires, relativement à la conduite que devront tenir respectivement leurs vaisseaux de Guerre publics et particuliers, à l'égard des Bâtiments qu'ils auront pris et amenés dans les ports des deux Puissances.

tributed in gratuities to the recaptors. 3, The restitution in the cases aforesaid shall be after due proof of property & Surety given for the part to which the recaptors are entitled. 4. The Vessels of war public & private of the two parties shall be reciprocally admitted with their prizes into the respective ports of each: but the said prizes shall not be discharged nor sold there until their legality shall have been decided according to the laws & regulations of the States to which the captor belongs, but by the judicatures of the place into which the prize shall have been conducted. 5. it shall be free to each party to make such regulations as they shall judge necessary for the conduct of their respective vessels of war public & private relative to the Vessels which they shall take & carry into the ports of the two parties.

Article 22. Lors que les Parties contractantes seront engagées en guerre contre un ennemi commun, ou qu'elles seront neutres toutes deux, les Vaisseaux de guerre de l'une, prendront, en toute occasion sous leur protection les navires de l'autre, qui font avec eux la même route, et ils les defendront, aussi long temps

Article 22. Where the parties shall have a common enemy, or shall both be neutral, the Vessels of war of each shall upon all occasions take under their protection the Vessels of the other going the same course, and shall defend such Vessels as long as they hold the same course against all force & violence, in the same manner as

qu'ils feront voile ensemble, contre toute force et violence et de la même maniere qu'ils protegeroient et défendroient les navires de leur propre nation.

Article 23. S'il survient une guerre entre les parties contractantes, les marchands de l'un des deux Etats qui resideront dans l'autre, auront la permission d'y rester encore neuf mois, pour recueillir leurs dettes actives et arranger leurs affaires; après quoi ils pourront partir en toute liberté et emporter tous leurs biens, sans être molestés ni empêchés. Les femmes et les enfans, les gens de lettres de toutes les facultés, les cultivateurs, artisans, Manufacturiers et Pêcheurs, qui ne sont point armés, et qui habitent des Villes, Villages ou places qui ne sont pas fortifiés, et en général tous ceux dont la vocation tend à la Subsistance et à l'avantage commun du genre humain, auront la liberté de continuer leurs professions respectives, et ne seront point molestés en leurs personnes, ni leurs Maisons, ou leurs biens incendiés, ou autrement detruits, ni leurs champs ravagés par les armées de l'ennemi au pouvoir du quel ils pourroient tomber par les évenemens de la guerre; mais Si l'on se trouve dans la necessité de prendre quelque chose de leurs propriétés pour l'usage de l'armée ennemie, la valeur en sera payée à un prix raisonnable. Tous les Vaisseaux marchands et com-

they ought to protect and defend Vessels belonging to the party of which they are.

Article 23. If war should arise between the two contracting parties, the merchants of either country then residing in the other shall be allowed to remain nine months to collect their debts & settle their affairs, and may depart freely carrying off all their effects, without molestation or hindrance: and all women & children, scholars of every faculty, Cultivators of the earth, artizans, manufacturers, and fishermen unarmed, and inhabiting, unfortified towns, villages or places & in general all others whose occupations are for the common subsistance & benifit of mankind shall be allowed to continue their respective employments, & shall not be molested in their persons, nor shall their houses or goods be burnt or otherwise destroyed nor their fields wasted by the armed force of the enemy into whose power by the events of war they may happen to fall: but if any thing is necessary to be taken from them for the use of such armed force, the same shall be paid for at a reasonable price. And all merchant & trading Vessels employed in exchanging the products of different places, & thereby rendering the necessaries. Conveniencies & comforts of

merçans, employés à l'échange des productions de differens endroits, et par consequent destinés a faciliter et repandre les nécessités, les commodités et les douceurs de la Vie, passeront librement et sans être molestés. Et les deux Puissances contractantes s'engagent à n'accorder aucune commission à des vaisseaux armés en course qui les autorisât à prendre ou à detruire ces sortes de vaisseaux marchands ou à interrompre le commerce.

Article 24. Afin d'adoucir le sort de Prisoñiers de guerre, et ne les point exposer à être envoyés dans des climats éloignés et rigoureux, ou resserrés dans des habitations étroites et malsaines, les deux Parties contractantes s'engagent solemnellement l'une envers l'autre, et à la face de l'univers, qu'elles n'adopteront aucun de ces usages; que les prisonniers qu'elles pourroient faire l'une sur l'autre ne seront transportés ni aux Indes Orientales, ni dans aucune contrée de l'Asie ou de l'Afrique, mais qu'on leur assignera en Europe ou en Amérique, dans les territoirs respectifs des Parties contractantes, un Séjour situé dans un Air sain; qu'ils ne seront point confinés dans des cachots, ni dans des prisons, ni dans des Vaisseaux de prison; qu'ils ne seront pas mis au fers, ni garotés, ni autrement privés de l'usage de leurs membres; que les officiers seront relâchés sur leur

human life more easy to be obtained & & more general, shall be allowed to pass free & unmolested. And neither of the contracting powers shall grant or issue any Commission to any private armed Vessels empowering them to take or destroy such trading Vessels or interrupt such commerce.

Article 24. And to prevent the destruction of prisoners of war by sending them into distant & inclement countries, or by crouding them into close & noxions places, the two contracting parties solemnly pledge themselves to each other & to the world that they will not adopt any such practice; that neither will send the prisoners whom they May take from the other into the East Indies or any other parts of asia or Africa, but that they shall be placed in some part of their dominions in Europe or America, in wholesome Situations, that they shall not be confined in dungeons, prisonships, nor prisons, nor be put into irons, nor bound, nor otherwise restrained in the use of their limbs, that the officers shall be enlarged on their paroles within convenient districts & have comfortable quarters, & the common men be disposed in cantonments open & extensive

parole d'honneur dans l'enceinte de certains districts qui leur seront fixés, et qu'on leur accordera des logemens commodes; que les simples Soldats seront distribués dans des cantonnemens ouverts, assez vastes pour prendre l'air et l'excercice, et qu'ils seront logés dans des barraques aussi spatieuses et aussi commodes que le sont celles des troupes de la Puissance au pouvoir de la quelle se trouvent les Prisoñiers. Que cette Puissance fera pourvoir journellement les officiers d'autant de rations, composées des mêmes Articles et de la même qualité, dont jouissent en nature ou en équivalent les officiers du même rang qui sont à son propre Service; qu'elle fournira également à tous les autres prisoñiers une ration pareille à celle qui est accordée au Soldat de sa propre Armée. Le montant de ces depenses sera payé par l'autre Puissance, d'après une liquidation de compte, à arrêter reciproquement pour l'entretien des prisonniers à la fin de la guerre; et ces comptes ne seront point confondus ou balancés avec d'autres comptes, ni la solde qui en est due, retenue comme compensation ou represailles, pour tel autre Article ou telle autre Prétention réelle ou supposée. Il sera permis à chacune des deux Puissances d'entretenir un Commissaire de leur choix dans chaque cantonnement des Prisoniers qui sont au pouvoir de l'autre; ces

enough for air & exercise, and lodged in barracks as roomly & good as are provided by the party in whose power they are for their own troops, that the officers shall also be daily furnished by the party in whose power they are with as many rations & of the same articles & quality as are allowed by them, either in Kind or by commutation, to Officers of equal rank in their own army, and all others shall be daily furnished by them with such ration as they allow to a common Soldier in their own Service; the value whereof shall be paid by the other party on a mutual adjustement of accounts for the Subsistence of prisoners at the close of the war. And the said accounts shall not be mingled with, or set off against any others, nor the ballances due on them be witheld as a Satisfaction or reprisal for any other article, or for any other cause real or pretended whatever: that each party shall be allowed to Keep a commissary of prisoners of their own appointment with every Separate cantonment of prisoners in possession of the other, which Commissary shall see the prisoners as often as he pleases, shall be allowed to receive and distribute whatever comforts may be sent to them by their friends, and shall be free to make his reports in open letters to those who employ him: but if any officer shall break his

commissaires auront la liberté de visiter les prisoñiers, aussi souvent qu'ils le desireront; ils pourront également recevoir et distribuer les douceurs que les parens ou amis des prisoniers leur feront parvenir; enfin il leur sera libre encore de faire leurs rapports par lettres ouvertes à ceux qui les employent. Mais si un officier manquoit à sa parole d'honneur, ou qu'un autre prisoñier sortit des limites qui auront été fixées à son Cantonnement, un tel officier ou un autre prisonnier sera frustré individuellement des avantages stipulés dans cet Article pour sa relaxation sur parole d'honneur ou pour son cantonnement. Les deux Puissances contractantes ont declaré en outre, que ni le prétexte que la guerre rompt les traités, ni tel autre motif quelconque, ne seront cencés annuller ou suspendre cet Article et le précédent; mais qu'au contraire le temps de la guerre est précisément celui pour lequel ils ont été stipulés, et durant lequel ils seront observés aussi saintement que les articles les plus universellement reconnus par le droit de la nature et des Gens.

Article 25. Les deux Parties contractantes se sont accordé mutuellement la faculté de tenir dans leurs ports respectifs des consuls, Vice-consuls, Agens et commissaires de leur choix et dont les fonctions seront determinées par un arrangement par-

parole, or any other prisoner shall escape from the limits of his cantonment, after they shall have been designated to him, such individual officer or other prisoner shall forfeit so much of the benefit of this article as provides for his enlargement on parole or cantonment. And it is declared that neither the pretence that war dissolves all treaties, nor any other whatever shall be considered as annulling or suspending this & the next preceding article but on the contrary that the State of war is precisely that for which they are provided, & during which they are to be as sacredly observed as the most acknowledged articles in the law of nature or nations.

Article 25. The two contracting parties grant to each other the liberty of having each in the ports of the other consuls, vice-Consuls, agents &. commissaries of their own appointment, whose functions shall be regulated by particular agreement whenever either

ticulier, lors que l'une des deux Puissances aura nommé à ces postes. Mais dans le cas que tel ou autre de ces consuls veuille faire le commerce, il sera soumis aux mêmes loix et usages, aux quels sont soumis les particuliers de sa nation à l'endroit où il réside.

party shall chuse to make such appointment, but if any such Consuls shall exercise commerce they shall be submitted to the same laws and usages to which the private individuals of their nation are submitted in the same place.

Article 26. Lors que l'une des deux parties contractantes accordera dans la suite quelque faveur particuliere en fait de Navigation ou de commerce à d'autres Nations, elle deviendra aussitôt commune à l'autre partie contractante, et celle-ci jouira de cette faveur, gratuitement, si la concession est gratuite, ou en accordant la même compensation si la concession est conditionelle.

Article 26. If either party shall hereafter grant to any other nation any particular favour in navigation or commerce, it shall immediately become common to the other party, freely where it is freely granted to such other nation, or on yeilding the compensation where such nation does the same.

Article 27. Sa Majesté le Roi de Prusse et les Etats Unis de l'Amérique sont convenus que le présent traité aura son plein effet pendant l'Espace de dix Ans, à compter du jour de l'échange des Ratifications, et que si l'expiration de ce terme arrivoit dans le cours d'une guerre entre eux, les articles ci-dessus stipulés pour regler leur conduite en temps de guerre, conserveront toute leur force, jusqu'à la conclusion du traité qui retablira la paix.

Le présent traité sera ratifié de part et d'autre, et les ratifications seront échangées dans l'espace d'une année, à compter du Jour de la Signature.

Article 27. His Majesty the King of Prussia & the United States of America agree that this treaty shall be in force during the term of ten years from the exchange of ratifications, & if the expiration of that term should happen during the course of a war between them, then the articles before provided for the regulation of their conduct during such a war shall continue in force until the conclusion of the treaty which shall reestablish peace, And that this treaty shall be ratified on both Sides, and the ratifications exchanged within one year from the day of its signature.

En foi de quoi les Plenipotentiaires sus nommés ont signé le présent Traité et y ont apposé le Cachet de leurs armes, aux lieux de leur domicile respectif, ainsi qu'il sera exprimé ci-dessous.

In Testimony Whereof the Plenipotentiaries before mentioned have hereto subscribed their names and affixed their Seals at the places of their respective residence and at the dates expressed under their several several Signatures.

F. G. de Thulemeier. a la Haye *le 10. Septembre 1785.* [Seal]

[Seal]	[Seal]	[Seal]
Th: Jefferson	B Franklin	John Adams.
Paris. *July 28. 1785.*	Passy, *July 9. 1785.*	London *August 5. 1785.*

NOTES

The signature of this treaty at four places on four dates was a highly unusual procedure. When the negotiations regarding the terms of the treaty had been concluded, Franklin was about to return to the United States (he left Paris on July 12, 1785), Jefferson was in Paris, Adams in London, and Baron de Thulemeier, the representative of Prussia, at The Hague. As a meeting to sign the treaty seemed impossible, the procedure adopted was proposed by Franklin and Jefferson to De Thulemeier (letter of May 26, 1785, Diplomatic Correspondence, 1783–1789, I, 580).

Franklin signed and sealed the treaty before the French text was written into its proper column in the duplicate originals. The circumstances of signature are detailed in various letters to be found in Diplomatic Correspondence, 1783–1789, I, 593–97.

The United States instrument of ratification is copied in 135 C. C. Papers, I; also in Journals, 1823 ed., IV, 639–43. Both texts were recited in the ratification; the record in 135 C. C. Papers so indicates, and a facsimile of the first and the last two pages of the original instrument, showing both texts, the French on the left, is now in the Department of State file, having been received from the German Foreign Office. Only the English is in Journals, 1823 ed.

Jay wrote (letter to Adams, June 6, 1786) that the ratification of the United States "for many months was delayed for want of a proper number of States in Congress to order and complete it" (Diplomatic Correspondence, 1783–1789, II, 657).

The instrument of ratification on behalf of Prussia recites the French text only.

The period allowed by Article 27 of the treaty for the exchange of ratifications was "one year from the day of its signature." Adams considered (rightly) that this meant one year from September 10, 1785, and regarded it as important that the exchange should be

made within that time (see his letter of July 30, 1786, Diplomatic Correspondence, 1783–1789, II, 671).

The Department of State file contains no protocol or other similar record of the exchange of ratifications. The date of exchange is usually stated as October, 1786, but this is erroneous. Adams gives the date in his letter to Jefferson of September 11, 1786 (C. F. Adams, Works of John Adams, VIII, 414); it is also reported in a letter of De Thulemeier of August 8, 1786 (copy from the German Foreign Office now in the Department of State file).

There appears to be no official record of any separate proclamation of this treaty. However, the United States instrument of ratification, embodying the English text, was published at the time (*e. g.*, broadside supplement to the Daily Advertiser, New York, June 6, 1786). The Department of State file now contains a facsimile of the newspaper print.

Accordingly, the instrument of ratification seems to have served as a proclamation and to have been regarded as such upon publication. As published it embodies the English text of the treaty and not the French; the preceding recital is: "which said treaty, written both in the American and French languages, is (in the American) in the words following, to wit" (see the same wording in Journals, 1823 ed., IV, 639).

Treaty Series, No. 244—1
8 Statutes at Large, 100–5

14

MOROCCO : JUNE 28 AND JULY 15, 1786

Treaty of Peace and Friendship, with additional article; also Ship-Signals Agreement. The treaty was sealed at Morocco with the seal of the Emperor of Morocco June 23, 1786 (25 Shaban, A. H. 1200), and delivered to Thomas Barclay, American Agent, June 28, 1786 (1 Ramadan, A. H. 1200). Original in Arabic. The additional article was signed and sealed at Morocco on behalf of Morocco July 15, 1786 (18 Ramadan, A. H. 1200). Original in Arabic. The Ship-Signals Agreement was signed at Morocco July 6, 1786 (9 Ramadan, A. H. 1200). Original in English.

Certified English translations of the treaty and of the additional article were incorporated in a document signed and sealed by the Ministers Plenipotentiary of the United States, Thomas Jefferson at Paris January 1, 1787, and John Adams at London January 25, 1787.

Treaty and additional article ratified by the United States July 18, 1787. As to the ratification generally, see the notes. Treaty and additional article proclaimed July 18, 1787.

Ship-Signals Agreement not specifically included in the ratification and not proclaimed; but copies ordered by Congress July 23, 1787, to be sent to the Executives of the States (Secret Journals of Congress, IV, 369; but see the notes as to this reference).

The following twenty-six pages of Arabic text are a reproduction of the pages of the original treaty; but they are arranged in left-to-right order of pagination. Then is printed the text of the document embodying the certified translations of the treaty and additional article, and thereafter the text of the Ship-Signals Agreement. Following those texts is a comment, written in 1930, on the English translation of 1786.

الحمد لله هذا تقييد شروط
الصلح التي جعلناها مع الماركانوس
وأثبتناها في هذا الدفتر ووضعنا
عليها طابعنا لتبقى مستمرة إن شاء
الله وكتبت في عاشر اكتوبر في الخامس
والعشرين من شعبان المبارك عام ومائتين وألف

ألشرط الأول أن هذه الشروط
المذكورة في هذا الدفتر وهي 1
خمسة وعشرون شرطا قد قبلت
من الجانبين وأكد سمعها وكيلهم
النائب طماس بركل الذي وقع من
عند اصحابه لما كانوا
وجهوه ليقف على امورهم وصلحهم
معنا

2 الشهب الثاني أنه متى
كانت الغزاة مع أي جنس كان
فلا تخرج سفينة من احدى الجانبين
وتعمل سنجق الغزو وتذهب
تغزو العدو اما من ههنا واما من
جهة الماركانوس

٣ الشرط الثالث انه متى
جعلت الغزاة مع اي جنس كان
وقبضت سفينة من أهل ذلك الجنس
ووجد فيها مسلما او نصرانيا
ولهم سلعة فانهم يسرحون بسلعهم
وحتى اذا كانوا حاملين سلعة لجنس
بيننا وبينه الغزوة فلا تؤخذ من ايديهم ولا
يكلمون فيهم ولهذا لما بيننا وبينهم من الصلح

4 ألشهر الرابع ذكروا بينهما
علامة يعرف بها بعضنا بعضا
في البحر ومهما لقي احدنا سفينة
الكفار لا يبحث عنها وانما يكفيه
كلام الرايس في شانها
مع سفر اخر

٥ اَلشَّرْطُ الْخَامِسُ أَنَّهُ مَتَى
تَلَاقَتِ السُّفُنُ فِي الْبَحْرِ وَكَانَتِ الْفُرْصَةُ
فَإِنَّ كُلَّ وَاحِدٍ مِنَ الْجِنْسَيْنِ لَا يَبْعَثُ
لِاخْتِبَارِ السَّفِينَةِ الَّتِي أَرَادَ اخْتِبَارَهَا
إِلَّا فَلُوكَةً وَاحِدَةً فِيهَا اثْنَانِ أَوْ ثَلَاثَةٌ
فَقَطْ وَيُفْهَمُ مَنْ خَرَجَتْ عِمَارَتُهُ وَأَفْسَدَتْ
شَيْئًا مِنْ إِحْدَى الْجِنْسَيْنِ مِنْ غَيْرِهِمْ سِوَى
فَإِنَّ صَاحِبَ الْعِمَارَةِ الَّتِي أَخْرَجَهَا يُصْلِحُ لِلْآخَرِ
مَا أَفْسَدَتْ لَهُ

6 الشرط السادس أنه متى
قبض المسلمون أهل جنسنا أو سلعتهم
وأتوا بهم لسيدنا نصره الله فإنه يسرح
وكذلك إذا قبضوهم مسلمون
من غير إيالتنا ودخلوا بهم لإحدى
مراسينا فإنهم يسرحون لأنهم في
أماننا ومصالحين معنا

7

الشرط السابع أنه متى
وقفت سفينة لاحدى مراكب الجانبين
تفتش كتابية أو غيرها فإنها
تفتش الكل من غير مشقة
ولا حرج

8 ألثامن ـــ فى ألتلامى أنه متى
وقع بآخر ألشيء شيئا وما لبث
إلى ألبر وقطعت وشقها حتى اضمحلت
ما أفسد منها فإنها متى أرادت تحمل
ذلك ألوقت ألنبي وقطعت فإنها
تحمله من غير طاكة واعنزها

والشرط التاسع أنه متى
جرت سفينة في ناحية من نواحينا
فإنها تبقى على حالها حتى تنظر ما يصلح
بها إما الخروج من موضع آخر
أو نقل السلع أو غير ذلك من الوجوه
التي تليق بها ولا يقربها أحد
لأنها في أماننا وكذلك إذا دخلت سفينة
للمرسى أو ألجأها ريح حتى دخلت للمرسى
فلا تكلف بنزول سلعها بل تبقى على الأمان
حتى تخرج برضاها

115605°—31—vol. 2——15

ألشرط ـــن العلامة أنه متى وقع
قتال من أخرى القطانيين مع بعض أجناس
النصارى وكان القتال فيما بين بعض
من القطانيين فإننا نعين بعضنا على
ذلك الجنس حتى يغلب أو يذهب
أو خرجت سفينة في واد نون أو غيره
فإن النصارى الذين بعهد الأمان حتى يصلوا
بلادهم إن شاء الله

11 الشرط الحادي عشر

أنه متى كانت القتالة بيننا وبين جنس

من أجناس النصارى وكنا بالمرسى

وأرادت سفينتنا الخروج من المرسى

وأرادت سفينة العدو تتبعها فلا تخرج

تتبعها حتى تمضي من الزمان أربعة

وعشرين ساعة وكذالك سفن المركانتش

إذا كانت بالمرسى وقت زمان القتالة وأرادت

الخروج فلا تتبعها سفينة حتى تمضي

اربعة وعشرين ساعة سواء كانت من

سفن المسلمين أم من سفن النصارى

12 ألشرط الثاني عشر أنه متى
وقفت سفينة لكم على احد مراسينا
فانها لا تفتش بل تبقى على حالها ومهما
كان بها أسير اهل بلادنا فانه لا ينزل
منه كرها وانما يطلب عامل تلك
البلاد الذي به السفينة من رب السفينة
قيمة ذلك الاسير

13 الشرط الثالث عشر أنه متى
وردت سفينة الكرك على أي مراسيه ووقفت
وأخرجت المدافع فإنها لا يخرج عليها
من تلك المرسى إلا مثل ما أخرجت من غير
زيادة ولا نقصان

14

ألشرط الرابع عشر أنّ
التجار يكونون على عادة تجار الصبنيول
ويكونون مميزين ويذهبون في البر
والمراسي حيث شاءوا ولا يتعرض لهم أحد
ويكونون مثل الجنس العزيز عندنا
في الوقت

دا الشرط الخامس عشر
أن التجار يكونون مشتغلين بالسبب
وإذا أرادوا أن يجعلوا من يقف معهم
أو خدام ما يأمرهم بذلك ولا يقلب وسق
سفينة إلى أخرى ولا تقف سفينة في
المرسى وإذا أرادوا أن يجعلوا من يعاونهم
على أمور الوسق أو غيرها فإنهم لا يعطون
سوى العدد الذي يعطون الأجناس من قبلهم

16 الشاهد السادس عشر انه
متى كانت الغزاة والجانبين فان الأسارى
يكونون أسارى راس براس فالراس بالراس
وسوى راسين بسوى راسين والبحر
بالبحر وهكذا وان لم يحصل
العدد بينهما فبعضهم في كل راس من الجانبين
مائة ريال بشرط ان يبقى الاسير من
الجانبين اكثر من سنة وحتى اذا اراد فداه
وكان في اوقات امر الجانبين فيعفيه
بالمائة ريال المذكورة

17 الفصل السابع عشر أن
التجار لا تكلف عليهم السلع ولا يشترون
إلا ما أرادوا وأعجبهم أنفسهم وكذلك
البيع إلا إذا كانت هناك مسايل
جارية فيها العادة مع من قبلهم من أجناس
النصارى يعملونها فلا باس بذلك

18 الشرط الثامن عشر أن
السلع التي توسق توزن وتقلب قبل وضعها
في السفينة لأجل أن تثقب السفينة
من أجل إذا اقفقفوا الريح بها كطربنك
وإذا كان كذلك فإن الذي جعل
الكطربنك هو الذي يؤاخذ بذلك
وحده على العادة الجارية به من قبله وأما
السفينة والسلع وما معها فإنها بريئة
من ذلك

وا الشرط التاسع عشر أنه
لا تتعوق سفينة في مرسى ولا تحمل شيئا
كرها إلا إذا كان عن طيب
نفس من رئيسها فإنه يشاور معه
على حمل ما أراد حمله

الشرط العشرون أنه مهمى جنا أحد من أهل جنسنا جناية أو من هو في خدمة سفننا فإنه يحكم فيه قونصوا جنسه وإذا احتاج القونصو إلى إعانة باشة البلاد يعينه على ذلك

21

الشرط الحادي والعشرون

أنه إذا قتل منهم نصراني أو العكس أو جرح
فإنه يحكم عليه بالقانون الشرعي من غير
زيادة ولا نقصان ويكون الحكم بمحضر
القونصو وإذا هرب قبل وقوع الحكم
فلا يؤاخذ به القونصو ولا بما جنى

22 ألشّاهد الثّاني والعشرين

أنّه مهما مات أحد من جنس الماركانوس

في بلدنا ولم يوص فإن قونصوه

هو الذي يقف على متاعه وكسبه وسلعته

وإن لم يكن قونصوا فتوضع عند

أمين حتّى يظهر من يستحقّها

وإذا كان عند أحد موروثه فتختصّ لورثته

من غير تعرّض أو أوصى على ميراثه لمن يدفع

ماله فلا تكلّم في ذلك لقونصوه

23 الشرط الثالث والعشرون

أن القونصوات يكونوا في أي مرسى

أرادوا ويكونوا موقرين مثل أجناس

من قبلهم من النصارى وإن تعامل

أحد من جنسهم مع مسلم بمال وأتلفه

له فلا يؤاخذ به القونصو ولا يضمنه

إلا إذا كان القونصو أعطى بذلك

خطا بيده فيتبعه وأما إذا لم يعطه خطا

بيده فلا كلام معه مثل جميع القونصوات

24 الشرط الرابع والعشرون

أنه مهما تنازع أحد في شيء من شروط
الصلح بأن ادعى أحد مسئلة وادعى الآخر
مسئلة وقال إنها ليست في الشروط
وطال النزاع بينهما فإن الصلح يبقى
على حاله ويبعث كل واحد منهما على من
يتبعه حتى إذا لم يوافق أحدهم ما في
الصلح وسمع منه كل الامتناع فإن أنكر له
تعمل حينئذ وجميع التجار تضرب لهم تسعة
أشهر أجلا إلى أن يرفعوا سلعهم وإذا انفصل
سيرنا على جنس من أجناس النصارى فتحرر من حملتهم.

ألشرط ـــــ الخامس والعشرون 25
أن هذا الصلح يبقى مستتما إن شاء الله
بحول الله وقوته مدة من خمسين سنة
وقد دفعنا هذه الأوراق بيد طماس
بركل النصر كونه في أول يوم من رمضان
المبارك عام مائتين وألف ـــــ

[Certified Translation of the Treaty and of the Additional Article, with Approval by Jefferson and Adams]

To all Persons to whom these Presents shall come or be made known—

Whereas the United States of America in Congress assembled by their Commission bearing date the twelvth day of May One thousand Seven hundred and Eighty four thought proper to constitute John Adams, Benjamin Franklin and Thomas Jefferson their Ministers Plenipotentiary, giving to them or a Majority of them full Powers to confer, treat & negotiate with the Ambassador, Minister or Commissioner of His Majesty the Emperor of Morocco concerning a Treaty of Amity and Commerce, to make & receive propositions for such Treaty and to conclude and sign the same, transmitting it to the United States in Congress assembled for their final Ratification, And by one other Commission bearing date the Eleventh day of March One thousand Seven hundred & Eighty five did further empower the said Ministers Plenipotentiary or a majority of them, by writing under their hands and Seals to appoint such Agent in the said Business as they might think proper with Authority under the directions and Instructions of the said Ministers to commence & prosecute the said Negotiations & Conferences for the said Treaty provided that the said Treaty should be signed by the said Ministers: And Whereas, We the said John Adams & Thomas Jefferson two of the said Ministers Plenipotentiary (the said Benjamin Franklin being absent) by writing under the Hand and Seal of the said John Adams at London October the fifth, One thousand Seven hundred and Eighty five, & of the said Thomas Jefferson at Paris October the Eleventh of the same Year, did appoint Thomas Barclay, Agent in the Business aforesaid, giving him the Powers therein, which by the said second Commission we were authorized to give, and the said Thomas Barclay in pursuance thereof, hath arranged Articles for a Treaty of Amity and Commerce between the United States of America and His Majesty the Emperor of Morocco, which Articles written in the Arabic Language, confirmed by His said Majesty the Emperor of Morocco & seal'd with His Royal Seal, being translated into the Language of the said United States of America, together with the Attestations thereto annexed are in the following Words, To Wit.

In the name of Almighty God,

This is a Treaty of Peace and Friendship established between us and the United States of America, which is confirmed, and which we have ordered to be written in this Book and sealed with our Royal Seal at our Court of Morocco on the twenty fifth day of the blessed Month of Shaban, in the Year One thousand two hundred, trusting in God it will remain permanent.

.1.

We declare that both Parties have agreed that this Treaty consisting of twenty five Articles shall be inserted in this Book and delivered to the Honorable Thomas Barclay, the Agent of the United States now at our Court, with whose Approbation it has been made and who is duly authorized on their Part, to treat with us concerning all the Matters contained therein.

.2.

If either of the Parties shall be at War with any Nation whatever, the other Party shall not take a Commission from the Enemy nor fight under their Colors.

.3.

If either of the Parties shall be at War with any Nation whatever and take a Prize belonging to that Nation, and there shall be found on board Subjects or Effects belonging to either of the Parties, the Subjects shall be set at Liberty and the Effects returned to the Owners. And if any Goods belonging to any Nation, with whom either of the Parties shall be at War, shall be loaded on Vessels belonging to the other Party, they shall pass free and unmolested without any attempt being made to take or detain them.

.4.

A Signal or Pass shall be given to all Vessels belonging to both Parties, by which they are to be known when they meet at Sea, and if the Commander of a Ship of War of either Party shall have other Ships under his Convoy, the Declaration of the Commander shall alone be sufficient to exempt any of them from examination.

.5.

If either of the Parties shall be at War, and shall meet a Vessel at Sea, belonging to the other, it is agreed that if an examination is to be made, it shall be done by sending a Boat with two or three Men only, and if any Gun shall be fired and injury done without Reason, the offending Party shall make good all damages.

.6.

If any Moor shall bring Citizens of the United States or their Effects to His Majesty, the Citizens shall immediately be set at Liberty and the Effects restored, and in like Manner, if any Moor not a Subject of these Dominions shall make Prize of any of the Citizens of America or their Effects and bring them into any of the Ports of His Majesty,

they shall be immediately released, as they will then be considered as under His Majesty's Protection.

.7.

If any Vessel of either Party shall put into a Port of the other and have occasion for Provisions or other Supplies, they shall be furnished without any interruption or molestation.

.8.

If any Vessel of the United States shall meet with a Disaster at Sea and put into one of our Ports to repair, she shall be at Liberty to land and reload her cargo, without paying any Duty whatever.

.9.

If any Vessel of the United States shall be cast on Shore on any Part of our Coasts, she shall remain at the disposition of the Owners and no one shall attempt going near her without their Approbation, as she is then considered particularly under our Protection; and if any Vessel of the United States shall be forced to put into our Ports, by Stress of weather or otherwise, she shall not be compelled to land her Cargo, but shall remain in tranquillity untill the Commander shall think proper to proceed on his Voyage.

.10.

If any Vessel of either of the Parties shall have an engagement with a Vessel belonging to any of the Christian Powers within gunshot of the Forts of the other, the Vessel so engaged shall be defended and protected as much as possible untill she is in safety; And if any American Vessel shall be cast on shore on the Coast of Wadnoon[1] or any Coast thereabout, the People belonging to her shall be protected, and assisted untill by the help of God, they shall be sent to their Country.

.11.

If we shall be at War with any Christian Power and any of our Vessels sail from the Ports of the United States, no Vessel belonging to the enemy shall follow untill twenty four hours after the Departure of our Vessels; and the same Regulation shall be observed towards the American Vessels sailing from our Ports.—be their enemies Moors or Christians.

[1] Or Ouadnoun, on the Atlantic coast, about latitude 29° N.

.12.

If any Ship of War belonging to the United States shall put into any of our Ports, she shall not be examined on any Pretence whatever, even though she should have fugitive Slaves on Board, nor shall the Governor or Commander of the Place compel them to be brought on Shore on any pretext, nor require any payment for them.

.13.

If a Ship of War of either Party shall put into a Port of the other and salute, it shall be returned from the Fort, with an equal Number of Guns, not with more or less.

.14.

The Commerce with the United States shall be on the same footing as is the Commerce with Spain or as that with the most favored Nation for the time being and their Citizens shall be respected and esteemed and have full Liberty to pass and repass our Country and Sea Ports whenever they please without interruption.

.15.

Merchants of both Countries shall employ only such interpreters, & such other Persons to assist them in their Business, as they shall think proper. No Commander of a Vessel shall transport his Cargo on board another Vessel, he shall not be detained in Port, longer than he may think proper, and all persons employed in loading or unloading Goods or in any other Labor whatever, shall be paid at the Customary rates, not more and not less.

.16.

In case of a War between the Parties, the Prisoners are not to be made Slaves, but to be exchanged one for another, Captain for Captain, Officer for Officer and one private Man for another; and if there shall prove a defficiency on either side, it shall be made up by the payment of one hundred Mexican Dollars for each Person wanting; And it is agreed that all Prisoners shall be exchanged in twelve Months from the Time of their being taken, and that this exchange may be effected by a Merchant or any other Person authorized by either of the Parties.

.17.

Merchants shall not be compelled to buy or Sell any kind of Goods but such as they shall think proper; and may buy and sell all sorts of Merchandise but such as are prohibeted to the other Christian Nations.

.18.

All goods shall be weighed and examined before they are sent on board, and to avoid all detention of Vessels, no examination shall afterwards be made, unless it shall first be proved, that contraband Goods have been sent on board, in which Case the Persons who took the contraband Goods on board shall be punished according to the Usage and Custom of the Country and no other Person whatever shall be injured, nor shall the Ship or Cargo incur any Penalty or damage whatever.

.19.

No vessel shall be detained in Port on any pretence whatever, nor be obliged to take on board any Article without the consent of the Commander, who shall be at full Liberty to agree for the Freight of any Goods he takes on board.

.20.

If any of the Citizens of the United States, or any Persons under their Protection, shall have any disputes with each other, the Consul shall decide between the Parties and whenever the Consul shall require any Aid or Assistance from our Government to enforce his decisions it shall be immediately granted to him.

.21.

If a Citizen of the United States should kill or wound a Moor, or on the contrary if a Moor shall kill or wound a Citizen of the United States, the Law of the Country shall take place and equal Justice shall be rendered, the Consul assisting at the Tryal, and if any Delinquent shall make his escape, the Consul shall not be answerable for him in any manner whatever.

22d

If an American Citizen shall die in our Country and no Will shall appear, the Consul shall take possession of his Effects, and if there shall be no Consul, the Effects shall be deposited in the hands of some Person worthy of Trust, untill the Party shall appear who has a Right to demand them, but if the Heir to the Person deceased be present, the Property shall be delivered to him without interruption; and if a Will shall appear, the Property shall descend agreeable to that Will, as soon as the Consul shall declare the Validity thereof.

.23.

The Consuls of the United States of America shall reside in any Sea Port of our Dominions that they shall think proper; And they shall be

respected and enjoy all the Privileges which the Consuls of any other Nation enjoy, and if any of the Citizens of the United States shall contract any Debts or engagements, the Consul shall not be in any Manner accountable for them, unless he shall have given a Promise in writing for the payment or fulfilling thereof, without which promise in Writing no Application to him for any redress shall be made.

.24.

If any differences shall arise by either Party infringing on any of the Articles of this Treaty, Peace and Harmony shall remain notwithstanding in the fullest force, untill a friendly Application shall be made for an Arrangement, and untill that Application shall be rejected, no appeal shall be made to Arms. And if a War shall break out between the Parties, Nine Months shall be granted to all the Subjects of both Parties, to dispose of their Effects and retire with their Property. And it is further declared that whatever indulgences in Trade or otherwise shall be granted to any of the Christian Powers, the Citizens of the United States shall be equally entitled to them.

.25.

This Treaty shall continue in full Force, with the help of God for Fifty Years.

We have delivered this Book into the Hands of the before-mentioned Thomas Barclay on the first day of the blessed Month of Ramadan, in the Year One thousand two hundred.

I certify that the annex'd is a true Copy of the Translation made by Issac Cardoza Nuñez, Interpreter at Morocco, of the treaty between the Emperor of Morocco and the United States of America.

THO[s] BARCLAY

Translation of the additional Article

Grace to the only God

I the underwritten the Servant of God, Taher Ben Abdelhack Fennish do certify that His Imperial Majesty my Master /whom God preserve/ having concluded a Treaty of Peace and Commerce with the United States of America has ordered me the better to compleat it and in addition of the tenth Article of the Treaty to declare "That, "if any Vessel belonging to the United States shall be in any of the "Ports of His Majesty's Dominions, or within Gunshot of his Forts, "she shall be protected as much as possible and no Vessel whatever

"belonging either to Moorish or Christian Powers with whom the "United States may be at War, shall be permitted to follow or engage "her, as we now deem the Citizens of America our good Friends.

And in obedience to His Majesty's Commands I certify this Declaration by putting my hand and Seal to it, on the Eighteenth day of Ramadan in the Year One thousand two hundred.

(Signed)

The Servant of the King my Master whom God preserve

TAHER BEN ABDELHACK[1] FENNISH

I Do Certify that the above is a True Copy of the Translation Made at Morocco by Isaac Cardoza Nunes, Interpreter, of a Declaration Made and Signed by Sidi Hage Tahar Fennish in addition to the Treaty between the Emperor of Morocco and the United States of America which Declaration the said Tahar Fennish Made by the Express Directions of His Majesty.

THO^{s} BARCLAY

Note, The Ramadan of the Year of the Hegira 1200 Commenced on the 28th June in the Year of our Lord 1786.

Now know Ye that We the said John Adams & Thomas Jefferson Ministers Plenipotentiary aforesaid do approve & conclude the said Treaty and every Article and Clause therein contained, reserving the same nevertheless to the United States in Congress assembled for their final Ratification.

In testimony whereof we have signed the same with our Names and Seals, at the places of our respective residence and at the dates expressed under our signatures respectively.

JOHN ADAMS. [Seal]

LONDON *January 25. 1787.*

TH: JEFFERSON [Seal]

PARIS *January 1. 1787.*

[1] The spelling in the original document is uncertain, but *Abdelhack* is correct, el-Hack or el-Haqq being one of the names of God.

[Ship-Signals Agreement]

The following Signals are agreed upon between Commodore Rais Farache, on the Part of His Majesty the Emperor of Morocco, and the Honorable Thomas Barclay Esquire Agent for the United States of America on their Part, to the End that the Vessels of both Parties may be known to each other at Sea.

For Vessels of two or of three Masts,

In the Day, a blue Pendant is to be hoisted on the End of the Main Yard, and in the Night a Lantern is to be hoisted on the same Place.

For Vessels of one Mast only,

In the Day, a blue Pendant is to be hoisted at the Mast-Head, and in the Night a Lantern is to be hoisted on the Ensign Staff.

Done at Morocco the Ninth day of the Month of Ramadan in the Year One thousand two hundred.

THO[s] BARCLAY

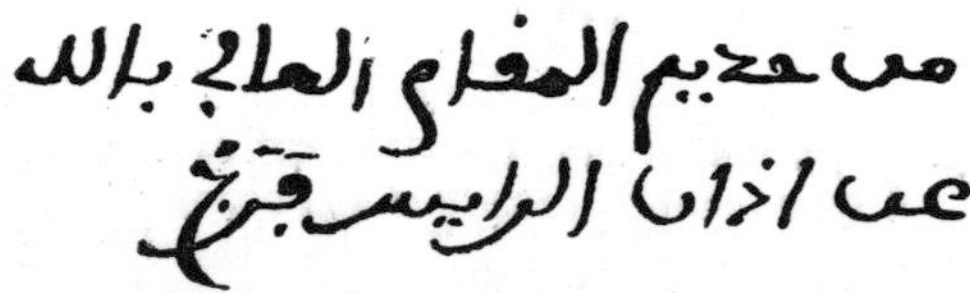

COMMENT OF DR. C. SNOUCK HURGRONJE

In the above two lines of Arabic script (very badly written) there are two gross errors: In the first line instead of *'aẓîm*, "great," which is evidently meant, there is written *'adîm*, which means "destitute of." In the second line the word *idhn*, "authorization," "permission," has a letter too many, by which it becomes *adhân*, meaning "call to prayer." The two necessary corrections being made, the words run as follows: "From the Great in Position, the High in God [*i. e.*, the Emperor]. By authorization: Rais [*i. e.*, captain] Faraj."

THE ENGLISH TRANSLATION OF 1786

The Arabic original of this treaty and the English translation thereof of 1786 have been examined by Dr. C. Snouck Hurgronje, of Leiden, whose comments and notes, and translation of various articles, are as follows:

[The Seal]

The inner circle of the seal contains the name "Muhammed, son of Abdallah, son of Isma'il, God is his protector and his Lord." The border of the seal contains the verse taken from the well-known poem in praise of the Prophet, called the Burdah, which verse occurs in several other seals of these North African documents: "He who takes the Apostle of God for his helper, if the lions encounter him in their jungles, they will withdraw."

[The Text]

Praise be to God! This is the written document of the articles of peace which we have established with the Americans [Marikanos] and which we have confirmed in this book and sealed with our seal, in order that they may remain permanent, if God please. Written in Murakush [Marrakesh] the twenty-fifth of the blessed month of Shaban of the year two hundred and thousand.

> I have given this literal translation of the introduction merely as a specimen, although it presents no essential difference from the translation of 1786. I have not thought it necessary to note all the merely formal differences occurring in the translation of the articles where they do not in the least affect the meaning.

The first article is that these articles mentioned in this book, being twenty-five articles, have been agreed upon by both parties. That took place in the presence of their agent, the Honorable Thomas Barclay, who came here from the side of the American States [Estados al-Marikanos] and whom they had sent to supervise their affairs and their treaty of peace with us.

The second article is that if there shall be war with any nation whatever, no ship of either of the parties shall sail out and take the colors of the enemy, going to help the enemy, neither from our side nor from that of the Americans.

The third article is that if war has been made with any nation whatever, and a ship has been captured from people belonging to that nation, and there shall be found on board a Moslem or a Christian with goods belonging to them, they shall be at liberty with their goods. Even if they were carrying goods belonging to a nation with whom we are at war [such goods] shall not be taken from their hands nor shall they be compelled to unload them, for the sake of the peace prevailing between us and them.

The fourth article. There shall be a signal [instead of "signal or pass" the original has only one word, *'alâmah,* meaning "signal," "sign," "token"] between us by which we may know each other at sea. Whenever one of us meets a warship, he shall not examine it, but the declaration of the commander shall suffice him concerning her [the warship] with other ships.

The fifth article. "If either of the parties shall be at war"—the original has only "if there shall be war."

The sixth article is that if Moslems shall capture people of our [meaning here the American] nation or their goods and bring them to our [here meaning of the Moroccans] Lord (may God give him victory!), he will set them at liberty. Likewise, if Moslems from other than our dominions shall capture them and bring them into any of our ports, they shall be set at liberty, because they are under our protection and on terms of peace with us.

The seventh article. Instead of "interruption" the original has a word meaning "difficulty".

The eighth article is that if any vessel meets with a disaster and runs ashore and unloads her cargo in order to repair, she shall be at liberty to reload her cargo whenever she likes without paying duty or anything.

The ninth article is that if any vessel shall be cast on shore on any part of our coasts, she will be left to herself that she may consider what suits her best, be it to sail out from [by] another place or to transfer her cargo, or whatever else may be convenient to her. Nobody shall approach her, as she is under our protection. Likewise, if a vessel enters a port or wind forces her to put into a port, she shall not be compelled to unload her cargo; on the contrary, she shall remain under our protection until she sails out by her own free will.

The tenth article is that if any of the parties shall have an engagement with any Christian nation, and the engagement takes place near a town of one of the parties, we shall help each other against that nation until she be defeated or have gone away; or if a vessel shall be cast ashore in Ouadnoun or in another place, the Christians being aboard shall be under [our] protection until they reach their country, if God please.

The eleventh article is that if we are at war with any Christian nation, and we shall be in a port and our ship intends to sail out of the port, and a ship of the enemy intends to pursue her, the latter shall not sail out in pursuit of her until twenty-four hours have elapsed; and likewise, ships of the Americans, if they are in a port during a war and they intend to sail out, no ship shall pursue her until twenty-four hours have elapsed, be they ships of the Mohammedans or of the Christians.

The twelfth article is that if a warship shall put into any of our ports, she shall not be examined but shall remain left to herself; and if there should be a fugitive prisoner on board her, he shall not be brought ashore by compulsion, nor shall the governor of the dominion where the ship stops demand from the commander of the ship the price of that prisoner.

> The thirteenth article is without any important difference from the translation of 1786.

The fourteenth article is that the commerce of the merchants shall be on the same footing as that of the Spaniards, and they shall be honored and go in the towns and seaports where they like, without anybody bothering them, and they shall be like the most favored nation with us for the time being.

The fifteenth article is that the merchants shall pursue their business, and if they wish to employ assistants or interpreters, they shall be free to do so. No cargo shall be transported from one ship into another, and no ship shall be detained in the port; and if they wish to employ people to assist them in matters concerning the cargo or otherwise, they shall not have to pay more than other nations used to pay before them.

> The sixteenth article has been well rendered in all essentials in the translation of 1786, but the words "are not to be made slaves" are not in the original, and the "Mexican dollar" is represented in Arabic by "reyal" only.

The seventeenth article is that the merchants shall not be compelled to buy merchandise, but such as they like to buy by their free consent. The same rule is to be applied to sale, except in cases concerning which there have prevailed customs with other Christian nations before them, who carried them [the goods?], in which cases there will be no difficulty. [The meaning of the latter stipulation is not clearly expressed in the Arabic text.]

The eighteenth article is that goods to be loaded shall be weighed and examined before they are brought on board, in order that the ship may not be detained because they have ascertained that there is contraband on board. Now if this be the case, then only he who brought the contraband shall be punished, according to the usage applied to others before him, but the ship and its cargo and what belongs to it shall be free from guilt. [Possibly the Arabic text intended to say what is said in the translation of 1786, but in that case the attempt has entirely failed. Thus there is no expression corresponding to "unless" of that translation.]

> The nineteenth article requires no correction.

The twentieth article is that if a person of our [can only mean here the American] nation or under our flag is guilty of misdemeanor, the

Consul of his nation shall pass sentence upon him. If the Consul wants the assistance of the officials of the Pasha of the place, it shall be granted to him.

The twenty-first article is that if there has been killed a Christian out of them or the reverse [*sic*] or has wounded him [*sic*], then he will be sentenced according to the rules of the Sacred [Mohammedan] Law, neither more nor less, and the trial is to take place in the presence of the Consul. If the delinquent escapes before having been sentenced, the Consul shall not be held responsible for him nor for the crime he committed. [The redaction of Article 21 is extremely inept.]

The twenty-second article is that if an American citizen shall die in our country and no will shall appear, their Consul shall supervise his estate and his goods [merchandise], and if there shall be no Consul, the effects shall be deposited in the hands of some person worthy of trust until the party shall appear who has a right to demand them, but if heirs of his are present, [the property] shall be given to the heirs without interference, or if he has designated in a will signed with his hand, the person to whom the property is to be delivered, then the question shall be submitted to the consideration of the Consul.

The twenty-third article is that the Consuls shall reside in any seaport they like, and they shall be respected like [consuls of] other Christian nations before them. If a person of their nation has had dealings with a Moslem concerning money, and he has caused it to be lost, the Consul shall not be held responsible for it, unless the Consul has given a written declaration to that effect, in which case he shall have to pay it. If he has not given such a declaration, then nobody has a claim upon him—like [this is the case with] all the consuls.

The twenty-fourth article is that if either party should protest concerning any articles of the peace treaty, so that one asserted a question and the other asserted a question and contended that this was not according to the article, and the controversy should last a long time, then peace is to be maintained and both parties have to argue the best they can. If in the end one of them does not agree to the treaty of peace and strenuously declines [or "if neither of them agrees to the treaty of peace and both strenuously decline"], so that war is declared [literally "put into action"], then nine months shall be granted to all the merchants to remove their goods. Whenever our Lord [*i. e.*, the Emperor of Morocco] shows a favor to any Christian nation, we [*i. e.*, the Americans] shall partake in it.

The twenty-fifth article is that this treaty of peace shall remain permanent, if God please, by God's might and power, a period from ["of" is evidently meant] fifty years. We have delivered this book to the above-mentioned Thomas Barclay on the first day of the blessed Ramadan of the year two hundred and thousand.

NOTES

The city of Morocco, where the treaty was signed, is now known as Marrakesh.

The dates given are those recited; some doubt is cast upon their accuracy, however, by a letter from Thomas Barclay, who negotiated the treaty with the Emperor of Morocco, addressed to Adams and Jefferson and dated at Morocco July 16, 1786, from which the following is extracted (Diplomatic Correspondence, 1783–1789, I, 814):

> The 13th instant the treaty was sent to me by the Effendi, since which some important alterations have been made, which the villany and carelessness of the Talbe Houdrani (to whom the drawing was committed) made necessary; and yesterday it was again delivered from Tahar Fennish, to whose hands the King committed the arrangement of the matter. It still wants an additional article, or rather a declaration, which his Majesty has permitted to be made in his name, but which he desired might not make a part of the treaty.

In a letter of June 26, 1786, Barclay had written, "the last draft of the treaty is made, and will probably be signed in a few days" (*ibid.*, 805).

The document signed by Jefferson and Adams, including the English translations of the treaty and of the additional article, is printed in full after the Arabic text of the treaty; following it is printed the Ship-Signals Agreement, with a comment on its two lines of Arabic script; then come the observations of Doctor Snouck Hurgronje regarding the English translation of 1786, with his own rendering of various articles.

The Original Documents

The original document signed by Jefferson and Adams is in 91 C. C. Papers, I, folios 213–31. The Department of State file contains a facsimile of that document, the original of the treaty, and the original of the Ship-Signals Agreement; but the original of the additional article has not been found and accordingly cannot be reproduced. As to this article, Barclay reported (letter to Adams and Jefferson, October 2, 1786, Diplomatic Correspondence, 1783–1789, II, 695):

> The original of the declaration made by Mr. Fennish could not be placed in the same book with the treaty sealed by the Emperor, the Moorish forms not permitting it; therefore, Mr. Fennish wrote it in another book, which I had placed in his hands, with a copy of the treaty for examination, in order that he might certify the verity of it, lest any accident should happen to the original; which book, with authenticated copies of the other papers, remains in my hands.

The original of the additional article appears to have been enclosed in a letter from Thomas Barclay to Jefferson, dated at Madrid December 4, 1786 (signed "copy" in 91 C. C. Papers, I, folios 211–12), from which the following is an extract:

> I now inclose you a Copy of the Declaration made by Tahar Fennish in addition to the 10th article of the Treaty with the Emperor of Morocco. It is in Arabic and sign'd by himself. the necessity of a Duplicate of that Declaration, did not appear obvious to me untill I got to Tangier, and within this hour it has reach'd me. you have also the Translation annex'd to it.

In the calendar of letters to Jefferson (Bulletin of the Bureau of Rolls and Library, No. 8, pt. 2, 36) this letter is listed "Press copy. 4°. 2 pages." The letter, which is in the Library of Congress (26 Thomas Jefferson Papers, folio 4477), is not a press copy, however; it is an original. There is no enclosure with it. In Diplomatic Correspondence, 1783–1789, II, 34, is printed a translation of the additional article, certified by Thomas Barclay under the date of the above-mentioned letter and referring to "the annexed declaration, in Arabic"; but that certified translation has not been found.

Note Regarding the Ratification

The United States instrument of ratification is copied in 135 C. C. Papers, I; also in Journals, 1823 ed., IV, 756–59. The two forms are not identical; the latter contains a paragraph mentioning the approval of the treaty by Jefferson and Adams which the former omits. Neither form mentions the Ship-Signals Agreement.

In the making of treaties, the procedure and customs of the various Barbary States differed somewhat *inter se* and were not in all respects those of usual diplomatic practice. Thus, in the present instance, the sealing on behalf of the Emperor of Morocco of the original treaty written in the "book," with the delivery thereof, was deemed a finality on the part of Morocco. The theory seems to have been somewhat similar to our notion of a unilaterally executed grant and its delivery, for the text in the "book" was not signed or sealed on behalf of the other party. It may be added that the "book" is literally a book, in leather covers, with the text running from the back leaf on alternate pages and the front pages blank.

The customs of Morocco were doubtless not known to Adams and Jefferson, for their commission to Barclay, following the language of their own commission from Congress (Diplomatic Correspondence, 1783–1789, I, 656–57), gave him authority only

> . . . under our directions and instructions, to commence and prosecute negotiations and conferences for the said treaty, with such person or persons on the part of the Emperor of Morocco as his Majesty shall appoint and empower for that purpose—
>
> Provided always, that the treaty in question shall be signed by us, but that preliminary articles thereto may, if previously approved by us, be signed by the said agent.

Indeed, such "missions by deputation" were criticized by Adams as "unknown to Courts and Ministers, and to the law of nations" (*ibid.*, II, 802); but the practice had been suggested by him (Wharton, Diplomatic Correspondence, VI, 692).

The signing by Jefferson and Adams of the certified translations was therefore properly a part of their report to Congress of the result of the negotiation entrusted to them and delegated by them to Thomas Barclay; but the agreement was already complete on the part of Morocco and awaited only the ratification of Congress, and doubtless notice thereof, to become complete on both sides.

As was reported from Morocco some fifty years later:

The Treaty, it will be observed, being sealed by the Emperor according to the diplomatic custom observed in this Empire, bears the form of a grant. Hence, it would be out of rule to deface the original with my signature or seal. I have therefore attached these to the copy and translation which will accompany the original, according to the usage observed by Diplomatic Agents in other parts of Barbary. (D. S., 5 Consular Despatches, Tangier, No. 39, October 11, 1836.)

The necessity of acceptance on the part of the United States was recognized, however, for Barclay wrote in one of his reports (letter to Adams and Jefferson, September 18, 1786, Diplomatic Correspondence, 1783–1789, II, 723):

I was asked to sign an acceptation of the articles on the part of the United States; but as the treaty was not drawn up in the form expected, I excused myself, (without, however, giving any offence,) referring Mr. Fennish to Congress and the Ministers.

A letter from Congress to the Emperor of Morocco notified the ratification of the treaty; the same letter indicates that it had been published and proclaimed (Secret Journals of Congress, IV, 365, July 23, 1787). With this letter the United States instrument of ratification was transmitted (Diplomatic Correspondence, 1783–1789, II, 44, 86). The letter and ratification were duly delivered to the Emperor of Morocco some time prior to August 17, 1788. The original of the letter of acknowledgment on the part of the Emperor of Morocco, dated that day and written in Arabic, is in the archives of the Department of State; and there is an Italian translation of it in 88 C. C. Papers, II, folio 524, as one of the enclosures to a letter ("triplicate") of November 5, 1788, from William Carmichael, Chargé d'Affaires at Madrid, to Jay. In that letter (printed in Diplomatic Correspondence, 1783–1789, III, 370) Carmichael calls the acknowledgment of the Emperor of Morocco "the ratification of the treaty," and similarly in his letter to Jefferson of November 3, 1788 (43 Thomas Jefferson Papers, folio 7423), and in his letter to Jay of December 2, 1788 ("duplicate" in 88 C. C. Papers, II, folios 588–89, with no enclosures; that letter is printed in Diplomatic Correspondence, 1783–1789, III, 381–82; see also the two letters of Francisco Chiappe, *ibid.*, 371–72). But, while doubtless a confirmation of the treaty, the letter of the Emperor of Morocco can hardly be deemed a ratification in any formal or technical sense.

The seal of the letter, which follows its opening phrases, is the same as that of the treaty; and as translated by Doctor Snouck Hurgronje, the letter reads thus:

In the name of God, the Compassionate, the Merciful, and there is no might nor power but in God, the Great, the High.

From the servant of God, Muhammed, son of Abdallah, may God bestow His favor upon him. Amen!

[Seal]

To the Great One of the American States [Estados Amarikanos], the President. Peace be on those who follow the right guidance [*i. e.*, the Mohammedan religion]! To come to the point: Your letter has reached us and also have reached us the

articles of the Treaty of Peace which you have sent us, and we are with you on terms of complete truce and peace. We have now written what you wanted us to write to Tunis and Tripoli, and all that you have asked from us shall be fulfilled, if God please. Greetings! Written in the middle in [the month Dhu] al-Qa'dah [Zu'lkadah] of the year two and two hundred and thousand 1202.

Doctor Snouck Hurgronje makes also the following comment on the letter:

Placing the seal at the head of the letter denotes great superiority in rank of the writer in comparison with that of the person to whom the letter is addressed.

"The Great One of . . ." is the title by which infidel rulers are addressed in letters from the Prophet. The greeting formula, "Peace be on those who follow the right guidance," is the classical one to be addressed to unbelievers, implying that they are not worth greeting.

Note Regarding Promulgation

There appears no official record of any separate proclamation of this treaty. The United States instrument of ratification, however, embodying the treaty and additional article in English, was published at the time (*e. g.*, the Daily Advertiser, New York, July 21, 1787). The Department of State file now contains a facsimile of the newspaper print.

Accordingly, the instrument of ratification seems to have served as a proclamation and to have been regarded as such upon publication. As published it follows the form in the Journals, referred to above, and recites that the treaty was "written in the Arabic language" and "translated into the language of the said United States of America"; it contains no mention of the Ship-Signals Agreement.

As stated above, copies of the Ship-Signals Agreement were, on July 23, 1787, ordered by Congress to be sent to the Executives of the States (Secret Journals of Congress, IV, 369, where the paper is called No. 6 instead of No. 7; see Diplomatic Correspondence, 1783–1789, II, 695). From that period to the present, however, the Ship-Signals Agreement seems never to have been printed, either in the diplomatic correspondence or elsewhere.

The Later Confirmation

A treaty with Morocco was there regarded as to some degree personal on the part of the ruling Emperor, at least to the extent of requiring confirmation or recognition by a successor. Accordingly, soon after the death of the then Emperor, in April, 1790, negotiations to that end were initiated (see American State Papers, Foreign Relations, I, 104, 128, 288–90); but conflicts regarding the succession to the throne of Morocco continued for some years; after these were ended, a letter was written by the succeeding Emperor, dated at Rabat August 19, 1795 (2 Safar, A. H. 1210), recognizing the treaty with his father. For the papers in the matter, including a translation of the confirming letter, see *ibid.*, 525–27.

115605°—31—vol. 2——17

Treaty Series, No. 84
8 Statutes at Large, 106-15

15

FRANCE : NOVEMBER 14, 1788

Convention Defining and Establishing the Functions and Privileges of Consuls and Vice Consuls, signed at Versailles November 14, 1788. Original in French.

Submitted to the Senate June 11, 1789. Resolution of advice and consent July 29, 1789. Ratified by the United States September 9, 1789. Ratified by France (according to the instrument of ratification) October 1, 1788. Ratifications exchanged at Paris January 6, 1790. (Protocol of exchange dated January 1, 1790.) Proclaimed April 9, 1790.

Convention entre le Roi très-Chrétien et les Etats-Unis de l'Amérique à l'effet de déterminer et fixer les fonctions et prérogatives des Consuls et Vice-Consuls respectifs.

Sa Majesté le Roi très-Chrétien et les Etats-Unis de l'Amérique s'étant accordés mutuellement par l'Art. XXIX du Traité d'Amitié et de Commerce[1] conclu entr'eux, la liberté de tenir dans leurs Etats et ports respectifs, des Consuls et Vice-Consuls, agens et commissaires, et voulant en conséquence déterminer et fixer d'une manière réciproque et permanente les fonctions et prérogatives des Consuls et Vice-Consuls qu'ils ont jugé convenable d'établir de préférence, Sa Majesté Très-chrétienne a nommé le Sieur Comte de Montmorin de St Herent, Maréchal de ses Camps et

[Translation]

Convention between His Most Christian Majesty and the United States of America, for the Purpose of Defining and Establishing the Functions and Privileges of Their Respective Consuls and Vice Consuls.

His Majesty the Most Christian King and the United States of America, having, by the twenty-ninth article of the Treaty of Amity and Commerce[1] concluded between them, mutually granted the liberty of having, in their respective states and ports, consuls, vice consuls, agents, and commissaries, and being willing, in consequence thereof, to define and establish, in a reciprocal and permanent manner, the functions and privileges of consuls and vice consuls, which they have judged it convenient to establish of preference, His Most Christian Majesty has nominated the Sieur

[1] Document 1.

armées, chevalier de ses ordres et de la Toison-d'Or, son Conseiller en tous ses Conseils, Ministre et Sécrétaire d'Etat et de ses Commandements et finances aïant le Département des Affaires Etrangères; et les Etats-Unis ont nommé le Sieur Thomas Jefferson, Citoyen des Etats-Unis de l'Amérique et leur Ministre Plénipotentiaire auprès du Roi, lesquels, après s'être communiqué leurs pleinpouvoirs respectifs sont convenus de ce qui suit:

Count of Montmorin, of St. Herent, Maréchal of his Camps and Armies, Knight of his Orders and of the Golden Fleece, his Counselor in all his Councils, Minister and Secretary of State and of his Commandments and Finances, having the Department of Foreign Affairs; and the United States have nominated the Sieur Thomas Jefferson, citizen of the United States of America and their Minister Plenipotentiary near the King; who, after having communicated to each other their respective full powers, have agreed on what follows:

Article 1er.

Les Consuls et Vice-Consuls nommés par le Roi très-chrétien et les Etats-Unis seront tenus de présenter leurs provisions selon la forme qui se trouvera établie respectivement par le Roi trés-chrétien dans ses Etats, et par le Congrès dans les Etats-Unis. On leur delivrera sans aucuns fraîx l'*Exequatur* nécessaire à l'éxercice de leurs fonctions, et sur l'exhibition qu'ils feront dudit *Exequatur*, les Gouverneurs, Commandants, chefs de justice, les Corps, Tribunaux ou autres officiers aïant autorité dans les ports et lieux de leurs Consulats, les y feront jouir aussitôt et sans difficulté des prééminences, autorité et privilèges accordés réciproquement, sans qu'ils puissent

Article 1.

The consuls and vice consuls named by the Most Christian King and the United States shall be bound to present their commissions according to the forms which shall be established respectively by the Most Christian King within his dominions and by the Congress within the United States. There shall be delivered to them, without any charges, the exequatur necessary for the exercise of their functions; and on exhibiting the said exequatur, the governors, commanders, heads of justice, bodies corporate, tribunals, and other officers having authority in the ports and places of their consulates, shall cause them to enjoy, immediately and without difficulty, the preeminences, au-

éxiger desdits Consuls et Vice-Consuls aucun droit sous aucun prétexte quelconque.

thority, and privileges reciprocally granted, without exacting from the said consuls and vice consuls any fee under any pretext whatever.

ART. 2ond

Les Consuls et Vice-Consuls et les personnes attachées á leurs fonctions, savoir leurs Chanceliers et Sécrétaires, jouiront d'une pleine et entière immunité pour leur Chancellerie et les papiers qui y seront renfermés. Ils seront éxemts de tout service persoñel, logement des gens de guerre, milice, guet, garde, tutelle, curatelle, ainsi que de tous droits, taxes, impositions et charges quelconques, á l'exception seulement des biens meubles et immeubles dont ils seroient propriétaires ou possesseurs, lesquels seront assujettis aux taxes imposées sur ceux de tous autres particuliers, et à tous égards ils demeureront sujets aux loix du paÏs comme les nationaux.

Ceux desdits Consuls et Vice-Consuls qui feront le Commerce seront respectivement assujettis à toutes les taxes, charges et impositions établies sur les autres négociants.

Ils placeront sur la porte extérieure de leurs Maisons les armes de leur souverain, sans que cette marque distinctive puisse donner auxdites Maisons le droit d'asîle, soit pour des personnes, soit pour des effets quelconques.

ARTICLE 2.

The consuls and vice consuls, and persons attached to their functions, that is to say, their chancellors and secretaries, shall enjoy a full and entire immunity for their chancery and the papers which shall be therein contained. They shall be exempt from all personal service, from soldiers' billets, militia, watch, guard, guardianship, trusteeship, as well as from all duties, taxes, impositions, and charges whatsoever, except on the estate, real and personal, of which they may be the proprietors or possessors, which shall be subject to the taxes imposed on the estates of all other individuals; and in all other instances they shall be subject to the laws of the land as the natives are.

Those of the said consuls and vice consuls who shall exercise commerce shall be respectively subject to all taxes, charges, and impositions established on other merchants.

They shall place over the outward door of their house the arms of their sovereign; but this mark of indication shall not give to the said house any privilege of asylum for any person or property whatsoever.

ART. 3.

Les Consuls et Vice-Consuls respectifs pourront établir des agens dans les différens ports et lieux de leurs Départements où le besoin l'éxigera; ces agens pourront être choisis parmi les négociants nationaux ou étrangers et munis de la Commission de l'un desdits Consuls. Ils se renfermeront respectivement à rendre aux Commercants, navigateurs et batiments respectifs, tous les services possible, et à informer le Consul le plus proche des besoins desdits Commercants, navigateurs et batiments, sans que lesdits agens puissent autrement participer aux immunités, droits et privilèges attribués aux Consuls et Vice-Consuls, et sans pouvoir sous aucun prétexte que ce soit, éxiger aucun droit ou émolument quelconque desdits Commerçants.

ARTICLE 3.

The respective consuls and vice consuls may establish agents in the different ports and places of their departments where necessity shall require. These agents may be chosen among the merchants, either national or foreign, and furnished with a commission from one of the said consuls. They shall confine themselves respectively to the rendering to their respective merchants, navigators, and vessels, all possible service, and to inform the nearest consul of the wants of the said merchants, navigators, and vessels, without the said agents otherwise participating in the immunities, rights, and privileges attributed to consuls and vice consuls, and without power, under any pretext whatever, to exact from the said merchants any duty or emolument whatsoever.

ART. 4.

Les Consuls et Vice-Consuls respectifs pourront établir une Chancellerie où seront déposés les délibérations, actes et procédures consulaires, ainsi que les testaments, obligations, contrats et autres Actes faits par les nationaux ou entr eux, et les effets délaissés par mort ou sauvés des naufrages.

Ils pourront en conséquence commettre à l'éxercice de ladite Chancellerie des personnes capables, les recevoir, leur faire prêter

ARTICLE 4.

The consuls and vice consuls respectively may establish a chancery where shall be deposited the consular determinations, acts, and proceedings, as also testaments, obligations, contracts, and other acts done by or between persons of their nation, and effects left by deceased persons or saved from shipwreck.

They may consequently appoint fit persons to act in the said chancery, receive and swear them in, commit to them the

serment, leur donner la garde du sceau et le droit de sceller les Commissions, jugements et autres actes consulaires, ainsi que d'y remplir les fonctions de Notaire et Greffiers du Consulat.

ART. 5.

Les Consuls et Vice-Consuls respectifs auront le droit exclusif de recevoir dans leur Chancellerie, ou à bord des batiments les déclarations et tous les autres actes que les Capitaines, patrons, Equipages, passagers et négociants de leur Nation, voudront y passer, même leur testament et autres dispositions de d.ère volonté, et les dispositions desdits actes duëment legalisés par lesdits Consuls ou Vice-Consuls, et munis du sceau de leur Consulat, feront foi en justice comme le feroient les Originaux dans tous les Tribunaux des Etats du Roi trèschrétien et des Etats-Unis.

Ils auront aussi, et exclusivement, en cas d' absence d'Éxécuteur testamentaire, Curateur ou héritiers légitimes, le droit de faire l'Inventaire, la liquidation et de procéder à la vente des effets mobiliers de la succession des sujets ou citoyens de leur nation qui viendront à mourir dans l'étenduë de leur Consulat. Ils y procéderont avec l'assistance de deux négocians de leur dite Nation, ou à leur défaut de tout autre à leur choix, et feront déposer dans leur Chancellerie

custody of the seal and authority to seal commissions, sentences, and other consular acts, and also to discharge the functions of notary and register of the consulate.

ARTICLE 5.

The consuls and vice consuls respectively shall have the exclusive right of receiving in their chancery, or on board of vessels, the declarations and all other the acts which the captains, masters, crews, passengers, and merchants of their nation may choose to make there, even their testaments and other disposals by last will; and the copies of the said acts, duly authenticated by the said consuls or vice consuls under the seal of their consulate, shall receive faith in law, equally as their originals would, in all the tribunals of the dominions of the Most Christian King and of the United States.

They shall also have, and exclusively, in case of the absence of the testamentary executor, administrator, or legal heir, the right to inventory, liquidate, and proceed to the sale of the personal estate left by subjects or citizens of their nation who shall die within the extent of their consulate; they shall proceed therein with the assistance of two merchants of their said nation, or for want of them, of any other at their choice, and shall cause to be deposited in their chancery the effects and

les effets et papiers desdites successions, sans qu'aucuns officiers militaires, de justice ou de police du païs, puissent les y troubler, ni y intervenir de quelque manière que ce soit, mais lesdits Consuls et Vice-Consuls ne pourront faire la délivrance des successions et de leur produit aux héritiers légitimes, ou à leurs Mandataires, qu'après avoir fait aquitter toutes les dettes que les défunts auront pû avoir contracteés dans le païs, à l'effet de quoi les créanciers auront droit de saisir lesdits effets dans leurs mains, de même que dans celles de tout autre individu quelconque, et en poursuivre la vente jusqu'au païement de ce qui leur sera légitimement dû; lorsque les dettes n'auront été contracteés par jugement, par acte ou par billet dont la signature sera reconnuë, le païement ne pourra en être ordonné, qu'en fournissant par le créancier caution suffisante et domiciliée de rendre Les sommes induëment perçües, principal, intérêts et fraîx; lesquelles cautions cependant demeureront duëment déchargées après une année en tems de paix, et deux en tems de guerre, si la demande en décharge ne peut être formée avant ces délais contre les Héritiers qui se présenteront. Et afin de ne pas faire injustement attendre aux héritiers les effets du défunt, les Consuls et Vice-Consuls feront annoncer sa mort dans quelqu'une

papers of the said estates; and no officer, military, judiciary, or of the police of the country, shall disturb them or interfere therein in any manner whatsoever. But the said consuls and vice consuls shall not deliver up the said effects nor the proceeds thereof, to the lawful heirs, or to their order, till they shall have caused to be paid all debts which the deceased shall have contracted in the country; for which purpose the creditors shall have a right to attach the said effects in their hands, as they might in those of any other individual whatever, and proceed to obtain sale of them till payment of what shall be lawfully due to them. When the debts shall not have been contracted by judgment, deed, or note, the signature whereof shall be known, payment shall not be ordered but on the creditor's giving sufficient surety, resident in the country, to refund the sums he shall have unduly received, principal, interest, and costs; which surety, nevertheless, shall stand duly discharged after the term of one year in time of peace and of two in time of war, if the demand in discharge cannot be formed before the end of this term against the heirs who shall present themselves.

And in order that the heirs may not be unjustly kept out of the effects of the deceased, the consuls and vice consuls shall

des gazettes qui se publient dans l'étenduë de leur Consulat, et qu'ils retiendront lesdits effets sous leurs mains pendant quatre mois pour répondre à toutes les demandes qui se présenteront: et ils seront tenus après ce délai, de délivrer aux héritiers l'excédent du montant des demandes qui auront été formées.

notify his death in some one of the gazettes published within their consulate, and that they shall retain the said effects in their hands four months to answer all demands which shall be presented; and they shall be bound after this delay to deliver to the persons succeeding thereto, what shall be more than sufficient for the demands which shall have been formed.

ART. 6.

Les Consuls et Vice-Consuls respectifs recevront les déclarations, protestations et raports de tous Capitaines et patrons de leur Nation respective pour raison d'avaries essuyées à la mer, et ces Capitaines et patrons remettront dans la Chancellerie desdits Consuls et Vice-Consuls les actes qu'ils auront faits dans d'autres ports pour les accidents qui leur seront arrivés pendant leur voyage. Si un sujet du Roi très-chrétien et un habitant des Etats-Unis ou un Etranger sont intéressés dans ladite cargaison, l'avarie sera règlée par les tribunaux du païs et non par les Consuls et Vice-Consuls; mais lorsqu'il n'y aura d'intéressés que les sujets ou citoyens de leur propre nation, les Consuls ou les Vice-Consuls respectifs nommeront des experts pour règler les dommages et avaries.

ARTICLE 6.

The consuls and vice consuls respectively shall receive the declarations, protests, and reports of all captains and masters of their respective nation on account of average losses sustained at sea; and these captains and masters shall lodge in the chancery of the said consuls and vice consuls, the acts which they may have made in other ports on account of the accidents which may have happened to them on their voyage. If a subject of the Most Christian King and a citizen of the United States, or a foreigner, are interested in the said cargo, the average shall be settled by the tribunals of the country and not by the consuls or vice consuls; but when only the subjects or citizens of their own nation shall be interested, the respective consuls or vice consuls shall appoint skilful persons to settle the damages and average.

ART. 7.

Dans le cas où par tempête ou autres accidents, des vaisseaux ou batiments français échoüeront sur les Côtes des Etats-Unis, et des vaisseaux et batiments des Etats-Unis échoüeront sur les Côtes des Etats de Sa Majesté très-chrétienne, le Consul ou le Vice-Consul le plus proche du lieu du naufrage pourra faire tout ce qu'il jugera convenable, tant pour sauver ledit vaisseau ou batiment, son chargement et apartenances, que pour le Magazinage et la sûreté des effets sauvés et marchandises. Il pourra en faire l'inventaire sans qu'aucuns officiers militaires, des Doüanes, de justice ou de police du païs, puissent s'y immiscer autrement que pour faciliter aux Consuls et Vice-Consuls, Capitaine et Equipage du vaisseau naufragé ou échoüé, tous les secours et faveurs qu'ils leur demanderont, soit pour la célérité et la sûreté du sauvetage et des effets sauvés, soit pour éviter tous désordres.

Pour prévenir même toute espèce de conflit et de discution dans lesdits cas de naufrage, il a été convenu que lorsqu'il ne se trouvera pas de Consul ou Vice-Consul pour faire travailler au sauvetage, ou que la résidence dudit Consul ou Vice-Consul, qui ne se trouvera pas sur le lieu du naufrage, sera plus éloignée dudit lieu que celle du Juge territorial

ARTICLE 7.

In cases where, by tempest or other accident, French ships or vessels shall be stranded on the coasts of the United States, and ships or vessels of the United States shall be stranded on the coasts of the dominions of the Most Christian King, the consul or vice consul nearest to the place of shipwreck shall do whatever he may judge proper, as well for the purpose of saving the said ship or vessel, its cargo, and appurtenances, as for the storing and the security of the effects and merchandise saved. He may take an inventory of them, without the intermeddling of any officers of the military, of the customs, of justice, or of the police of the country, otherwise than to give to the consuls, vice consuls, captain, and crew of the vessel shipwrecked or stranded, all the succor and favor which they shall ask of them, either for the expedition and security of the saving and of the effects saved, as to prevent all disturbance.

And in order to prevent all kind of dispute and discussion in the said cases of shipwreck, it is agreed that when there shall be no consul or vice consul to attend to the saving of the wreck, or that the residence of the said consul or vice consul (he not being at the place of the wreck) shall be more distant from the said place than that of the com-

compétent, ce dernier fera procéder sur le champ avec toute la célérité, la sûreté et les précautions prescrites par les loix respectives, sauf audit Juge territorial à se retirer, le Consul ou Vice-Consul survenant, et à lui remettre l'expédition des procédures par lui faites dont le Consul ou Vice-Consul lui fera rembourser les fraîx ainsi que ceux du sauvetage.

Les marchandises et effets sauvés devront être déposés à la Doüane ou autre lieu de sûreté le plus prochain, avec l'Inventaire qui en aura été dressé par le Consul ou Vice-consul, ou en leur absence par le Juge qui en aura connu, pour lesdits effets et marchandises être ensuite délivrés, après le prélevement des fraix et sans forme de procès, aux propriétaires qui, munis de la mainlevée du Consul ou Vice-Consul le plus proche, les réclameront par eux-mêmes ou par leurs mandataires, soit pour réexporter les marchandises, et dans ce cas, elles ne païeront aucune espèce de droits de sortie, soit pour les vendre dans le paîs, si elles n'y sont pas prohibées, et dans ce d^er cas lesd^tes marchandises se trouvant avariées, on leur accordera une modération sur les droits d'entrée, proportionné au dommage souffert, lequel sera constaté par le procès verbal dressé lors du naufrage ou l'échoüement.

petent judge of the country, the latter shall immediately proceed therein, with all the dispatch, certainty, and precautions prescribed by the respective laws; but the said territorial judge shall retire on the arrival of the consul or vice consul and shall deliver over to him the report of his proceedings, the expenses of which the consul or vice consul shall cause to be reimbursed to him, as well as those of saving the wreck.

The merchandise and effects saved shall be deposited in the nearest customhouse, or other place of safety, with the inventory thereof, which shall have been made by the consul or vice consul, or by the judge who shall have proceeded in their absence, that the said effects and merchandise may be afterwards delivered (after levying therefrom the costs) and without form of process, to the owners, who, being furnished with an order for their delivery from the nearest consul or vice consul, shall reclaim them by themselves, or by their order, either for the purpose of reexporting such merchandise, in which case they shall pay no kind of duty of exportation, or for that of selling them in the country, if they be not prohibited there, and in this last case the said merchandise, if they be damaged, shall be allowed an abatement of entrance duties proportioned to the damage they have sustained, which shall be

ascertained by the affidavits taken at the time the vessel was wrecked or struck.

Art. 8.

Les Consuls ou Vice-Consuls éxerceront la police sur tous les batimens de leurs Nations respectives, et auront à bord desdits batimens tout pouvoir et jurisdiction en matière civile dans toutes les discutions qui pourront y survenir; ils auront une entière inspection sur lesdits batiments, leurs équipages et les changements et remplacements à y faire; pour quel effet ils pourront se transporter à bord desdits batiments toutes les fois qu'ils le jugeront nécessaire; bien entendu que les fonctions ci-dessus énoncées seront concentrées dans l'intérieur des batiments et qu'elles ne pourront avoir lieu dans aucun cas qui aura quelque raport avec la police des ports où lesdits batiments se trouveront.

Article 8.

The consuls or vice consuls shall exercise police over all the vessels of their respective nations and shall have on board the said vessels all power and jurisdiction in civil matters, in all the disputes which may there arise; they shall have an entire inspection over the said vessels, their crew, and the changes and substitutions there to be made, for which purpose they may go on board the said vessels whenever they may judge it necessary. Well understood that the functions hereby allowed shall be confined to the interior of the vessels, and that they shall not take place in any case which shall have any interference with the police of the ports where the said vessels shall be.

Art. 9.

Les Consuls et Vice-Consuls pourront faire arrêter les Capitaines Officiers-mariniers, matelots et toutes autres personnes faisant partie des Equipages des batiments de leurs nations respectives qui auroient déserté desdits batimens pour les renvoyer et faire transporter hors du païs. Auquel effet lesdits Consuls et Vice-Consuls s'addresseront aux tribunaux, juges et officiers compétents, et leur feront par écrit la

Article 9.

The consuls and vice consuls may cause to be arrested the captains, officers, mariners, sailors, and all other persons, being part of the crews of the vessels of their respective nation, who shall have deserted from the said vessels, in order to send them back and transport them out of the country; for which purpose the said consuls and vice consuls shall address themselves to the courts, judges, and officers competent,

demande desdits déserteurs, en justifiant, par l'exhibition des Registres du Batiment ou Rôle d'Equipage, que ces hommes faisoient partie des susdits Equipages. Et sur cette demande ainsi justifiée, sauf toutefois la preuve contraire, l'extradition ne pourra être refusée, et il sera donné toute aide et assistance auxdits Consuls et Vice-Consuls pour la recherche, saisie et arrestation des susdits déserteurs, lesquels seront même détenus et gardés dans les prisons du païs, à leur réquisition et à leurs fraîx, jusqu'à ce qu'ils aïent trouvé occasion de les renvoyer. Mais s'ils n'étoient renvoyés dans le délai de trois mois à compter du jour de leur Arrêt, ils seront élargis et ne pourront plus être arrêtés pour la même cause.

ART. 10.

Dans le cas où les sujets ou citoyens respectifs auront commis quelque crime ou infraction de la tranquillité publique, ils seront justiciables des Juges du païs.

ART. 11.

Lorsque lesdits coupables feront partie de l'Equipage de l'un des batiments de leur nation, et se seront retirés à bord desdits navires, ils pourront y être saisis et arrêtés par l'ordre des Juges territoriaux: ceux-ci en préviendront le Consul ou Vice-Consul, lequel pourra se rendre à bord

and shall demand the said deserters in writing, proving by an exhibition of the registers of the vessel or ship's roll that those men were part of the said crews; and on this demand so proved (saving, however, where the contrary is proved) the delivery shall not be refused; and there shall be given all aid and assistance to the said consuls and vice consuls for the search, seizure, and arrest of the said deserters, who shall even be detained and kept in the prisons of the country, at their request and expense, until they shall have found an opportunity of sending them back. But if they be not sent back within three months, to be counted from the day of their arrest, they shall be set at liberty and shall be no more arrested for the same cause.

ARTICLE 10.

In cases where the respective subjects or citizens shall have committed any crime or breach of the peace, they shall be amenable to the judges of the country.

ARTICLE 11.

When the said offenders shall be a part of the crew of a vessel of their nation and shall have withdrawn themselves on board the said vessel, they may be there seized and arrested by order of the judges of the country. These shall give notice thereof to the consul or vice consul, who may

s'il le juge à-propos: mais cette prévenance ne pourra en aucun cas retarder l'éxécution de l'ordre dont il est question. Les personnes arrêtées ne pourront ensuite être mises en liberté qu'après que le Consul ou Vice-Consul en aura été prévenu; et elles lui seront remises, s'il le requiert, pour être reconduites sur les batiments où elles auront été arrêtées, ou autres de leur Nation, et être renvoyeés hors du païs.

ART. 12.

Tous différends et procès entre les sujets du Roi très-chrétien dans les Etats-Unis ou entre les citoyens des Etats-Unis dans les Etats du Roi très-chrétien, et notamment toutes les discutions relatives aux salaires et conditions des engagements des Equipages des batiments respectifs, et tous différends de quelque nature qu'ils soient qui pourroient s'élever entre les hommes desdits Equipages ou entre quelques uns d'eux et leurs Capitaines, ou entre les Capitaines de divers batiments nationaux, seront terminés par les Consuls et Vice-Consuls respectifs, soit par un renvoi par devant des arbitres, soit par un jugement sommaire et sans fraîx. Aucun officier territorial civil ou militaire ne pourra y intervenir ou prendre une part quelconque à l'affaire, et les apels desdits jugements consulaires seront portés devant les tribunaux de france

repair on board if he thinks proper; but this notification shall not in any case delay execution of the order in question. The persons arrested shall not afterwards be set at liberty until the consul or vice consul shall have been notified thereof; and they shall be delivered to him, if he requires it, to be put again on board of the vessel on which they were arrested, or of others of their nation, and to be sent out of the country.

ARTICLE 12.

All differences and suits between the subjects of the Most Christian King in the United States, or between the citizens of the United States within the dominions of the Most Christian King, and particularly all disputes relative to the wages and terms of engagement of the crews of the respective vessels, and all differences, of whatever nature they be, which may arise between the privates of the said crews, or between any of them and their captains, or between the captains of different vessels of their nation, shall be determined by the respective consuls and vice consuls, either by a reference to arbitrators or by a summary judgment, and without costs.

No officer of the country, civil or military, shall interfere therein or take any part whatever in the matter; and the appeals from the said consular sentences shall be

ou des Etats-Unis qui doivent en connaître.

ART. 13.

L'utilité générale du Commerce aïant fait établir dans les Etats du Roi très-chrétien des tribunaux et des formes particulières pour accélerer la décision des affaires de Commerce, les négocians des Etats-Unis jouiront du bénéfice de ces Etablissements, et le Congrès des Etats-Unis pourvoira de la manière la plus conforme à ses loix, à l'établissement des avantages équivalents en faveur des négociants français pour la prompte expédition et décision des affaires de la même nature.

ART. 14.

Les sujets du Roi très-chrétien et les citoyens des Etats-Unis qui justifieront authentiquement être du Corps de la Nation respective jouiront en conséquence de l'éxemption de tout Service personnel dans le lieu de leur établissement.

ART. 15.

Si quelqu'autre Nation acquiert en vertu d'une Convention quelconque un traitement plus favorable relativement aux prééminences, pouvoirs, autorité et privilèges consulaires, les Consuls

carried before the tribunals of France or of the United States, to whom it may appertain to take cognizance thereof.

ARTICLE 13.

The general utility of commerce having caused to be established within the dominions of the Most Christian King particular tribunals and forms for expediting the decision of commercial affairs, the merchants of the United States shall enjoy the benefit of these establishments; and the Congress of the United States will provide, in the manner the most conformable to its laws, for the establishment of equivalent advantages in favor of the French merchants, for the prompt dispatch and decision of affairs of the same nature.

ARTICLE 14.

The subjects of the Most Christian King and citizens of the United States who shall prove by legal evidence that they are of the said nations respectively, shall in consequence enjoy an exemption from all personal service in the place of their settlement.

ARTICLE 15.

If any other nation acquires, by virtue of any convention whatever, a treatment more favorable with respect to the consular preeminences, powers, authority, and privileges, the consuls and vice

et Vice-Consuls du Roi très-chrétien ou des Etats-Unis réciproquement y participeront aux termes stipulés par les Articles deux, trois et quatre du Traité d'amitié et de Commerce[1] conclu entre le Roi très-chrétien et les Etats-Unis.

consuls of the Most Christian King or of the United States reciprocally shall participate therein, agreeable to the terms stipulated by the second, third, and fourth articles of the Treaty of Amity and Commerce[1] concluded between the Most Christian King and the United States.

ART. 16.

La présente Convention aura son plein effet pendant l'espace de douze ans, à-compter du jour de l'échange des Ratifications, lesquelles seront données en bonne forme et échangées de part et d'autre dans l'espace d'un an ou plustôt si faire se peut.

En foi de quoi, Nous Ministres Plénipotentiaires, avons signé la présente Convention, et y avons fait apposer le cachet de nos armes.

Fait à Versailles le 14 Novembre mil sept cent quatre-vingt-huit.

L. C. DE MONTMORIN
[Seal]
TH: JEFFERSON
[Seal]

ARTICLE 16.

The present convention shall be in full force during the term of twelve years, to be counted from the day of the exchange of ratifications, which shall be given in proper form and exchanged on both sides within the space of one year, or sooner if possible.

In faith whereof we, Ministers Plenipotentiary, have signed the present convention and have thereto set the seal of our arms.

Done at Versailles the fourteenth of November, one thousand seven hundred and eighty-eight.

L. C. DE MONTMORIN
[Seal]
TH: JEFFERSON
[Seal]

[1] Document 1.

NOTES

Except for some treaties with Indian tribes, this is the first treaty ever submitted to the Senate of the United States. While the date of the signature, November 14, 1788, was subsequent to the going into force of the Constitution and to the resolution of Congress for elections thereunder (September 13, 1788), it was prior to the date fixed for the beginning of the new régime (March 4, 1789).

The resolution of advice and consent of the Senate, under date of July 29, 1789, and attested by Sam. A. Otis, Secretary, is thus written in D. S., 122 C. C. Papers, Resolve Book, folio 146:

> The Senate having duly considered the "Convention between his Most Christian Majesty and the United States of America, for the purpose of defining and establishing the Functions and Privileges of their respective Consuls and Vice Consuls"—transmitted to the Senate by the President of the United States, thro' the Secretary for Foreign Affairs—
>
> Resolved Unanimously, That the Senate do consent to the said Convention, and advise the President of the United States to Ratify the same.
>
> Ordered, That the Secretary of the Senate make the above communication to the President of the United States.

The wording of the last paragraph differs somewhat from that of the resolution as printed in Executive Journal, I, 8–9, which reads: "*Ordered*, That the Secretary of the Senate carry an attested copy of the above resolution to the President of the United States."

Thus the present practice of the Senate, which is to send to the President an attested resolution of its action on a treaty, has this original precedent.

The Ratifications

There is now in the Department of State file a facsimile of the United States instrument of ratification, obtained from the French archives. It has the signature of Washington and is under the Great Seal, but is not attested. The date thereof, September 9, 1789, has hitherto been lacking. The delay in the ratification, from July 29, 1789, the date of the Senate resolution, is explained by the following instructions which were sent by Jay to William Short, Chargé d'Affaires at Paris, under date of September 17:

> It was not until very lately that all Doubts respecting the Seal of the United States were removed, and this Circumstance will account for the Ratification of the Consular Convention having been postponed until then. You will now receive it herewith enclosed, and it is the Desire of the President that you present it for Exchange to the Minister without Delay, and transmit the one you will receive on their Part by the first good Opportunity, that as soon as it shall arrive the Convention may be published and take Effect. (D. S., 121 C. C. Papers, Foreign Letters, folios 325–26.)

October 1, 1788, is the date appearing in the French instrument of ratification. It is certainly erroneous, as the treaty was signed on November 14, 1788. The letter of William Short, quoted below, does not make the matter wholly clear; but seemingly the ratification was prepared at or about the time that the treaty was signed, with perhaps a space left for the date, which was erroneously filled in later.

There are other points to be mentioned regarding the French instrument of ratification. Its concluding words are "Donné à Versailles le premier octobre l'an de grace mil sept-cent quatre-vingt-huit, et de notre règne le quatorzième." Here there is clearly an error, for Louis XVI succeeded to the throne of France on May 10, 1774; the autumn of 1788 was therefore in the fifteenth year of his reign.

Furthermore, in the opening language of the French instrument of ratification, after the words "signé le 14 Novembre de," appears an erasure, blank and about one and one-half inches in length, followed by "à Versailles." What was originally there written is difficult to imagine; the space would permit the insertion of about eleven letters of the script used. There is an equivalent blank in a translation, in the handwriting of Jefferson, which is in the Department of State file.

The Exchange of Ratifications

January 6, 1790, appears to be the date of the exchange of ratifications, according to the letter of William Short, Chargé d'Affaires, dated that day at Paris and quoted below. Doubtless the exchange took place at the time of the signature of the protocol of exchange; that date was subsequent to the term of one year after signature prescribed in Article 16 of the treaty.

> I have at length received the ratification of the consular convention & signed the article of exchange, both of which I have the honor of forwarding to you by the way of Havre. The ratification was made out last year at the time of the convention being signed & remained in one of the bureaux unknown to the minister, where it only waited his signature. I mention the circumstance that it may explain to you the date & at the same time the delay. The article of exchange by which the duration of the convention is to be calculated is dated the first day of the year although signed only to-day. (D. S., 1 Despatches, France, No. 16, January 6, 1790.)

No original of the protocol of exchange is in the Department of State file, which contains, however, a translation thereof by John Pintard and also a facsimile of the original, obtained from the French archives.

The Translation

The basis of the translation of the convention which is here printed is that enclosed by Jefferson in his elaborate report to Jay of November 14, 1788, the day of the signature of the treaty (Diplomatic Correspondence, 1783–1789, II, 193–231). In that report, at page 195 Jefferson wrote:

> I add No. 5, the copy of a translation which I have put into their [the French] hands, with a request that if they find any passages, in which the sense of the original is not faithfully rendered, they will point them out to me; otherwise, we may consider it as having their approbation. This and the [unratified] convention of [July 29,] 1784 (marked No. 1) are placed side by side, so as to present to the eye, with less trouble, the changes made; and I enclose a number of printed copies of them for the use of the members who will have to decide on the ratification. It is desirable that the ratification should be sent here for exchange as soon as possible.

There seems to be no doubt that that translation of the two conventions, printed in parallel columns, with the convention of 1788 on the right, was before the Senate (Executive Journal, I, 7). The paper, which is entirely in English, although both conventions—that of 1784, which did not go into force, and that of 1788—were signed in French only, may now be found in 47 C. C. Papers, folios 249–58. That copy of the printed translation of the 1788 convention has various written corrections or changes, probably made pursuant to the directions given by the Senate to Jay on June 17, 1789, to "examine the translation of the Consular Convention, and report his opinion as to its fidelity." A facsimile of the corrected print is in the Department of State file; the translation, as so altered, is that which is in the Statutes at Large and which has been generally used since. It is the one here printed.

The convention of November 14, 1788, was a revision of the convention of July 29, 1784, which had proved unacceptable to Congress and had not been ratified. The original of the 1784 convention is in 47 C. C. Papers, folios 219–35. The date in that original is July 29, 1783, a very strange error, as there is no doubt whatever that the year was 1784. There is a translation of the 1784 convention in Secret Journals of Congress, IV, 146–58.

The Proclamation

The original proclamation of April 9, 1790, has not been found, and there appears no official record thereof; but it was published at the time (*e. g.*, the Daily Advertiser, New York, April 12, 1790). A facsimile of the newspaper print is now in the Department of State file. That print shows that the proclamation was in customary form, under the Great Seal, signed by Washington, and attested by Jefferson as Secretary of State. There is no indication in its recitals that the convention was signed in French; and the text set forth is the English translation above mentioned and here printed.

Treaty Series, No. 105
8 Statutes at Large, 116-30

16

GREAT BRITAIN : NOVEMBER 19, 1794

The Jay Treaty. Treaty of Amity, Commerce, and Navigation, signed at London November 19, 1794, with additional article. Original in English.

Submitted to the Senate June 8, 1795. Resolution of advice and consent, on condition, June 24, 1795. Ratified by the United States August 14, 1795. Ratified by Great Britain October 28, 1795. Ratifications exchanged at London October 28, 1795. Proclaimed February 29, 1796.

Treaty of Amity Commerce and Navigation, between His Britannick Majesty;—and The United States of America, by Their President, with the advice and consent of Their Senate.

His Britannick Majesty and the United States of America, being desirous by a Treaty of Amity, Commerce and Navigation to terminate their Differences in such a manner, as without reference to the Merits of Their respective Complaints and Pretensions, may be the best calculated to produce mutual satisfaction and good understanding: And also to regulate the Commerce and Navigation between Their respective Countries, Territories and People, in such a manner as to render the same reciprocally beneficial and satisfactory; They have respectively named their Plenipotentiaries, and given them Full powers to treat of, and conclude, the said Treaty, that is to say; His Brittanick Majesty has named for His Plenipotentiary, The Right Honourable William Wyndham Baron Grenville of Wotton, One of His Majesty's Privy Council, and His Majesty's Principal Secretary of State for Foreign Affairs; and The President of the said United States, by and with the advice and Consent of the Senate thereof, hath appointed for Their Plenipotentiary The Honourable John Jay, Chief Justice of the said United States and Their Envoy Extraordinary to His Majesty, who have agreed on, and concluded the following Articles

Article 1.

There shall be a firm inviolable and universal Peace, and a true and sincere Friendship between His Britannick Majesty, His Heirs and Successors, and the United States of America; and between their

respective Countries, Territories, Cities, Towns and People of every Degree, without Exception of Persons or Places.

ARTICLE 2.

His Majesty will withdraw all His Troops and Garrisons from all Posts and Places within the Boundary Lines assigned by the Treaty of Peace[1] to the United States. This Evacuation shall take place on or before the first Day of June One thousand seven hundred and ninety six, and all the proper Measures shall in the interval be taken by concert between the Government of the United States, and His Majesty's Governor General in America, for settling the previous arrangements which may be necessary respecting the delivery of the said Posts: The United States in the mean Time at Their discretion extending their settlements to any part within the said boundary line, except within the precincts or Jurisdiction of any of the said Posts. All Settlers and Traders, within the Precincts or Jurisdiction of the said Posts, shall continue to enjoy, unmolested, all their property of every kind, and shall be protected therein. They shall be at full liberty to remain there, or to remove with all or any part of their Effects; and it shall also be free to them to sell their Lands, Houses, or Effects, or to retain the property thereof, at their discretion; such of them as shall continue to reside within the said Boundary Lines shall not be compelled to become Citizens of the United States, or to take any Oath of allegiance to the Government thereof, but they shall be at full liberty so to do, if they think proper, and they shall make and declare their Election within one year after the Evacuation aforesaid. And all persons who shall continue there after the expiration of the said year, without having declared their intention of remaining Subjects of His Britannick Majesty, shall be considered as having elected to become Citizens of the United States.

ARTICLE 3.

It is agreed that it shall at all Times be free to His Majesty's Subjects, and to the Citizens of the United States, and also to the Indians dwelling on either side of the said Boundary Line freely to pass and repass by Land, or Inland Navigation, into the respective Territories and Countries of the Two Parties on the Continent of America (the Country within the Limits of the Hudson's Bay Company only excepted) and to navigate all the Lakes, Rivers, and waters thereof, and freely to carry on trade and commerce with each other. But it is

[1] Document 11.

understood, that this Article does not extend to the admission of Vessels of the United States into the Sea Ports, Harbours, Bays, or Creeks of His Majesty's said Territories; nor into such parts of the Rivers in His Majesty's said Territories as are between the mouth thereof, and the highest Port of Entry from the Sea, except in small vessels trading bonâ fide between Montreal and Quebec, under such regulations as shall be established to prevent the possibility of any Frauds in this respect. Nor to the admission of British vessels from the Sea into the Rivers of the United States, beyond the highest Ports of Entry for Foreign Vessels from the Sea. The River Mississippi, shall however, according to the Treaty of Peace [1] be entirely open to both Parties; And it is further agreed, That all the ports and places on its Eastern side, to whichsoever of the parties belonging, may freely be resorted to, and used by both parties, in as ample a manner as any of the Atlantic Ports or Places of the United States, or any of the Ports or Places of His Majesty in Great Britain.

All Goods and Merchandize whose Importation into His Majesty's said Territories in America, shall not be entirely prohibited, may freely, for the purposes of Commerce, be carried into the same in the manner aforesaid, by the Citizens of the United States, and such Goods and Merchandize shall be subject to no higher or other Duties than would be payable by His Majesty's Subjects on the Importation of the same from Europe into the said Territories. And in like manner, all Goods and Merchandize whose Importation into the United States shall not be wholly prohibited, may freely, for the purposes of Commerce, be carried into the same, in the manner aforesaid, by His Majesty's Subjects, and such Goods and Merchandize shall be subject to no higher or other Duties than would be payable by the Citizens of the United States on the Importation of the same in American Vessels into the Atlantic Ports of the said States. And all Goods not prohibited to be exported from the said Territories respectively, may in like manner be carried out of the same by the Two Parties respectively, paying Duty as aforesaid

No Duty of Entry shall ever be levied by either Party on Peltries brought by Land, or Inland Navigation into the said Territories respectively, nor shall the Indians passing or repassing with their own proper Goods and Effects of whatever nature, pay for the same any Impost or Duty whatever. But Goods in Bales, or other large Packages unusual among Indians shall not be considered as Goods belonging bonâ fide to Indians.

[1] Document 11.

No higher or other Tolls or Rates of Ferriage than what are, or shall be payable by Natives, shall be demanded on either side; And no Duties shall be payable on any Goods which shall merely be carried over any of the Portages, or carrying Places on either side, for the purpose of being immediately reimbarked, and carried to some other Place or Places. But as by this Stipulation it is only meant to secure to each Party a free passage across the Portages on both sides, it is agreed, that this Exemption from Duty shall extend only to such Goods as are carried in the usual and direct Road across the Portage, and are not attempted to be in any manner sold or exchanged during their passage across the same, and proper Regulations may be established to prevent the possibility of any Frauds in this respect.

As this Article is intended to render in a great Degree the local advantages of each Party common to both, and thereby to promote a disposition favourable to Friendship and good neighbourhood, It is agreed, that the respective Governments will mutually promote this amicable Intercourse, by causing speedy and impartial Justice to be done, and necessary protection to be extended, to all who may be concerned therein.

ARTICLE 4.

Whereas it is uncertain whether the River Mississippi extends so far to the Northward as to be intersected by a Line to be drawn due West from the Lake of the woods in the manner mentioned in the Treaty of Peace [1] between His Majesty and the United States, it is agreed, that measures shall be taken in Concert between His Majesty's Government in America, and the Government of the United States, for making a joint Survey of the said River, from one Degree of Latitude below the falls of St Anthony to the principal Source or Sources of the said River, and also of the parts adjacent thereto, And that if on the result of such Survey it should appear that the said River would not be intersected by such a Line as is above mentioned; The two Parties will thereupon proceed by amicable negotiation to regulate the Boundary Line in that quarter as well as all other Points to be adjusted between the said Parties, according to Justice and mutual Convenience, and in Conformity, to the Intent of the said Treaty.

---

[1] Document 11.

Article 5.

Whereas doubts have arisen what River was truly intended under the name of the River St Croix mentioned in the said Treaty of Peace[1] and forming a part of the boundary therein described, that question shall be referred to the final Decision of Commissioners to be appointed in the following Manner—Viz—

One Commissioner shall be named by His Majesty, and one by the President of the United States, by and with the advice and Consent of the Senate thereof, and the said two Commissioners shall agree on the choice of a third, or, if they cannot so agree, They shall each propose one Person, and of the two names so proposed one shall be drawn by Lot, in the presence of the two original Commissioners. And the three Commissioners so appointed shall be Sworn impartially to examine and decide the said question according to such Evidence as shall respectively be laid before Them on the part of the British Government and of the United States. The said Commissioners shall meet at Halifax and shall have power to adjourn to such other place or places as they shall think fit. They shall have power to appoint a Secretary, and to employ such Surveyors or other Persons as they shall judge necessary. The said Commissioners shall by a Declaration under their Hands and Seals, decide what River is the River St Croix intended by the Treaty. The said Declaration shall contain a description of the said River, and shall particularize the Latitude and Longitude of its mouth and of its Source. Duplicates of this Declaration and of the Statements of their Accounts, and of the Journal of their proceedings, shall be delivered by them to the Agent of His Majesty, and to the Agent of the United States, who may be respectively appointed and authorized to manage the business on behalf of the respective Governments. And both parties agree to consider such decision as final and conclusive, so as that the same shall never thereafter be called into question, or made the subject of dispute or difference between them.

Article 6.

Whereas it is alledged by divers British Merchants and others His Majesty's Subjects, that Debts to a considerable amount which were bonâ fide contracted before the Peace, still remain owing to them by Citizens or Inhabitants of the United States, and that by the operation of various lawful Impediments since the Peace, not only the full

[1] Document 11.

recovery of the said Debts has been delayed, but also the Value and Security thereof, have been in several instances impaired and lessened, so that by the ordinary course of Judicial proceedings the British Creditors, cannot now obtain and actually have and receive full and adequate Compensation for the losses and damages which they have thereby sustained: It is agreed that in all such Cases where full Compensation for such losses and damages cannot, for whatever reason, be actually obtained had and received by the said Creditors in the ordinary course of Justice, The United States will make full and complete Compensation for the same to the said Creditors; But it is distinctly understood, that this provision is to extend to such losses only, as have been occasioned by the lawful impediments aforesaid, and is not to extend to losses occasioned by such Insolvency of the Debtors or other Causes as would equally have operated to produce such loss, if the said impediments had not existed, nor to such losses or damages as have been occasioned by the manifest delay or negligence, or wilful omission of the Claimant.

For the purpose of ascertaining the amount of any such losses and damages, Five Commissioners shall be appointed and authorized to meet and act in manner following—viz—Two of them shall be appointed by His Majesty, Two of them by the President of the United States by and with the advice and consent of the Senate thereof, and the fifth, by the unanimous voice of the other Four; and if they should not agree in such Choice, then the Commissioners named by the two parties shall respectively propose one person, and of the two names so proposed, one shall be drawn by Lot in the presence of the Four Original Commissioners. When the Five Commissioners thus appointed shall first meet, they shall before they proceed to act respectively, take the following Oath or Affirmation in the presence of each other, which Oath or Affirmation, being so taken, and duly attested, shall be entered on the Record of their Proceedings,—viz.—I. A: B: One of the Commissioners appointed in pursuance of the 6th Article of the Treaty of Amity, Commerce and Navigation between His Britannick Majesty and The United States of America, do solemnly swear (or affirm) that I will honestly, diligently, impartially, and carefully examine, and to the best of my Judgement, according to Justice and Equity decide all such Complaints, as under the said Article shall be preferred to the said Commissioners: and that I will forbear to act as a Commissioner in any Case in which I may be personally interested.

Three of the said Commissioners shall constitute a Board, and shall have power to do any act appertaining to the said Commission,

provided that one of the Commissioners named on each side, and the Fifth Commissioner shall be present, and all decisions shall be made by the Majority of the Voices of the Commissioners then present. Eighteen Months from the Day on which the said Commissioners shall form a Board, and be ready to proceed to Business are assigned for receiving Complaints and applications, but they are nevertheless authorized in any particular Cases in which it shall appear to them to be reasonable and just to extend the said Term of Eighteen Months, for any term not exceeding Six Months after the expiration thereof. The said Commissioners shall first meet at Philadelphia, but they shall have power to adjourn from Place to Place as they shall see Cause.

The said Commissioners in examining the Complaints and applications so preferred to them, are impowered and required in pursuance of the true intent and meaning of this article to take into their Consideration all claims whether of principal or interest, or balances of principal and interest, and to determine the same respectively according to the merits of the several Cases, due regard being had to all the Circumstances thereof, and as Equity and Justice shall appear to them to require. And the said Commissioners shall have power to examine all such Persons as shall come before them on Oath or Affirmation touching the premises; and also to receive in Evidence according as they may think most consistent with Equity and Justice all written Depositions, or Books or Papers, or Copies or Extracts thereof. Every such Deposition, Book or Paper or Copy or Extract being duly authenticated either according to the legal Forms now respectively existing in the two Countries, or in such other manner as the said Commissioners shall see cause to require or allow.

The Award of the said Commissioners or of any three of them as aforesaid shall in all Cases be final and conclusive, both as to the Justice of the Claim, and to the amount of the Sum to be paid to the Creditor or Claimant.—And the United States undertake to cause the Sum so awarded to be paid in Specie to such Creditor or Claimant without deduction; and at such Time or Times, and at such Place or Places, as shall be awarded by the said Commissioners, and on Condition of such Releases or assignments to be given by the Creditor or Claimant as by the said Commissioners may be directed; Provided always that no such payment shall be fixed by the said Commissioners to take place sooner then twelve months from the Day of the Exchange of the Ratifications of this Treaty.

ARTICLE 7.

Whereas Complaints have been made by divers Merchants and others, Citizens of the United States, that during the course of the War in which His Majesty is now engaged they have sustained considerable losses and damage by reason of irregular or illegal Captures or Condemnations of their vessels and other property under Colour of authority or Commissions from His Majesty, and that from various Circumstances belonging to the said Cases adequate Compensation for the losses and damages so sustained cannot now be actually obtained, had and received by the ordinary Course of Judicial proceedings; It is agreed that in all such Cases where adequate Compensation cannot for whatever reason be now actually obtained, had and received by the said Merchants and others in the ordinary course of Justice, full and Complete Compensation for the same will be made by the British Government to the said Complainants. But it is distinctly understood, that this provision is not to extend to such losses or damages as have been occasioned by the manifest delay or negligence, or wilful omission of the Claimant.

That for the purpose of ascertaining the amount of any such losses and damages Five Commissioners shall be appointed and authorized to act in London exactly in the manner directed with respect to those mentioned in the preceding Article, and after having taken the same Oath or Affirmation (mutatis mutandis). The same term of Eighteen Months is also assigned for the reception of Claims, and they are in like manner authorised to extend the same in particular Cases. They shall receive Testimony, Books, Papers and Evidence in the same latitude, and exercise the like discretion, and powers respecting that subject, and shall decide the Claims in question, according to the merits of the several Cases, and to Justice Equity and the Laws of Nations. The award of the said Commissioners or any such three of them as aforesaid, shall in all Cases be final and conclusive both as to the Justice of the Claim and the amount of the Sum to be paid to the Claimant; and His Britannick Majesty undertakes to cause the same to be paid to such Claimant in Specie, without any Deduction, at such place or places, and at such Time or Times as shall be awarded by the said Commissioners and on Condition of such releases or assignments to be given by the Claimant, as by the said Commissioners may be directed.

And whereas certain merchants and others, His Majesty's Subjects, complain that in the course of the war they have sustained Loss and Damage by reason of the Capture of their Vessels and Merchandize

taken within the Limits and Jurisdiction of the States, and brought into the Ports of the same, or taken by Vessels originally armed in Ports of the said States:

It is agreed that in all such cases where Restitution shall not have been made agreably to the tenor of the letter from Mr Jefferson to Mr Hammond dated at Philadelphia September 5th 1793. A Copy of which is annexed [1] to this Treaty, the Complaints of the parties shall be, and hereby are referred to the Commissioners to be appointed by virtue of this article, who are hereby authorized and required to proceed in the like manner relative to these as to the other Cases committed to them, and the United States undertake to pay to the Complainants or Claimants in specie without deduction the amount of such Sums as shall be awarded to them respectively by the said Commissioners and at the times and places which in such awards shall be specified, and on Condition of such Releases or assignments to be given by the Claimants as in the said awards may be directed: And it is further agreed that not only the now existing Cases of both descriptions, but also all such as shall exist at the Time, of exchanging the Ratifications of this Treaty shall be considered as being within the provisions intent and meaning of this article.

Article 8.

It is further agreed that the Commissioners mentioned in this and in the two preceding articles shall be respectively paid in such manner, as shall be agreed between the two parties, such agreement being to be settled at the Time of the exchange of the Ratifications of this Treaty.[2] And all other Expences attending the said Commissions shall be defrayed jointly by the Two Parties, the same being previously ascertained and allowed by the Majority of the Commissioners. And in the case of Death, Sickness or necessary absence, the place of every such Commissioner respectively, shall be supplied in the same manner as such Commissioner was first appointed, and the new Commissioners shall take the same Oath, or Affirmation, and do the same Duties.

Article 9.

It is agreed, that British Subjects who now hold Lands in the Territories of the United States, and American Citizens who now hold Lands in the Dominions of His Majesty, shall continue to hold them according to the nature and Tenure of their respective Estates and

[1] The copy of the letter follows the signatures to the treaty.
[2] See the note regarding Article 8.

Titles therein, and may grant Sell or Devise the same to whom they please, in like manner as if they were Natives; and that neither they nor their Heirs or assigns shall, so far as may respect the said Lands, and the legal remedies incident thereto, be regarded as Aliens.

ARTICLE 10.

Neither the Debts due from Individuals of the one Nation, to Individuals of the other, nor shares nor monies, which they may have in the public Funds, or in the public or private Banks shall ever, in any Event of war, or national differences, be sequestered, or confiscated, it being unjust and impolitick that Debts and Engagements contracted and made by Individuals having confidence in each other, and in their respective Governments, should ever be destroyed or impaired by national authority, on account of national Differences and Discontents.

ARTICLE 11.

It is agreed between His Majesty and the United States of America, that there shall be a reciprocal and entirely perfect Liberty of Navigation and Commerce, between their respective People, in the manner, under the Limitations, and on the Conditions specified in the following Articles.

ARTICLE 12.[1]

His Majesty Consents that it shall and may be lawful, during the time hereinafter Limited, for the Citizens of the United States, to carry to any of His Majesty's Islands and Ports in the West Indies from the United States in their own Vessels, not being above the burthen of Seventy Tons, any Goods or Merchandizes, being of the Growth, Manufacture, or Produce of the said States, which it is, or may be lawful to carry to the said Islands or Ports from the said States in British Vessels, and that the said American Vessels shall be subject there to no other or higher Tonnage Duties or Charges, than shall be payable by British Vessels, in the Ports of the United States; and that the Cargoes of the said American Vessels, shall be subject there to no other or higher Duties or Charges, than shall be payable on the like Articles, if imported there from the said States in British vessels.

And His Majesty also consents that it shall be lawful for the said American Citizens to purchase, load and carry away, in their said vessels to the United States from the said Islands and Ports, all such articles being of the Growth, Manufacture or Produce of the said Islands, as may now by Law be carried from thence to the said States

[1] This article was in part suspended by the additional article.

in British Vessels, and subject only to the same Duties and Charges on Exportation to which British Vessels and their Cargoes are or shall be subject in similar circumstances.

Provided always that the said American vessels do carry and land their Cargoes in the United States only, it being expressly agreed and declared that during the Continuance of this article, the United States will prohibit and restrain the carrying any Melasses, Sugar, Coffee, Cocoa or Cotton in American vessels, either from His Majesty's Islands or from the United States, to any part of the World, except the United States, reasonable Sea Stores excepted. Provided also, that it shall and may be lawful during the same period for British vessels to import from the said Islands into the United States, and to export from the United States to the said Islands, all Articles whatever being of the Growth, Produce or Manufacture of the said Islands, or of the United States respectively, which now may, by the Laws of the said States, be so imported and exported. And that the Cargoes of the said British vessels, shall be subject to no other or higher Duties or Charges, than shall be payable on the same articles if so imported or exported in American Vessels.

It is agreed that this Article, and every Matter and Thing therein contained, shall continue to be in Force, during the Continuance of the war in which His Majesty is now engaged; and also for Two years from and after the Day of the signature of the Preliminary or other Articles of Peace by which the same may be terminated

And it is further agreed that at the expiration of the said Term, the Two Contracting Parties will endeavour further to regulate their Commerce in this respect, according to the situation in which His Majesty may then find Himself with respect to the West Indies, and with a view to such Arrangements, as may best conduce to the mutual advantage and extension of Commerce. And the said Parties will then also renew their discussions, and endeavour to agree, whether in any and what cases Neutral Vessels shall protect Enemy's property; and in what cases provisions and other articles not generally Contraband may become such. But in the mean time their Conduct towards each other in these respects, shall be regulated by the articles hereinafter inserted on those subjects.

Article 13.

His Majesty consents that the Vessels belonging to the Citizens of the United States of America, shall be admitted and Hospitably received in all the Sea Ports and Harbours of the British Territories in the East Indies: and that the Citizens of the said United States,

may freely carry on a Trade between the said Territories and the said United States, in all articles of which the Importation or Exportation respectively to or from the said Territories, shall not be entirely prohibited; Provided only, that it shall not be lawful for them in any time of War between the British Government, and any other Power or State whatever, to export from the said Territories without the special Permission of the British Government there, any Military Stores, or Naval Stores, or Rice. The Citizens of the United States shall pay for their Vessels when admitted into the said Ports, no other or higher Tonnage Duty than shall be payable on British Vessels when admitted into the Ports of the United States. And they shall pay no other or higher Duties or Charges on the importation or exportation of the Cargoes of the said Vessels, than shall be payable on the same articles when imported or exported in British Vessels. But it is expressly agreed, that the Vessels of the United States shall not carry any of the articles exported by them from the said British Territories to any Port or Place, except to some Port or Place in America, where the same shall be unladen, and such Regulations shall be adopted by both Parties, as shall from time to time be found necessary to enforce the due and faithfull observance of this Stipulation: It is also understood that the permission granted by this article is not to extend to allow the Vessels of the United States to carry on any part of the Coasting Trade of the said British Territories, but Vessels going with their original Cargoes, or part thereof, from one port of discharge to another, are not to be considered as carrying on the Coasting Trade. Neither is this Article to be construed to allow the Citizens of the said States to settle or reside within the said Territories, or to go into the interior parts thereof, without the permission of the British Government established there; and if any transgression should be attempted against the Regulations of the British Government in this respect, the observance of the same shall and may be enforced against the Citizens of America in the same manner as against British Subjects, or others transgressing the same rule. And the Citizens of the United States, whenever they arrive in any Port or Harbour in the said Territories, or if they should be permitted in manner aforesaid, to go to any other place therein, shall always be subject to the Laws, Government and Jurisdiction, of what nature, established in such Harbour, Port or Place according as the same may be: The Citizens of the United States, may also touch for refreshment, at the Island of S[t] Helena, but subject in all respects to such regulations, as the British Government may from time to time establish there.

Article 14.

There shall be between all the Dominions of His Majesty in Europe, and the Territories of the United States, a reciprocal and perfect liberty of Commerce and Navigation. The people and Inhabitants of the Two Countries respectively, shall have liberty, freely and securely, and without hindrance and molestation, to come with their Ships and Cargoes to the Lands, Countries, Cities, Ports Places and Rivers within the Dominions and Territories aforesaid, to enter into the same, to resort there, and to remain and reside there, without any limitation of Time: also to hire and possess, Houses and warehouses for the purposes of their Commerce; and generally the Merchants and Traders on each side, shall enjoy the most complete protection and Security for their Commerce; but subject always, as to what respects this article, to the Laws and Statutes of the Two Countries respectively.

Article 15.

It is agreed, that no other or higher Duties shall be paid by the Ships or Merchandize of the one Party in the Ports of the other, than such as are paid by the like vessels or Merchandize of all other Nations. Nor shall any other or higher Duty be imposed in one Country on the importation of any articles, the growth, produce, or manufacture of the other, than are or shall be payable on the importation of the like articles being of the growth, produce or manufacture of any other Foreign Country. Nor shall any prohibition be imposed, on the exportation or importation of any articles to or from the Territories of the Two Parties respectively which shall not equally extend to all other Nations.

But the British Government reserves to itself the right of imposing on American Vessels entering into the British Ports in Europe a Tonnage Duty, equal to that which shall be payable by British Vessels in the Ports of America: And also such Duty as may be adequate to countervail the difference of Duty now payable on the importation of European and Asiatic Goods when imported into the United States in British or in American Vessels.

The Two Parties agree to treat for the more exact equalization of the Duties on the respective Navigation of their Subjects and People in such manner as may be most beneficial to the two Countries. The arrangements for this purpose shall be made at the same time with those mentioned at the Conclusion of the 12th Article of this Treaty, and are to be considered as a part thereof. In the interval it is agreed, that the United States will not impose any new or additional Tonnage

Duties on British Vessels, nor increase the now subsisting difference between the Duties payable on the importation of any articles in British or in American Vessels.

ARTICLE 16.

It shall be free for the Two Contracting Parties respectively, to appoint Consuls for the protection of Trade, to reside in the Dominions and Territories aforesaid; and the said Consuls shall enjoy those Liberties and Rights which belong to them by reason of their Function. But before any Consul shall act as such, he shall be in the usual forms approved and admitted by the party to whom he is sent, and it is hereby declared to be lawful and proper, that in case of illegal or improper Conduct towards the Laws or Government, a Consul may either be punished according to Law, if the Laws will reach the Case, or be dismissed or even sent back, the offended Government assigning to the other, Their reasons for the same.

Either of the Parties may except from the residence of Consuls such particular Places, as such party shall judge proper to be so excepted.

ARTICLE 17.

It is agreed that, in all Cases where Vessels shall be captured or detained on just suspicion of having on board Enemy's property or of carrying to the Enemy, any of the articles which are Contraband of war; The said Vessel shall be brought to the nearest or most convenient Port, and if any property of an Enemy, should be found on board such Vessel, that part only which belongs to the Enemy shall be made prize, and the Vessel shall be at liberty to proceed with the remainder without any Impediment. And it is agreed that all proper measures shall be taken to prevent delay, in deciding the Cases of Ships or Cargoes so brought in for adjudication, and in the payment or recovery of any Indemnification adjudged or agreed to be paid to the masters or owners of such Ships.

ARTICLE 18.

In order to regulate what is in future to be esteemed Contraband of war, it is agreed that under the said Denomination shall be comprized all Arms and Implements serving for the purposes of war by Land or Sea; such as Cannon, Muskets, Mortars, Petards, Bombs, Grenades Carcasses, Saucisses, Carriages for Cannon, Musket rests, Bandoliers, Gunpowder, Match, Saltpetre, Ball, Pikes, Swords, Headpieces Cuirasses Halberts Lances Javelins, Horsefurniture, Holsters, Belts

and, generally all other Implements of war, as also Timber for Ship building, Tar or Rosin, Copper in Sheets, Sails, Hemp, and Cordage, and generally whatever may serve directly to the equipment of Vessels, unwrought Iron and Fir planks only excepted, and all the above articles are hereby declared to be just objects of Confiscation, whenever they are attempted to be carried to an Enemy.

And Whereas the difficulty of agreeing on the precise Cases in which alone Provisions and other articles not generally contraband may be regarded as such, renders it expedient to provide against the inconveniences and misunderstandings which might thence arise: It is further agreed that whenever any such articles so becoming Contraband according to the existing Laws of Nations, shall for that reason be seized, the same shall not be confiscated, but the owners thereof shall be speedily and completely indemnified; and the Captors, or in their default the Government under whose authority they act, shall pay to the Masters or Owners of such Vessels the full value of all such Articles, with a reasonable mercantile Profit thereon, together with the Freight, and also the Demurrage incident to such Detension.

And Whereas it frequently happens that vessels sail for a Port or Place belonging to an Enemy, without knowing that the same is either besieged, blockaded or invested; It is agreed, that every Vessel so circumstanced may be turned away from such Port or Place, but she shall not be detained, nor her Cargo, if not Contraband, be confiscated; unless after notice she shall again attempt to enter; but She shall be permitted to go to any other Port or Place She may think proper: Nor shall any vessel or Goods of either party, that may have entered into such Port or Place before the same was besieged, blockaded or invested by the other, and be found therein after the reduction or surrender of such place, be liable to confiscation, but shall be restored to the Owners or proprietors thereof.

Article 19.

And that more abundant Care may be taken for the security of the respective Subjects and Citizens of the Contracting Parties, and to prevent their suffering Injuries by the Men of war, or Privateers of either Party, all Commanders of Ships of war and Privateers and all others the said Subjects and Citizens shall forbear doing any Damage to those of the other party, or committing any Outrage against them, and if they act to the contrary, they shall be punished, and shall also be bound in their Persons and Estates to make satisfaction and reparation for all Damages, and the interest thereof, of whatever nature the said Damages may be.

For this cause all Commanders of Privateers before they receive their Commissions shall hereafter be obliged to give before a Competent Judge, sufficient security by at least Two responsible Sureties, who have no interest in the said Privateer, each of whom, together with the said Commander, shall be jointly and severally bound in the Sum of Fifteen hundred pounds Sterling, or if such Ships be provided with above One hundred and fifty Seamen or Soldiers, in the Sum of Three thousand pounds sterling, to satisfy all Damages and Injuries, which the said Privateer or her Officers or Men, or any of them may do or commit during their Cruize contrary to the tenor of this Treaty, or to the Laws and Instructions for regulating their Conduct; and further that in all Cases of Aggressions the said Commissions shall be revoked and annulled.

It is also agreed that whenever a Judge of a Court of Admiralty of either of the Parties, shall pronounce sentence against any Vessel or Goods or Property belonging to the Subjects or Citizens of the other Party a formal and duly authenticated Copy of all the proceedings in the Cause, and of the said Sentence, shall if required be delivered to the Commander of the said Vessel, without the smallest delay, he paying all legal Fees and Demands for the same.

Article 20.

It is further agreed that both the said Contracting Parties, shall not only refuse to receive any Pirates into any of their Ports, Havens, or Towns, or permit any of their Inhabitants to receive, protect, harbour conceal or assist them in any manner, but will bring to condign punishment all such Inhabitants as shall be guilty of such Acts or offences.

And all their Ships with the Goods or Merchandizes taken by them and brought into the port of either of the said Parties, shall be seized, as far as they can be discovered and shall be restored to the owners or their Factors or Agents duly deputed and authorized in writing by them (proper Evidence being first given in the Court of Admiralty for proving the property,) even in case such effects should have passed into other hands by Sale, if it be proved that the Buyers knew or had good reason to believe, or suspect that they had been piratically taken.

Article 21.

It is likewise agreed that the Subjects and Citizens of the Two Nations, shall not do any acts of Hostility or Violence against each other, nor accept Commissions or Instructions so to act from any Foreign Prince or State, Enemies to the other party, nor shall the

Enemies of one of the parties be permitted to invite or endeavour to enlist in their military service any of the Subjects or Citizens of the other party; and the Laws against all such Offences and Aggressions shall be punctually executed. And if any Subject or Citizen of the said Parties respectively shall accept any Foreign Commission or Letters of Marque for Arming any Vessel to act as a Privateer against the other party, and be taken by the other party, it is hereby declared to be lawful for the said party to treat and punish the said Subject or Citizen, having such Commission or Letters of Marque as a Pirate.

Article 22.

It is expressly stipulated that neither of the said Contracting Parties will order or Authorize any Acts of Reprisal against the other on Complaints of Injuries or Damages until the said party shall first have presented to the other a Statement thereof, verified by competent proof and Evidence, and demanded Justice and Satisfaction, and the same shall either have been refused or unreasonably delayed.

Article 23.

The Ships of war of each of the Contracting Parties, shall at all times be hospitably received in the Ports of the other, their Officers and Crews paying due respect to the Laws and Government of the Country. The officers shall be treated with that respect, which is due to the Commissions which they bear. And if any Insult should be offered to them by any of the Inhabitants, all offenders in this respect shall be punished as Disturbers of the Peace and Amity between the Two Countries.

And His Majesty consents, that in case an American Vessel should by stress of weather, Danger from Enemies, or other misfortune be reduced to the necessity of seeking Shelter in any of His Majesty's Ports, into which such Vessel could not in ordinary cases claim to be admitted; She shall on manifesting that necessity to the satisfaction of the Government of the place, be hospitably received, and be permitted to refit, and to purchace at the market price, such necessaries as she may stand in need of, conformably to such Orders and regulations as the Government of the place, having respect to the circumstances of each case shall prescribe. She shall not be allowed to break bulk or unload her Cargo, unless the same shall be bonâ fide necessary to her being refitted. Nor shall be permitted to sell any part of her Cargo, unless so much only as may be necessary to defray her expences, and then not without the express permission of the Govern-

ment of the place. Nor shall she be obliged to pay any Duties whatever, except only on such Articles, as she may be permitted to sell for the purpose aforesaid.

Article 24.

It shall not be lawful for any Foreign Privateers (not being Subjects or Citizens of either of the said Parties) who have Commissions from any other Prince or State in Enmity with either Nation, to arm their Ships in the Ports of either of the said Parties, nor to sell what they have taken, nor in any other manner to exchange the same, nor shall they be allowed to purchase more provisions than shall be necessary for their going to the nearest Port of that Prince or State from whom they obtained their Commissions.

Article 25.

It shall be lawful for the Ships of war and Privateers belonging to the said Parties respectively to carry whithersoever they please the Ships and Goods taken from their Enemies without being obliged to pay any Fee to the Officers of the Admiralty, or to any Judges whatever; nor shall the said Prizes when they arrive at, and enter the Ports of the said Parties be detained or seized, neither shall the Searchers or other Officers of those Places visit such Prizes (except for the purpose of preventing the Carrying of any part of the Cargo thereof on Shore in any manner contrary to the established Laws of Revenue, Navigation or Commerce) nor shall such Officers take Cognizance of the Validity of such Prizes; but they shall be at liberty to hoist Sail, and depart as speedily as may be, and carry their said Prizes to the place mentioned in their Commissions or Patents, which the Commanders of the said Ships of war or Privateers shall be obliged to shew. No Shelter or Refuge shall be given in their Ports to such as have made a Prize upon the Subjects or Citizens of either of the said Parties; but if forced by stress of weather or the Dangers of the Sea, to enter therein, particular care shall be taken to hasten their departure, and to cause them to retire as soon as possible. Nothing in this Treaty contained shall however be construed or operate contrary to former and existing Public Treaties with other Sovereigns or States. But the Two parties agree, that while they continue in amity neither of them will in future make any Treaty that shall be inconsistent with this or the preceding article.

Neither of the said parties shall permit the Ships or Goods belonging to the Subjects or Citizens of the other to be taken within Cannon Shot of the Coast, nor in any of the Bays, Ports or Rivers of their

Territories by Ships of war, or others having Commission from any Prince, Republic or State whatever. But in case it should so happen, the party whose Territorial Rights shall thus have been violated, shall use his utmost endeavours to obtain from the offending Party, full and ample satisfaction for the Vessel or Vessels so taken, whether the same be Vessels of war or Merchant Vessels.

Article 26.

If at any Time a Rupture should take place (which God forbid) between His Majesty and the United States, the Merchants and others of each of the Two Nations, residing in the Dominions of the other, shall have the privilege of remaining and continuing their Trade so long as they behave peaceably and commit no offence against the Laws, and in case their Conduct should render them suspected, and the respective Governments should think proper to order them to remove, the term of Twelve Months from the publication of the order shall be allowed them for that purpose to remove with their Families, Effects and Property, but this Favor shall not be extended to those who shall act contrary to the established Laws, and for greater certainty it is declared that such Rupture shall not be deemed to exist while negotiations for accommodating Differences shall be depending nor until the respective Ambassadors or Ministers, if such there shall be, shall be recalled, or sent home on account of such differences, and not on account of personal miscondut according to the nature and degrees of which both parties retain their Rights, either to request the recall or immediately to send home the Ambassador or Minister of the other; and that without prejudice to their mutual Friendship and good understanding.

Article 27.

It is further agreed that His Majesty and the United States on mutual Requisitions by them respectively or by their respective Ministers or Officers authorized to make the same will deliver up to Justice, all Persons who being charged with Murder or Forgery committed within the Jurisdiction of either, shall seek an Asylum within any of the Countries of the other, Provided that this shall only be done on such Evidence of Criminality as according to the Laws of the Place, where the Fugitive or Person so charged shall be found, would justify his apprehension and commitment for Tryal, if the offence had there been committed. The Expence of such apprehension and Delivery shall be borne and defrayed by those who make the Requisition and receive the Fugitive.

ARTICLE 28.

It is agreed that the first Ten Articles of this Treaty shall be permanent and that the subsequent Articles except the Twelfth shall be limited in their duration to Twelve years to be computed from the Day on which the Ratifications of this Treaty shall be exchanged, but subject to this Condition that whereas the said Twelfth Article will expire by the Limitation therein contained at the End of two years from the signing of the Preliminary or other Articles of Peace, which shall terminate the present War, in which His Majesty is engaged; It is agreed that proper Measures shall by Concert be taken for bringing the subject of that article into amicable Treaty and Discussion so early before the Expiration of the said Term, as that new Arrangements on that head may by that Time be perfected and ready to take place. But if it should unfortunately happen that His Majesty and the United States should not be able to agree on such new Arrangements, in that Case, all the Articles of this Treaty except the first Ten shall then cease and expire together.

Lastly. This Treaty when the same shall have been ratified by His Majesty, and by The President of the United States, by and with the advice and Consent of Their Senate, and the respective Ratifications mutually exchanged, shall be binding and obligatory on His Majesty and on the said States, and shall be by Them respectively executed and observed with punctuality, and the most sincere regard to good Faith. And Whereas it will be expedient in order the better to facilitate Intercourse and obviate Difficulties that other Articles be proposed and added to this Treaty, which Articles from want of time and other circumstances cannot now be perfected; It is agreed that the said Parties will from Time to Time readily treat of and concerning such Articles, and will sincerely endeavour so to form them, as that they may conduce to mutual convenience, and tend to promote mutual Satisfaction and Friendship; and that the said Articles after having been duly ratified, shall be added to, and make a part of this Treaty.

In Faith whereof We the Undersigned, Ministers Plenipotentiary of His Majesty The King of Great Britain; and the United States of America, have signed this present Treaty, and have caused to be affixed thereto, the Seal of Our Arms.

Done at London, this Nineteenth Day of November, One thousand seven hundred and ninety Four.

GRENVILLE [Seal] JOHN JAY [Seal]

[Annexed Copy of the Letter Mentioned in Article 7]

PHILADELPHIA *Septr 5th 1793.*

SIR, I am honored with yours[1] of August 30th Mine[1] of the 7th of that Month assured you that measures were taken for excluding from all further Asylum in our Ports Vessels armed in them to Cruize on Nations with which we are at Peace; and for the restoration of the Prizes the Lovely Lass, Prince William Henry, and the Jane of Dublin, and that should the measures for restitution fail in their Effect, The President considered it as incumbent on the United States to make compensation for the Vessels.

We are bound by our Treaties[2] with Three of the Belligerent Nations, by all the means in our Power to protect and defend their Vessels and Effects in our Ports, or waters, or on the Seas near our Shores and to recover and restore the same to the right owners when taken from them. If all the means in our Power are used, and fail in their Effect, we are not bound, by our Treaties with those Nations to make Compensation.

Though we have no similar Treaty with Great Britain, it was the opinion of the President that we should use towards that Nation the same rule, which, under this Article, was to govern us with the other Nations; and even to extend it to Captures made on the High Seas, and brought into our Ports; if done by Vessels, which had been armed within them.

Having for particular reasons, forbore to use all the means in our power for the restitution of the three vessels mentioned in my Letter[1] of August 7th The President thought it incumbent on the United States to make Compensation for them; and though nothing was said in that Letter of other Vessels taken under like Circumstances and brought in after the 5th of June, and before the date of that Letter, yet when the same forbearance had taken place it was and is his opinion that Compensation would be equally due.

As to Prizes made under the same Circumstances, and brought in after the date of that Letter the President determined, that all the means in our power, should be used for their restitution. If these fail as we should not be bound by our Treaties to make Compensation to the other Powers, in the analagous Case, he did not mean to give an opinion that it ought to be done to Great Britain: But still

[1] See the note regarding Jefferson's letter of September 5, 1793.

[2] With France, Document 1, Article 6; with the Netherlands, Document 5, Article 5; with Prussia, Document 13, Article 7.

if any Cases shall arise subsequent to that date, the circumstances of which shall place them on similar ground with those before it, the President would think Compensation equally incumbent on the United States.

Instructions are given to the Governors of the different States to use all the means in their Power for restoring Prizes of this last description found within their Ports. Though they will of course take measures to be imformed of them, and the General Government has given them the aid of the Custom-house Officers for this purpose, yet you will be sensible of the importance of multiplying the Channels of their Information as far as shall depend on yourself, or any person under your direction, in order that the Governors may use the means in their power, for making restitution. Without knowledge of the Capture they cannot restore it. It will always be best to give the notice to them directly: but any information which you shall be pleased to send to me also, at any time, shall be forwarded to them as quickly as distance will permit.

Hence you will perceive Sir, that, The President contemplates restitution or Compensation in the Case before the 7th August, and after that date restitution if it can be effected by any means in our power: And that it will be important that you should substantiate the fact, that such prizes are in our Ports or waters.

Your List of the Privateers illicitly armed in our ports, is, I believe Correct.

With respect to losses by detension, waste Spoilation sustained by vessels taken as before mentioned between the dates of June 5th and August 7th it is proposed as a provisional measure, that the Collector of the Customs of the district, and the British Consul, or any other person you please, shall appoint persons to establish the Value of the Vessel and Cargo, at the time of her Capture and of her arrival in the port into which She is brought, according to their value in that Port. If this shall be agreable to you, and you will be pleased to signify it to me with the Names of the Prizes understood to be of this description Instructions will be given accordingly to the Collector of the Customs where the respective Vessels are.

I have the Honor to be &c

(Signed) Thos. Jefferson.

Additional Article

It is further agreed between the said contracting parties, that the operation of so much of the twelfth Article of the said Treaty as

respects the trade which his said Majesty thereby consents may be carried on between the United States and his Islands in the West Indies, in the manner and on the terms and conditions therein specified, shall be suspended.

NOTES

There is no signed original of the Jay Treaty in the Department of State file.

That John Jay sent two originals of this treaty to the United States is clear from his despatches. That only two originals were transmitted seems equally certain. If a third original had been transmitted, the records of the time would mention it; but they do not.

The first of the two originals which Jay did send went from Falmouth by the packet *Tankerville*, which had been detained a week or more for the purpose of taking the treaty. Jay wrote on November 19, 1794, the date of signature:

> The long expected Treaty accompanies this letter;—a probability of soon concluding it has caused the Packet to be detained for more than a week. (D. S., 1 Despatches, Great Britain, No. 22, duplicate.)

And on November 21 he wrote:

> On the 19th Inst. a Treaty was signed. The next Day it was, together with my Letters to you No 21–22–& 23, dispatched to the Packet at Falmouth, which had been detained. (*Ibid.*, No. 24.)

The example sent by the packet was lost; it is reported to have been "cast into the sea to escape French hands" (Conway, Omitted Chapters of History Disclosed in the Life and Papers of Edmund Randolph, 233–34, 293). Grenville wrote of the unfortunate "loss" of the packet, misspelled *Tankenville* (Correspondence and Public Papers of John Jay, 1794–1826, IV, 174). The press of the period recounts that the *Tankerville*, on account of bad weather, did not sail from Falmouth until December 14, and that she was taken by a French brig near the West Indies and burned (the Evening Mail, London, December 3–5 and 15–17, 1794, and April 20–22, 1795).

As to the second original, Jay wrote in his despatch of November 21:

> I now send you duplicates of them all, by Mr [David] Blaney, a Gentleman of Virginia, recommended to me by Gov. Lee. The earliest advices from you will be expedient.

That only two originals were sent by Jay appears from his letter of December 10, 1794 (D. S., 1 Despatches, Great Britain, No. 26, duplicate), from which the following is extracted:

> As the Treaty concluded on the 19th of last month, was sent by the Packet, and a Duplicate was committed to the Care of Mr Blaney who sailed in a Vessel for Virginia commanded by Captn Vickary, I flatter myself it will arrive before you receive this Letter. . . . The Treaty may possibly not arrive so soon, as that the Ratification will reach this place before my Departure;—especially, as not only the Packet but also Mr Blaney were detained a considerable Time by contrary Winds.

It appears that Captain Blaney left London on December 17, sailing by the *Thomas* (Captain Vickery), and reached Norfolk on February 27, going to Philadelphia by way of Baltimore (Boston Gazette, March 23, 1795).

Blaney's arrival was reported in the letter of Edmund Randolph (Secretary of State) to Jay of March 8, 1795 (D. S., 2 Instructions, U. S. Ministers, 327–28), as follows:

> At 7 o'Clock yesterday evening, Mr Blaney delivered to me the very important dispatches, which you had consigned to his care. He arrived at Norfolk eight days ago, after having been beaten off from the Capes of Virginia for some weeks by strong winds. His charge was in good order, and the seals and envelope were unviolated.

It was this original, delivered by Blaney, which was sent to the Senate on June 8; for the message of Washington says that it had been received by the Secretary of State on March 7 (Executive Journal, I, 178).

There can be no doubt that that same original was used, after its return from the Senate, to form part of the original United States instrument of ratification, which was transmitted to London and was there exchanged for the British instrument of ratification on October 28, 1795; accordingly the Department of State archives do not, and seemingly since 1795 have not, contained a signed original of the Jay Treaty. There is, however, now in the file a facsimile of the United States instrument of ratification which is in the British archives; as that instrument includes as a part thereof the original signed treaty, the facsimile is in part a facsimile of that original; and the text here printed is taken therefrom. It differs from the text heretofore usually printed only in matters of spelling, punctuation, capitalization, and paragraphing. In the signed treaty, as here, the copy of Jefferson's letter of September 5, 1793, follows the signatures; the additional article was, as hereafter noted, the result of the later action of the Senate.

The procedure adopted in 1795 regarding the ratification of the Jay Treaty by the United States was a most unusual one. While two originals of the treaty had been sent to the United States by Jay, it was known that one of them had been lost. One had arrived; and that original was a document of the highest importance, belonging to the United States. Every consideration required that it be retained in the archives of the Government. To return it to London as a part of the United States instrument of ratification was not only unnecessary, but a gravely imprudent step; it was unnecessary, for international procedure requires merely the copying of the text of a treaty into an instrument of ratification which is to be delivered to the other party; it was imprudent, as it deprived this Government of possession of the best evidence of the text of one of its most essential treaties, a treaty which was constantly a matter of diplomatic discussion up to the war of 1812, which was of practical and historical importance for generations thereafter, and which, indeed, was before the Supreme Court of the United States for consideration as late as 1929.

Of course the text of the treaty has always been available here; it is written in full in D. S., 2 Despatches, Great Britain, at pages 131–68; it was printed at the time—"a printed and authentic copy of the treaty and of the advice of the Senate" was among the papers transmitted to John Quincy Adams on August 25, 1795 (D. S., 3 Instructions, U. S. Ministers, 27); and the treaty was duly proclaimed; but the primary document was sent to London.

It seems that it was expected at the Department of State that the British instrument of ratification would itself include an original signed treaty; expressions in various letters to Deas in 1796 (D. S., 3 Instructions, U. S. Ministers, 95, 99–100, 104) indicate this fact: "the treaty itself, with the ratification, has not yet arrived" (January 15); "nothing but the Treaty itself with the ratification signed by the King's own hand, and further authenticated by annexing thereto the Great Seal of the Kingdom, would be proper for such a purpose" (January 25); "the treaty itself with the King's ratification" (February 27). But even if that expectation had been a reasonable one, as it was not, it was foolhardy to trust to the then risk of transportation overseas a single instrument of ratification including the only original of the treaty which the Government of the United States possessed; and that transportation risk was a serious one, as the loss of the *Tankerville* had just shown. If the United States ratification had not safely reached London, as it did, in October, 1795, the Jay Treaty could hardly have gone into force until the following spring at the earliest.

Furthermore, while it might properly have been thought that the British instrument of ratification, although not including a signed original of the treaty, would be a perfect evidence of the exact text, still that expectation would not, in this particular case, have been justified by the fact; for, as is noted hereafter, the British ratification is a quite imperfect paper.

The Department of State file of the Jay Treaty also contains the British instrument of ratification of October 28, 1795, and the original proclamation of the treaty, dated February 29, 1796. It does not include any protocol or other original record of the exchange of ratifications; but with the facsimile of the United States instrument of ratification is a facsimile of a certificate of the exchange of ratifications on October 28, 1795. It is signed by William Allen Deas, Chargé d'Affaires of the United States, and is dated November 5, 1795. An initialed copy in the handwriting of Deas is in D. S., 3 Despatches, Great Britain, November 5, 1795.

Note Regarding Submission to the Senate

Some historians have thought that the Jay Treaty was for some four months withheld from the Senate. Such was not the case. It was widely reported and well known in the United States in the first days of February, 1795, that a treaty with Great Britain had been signed at London on the previous November 19; but its terms were not disclosed, and the treaty was not received at the Department of State until the evening of March 7, 1795, three and one-half months after

its signature. The Senate was not then in session; a call for an extra session had previously (on March 3) been issued; the date set by that call was June 8, 1795; and on that day the treaty was sent to the Senate by President Washington. No earlier date of submission was possible unless another and earlier extra session of the Senate had been called for the purpose.

Jefferson's Letter of September 5, 1793

In this letter of Secretary of State Jefferson to George Hammond, Minister of Great Britain to the United States, reference is made to two earlier letters, one written by Jefferson to Hammond on August 7, 1793, the text of which (from D. S., 5 Domestic Letters, 218) follows:

The Minister Plenipoy of Great Britain

Philadelphia, 7th August 1793

Sir/A constant expectation of carrying into full effect the declaration of the President, against permitting the armament of vessels within the ports of the United States, to cruize on nations with which they are at peace, has hitherto prevented my giving you a final answer on the subject of such vessels and their prizes. Measures to this effect are still taking, and particularly for excluding from all further Asylum in our ports, the vessels so armed, and for the restoration of the prizes, the Lovely Lass, the Prince William Henry and the Jane of Dublin, taken by them: and I am authorized, in the mean time to assure you, that should the measures for restoration fail in their effect, the President considers it as incumbent on the United States to make compensation for the Vessels. I have the honor to be, with great respect, Sir, &ca

Th: Jefferson

The other was the letter of Hammond to Jefferson of August 30, 1793 (original in D. S., 1 Notes from the British Legation), which reads thus:

Philadelphia 30h August 1793

Sir. Several communications having at different times passed between you and myself, both in conversation and in writing, on the subject of the prizes made by the French privateers, fitted out in the ports of the United States; I have thought it expedient, for the sake of perspicuity and of avoiding future misunderstanding, to reduce the result of those communications under one point of view, and to request you, Sir, to have the goodness to inform me, whether my conception of the intentions of this government in this respect be accurate.

I understand—that all captures, made subsequently to the 7th of June and *antecedently* to the 7th of August, by any vessel, fitted out, armed and equipped, in the ports of the United States, are either to be restored by the captors, or a compensation for their full value, is to be paid, to their owners, by the government of the United States—and that all prizes, made by vessels of this description *subsequently* to the 7th of August, are to be seized and immediately restored by the government of the United States, or, if the restitution cannot be effected, a compensation for their value is to be paid in the same manner as in the former case.

If this statement be correct, I wish, Sir, farther to be acquainted—whether an official communication of any capture, that has been or may hereafter be made under the circumstances abovementioned, will be necessary on my part to substantiate the fact—or whether the circular instructions, which, as I infer from the public prints, have been transmitted to the Collectors of the Customs in the different ports of the United States, will obviate that necessity.

There is another point connected with the foregoing, upon which also I am extremely solicitous to obtain some early information. Being convinced that

the determination of this government upon these subjects has been dictated by a sincere desire to redress, as far as was possible, the injuries that individuals might suffer from acts of rapine and plunder committed by the privateers, which have been fitted out in it's ports, in violation of it's authority—I presume that the effects of that desire, are not to be limited to the simple restitution of the prizes, but are farther to be extended to the procuring of a reparation for any loss, which the vessels captured or their cargoes may sustain, from detention, waste, or spoliation. Under the influence of this conviction therefore, I shall be infinitely obliged to you, Sir, if you will prescribe the mode, that may appear to the executive government of the United States the most satisfactory, and the best adapted to the ascertainment of the real amount of the damages, which may, in any instance, arise from the causes I have just recited.

I annex to this letter a list of privateers, which, according to the information I have received, have been all fitted out, armed and equipped in ports of the United States; and I have the honor to be, with sentiments of great respect, Sir,

Your most obedient, humble Servant,

GEO. HAMMOND.

Mr JEFFERSON.

List of privateers, fitted out, armed and equipped, in Ports of the United States.

L'Anti-George*	Savannah
Le Citoyen Genet Le Sans culotte Le Vainqueur de la Bastille	Charleston.
La Caramagnde	River Delawar.
Le petit Democrat	Philadelphia
Le Republicain † Le Roland	Boston.

* lost † taken

NOTE REGARDING THE ADDITIONAL ARTICLE

The additional article was added pursuant to the Senate resolution of advice and consent of June 24, 1795. No attested copy of that resolution is in the Department of State file; as printed in the Executive Journal, I, 186, it reads:

Resolved, (two-thirds of the Senate concurring therein,) That they do consent to, and advise the President of the United States, to ratify the treaty of amity, commerce, and navigation, between his Britannic Majesty and the United States of America, concluded at London, the 19th day of November, 1794, on condition that there be added to the said treaty an article, whereby it shall be agreed to suspend the operation of so much of the 12th article, as respects the trade which his said Majesty thereby consents may be carried on, between the United States and his islands in the West Indies, in the manner, and on the terms and conditions therein specified.

And the Senate recommend to the President to proceed, without delay, to further friendly negotiations with his Majesty, on the subject of the said trade, and of the terms and conditions in question.

The form of the Senate resolution, being then without precedent, caused doubt as to the procedure necessary for ratification on the part of the United States. On July 21, 1795, Randolph wrote as follows:

By a past opportunity, I did myself the honor of sending to you a printed copy of the proposed Treaty between the United States and Great-Britain. With it was bound up a copy of the act of our Senate. The want of precedent for such a mode of ratification; the doubts, whether they meant to sit in judgment again upon the article, to be added; whether the President can ratify without re-

submitting the new article to them; whether he can ratify before he himself inspects the new article, after it shall have been assented to by the British King; and what effect the suspension of the 12th article will have upon all those, subsequent to the 10th; create difficulties and delays, even independent of the *real merits* of the Treaty. (D. S., 3 Instructions, U. S. Ministers, 13.)

The additional article was recited textually in each instrument of ratification, but was not otherwise drawn up or signed; in 8 Statutes at Large, 130, the date thereof is given erroneously as May 4, 1796; reference thereto in the British instrument of ratification is in the following language:

Whereas a certain additional Article has on the Part of the said United States been proposed to be annexed to the said Treaty as a Part thereof, to which Addition We are willing to consent, the said Treaty and Additional Article being in the Words following.

In the United States instrument of ratification the language following the text of the letter of Jefferson is this:

And Whereas the Senate of the United States did, by their resolution on the twenty fourth day of June, in the Year of our Lord 1795 (all the Senators of the United States being then present, and two thirds thereof concurring) "consent to, "and advise the President of the United States, to ratify the treaty of amity, "commerce and navigation, between his Britannick Majesty and the United "States of America, concluded at London the 19th day of November 1794, on "condition that there be added to the said Treaty, an article whereby it shall be "agreed to suspend the operation of so much of the 12th Article as respects the "trade, which his said Majesty thereby consents may be carried on between the "United States and his Islands in the West Indies, in the manner, and on the "terms and conditions therein specified."

And Whereas it will satisfy and be conformable with the said Advice and consent of the Senate, if there be added to the said Treaty an Article in the following Words, that is to say; "Additional Article—

"It is further agreed between the said contracting parties, that the operation "of so much of the twelfth Article of the said Treaty as respects the trade which "his said Majesty thereby consents may be carried on between the United "States and his Islands in the West Indies, in the manner and on the terms and "conditions therein specified, shall be suspended."

Now therefore I George Washington, President of the United States of America, having seen and considered the Treaty and additional Article aforesaid, do in pursuance of the aforesaid advice and consent of the Senate of the United States of America, by these presents, ratify accept and confirm the said Treaty and the said Additional Article, as the same are herein before set forth.

And I do moreover hereby declare, that the said Treaty, and the said additional Article form together one Instrument and are a Treaty between the United States of America and his Britannic Majesty, made by the President of the United States by and with the advice and consent of the Senate thereof.

For the greater Testimony and Validity of all which, I have caused the Great Seal of the United States of America to be affixed to these presents and have signed the same with my Hand.

Given at the City of Philadelphia, the fourteenth day of August, in the Year one thousand seven hundred and ninety five, and of the Independence of the United States of America, the Twentieth.

Note Regarding the British Ratification

Aside from minor matters of punctuation, etc., the language of the treaty provisions in the British instrument of ratification varies in thirty or more instances from that of the signed treaty; moreover,

the former does not contain the treaty heading, and it inserts a heading to the letter of Jefferson to Hammond of September 5, 1793. Most of the variances between the two documents are not very material, but at least one is. The treaty text in the British ratification was obviously very carelessly copied, notably in the first paragraph of Article 18. There could have been no scrupulous comparison of the documents upon the exchange of ratifications, as is customary.

Note Regarding the Exchange of Ratifications

Elaborate instructions were drawn up at Philadelphia regarding the exchange of ratifications. It was intended that these should be carried out by John Quincy Adams, then at The Hague; but Deas, the Chargé at London, was instructed to proceed if Adams did not arrive by October 20 (see D. S., 3 Instructions, U. S. Ministers, 24–32, letters to Adams of August 14 and 25, and letters to Deas of August 15 and 25; the letters of August 14 and 15 are signed by Randolph, the others by Pickering). The language of the letter of August 25 to Deas correctly describes the United States instrument of ratification as including the original treaty:

> The packet to your care herewith transmitted, addressed to John Quincy Adams Esq[r] contains the treaty of amity, commerce and navigation between the United States and Great Britain, ratified by the President.

The various letters were not received in London until October 3 and 8 (D. S., 3 Despatches, Great Britain, letter from Deas of October 13, 1795). As Adams had not arrived in London, Deas sent Grenville a copy of the ratification on October 23 (*ibid.*, letter from Deas of that date). There appears to have been no discussion between Grenville and Deas regarding the additional article. As to this, Adams, who reached London on November 11, wrote:

> The additional Article, suspending the clause in the twelfth article according to the ratification of the Senate, was agreed to without difficulty. (D. S., 1 Despatches, Netherlands, 258, November 14, 1795.)

The despatch of Deas of October 28, 1795 (D. S., 3 Despatches, Great Britain), reported the exchange of ratifications on that day and enclosed a copy of the British ratification. That despatch is endorsed as received on December 28, 1795.

The original British instrument of ratification did not arrive, however, until April 22, 1796, when it was received from Thomas Pinckney; it is endorsed as received on that date (see D. S., 3 Instructions, U. S. Ministers, 123, letter to Pinckney of April 23, 1796). Various letters to Deas complained of the delay as preventing proclamation and communication to Congress (*ibid.*, 95, 99–100, 104–7, January 15 and 25, February 27, and March 9, 1796). The letter of February 27 says that a copy of the treaty, "with the ratifications of the King of Great Britain and of the President," had arrived a month earlier at Charleston and had all been printed in the news-

papers; the letter of March 9 states that "the President at length directed the treaty with Great Britain to be promulgated, on the evidence of its ratification by his Britannic Majesty contained in your letter of October 28th."

Note Regarding Article 8

No "such agreement" as that "to be settled" pursuant to Article 8 of the treaty was entered into upon the exchange of ratifications as therein provided (D. S., 3 Despatches, Great Britain, letter of Deas of October 28, 1795). Subsequently an informal understanding regarding the payment of the Commissioners was reached by the two Governments (see D. S., 1 Despatches, Netherlands, 260–78, 283–89, letters of John Quincy Adams of November 27 and December 5 and 19, 1795; D. S., 3 Instructions, U. S. Ministers, 131–34, Pickering to Pinckney, May 23, 1796; also act of May 6, 1796, 1 Statutes at Large, 459).

Note Regarding the Proclamation

As has been stated above, the original proclamation, dated February 29, 1796, signed by Washington, attested by Timothy Pickering as Secretary of State, and with the Great Seal, is in the treaty file. Its treaty text is an accurate copy of the language of the original treaty which is embodied in the United States instrument of ratification, although it differs from that text in matters of spelling, punctuation, capitalization, and paragraphing. Following the signatures to the treaty is copied the letter of Jefferson to Hammond of September 5, 1793, and then the additional article.

It appears that the proclamation is the source of the text printed in 8 Statutes at Large and other treaty collections.

Treaty Series, No. 1
8 Statutes at Large, 133–37

17

ALGIERS : SEPTEMBER 5, 1795

Treaty of Peace and Amity, signed at Algiers September 5, 1795 (21 Safar, A. H. 1210). Original in Turkish.

Submitted to the Senate February 15, 1796. Resolution of advice and consent March 2, 1796. Ratified by the United States March 7, 1796. As to the ratification generally, see the notes. Proclaimed March 7, 1796.

The following twenty-three pages of Turkish are a reproduction of the pages of the original treaty; but they are arranged in left-to-right order of pagination. They are followed first by the English translation signed by Joseph Donaldson, jr., and by the text of the approval of David Humphreys, each as written in that same document; then is printed the English translation of 1930.

فصل
١

ابتداکی فصلك قول وقراری اولدرکه کشینو بیك ایکینوز اون سنه سنه دن بری
حالا مریکان خیر سھی ی یالتالرینه متصرف دوستمز جورج ووا شنتون صاحب الدولت اولان
نام مریکا ماکی ایله رجا جمهور جمهور ضرایر غریبه صاحب نیشا حضرتلرینك رای و
سعادتلو حسن پاشا یسر الله له مایرید ومبا یشا وسایر اوداباب دیوان وجمله عساکر
منصوره اغاسی وقول کتخداسی وسایر اتفاقیله بو صلح وصلاح جمهورمتینك
منصوره وجانبینك رعایا الرعا اتفاقیله مصلحتی مخالف ومغایر
وحکم اولوب ثابت اولمشدر بعد الیوم ثابت قائما مستمر اولسه والسلام
وفا سنه ایده جك ... سوز قائما مشدد
محرم الحرام ٢١ ص ١٢١١

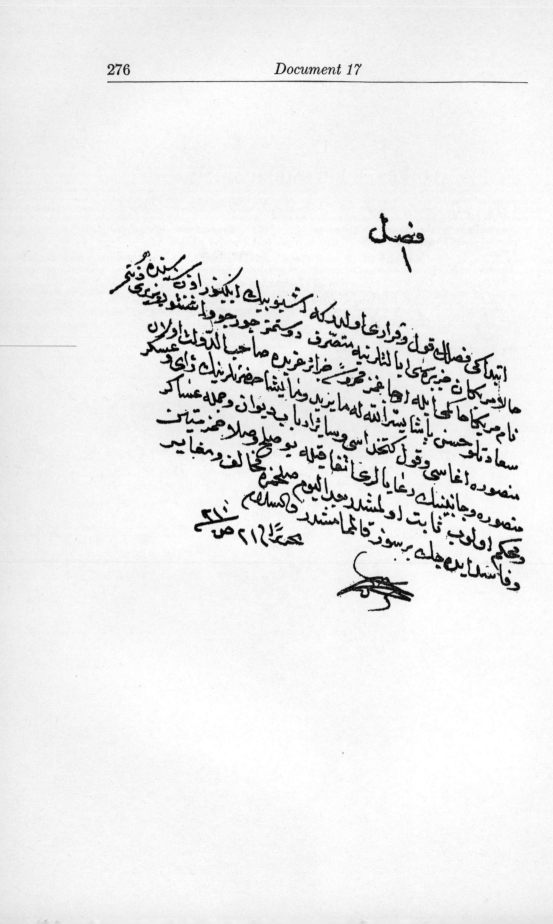

فصل ۲

ایکنجی فصلک قولو قراری اولدرکه امریکان حاکمی دوستمیزینه بکیلری
کرک بیوک وکرک کوچک وکذلک انلرین حکمنده اولان رعایاسنک
بکیلری محروسه جزایر اسکله سی ویاخود تحت حکمنده اولان اسکله لرده
وارد اولدقلرنده عادت قدیم اوزره اوتوردیغم ما ایدقلرندن عقد
سائر انکلیز وفلمنک وسوید یازدکلرندن ویرم کلدوکی وانلره اولنیه
اوضان کمرک نوز غروشدن بش غروش کمرک آلنه زیاده طلب اولنیه
دفی بوددکه ما تلیان دبقلرینه بنه کمیه قویوب تورملک
مراد ایدکلرنده بکسنه انلردن برشیئ طلب ایلمیه ومزبور اسکله لرده
بکسنه انلری اجفدوبالی قومیه لردا استلمم

۲۱ صفر ۱۲۱۰

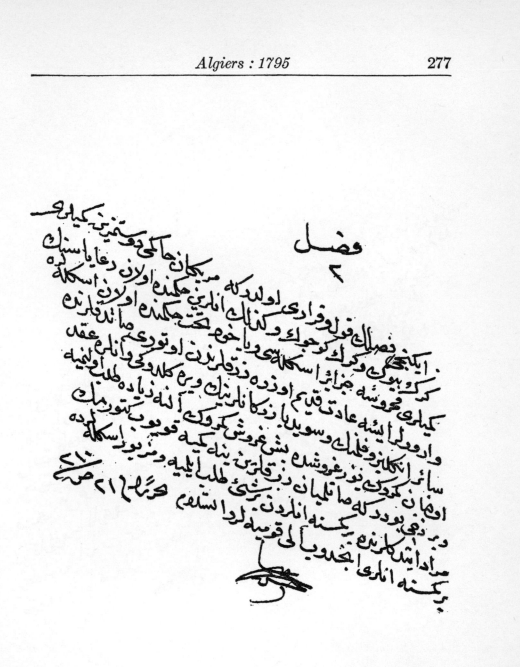

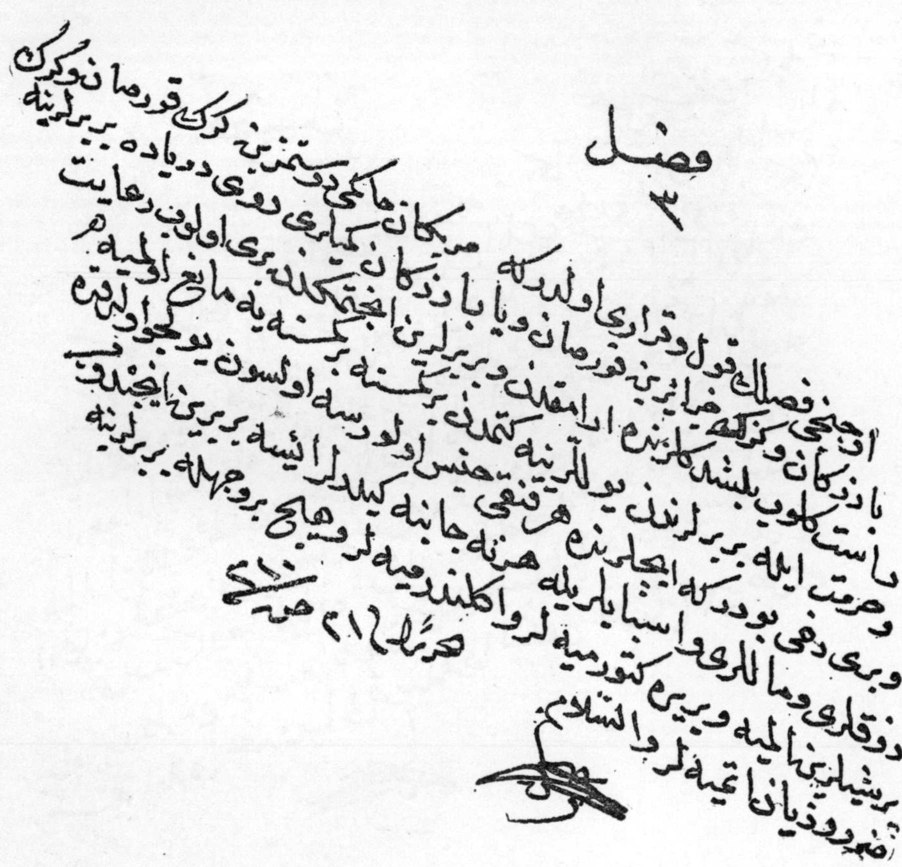

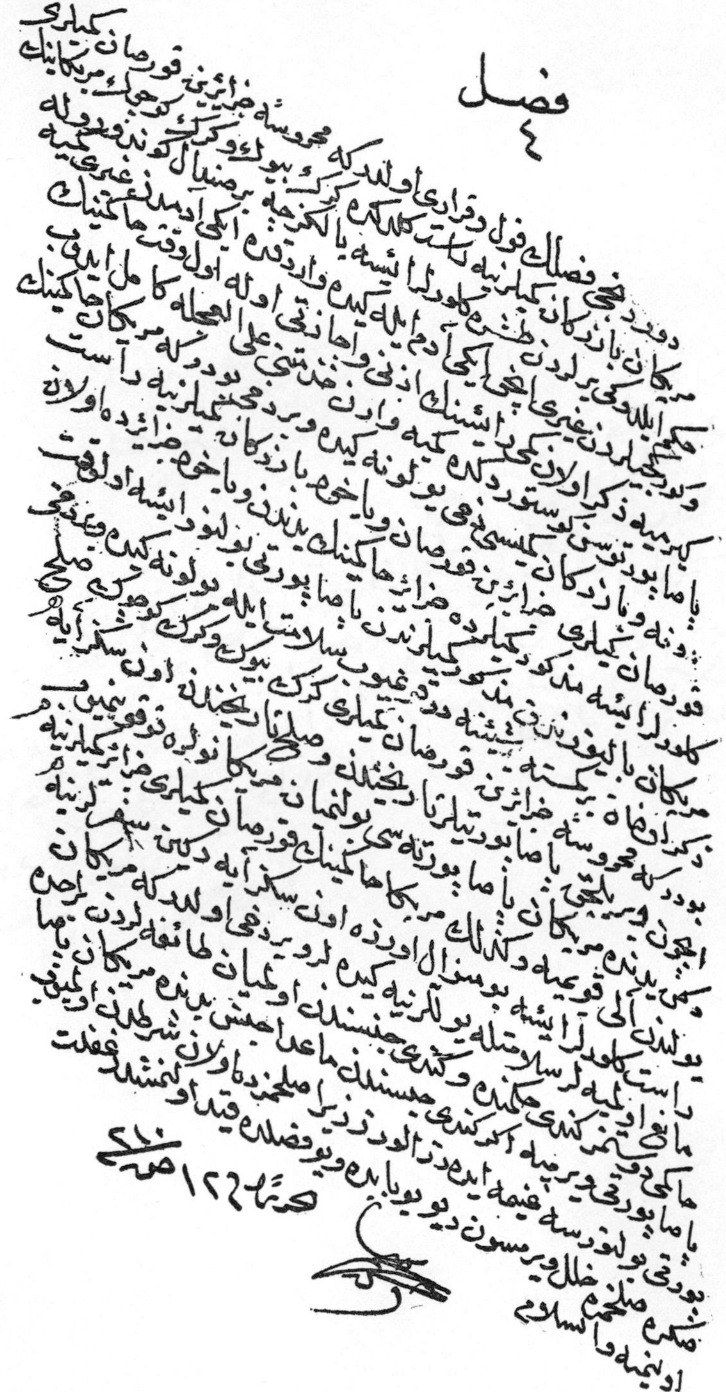

فصل ٤

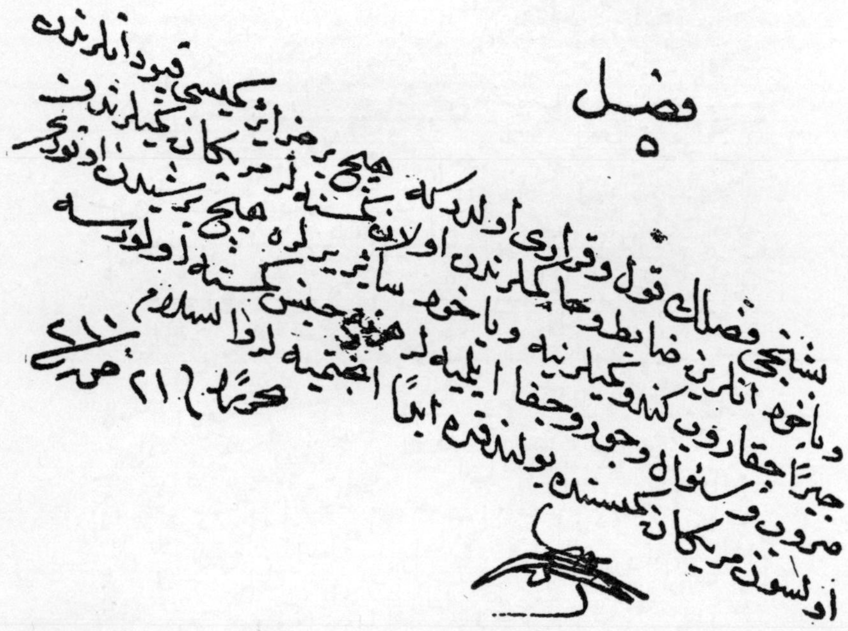

فصل ٦

التنجي فصلك قول وقراري اولدركه مريكان حاكمنك وياخود آتنك
حكمنده اولان رعايا سنك كيميلرندن بري جزاير حكم ايلدوكي ملكتلرينه يا كيلرينه
باشلنده قرع اولوب پاره لنسه اصلا وقطعا كندولرين ماللرين لي ذرقلرني
هيچ بر كمسنه بيلرينه الوب نغما وغنيمت ايتميه وبردخي نوددكه
بويله برايش واقع اولور ايسه كمركه دزقلري التميوب وادملرينه برضرر
اتيه لروجزايرينه تعب حكمنده اولان يرلرده بو منوال اوزره برايش ظهور
ايد ايشه ممكن اولدقجه على قدر الطاقه چالشوب معاونت ايدوب
دوستلوغي اجرا ايدرلر وذرقلرينه قوروب منفعه امداد ايدرلر والسلام

٢١ صفر سنه ١٢١٠

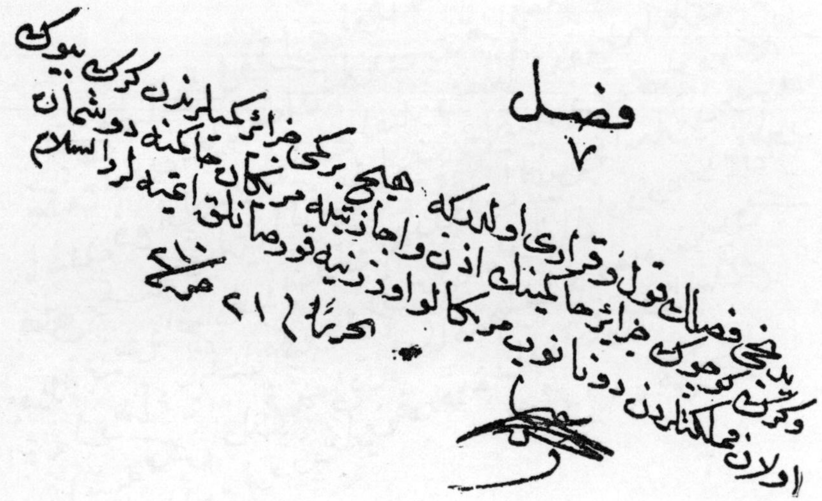

فصل ۷

یدنجی فصلك قول وقراری اولدرکه هیچ برگمی جزائر گمیلرندن کرک بیوك
وکرك کوچك جزائر حاکمینك اذن واجازتیله مریکان حاکمنه دوشمان
اولان مملکتلردن دونانوب مریکالو اوادنیه قورصانلق ایتمیه لر واسلام

تحریرا فی ۲۱ محرم

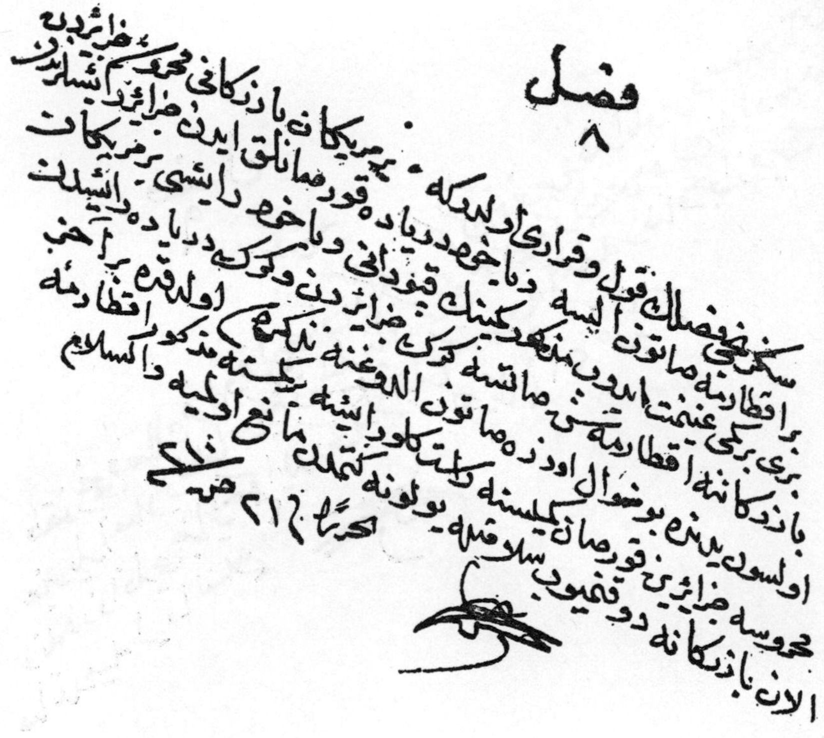

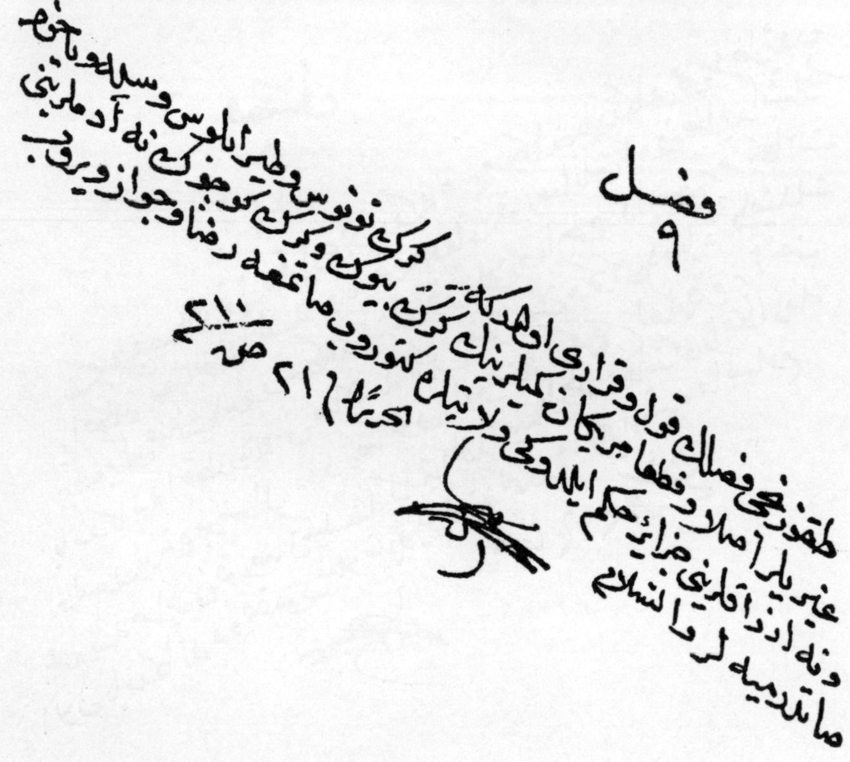

فصل ۱۰

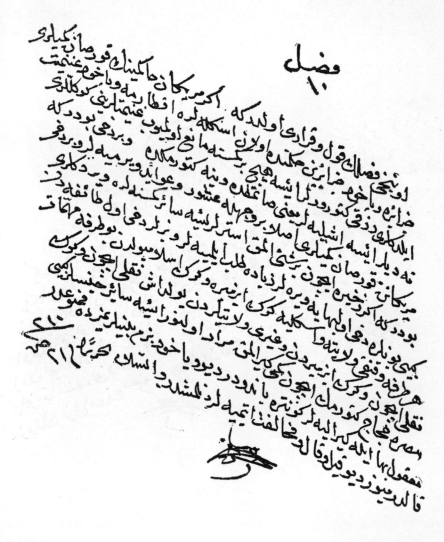

فصل
١١

اون برنجی فصلک قول و قراری اولدر که مریکانه حاکمی دوستمزینه قورصان
کمیلری محروسه جزایر اوکونه کلوب تیمور براقدقده محروسه جزایردن کرکی
مریکان و کرک غیری جنسدن اکر بر اسیر قاچوب وارور قورصان کمیسنه
فرارا وصول اولوب محروسه جزایر حاکمی مزبور قچق اسیری طلبایلیه و طلب
اولندقده مزبور قورصان کمیسنک قپودانی دخی البته کمیسندن اول فرار
ایدن اسیری چقاروب ویره و اکر قچق اسیر تونوب ویرمیوب
کافر نقاسنه دخی واروب ایشه اول حاکمک حضورینه قپودانی تکرار دونوب جزایره
کتورمک قولی اودنه قطع کلام و شرط اد نمشدر والسلام

تحریرا ۲۱ صفر

فصل
١٢

اون ایکنجی فصلك قول وقراری اولدیکه شمدن صکره مریکان حاکمینك
رعایاسی فراشی حکم ایلیه وکیجی یرلرده نه الوزدونه صاتلوردونه اسیر اولور
ویردیکی بوددکه مریکان حاکمی ایله بارشق اولدوغندن اوتوری کوکلی
اوکینجه البته اسیرلرینی قورتردنلیه خصوص مزبور اچون مراد ایلدوکی
زمانه اوچون تکه اسیرلرین خصم واقربالری مروت وغیریلرندن اوله
ویردیکی بوددکه قورترمغه برو عدد زمان اولمیه ودخی نه مقداری معقول
کوردو لرئیسه اول دخی حسنه حال ایله اسیرلرین بهالرندن اوتوری افندیلریله
سویلشله وترك هیچ برکمسنه البته اسیرلریکزی فلان بهایه ویر
دیمیه ودنلیه افندیلرینه شخص غیرینك اولسون وکرك پاشانك اولسون
ولکن مریکان رئیسه کلدی قورتللقلری وقت عادت قدیم اوزره
ینجه او مریکان حاکمینك طائفه سائر اجناس مطلب اولنمیه جبیسك
ویردیکی بوددکه مریکان ضرایقورصانلری بولنورسه اسیر اولوردوغی
بربسینك تکنه سنده بولنورسه یا ماونده بولنمزسه اسیر
بولنان مریکان طائفه واکریدینن یا ماونده
وورقه برضرر اولمز
ومالی التور والسلام

تحریرا ٢١ صفر

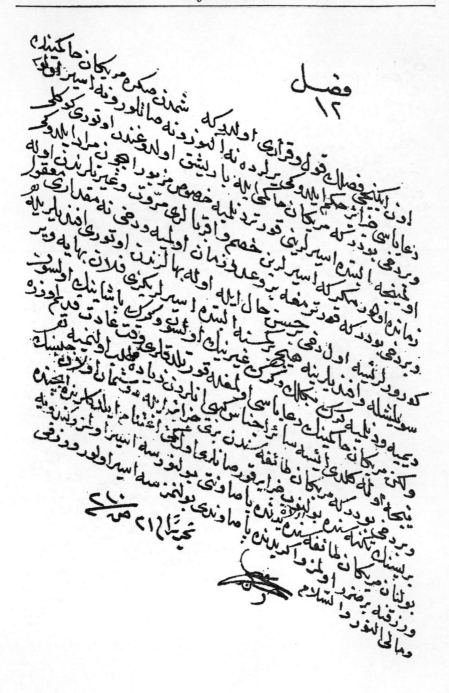

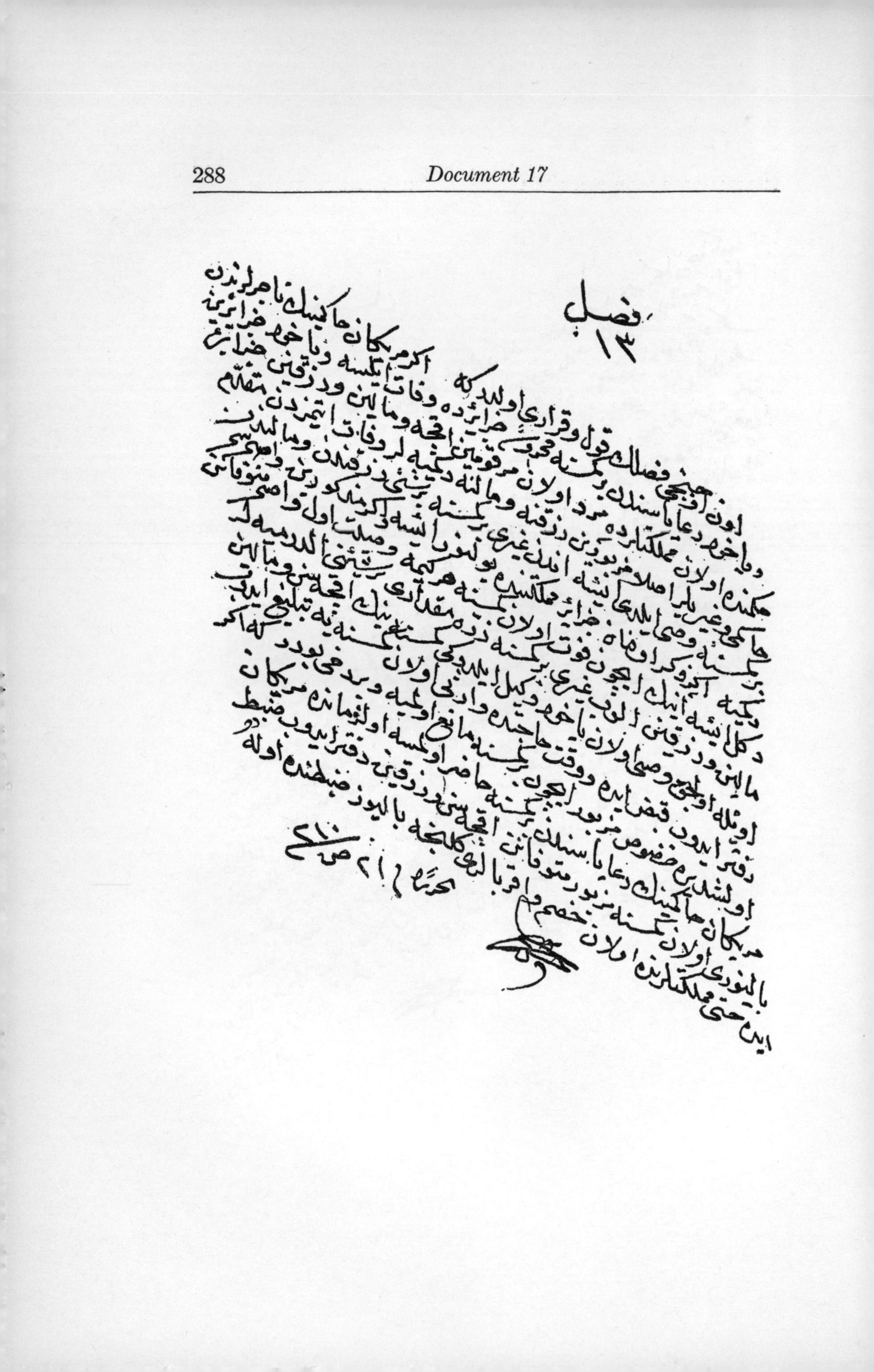

فصل ١٣

فصل
١٤

اون دوردنجی فصلك قول وقراری اولدیرکه جزایرنه کندوکندم ونه حکم ایلدوکجه
اده مریکانا مرلرینه نقلت ایدوب کوکلی استدوکی دذقی اللددمیه لر الحقه
شکلاری استدوکی زنقی اله لر ودکی بودرکه جزایریه اسکله لرینه کلان
سوکلرینه نورو ونقلت ایدوب استدکلری دذقی کیمسی ایجنه قومیه لر وبر
میکانته نه مریکانه یا ایبوزی ذنه غیریسی مریکانه رعایا اسندن بریسی بورجلو
ذی بودرکه قددتی اولمسه مذکوردن بورجندن اوتوری برغیریسنه یا بشوب
اولسه اودرسوکلی اولوب وبورجلویه برقاج کمسته کفیل اولدوا اسلام
اودنلدرمیه لرمکر

صح
محرم سنه ١٢١٠

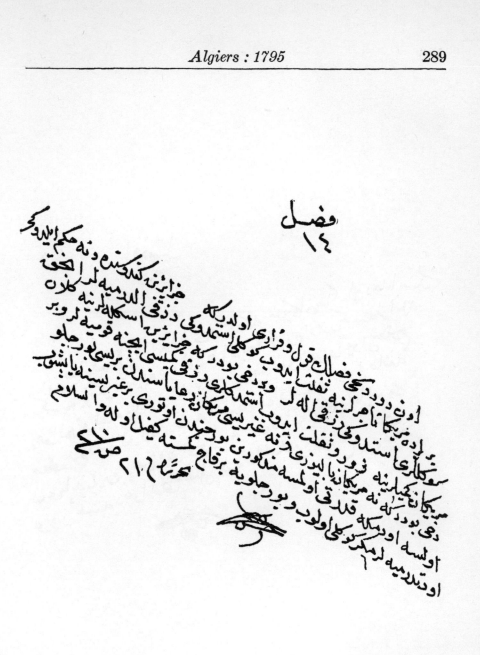

فصل
١٥

اون بشنجی فصلک قول وقراری اولدرکه مریکان حاکمینک رعایاسندن
بر کسنه بر مسلمان ایله ویاخود جزائرینه حکمنده اولان کسنه لر ایله
دعوالری اولسه مذکورلرینک دعوالری دوتلو دایی ودیوان محترم
حضورنده فصل اولنه بر غیری کسنه دن اولنمیه واکر اوله طائفه
کندی مابینلرنده دعوالری اولورسه اول زمان مریکان بالیوزی
اولان کسنه دعوالرینی فصل ایلیه والسلام تحریرا ٢١ ص ١٢١٠

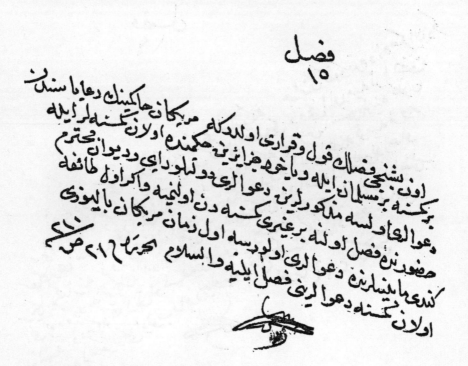

فصل
١٦

اون التنجی فصلك قول وقراری اولدرکه حالیا احتمال اولدرکه مریکان
حاکمنك قوللرندن برکسنه برمسلمان ایله قوغا ایدوب بربرین یاره لیوب
ویا قتل ایدرلر ایسه بربرینه مملکتی شریعتی هرنه حکم ایدر ایسه یعنی
سائرلره کوره جزا ویریله واما برمریکان برمسلمانی اولدرسه
واولدردکدن صکره قاجوب قورتلور ایسه جزائرده اولان مریکان
بالیوزینه ونه انلردن اولنلره بروجهله عقوبت ایدوب انجیتمیه لر

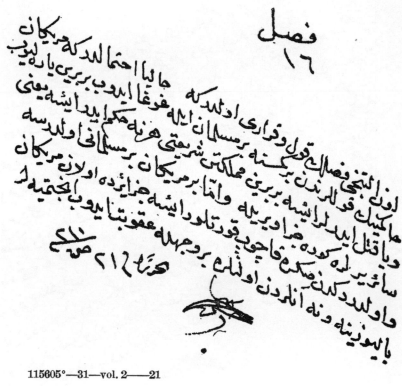

فصل
۱۷

اون یدنجی فصلك قول وقراری اولدرکه مریکان بالیوزی اولان کمسنه
شمدیکی حالده وکلجك زمانده هرکیم اولور ایسه اولسون دائما قودسوز
کوزنجه بجنده وهیچ برکمسنه نه کندویه ونه دزقنه دوتنوب اغتیمیه
ومردقی، بودوکه هر کیمی دیلر ایسه ترجمان ایدر وکذلك سمسار ایدر
دمردقی بوسکه هر زمانده برکیمیه گیتمك مراد ایدر ایسه ویاخود
ویردقی بوجانی راحت ایتمك مراد ایدر ایسه برکمسنه مانع اولمیه
هشنده ده طریقنجه آیین عاطله‌سن اجرا ایتمکه بریوسر کوستوریله
ودخی انلرین ایچون کندولره لازم بر پاپاس ودخی ساکن اوله ومحروس
ودخی تعلیم فن اسیرلری کرك بکلك وکرك سایر کمسنه لرده
هذا یرده بولنان مریکان اسیرلری طریقنجه آیین باطله لرینی اجرا
اولانلر قونصولو اوینه وارمغه افندیلری مانع اولمیه
ایتمکه کرك واردیان باشی وکرك

تحریرا فی ۲۱ صفر ۱۲۱۰

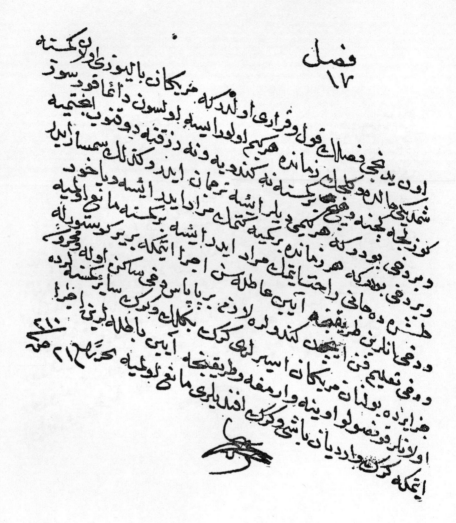

فصل
١٨

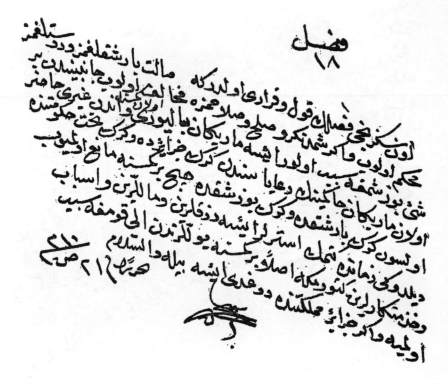

فصل
١٩

اون طقوزنجی فصلك قول وقراری اولدركه مریكان حاكمینك رعایاسندن

بركمسنه هرنه مملكته [illegible] ایمن ویاخود كلوردكن وهرقنقی اجناسندن بر

جنس اولوردسه نه كندوسنه ونه رزقنه ونه ماله ونه اسبابنه ونه یوكنه دست كلدكلری یرلرده

خدمتكارینه جزائركیلری كرك یوك دكرك وشمالی اولان كمسنه

اغتیه لرو كذلك آكدنیز جزائرلی مریكان حاكمینك وزرلری و اقچه لری

لرینك كیلرینی بولنور ایسه ذكر اولنان كشیلرینی مالاری وزرلری كمنظر ایله

وخدمتكارلری املاو قطعا المخلیه مذكورلرینك اشیالرینه

بغلیوب دائما دوستلق یوزی كوستروله والسلام

صحیح

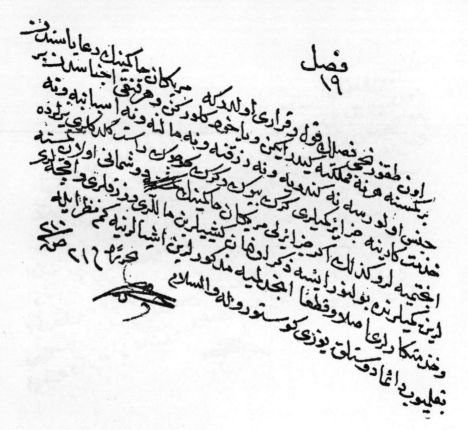

فصل ٢٠

یکرمنجی فصلك قول وقراری اولدیکه هرزمانده مریکان قرالی دونانمه سنه
بر قپوداناسی جزائر اوکونه کلوب کورندکی زمانده مریکان بالیوزی اوردن
کمسنه وار دیو حاکمه خبر ویردکدن صکره مذکور قپودانه امان اولونوب قپود
براقدقده بر حاکمی اولان کمسنه دکرلوفاه مریکان حاکمینه حرمة ورعایة
خطر جون برجلردن یکرمی بر پاره طوب اتمه امر ایلیه واتله اندن صکره
مریکان حاکمینک قپوداناسی اولان کمسنه ذکرلوفاه طوب عددیجه دخی جواب
ایدوب اول مقداری طوب اته دخی بو کیفیه قواللری اولوبیه قدیم الله حرمة عادت
اوقدده مونه لهذه بیلا والسلام

فی ٢١ صفر سنة ١٢١٠

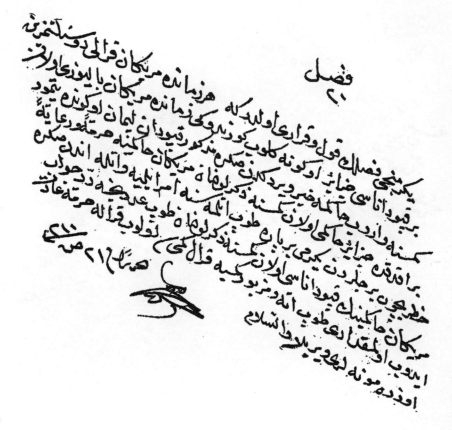

فصل
۲۱

يكرمى برنجى فصلك قول وقرار اولديكه مريكانه باليوزى اولان كمسنه
ادينه خرج اولنجق ماكولات ومشروبات وسائر مهمات وهدايا كبى بو
مقوله اشيالردن كمرك ومكس طلب اولنميه والسلام تحريرا ۱۲ ۲ [illegible]

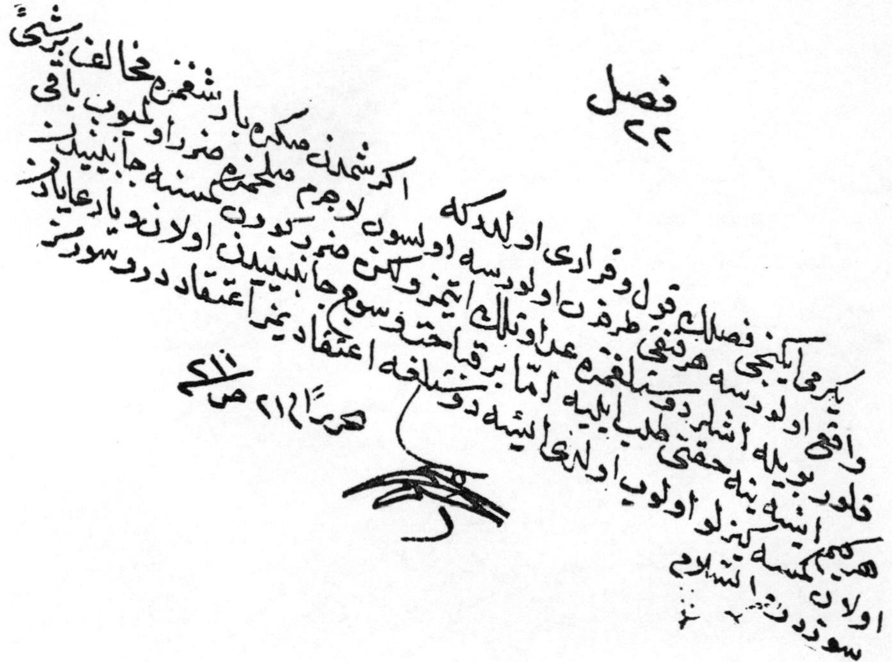

فصل ٢٢

بکرمی ایکنجی فصلک قول وقراری اولدرکه اکر شمدن صکره بارشغمزه مخالف بر شی
واقع اولورسه هر قنقی طرفدن اولورسه اولسون لاجرم صلحمز ضرر اولمیوب باقی
قالور بویله اشلرده مستلقمز عداوتلک ایتمز ولکن ضرب توب جانبیندن
انسه بینه حقی طلب ایلیه اما بر قباحت وسوء جانبیندن اولانه دیار عایدن
هر کیم کسه کیزلو اولوب اولنه عائشه دو تلغه اعتقادیمز اعتقاد در وسوزمز
اولان سوزدن والسلام

فی ۲۱ صفر ۱۲۱۰

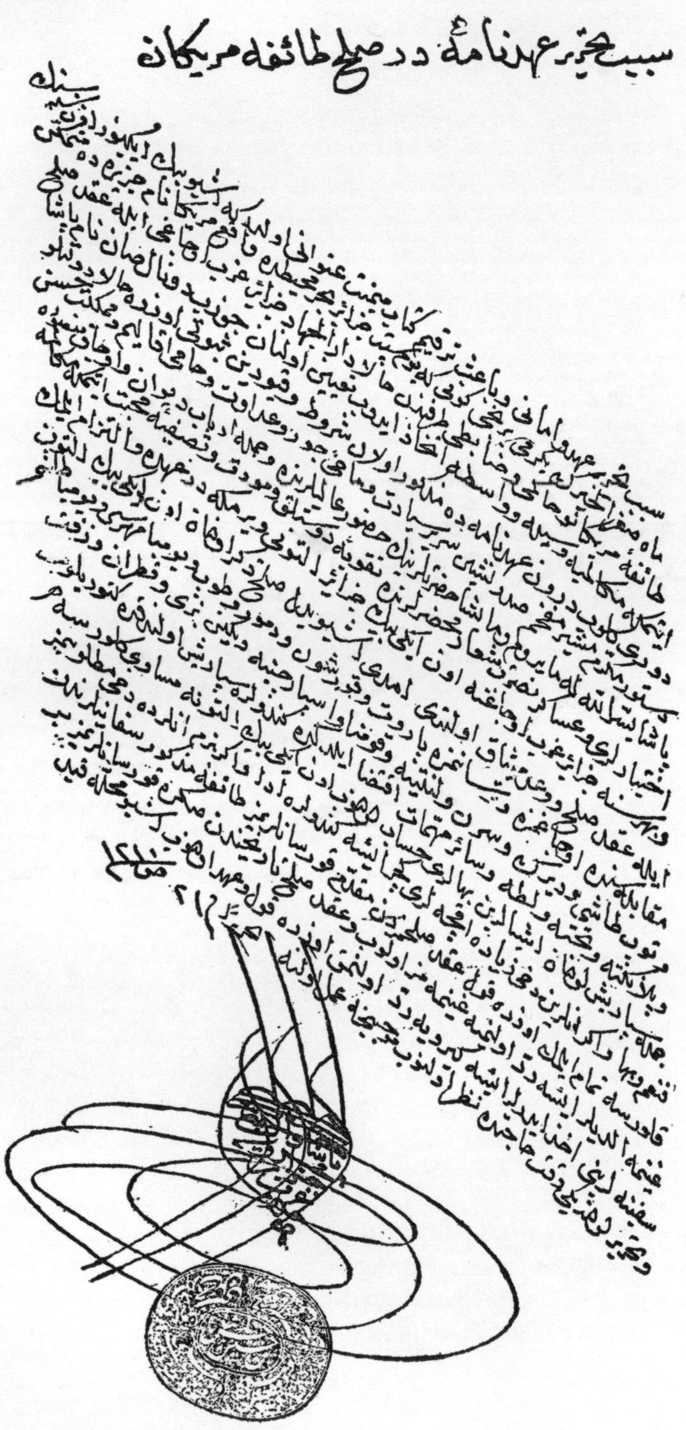
سبب تحریر عهدنامه در صلح طائفهٔ مریکان

[Translation]

Article 1st

From the date of the Present Treaty there shall subsist a firm and Sincere Peace and Amity between the President and Citizens of the United States of North America and Hassan Bashaw Dey of Algiers his Divan and Subjects the Vessels and Subjects of both Nations reciprocally treating each other with Civility Honor and Respect

Article ye 2d

All Vessels belonging to the Citizens of the United States of North America Shall be permitted to enter the Different ports of the Regency to trade with our Subjects or any other Persons residing within our Jurisdiction on paying the usual duties at our Custom-House that is paid by all nations at Peace with this Regency observing that all Goods disembarked and not Sold here shall be permitted to be reimbarked without paying any duty whatever either for disembarking or embarking all naval & Military Stores Such as Gun-Powder Lead Iron Plank Sulphur Timber for building Tar pitch Rosin Turpentine and any other Goods denominated Naval and Military Stores Shall be permitted to be Sold in this Regency without paying any duties whatever at the Custom House of this Regency

Article 3d

The Vessels of both Nations shall pass each other without any impediment or Molestation and all Goods monies or Passengers of whatsoever Nation that may be on board of the Vessels belonging to either Party Shall be considered as inviolable and shall be allowed to pass unmolested

Article 4th

All Ships of War belonging to this regency on meeting with Merchant Vessels belonging to Citizens of the United States shall be allowed to Visit them with two persons only beside the rowers these two only permitted to go on board said vessel without obtaining express leave from the commander of said Vessel who shall compare the Pass-port and immediately permit said Vessel to proceed on her Voyage unmolested All Ships of War belonging to the United States of North America on meeting with an Algerine Cruiser and Shall have seen her pass port and Certificate from the Consul of the United States of North America resident in this Regency shall be permittd to proceed on her cruise unmolested no Pass-port to be Issued to any Ships but such as are Absolutely the Property of Citizens of the

United States and Eighteen Months Shall be the term allowed for furnishing the Ships of the United States with Pass-ports

Article 5th

No Commander of any Cruiser belonging to this Regency shall be allowed to take any person of whatever Nation or demomination out of any Vessel belonging to the United States of North America in order to Examine them or under pretence of making them confess any thing desired neither shall they inflict any corporal punishment or any way else molest them

Article 6th

If any Vessel belonging to the United States of North America shall be Stranded on the Coast of this Regency they shall receive every possible Assistance from the Subjects of this Regency all goods saved from the wreck shall be Permitted to be Reimbarked on board of any other Vessel without Paying any Duties at the Custom House

Article 7th

The Algerines are not on any pretence whatever to give or Sell any Vessel of War to any Nation at War with the United States of North America or any Vessel capable of cruising to the detriment of the Commerce of the United States

Article ye 8th

Any Citizen of the United States of North America having bought any Prize condemned by the Algerines shall not be again captured by the Cruisers of the Regency then at Sea altho they have not a Pass-Port a Certificate from the Consul resident being deemed Sufficient untill such time they can procure such Pass-Port

Article ye 9th

If any of the Barbary States at War with the United States of North America shall capture any American Vessel & bring her into any of the Ports of this Regency they shall not be Permitted to sell her but Shall depart the Port on Procuring the Requisite Supplies of Provision

Article ye 10th

Any Vessel belonging to the United States of North America, when at War with any other Nation shall be permitted to send their Prizes into the Ports of the Regency have leave to Dispose of them with out Paying any duties on Sale thereof All Vessels wanting Provisions or refreshments Shall be permitted to buy them at Market Price

Article ye 11th

All Ships of War belonging to the United States of North America on Anchoring in the Ports of ye Regency shall receive the Usual presents of Provisions & Refreshments Gratis should any of the Slaves of this Regency make their Escape on board said Vessels they shall be immediately returned no excuse shall be made that they have hid themselves amongst the People and cannot be found or any other Equivocation

Article ye 12th

No Citizen of ye United States of North America shall be Oblidged to Redeem any Slave against his Will even Should he be his Brother neither shall the owner of A Slave be forced to Sell him against his Will but All Such agreements must be made by Consent of Parties. Should Any American Citizen be taken on board an Enemy-Ship by the Cruisers of this Regency having a Regular pass-port Specifying they are Citizens of the United States they shall be immediately Sett at Liberty. on the Contrary they having no Passport they and their Property shall be considered lawfull Prize as this Regency Know their friends by their Passports

Article ye 13th

Should any of the Citizens of the United States of North America Die within the Limits of this Regency the Dey & his Subjects shall not Interfere with the Property of the Deceased but it Shall be under the immediate Direction of the Consul unless otherwise disposed of by will Should their be no Consul, the Effects Shall be deposited in the hands of Some Person worthy of trust untill the Party Shall Appear who has a Right to demand them, when they Shall Render an Account of the Property neither Shall the Dey or Divan Give hinderence in the Execution of any Will that may Appear

Article 14th

No Citizen of the United States of North America Shall be oblidged to purchase any Goods against his will but on the contrary shall be allowed to purchase whatever it Pleaseth him. the Consul of the United States of North America or any other Citizen shall not be answerable for debts contracted by any one of their own Nation unless previously they have Given a written Obligation so to do. Shou'd the Dey want to freight any American Vessel that may be in the Regency or Turkey said Vessel not being engaged, in consequence of the friendship subsisting between the two Nations he expects to

have the preference given him on his paying the Same freight offered by any other Nation

ARTICLE YE 15th

Any disputes or Suits at Law that may take Place between the Subjects of the Regency and the Citizens of the United States of North America Shall be decided by the Dey in person and no other, any disputes that may arise between the Citizens of the United States, Shall be decided by the Consul as they are in Such Cases not Subject to the Laws of this Regency

ARTICLE YE 16th

Should any Citizen of the United States of North America Kill, wound or Strike a Subject of this Regency he Shall be punished in the Same manner as a Turk and not with more Severity should any Citizen of the United States of North America in the above predicament escape Prison the Consul Shall not become answerable for him

ARTICLE YE 17th

The Consul of the United States of North America Shall have every personal Security given him and his houshold he Shall have Liberty to Exercise his Religion in his own House all Slaves of the Same Religion shall not be impeded in going to Said Consul's House at hours of Prayer the Consul shall have liberty & Personal Security given him to Travil where ever he pleases within the Regency. he Shall have free licence to go on board any Vessel Lying in our Roads when ever he Shall think fitt. the Consul Shall have leave to Appoint his own Drogaman & Broker

ARTICLE YE 18th

Should a War break out between the two Nations the Consul of the United States of North America and all Citizens of Said States Shall have leave to Embark themselves and property unmolested on board of what Vessel or Vessels they Shall think Proper

ARTICLE YE 19th

Should the Cruisers of Algiers capture any Vessel having Citizens of the United States of North America on board they having papers to Prove they are Really so they and their property Shall be immediately discharged and Shou'd the Vessels of the United States capture any Vessels of Nations at War with them having Subjects of this Regency on board they shall be treated in like Manner

ARTICLE YE 20th

On a Vessel of War belonging to the United States of North America Anchoring in our Ports the Consul is to inform the Dey of her arrival and She shall be Saluted with twenty one Guns which she is to return in the Same Quanty or Number and the Dey will Send fresh Provisions on board as is Customary, Gratis

ARTICLE YE 21st

The Consul of ye United States of North America shall not be required to Pay duty for any thing he brings from a foreign Country for the Use of his House & family

ARTICLE YE 22d

Should any disturbance take place between the Citizens of ye United States & the Subjects of this Regency or break any Article of this Treaty War shall not be Declared immediately but every thing shall be Searched into regularly. the Party Injured shall be made Repairation

On the 21st of ye Luna of Safer 1210 corrisponding with the 5th September 1795 Joseph Donaldson Junr on the Part of the United States of North America agreed with Hassan Bashaw Dey of Algiers to Keep the Articles Contained in this Treaty Sacred and inviolable which we the Dey & Divan Promise to Observe on Consideration of the United States Paying annually the Value of twelve thousand Algerine Sequins[1] in Maritime Stores Should the United States forward a Larger Quantity the Over-Plus Shall be Paid for in Money by the Dey & Regency any Vessel that may be Captured from the Date of this Treaty of Peace & Amity shall immediately be deliver'd up on her Arrival in Algiers

Sign'd VIZIR HASSAN BASHAW
JOSEPH DONALDSON Jun

To all to whom these Presents shall come or be made known.

Whereas the Underwritten David Humphreys hath been duly appointed Commissioner Plenipotentiary, by Letters Patent under the Signature of the President and Seal of the United States of America, dated the 30th of March 1795, for negociating & concluding a Treaty of Peace with the Dey and Governors of Algiers; Whereas by Instructions given to him on the part of the Executive, dated the 28th of March & 4th of April 1795, he hath been farther authorised

[1] Or $21,600.

to employ Joseph Donaldson Junior on an Agency in the said business; whereas by a Writing under his hand and seal, dated the 21st of May 1795, he did constitute & appoint Joseph Donaldson Junior Agent in the business aforesaid; and the said Joseph Donaldson Junior did, on the 5th of September 1795, agree with Hassan Bashaw Dey of Algiers, to keep the Articles of the preceding Treaty sacred and inviolable.

Now Know ye, that I David Humphreys, Commissioner Plenipotentiary aforesaid, do approve & conclude the said Treaty, and every article and clause therein contained, reserving the same nevertheless for the final Ratification of the President of the United States of America, by and with the advice and consent of the Senate of the said United States.

In testimony whereof I have signed the same with my hand and seal, at the City of Lisbon this 28th of November 1795.

[Seal] DAVID HUMPHREYS.

THE TRANSLATION OF 1930

The Turkish text of the original treaty which is reproduced above has been examined by Dr. J. H. Kramers, of Leiden, in collaboration with Dr. C. Snouck Hurgronje. The new translation of the Turkish made by Doctor Kramers, with his notes thereon, is printed below, following this general comment of Doctor Kramers on the text:

As the 1795 English translation of nearly all the articles of this treaty discloses considerable difference from the Turkish text, a complete new English translation has been given.

The treaty is written in excellent Turkish and does not show any sign of being a translation from an Arabic original.

It seems that the last page of Turkish text of the document was originally the beginning of the treaty, for it contains the preambulary stipulations to the articles of the treaty, as is also the case in the treaty with Algiers of 1816 (Document 37). Accordingly the translation begins with those introductory clauses.

[Translation]

Reason for the Drawing Up of the Peace Treaty with the American People

The reason for the drawing up of this treaty and the motive for the writing of this convention of good omen, is that on Saturday, the twenty-first day of the month of Safar of this year 1210,[1] there have

[1] In the chronological tables 21 Safar, A. H. 1210, corresponds to September 6, 1795, which was a Sunday. In this case, however, 21 Safar, A. H. 1210, no doubt answers to September 5, 1795.

been negotiations for a treaty of peace between the ruler and commander of the American people, living in the island called America among the isles of the ocean, and the frontier post of the holy war, the garrison [1] of Algiers. To this purpose has been appointed as his Ambassador,[2] Joseph Donaldson, who has, in confirmation of the articles and paragraphs of the present treaty, strengthened the mutual friendship and good understanding in the exalted presence of His Excellency the noble Vizier and powerful Marshal who sits on the throne of lordship, the destructor of tyranny and injustice and the protector of the country, Hassan Pasha—may God grant to him what he wishes; and in the presence of all the members of the Divan, of the chiefs of the victorious garrison, and of the victorious soldiers. This peace treaty has been concluded, together with the contractual promise to give annually to the garrison of Algiers 12,000 Algerian gold pieces, provided that, in equivalence of these 12,000 gold pieces, being the price of the peace, there may be ordered and imported for our garrison and our arsenal, powder, lead, iron, bullets, bombshells, bomb stones, gun stones, masts, poles, yards, anchor chains, cables, sailcloth, tar, pitch, boards, beams, laths, and other necessaries, provided that the price of all the ordered articles shall be accounted for, so that, if this is equal to 12,000 gold pieces, it shall be all right, but if the price of the articles is higher, it shall be paid to them,[3] and if there remains something to our credit, they promise to complete it. If, before the conclusion of our peace, our vessels of war have captured vessels of the said nation, these shall not be restored and shall remain our prizes, but if our war vessels capture one of their ships after the date of the conclusion of the peace treaty, it is promised that this ship shall be given back.

All this has been put down in the present document, which shall be consulted whenever needed and according to which both parties shall act.

21 Safar, 1210.

[Tughra [4] of HASSAN PASHA]
[Seal of HASSAN PASHA]

ARTICLE 1.

The statements of the first article are that in this year 1210 an agreement has been reached between the ruler of America, George Washington, President, our friend and actually the Governor of the States of the island of America, and the lord of our well-preserved garrison of Algiers, His Highness Hassan Pasha—may God grant to him what he wishes—the Dey, together with the Agha of his victorious army, his minister, all the members of the Divan, and all his

[1] "Garrison" renders the Turkish word "odgiak," which means originally "a hearth" and, as a military term, "a regiment" of the Janizaries.

[2] The Turkish text has here "pashador," which seems to be an attempt to render the word "ambassador."

[3] That is, the difference shall be paid to the Americans.

[4] "Tughra" is the "name sign," a kind of calligraphic monogram in which a ruler's names are inscribed. The tughra takes the place of the signature.

victorious soldiers, and equally between the subjects of both parties. According to this agreement our peace and friendship shall be steady and has been confirmed. After this date nothing has been left that is contrary to our peace or that may disturb it.[1]

21 Safar, 1210.

ARTICLE 2.

The statements of the second article are that when large or small ships belonging to our friend the ruler of America, and equally ships belonging to his subjects, arrive in the port of Algiers or in other ports dependent on Algiers, and they sell from their goods according to the ancient usage, there shall be taken a duty of 5 piasters from every 100 piasters, in the same way as this is paid, according to the treaties, by the English, the Dutch, and the Swedes, and that no more shall be taken. Also that if they wish to take back their unsold goods and reembark them, nobody shall require anything from them, and equally that nobody in the said ports shall do them harm or lay hand upon them.

21 Safar, 1210.

ARTICLE 3.

The statements of the third article are that if war vessels or merchant vessels belonging to our friend the American ruler meet on the open sea with war vessels or merchant vessels belonging to Algiers, and they become known to each other, they shall not be allowed to search or to molest each other, and that none shall hinder the other from wending its own way with honor and respect. Also, that whatever kind of travelers there are on board, and wherever they go with their goods, their valuables, and other properties, they shall not molest each other or take anything from each other, nor take them to a certain place and hold them up, nor injure each other in any way.

21 Safar, 1210.

ARTICLE 4.

The statements of the fourth article are that if war vessels of Algiers meet with American merchant vessels, large or small, and this happens out of the places under the rule of America, there shall be sent only a shallop, in which, besides the rowers, two persons shall take place; on their arrival no more than two persons shall go on board the ship, the commander of the said ship having to give permission, and after the showing of the Government passport, these persons shall perform quickly the formalities with regard to the ship, and return, after which the merchant vessel shall wend its own way.

Further, that if war vessels of the American ruler meet with war vessels or merchant vessels of Algiers, and these vessels are in possession of a passport delivered by the ruler of Algiers or the American Consul residing in Algiers, nobody may touch anything belonging to the said vessel, but it shall wend its way in peace.

---

[1] Each article concludes with the word "salaam," salutation or peace, which has been left untranslated.

Further, that the war vessels of Algiers, large or small, shall not touch Americans not possessed of American passports within a period of eighteen months after the date of the passports given by reason of the peace treaty and after the date of the peace treaty,[1] and they shall not hinder them from going their way. Equally, if the war vessels of the American ruler meet with Algerian ships, they shall not prevent them from continuing their journey in the same way, within a period of eighteen months, but they shall wend peacefully their way.

Further that our friend the American ruler shall not give a passport to any crew not being under his rule and not belonging to his own people; if an American passport is found in the hands of a crew not belonging to his own people, we shall take them as prize, for this is not covered by the stipulations of this peace treaty. This has been expressly stated in this article in order to prevent a rupture of peace; so it shall not be neglected.

21 Safar, 1210.

ARTICLE 5.

The statements of the fifth article are that none of the captains of Algerian ships or of their officers or commanders shall take anybody by force from American ships into their own ships or bring such a person to other places, that they shall not interrogate them on account of anything or do them harm, whatever kind of people they may be; as long as these are on American ships, they shall not molest them.

21 Safar, 1210.

ARTICLE 6.

The statements of the sixth article are that if a ship of the American ruler or belonging to his subjects shall be stranded on one of the coasts of the territory under Algerian rule and is wrecked, nobody shall take anything from their properties or goods or plunder them.

Also, that if such a thing should happen, their goods shall not be taken to the customhouse, nor shall there be done any damage to their people, and if a similar thing should happen in the places that are under the rule of Algiers, the inhabitants shall do anything in their power to give every possible aid and assistance and help them to bring their goods on dry places.

21 Safar, 1210.

ARTICLE 7.

The statements of the seventh article are that no Algerian ship, small or large, shall, with the permission and the authority of the ruler of Algiers, be equipped from countries at war with the ruler of America and commit acts of war against the Americans.

21 Safar, 1210.

---

[1] This is a literal translation, but the sense is not very clear. The words "of the passports given by reason of the peace treaty" seem to be superfluous.

115605°—31—vol. 2——22

ARTICLE 8.

The statements of the eighth article are that if an American merchant buys a prize in Algiers, or if an Algerian cruiser captain who has taken a prize on the open sea sells his prize to an American merchant, either in Algiers or on the sea, so that it is bought immediately from the captain, and there is drawn up a document concerning this sale, and if he meets afterwards another war vessel from Algiers, nobody shall molest the merchant who has bought this prize, nor shall he prevent him from wending peacefully his way.

21 Safar, 1210.

ARTICLE 9.

The statements of the ninth article are that the inhabitants of Tunis, Tripoli, Sale, or others shall in no wise bring the people or the goods of American ships, large or small, to the territory under the rule of Algiers, nor shall there be given permission to sell them nor shall they be allowed to be sold.

21 Safar, 1210.

ARTICLE 10.

The statements of the tenth article are that if the warships of the American ruler bring to Algiers, or to ports under Algerian rule, prizes or goods captured by them, nobody shall hinder them from doing with their booty as they wish, namely, selling it or taking it with them.

Also, that American war vessels shall not pay any tithes or duties whatever.

Further, that if they wish to buy anything for provisions, the inhabitants shall give it to them at the same price as they sell it to others and ask no more.

Likewise, if those people want to charter ships for the transport of goods to whatever region, province, or port, be it to Smyrna or from Constantinople to this region, or for the transport of travelers from Smyrna or other provinces, or in order to convey pilgrims to Egypt, they may charter those ships at reasonable prices, in the same way as other peoples, and from our side they shall not be opposed by pretexts such as that it is contraband or that it is not allowed among us, so that we do not allow those ships to leave.

21 Safar, 1210.

ARTICLE 11.

The statements of the eleventh article are that if war vessels belonging to our friend the American ruler come to anchor in front of Algiers, and a slave, being an American or of another nationality, takes refuge on board the said war vessel, the ruler of Algiers may claim this slave, at which request the commander of the war vessel shall make this fugitive slave leave his ship and deliver him into the presence of the ruler of Algiers. If the slave is not to be found and reaches a country of unbelievers, the commander of the ship shall pledge his word that he shall return and bring him to Algiers.

21 Safar, 1210.

Article 12.

The statements of the twelfth article are that from this time onward the subjects of the American ruler shall not be bought, nor sold, nor taken as slaves, in the places under the rule of Algiers.

Also, that since there is friendship with the American ruler, he shall not be obliged to redeem against his will slaves belonging to him, but that this shall be done at the time he likes and that it shall depend on the generosity and the solicitude of the friends and relations of the slaves.

Further, that there shall be put no term or time for the redeeming of prisoners, that the amount which shall be found convenient shall be paid in due order, and that there shall be negotiations about the price with the masters of the slaves; nobody shall oblige the masters to sell their slaves at an arbitrary price, whether they be slaves of the State, of others, or of the Pasha; but if the redeemed persons are American subjects, there shall not be asked of them more than of other nations in similar circumstances.

Also, that if the Algerian vessels of war capture a ship belonging to a nation with which they are at war, and there are found Americans among the crew of this ship, these shall not be made slaves if they are in possession of a pass,[1] nor shall there be done harm to their persons and goods; but if they are not in possession of a pass[1] they shall be slaves and their goods and properties shall be taken.

21 Safar, 1210.

Article 13.

The statements of the thirteenth article are that if one of the merchants of the American ruler or one of his subjects shall die in Algiers or in one of the dependencies of Algiers, the ruler of Algiers or other persons shall not touch in any way the deceased's money, property, or goods; if he has designated before his death an executor, nobody else shall touch any part of his property or goods, either if the executor mentioned is present in Algiers or if he is not there. Accordingly, the person designated as executor by the deceased shall take the properties and the goods, and nobody else shall touch the slightest part of it; so shall it be. The executor or the person delegated by him as his representative shall make an inventory of his money and property, take possession of it, and forward it in due time to the heir.

Further, that if no subject of the American ruler is present, the American Consul shall made an inventory of the said deceased's money and goods and take possession of them and keep them in charge until the arrival of his relations living in their own country.

21 Safar, 1210.

Article 14.

The statements of the fourteenth article are that neither in Algiers itself nor in its dependencies shall the American merchants be obliged

[1] The Turkish has "passavant."

to purchase goods which they do not desire, but they shall be free to purchase the goods they desire.

Also, that the ships visiting the ports of Algiers shall not be molested in this way—that goods which they do not wish be put into the ships.

Further, that neither the American Consul nor anyone else, in case an American subject is unable to pay his debts, shall be held responsible for those debts and be obliged to pay, unless some persons, according to their free will, are bound for the debtor.

21 Safar, 1210.

Article 15.

The statements of the fifteenth article are that if one of the subjects of the American ruler has a suit at law with a Mohammedan or with some one subjected to the rule of Algiers, the said suit at law shall be settled in the presence of His Excellency the Dey and the honored Divan, without intervention of anybody else. If there occurs a suit at law among those people themselves, the American Consul shall decide their disputes.

21 Safar, 1210.

Article 16.

The statements of the sixteenth article are that should one of the subjects of the American ruler have a fight with a Mohammedan, so that one wounds the other or kills him, each one shall be punished according to the prescriptions of the law of his own country, that is, according to the custom in all other places. If, however, an American kills a Mohammedan and flies and escapes after the murder, neither the American Consul in Algiers nor other Americans shall be compelled to answer for him.

21 Safar, 1210.

Article 17.

The statements of the seventeenth article are that the American Consul, now and in future, without regard to who he is, shall be free to circulate without fear, while nobody shall molest his person or his goods.

Also, that he may appoint anyone whom he desires as dragoman or as broker.

Also, that whenever he wishes to go on board a ship or to take a walk outside, nobody shall hinder him.

Further, that a place shall be designated for the practice of their void religious ceremonies, that a priest whom they need for their religious instruction may dwell there, and that the American slaves present in Algiers, either belonging to the Government or to other people, may go to the house of the Consul and practice their vain religious ceremonies without hindrance from the chief slave guard or from their masters.

21 Safar, 1210.

ARTICLE 18.

The statements of the eighteenth article are that now there reigns between us peace and friendship, but that if in future there should occur a rupture of our present state of peace and friendship, and there should be caused trouble on both sides, the American Consul, and besides him the subjects of the American ruler either in Algiers or in its dependencies, may not be hindered either in peace or in trouble, and that whenever they wish to leave, nobody shall prevent them from leaving with their goods, properties, belongings, and servants, even if such a person be born in the country of Algiers.

21 Safar, 1210.

ARTICLE 19.

The statements of the nineteenth article are that a subject of the American ruler, to whatever country he goes or from whatever country he comes, and to whatever kind of people he belongs, shall not be molested in his person, goods, property, belongings, or servants, in case he meets with Algerian vessels, large or small.[1] Equally, if an Algerian is found on board a ship belonging to enemies of the American ruler, they shall not be molested in any way in their person, their property, their goods, their money, or their servants, but the properties of these people shall not be regarded with disdain, and they shall always be treated in a friendly manner.

21 Safar, 1210.

ARTICLE 20.

The statements of the twentieth article are that every time that a naval commander of the American King, our friend, arrives off Algiers, the American Consul shall inform the commander as soon as the vessel is seen; after the said captain has anchored before the port, the commander of Algiers shall, in honor of the American ruler, order a salute of twenty-one guns from the citadel, after which the captain of the American ruler shall answer gun for gun, and, as the said vessel is a vessel of the King, there shall be given provisions according to the custom, in honor of the King.

21 Safar, 1210.

ARTICLE 21.

The statements of the twenty-first article are that there shall not be asked duty and taxes for goods that are destined for the house of the American Consul, consisting of eatables, drinkables, other necessaries, and presents.

21 Safar, 1210.

ARTICLE 22.

The statements of the twenty-second article are that if there occurs from this time onward a disturbance of our peaceful relations,

---

[1] The Turkish text does not mention the condition that these Americans and their goods are on ships belonging to enemies of Algiers, but this, of course, is the meaning.

from whatever side this happens, this shall not rupture our peace, but the peace shall be maintained and our friendship shall not be disturbed. The person injured, to whatever party he belongs, shall claim justice. If, however, the fault and the guilt are on both sides, or on the side of a subject, and the matter is kept secret,[1] our belief in our friendship shall remain and our word shall remain as good as ever.

21 Safar, 1210.

NOTES

The original of this treaty is in Turkish, not in Arabic as stated in the proclamation. The articles which are written in English on pages of the original document are a translation, signed by Joseph Donaldson, jr., who negotiated the treaty at Algiers.

There is an interesting account of the negotiations, entitled "Narrative of the proceedings of Joseph Donaldson Esq[e]," written by Richard O'Brien, afterwards Consul General at Algiers, in D. S., 1 Archives, Tunis, 1793–1801 (a volume from the consular archives at Tunis), where O'Brien gives this account of himself:

> Late Master of the Ship Dauphin, of Philadelphia, but was Captured the 30th of July 1785. fifty leagues to the Westward of Lisbon, by an Algerine Corsair of 34 Guns & 450 men—& Remained in Captivity untill the 11th of September 1795 Redeemed in Consequence, of the Peace made by the United States, with Algiers.

The report of Donaldson on the treaty, dated September 7, 1795 (D. S., 1 Consular Despatches, Algiers), is somewhat confused and in certain respects obscure; but he mentions that the text was in Turkish, saying that James Leander Cathcart, who was one of the American captives and was chief Christian clerk of the Dey of Algiers, "returned to me with Articles of a Treaty in Turkish & then Englished, which Proves to be that of the Sweedes." The Swedish treaty here referred to is the Treaty of Peace and Commerce with Algiers of April 25/May 5, 1792, which was a renewal, with additions, of a treaty of April 5/16, 1729. For the Swedish text and a French translation, see Von Martens, Recueil des principaux traités, 1st ed., VI, 296–311; 2d ed., V, 316–31. The substance of each of the respective twenty-two articles of the Swedish and American treaties is in general similar.

The date of the treaty is stated above in the two calendars according to the original documents, namely, Saturday, September 5, 1795, and 21 Safar, A. H. 1210. According to the chronological tables the Mohammedan date corresponds to September 6, 1795; however, the mention of the day of the week (see the opening phrase of the translation of 1930) fixes the date definitively, and in this case there is no doubt that 21 Safar, A. H. 1210, answers to September 5, 1795. From the report of Donaldson above mentioned it appears that the money bargain, to which the negotiations in reality wholly related, was

[1] This passage is not very clear in the Turkish text.

struck on Saturday, September 5, and the treaty was delivered by Cathcart to Donaldson "the next morning."

However, a more complete and perhaps more accurate account of the negotiations is that of Cathcart, as written in The Captives, 158–95. Certainly Cathcart had at least as much to do with the bargain struck to pay $585,000 for the treaty and the ransom of the American captives as Donaldson had, and indeed, according to Cathcart, much more. He gives September 3, 1795, as the date of the arrival of Donaldson at Algiers and September 5 as the date of the verbal money agreement, the proclamation of peace, and the salute to the American flag; and on September 7 he says (page 191):

This afternoon I received the treaty in Turkish from the Secretary of State, and with the translation in English which was made and written by me, and collated with the original in twenty-three articles, and the four passports before mentioned, I took to Mr. Donaldson.

The Original Treaty

The documentary form of the original treaty in the Department of State file, the only original paper which it contains, is unusual. The document is composed of sixteen sheets of paper approximately ten inches wide and fourteen inches long, folded once, evenly, lengthwise; these sheets are held together by a ribbon which is tied along the center fold; so that, as folded, the treaty looks like a long pamphlet of thirty-two narrow leaves or sixty-four narrow pages. Neither the sheets nor the pages are numbered; but taking the pages as if they were numbered, the articles appear (beginning at page 16) in left-to-right order of pagination, one on a page, the English on the left pages, the Turkish on the right; these are followed by the final clause of the English translation of 1795 with the signature of Donaldson and, opposite thereto, the corresponding Turkish text with its signature and seal; next and last is written the confirmation or approval of Col. David Humphreys, then Minister to Portugal; and on page 14 is written, in English, the long way of the page from foot to top:

A Treaty of Peace & Amity concluded this Present Day Jima artasi y[e] twenty first of the Luna Safer year of the Hegira 1210 Corrisponding with Saturday the fifth of September One thousand Seven Hundred & Ninety five between Hassan Bashaw Dey of Algiers his Divan and Subjects and George Washington President of the United States of North America and the Citizens of y[e] Said United States.

Finally there is a later endorsement on page 1 of the document giving the date of Senate action.

Whether the present arrangement of the sheets that compose the treaty document is the original arrangement thereof is very doubtful; the internal evidence leads to the view that this present arrangement of the document is that which it had when it left the hands of Donaldson; but it may well be that when the treaty was first written in Turkish and before it was "Englished," as Donaldson says, the articles were arranged in the usual Turkish right-to-left order of pagination. The point is quite unimportant except that it is now impossible to say definitely whether the clause which has always been

printed as the final clause of the treaty (according to the English translation of 1795) was not in reality a preamble. That Donaldson regarded it as a final clause is clear from the position of his signature; but as the translation of 1930 shows, it reads like a preamble and may well have been one.

However, in the reproduction of the Turkish text above, the clause appears at the end, corresponding with the English translation of 1795 and with the original document in its present arrangement.

The translation which is first printed above is that which is written in the treaty document and which was then signed by Donaldson. It is that which is in the Statutes at Large and elsewhere generally. The style of that translation as here printed follows the original document literally, except that punctuation which has been inserted in the first four articles of the document in a different-colored ink and in a different hand, apparently at a later date, is here omitted. Following that translation is the certificate or approval of Humphreys. Then is printed the translation of the Turkish which was made in 1930 by Dr. J. H. Kramers, of Leiden. As shown by the translation of 1930, the discrepancies between the original Turkish and the translation of 1795 are numerous; and in some articles, such as 10, 11, and 14, the differences are striking.

Other Originals

It appears that there was another original of this treaty in the files of the Consulate at Algiers. After the treaty had been in force for nearly seventeen years, a rupture took place and Tobias Lear, Consul General, and all other Americans then in Algiers, were expelled from the country on July 25, 1812. One of the demands of the Dey of Algiers at that time, which he successfully enforced, was that the yearly tribute of $21,600 stipulated in the treaty should be calculated according to Mohammedan and not to Christian years. While the money settlement was being arranged, the Dey sent by messenger to Lear for "the original Treaty, (in English and Turkish,)" so that he "might see the time when the said Treaty was ratified, the terms &c," and Lear delivered it "without hesitation, supposing that the Dey might wish to see something in it, or that he might compare it with that which was in the Palace"; but the Dey refused to return the treaty, sending word "he should retain the Treaty, as was the custom in Algiers, when a Consul was sent away on account of his Government" (report of Lear, July 24, 1812, and letter to the Secretary of State, July 29, 1812, D. S., 8 Consular Despatches, Algiers; see also Laws of the United States, Bioren & Duane ed., I, 288–89).

According to Cathcart (The Captives, 221–23), there were, in all, four originals of the treaty, two executed at the time of the agreement and two others by October 1, 1795; these were intended to be delivered as follows (*ibid.*, 221): "one to be sent to the Secretary of State, one to Col. Humphreys, one to remain in the Consulate, and one in the palace."

Note Regarding Ratification

Some observations regarding the practice as to treaties with the Barbary States are to be found in the notes to the treaty with Morocco of 1786 (Document 14).

There is no duplicate or written copy of the United States instrument of ratification in the Department of State file. The text of the instrument, however, was published at the time (*e. g.*, Claypoole's American Daily Advertiser, Philadelphia, March 10, 1796). In form the document, dated March 7, 1796, is at once a ratification and a proclamation. It mentions the treaty as "written in the Arabic language, being translated into the language of the United States," and includes the translation signed by Donaldson and also the approval of Humphreys. A facsimile of the newspaper print is now in the Department of State file.

On April 13, 1796, the instrument of ratification was forwarded to Humphreys (D. S., 3 Instructions, U. S. Ministers, 117–20). The instrument was received by Humphreys on June 17, 1796, and was forwarded by him to Robert Montgomery, Agent at Alicante, for transmission to Joel Barlow, Consul General at Algiers (D. S., 3 Despatches, Spain, No. 50, June 22, 1796).

Accordingly it seems probable that the Dey of Algiers was notified by Barlow of the ratification shortly thereafter, perhaps during the negotiations and discussions of July, 1796; and it is even possible that the United States instrument of ratification was then delivered; in his report of September 7, 1795, Donaldson wrote, "the Dey recommends a Frigate being sent here with the ratification as it is on Secret Questions usual to return the Salute which is always fired from the Castle Fort." But doubt on the point must remain in view of statements subsequently made regarding the practice of Algiers; thus Charles O. Handy, Secretary to the Mission of 1816 to Algiers, in a letter to Commodore Chauncey of December 30, 1816 (D. S., 9 Consular Despatches, Algiers) wrote:

> The Treaties which Algiers has heretofore had with the Maratime Powers of Europe, appear more in the light of capitulations made with their respective Consuls, acting with plenary Powers, than with their Governments of whose sentiments they are only the authorized organs. Consequently the rejection, or ratification, of such Treaties, is never with the Regency a subject of interest, or importance. From the long and unvaried custom, arbitrarily adopted, and resolutely pursued, by this Barbary State, they never have, & probably never will, recognize, the approbation of a Government, as essential to the completion and execution of a Treaty. Our Treaty in June 1815 they refused to receive after it had been approved of by the President & Senate, alledging as a reason therefor, that the Algerine Regency never had acknowledged the necessity of such a measure & would never be governed by it in any manner whatever.

Not very important in this case, however, were treaty formalities and treaty procedure. The existence and execution of the treaty, from the viewpoint of the Dey of Algiers, depended wholly upon the receipt by him of the large payments by the United States stipulated *dehors* the treaty. The delay in the transmittal of the amounts promised on the signature of the agreement caused added and

successful demands for more; the statement of Cathcart (The Captives, 220–21) is that "had the funds arrived as the Dey expected, it would have prevented all the trouble, anxiety and enormous expense which occurred afterwards, which at least doubled the original price promised for peace and the ransom of our brethern in captivity." (See the papers with the message of President Washington of January 9, 1797, American State Papers, Foreign Relations, I, 553–58.)

Not until July 8, 1796, were the survivors of the American captives who had been held in miserable slavery in Algiers released. Joel Barlow reported that six of them had in the previous few weeks died of the plague, which "still rages with such violence in the town"; and he added:

> Our people have conducted themselves in general with a degree of patience and decorum which would become a better condition than that of slaves. . . .
>
> Several of them are probably rendered incapable of gaining a living. One is in a state of total blindness; another is reduced nearly to the same condition; two or three carry the marks of unmerciful treatment in ruptures produced by hard labour; and others have had their constitutions injured by the plague. Some of these are doubtless objects of the charity of their countrymen. (D. S., 2 Consular Despatches, Algiers, No. 8, July 12, 1796.)

The treaty was bought by the United States; and it was the price paid and payable, which the Treasury estimated at $992,463.25, and not any instrument of ratification, which made the treaty a realty.

The practical difficulties of the situation were officially recognized at the time; under date of June 8, 1796, the following notice or press release, signed by the Secretary of State, was issued, entitled "Caution to Merchants and other Citizens of the United States" (text from D. S., 9 Domestic Letters, 158; the notice was published in the press, *e. g.*, Claypoole's American Daily Advertiser, Philadelphia, June 10, 1796):

> The advices received by Captain O'Brien from Col? Humphreys at Lisbon, shew that the temporary obstacles to a fulfilment of the stipulations on the part of the United States with the Dey and Regency of Algiers are not yet removed. The treaty itself being put in jeopardy, by these unexpected delays, the safety of American vessels entering the Mediterranean has become extremely precarious. It should also be remembered, that no treaty has ever yet been made between the United States and the Governments of Tunis and Tripoli. Merchants and other citizens of the United States, will hence see the hazard to which they will expose their property and the liberty of their fellow citizens, by engaging, in the present state of things, in commerce within the straights of Gibraltar.

Indeed, years elapsed before the stipulations of 1795 and 1796 could be fulfilled by the United States. They are discussed at some length in the instructions to O'Brien, given when he went as Consul General to Algiers in 1798 (D. S., 4 Instructions, U. S. Ministers, 188–93, December 29, 1797). The following extracts therefrom will serve to show their nature:

> The Crescent Frigate in which you are to embark, you will deliver to the Dey and Regency, for whom it has been constructed and equipped, conformably to the stipulation of M! Barlow. . . .

The Schooner Hamdullah, which has lately sailed with Stores for Algiers is also to be delivered to the Dey. . . . This Schooner has been purchased, and the Schooner Lelah Eisha is now building here, for the Dey, in the expectation that they will not only soothe him under the past delays & disappointments in the fulfilment of our stipulations, but serve as acceptable substitutes for the stipulated, masts, Yards, and heavy planks, which are so costly and difficult to procure, and so exceedingly expensive to transport—the former, when delivered at Algiers will cost the United States perhaps thirty times their estimated price in the stipulations. You will, therefore, exert all your talents to effect these objects. And for your full information concerning them, the copies of the original agreement and of the articles for the annual presents, and of the Invoices of articles furnished in pursuance thereof, are herewith delivered to you. We shall be anxious to receive the details of your negotiations in this business & their result.

The Passports

The original treaty was brought to the United States by Capt. Richard O'Brien; one of the four passports mentioned by Cathcart as having been delivered with the treaty on September 7, 1795 (The Captives, 191), and very likely the one used by O'Brien, is in the archives of the Department of State; it has the seal and also the tughra or name sign of Hassan Pasha, Dey of Algiers; and as translated by Doctor Kramers from the Turkish, it reads as follows:

The reason of the writing of this document is this: On the 23d of the month of Safar, 1210. The bearer of the present document, belonging to the American people, that has now concluded a peace treaty with the frontier-post of the holy war, Algiers, has desired a passport for himself as well as for the ship on board which he is and for all the sailors, being Americans, for the period of a year after the date of this document, in order that, when navigating and passing on sea, if they meet with war vessels of Algiers or of Tunis the well-preserved, or of Tripoli, these shall not lay hand on his ship or on his crew or his load and cargo, or molest him. According to this demand of security this passport has been drawn up and written and given into his hands. Therefore, if the war vessels of Algiers, when meeting, do him any harm or molestation, those people shall be punished severely, and if he meets with molestation from the war vessels of Tunis or Tripoli, they shall be punished by the intermediary of their officers. In order to state this, this passport has been given as a proof into his hands, so that it may be produced and used in time of need.

Written in the last days of Safar, 1210.
Frontier of Algiers the well-preserved.

Treaty Series, No. 325
8 Statutes at Large, 138–53

18

SPAIN : OCTOBER 27, 1795

Treaty of Friendship, Limits, and Navigation, signed at San Lorenzo el Real October 27, 1795. Original in English and Spanish. Submitted to the Senate February 26, 1796. Resolution of advice and consent March 3, 1796. Ratified by the United States March 7, 1796. Ratified by Spain April 25, 1796. Ratifications exchanged at Aranjuez April 25, 1796. Proclaimed August 2, 1796.

His Catholic Majesty and the United States of America desiring to consolidate on a permanent basis the Friendship and good correspondence which happily prevails between the two Parties, have determined to establish by a convention several points, the settlement whereof will be productive of general advantage and reciprocal utility to both Nations.

Deseando S. M. Catolica y los Estados Unidos de America consolidar de un modo permanente la buena correspondencia y amistad que felizmente reyna entre ambas Partes, han resuelto fixar por medio de un Convenio varios puntos de cuyo arreglo resultará un beneficio general, y una utilidad reciproca â los dos Paises.

With this intention his Catholic Majesty has appointed the most Excellent Lord Don Manuel de Godoy and Alvarez de Faria, Rios, Sanchez Zarzosa, Prince de la Paz Duke de la Alcudia Lord of the Soto de Roma and of the State of Albalá: Grandee of Spain of the first class: perpetual Regidor of the Citty of Santiago: Knight of the illustrious Order of the Golden Fleece, and Great Cross of the Royal and distinguished Spanish order of Charles the III. Commander of Valencia del Ventoso, Rivera, and Aceuchal in that of Santiago: Knight

Con esta mira han nombrado S. M. Catolica al Excelentisimo S.or D.n Manuel de Godoy, y Alvarez de Faria, Rios, Sanchez Zarzosa, Principe de la Paz, Duque de la Alcudia: Señor del Soto de Roma, y del Estado de Albalá: Grande de España de primera clase: Regidor perpetuo de la Ciudad de Santiago: Caballero de la insigne Orden del Toyson de Oro: Gran Cruz de la Real y distinguida Orden Española de Carlos III. Comendador de Valencia del ventoso, Rivera, y Aceuchal en la de Santiago: Caballero Gran Cruz de

and Great Cross of the religious order of St John: Counsellor of State: First Secretary of State and Despacho: Secretary to the Queen: Superintendant General of the Posts and High Ways: Protector of the Royal Academy of the Noble Arts, and of the Royal Societies of natural history, Botany, Chemistry, and Astronomy: Gentleman of the King's Chamber in employement: Captain General of his Armies: Inspector and Major of the Royal Corps of Body Guards &a &a &a and the President of the United States with the advice and consent of their Senate, has appointed Thomas Pinckney a Citizen of the United States, and their Envoy Extraordinary to his Catholic Majesty. And the said Plenipotentiaries have agreed upon and concluded the following Articles.

la Religion de Sn Juan: Consegero de Estado: primer Secretario de Estado y del Despacho: Secretario de la Reyna Nra Sra Superintendente general de Correos y Caminos: Protector de la Rl Academia de las Nobles Artes, y de los Rles Gabinere de Historia natural, Jardin Botanico, Laboratorio Chîmico, y Observatorio Astronomico: Gentilhombre de Camara con exercicio: Capitan General de los Reales Exercitos: Inspector, y Sargento Mayor del Rl Cuerpo de Guardias de Corps. &a &a &a y el Presidente de los Estados Unidos con el consentimiento y aprobacion del Senado à Dn Tomas Pinckney Ciudadano de los mismos Estados y su Enviado Extraordinario cerca de S. M. Catholica. Y ambos Plenipotenciarios han ajustado y firmado los Articulos siguientes.

Art. I.

There shall be a firm and inviolable Peace and sincere Friendship between His Catholic Majesty his successors and subjects, and the United Estates and their Citizens without exception of persons or places.

Art. I.

Habrá una Paz solida ê inviolable y una amistad sincera entre S. M. Catolica sus succesores y subditos, y los Estados Unidos y sus Ciudadanos, sin excepcion de personas ô lugares.

Art. II.

To prevent all disputes on the subject of the boundaries which separate the territories of the two High contracting Parties, it is hereby declared and agreed as follows: to wit: The Southern boundary of the United States

Art. II.

Para evitar toda disputa en punto â los limites que separan los territorios de las dos Altas Partes Contratantes, se han convenido, y declarado en el presente articulo lo siguiente: â saber. Que el Limite Meridional de los Estados

which divides their territory from the Spanish Colonies of East and West Florida, shall be designated by a line beginning on the River Mississipi at the Northermost part of the thirty first degree of latitude North of the Equator, which from thence shall be drawn due East to the middle of the River Apalachicola or Catahouche, thence along the middle thereof to its junction with the Flint, thence straight to the head of St Mary's River, and thence down the middle there of to the Atlantic Occean. And it is agreed that if there should be any troops, Garrisons or settlements of either Party in the territory of the other according to the above mentioned boundaries, they shall be withdrawn from the said territory within the term of six months after the ratification of this treaty or sooner if it be possible and that they shall be permitted to take with them all the goods and effects which they possess.

Unidos que sepára su territorio de el de las Colonias Españolas de la Florida Occidental y de la Florida Oriental se demarcará por una linea que empieze en el Rio Misisipi en la parte mas septentrional del grado treinta y uno al Norte del Equador, y qe desde alli siga en derechura al Este hasta el medio del Rio Apalachicola ô Catahouche, desde alli por la mitad de este Rio hasta su union con el Flint, de alli en derechura hasta el nacimiento del Rio Sta Maria, y de alli baxando por el medio de este Rio hasta el Occeano Atlantico. Y se han convenido las dos Potencias en que si hubiese tropa, Guarniciones, ô Establecimientos de la una de las dos Partes en el territorio de la otra segun los limites que se acaban de mencionar, se retirarán de dicho territorio en el termino de seis meses despues de la ratificacion de este Tratado, ô antes si fuese posible, y que se les permitirá llevar consigo todos los bienes y efectos qe posean.

ART. III.

In order to carry the preceding Article into effect one Commissioner and one Surveyor shall be appointed by each of the contracting Parties who shall meet at the Natchez on the left side of the River Mississipi before the expiration of six months from the ratification of this convention, and they shall proceed to run and mark this boundary according to

ART. III.

Para la execucion del articulo antecedente se nombrarán por cada una de las dos Altas Partes contratantes un Comisario y un Geometra qe se juntarán en Natchez en la orilla izquierda del Misisipi antes de expirar el termino de seis meses despues de la ratificacion de la convencion presente, y procederán à la demarcacion de estos limites conforme à lo estipu-

the stipulations of the said Article. They shall make Plats and keep journals of their proceedings which shall be considered as part of this convention, and shall have the same force as if they were inserted therein.[1] And if on any account it should be found necessary that the said Commissioners and Surveyors should be accompanied by Guards, they shall be furnished in equal proportions by the Commanding Officer of his Majesty's troops in the two Floridas, and the Commanding Officer of the troops of the United States in their Southwestern territory, who shall act by common consent and amicably, as well with respect to this point as to the furnishing of provissions and instruments and making every other arrangement which may be necessary or useful for the execution of this article.

lado en el articulo anterior. Levantarán planos, y formarán Diarios de sus operaciones que se reputarán como parte de este Tratado, y tendran la misma fuerza que si estubieran insertas en el.[1] Y si por qualquier motivo se creyese necesario que los dichos Comisarios y Geometras fuesen acompañados con Guardias, se les darán en numero igual por el General que mande las tropas de S. M. en las dos Floridas, y el Comandante de las tropas de los Estados Unidos en su territorio del sudoeste, que obrarán de acuerdo y amistosamente asi en este punto, como en el de apronto de viveres ê instrumentos, y en tomar qualesquiera otras disposiciones necesarias para la execucion de este articulo.

Art. IV.

It is likewise agreed that the Western boundary of the United States which separates them from the Spanish Colony of Louissiana, is in the middle of the channel or bed of the River Mississipi from the Northern boundary of the said States to the completion of the thirty first degree of latitude North of the Equator; and his Catholic Majesty has likewise agreed that the navigation of the said River in its whole breadth

Art. IV.

Se han convenido igualmente que el Limite Occidental del territorio de los Estados Unidos q^e^ los separa de la Colonia Española de la Luisiana, está en medio del Canal ô Madre del Rio Misisipi, desde el limite septentrional de dichos Estados hasta el complemento de los treinta y un grados de latitud al Norte del Equador; y S. M. Catolica ha convenido igualmente en que la navegacion de dicho Rio en toda

[1] See the note regarding Article 3.

from its source to the Occean shall be free only to his Subjects, and the Citizens of the United States, unless he should extend this privilege to the Subjects of other Powers by special convention.

ART. V.

The two High contracting Parties shall by all the means in their power maintain peace and harmony among the several Indian Nations who inhabit the country adjacent to the lines and Rivers which by the preceeding Articles form the boundaries of the two Floridas; and the beter to obtain this effect both Parties oblige themselves expressly to restrain by force all hostilities on the part of the Indian Nations living within their boundaries: so that Spain will not suffer her Indians to attack the Citizens of the United States, nor the Indians inhabiting their territory; nor will the United States permit these last mentioned Indians to commence hostilities against the Subjects of his Catholic Majesty, or his Indians in any manner whatever.

And whereas several treaties[1] of Friendship exist between the two contracting Parties and the said Nations of Indians, it is hereby agreed that in future no treaty of alliance or other whatever (except treaties of Peace) shall be made by either Party with the

su extension desde su orilla hasta el Occeano, será libre solo â sus subditos, y á los Ciudadanos de los Estados Unidos, â menos que por algun tratado particular haga extensiva esta libertad à subditos de otras Potencias.

ART. V.

Las dos Altas Partes contratantes procurarán por todos los medios posibles mantener la paz, y buena armonía entre las diversas Naciones de Indios que habitan los terrenos adyacentes â las lineas y Rios que en los articulos anteriores forman los limites de las dos Floridas; y para conseguir mejor este fin se obligan expresamente ambas Potencias à reprimir con la fuerza todo genero de hostilidades de parte de las Naciones Indias que habitan dentro de la linea de sus respectivos limites: de modo que ni la España permitirá que sus Indios ataquen â los qe vivan en el territorio de los Estados Unidos ô â sus ciudadanos; ni los Estados qe los suyos hostilizen â los Subditos de S. M. Catolica ô â sus Indios de manera alguna.

Exîstiendo varios tratados[1] de amistad entre las expresadas Naciones y las dos Potencias, se ha convenido en no hacer en lo venidero alianza alguna ô tratado (excepto los de Paz) con las Naciones de Indios que habitan dentro de los limites de la otra

[1] See the note regarding Article 5.

Indians living within the boundary of the other; but both Parties will endeavour to make the advantages of the Indian trade common and mutualy beneficial to their respective Subjects and Citizens observing in all things the most complete reciprocity: so that both Parties may obtain the advantages arising from a good understanding with the said Nations, without being subject to the expence which they have hitherto occasioned.

parte; aunque procurarán hacer comun su comercio en beneficio amplio de los Subditos y Ciudadanos respectivos, guardandose en todo la reciprocidad mas completa: de suerte qe sin los dispendios que han causado hasta ahora dichas Naciones á las dos Partes contratantes consigan ambas todas las ventajas qe debe producir la armonía con ellas.

Art. VI.

Each Party shall endeavour by all means in their power to protect and defend all Vessels and other effects belonging to the Citizens or Subjects of the other, which shall be within the extent of their jurisdiction by sea or by land, and shall use all their efforts to recover and cause to be restored to the right owners their Vessels and effects which may have been taken from them within the extent of their said jurisdiction whether they are at war or not with the Power whose Subjects have taken possession of the said effects.

Art. VI.

Cada una de las dos Partes contratantes procurará por todos los medios posibles protexer y defender todos los Buques y qualesquiera otros efectos pertenecientes â los Subditos y Ciudadanos de la otra que se hallen en la extension de su jurisdiccion por Mar ô por Tierra; y empleará todos sus esfuerzos para recobrar y hacer restituir â los Propietarios lexitimos los Buques y Efectos que se les hayan quitado en la extension de dicha jurisdiccion estén ô no en guerra con la Potencia cuyos subditos hayan interceptado dichos Efectos.

Art. VII.

And it is agreed that the Subjects or Citizens of each of the contracting Parties, their Vessels, or effects shall not be liable to any embargo or detention on the part of the other for any military expedition or other public or

Art. VII.

Se ha convenido que los Ciudadanos y Subditos de una de las Partes contratantes, sus Buques, ô efectos no podran sugetarse â ningun embargo ô detencion de parte de la otra, â causa de alguna expedicion militar, uso publico, ô

private porpose whatever; and in all cases of seizure, detention, or arrest for debts contracted or offences commited by any Citizen or Subject of the one Party within the jurisdiction of the other, the same shall be made and prosecuted by order and authority of law only, and according to the regular course of proceedings usual in such cases. The Citizens and Subjects of both Parties shall be allowed to employ such Advocates, Sollicitors, Notaries, Agents, and Factors, as they may judje proper in all their affairs and in all their trials at law in which they may be concerned before the tribunals of the other Party, and such Agents shall have free access to be present at the proceedings in such causes, and at the taking of all examinations and evidence which may be exhibited in the said trials.

particular de qualquiera que sea; y en los casos de aprehension, detencion, ô arresto bien sea por deudas contrahidas û ofensas cometidas por algun Ciudadano ô Subdito de una de las Partes contratantes en la jurisdiccion de la otra, se procederá unicamente por orden y autoridad de la Justicia, y segun los tramites ordinarios seguidos en semejantes casos. Se permitira à los Ciudadanos y Subditos de ambas Partes emplear los Abogados, Procuradores, Notarios, Agentes, ô Factores que juzguen mas à proposito en todos sus asuntos y en todos los Pleytos qe podrán tener en los Tribunales de la otra Parte, â los quales se permitirá igualmente el tener libre acceso en las causas, y estar presentes â todo exâmen y testimonios que podran ocurrir en los Pleytos.

Art. VIII.

In case the Subjects and inhabitants of either Party with their shipping whether public and of war or private and of merchants be forced through stress of weather, pursuit of Pirates, or Enemis, or any other urgent necessity for seeking of shelter and harbor to retreat and enter into any of the Rivers, Bays, Roads, or Ports belonging to the other Party, they shall be received and treated with all humanity, and enjoy all favor, protection and help, and they shall be permitted to re-

Art. VIII.

Quando los Subditos y habitantes de la una de las dos Partes contratantes con sus Buques bien sean publicos y de guerra, bien particulares ô mercantiles se viesen obligados por una tempestad, por escapar de Piratas ô de Enemigos, ô por qualquiera otra necesidad urgente â buscar refugio y abrigo en alguno de los Rios, Bahias, Radas, ô Puertos de una de las dos Partes, serán recibidos, y tratados con humanidad, y gozaran de todo fabor, proteccion y socorro, y les será licito prove-

fresh and provide themselves at reasonable rates with victuals and all things needful for the sustenance of their persons or reparation of their Ships, and prosecution of their voyage; and they shall no ways be hindered from returning out of the said Ports, or Roads, but may remove and depart when and whither they please without any let or hindrance.

erse de refrescos, viveres y demas cosas necesarias para su sustento, para componer los Buques, y continuar su viage, todo mediante un precio equitativo; y no se les detendrá ô impedirá de modo alguno el salir de dichos Puertos ô Radas, antes bien podran retirarse y partir como y quando les pareciere sin ningun obstaculo ô impedimento.

ART. IX.

All Ships and merchandize of what nature soever which shall be rescued out of the hands of any Pirates or Robbers on the high seas shall be brought into some Port of either State and shall be delivered to the custody of the Officers of that Port in order to be taken care of and restored entire to the true proprietor as soon as due and sufficient proof shall be made concerning the property there of.

ART. IX.

Todos los Buques y mercaderias de qualquiera naturaleza que sean que se hubiesen quitado à algunos Piratas en Alta Mar, y se traxesen à algun Puerto de una de las dos Potencias, se entregarán alli â los Oficiales ô Empleados en dicho Puerto â fin de que los guarden y restituyan integramente â su verdadero propietario luego que hiciese constar debida y plenamente que era su legitima propiedad.

ART. X.

When any Vessel of either Party shall be wrecked, foundered, or otherwise damaged on the coasts or within the dominion of the other, their respective Subjects or Citizens shall receive as well for themselves as for their Vessels and effects the same assistence which would be due to the inhabitants of the Country where the damage happens, and shall pay the same charges and dues only as the said inhabitants

ART. X.

En el caso de que un Buque perteneciente à una de las dos Partes contratantes naufragase, varase, ô sufriese alguna avería en las Costas ô en los dominios de la otra, se socorrerá â los Subditos ô Ciudadanos respectivos, asi â sus personas, como â sus Buques y efectos, del mismo modo que se haría con los habitantes del Pais donde suceda la desgracia, y pagaran solo las mismas cargas y derechos q^e se hubieran exĩgido

would be subject to pay in a like case: and if the operations of repair should require that the whole or any part of the cargo be unladen they shall pay no duties, charges, or fees on the part which they shall relade and carry away.

Art. XI.

The Citizens and Subjects of each Party shall have power to dispose of their personal goods within the jurisdiction of the other by testament, donation, or otherwise; and their representatives being Subjects or Citizens of the other Party shall succeed to their said personal goods, whether by testament or ab intestato and they may take possession thereof either by themselves or others acting for them, and dispose of the same at their will paying such dues only as the inhabitants of the Country wherein the said goods are shall be subject to pay in like cases, and in case of the absence of the representatives, such care shall be taken of the said goods as would be taken of the goods of a native in like case, until the lawful owner may take measures for receiving them. And if question shall arise among several claimants to which of them the said goods belong the same shall be decided finally by the laws and Judges of the Land wherein the said goods are. And where on the death of any person hold-

de dichos habitantes en semejante caso. y si fuese necesario para componer el Buque qe se descargue el cargamento en todo ô en parte, no pagarán impuesto alguno, carga, ô derecho de lo que se buelva â embarcar para ser exportado.

Art. XI.

Los Ciudadanos ô Subditos de una de las dos Partes contratantes, tendran en los Estados de la otra la libertad de disponer de sus bienes personales bien sea por testamento, donacion, û otra manera, y si sus herederos fuesen Subditos ô Ciudadanos de la otra Parte contratante, sucederán en sus bienes ya sea en virtud de testamento ô ab intestato y podran tomar posesion bien en persona ô por medio de otros que hagan sus veces, y disponer como les pareciere sin pagar mas derechos que aquellos qe deben pagar en semejante caso los habitantes del Pais donde se verificase la herencia. Y si estubiesen ausentes los herederos se cuydará de los bienes que les hubiesen tocado, del mismo modo que se hubiera hecho en semejante ocasion con los bienes de los naturales del Pais, hasta que el legitimo Propietario haya aprobado las disposiciones para recoger la herencia. Si se suscitasen disputas entre diferentes competidores que tengan derecho â la herencia, seran determinadas en ultima instancia segun las leyes y por los Jueces

ng real estate within the territories of the one Party, such real estate would by the laws of the Land descend on a Citizen or Subject of the other were he not disqualified by being an alien, such subject shall be allowed a reasonable time to sell the same and to withdraw the proceeds without molestation, and exempt from all rights of detraction on the part of the Government of the respective states.

del Pais en que vacase la herencia. Y si por la muerte de alguna persona que poseyese bienes raizes sobre el territorio de una de las Partes contratantes, estos bienes raizes llegasen à pasar segun las leyes del Pais à un Subdito ô Ciudadano de la otra Parte, y este por su calidad de extrangero fuese inhabil para poseerlos, obtendra un termino conveniente para venderlos y recoger su producto, sin obstaculo, exento de todo derecho de retencion de parte del Gobierno de los Estados respectivos.

Art. XII.

The merchant Ships of either of the Parties which shall be making into a Port belonging to the enemy of the other Party and concerning whose voyage and the species of goods on board her there shall be just grounds of suspicion shall be obliged to exhibit as well upon the high seas as in the Ports and havens not only her passports but likewise certificates expressly shewing that her goods are not of the number of those which have been prohibited as contraband.

Art. XII.

A los Buques mercantes de las dos Partes q[e] fuesen destinados à Puertos pertenecientes â una Potencia enemiga de una de las dos, cuyo viage y naturaleza del cargamento diese justas sospechas, se les obligará à presentar bien sea en alta Mar bien en los Puertos y Cabos no solo sus pasaportes sino tambien los certificados que probarán expresamente que su cargamento no es de la especie de los que están prohibidos como de contrabando.

Art. XIII.

For the beter promoting of commerce on both sides, it is agreed that if a war shall break out between the said two Nations one year after the proclamation of war shall be allowed to the merchants in the Cities and Towns where they shall live for collect-

Art. XIII.

A fin de faborecer el comercio de ambas Partes se ha convenido que en el caso de romperse la guerra entre las dos Naciones, se concedera el termino de un año despues de su declaracion á los Comerciantes en las Villas y Ciudades que habitan, para juntar

ing and transporting their goods and merchandizes, and if any thing be taken from them, or any injury be done them within that term by either Party, or the People or Subjects of either, full satisfaction shall be made for the same by the Government.

Art. XIV.

No subject of his Catholic Majesty shall apply for or take any commission or letters of marque for arming any Ship or Ships to act as Privateers against the said United States or against the Citizens, People, or inhabitants of the said United States, or against the property of any of the inhabitants of any of them, from any Prince or State with which the said United States shall be at war.

Nor shall any Citizen, Subject, or Inhabitant of the said United States apply for or take any commission or letters of marque for arming any Ship or Ships to act as Privateers against the subjects of his Catholic Majesty or the property of any of them from any Prince or State with which the said King shall be at war. And if any person of either Nation shall take such commissions or letters of marque he shall be punished as a Pirate.

Art. XV.

It shall be lawful for all and singular the Subjects of his Catholic Mayesty, and the Citizens

y transportar sus mercaderias, y si se les quitase alguna parte de ellas ô hiciese algun daño durante el tiempo prescrito arriba por una de las dos Potencias, sus Pueblos ô Subditos, se les dará en este punto entera satisfaccion por el Gobierno.

Art. XIV.

Ningun Subdito de S. M. Catolica tomará encargo ô patente para armar Buque ô Buques q^e obren como Corsarios contra dichos Estados Unidos, ô contra los Ciudadanos, Pueblos, y habitantes de los mismos, ô contra su propiedad ô la de los habitantes de alguno de ellos de qualquier Principe que sea con quien estubieren en guerra los Estados Unidos.

Igualmente ningun Ciudadano ô habitante de dichos Estados Unidos pedirá ô acceptará encargo ô patente para armar algun Buque ô Buques con el fin de perseguir los Subditos de S. M. Catolica, ô apoderarse de su propiedad, de qualquier Principe ô Estado que sea con quien estubiese en guerra S. M. Catolica. Y si algun individuo de una ô de otra Nacion tomase semejantes encargos ô patentes sera castigado como Pirata.

Art. XV.

Se permitirá à todos y â cada uno de los Subditos de S. M. Catolica; y â los Ciudadanos

People, and inhabitants of the said United States to sail with their Ships with all manner of liberty and security, no distinction being made who are the propietors of the merchandizes laden thereon from any Port to the Places of those who now are or hereafter shall be at enmity with his Catholic Majesty or the United States. It shall be likewise lawful for the Subjects and inhabitants aforesaid to sail with the Ships and merchandizes aforementioned, and to trade with the same liberty and security from the Places, Ports, and Havens of those who are Enemies of both or either Party without any opposition or disturbance whatsoever, not only directly from the Places of the Enemy aforementioned to neutral Places but also from one Place belonging to an Enemy to another Place belonging to an Enemy, whether they be under the jurisdiction of the same Prince or under several, and it is hereby stipulated that Free Ships shall also give freedom to goods, and that every thing shall be deemed free and exempt which shall be found on board the Ships belonging to the Subjects of either of the contracting Parties although the whole lading or any part thereof should appartain to the Enemies of either; contraband goods being always excepted. It is also agreed that the same liberty be extended to persons who are on board a free Ship, so that, although they be

Pueblos y habitantes de dichos Estados q^{e} puedan navegar con sus Embarcaciones con toda libertad y seguridad, sin que haya la menor excepcion por este respeto aunque los propietarios de las mercaderias cargadas en las referidas embarcaciones vengan del Puerto que quieran y las traygan destinadas â qualquiera Plaza de una Potencia actualmente enemiga ô q^{e} lo sea despues asi de S. M. Catolica como de los Estados Unidos. Se permitirá igualmente à los Subditos y habitantes mencionados navegar con sus Buques y mercaderias, y frequëntar con igual libertad y seguridad las Plazas y Puertos de las Potencias enemigas de las Partes contratantes ô de una de ellas sin oposicion û obstaculo, y de comerciar no solo desde los puertos del dicho enemigo à un Puerto neutro directamente, sino tambien desde uno enemigo â otro tal bien se encuentre bajo su jurisdicion ô bajo la de muchos; y se estipula tambien por el presente tratado que los Buques libres asegurarán igualmente la libertad de las mercaderias, y que se juzgaran libres todos los efectos que se hallasen â bordo de los Buques que perteneciesen â los Subditos de una de las Partes contratantes, aun quando el cargam^{to} por entero ô parte de el fuese de los enemigos de una de las dos; bien entendido sin embargo q^{e} el contrabando se exceptua siempre. Se ha convenido asi-

Enemies to either Party they shall not be made Prisoners or taken out of that free Ship unless they are Soldiers and in actual service of the Enemies.

mismo que la propia libertad gozarán los sugetos que pudiesen encontrarse â bordo del Buque libre aun quando fuesen enemigos de una de las dos Partes contratantes, y por lo tanto no se les podra hacer Prisioneros ni separarlos de dichos Buques, â menos qᵉ no tengan la qualidad de Militares, y esto hallandose en aquella sazon empleados en el servicio del enemigo.

Art. XVI.

This liberty of navigation and commerce shall extend to all kinds of merchandizes excepting those only which are distinguished by the name of contraband; and under this name of contraband or prohibited goods shall be comprehended arms, great guns, bombs, with the fusees, and other things belonging to them, cannon ball, gun powder, match, pikes, swords, lances, speards, halberds, mortars, petards, granades, salpetre, muskets, musket ball bucklers, helmets, breast plates, coats of mail, and the like kind of arms proper for arming soldiers, musket rests, belts, horses with their furniture and all other warlike instruments whatever. These merchandizes which follows shall not be reckoned among contraband or prohibited goods; that is to say, all sorts of cloths and all other manufactures woven of any wool, flax, silk, cotton, or any other materials whatever, all kinds of wearing aparel together

Art. XVI.

Esta libertad de navegacion y de comercio debe extenderse â toda especie de mercaderias, exceptuando solo las que se comprehenden bajo el nombre de contrabando ô de mercaderias prohibidas: quales son las armas, cañones, bombas con sus mechas y demas cosas pertenecientes â lo mismo: balas, polvora, mechas, picas espadas, lanzas, dardos, alabardas, morteros, petardos, granadas, salitre, fusiles, balas escudos casquetes, corazas, cotas de malla, y otras armas de esta especie propias para armar â los Soldados. Portamosquetes, bandoleras, Caballos, con sus armas y otros instrumentos de guerra sean los que fueren. Pero los generos y mercaderias que se nombrarán ahora, no se comprehenderán entre los de contrabando ô cosas prohibidas: â saber, toda especie de paños y qualesquiera otras telas de lana, lino, Seda, algodon, û otras qualesquiera materias, toda especie de

with all species whereof they are used to be made, gold and silver as well coined as uncoined, tin, iron, latton, copper, brass, coals, as also wheat, barley, oats, and any other kind of corn and pulse: tobacco and likewise all manner of spices, salted and smoked flesh, salted fish, cheese and butter, beer, oils, wines, sugars, and all sorts of salts, and in general all provisions which serve for the sustenance of life. Furthermore all kinds of cotton, hemp, flax, tar, pitch, ropes, cables, sails, sail cloths, anchors, and any parts of anchors, also ships masts, planks, wood of all kind, and all other things proper either for building or repairing ships, and all other goods whatever which have not been worked into the form of any instrument prepared for war by land or by sea, shall not be reputed contraband, much less such as have been already wrought and made up for any other use: all which shall be wholy reckoned among free goods, as likewise all other merchandizes and things which are not comprehended and particularly mentioned in the foregoing enumeration of contraband goods: so that they may be transported and carried in the freest manner by the subjects of both parties, even to Places belonging to an Enemy, such towns or Places being only excepted as are at that time besieged, blocked up, or invested. And except the cases in which any Ship of war

vestidos con las telas de que se acostumbran hacer, el oro y la plata labrada en moneda ô no, el estaño yerro, laton, cobre, bronce, carbon, del mismo modo que la cevada, el trigo, la avena, y qualesquiera otro genero de legumbres: el tabaco y toda la especieria, carne salada y ahumada, pescado salado, queso y manteca, cerveza, aceytes, vinos, azucar y toda especie de sal, y en general todo genero de provisiones que sirven para el sustento de la vida. Ademas toda especie de algodon cañamo, lino, alquitran, pez, cuerdas, cables, velas, telas para velas, ancoras, y partes de que se componen, mastiles, tablas, maderas de todas especies, y qualesquiera otras cosas que sirvan para la construccion y reparacion de los Buques, y otras qualesquiera materias que no tienen la forma de un instrumento preparado para la guerra por tierra ô por mar no seran reputadas de contrabando, y menos las que estan ya preparadas para otros usos. Todas las cosas que se acaban de nombrar deben ser comprehendidas entre las mercaderias libres, lo mismo que todas las demas mercaderias y efectos que no estan comprehendidos y nombrados expresamente en la enumeracion de los generos de contrabando: de manera que podran ser transportados y conducidos con la mayor libertad por los Subditos de las dos Partes contratantes, á las Plazas enemigas,

or Squadron shall in consequence of storms or other accidents at sea be under the necessity of taking the cargo of any trading Vessel or Vessels, in which case they may stop the said Vessel or Vessels and furnish themselves with necessaries, giving a receipt in order that the Power to whom the said ship of war belongs may pay for the articles so taken according to the price thereof at the Port to which they may appear to have been destined by the Ship's papers: and the two contracting Parties engage that the Vessels shall not be detained longer than may be absolutely necessary for their said Ships to supply themselves with necessaries: that they will immediately pay the value of the receipts: and indemnify the proprietor for all losses which he may have sustained in consequence of such transaction.

exceptuando sin embargo las qe se hallasen en la actualidad sitiadas, bloqueadas, ô embestidas. Y los casos en que algun Buque de Guerra, ô Esquadra que por efecto de avería û otras causas se halle en necesidad de tomar los efectos que conduzca el Buque ô Buques de comercio, pues en tal caso podra detenerlos para aprovisionarse y dar un recibo para que la Potencia cuyo sea el Buque que tome los efectos, los pague segun el valor que tendrian en el Puerto adonde se dirigiese el propietario segun lo expresen sus cartas de navegacion: obligandose las dos Partes contratantes â no detener los Buques mas de lo que sea absolutamente necesario para aprovisionarse, pagar inmediatamente los recibos, y â indemnizar todos los daños qe sufra el propietario â consequencia de semejante suceso.

Art. XVII.

To the end that all manner of dissentions and quarels may be avoided and prevented on one side and the other, it is agreed that in case either of the Parties hereto should be engaged in a war, the ships and Vessels belonging to the Subjects or People of the other Party must be furnished with sea letters or passports expressing the name, property, and bulk of the Ship, as also the name and place of habitation of the master or commander of the said

Art. XVII.

A fin de evitar entre ambas Partes toda especie de disputas y quejas, se ha convenido qe en el caso de que una de las dos Potencias se hallase empeñada en una guerra, los Buques y Bastimentos pertenecientes à los Subditos ô Pueblos de la otra, deberan llevar consigo patentes de Mar ô pasaportes que expresen el nombre, la propiedad, y el porte del Buque, como tambien el nombre y morada de su dueño y Comandante de dicho Buque, para que de este

Ship, that it may appear thereby that the Ship really and truly belongs to the Subjects of one of the Parties; which passport shall be made out and granted according to the form [1] annexed to this Treaty. They shall likewise be recalled every year, that is, if the ship happens to treurn home within the space of a year. It is likewise agreed that such ships being laden, are to be provided not only with passports as above mentioned but also with certificates containing the several particulars of the cargo, the place whence the ship sailed, that so it may be known whether any forbidden or contraband goods be on board the same; which certificates shall be made out by the Officers of the place whence the ship sailed in the accustomed form; and if any one shall think it fit or adviseable to express in the said certificates the person to whom the goods on board belong he may freely do so: without which requisites they may be sent to one of the Ports of the other contracting Party and adjudged by the competent tribunal according to what is above set forth, that all the circumstances of this omission having been well examined, they shall be adjudged to be legal prizes, unless they shall give legal satisfaction of their property by testimony entirely equivalent.

modo conste que pertenece real y verdaderam^te^ â los Subditos de una de las dos Partes contratantes; y que dichos pasaportes deberan expedirse segun el modelo [1] adjunto al presente tratado. Todos los años deberán renovarse estos pasaportes en el caso de que el Buque buelva â su Pais en el espacio de un año. Igualmente se ha convenido en que los Buques mencionados arriba si estubiesen cargados, deberán llevar no solo los pasaportes sino tambien certificados que contengan el pormenor del cargamento, el lugar de donde ha salido el Buque, y la declaracion de las mercaderias de contrabando q^e^ pudiesen hallarse â bordo; cuyos certificados deberán expedirse en la forma acostumbrada por los Oficiales empleados en el Lugar de donde el Navio se hiciese â la vela; y si se juzgase util y prudente expresar en dichos pasaportes la persona propietaria de las mercaderias se podra hacer libremente: sin cuyos requisitos sera conducido à uno de los Puertos de la Potencia respectiva y juzgado por el tribunal competente con arreglo â lo arriba dicho, para que exâminadas bien las circunstancias de su falta sea condenado por de buena presa si no satisfaciese legalmente con los testimonios equivalentes en un todo.

[1] No form of passport is annexed to the treaty; see the note regarding Articles 17 and 18.

ART. XVIII.

If the Ships of the said subjects, People or inhabitants of either of the Parties shall be met with either sailing along the Coasts on the high Seas by any Ship of war of the other or by any Privateer, the said Ship of war or Privateer for the avoiding of any disorder shall remain out of cannon shot, and may send their boats aboard the merchant Ship which they shall so meet with, and may enter her to number of two or three men only to whom the master or Commander of such ship or vessel shall exhibit his passports concerning the property of the ship made out according to the form[1] inserted in this present Treaty: and the ship when she shall have shewed such passports shall be free and at liberty to pursue her voyage, so as it shall not be lawful to molest or give her chace in any manner or force her to quit her intended course.

ART. XVIII.

Quando un Buque perteneciente â los dichos Subditos, Pueblos, y habitantes de una de las dos Partes fuese encontrado navegando â lo largo de la Costa ô en plena Mar por un Buque de Guerra de la otra, ô por un corsario, dicho Buque de guerra ô corsario â fin de evitar todo desorden se mantendrá fuera del tiro de cañon, y podra enviar su Chalupa â bordo del Buque mercante, hacer entrar en el dos ô tres hombres â los quales enseñará el Patron, ô Comandante del Buque sus pasaportes y demas documentos que deberan ser conformes â lo prevenido[1] en el presente tratrado, y probará la propiedad del Buque: y despues de haber exhibido semejante pasaporte, y documentos, se les dejará seguir libremente su viage sin que les sea licito el molestarles ni procurar de modo alguno darle caza û obligarle à dejar el rumbo q^e^ seguía.

ART. XIX.

Consuls shall be reciprocally established with the privileges and powers which those of the most favoured Nations enjoy in the Ports where their consuls reside, or are permitted to be.

ART. XIX.

Se establecerán Consules reciprocamente con los privilegios y facultades que gozaren los de las Naciones mas faborecidas en los Puertos donde los tubieren estas ô les sea licito el tenerlos.

ART. XX.

It is also agreed that the inhabitants of the territories of each

ART. XX.

Se ha convenido igualmente que los habitantes de los territorios de

[1] No form of passport is inserted in the treaty; see the note regarding Articles 17 and 18.

Party shall respectively have free access to the Courts of Justice of the other, and they shall be permitted to prosecute suits for the recovery of their properties, the payment of their debts, and for obtaining satisfaction for the damages which they may have sustained, whether the persons whom they may sue be subjects or Citizens of the Country in which they may be found, or any other persons whatsoever who may have taken refuge therein; and the proceedings and sentences of the said Court shall be the same as if the contending parties had been subjects or Citizens of the said Country.

una y otra Parte respectivamente seran admitidos en los tribunales de Justicia de la otra Parte, y les sera permitido el entablar sus Pleytos para el recobro de sus propiedades, pago de sus deudas, y satisfaccion de los daños que hubieren recibido bien sean las personas contra las quales se quejasen Subditos ô Ciudadanos del Pais en el que se hallen, ô bien sean qualesquiera otros sugetos que se hayan refugiado alli; y los Pleytos y sentencias de dichos tribunales seran las mismas que hubieran sido en el caso de que las Partes litigantes fuesen Subditos ô Ciudadanos del mismo Pais.

Art. XXI.

In order to terminate all differences on account of the losses sustained by the Citizens of the United States in consequence of their vessels and cargoes having been taken by the Subjects of his Catholic Majesty during the late war between Spain and France, it is agreed that all such cases shall be referred to the final decision of Commissioners to be appointed in the following manner. His Catholic Majesty shall name one Commissioner, and the President of the United States by and with the advice and consent of their Senate shall appoint another, and the said two Commissioners shall agree on the choice of a third, or if they cannot agree so they shall each propose one

Art. XXI.

A fin de concluir todas las disensiones sobre las perdidas que los Ciudadanos de los Estados Unidos hayan sufrido en sus Buques y cargamentos apresados por los Vasallos de S. M. Catolica durante la guerra que se acaba de finalizar entre España y Francia se ha convenido que todos estos casos se determinarán finalm.[te] por Comisarios que se nombrarán de esta manera. S. M. Catolica nombrará uno, y el Presidente de los Estados Unidos otro con consentimiento y aprobacion del Senado, y estos dos Comisarios nombrarán un tercero de comun acuerdo: pero si no pudiesen acordarse cada uno nombrará una persona, y sus dos nombres puestos en suerte se sacarán en presencia de los dos

person, and of the two names so proposed one shall be drawn by lot in the presence of the two original Commissioners, and the person whose name shall be so drawn shall be the third Commissioner, and the three Commissioners so appointed shall be sworn impartially to examine and decide the claims in question according to the merits of the several cases, and to justice, equity, and the laws of Nations. The said Commissioners shall meet and sit at Philadelphia and in the case of the death, sickness, or necessary absence of any such commissioner his place shall be supplied in the same manner as he was first appointed, and the new Commissioner shall take the same oaths, and do the same duties. They shall receive all complaints and applications, authorized by this article during eighteen months from the day on which they shall assemble. They shall have power to examine all such persons as come before them on oath or affirmation touching the complaints in question, and also to receive in evidence all written testimony authenticated in such manner as they shall think proper to require or admit. The award of the said Commissioners or any two of them shall be final and conclusive both as to the justice of the claim and the amount of the sum to be paid to the claimants; and his Catholic Majesty

Comisarios, resultando por tercero aquel cuyo nombre hubiese salido el primero. Nombrados asi estos tres Comisarios, jurarán que exâminarán y decidirán con inparcialidad las quejas de que se trata segun el merito de la diferencia de los casos, y segun dicten la justicia, equidad, y derecho de gentes. Dichos Comisarios se juntarán y tendran sus sesiones en Filadelfia, y en caso de muerte, enfermedad, ô ausencia precisa se reemplazará su plaza de la misma manera que se eligió, y el nuevo Comisario hará igual juramento y exercerá iguales funciones. En el termino de diez y ocho meses contados desde el dia en que se junten, admitirán todas las quejas y reclamaciones autorizadas por este articulo. Asimismo tendran autoridad para exâminar baxo la sancion del juramento â todas las personas que ocurran ante ellos sobre puntos relativos â dichas quejas, y recibirán como evidente todo testimonio escrito que de tal manera sea autentico que ellos lo juzguen digno de pedirle ô admitirle. La decision de dichos Comisarios ô de dos de ellos sera final y concluyente tanto por lo q[e] toca â la justicia de la queja como por lo que monte la suma que se deba satisfacer â los demandantes, y S. M. Catolica se obliga â hacer las pagar en especie sin rebaxa, y en las epocas lugares, y baxo las condiciones que se decidan por los Comisarios.

undertakes to cause the same to be paid in specie without deduction, at such times and Places and under such conditions as shall be awarded by the said Commissioners.

ART. XXII.

The two high contracting Parties hopping that the good correspondence and friendship which happily reigns between them will be further increased by this Treaty, and that it will contribute to augment their prosperity and opulence, will in future give to their mutual commerce all the extension and favor which the advantage of both Countries may require; and in consequence of the stipulations contained in the IV. article his Catholic Majesty will permit the Citizens of the United States for the space of three years from this time to deposit their merchandize and effects in the Port of New Orleans, and to export them from thence without paying any other duty than a fair price for the hire of the stores, and his Majesty promises either to continue this permission if he finds during that time that it is not prejudicial to the interests of Spain, or if he should not agree to continue it there, he will assign to them on another part of the banks of the Mississipi an equivalent establishment.

ART. XXII.

Esperando las dos Altas partes contratantes que la buena correspondencia y amistad que reyna actualmente entre si se estrechará mas y mas con el presente tratado, y que contribuirá à aumentar su prosperidad y opulencia, concederán reciprocamente en lo succesivo al comercio todas las ampliaciones ô fabores que exîgiese la utilidad de los dos Paises; y desde luego à consequencia de lo estipulado en el articulo IV. permitirá S. M. Catolica por espacio de tres años â los Ciudadanos de los Estados Unidos que depositen sus mercaderias y efectos en el Puerto de Nueva Orleans, y que las extraigan sin pagar mas derechos qᵉ un precio justo por el alquiler de los Almacenes ofreciendo S. M. continuar el termino de esta gracia si se experimentase durante aquel tiempo que no es perjudicial â los intereses de la España, ô sino conviniese su continuacion en aquel Puerto proporcionará en otra parte de las orillas del Rio Misisipi un igual establecimiento.

ART. XXIII.

The present Treaty shall not be in force untill ratified by the Contracting Parties, and the ratifications shall be exchanged in six months from this time, or sooner if possible.

In Witness whereof We the underwritten Plenipotentiaries of His Catholic Majesty and of the United States of America have signed this present Treaty of Friendship, Limits and Navigation and have thereunto affixed our seals respectively.

Done at San Lorenzo el Real this seven and twenty day of October one thousand seven hundred and ninety five.

THOMAS PINCKNEY
[Seal]
EL PRINCIPE DE LA PAZ
[Seal]

ART. XXIII.

El presente tratado no tendrá efecto hasta que las Partes contratantes le hayan ratificado, y las ratificaciones se cambiarán en el termino de seis meses, ô antes si fuese posible contando desde este dia.

En fe de lo qual Nosotros los infraescritos Plenipotenciarios de S. M. Catolica y de los Estados Unidos de America hemos firmado en virtud de nuestros plenos poderes este tratado de Amistad, Limites, y Navegacion, y le hemos puesto nuestros sellos respectivos.

Hecho en San Lorenzo el Real á veinte y siete de Octubre de mil setecientos noventa y cinco.

THOMAS PINCKNEY
[Seal]
EL PRINCIPE DE LA PAZ
[Seal]

NOTES

There are two originals of this treaty in the Department of State file; no differences between them have been noticed; the text here printed has been collated with that one of them which forms a part of the proclamation and which is indorsed as received on April 12, 1796. The other was received on February 22, 1796, and is so indorsed; it is the example sent to the Senate (D. S., 3 Instructions, U. S. Ministers, 103, letter to Pinckney of February 27, 1796); from it the signature and seal of El Principe de la Paz, following the Spanish text, have been cut away.

The Department of State file now contains a facsimile of the United States instrument of ratification, obtained from the Spanish archives; it is in usual form, including both English and Spanish texts. A draft of the instrument, bearing the same date, March 7, 1796, is in D. S., Miscellaneous Letters, January–April, 1796.

The treaty was not received by the Department of State until February 22, 1796. The effort made to accomplish the exchange of ratifications by the date fixed by Article 23 of the treaty six months

from the date of signature, or April 27, 1796, was successful. In a letter to Charles Rutledge of March 10, 1796 (D. S., 3 Instructions, U. S. Ministers, 111), Pickering wrote:

> To guard against accidents from the danger of the seas, three ratified copies of the treaty will be sent addressed to you. For the same reason it will be proper for you to obtain at least duplicate copies, each formally ratified by the King, one of which you will forward to this office by the earliest good opportunity; and retain the other until a conveyance offers by some American citizen of reputation who shall be returning to this Country. And because the President desires to receive the earliest possible authentic information of the ratification by his Catholic Majesty, you will, besides forwarding at least one copy of the treaty with the original ratification thereon by the King, transmit to this office, by three separate conveyances, three original certificates of the exchange of the ratifications, under the hand and seal of the Spanish minister with whom the exchange shall be made. Of this mode of giving certificates we have an example in the case of the exchange of the ratifications of the late treaty between the United States and Great Britain: and the forms of the certificates proper to be used on this occasion you will find inclosed. One such certificate given by you, on the part of the United States, to the Spanish minister, will suffice: but three originals will be proper for you to receive from him, because of the hazard of failure in crossing the sea.
>
> The letter of credence from the President to his Catholic Majesty declares your special powers to exchange the ratifications. The original and a copy of that letter are inclosed.

The certificate of the exchange of ratifications was executed in triplicate at Aranjuez on the date of the exchange. An original is in the Department of State file, which contains also the Spanish instrument of ratification; this was received at Philadelphia on July 30, 1796 (D. S., 3 Instructions, U. S. Ministers, 218), and the proclamation was issued three days later.

The original proclamation is in the Department of State file; inclusion of a duplicate original of the treaty was not usual in the early practice, but otherwise the document is in the customary form.

Note Regarding Articles 17 and 18

Each of these articles speaks of sea letters or passports "according to the form annexed to" or "inserted in" the treaty; but no such form is part of either of the two originals of the treaty in the Department of State file or of either instrument of ratification; the protocol of exchange of ratifications makes no mention of any form of passport or sea letter; and no such form is set forth in the proclamation of the treaty. It may be said here that in the records of the period the expressions "passport" and "sea letter" were interchangeably used as meaning the same kind of paper.

The omission of the form of passport from the treaty when signed was deliberate; the reason given was doubtless inadequate, but Pinckney is explicit on the point in his letter from Paris of December 18, 1795 (received May 12, 1796; D. S., 6 Despatches, Spain; copy in D. S., 4 Despatches, Great Britain, 354):

> Not being furnished with a copy of the Sea Letter issued by the President I could not annex it to the treaty as I had intended in pursuance of the provision

in the 17th Article—You will no doubt, Sir, have observed & supplied that deficiency—it will likewise be *essential* in case the treaty should be ratified to send proper powers to whoever may be charged with the Exchange of the ratifications in Spain.

The omission of any form of passport or sea letter from the treaty had consequences which were elaborately discussed in *The Amiable Isabella*, 6 Wheaton, 1–101.

There is no doubt, however, that the deliberate omission of the form from the treaty was well known to the Department of State from the above-quoted despatch of Pinckney of December 18, 1795.

Pinckney's letter of December 18, 1795, was answered on May 23, 1796 (D. S., 3 Instructions, U. S. Ministers, 131). The ratification by the United States had, of course, already been sent to Spain, and indeed had been delivered on the previous April 25. The only reference to the point in the instruction was this paragraph:

With the treaty with Spain ratified by the President, were transmitted to Mr Rutledge the necessary powers to exchange the ratifications with the Spanish Minister.

That forms were agreed on and exchanged between the two Governments shortly after the going into force of the treaty is almost equally certain.

In earlier treaty editions (Davis, 780–81, Haswell, 1012, and Malloy, II, 1647), reference is made to the fact that in Volume III (not Volume II) of a collection of Spanish treaties printed at Madrid in 1801 (not 1800), at pages 429–31 (Coleccion de los tratados de paz), there appear two forms of Spanish sea letters as annexes to the treaty text. These are also printed in 6 Wheaton, 97–101. In the English version of the memoirs of the Prince of the Peace (Memoirs of Don Manuel de Godoy) are to be found nearly accurate English translations of those Spanish forms of sea letters, which are there called "models of passports or naval patents"; it seems from that work that those forms, with the text of the treaty, were embraced in an ordinance or decree of September 4, 1796 (*ibid.*, II, 402–18). There is no copy of that document in the Spanish edition of the memoirs of Godoy.

With the note of Davis above mentioned, which remarks that "no explanation of these facts has ever been discovered," there is printed also a letter from Jacob Wagner to the Secretary of State under date of November 3, 1814 (original in D. S., Miscellaneous Letters, October–December, 1814), in which he says:

Averse to a correspondence with the writer of the enclosed letter, but willing to answer the object for public purposes, I take the liberty of doing it to you.

No form of a passport was annexed to the treaty with Spain, though referred to in one of the articles as annexed. To remedy this defect, the Secretary of State agreed with the Chevalier (now Marquis) Yrujo, Envoy of Spain, upon a form which has been constantly printed in the Spanish language, in the sea-letters issued to American vessels. It was closely translated from one of the other passports in the ordinary formulary, under the inspection of the Chevalier. From which of them I do not recollect—most probably it was from that contained in the treaty with Great Britain. My knowledge of the matter is the more certain from having had some agency in it.

I suppose there must be something in the correspondence of the Department of State *in perpetuam rei memoriam;* but as it passed about 18 years ago I cannot refer to it from memory.

Among the printed State-Papers I collected and had bound together, when employed in the Department of State, was a quarto volume, comprehending an official copy of the treaty as promulged by the Spanish Sovereign. If the volume remains in the office, it may be consulted with advantage, as it embraces a variety of passports prescribed in consequence of the treaty and probably adopts and sanctions the one agreed upon at Philadelphia, as above explained.

The precise position of Wagner in the Department of State in 1796–97 does not appear; but he was Chief Clerk from February 8, 1798, to March 31, 1807. Wagner's letter was written in response to a letter to him from J. B. Colvin dated November 2, 1814, which Wagner enclosed to the Secretary of State. Colvin was then editor of the Bioren and Duane edition of the laws of the United States. There is a brief note to Article 17 of the treaty in Volume I of that edition (printed in 1815), at page 274, based seemingly on Wagner's letter.

Wagner's recollection, nearly eighteen years after the event, was somewhat at fault. The form of the United States passport under the Spanish treaty was certainly not taken from any "treaty with Great Britain," for there was no such form to take; however, Wagner's statement that the two Governments agreed "upon a form which has been constantly printed in the Spanish language, in the sea-letters issued to American vessels," is confirmed by the following note of February 24, 1797, from the Minister of Spain to Colonel Pickering, the original of which is in D. S., 1A Notes from the Spanish Legation:

The Chevalier d'Yrujo presents his Compliments to Colonel Pickering, and has just received the Copy of the passports or Sea letters, agreed on by our Treaty. The Chevalier will have immediately a Translation made in Spanish, which he will send to the Secretary of State to be printed.

In the printed Copies received from Madrid, of the Treaty, there is only the model of the Sea letters given by the King of Spain, and as it will be convenient to have a Copy in the office of the Secretary of State the Chevalier d'Yrujo takes the liberty of sending one to Colonel Pickering, at the same time the Chevalier will keep in his office the printed Copy of the American sea letters, which he has just sent him

From the above note it is clear that D'Yrujo had received from Pickering the United States printed form of sea letter in English; he was translating that form into Spanish for printing by this Government; and he transmitted a copy of the Spanish forms. The agreement between the two Governments, while informal, was thus complete.

There seems no reason to doubt that the Spanish forms transmitted to Pickering by D'Yrujo were those embodied in the Spanish decree and referred to above. Just what United States form was printed in Spanish by this Government is not so certain. The "quarto volume" mentioned in the last paragraph of the letter of Wagner above quoted has not been found; but it is highly probable that that United States form was similar to one which was in use in the early

part of the nineteenth century, some original examples of which are in the Manuscript Division of the Library of Congress. The earliest in date is of 1805; others, issued during the next few years, are in the archives of the Department of State.

The form of document just mentioned was based in part on the provisions of the treaty with the Netherlands of 1782 (Document 5), to which there are annexed three forms of ship's documents, the first being called a passport, the second a certificate, and the third a sea letter; it was printed in four languages, French, Spanish, English, and Dutch, in parallel columns. At the top of the sheet, in the English and the Dutch, is the first form annexed to the treaty with the Netherlands and there called a passport; this is followed by the signatures of the President and the Secretary of State, with the Great Seal, and the countersignature of the collector of the port; then follows the third form from the treaty with the Netherlands, in the four languages, with the signature of the official before whom the oath was taken. But in the first part of the document, the passport proper, the French and the Spanish are quite different in their wording from the English and the Dutch; they contain the provisions of the form annexed to the Treaty of Amity and Commerce with France of February 6, 1778 (Document 1), and included in Article 4 of the convention of September 30, 1800 (Document 25). It appears that passports under the French treaty had earlier been issued in English and that Jefferson, as Secretary of State, had in 1793 made some slight changes in their wording (American State Papers, Foreign Relations, II, 302).

That the above-described document embodied the wording sent by D'Yrujo to Pickering on February 24, 1797, is very likely, particularly in view of Wagner's later statement that it had "been constantly printed in the Spanish language, in the sea-letters issued to American vessels."

At the same time there was also in current use a much shorter form of passport. There are numerous original examples extant, some in the archives of the Department of State and others in the Manuscript Division of the Library of Congress. Some of these are dated as early as 1802, and there is one which, while mutilated, could not have been later than 1801; and this form continued in use at least as late as 1841, for among the examples in the archives of the Department of State is one signed in blank by John Tyler and Daniel Webster.

This short form is in English only. It is an engraved parchment, and all the examples which have been seen are cut or indented at the top. It appears that this form was prepared under the statute of June 1, 1796 (1 Statutes at Large, 489–90). It was issued under the Great Seal, with the signatures of the President and of the Secretary of State and a further signature by the collector of the port. A letter of Pickering of August 16, 1796, transmits twenty-four such passports to President Washington "to be completed by your signature" (D. S., Miscellaneous Letters, August-December, 1796).

The reference in the letter of Pinckney above quoted of December 18, 1795, to "the Sea Letter issued by the President," is perhaps to a form prepared by John Jay and approved by Washington late in the year 1789 (D. S., 130 C. C. Paper, Passports, folios 13–14). That form of 1789 replaced a still earlier form under the resolution of the Continental Congress of February 12, 1788 (*ibid.*, folios 1–3). The form of 1789 was similar to that of 1796 in its requirements of signatures and seal.

Note Regarding Article 3

The Commissioner of the United States to run the line under Article 3 was Andrew Ellicott. Two volumes of his papers, including his journal for about two months of 1799 and correspondence with the Secretary of State and other officials, Spanish and American, are in the archives of the Department of State. Some of the correspondence is printed in American State Papers, Foreign Relations, II, 20–27, 78–87. The Journal of Andrew Ellicott, which covers the entire period of his work, from 1796 to 1800, with six maps, was printed in Philadelphia in 1803; following the journal proper is an appendix of "Astronomical, and Thermometrical Observations," with eight plates. This appendix (seemingly with only one plate) had been separately printed in Philadelphia in 1801.

However, the original report (or reports) of the Commissioners under Article 3 and their map (or maps) of the boundary are not to be found in the archives of the Department of State. It appears from a letter of Albert Gallatin, dated at New York February 18, 1830 (original in the archives of the Department of State), that while he was Secretary of the Treasury (1801–1813) they had been loaned for use in the Land Office and that thereafter they (or at least the map) had been loaned to "a Committee of Congress." Gallatin's letter enclosed Ellicott's manuscript of "observations to accompany the Map of part of the Mississippi River; the southern boundary of the United States; and the coast of West Florida" (which was used in parts of the book of 1803), and also a copy of the book of 1801.

Note Regarding Article 5

It is not possible to state positively just what treaties between the United States and the Indian nations in question were then in force; those that had previously been made are the following: with the Cherokee, November 28, 1785 (a treaty of 1783 is mentioned in American State Papers, Indian Affairs, I, 326, but this was probably with the State of Virginia); with the Choctaw, January 3, 1786; with the Chickasaw, January 10, 1786; with the Creeks, August 7, 1790; with the Cherokee, July 2, 1791, February 17, 1792, and June 26, 1794. The texts of those treaties are in Kappler, Indian Affairs; Laws and Treaties, II, 8–16, 25–34.

There were also secret articles of the treaty with the Creeks of 1790, the original of which is in the Department of State archives; their provisions are summarized in the work of Samuel Flagg Bemis,

Pinckney's Treaty, at pages 200–1; the first of those articles received the assent of the Senate during the negotiations (Executive Journal, I, 55–6); but with that exception it seems that the text of the six secret articles has not heretofore b en published. They read as follows:

Article 1st—The commerce necessary for the Creek nation shall be carried on through the ports, and by the citizens of the United States, if substantial and effectual arrangements shall be made for that purpose by the United States, on or before the first day of August one thousand seven hundred and ninety two—In the mean time, the said commerce may be carried on through its present channels and according to its present regulations.

And whereas the trade of the said Creek nation is now carried on wholly or principally through the territories of Spain and obstructions thereto may happen by war or prohibitions of the Spanish government:

It is therefore agreed between the said parties that in the event of any such obstructions happening it shall be lawful for such persons as the President of the United States shall designate to introduce into and transport through the territories of the United States to the country of the said Creek nation, any quantity of goods wares and merchandize not exceeding in value in any one year Sixty thousand dollars, and that free from any duties or impositions whatsoever, but subject to such regulations for guarding against abuse, as the United States shall judge necessary; which privilege shall continue as long as such obstructions shall continue.

Article 2'nd—The United States also agree to allow to each of the great medal chiefs herein after named, a commission, a great medal with proper ornaments, and each one hundred dollars annually for themselves and the other beloved men of their towns respectively—to wit—

Of the Upper Creeks—The Chiefs the Oakfuskees, Tuckabatchees, and the present Talissee King of the half-way house.

Of the lower Creeks—The Chiefs of the Cusitahs and Cowetas— And—

Of the Semanolees—The Chief of Micasukee—

Article 3'rd—In order to effect a consolidation of the interests of the United States and the Creek nation, it is hereby stipulated that Alexander McGillivray the beloved Chief of the said nation shall also be constituted the Agent of the United States in the said nation with the rank of Brigadier General and the pay of one thousand two hundred dollars per annum, on his taking the usual oaths required by law.

Article 4th—And the said Alexander McGillivray hereby stipulates to use his highest exertions to endeavor to cultivate the firmest friendship between the United States and the said Creek nation.

Article 5th—The United States agree to educate and clothe such of the Creek youth as shall be agreed upon, not exceeding four in number at any one time.

Article 6th—These secret articles shall take effect and be obligatory on the contracting parties as soon as the same shall have been ratified by the President of the United States, with the advice and consent of the Senate of the United States.

An account of the relations between Spain and the Indian nations, by Jane M. Berry, with citations of various treaties, is in The Mississippi Valley Historical Review, III, 462–77. Two of the Spanish treaties, that with the Talapuche of June 1, 1784, and that with the Chickasaw and Choctaw of May 14, 1790, are printed in American State Papers, Foreign Relations, I, 278–80. Texts (in Spanish) of three treaties made by Spain are in Serrano y Sanz, España y los Indios Cherokis y Chactas (Seville, 1916), 82–92; these are a treaty

with the Choctaw of July 14, 1784, a treaty with the Choctaw and Chickasaw of May 10, 1793, and a treaty with the Chickasaw and various other nations of October 28, 1793. In Documentos históricos de la Florida y la Luisiana (Madrid, 1912) is the text (in Spanish) of a treaty with the Chickasaw and Choctaw of May 14, 1792 (436–39); and the book of Doctor Bemis, cited above, discusses the relations of both countries with the Indian tribes in Chapters II and IX; see also generally, The Spanish-American Frontier, 1783–1795, by Arthur Preston Whitaker.

Treaty Series, No. 106
8 Statutes at Large, 130–31

19

GREAT BRITAIN : MAY 4, 1796

Explanatory Article to Article 3 of the Jay Treaty (Document 16), signed at Philadelphia May 4, 1796. Original in English. Submitted to the Senate May 5, 1796. Resolution of advice and consent May 9, 1796. Ratified by the United States May 9, 1796. Ratified by Great Britain July, 1796. Ratifications exchanged at Philadelphia October 6, 1796. Proclaimed November 4, 1796.

Explanatory Article.

Whereas by the third Article of the treaty of amity, commerce and navigation concluded at London on the nineteenth day of November, one thousand seven hundred and ninety four, between his Britannic Majesty and the United States of America, it was agreed that it should at all times be free to his Majesty's subjects and to the Citizens of the United States, and also to the Indians dwelling on either side of the boundary-line assigned by the treaty of peace to the United States, freely to pass and repass by land or inland navigation, into the respective territories and Countries of the two contracting parties, on the continent of America (the country within the limits of the Hudson's bay company only excepted) and to navigate all the Lakes, rivers and waters thereof, and freely to carry on trade and commerce with each other, subject to the provisions and limitations contained in the said Article: And Whereas by the eighth Article of the treaty of peace and friendship [1] concluded at Greenville on the third day of August, one thousand seven hundred and ninety five, between the United States and the Nations or tribes of Indians called the Wyandots, Delawares, Shawanoes, Ottawas, Chippewas, Putawatimies, Miamis, Eel-River, Weeas, Kickapoos, Piankashaws, and Kaskaskias, it was stipulated that no person should be permitted to reside at any of the towns or hunting Camps of the said Indian tribes as a trader, who is not furnished with a licence for that purpose, under the authority of the United States: Which latter stipulation has excited doubts whether in its operation it may not interfere with the due execution of the said third

[1] For the text of this treaty, see Kappler, Indian Affairs; Laws and Treaties, II, 39–45; or 7 Statutes at Large, 49–54.

Article of the treaty of amity, commerce and navigation: And it being the sincere desire of his Britannic Majesty and of the United States that this point should be so explained as to remove all doubts, and promote mutual satisfaction and friendship: And for this purpose his Britannic Majesty having named for his Commissioner, Phineas Bond Esquire his Majesty's Consul-General for the middle and southern States of America (and now his Majesty's chargé d'affaires to the United States) and the President of the United States having named for their Commissioner Timothy Pickering Esquire, Secretary of State of the United States, to whom, agreeably to the laws of the United States he has intrusted this negotiation; They the said Commissioners, having communicated to each other their full powers, have in virtue of the same, and conformably to the spirit of the last Article of the said treaty of Amity, Commerce, and Navigation, entered into this explanatory Article, and do by these presents explicitly Agree and declare, That no stipulations in any treaty subsequently concluded by either of the contracting parties with any other State or Nation, or with any Indian tribe, can be understood to derogate in any manner from the rights of free intercourse and commerce secured by the aforesaid third Article of the treaty of Amity, commerce and navigation, to the subjects of his Majesty and to the Citizens of the United States and to the Indians dwelling on either side of the boundary-line aforesaid; but that all the said persons shall remain at full liberty freely to pass and repass by land or inland navigation, into the respective territories and countries of the contracting parties, on either side of the said boundary-line, and freely to carry on trade and commerce with each other, according to the stipulations of the said third Article of the treaty of Amity, Commerce and Navigation.

This explanatory Article, when the same shall have been ratified by his Majesty, and by the President of the United States by and with the advice and consent of their Senate, and the respective ratifications mutually exchanged, shall be added to and make a part of the said treaty of amity, commerce and navigation, and shall be permanently binding upon his Majesty and the United States.

In Witness whereof We the said Commissioners of his Majesty the King of Great Britain and the United States of America, have signed this present explanatory Article, and thereto affixed our seals.

Done at Philadelphia, this fourth day of May—, in the Year of our Lord, one thousand seven hundred and ninety six.

P. Bond [Seal] Timothy Pickering [Seal]

NOTES

The British instrument of ratification does not give the exact date of its execution; the month and year are given, but the place for the day of the month is blank.

A facsimile of the United States instrument of ratification in the British archives is now in the Department of State file. It includes a signed original of the treaty; so the agreement was signed at least in triplicate, for there is an original in the Department of State file, from which the text here printed is taken.

With the facsimile of the ratification is a facsimile of a certificate, signed by Pickering on October 6, 1796, and under the seal of the Department of State, acknowledging the delivery of the British instrument of ratification on that date. A copy of this paper is in D. S., 9 Domestic Letters, 322; and at page 345 is a copy of a similar certificate, executed on the same day by Bond (the original of which has not been found), from which it appears that the United States instrument of ratification was delivered to him on May 9, 1796, the date of its execution; and it seems that a duplicate was delivered on May 10 (*ibid.*, 111); but the exchange of ratifications was completed on October 6, 1796.

The original proclamation has not been found; the text of the treaty itself was published at the time; it is in The Laws of the United States, Folwell ed., II, 496–98 (printed in 1796); that edition was official in the strict sense, as it was issued pursuant to the act of March 3, 1795 (1 Statutes at Large, 443); but no print of the proclamation, as such, has been noticed except that printed in English, with a French translation, in Martens, Recueil des principaux traités, 1st ed., VI, 600–5, and 2d ed., V, 696–703. The proclamation appears to have been in the usual form, with the signature of President Washington, the attest of Pickering as Secretary of State, and the Great Seal.

Treaty Series, No. 358
8 Statutes at Large, 154–56

20

TRIPOLI : NOVEMBER 4, 1796, AND JANUARY 3, 1797

Treaty of Peace and Friendship, signed at Tripoli November 4, 1796 (3 Jumada I, A. H. 1211), and at Algiers January 3, 1797 (4 Rajab, A. H. 1211). Original in Arabic.

Submitted to the Senate May 29, 1797. (Message of May 26, 1797.) Resolution of advice and consent June 7, 1797. Ratified by the United States June 10, 1797. As to the ratification generally, see the notes. Proclaimed June 10, 1797.

The following fourteen pages of Arabic are a reproduction of the text in the original treaty book, first the pages of the treaty in left-to-right order of pagination, and then the "receipt" and the "note" mentioned, according to the Barlow translation, in Article 10. Following the Arabic and in the same order, is the translation of Joel Barlow as written in the treaty book—the twelve articles of the treaty, the "receipt," and the "note"; and after these is the approval of David Humphreys from the same document, which is fully described in the notes. Following those texts is the annotated translation of 1930.

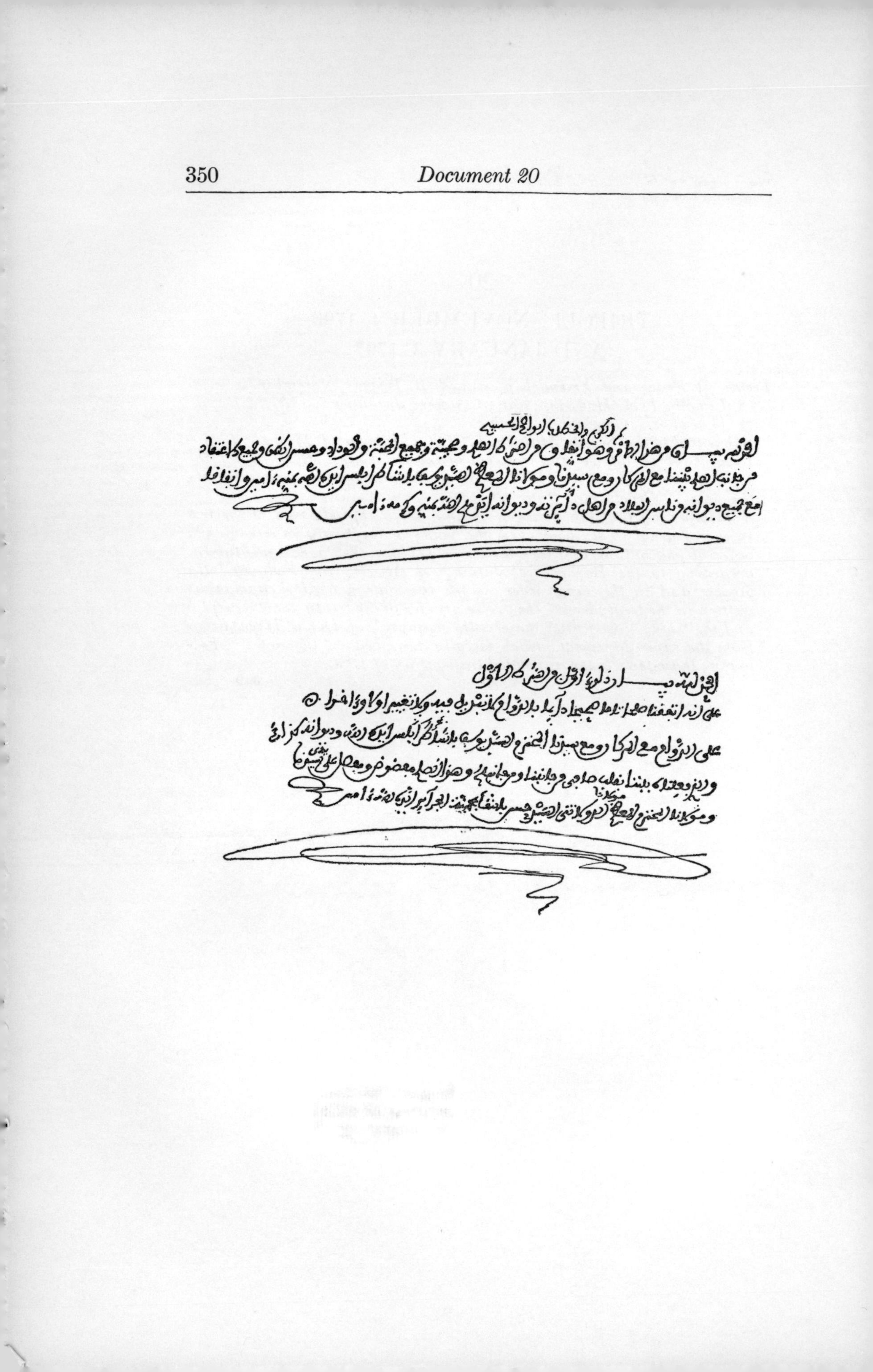

[illegible]

[illegible]

أعجبنا ان بيـــان ذلك حتى اتفق كل الاثنين   فوافقنا

على انه جميع الصلح عند ان يكون في مراكب الميركان لا يغير ويكبس عليهم الحرم ومن مراكب البحر

وكذلك مراكب كل البحر حتى يكون بالاسلام لا ينغروا عليهم احد ومراكب الميركان من الغرباء وهكذا

كلام عندنا وكلام عندكم

مرهم فبرابر ١٠ ثنية

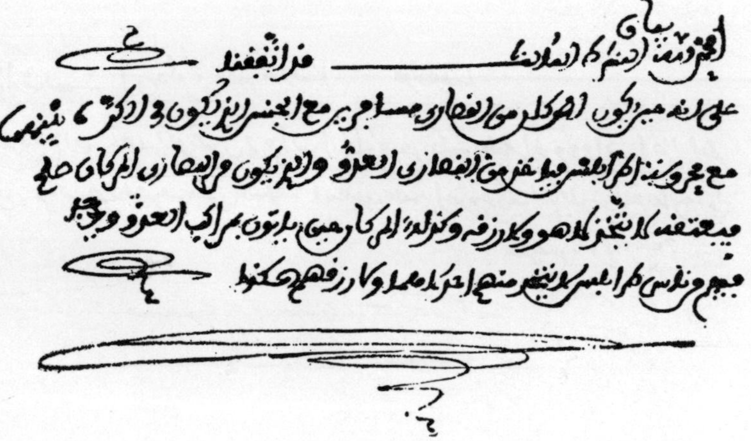

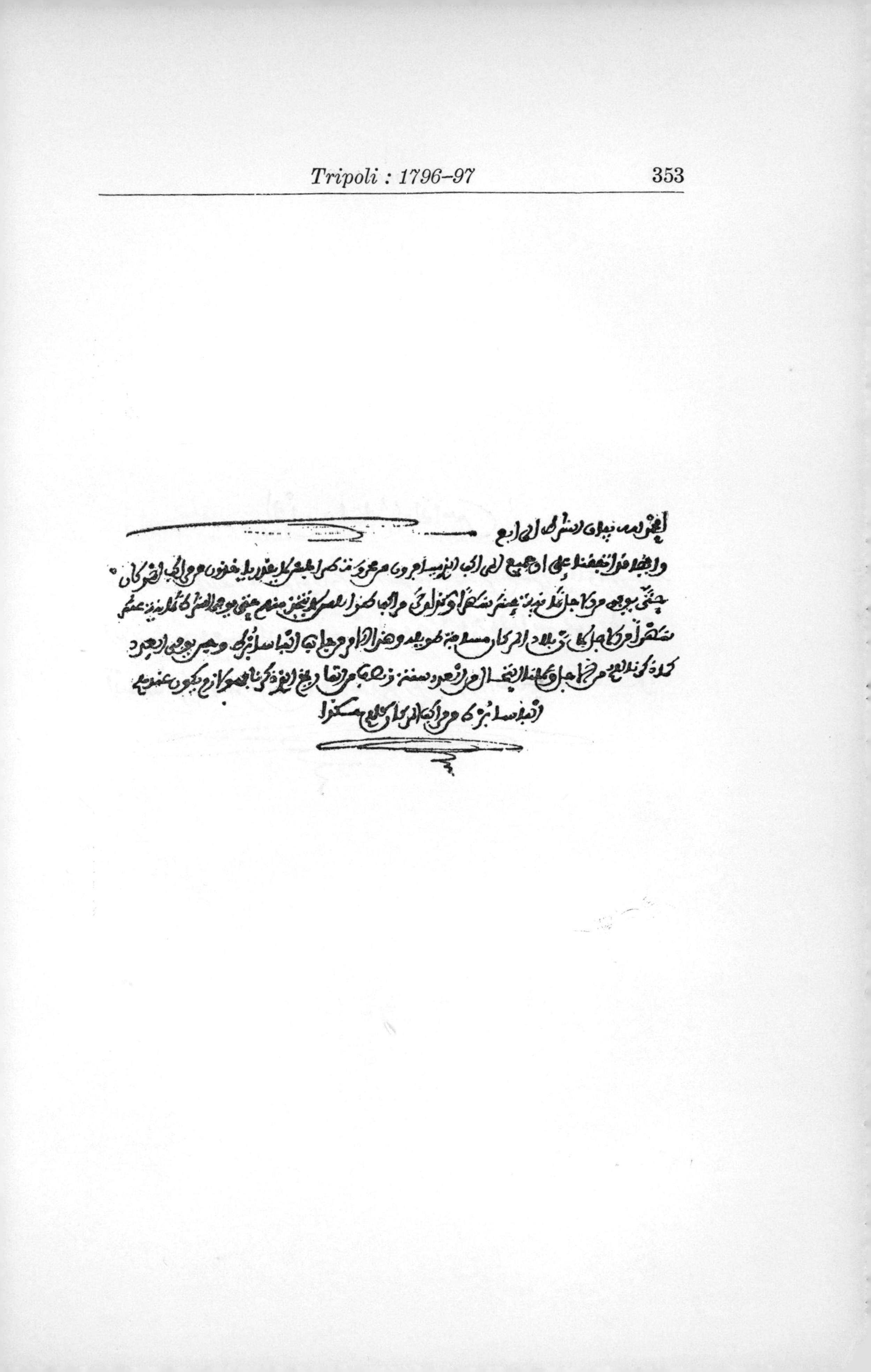

[illegible]

[illegible]

[illegible]

[illegible]

[illegible]

[illegible]

[illegible]

الحمد لله [illegible] الخامس

قد اتفقنا على انه من جنس [illegible] كان اذا اشترى واعتبه من الجنس الذي كان بالمكان [illegible]

الذي يشترى وهذا ينبغي [illegible] بيننا [illegible] كان في المكان نفسه تجوز [illegible]

[illegible] من [illegible] الذي يشترى والغنيمة [illegible]

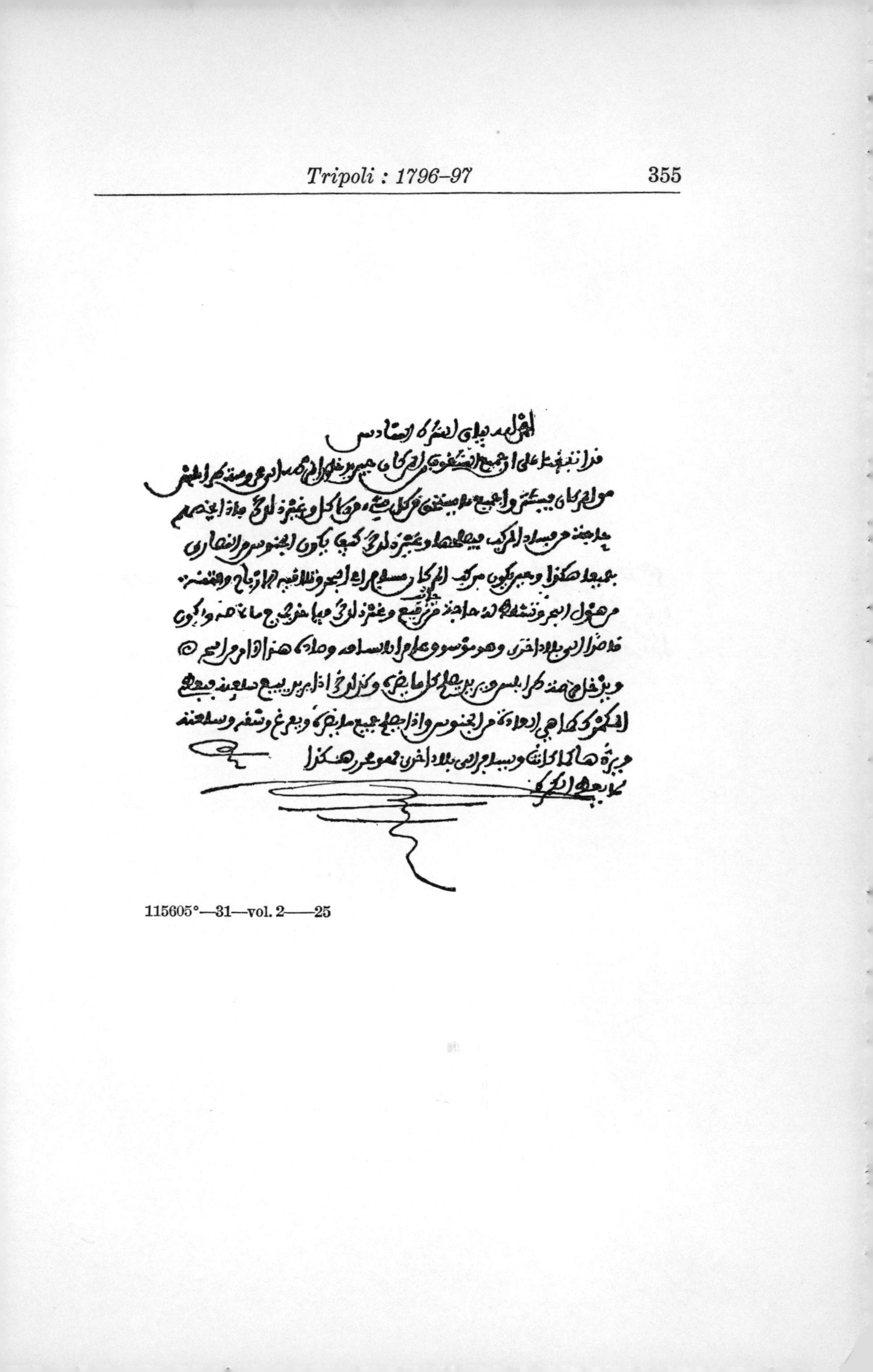

115605°—31—vol. 2——25

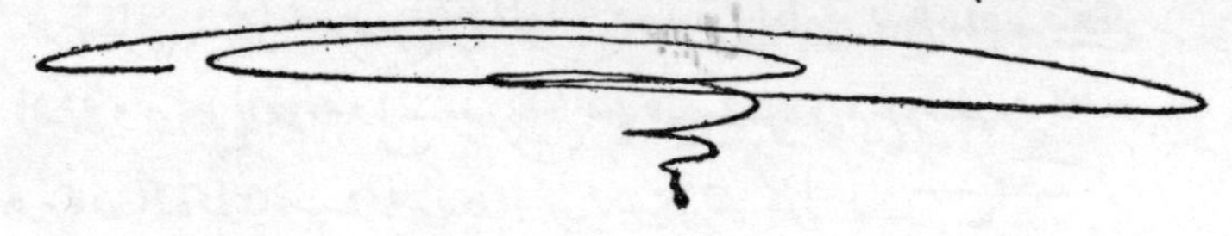

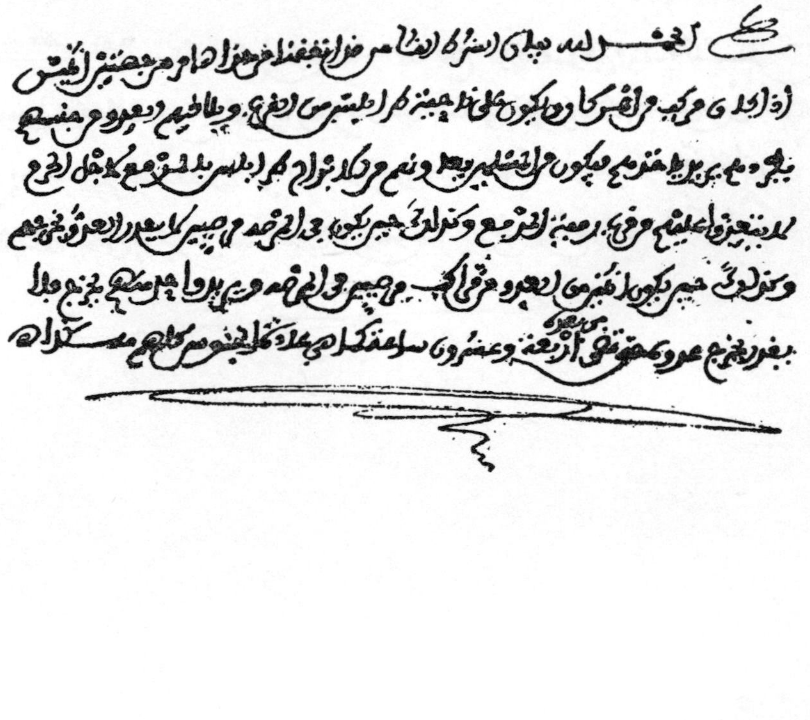

[illegible] اتفقنا على ان جميع [illegible]

[illegible] بالسلطة [illegible]

[illegible] كلهم [illegible]

[illegible] كلهم [illegible]

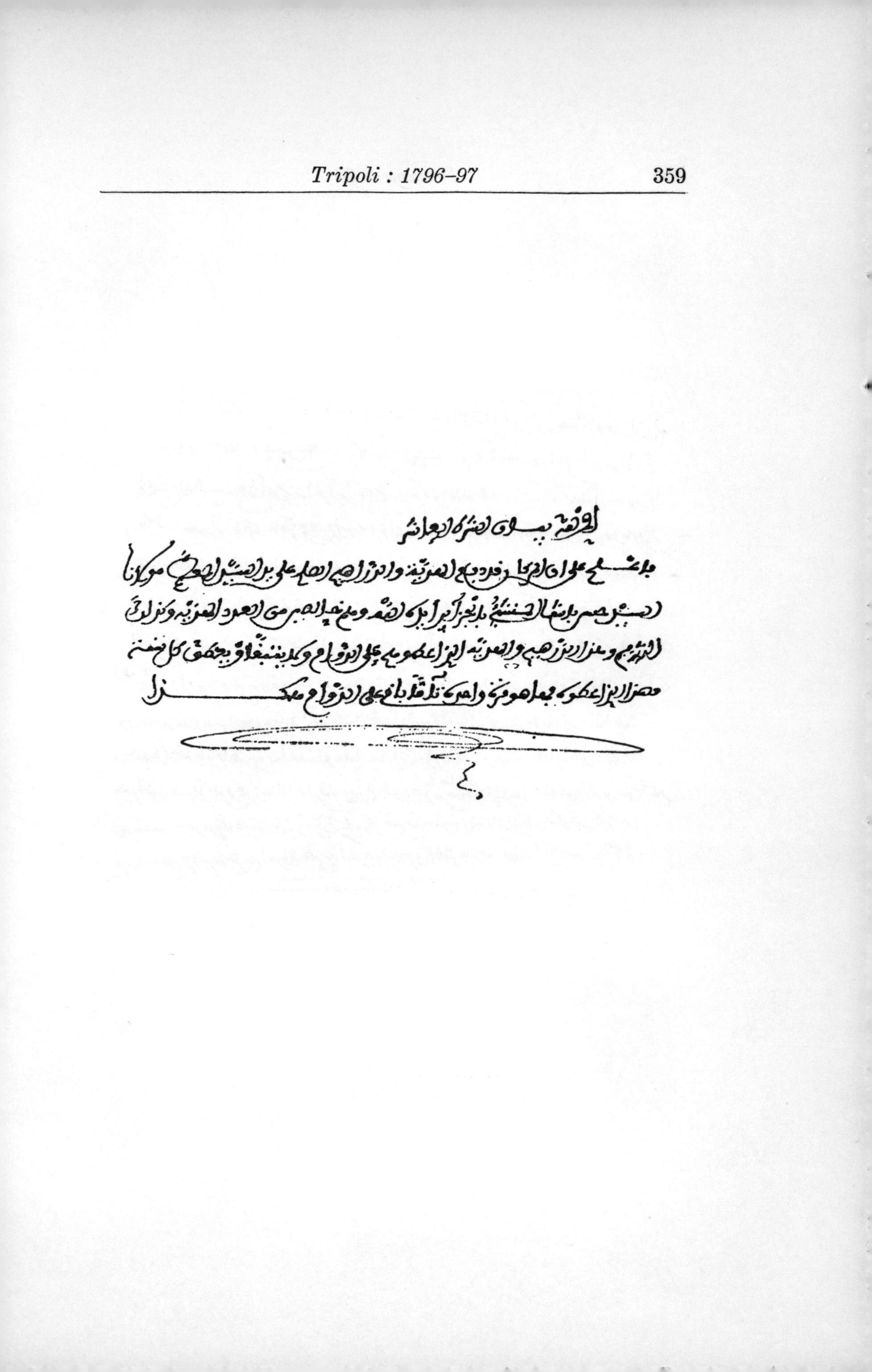

الورقة بيان الشرط العاشر

[illegible]

[illegible]

[illegible]

[illegible]

الحمد لله

الذي [illegible] الاستقلال [illegible] بالاستيلاء على الخير والرشاد، ويكون منه الكلام فيه اصلاح

البلاد والعباد، حتى وضعت [illegible] الاشياء في محلها، وكان [illegible] على بن ابراهيم [illegible]

[illegible] بمحروسة الجزائر ابن [illegible] و[illegible] على فعل الخيرات [illegible] الولاء و[illegible]

وكل [illegible] في جميع اموره، واعتمد [illegible] في [illegible]، و[illegible] بالخير

هذا [illegible] بالخير [illegible] افضال، و[illegible] على [illegible] من محبة الخير و[illegible]

و[illegible] [illegible] بمحروسة [illegible] ابن [illegible] و[illegible] امير

[illegible] و[illegible] الاعمال [illegible] الاعمال و[illegible] تكون محمودة [illegible] والفعال

[illegible] امير [illegible] والدعاء [illegible]

و[illegible] الخير بقبول النصائح و[illegible] على [illegible]

و[illegible] [illegible] و[illegible] [illegible] [illegible]

[illegible] يكون [illegible] بمحروسة [illegible] [illegible] يكون [illegible] [illegible]

و[illegible] [illegible] و[illegible] [illegible] [illegible]

[illegible] على [illegible] [illegible]

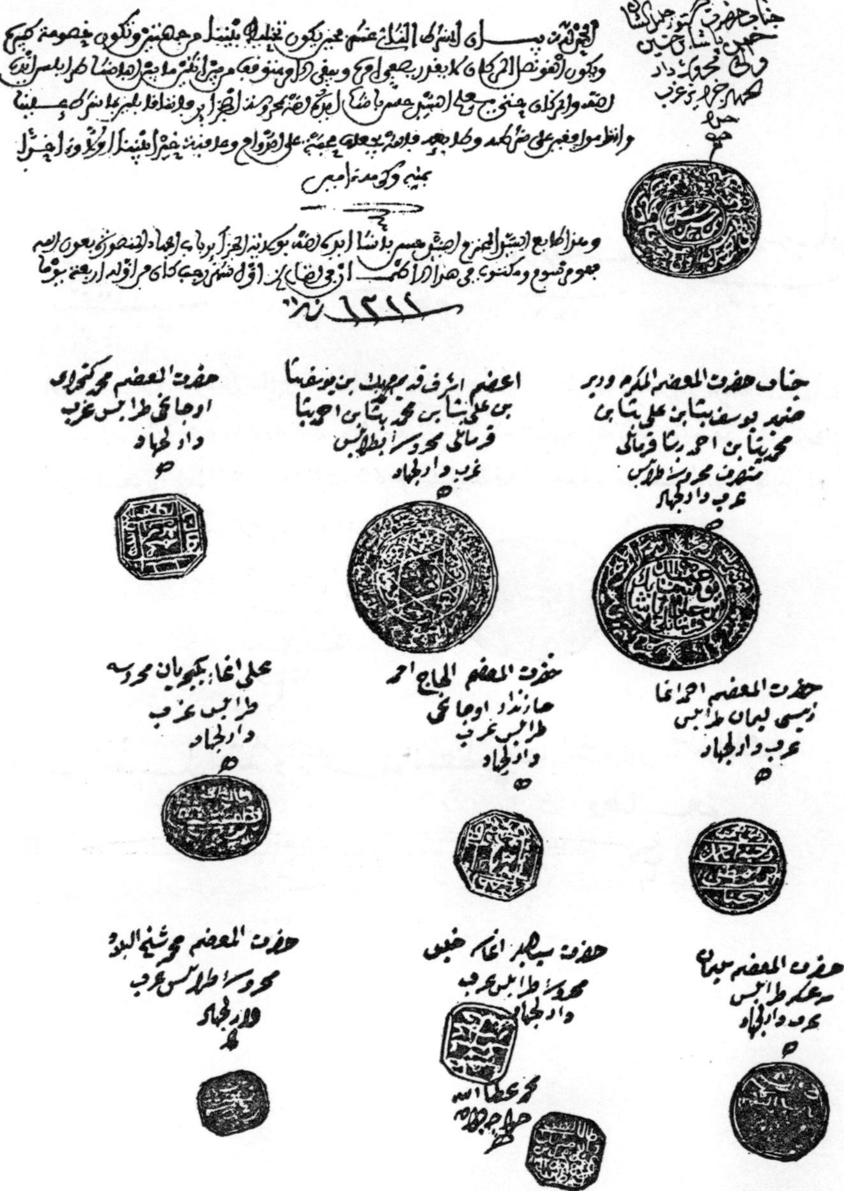

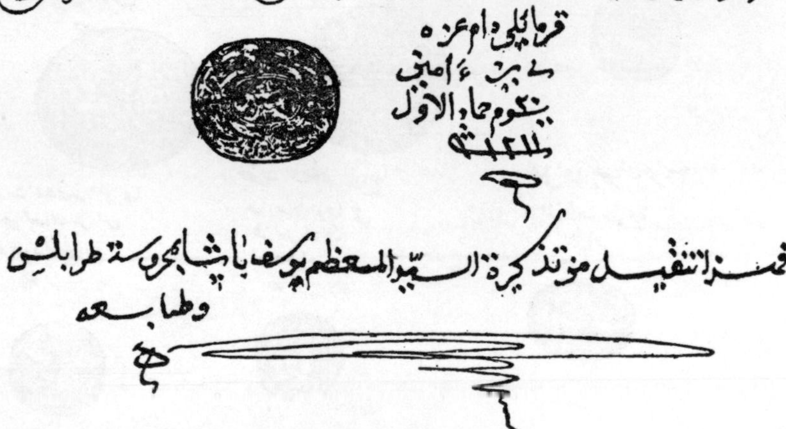

اربعين الف دورو 40000 — ساعة ١٣ — خاتم ٥ — دراع ملف ١٤٠ — تفصيلة سرسار ٤

الحمد لله بيان ما [illegible] الى ابن ابراهيم الحركات وصل الينا اربعين الف دورو وثلاثة
عشر ساعة [illegible] ذهب [illegible] وخمسة خواتم منهم ثلاثة الماس وواحد [illegible] وواحد [illegible] ساعة ومائة
واحدى واربعون ذراعا ملف واربعة تفصيلات سرسار [illegible] من جانب [illegible] يوسف باشا [illegible] الحركات والسلام

قرمانلي دام عزه
[illegible]
[illegible] جمادى الاول
[illegible]

وهذا التفصيل من تذكرة السيد المعظم يوسف باشا محروسة طرابلس
وطابعه

لحمد لله هذه تذكرة وبيان ما ينبغي دفعه المركان من جانب الفصل من العون اللازم ما فيه اثني عشر الفا
ريالة صور وكذلك اشبر شبيات ومما خمسة وعلاهم من ثمانية بو الكطات وايضا كومة ومما ثلاثة
من عشر نبو الكطات لكل واحدة وايضا فيه اخمسة وعشرون برمل وكذلك بمبكة خمسة وعشرون
برمل وكذلك از جينية عشرة براميل وايضا لوح زونبل خمسمائة وكذلك لوح بير ايضا منه خمسمائة
وايضا امواد ومما عشرة وكذلك لنطينية اثني عشر وايضا باز للقلاع في لونة ومما خمسون نفخة
وايضا مخالطة ومما اربعة هذا الذي ينبغي بدفعه المركان من هذا العهد المذكور كما ذكر وبعد خبر بانني
تعونصل ناجية بيلاده فيما نوى بالجميع الذي كان وهذا العون حين يفرغ الحمل ويقدم البشر اضنه ان شاء الله
تعلى بمنه امين ومكتوبا يد تمام ونفذ اول شهر رجب هذا الذي تسع عشر مئتين ١٢١١ سنة

[Translation]

Treaty of Peace and Friendship between the United States of America and the Bey and Subjects of Tripoli of Barbary.

ARTICLE 1.

There is a firm and perpetual Peace and friendship between the United States of America and the Bey and subjects of Tripoli of Barbary, made by the free consent of both parties, and guaranteed by the most potent Dey & regency of Algiers.

ARTICLE 2.

If any goods belonging to any nation with which either of the parties is at war shall be loaded on board of vessels belonging to the other party they shall pass free, and no attempt shall be made to take or detain them.

ARTICLE 3.

If any citizens, subjects or effects belonging to either party shall be found on board a prize vessel taken from an enemy by the other party, such citizens or subjects shall be set at liberty, and the effects restored to the owners.

ARTICLE 4.

Proper passports are to be given to all vessels of both parties, by which they are to be known. And, considering the distance between the two countries, eighteen months from the date of this treaty shall be allowed for procuring such passports. During this interval the other papers belonging to such vessels shall be sufficient for their protection.

ARTICLE 5

A citizen or subject of either party having bought a prize vessel condemned by the other party or by any other nation, the certificate of condemnation and bill of sale shall be a sufficient passport for such vessel for one year; this being a reasonable time for her to procure a proper passport.

ARTICLE 6

Vessels of either party putting into the ports of the other and having need of provissions or other supplies, they shall be furnished at the market price. And if any such vessel shall so put in from a disaster at sea and have occasion to repair, she shall be at liberty to land and reembark her cargo without paying any duties. But in no case shall she be compelled to land her cargo.

ARTICLE 7.

Should a vessel of either party be cast on the shore of the other, all proper assistance shall be given to her and her people; no pillage shall be allowed; the property shall remain at the disposition of the owners, and the crew protected and succoured till they can be sent to their country.

ARTICLE 8.

If a vessel of either party should be attacked by an enemy within gun-shot of the forts of the other she shall be defended as much as possible. If she be in port she shall not be seized or attacked when it is in the power of the other party to protect her. And when she proceeds to sea no enemy shall be allowed to pursue her from the same port within twenty four hours after her departure.

ARTICLE 9.

The commerce between the United States and Tripoli,—the protection to be given to merchants, masters of vessels and seamen,—the reciprocal right of establishing consuls in each country, and the privileges, immunities and jurisdictions to be enjoyed by such consuls, are declared to be on the same footing with those of the most favoured nations respectively.

ARTICLE 10.

The money and presents demanded by the Bey of Tripoli as a full and satisfactory consideration on his part and on the part of his subjects for this treaty of perpetual peace and friendship are acknowledged to have been recieved by him previous to his signing the same, according to a reciept which is hereto annexed, except such part as is promised on the part of the United States to be delivered and paid by them on the arrival of their Consul in Tripoly, of which part a note is likewise hereto annexed. And no pretence of any periodical tribute or farther payment is ever to be made by either party.

ARTICLE 11.

As the government of the United States of America is not in any sense founded on the Christian Religion,—as it has in itself no character of enmity against the laws, religion or tranquility of Musselmen,—and as the said States never have entered into any war or act of hostility against any Mehomitan nation, it is declared by the parties that no pretext arising from religious opinions shall ever produce an interruption of the harmony existing between the two countries.

Article 12.

In case of any dispute arising from a violation of any of the articles of this treaty no appeal shall be made to arms, nor shall war be declared on any pretext whatever. But if the Consul residing at the place where the dispute shall happen shall not be able to settle the same, an amicable referrence shall be made to the mutual friend of the parties, the Dey of Algiers, the parties hereby engaging to abide by his decision. And he by virtue of his signature to this treaty engages for himself and successors to declare the justice of the case according to the true interpretation of the treaty, and to use all the means in his power to enforce the observance of the same.

Signed and sealed at Tripoli of Barbary the 3ᵈ day of Jumad in the year of the Higera 1211—corresponding with the 4ᵗʰ day of Novʳ 1796 by

Jussuf Bashaw Mahomet *Bey*
Mamet—*Treasurer*
Amet—*Minister of Marine*
Amet—*Chamberlain*
Ally—*Chief of the Divan*
Soliman *Kaya*
Galil—*Genˡ of the Troops*
Mahomet—*Comᵗ of the city*
Mamet—*Secretary*

Signed and sealed at Algiers the 4ᵗʰ day of Argib 1211—corresponding with the 3ᵈ day of January 1797 by

Hassan Bashaw *Dey*

and by the Agent plenipotentiary of the United States of America

[Seal] Joel Barlow

[The "Receipt"]

Praise be to God &c—

The present writing done by our hand and delivered to the American Captain OBrien makes known that he has delivered to us forty thousand Spanish dollars,—thirteen watches of gold, silver & pinsbach,—five rings, of which three of diamonds, one of saphire and one with a watch in it,—one hundred & forty piques of cloth, and four caftans of brocade,—and these on account of the peace concluded with the Americans.

Given at Tripoli in Barbary the 20ᵗʰ day of Jumad 1211, corresponding with the 21ˢᵗ day of Novʳ 1796—

(Signed) Jussuf Bashaw—*Bey*
whom God Exalt

The foregoing is a true copy of the reciept given by Jussuf Bashaw—Bey of Tripoli—

(Signed) HASSAN BASHAW—*Dey of Algiers.*

The foregoing is a literal translation of the writing in Arabic on the opposite page

JOEL BARLOW

[The "Note"]

On the arrival of a consul of the United States in Tripoli he is to deliver to Jussuf Bashaw Bey—

twelve thousand Spanish dollars
five hawsers—8 Inch
three cables—10 Inch
twenty five barrels tar
twenty five d° pitch
ten d° rosin
five hundred pine boards
five hundred oak d°
ten masts (without any measure mentioned, suppose for vessels from 2 to 300 ton)
twelve yards
fifty bolts canvas
four anchors

And these when delivered are to be in full of all demands on his part or on that of his successors from the United States according as it is expressed in the tenth article of the following treaty. And no farther demand of tributes, presents or payments shall ever be made.

Translated from the Arabic on the opposite page, which is signed & sealed by Hassan Bashaw Dey of Algiers—the 4th day of Argib 1211—or the 3^{d} day of Jany 1797—by—

JOEL BARLOW

[Approval of Humphreys]

To all to whom these Presents shall come or be made known.

Whereas the Underwritten David Humphreys hath been duly appointed Commissioner Plenipotentiary by Letters Patent, under the Signature of the President and Seal of the United States of America, dated the 30th of March 1795, for negociating and concluding a Treaty of Peace with the Most Illustrious the Bashaw, Lords and Governors of the City & Kingdom of Tripoli; whereas by a Writing under his Hand and Seal dated the 10th of February 1796, he did (in

conformity to the authority committed to me therefor) constitute and appoint Joel Barlow and Joseph Donaldson Junior Agents jointly and seperately in the business aforesaid; whereas the annexed Treaty of Peace and Friendship was agreed upon, signed and sealed at Tripoli of Barbary on the 4th of November 1796, in virtue of the Powers aforesaid and guaranteed by the Most potent Dey and Regency of Algiers; and whereas the same was certified at Algiers on the 3d of January 1797, with the Signature and Seal of Hassan Bashaw Dey, and of Joel Barlow one of the Agents aforesaid, in the absence of the other.

Now Know ye, that I David Humphreys Commissioner Plenipotentiary aforesaid, do approve and conclude the said Treaty, and every article and clause therein contained, reserving the same nevertheless for the final Ratification of the President of the United States of America, by and with the advice and consent of the Senate of the said United States.

In testimony whereof I have signed the same with my Name and Seal, at the City of Lisbon this 10th of February 1797.

[Seal] David Humphreys.

THE ANNOTATED TRANSLATION OF 1930

The Arabic text of the original treaty book with the Barlow translation, as well as the Cathcart copy (described below), and also the Italian translation in the Department of State file, have been examined by Dr. C. Snouck Hurgronje, of Leiden.

The annotated translation of the Arabic, the work of Doctor Snouck Hurgronje, follows. The order of arrangement is that there comes first what may be called the treaty proper, then the "receipt," and then the "note," followed by an account of the seals used.

[Translation of the Treaty]

Praise be to God! Declaration from [*sic*] this noble affair and this clear and important speech, being the agreement consisting of the articles of peace and fellowship and all friendship and love and good trust and all confidence on account of the peace treaty between us with the Americans and [*sic*] with our Lord and Master the exalted Lord Yussuf Pasha of Tripoli, may God strengthen him by His grace, amen! and in agreement with his whole Divan, the whole population of his regency and his Divan, may God strengthen them by His grace and His favor, amen!

Praise be to God! Declaration thereof from the first article. That we have agreed upon a perfect, valid, everlasting peace, without

modification or change from the beginning to the end, in permanency, with the Americans and [*sic*] with our honored Lord, the Lord Yussuf Pasha of Tripoli, may God strengthen him and likewise his Divan, and what we have arranged between us [has been arranged] with a pure heart from our side and from their side. This treaty of peace has been displayed [the Arabic word here used generally denotes "to break a seal," or something of that sort] and worked out in detail by our honored and exalted Master, our supreme [the word here used is uncommon; it may have the meaning of sovereign] Master, the Lord Yussuf Pasha, in the protected [*i. e.*, by God] Algiers, may God strengthen him by His grace, amen!

Praise be to God! Declaration thereof: the second article. We have agreed concerning all goods carried by ships of the Americans, that it shall not be lawful to seize them from [on] the part of Tripoli ships; and likewise ships of Tripoli carrying goods, no American warship shall commit inimical acts against them. Thus it shall be with us and with them, from both of the two [*sic*] sides.

Glory be to God! Declaration of the third article. We have agreed that if American Christians are traveling with a nation that is at war with the well-preserved Tripoli, and he [evidently the Tripolitan] takes [prisoners] from the Christian enemies and from the American Christians with whom we are at peace [the Arabic sentence is here most confused], then he sets him [*sic*] free; neither he nor his goods shall be taken. Likewise, the Americans, when they take [literally "bring"] ships of their enemies and there are on board people from Tripoli, they shall not take one of them nor their goods. Thus! [This word, occurring at the end of several articles, seems to take the place of a full stop.]

Praise be to God! Declaration of the fourth article. We have also agreed concerning all the ships sailing out from the well-preserved Tripoli, that they [evidently the Tripolitans] are not allowed to take any of the American ships until a term of eighteen months shall have expired, and likewise there shall not be taken any of the Tripolitan ships until the condition of eighteen months shall be fulfilled, because the country of the Americans is at a great distance. This stipulation is connected with the passports; when the number of months of the term that we have mentioned shall be complete, and we have observed the term of one year and a half, beginning by the date which we have mentioned, then all the ships of the Americans must have passports. Thus.

Praise be to God! Declaration of the fifth article. We have agreed that, if persons of the American nation have bought a prize from the nation which has been by correspondence [writing] that they have bought it [apart from the obscurity of this Arabic sentence, it seems that some words after "nation" have been omitted], then the written document shall be valid between us from both sides, because the cor-

respondence has the validity of a passport, and the term shall be of one year from the date of their buying the prize. Thus.

Praise be to God! Declaration of the sixth article. We have agreed that all American vessels putting into the port of the well-preserved Tripoli, of the Americans [*sic*], shall buy anything they are entitled to, provisions and other things. If the ship has suffered any damage, she shall repair it and so forth, like all the other Christian nations. And if an American ship, while sailing, has encountered winds or heavy storm at sea and is shipwrecked, and she is in want of lifting [?] or of anything else, she shall take whatever is necessary [or "whatever belongs to her"], and if she is bound to another country, being full of cargo, while such a misfortune befell her at sea, and she put into the port of Tripoli in order to repair all her damages, [she shall be allowed to do so]. And if she wants to sell her merchandise, she shall pay the customs according to the custom of other [Christian] nations. But if she has repaired all her damages and discharged her load and merchandise, and then reloads it again as it was before, [the cargo] shall be free. Thus.

Praise be to God! Declaration of the seventh article. We have agreed that if any vessel of the Americans is shipwrecked or damaged on the shore of Tripoli, the Moslems shall assist them until their goods are completely recovered from him who withholds. And if the vessel has merchandise or anything else, the Moslems shall be with them guarding the goods from thieves [deceivers] and shall watch over them until they have finished their affairs. Thus.

Praise be to God! Declaration of the eighth article. We have agreed upon this matter from both the two [*sic*] sides. If there is an American ship in the neighborhood of the Tripoli shore, and an enemy of their own kind [*i. e.*, a Christian enemy] encounters them and pursues them, trying to take them, then they shall be assisted from the side of the Moslems with guns from the forts of Tripoli for their defense [?], that they commit no hostility against them within gunshot. Likewise, if they are in the port, lying at anchor, the enemy shall not be allowed to expel them. Likewise, if there are at anchor in the port two ships [belonging to nations] which are at enmity with each other, and one of them wishes to sail out, then her enemy shall not be allowed to sail out within twenty-four hours, as is the custom of all the [Christian] nations. Thus.

Praise be to God! Declaration of the ninth article. We have agreed that all the tradesmen and likewise the merchants [the two words used here are the Arabic *musabbibîn* and the foreign word *merkantiyye;* perhaps it is simply a pleonastic expression, or perhaps two different classes of commercial people are meant] of the American nation who bring merchandise to the well-preserved Tripoli, and likewise the captains and sailors, shall have to pay the customs as all the [Christian] nations pay them, and as it is the custom, and the Consul of the Americans shall continue doing his official duty as it is done

by all the [Christian] nations, namely, the kiss of the Feast and of the [*mifḍâ*?]. Thus.

> The word not transalted (*mifḍâ*, or something like it), is of uncertain reading; the Italian translation renders it by "godimento." It may have denoted some periodical, probably annual, entertainment or feast of non-religious character, at which the authorities had to pay a complimentary visit to the Sultan. The "Feast" seems to denote that of the 1st of Shawwal, the conclusion of the Ramadan fasting. I guess that on such occasions the consuls had to "kiss" the Pasha's cloak or even the floor in front of His Highness, and most probably they were obliged to accompany that act of reverence with the offering of costly presents.

Praise be to God! Declaration of the tenth article. Be it known that the Americans have paid the present and the money for the peace treaty on the hand of the exalted Lord, our Master, the Lord Hassan Pasha, who [*al-munshî*?] in Algiers, may God strengthen him, and they are now acquitted of the number of presents [literally "the number, the present"] and likewise of the money, and this money and these presents they have given [shall be counted] forever, and they shall not continue to pay every year. This which they have given shall be at once complete, remaining forever. Thus.

> The word not translated, probably to be read *al-munshî*, seems to be the equivalent of "residing" or "governing," but is not used in that sense in common Arabic.
>
> The eleventh article of the Barlow translation has no equivalent whatever in the Arabic. The Arabic text opposite that article is a letter from Hassan Pasha of Algiers to Yussuf Pasha of Tripoli. The letter gives notice of the treaty of peace concluded with the Americans and recommends its observation. Three fourths of the letter consists of an introduction, drawn up by a stupid secretary who just knew a certain number of bombastic words and expressions occurring in solemn documents, but entirely failed to catch their real meaning. Here the only thing to be done by a translator is to try to give the reader an impression of the nonsensical original:

Praise be to God, who inspires the minds of rulers with causes of well-being and righteousness! The present matter may be in the interest of the land and the servants [of God], in order that things may be put in their place. This whole affair has been opened [by omission of one letter the Arabic reads "victories" instead of "opened"] by the intermediary of the exalted, honored Prince, the Lord Hassan Pasha, in the protected [by God] Algiers, may God strengthen him and give him victory and help him in accomplishing good things; thus in the beginning and in the end, and may the acquiescence in his order take place by considering all his affairs, and may his en-

deavor repose on the fitness of his reflection. So may God make it, the beginning of this peace, a good and graceful measure and an introduction having for result exaltation and glorification, out of love for our brother and friend and our most beloved, the exalted Lord Yussuf Pasha, [here follows the same word as in Article 10: *al-munshî*?, "residing" or "governing"] in the well-protected [by God] Tripoli, may God strengthen him by His grace and His favor, amen! Because our interests are one and united, because our aim is that acts may succeed by overflowing justice, and the observance [of duty?; of treaties?; of the Sacred Law?] becomes praiseworthy by facts entirely, amen! by making successful safety and security by permanence of innumerable benefits and pure and unmixed issue. Prosperity accompanies highness and facilitation of good by length of the different kinds of joy makes permanent. Praise be to God for the comprehensive benefit and your perfect gifts, may God make them permanent for us and for you, thus till the day of resurrection and judgment, as long as times last, amen!

Further, if there are American people coming to the well-protected Tripoli, they wish to be, by your carefulness, honored [and free] from all disagreements as are, indeed, all the [Christian] nations, so that nobody molests them and no injury befalls them; and likewise people from Tripoli, if they proceed to the country of the Americans, they shall be honored, elevated upon the heads, nobody molesting or hindering them until they travel [homeward] in good state and prosperity. Thus. And greetings!

Praise be to God! Declaration of the twelfth article. If there arises a disturbance between us on both sides, and it becomes a serious dispute, and the American Consul is not able to make clear [settle] his affair, and [then] the affair shall remain suspended between them both, between the Pasha of Tripoli, may God strengthen him, and the Americans, until the Lord Hassan Pasha, may God strengthen him, in the well-protected Algiers, has taken cognizance of the matter. We shall accept whatever decision he enjoins on us, and we shall agree with his condition and his seal [*i. e.*, the decision sealed by him]; may God make it all permanent love and a good conclusion between us in the beginning and in the end, by His grace and favor, amen!

[Translation of the "Receipt"]

forty thousand duros	watches	seal rings	ells of cloth	*sersâr*[?] garments
40,000	13	5	140	4

Praise be to God! Explanation: This is our memorandum delivered to [in the hand of] its bearer, the Captain Ibrahîm [*sic*], the American: We have received forty thousand royal duros and thirteen watches, some of them gold, some silver, some *tumbâk*, and five seal rings, three of which diamond, one sapphire, one with a watch in it, hundred and forty one [*sic*] ells of cloth, and four *sersâr* [?] garments. That is on account of the peace treaty of His [God's] servant, Yussuf

Pasha, with the Americans and the completeness [perhaps the last word means only that the memorandum is hereby finished].

The seal, badly imprinted on this "receipt," is the same as the topmost of those which follow Article 12 of the treaty; it represents the signature of Hassan Pasha.

On the right side of the seal there are four small lines of script, written by the same hand that wrote the names of the goods and the figures at the top of the page, and the two lines under the seal, but a hand other than that which wrote the three lines of text. Those four lines of script read as follows: "Karamaïli [*sic*], may his glory last, amen! 20th day of Jumada al-awwal, year 1211." The last two lines read: "This is the copy from [*sic*] the memorandum of the exalted Lord Yussuf Pasha, in the well-preserved Tripoli, and his seal.

The word used for "silver" (*fejra*) is uncommon, although not altogether unknown. The word corresponding to "pinsback" in the Barlow translation is *tumbâk*, which may be derived from Portuguese "tambaca" (from Malay "tembâga"), which denotes copper and a certain number of alloys of that metal. That word is derived from the Sanskrit; the thus-named alloy of copper and zinc used to be imported from Indo-Chinese countries (see Hobson-Jobson—A Glossary of Colloquial Anglo-Indian Words and Phrases, 929, and the references in Note A of that work, List of Glossaries, *in verbo*).

The 20th day of Jumada I, A. H. 1211, coincided with November 21, 1796, or thereabout.

"Karamaïli" is probably a corruption of the clan-name, "Karamanli," which occurs several times in the signatures to the treaty, *e. g.*, in the signature of Yussuf Pasha of Tripoli, but not in that of Hassan Pasha of Algiers; so it seems to be here not an adscript to the seal of Hassan Pasha, but rather a substitute for the seal of Yussuf Pasha; but even then it remains an enigma why he did not seal this receipt and why his name should have been written so incompletely, with the essential elements lacking.

[Translation of the "Note"]

Praise be to God! This is a memorandum and a statement of what the Americans are still obliged to pay on account of the peace treaty: The amount of money being the value of twelve thousand royal duros; and likewise hawsers, being five, eight inches thick; and also cables, being three, each ten inches thick; and also tar, twenty-five barrels; and also pitch, twenty-five barrels; and likewise rosin, ten barrels; and also boards of *rubel* [this denotation of a sort of wood is unknown to me; it is not the common Arabic word for oak], five hundred; and likewise boards of *binu flamank* [also unknown to me; *flamank* means Dutch; perhaps "Dutch pine" is meant], five hundred; and also masts, being ten; and likewise yards, twelve; and also canvas for sails [the text adds the qualification *dhî lamûnah*, which I cannot explain], fifty pieces; and also anchors,

being four. This is what the Americans are still obliged to pay in this mentioned number as has been mentioned [*sic*] and afterwards, when the Consul comes from his country, they shall have to bring all that we have mentioned, amounting to this number, when he arrives at the well-preserved Tripoli, may God protect her by His grace, amen! Contained [certified?] completely on the first day of Rajab in this above-mentioned rescript, year 1211.

The seal imprinted on this "note" is illegible; it is, however, the seal of Hassan Pasha, Dey of Algiers, and the same as the topmost of those which follow Article 12 of the treaty, where the imprint is clearer.

The "4th" of Rajab is not in the Arabic text. The 1st of Rajab, 1211, may have corresponded to December 31, 1796, or to January 1, 1797; but compare "four days from the beginning" in the lines written at the left of the seal of Hassan Pasha, following Article 12 of the treaty, which are translated below in the account of the seals. The Arabic rendering of "1st Rajab" may also mean "beginning of Rajab."

Account of the Seals

The eleven seals will be explained here, beginning with the topmost, after which the three horizontal rows (of three, three, and four seals respectively) are treated, proceeding from the right side to the left.

The superscriptions are not signatures (the seals themselves being considered as such), but each of them denotes the name and title or function of the owner of the seal at the top of which it is written. All these superscriptions, except that of the topmost seal, are in the handwriting of one and the same secretary; the exception is probably owing to the fact that the seal of Hassan Pasha, with its superscription, was affixed in Algiers, not, like the other ten, in Tripoli. The writer of the ten superscriptions follows the eastern method of using diacritical points, whereas all the other pages, and also Article 12, are written in the western (Maghrebin) manner.

First superscription. "His Worship the Eminent Hassan Pasha, son of Husein, Wâlî [governor] of the well-protected Gate of Holy War, Algiers of the West."

The seal. The central oval contains the name of Hassan Pasha, son of Husein, and around the oval are two verses which may be rendered as follows:

My God, Thou art the Giver of grace and favors
And I am the committer of sins; so forgive me.

My Lord! full is my trust in Thee,
So make true, O my God, my good trust!

At the left of this topmost seal there are two lines written by the same hand as Article 12, which wrote also all the other articles and

which is different from the hands of both writers of the superscriptions. These lines read as follows: "And this is the seal of the honored Lord, the Lord Hassan Pasha, may God strengthen him, in the vilayet [province] of Algiers, dominion of Holy War, may she be victorious by the help of God. It [referring, as it seems, to the whole treaty] has been fixed and written down in this document [the word *itmân*, translated here by "document," is rather uncommon and means properly something like "assurance" or "certification"] at the date of the beginning of the month of Rajab, four days from the beginning. Year 1211."

Second superscription. "His Excellency the Exalted, the Honorable Wezîr [after *Wezîr* there is a word which I cannot exactly identify] Yussuf Pasha, son of Ali Pasha, son of Muhammed Pasha, son of Ahmed Pasha Karamanli [see above, the notes to the translation of the 'receipt'], Mutesarrif [this word denotes in the Turkish administration a rank inferior to that of Wâlî, 'subgovernor,' governing a sanjak, being a part of a vilayet, governed by a Wâlî] of the well-preserved Tripoli of the West, dominion of Holy War."

The seal. In the central oval: "His [God's] servant, Yussuf Bey, son of Ali Pasha Karamanli, 1195" (probably the Hegira year of his nomination). Around the oval are two verses from the well-known Burdah (the poem in praise of the Prophet), running thus: "He who takes the Apostle of God for his helper, if the lions encounter him in their jungles, they will withdraw." "You never see a friend of his [the Apostle's] but victorious, nor an enemy of his but crushed!"

Third superscription. "The Right Honorable Kadîm Muhammed Bey, son of Yussuf Pasha, son of Ali Pasha, son of Muhammed Pasha, son of Ahmed Pasha Karamanli, in the well-protected Tripoli of the West, dominion of Holy War."

The seal. The inner circle certainly contains the names mentioned in the superscription, but the letters are intertwined so as to make up a calligraphic puzzle of the sort favorite with Arabic seal-engravers. I have read only some of the names, and it seemed hardly worth while to decipher the whole. The outer circle contains the first of the two verses occurring around the oval of the seal last above described.

Fourth superscription. "The Exalted Muhammed, Kethoda-i-Ojaghy ['chief of the garrison'; may also denote 'chief of the place'] of Tripoli of the West, dominion of Holy War."

The seal. Inner square: "Muhammed, son of Abdallah." Around the square: "Seeking [asking for] the grace of God." There is still one word more, of the reading of which I am not quite sure.

Fifth superscription. "The Exalted Ahmed Agha, chief of the port of Tripoli of the West, dominion of Holy War."

The seal. "Hoping for His [God's] grace, which is worthy of being hoped for. Ahmed, son of Mustapha, son of Ahmed. Year 1201."

Sixth superscription. "The Exalted al-Hâjj [title of those who have performed the pilgrimage to Mecca] Ahmed, treasurer of the garrison [or place] of Tripoli of the West, dominion of Holy War."

The seal. "His [God's] servant, who seeks His Grace, al-Hâjj Ahmed, treasurer."

Seventh superscription. "Ali, Agha [commander] of the Janizaries of the well-protected Tripoli of the West, dominion of Holy War."

The seal. "His [God's] servant, seeking God's powerful grace, Ali, son of . . . [illegible] Year 1200."

Eighth superscription. "The Exalted Suleyman, Seraskar [commander of the army] of Tripoli of the West, dominion of Holy War."

The seal. "Seeking God's grace, Suleyman . . . "(other words illegible).

Ninth superscription. "The Exalted the Agha [commander] of the Sipahis [soldiers; perhaps the infantry is meant], Khalîl, in the well-protected Tripoli of the West, dominion of Holy War."

The seal. "The proprietor [*i. e.*, of this seal], His [God's] servant, Muhammed Khalîl."

Tenth superscription. Muhammed Atâ Allah, secretary of the town.

The seal. "Seeking forgiveness and safeguard, His [God's] servant, Muhammed, son of Al-Hâjj Atâ allah Kabtân."

Eleventh superscription. "The Honorable Muhammed, sheik of the town [or 'of the country'], the well-protected Tripoli, dominion of Holy War."

The seal. "Seeking . . . Muhammed . . ." (the rest illegible).

NOTES

The two dates and places given for the signature of the treaty (Tripoli, November 4, 1796, and Algiers, January 3, 1797) are explained by the fact that the provisions of the agreement with the Pasha of Tripoli were deemed to be to some extent at least under the protection or guaranty of the Dey of Algiers and made with his approval. So after the completion of the negotiations at Tripoli by Capt. Richard O'Brien, the agreement was taken to Algiers for the signature and seal of the Dey of Algiers; and consequently the various signatures and certificates of Joel Barlow, Consul General at Algiers, which are hereafter mentioned, became a part of the record.

There are four documents in the Department of State file of this treaty.

The Original Treaty

The first to be noted is that which contains the original treaty. It is a book in the literal sense. There are fourteen pages of Arabic text; all of these are right-hand pages. In the Arabic order, the first of them is the "note" of the money and presents, mentioned, accord-

ing to the Barlow translation, in Article 10 of the treaty; the second is the "receipt," also mentioned in that article, and this page, like the first, is sealed with the seal of the Dey of Algiers. Then come the twelve pages of the treaty; the preamble is on the first of these with Article 1; and there is one article on a page, except that the script on the page between Articles 10 and 12, is, as fully explained in the annotated translation of 1930, not an article at all. The last of those twelve pages has also the seals and superscriptions, of which there are eleven in all, including one for the Dey of Algiers. The fourteen pages of Arabic text are reproduced above in left-to-right order of pagination; but the twelve treaty pages come first and then the "receipt" and then the "note."

In the original treaty book, on the corresponding fourteen left-hand pages, each signed or initialed by Joel Barlow, Consul General at Algiers, is a purported English translation of the Arabic of the respective pages opposite.

It is the Barlow translation which is here printed following the Arabic text and in the same order, first the twelve articles of the treaty, then the "receipt" and the "note," after which is the approval of Col. David Humphreys, then Minister at Lisbon, dated February 10, 1797, as written in the original document.

The Barlow translation of the treaty proper is that which has been printed in all official and unofficial treaty collections ever since it appeared in the Session Laws of the first session of the Fifth Congress, in 1797, and in The Laws of the United States, Folwell ed., IV, 44–48, printed in 1799; but in those treaty collections, as, for example, in 8 Statutes at Large, 154–56, the "receipt" and the "note" (there called "notice") are omitted; and the first source of the texts of those collections was clearly a now missing copy, as is shown by the fact that they include a certification of the text as a copy; that certification is signed by Joel Barlow under date of January 4, 1797, and it is neither in the original document nor in the Cathcart copy, which is particularly described below.

Returning to the original document and still observing the reverse or Arabic order, the next page has written on it a certificate in Spanish regarding the signatures and seals, which reads as follows:

Nos D[n] Gerardo Joseph de Souza Caballero Profeso en la orden de Christo, Consul General y Encargado de Negocios por Su Magestad Catholica en esta Ciudad y Reyno de tripoly de Berberia.

Certificamos que las antecedentes firmas y sellos son los verdaderos de los Sugetos que firman todos los Documentos de Paz que se hacen con las Naciones Christianas y son:—

Issuf Baxá: Mohamet Bey: Mamet Keya: Amet Rais de Marina: Amet Gamadar: Aly Haga del Divan: Soliman Kaya: Galil Bachi Aga: Mohamet Chegue de la Ciudad: Mamet Cocha: y por fé de la verdad lo firmo de mi propia mano, sellado del Real sello de este Consulado de España, en tripoly de Berberia a los quatro dias del mes de Noviembre de Mil siete Cientos noventa y seis.

[Seal] Gerardo Joseph de Souza

Affixed to the same page is the following translation of that Spanish certificate:

We Don Gerardo Joseph de Souza Knight of the order of Christ, Consul General and Chargé des Affaires of his Catholic Majesty in this City and Kingdom of Tripoli of Barbary.

Certify That the foregoing signatures and seals are those of the persons who sign all treaties of peace which are concluded with Christian Nations. They are

Jussuf Bashaw	*Mahomet Bey*
Mamet	*Treasurer*
Amet	*Minister of Marine*
Amet	*Chamberlain*
Ally	*Chief of the Divan*
Soliman	*Kaya*
Galil	*General of the Troops*
Mohamet	*Com^t. of the City*
Mamet	*Secy*

In faith of which I sign these presents with my own hand. Sealed with the royal seal of this Consulate of Spain, in Tripoli of Barbary on the 4th of November 1796

(L. S.) signed GERARDO JOSEPH DE SOUZA

On the next (preceding) page of the original treaty book is the following certificate regarding the signature and seal of the Dey of Algiers:

I Joel Barlow, agent and consul general of the United States of America for the city and Kingdom of Algiers, certify and attest that the seal standing uppermost on the page next but two preceding this [in the Arabic order] is that of the Regency of Algiers and that the signature above it is that of Hassan Bashaw Dey.

In testimony whereof I sign these presents with my hand and affix thereto the seal of the consulate of the United States at Algiers this 4th day of January 1797.

[Seal] JOEL BARLOW

To that same page of the book is affixed a sheet of note paper; the first portion of the writing thereon by Capt. Richard O'Brien, who had negotiated the treaty at Tripoli and who had previously for some years been a prisoner in Algiers, reads thus:

Recapitulation of the Terms of Peace of the United States of America with the Bashaw of Tripolia november the 4th 1796. Concluded.

	Drs.
For the Peace and the Redemption of 4 Captives	40000.
Given to the Bashaw as presents agreeable to the list amounting to	3486.
To be given for the Peace and Consolary presents	12000.
For the Services of al Signior Farfaro	2000.
For the Ries of the Marine	1000.

Requisite with the Consul, 200 piques of Cloth.

Remarkd and Certifyed by me. RICHd OBRIEN in Tripolia november the 4th 1796.

Following this, on the same affixed sheet, is this certificate in Spanish:

Dn Gerardo Josef de Sousa, Cavro profeso en la Orñ. de Christo, Consul Grâl. y Encargado de negocios de S. M. C. serca del Baxa de Tripoly de Berberia.

Certefico que la Cüenta que antecede formada y accinada por el Capitan Ricardo Obrien individuo Americano, y Acomisinado en esta Capital pa la con-

firmasion de Paz entre su Nacion, y esta Regencia; és sierta, verdadera, y conforme su distribucion a los particulares que expresa: en los que intervine, a instancias del mencionado Obrien. En fee de lo qual sele dá el pres^te^ sellado Con el R^l^ sello de este Consulado, y firmado de mi propia mano: en Tripoly de Berber^a^ a quatro de Nov^re^ de mil setecientos noventa y seis.

[Seal] Gerardo Joseph de Souza

Also affixed to the same page of the treaty book is the following translation of the foregoing certificate:

We Don Gerardo Josef de Souza Knight of the Order of Christ, Consul General and Chargé des Affaires of his Catholic Majesty near the Bey of Tripoli of Barbary

Certify that the foregoing account, formed and entered into by Captain Richard OBrien, an American Citizen, and Commissioner in this Capital for concluding peace between his Nation and this Regency, is accurate, true and conformable to the distribution to the individuals therein mentioned: to which I was a witness at the request of the said OBrien.

In faith whereof I have sealed these presents with the royal Seal of this Consulate, and signed the same with my hand in Tripoly of Barbary the 4th of November 1796.

(L. S.) Gerardo Joseph de Souza

On the next two (preceding) pages of the original treaty book appears the approval of Col. David Humphreys, then Minister to Portugal, dated at Lisbon February 10, 1797.

It is to be added that most of the pages of the original treaty book are quite stained.

The Cathcart Copy

The second document in the Department of State file to be noted is a very similar book, containing a copy of the treaty certified by the Dey of Algiers and also by Barlow; this latter book may be called the Cathcart copy. Something should be said about James Leander Cathcart and the book itself, before noting the differences between the Cathcart copy and the original treaty book.

Cathcart was born in Scotland on June 1, 1767; he had been a midshipman on the frigate *Confederacy* of the Continental forces; while a seaman on the schooner *Maria* from Boston he had been taken prisoner by the Algerines in 1785. He became chief Christian clerk to the Dey of Algiers and returned to the United States during the negotiations with Algiers in 1796. Cathcart was commissioned Consul at Tripoli on July 10, 1797; but his instructions were not written until December 20, 1798, his letter of credence being dated the next day; and he did not reach Tripoli as Consul until April 5, 1799.

That Cathcart had with him in Tripoli the book which is here given his name is certain. Where it had been before that is uncertain, but probably Cathcart took it with him from Algiers in 1799, for he says in one of his letters that he found no document at all, not even a copy of the treaty, in the office at Tripoli. That the Cathcart copy was prepared at the same time as the original treaty book is conclusively established both by its appearance and by the internal evidence of its contents; but there is nothing to show when it was received by the Department of State.

The differences between the Cathcart copy and the original treaty book will now be noted.

The fourteen pages of the Arabic in the original are (with absolutely insignificant differences) the same in the Cathcart copy, *except* that the copy lacks all the seals and superscriptions of the original, and *except* that the copy has on four of its pages, under the Arabic, a seal of red wax impressed with the monogram "JLC," the seal of Cathcart. The English written opposite the fourteen pages of the Arabic in the copy and signed or initialed, as in the original, by Joel Barlow on each page, is in substance in the copy the same as in the original. There are some variances, but none of them is very material. However, on the first page of the English, which is the "note" mentioned in Article 10 of the treaty, there are certain annotations of Cathcart, as follows:

(*a*) Referring to the pine and oak boards: "3 inch of the longest & best sort for deck planks planks fit for ship building. Thus saith the Bashaw. Cathcart."

(*b*) Referring to the masts and yards: "fit for vessels from 2 to 300 Tons."

(*c*) Referring to the canvas: "the Bashaw insisted upon having 50 bales of Canvas with 12 pieces or bolts in each bale. Cathcart."

(*d*) At the foot of the page the following: "In April 1799, I gave the Bashaw 10,000 Spanish dollars for the above list of stores & 8,000 for a brig of War of ten guns promised him by Cap^{tn} OBrien this sum being in full of all demands for ever. Cathcart."

On the next page of the English of the copy, which is a translation of the receipt for the money and presents, someone (perhaps Cathcart) has added three words (here italicized) to the transcription of the signature by Barlow, so that it reads, "Jussuf Bashaw—Bey—whom God exalt *upon a Gibbet*."

It is in respect of the pages following, or as would be said here, preceding, the fourteen Arabic and corresponding English pages above mentioned, that the differences between the original treaty book and the copy are more notable. In the copy the following are omitted: (*a*) the certificate of the Spanish Consul General regarding the signatures and seals, and the translation thereof; (*b*) the certificate of Barlow regarding the seal of the Dey of Algiers; (*c*) the account of O'Brien, with the certificate appended thereto and the translation thereof; (*d*) the approval of Humphreys.

There are, however, in the Cathcart copy three written pages which are not in the original treaty book; and those three pages follow, or, as would be said here, precede directly the above-mentioned fourteen pages.

The first of the three is in Arabic under the seal of Hassan Pasha, Dey of Algiers; it is in the nature of a certificate, dated January 3, 1797; Doctor Snouck Hurgronje writes that "the text is drawn up in a very bad style" and gives this translation thereof:

Praise be to God! Declaration that this speech and this copy is from two documents [here again the word *itmân* is used; see the account of the seals, above] containing that [same text] in the same words exactly as in the [document] seal[ed]

by the exalted, the honored Lord Hassan Pasha, residing [governing?; see the annotated translation of Article 10 of this treaty] in Algiers, and this peace treaty has been authorized at his hands, consisting of a full [complete] peace treaty forever, may God make his days last and give him victory and make him continue in life with fulness of enjoyments; and likewise sealed by the exalted, the Lord Yussuf Pasha in the well-protected Tripoli, may God strengthen him; and likewise sealed by all the chief officers of his Government and the members of his Divan. We have put them [evidently the articles of peace are meant] in writing completely in the mentioned rescript in the two documents [*itmâns*], and likewise the seal of the exalted, the Lord Hassan Pasha in the vilayet of Algiers, the Gate of Holy War, may she be victorious by the help of God. Thus it has been put down and written in the two documents, at the date of the beginning of the month Rajab, four days from the beginning, in the year 1211.

The second of the three pages is opposite the foregoing and has the following in English:

I Joel Barlow, agent and consul general of the United States of America for the city and Kingdom of Algiers, certify and attest that the foregoing is a true copy of the treaty between the United States of America & the Bey and subjects of Tripoli, and of the several papers accompanying the same. And that the writing in Arabic on the page opposite to this is a certificate of the Dey of Algiers similar to what is here written by me.

In testimony whereof I sign these presents with my hand and affix thereto the seal of the Consulate of the United States—at Algiers this 3d day of January 1797.

[Seal] Joel Barlow

Then comes another (the final) page, in Arabic text, without any English translation or equivalent at all. It has an Arabic seal at the top and under the Arabic text the same red-wax seal of Cathcart as elsewhere. The following translation of that page of Arabic shows that it is in the nature of a confirmation or approval of the treaty on the part of Mustapha Pasha, who became Dey of Algiers upon the death of Hassan on May 15, 1798 (D. S., 3 Consular Despatches, Algiers, letter of Richard O'Brien of July 1, 1798; 7 *ibid.*, letter of Tobias Lear of January 25, 1807). While the Arabic seal is illegible, comparison shows that it is the seal of Mustapha Pasha. Doctor Snouck Hurgronje writes that "the text is drawn up in an abominable style similar to that of the letter which is in place of Article 11 of the treaty"; he mentions that at the right side of the seal are the words, "Praise be to God alone!"; and he gives this translation of the page:

Be that known to whosoever takes cognizance of our rescript concerning this noble affair and this important, clear speech from His [God's] granting success by His grace and His favor, to the results of acts and may He make prosperous by His bounty the end and the present! The right honorable the Lord Mustapha Pasha, may God strengthen him, amen! The reason is that we have now written down our rescript concerning the agreement and all the articles which have been signed by Yussuf Pasha in the well-protected Tripoli with the Americans, and we accord with their having concluded a full [complete] peace, and we assent to this agreement written down here and to take upon ourselves that contract and that assent exactly as that is contained [in the documents], without any alteration, modification, or change being made in this affair. Greetings!

And this comes from him who has written by authorization of the exalted, the most faithful and blessed, the Lord Mustapha Pasha, may God strengthen him, amen!

At the date of two days from [*sic*] Zu'lkadah in the end of it, year 1212.

On the authority of Doctor Snouck Hurgronje it is to be added that the above formula of dating is quite uncommon; it might denote either 2 or 28 Zu'lkadah. In the latter case the words "in the end of it" would refer to the month; otherwise, to the year. But the date here intended is 28 Zu'lkadah, A. H. 1212; for by the chronological tables the equivalent date is May 14, 1798, and in this case May 15, 1798, the date of the accession of Mustapha Pasha.

The Italian Translation

The third document in the Department of State file to be noted, is a translation of the treaty into Italian, a language then much in use in Tripoli. The translation covers not only the twelve articles of the treaty proper, but the receipt and note as well; and also the two Arabic pages of the Cathcart copy which are not in the original treaty book; so the translator had before him the Cathcart copy.

This translation was not made by Cathcart; it is not in his writing; he would naturally have written in English; and further it appears from his journal of the Tripoli negotiations of 1799 that he did not read Arabic, although he seems to have been familiar with Turkish and Italian. But that the translation was made for him and under his direction is clear, for on the cover page is written, over his full signature:

> Literal translation of the Treaty between the United States of America & the Regency of Tripoli in Barbary—the translation in English sign'd by Joel Barlow Esq[r] on the 26th of November 1796 being extremely erroneous.

Undoubtedly this refers to the Barlow translation in the certified copy which Cathcart had, here called the Cathcart copy, which, as above set forth, is now in the Department of State file. (The Barlow translation in the original treaty book is almost identical.) The date given for the Barlow translation, November 26, 1796, is approximately, and may even be quite, correct; for strictly speaking, that translation is not, *as a translation*, dated at all.

The Italian translation is a pamphlet with one page of Italian script for each page of the Arabic of the Cathcart copy. When the Italian translation of the treaty was received at the Department of State does not appear. It seems not to have been rendered into English; but as hostilities were begun by Tripoli in May, 1801, after threats for a year earlier, the actual terms of the treaty became, not long after the arrival of Cathcart in Tripoli in 1799, of little practical importance. The content of the Italian translation is discussed below.

The United States Ratification and Proclamation

The fourth document in the Department of State file, and the last to be noted, is at once the United States instrument of ratification and the proclamation, dated June 10, 1797.

In its combination of what are ordinarily two separate papers, that document is of unusual form. It is under the Great Seal and is

signed by Adams and attested by Pickering as Secretary of State; but before the testimonium clause is this paragraph of ratification and proclamation:

Now be it known, That I John Adams, President of the United States of America, having seen and considered the said Treaty do, by and with the advice and consent of the Senate, accept, ratify, and confirm the same, and every clause and article thereof. And to the End that the said Treaty may be observed and performed with good Faith on the part of the United States, I have ordered the premises to be made public; And I do hereby enjoin and require all persons bearing office civil or military within the United States, and all others citizens or inhabitants thereof, faithfully to observe and fulfil the said Treaty and every clause and article thereof.

The text embodied in the paper after the words, "which Treaty written in the Arabic Language, being translated into the Language of the United States, is in the words following to wit," is almost exactly the same as that in the Statutes at Large, which was perhaps copied from the instrument now described. Accordingly the provisions of the twelve articles appear in the document as written by Barlow in English in the original treaty book; so do the signatory names, although the copyist of them made a slip or two. The Barlow certification of January 4, 1797, which was doubtless contained in a now missing copy, is included, as is also the Humphreys approval or confirmation; but the receipt and the note, each of which Article 10 (according to the Barlow translation) in terms makes a part of the treaty, are not otherwise mentioned.

Thus the proclamation was immediate with the ratification and did not await any such formality as notice to the Bey of Tripoli of the ratification of the treaty by the United States. The treaty, like the treaty with the Dey of Algiers of 1795 (Document 17), had been bought; and, as much of the purchase price had already been paid, any subsequent item of procedure was doubtless considered to be of comparatively little importance.

Note Regarding the Arabic Text

The original here reproduced consists of the fourteen Arabic pages of the original treaty book heretofore described. The two Arabic pages of the certified or Cathcart copy, to which reference has been made in these notes, are not, as such, reproduced.

Note Regarding the Barlow Translation

The translation first printed is that of Barlow as written in the original treaty book, including not only the twelve articles of the treaty proper, but also the receipt and the note mentioned, according to the Barlow translation, in Article 10. The signature of Barlow is copied as it occurs, but not his initials, which are on every page of the fourteen which is not signed. The Humphreys approval or confirmation follows the translation; but the other writings, in English and Spanish, in the original treaty book, are not printed with the translation but only in these notes.

It is to be remembered that the Barlow translation is that which was submitted to the Senate (American State Papers, Foreign Relations, II, 18–19) and which is printed in the Statutes at Large and in treaty collections generally; it is that English text which in the United States has always been deemed *the* text of the treaty.

As even a casual examination of the annotated translation of 1930 shows, the Barlow translation is at best a poor attempt at a paraphrase or summary of the sense of the Arabic; and even as such its defects throughout are obvious and glaring. Most extraordinary (and wholly unexplained) is the fact that Article 11 of the Barlow translation, with its famous phrase, "the government of the United States of America is not in any sense founded on the Christian Religion," does not exist at all. There is no Article 11. The Arabic text which is between Articles 10 and 12 is in form a letter, crude and flamboyant and withal quite unimportant, from the Dey of Algiers to the Pasha of Tripoli. How that script came to be written and to be regarded, as in the Barlow translation, as Article 11 of the treaty as there written, is a mystery and seemingly must remain so. Nothing in the diplomatic correspondence of the time throws any light whatever on the point.

A further and perhaps equal mystery is the fact that since 1797 the Barlow translation has been trustfully and universally accepted as the just equivalent of the Arabic. Its text was not only formally proclaimed as such but has been continuously printed and reprinted as such; and yet evidence of the erroneous character of the Barlow translation has been in the archives of the Department of State since perhaps 1800 or thereabouts; for in the handwriting of James Leander Cathcart is the statement quoted above that the Barlow translation is "extremely erroneous"; and while the Italian translation of the Arabic text on which that endorsement appears, presents its own linguistic difficulties, largely owing to its literal rendering and its consequent non-literary character as Italian, it is none the less in essence a reasonable equivalent of the Arabic. Indeed, allowing for the crudeness of the original Arabic and the changes which always result from a retranslation, it may be said that a rendering of the Italian translation into English gives a result which is in general not dissimilar from the English translation of Doctor Snouck Hurgronje of 1930; and of course the most cursory examination of the Italian translation would show (assuming the Italian to be even an approximation of the Arabic), that the Barlow translation, as Cathcart wrote, was "extremely erroneous"; but nothing indicating that the Italian translation was even consulted has been found, and it does not appear that it was ever before 1930 put into English. Some account of the Italian translation as a document is given above.

Note Regarding Ratification

From the point of view of the rulers of Tripoli, the validity and effective character of the treaty depended on the receipt of those things promised in the "note," which were to be delivered "on the

arrival of an American Consul in Tripoli." What had been delivered on the negotiation of the treaty as set forth in O'Brien's account, was merely a part of an uncompleted whole.

When Cathcart, as the American Consul, arrived at Tripoli on April 5, 1799, the stores agreed to be delivered, and at least part of which had been shipped, had not arrived. They were thought to have been lost or captured. Cathcart was quite willing to agree upon a money equivalent; but he was met with an added demand of the Pasha of Tripoli for a brig alleged to have been promised by O'Brien at the time of the signing of the treaty. The negotiations following, during the course of which the Pasha of Tripoli declared that he did not consider himself obliged to fulfil the treaty, were very lively; but with the help of Dr. Bryan McDonogh, whom the Pasha wrote of as "our Doctor," the whole matter was finally adjusted for $18,000 on April 10, 1799. There is a full and interesting account of the proceedings in Cathcart's "Journal of the negotation and ratification of the Treaty between the United States of America and the Regency of Tripoli in Barbary" (D. S., 2 Consular Despatches, Algiers).

"A ratified copy of the Treaty with Tripoli" was one of the enclosures with the instructions to Cathcart of December 20, 1798 (D. S., 5 Instructions, U. S. Ministers, 25–30); very likely the ratification embraced the copy certified by Barlow under date of January 4, 1797, for, as above mentioned, the proclamation includes that certification, which is also printed in the Statutes at Large. While the original ratification remained in the hands of Cathcart (Tripoli . . . Letter Book by James Leander Cathcart, 270, 285), it is possible that a copy thereof was delivered upon the settlement of April 10, 1799, and further possible that there was something almost in the nature of an exchange of ratifications of the treaty on or about April 10, 1799, the day of the agreed settlement. A letter from the Pasha of Tripoli to President Adams of April 15, 1799 (translation from the Italian in D. S., 1 Consular Despatches, Tunis), concludes thus:

> Whereby we have consummated the Peace which shall, on our side, be inviolate, provided You are Willing to treat us as You do other Regencies, without any difference being made between Us. Which is the whole of what We have, at present, to say to You, wishing you at the same time the most unlimited prosperity.

Treaty Series, No. 360
8 Statutes at Large, 157–61

21

TUNIS : AUGUST 28, 1797, AND MARCH 26, 1799

Treaty of Peace and Friendship, signed at Tunis August 28, 1797, and, with alterations, March 26, 1799. Original in Turkish.
Submitted to the Senate February 21, 1798. Resolution of advice and consent, on condition, March 6, 1798. Resubmitted to the Senate December 13, 1799. Resolution of advice and consent to altered Articles 11, 12, and 14, December 24, 1799. Ratified by the United States January 10, 1800. As to the ratification generally, see the notes. Not proclaimed (semble), but see the notes as to publication.
The following pages of Turkish are a reproduction of the articles of the original of the altered treaty; but they are arranged in left-to-right order of pagination, and of necessity the Turkish script runs lengthways of the pages. They are followed by the French translation which is written in the original document and the English translation which is in the Department of State file; after the translations is the approval of Humphreys of the treaty as first signed, and then the approval of Eaton and Cathcart of the altered treaty, as copied in the original. Following those texts is a comment on the French translation, written in 1930.

هو المعين

جناب کهداننده کون ومکان وزینتبخشنده زمین واسمان جل شانه حضرتلرینک عنایت علیه عظما ونعمت جلیله کبرالرینه مقارنت ایله
حالا سریر آرای تختگاه سلطنت عثمانی ومتکا پیرای اریکه مسند خلافت اولان خورشید آسمان دولت ومهر جهان افروز اوج سلطنت شوکتلو
مهابتلو عظمتلو قدرتلو سلطان البرین وخاقان البحرین السلطان ابن السلطان غازی سلیم خان ابن السلطان غازی مصطفی خان خلد الله
ملکه وسلطنته الی آخر الدوران حضرتلرینک حسن نظر پادشاهانه لری وبرکاتیه زمان معدلت نشان شهنشاهانه لرنده حالا دار الجهاد
محروسه تونس اوجاغی محافظی ووالی ایالت تونس ومیر لواسی اولان دولتلو سعادتلو حمودة پاشا باشابک اطال الله عمره واقباله وادام سلطنته واجلاله
واوجاغ منصوره دایسی ساحتلو ابراهیم دای ووکیل خرج اغاسی سلیمان اغا واهالی دیوان واوجاق اختیارلری بالاتفاق حالا مرقان
طائفه سنک سرکرده وحاکمی اولان افتخار الامراء الملة المسیحیة مختار الکبراء الطائفة العیسویة آدامس دوستمز ختمت عواقبه بالخیر والرشاد بیننده منعقد
اولان صلح وصلاح وعهد وپیمانی مکالمه وربط قوی بند ایدوب بنهاده اولان بروده لی مودة تبدیل ایتمکه مرقان سرکرده مشار الیه طرفندن مأذون
حالا تونس اوجاغنده مقیم فرانچه طائفه سی تجارتلری جوزاب فامیس باذکان وساطتیله صلح مذکور بالمکالمه تنظیم وعقد اولنان رشته مصالحه
شروط وقیود وعهودی تشیید اساسی یکرمی اوچ ماده اوزرینه بناء وربط وقید اولنوب باعبارتها ایزیده تحریر وتسطیر اولنمغین طرفیندن مرعی ودستور
العمل طوتیلوب مغایر شروط معاهده حرکات بروجهیه جواز وجهت ویرلمیه

الشرط الاول

محروسهٔ تونس دولتی ایله طائفهٔ مرقان بیننده صلح وصلاح علی الدوام والاستمرار اولوب مرور ازمنه واعوام وطول مدت ایله تبدیل وتغییر اولنمیوب همان محبت ومودت والفت امتداد وازدیاد اوده

الشرط الثانی

ایکی طرفدن بری دشمانه غالب کلوب واخذ وکرفت واغتنام ایسه وددری غنیمه ده توتسلونلر اموال واشیاسی بولنسه غنیمه ده بولنان توتسلونلر اموال واشیاسنی طائفهٔ مرقان صاحبنه تماما رد وتسلیم ایده وکذلک تونس دونتنه قورصان سفینه‌لری اغتنام ایدیکی غنیمه‌سنده بولنان مرقان طائفه‌سنک اموال واشیاسنی صاحب مال اولان مرقانلویه بعد الاثبات تماما رد وتسلیم ایده

الشرط الثالث

طائفهٔ مریقان سفینه‌لرنده تونس دولتی دشمانلری ماللرندن هر نه بولنورسه وکذلک تونس سفینه‌لرنده طائفهٔ مذکوره دشمانلری ماللرندن هر نه بولنورسه طرفینی سفینه‌لرینه اکراماً واحتراماً دوست سلط اولنمیوب تونسلو طرفندن مریقان سفینه‌سنه و مریقان طائفه‌سی طرفندن تونس سفینه‌سنه مال عدوندن اخذ ایچون تعدی اولنمیه ایکی جانبی سفینه‌لرینه حرمتی ایچون طرفینه مأمور اوله

الشرط الرابع

ایکی طرف بر جانب سفینه‌لرینه پاصه‌پورطه اعطا ایده‌که هیچ من فائده بربرلرینه داخل اولدقلرنده تحصیل معرفت حاصل اوله و طائفهٔ مریقان ایچون اون سکز ای مقداری مدت تعیین اولنه احضارنسنه ایچون و مدت مذکوره اثناسنده ابتداء مدتدن انتهاسنه دکین حامل پاصه‌پورطه تحمل اولنه بعد مسافه ایچون و تنسنه توقف اولنمیه و مدت مذکوره تجاوز ایدرکه طائفهٔ مذکوره احضارنسنه تکلیف اولنه

الشرط الخامس

دوی و دیاده قورسانز مرخان قورسانته داسف کلوب مرافعی اولسه و مرخان قورسانلری معینده جنس مرخانلردن بازرکان تکنه لری قورسانز اول مرخان
بازرکانی تکنه لرینه دست درازلق ایتمیه و اندن بعد بو وجهله طلب ایتمه همان قوربان تکنه فرماندانی شبهه سوز ایتدیرمه و قوماندانی مرخوم هر نکو افاده
ایدر ایسه کلامنی تصدیق ایده قورخینه لری بوزولمامق ایچون و کذلک مرخان طائفه قورسانلری قورسانز سفینه لرینه موافقی اولدقده معیننده بازرکانی
تکنه لری بولنور مرخان قوماندانی برنسنه سؤال ایتمیه قورسانز قوماندانیه مکالمه ایتمیه جنبهاده ذکر اولنان منوال اوزره اولنه

الشرط السادس

قورسانز تکنه لرندن بر قورسانز مرخان جنسندن اولان بر بازرکان تکنه سنه اکر موافقی اولسه بازرکان سفینه سی فلوکه سنی کوندرده و قوربان قبودانی عادت قدیمه دن
خارج اندن برنسنه اخذ ایتمیه و عادت قدیمه مغایر اولان اشیادن برنسنه ایتسه بو جانبده محکم حقنده کلنجه جزاسی ترتیب اولنه و کذلک جنس
مرخان قورسانی و اونمزلو بازرکان تکنه لرندن بر تکنه یه راست کلوب موافقی اولدقده ذکر اولنان منوال اوزره ایتمیه و مرخانلو قوربان سفینه سنه بر اسیر فراد
ایسه اول سفینه نک اسیری اندرملری خصوصی قونسلوسندن طلب اولنه و کذلک قورسانزه فرار ایدن اسیر اندیر یوب و اخراج اولنه و بازرکان سفینه
اصلا کسنه نک منعه ایتمزلر و اکر بازرکان سفینه سنه بر اسیر فرار ایتسه و اول سفینه اسیری آلیه فرار ایسه بعد الثبوت اسیر و یا خود بهاسی قونسلوسدن طلب اولنور

الشرط السابع

جنس مرقومدن بر سنه اوجاقلو مخصوص مرزه بر قطعه اقطارمه غنیمه اشترا ایسه مشتریسی مبتی بر سنه تمامنه دکین مدت ایله طرفمزدن بر قطعه مرور نامه تحریر اولنوب
دخی دیاده قورسانمزدن حمایت وصیانت اولنمق ایچون وطرفمزدن ویریلان مرور نامه مقفصانجه قونصلوس دخی کونترهٔ تحریر واعطا ایلرو ویریلان تعید
حسبیه ولو بندن اکا ایصه بورط کتوردملوی متعذر اولمغنه مسافهٔ بعیده اولدیغنچون واکر مدت مذکوره بر سنه تمامندن صکره ولا تقتدن بعید بوبورد
کلمسه وبر سنه مرور دن صکره قورسانمز اکا راست کلور مرفقی اولسه کرک سفینه یی وکرک دروننده اولانلری ونصادالرکیـــ اخذ وکرفت
واغتنام ایدر

الشرط الثامن

اکر ایکی طرف سفاینلرندن بر سفینه حسب الاقتضا ایکی طرف لیمانلرینه دخولی لازم کلوب ویاخود داخل اولان سفینه سنه متعلق بعض الات وادوات
وغیر ذلک مصالح لازمه سنی رؤیت ایچون محتاج اولدیغی شیلدن منع اولنمیه واهل بلد بیننده سعر جاری اودوزه اشترا ایده واکر سفینهٔ اهلوب
صوایدوب وصاحب سفینه قبطانی واصحابی مراد ایسه سفینه سندن دزفتی خرجی اندروب وبعد الاصلاح دزفتی سفینه سنه اعاده وتحمیل
ایدکن کرکچی ویاغیره طرفندن رسم کرکلو طلب اولنمیه واعاده ایدنلرلو اجرتلری ادا اولنه

الشرط التاسع

ایکی طرفك سفینه لرندن بر سفینه ایکی جانب مملکتلرینده بقضاء الله تعالی باشدن قره اولسه ویا بادو لندن شکست اولنسه اول ولایتلرك حاکملری اول دزدن
اخراجی ممکن اولان دزخلو اخراجنه سعی واعانت ایدوب اوزرینه تعدی ایتدرمیز واصحاب مال خدمت ایدنلره اجرتلرینی اداء واعطا ایدر

الشرط العاشر

ایکی طرفك سفاینلرندن بر سفینه طرفین لیمانلرندن بر لیمانه داخل اولسه وطوپ منزلی بر ده بولنسه کوچك بندوکی قدر دشمانندن حمایت وصیانت ایدر
واکر اول مکاندن سفر ایتسه دشمانی اولان سفینه قالقوب ذهابنه اذن ورخصت ویرلمز تاکه فرق سکز ساعت مرور ایده وکذلك بولندیغی لیمانه قریب
برشقه لیمانده دشمانی سفینه اولسه سنوح اولنمز تاکه ذکر اولنان فرق سکز ساعت مرور ایده

الشرط الحادی عشر

مرجان طائفه سنك بكلو سفينه لرى تونس قبانته كلدكده قونسلوسي كلوب مذكور سفينه ايچون قومه لي طوب اطلمق استرسه مطلوب ايدكي مقداري
قومه لي طوب اطلوب و اكر قونسلوس استرسه طوب اطلميه فاما قونسلوس طوب اطلمسني استرسه مطلوب ايدكي مقدار طوب اطلوب هر مقدار طوب اطلور
عدد بچه برر وارل بارود مرجان تكنه ويره كذلك تونس قرسانى دخى مرجان قبانته وارد دخى برمنوال محرر اوله

الشرط الثاني عشر

مرفان طائفه سندن اولان تجار محروسه تونس مملکتنه کلدکلرده غیر اجناس دول تجارلری عادتلری اوزره اجرا اولنه و اکر جنس مرفان تجارلرندن برکسنه
دولت مصالح لازمه سیچون و لازم لو بعض لیمانلرینه توجه و عزیمت ایتمك مراد ایتسه منع اولنمیه و معیتنده ترجمانلق ایدر کسنه کندوسی و یاخود کندو
ایچون خدمتکار کتورسه کذلك منع اولنمیه الا مکرکه غیر اجناس دول اوزرینه حاکم طرفندن عوق و منع واقع اوله اندرده غیر یلری کبی منع و عوق
اولنه لر و اکر تجار مز ولایت مرفانه توجه و عزیمت ایتسه لر ذکر اولنان منوال اوزره اوله و اکر تونس اهالیسی تجارلرندن برکسنه مرفان طائفه سندن برسفینه
استیجار و درونینه ذرق تجار وضع و تحمیل ایتسه و بعد التحمیل اول ذخایری طشره اخراج و یاخود برشقه سفینه یه نقل و تحویل مراد ایتسه خصوص مذکوره طرفین
اذن و یرلمز تاکه جماعت تجار و ارباب قبیله قتنده مرافعه و تحاکم ایده لر و بعد التحاکم جماعت تجار و ارباب قبیله اندر نه منوال اوزره حکم ایدرلر ایسه قضیه ده
حکم تجار اوزره عمل اولنه و مرفان طائفه سندن اولان سفینه لری لیمانلرمزده عوق و تأخیر اولنمیه الا مکرکه جمیع اجناس سفاینلری قورسان ایچون و یا برغیری نسنه
ایچون عوق و منع اولندقده اول زمان اندرده برشقه لری کبی عوق و منع اولنه لر و اما بکلکه کیره سفینه لرینه عوق و منع اولنمقدن برشی لازم کلمز و ایکی جانب
اهالیلری طرفندن و اونلرمز حاکملر تحت نظرنده اوله و بولندیغی ولایتده حاکمی آکا حکم ایده و حاکمدن غیری کمسنه اندر حکم و تعرض ایتمیه و اکر خصوص مذکوری ولایت
حاکمی حق اوزره فصل ایده مزسه مدعی و مدعا علیهی احقاق حق ایچون طرفمزه ارسال ایتمیه و اکر جانب سپاهیدن ایچون طائفه مرفاندن بر بازرکان تکمه اکر مده اولنوب اقتضا
ایتسه بیلیه طرفندن طائفه مرسومدن بازرکان سفینه سی استیجار اولنوب اقتضا ایدن تولی حاکملر مرادی اوزره سفینه قپودانه ویریله و خصوص مذکور ایچون سفینه
قپودانی ابا و امتناع ایتمیه

الشرط الثالث عشر

اکر مرفان طائفه سنك تجار سفینه لرینه بزه دشمان اولان اجناس مختلف تونس اسیر اولنمز اول شرطیله که مرفان طائفه سنك تمتعی اقل اوله
واکر تونسك زیاده بولنور ایسه اسیر اولنورلر شبو شرط بحریه لر حقنده در فاما تجار ویولجی اولسه لر نه مقدار اولورلر ایسه دخی اولنمز

الشرط الرابع عشر

محمیه تونس تجارندن بری هر قنغی طائفه نك سنجاغی سفینه سنه اولورلر ایسه اولسون مرفان ولایتنه تونس ولایتی متاعی کوتورسه مرفان ولایتنده اجناس
سائره یه هر قنغیسی قبیل کمرک ویررلر ایسه تونس تجاری دخی اول مقدار کمرک ویره و یوزده قاج کمرک ویررلر ایسه کذلك مرفان تجاری دخی کندو ولایتی متاعی
کندو سنجاغی سفینه سیله تونسه ومحفظه سنه کتوردکده اول مقدار کمرک ویره فاما مرفان تجارندن بری کندو ولایتی مرفه سنی ویاخود آخر جنس ولایتلردن
طائفه سائره سنجاغی سفینه سیله دوق کتورسه یوزده اوچ کمرک ویره واکر طائفه سائره تجاری کندو ولایتندن ویاخود مرفه سنی مرفان سنجاغی سفینه سیله
دوق کتورسه یوزده اوچ کمرک ویره

الشرط الخامس عشر

طائفهٔ مرقان تجاری ولایتمزده تجارت ایدنلر و اندن بیع و شرادن کسنه منع ایمیه و غیری تجارلرکبی بیع و شرا ایدلر انجق همان خمر مقوله مسکراتی تجارت
ایتمیلر و مرقان تجارندن برکسنه کونشم باشنده اولان اشیادن برشی ایه ولایتنه عادلی اوزره حاکم انلر حقندن کله و اگر دشمله بحریه لر کونشم باشنده
اولان اشیادن سفینه لرینه تحمیل ایدرلر اول مقوله فعله مباشرت و اقدام ایدن کسنه یه حکم شدید اولنه و انلر غیرسی خصوص مذکور ایچون مدافعه اولنمیه و بر بحرده
مرعی قاعدهٔ الحاق فصل اشمسنده سفینه و بادرونده اولان رزق عرق و ناخذ و محافظت اولنمه حفظ اول محلی ابراز ایدن کسنه طلب اولنوب محکم حقنده کننه
سفاین خصوصاتلرینه برکسنه طرفندن تطلیع رزق ایچون غصب و ابرام اولنمیه الا مکر که قپودان ایچه کراده انفصالده صکره تحمیل اولنه

الشرط السادس عشر

مرقان سفینه سی هلاک الوار لیمانده و یا دکزده محفاتنده اولان غیری لیمانه اگر داخل اولسه انلر اوزرینه حکم انفراغ قرانلر سفینه لری کبی اولوب اگر کلور کلودر
بو کمی بوشالتدیغی حالده اون یدی بحق دیال انفراغ ویرد و اگر بوکونی افراغدن صکره ینه تحمیل اولنور ایسه لاجل التحمیل عدد مذکور مقداری عدد زیاده اولنور
و اگر بوش کلور ایسه انفراجدن برشی لازم کلمز و کذلک بوش کیدر ایسه دخی برشی لازم کلمز

الشرط السابع عشر

جانبین قونسلوس نصب ایتمك مراد ایدرلر ایسه منع وتعرض اولنماز الا مکرکه قونسلوسلری عادت قدیمه مستحسنه یه مغایر سنه صادر اوله اول زمانده حاکمه
العموم والامنا واولیجب حاکمی انی عزل وتبدیل ویرینه بشقه کمسنه یی قونسلوس نصب ایده وقونسلوس اهل وعیالی واتباعی حاکمان تحت نظارتی اوله
وقونسلوس خانه سنه ماکولات ومشروبات وملبوساتدن غیری تجارت ایچون رزق کتورسه عادت جاری اولدوغی کمرکه ویره

الشرط الثامن عشر

اکر ایکی طرف رعایاسندن بر ودیعه آخرده بعض کمسنه اوزرینه دین ترتب ایسه قونسلوسلری ویاخود وکیللری ویا ابناء جنسندن وغیریلردن اول دین طلب اولنمیه
اماکه اکر قونسلوس ویاخود وکیل ویا غیریلری خط یدیله یادوب ضامن اولسه لر ضمانات خط یدی موجبنجه اول وقتده مذکور مطالبه اولنور

الشرط التاسع عشر

ایکی طرف رعایاسندن برکسنه بلاد آخرده وفات ایسه جمیع مخلفات ومتروکاتی قونصلوسی ویاخود وکیلی ضبط ودفتره قید ومستحقنه اعطا وتسلیم ایده
واول ولایت حاکمی طرفندن انلرک اوزرینه تسلط ایتملو یوقدر واکر قونصلوسی ویاخود وکیلی اولمیان ولایتده وفات ایدرسه اول ولایتلو
بیوککی اولان کسنه انلرک جمله مخلفات ومتروکاتی ضبط وذمامه قید وتحریر وبعده قونصلوسنه ویاخود وکیلنه ارسال ایده

الشرط العشرون

طرفینک جانبندن اولان قونصلوس ویاخود وکیل بلاد آخرده ابناء جنسی وابناء ملتی اوزرینه حاکم اولوب واکر تنفیذ حکمی ایچون اول ولایت حاکمندن مدد
واعانت طلب ایدرسه ولایتلو حاکمی خصوص مزبور ایچون یاردم ومدد واعانت ایده

الشرط الحادی والعشرون

ایکی طرف رعایاسندن برکسنه فریق آخرین بعض کسنه اوزرینه تعدی وجرم وجنایت ایسه یرالایق وضرب ویاخود قتل وغیری نسنه یه مجبر اولور
حاکمی اول جنایت ایدن کسنه یی کرکی کبی حکم ایده کندو دعویسنده اولنلره حکم ایندوکی کبی قونصلوسلر ویاخود وکیللری حضورنده اوله واکر
فاعل هرب فرار ایدرسه قونصلوس ویاخود وکیل انلر ایچون مطالبه اولنمیه

الشرط الثانی والعشرون

ایکی طرفدن بعض کسنه لر بو آخرده متعلقات تجارتدن وغیری نسنه یه برشیده نزاع ومخاصمه ایسه قونصلوس ویاخود وکیل انلر ایچون معا
حاضر اوله که اهل حکم قتنده حضورنده قضیه لری ما بینلرنده انفصال وخصاملری قطع اوله واکر برینه کسنه کوندرملو مراد ایدرسه
انلر ایچون برینه آدم کوندرملو وارد در

الشرط الثالث والعشرون

تونس حاكمی طرفندن جماعت مرقاتن اوزرينه نوعًا نفسانيت ويا خود اثلدن واقع اولسه وشروط مصالحه يه منابعت واقع اولسه بر نهاده خصوصنه كيره

عجبه مبادرت اولنيه بلكه بو خصوصده تأنی كوركدكه نا كه مابينلرنده مراجعت واقع اوله وحرارت نفس ساكن اوله وشايد مابينلرنده هو

واقع اوله وبو تأنی ومراجعتدن صكره هدنه واقع اولدوغی امر تمام اولمق ومراد ومقصود حاصل اولور والا حال كما كان باقی قلور فرنج

آخره برسنه مقداری اجل ومدت ويريه اموالن جمع ايتمك ايچون وترتيب اموری ايچون دولتلرينه چقار وبرسنه مدتدن صكره مرادلری اولور

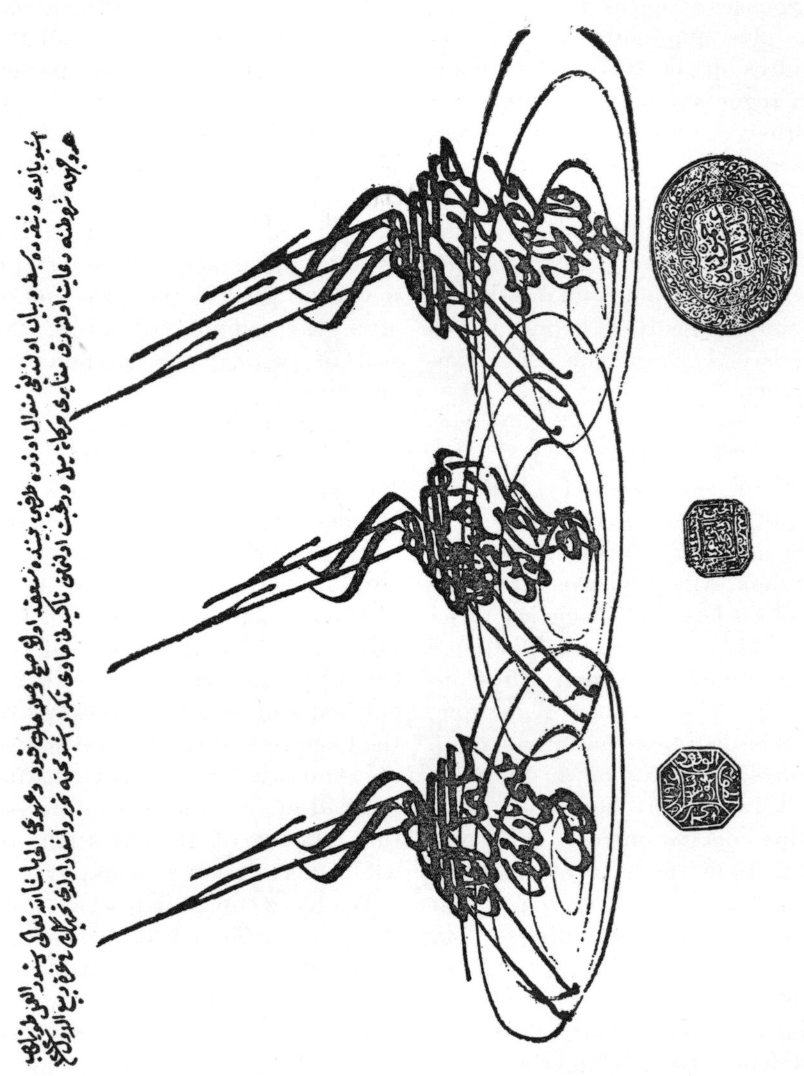

[Translation]

Dieu Infini.

Sous les auspices du plus grand, du plus puissant de tous les Princes de la Nation Ottomane qui regne sur la terre, notre tres glorieux et tres Auguste Empereur qui commande les deux terres et les deux mers, Selim Kan,[1] le Victorieux, fils de Sultan Moustafa, que Dieu prospere son royaume, jusqu'à la fin des siecles, le Soutien des Rois, le Sceau de la Justice, L'Empereur des Empereurs.

Le tres Illustre et tres Magnifique Prince Hamouda Pacha, Bey qui commande l'Odgiak de Tunis, le sejour de la felicité, et le tres honnoré Ibrahim Dey et Soliman, Aga des Janissaires et le Chef du Divan, et tous les Vieux de l'Odgiak et le tres Distingué et Honnoré President du Congres des Etats Unis d'Amerique, le plus distingué parmi ceux qui professent la religion du Messiah, dont la fin soit heureuse; Nous avons conclus entre nous le present traité de paix et d'amitié, dont tous les articles qui y sont contenus ont été dirigés par l'entremise de Joseph Etienne Famin, Negociant Français resident a Tunis, Chargé d'Affaires des Etats Unis d'Amerique, lesquels pactes et conditions sont fondees en vingt trois Articles, ecrits et conçus de maniere a ne laisser aucune Doute sur leur

[Translation]

God is infinite.

Under the auspices of the greatest, the most powerful of all the princes of the Ottoman nation who reign upon the earth, our most glorious and most august Emperor, who commands the two lands and the two seas, Selim Khan[1] the victorious, son of the Sultan Moustafa, whose realm may God prosper until the end of ages, the support of kings, the seal of justice, the Emperor of emperors.

The most illustrious and most magnificent Prince Hamuda Pasha, Bey, who commands the Odgiak of Tunis, the abode of happiness; and the most honored Ibrahim Dey; and Suleiman, Agha of the Janizaries and chief of the Divan; and all the elders of the Odgiak; and the most distinguished and honored President of the Congress of the United States of America, the most distinguished among those who profess the religion of the Messiah, of whom may the end be happy.

We have concluded between us the present Treaty of Peace and Friendship, all the articles of which have been framed by the intervention of Joseph Stephen Famin, French merchant resident at Tunis, Chargé d'Affaires of the United States of America; which stipulations and conditions are comprised in twenty-three arti-

[1] Selim III, Sultan of Turkey from 1789 to 1807.

contenû et de façon a ne pouvoir y contrevenir.

Article Premier

Il y a paix perpetuelle et constante entre les Etats Unis d'Amerique et le Magnifique Pacha Bey de Tunis, ainsi qu'une Amitie permanente qui s'augmentera toujours d'avantage.

Article Second

Si un Batiment de guerre des deux nations fait une prise de navire ennemi sur lequel il se trouve des effets, proprietés et sujets des deux parties contractantes, on doit les rendre en entier; le Bey rendra les proprietés et sujets des Etats Unis, et ces derniers rendront le reciproque; bien entendû que de part et d'autre, il devra être prouvé la legitimité des objets reclamés.

Article Troisieme

Telle sort de marchandise appartenante à quelque nation qui se trouve en guerre avec une des parties contractantes et chargées a bord des batiments de l'autre, dites marchandises passeront sans etre molestées et sans qu'il se puisse attenter de les prendre ou detenir.

Article Quatrieme

Il sera donné de part & d'autres des suffisants Passeports, aux

cles, written and expressed in such manner as to leave no doubt of their contents, and in such way as not to be contravened.

Article 1.

There shall be a perpetual and constant peace between the United States of America and the magnificent Pasha, Bey of Tunis, and also a permanent friendship, which shall more and more increase.

Article 2.

If a vessel of war of the two nations shall make prize of an enemy vessel in which may be found effects, property, and subjects of the two contracting parties, the whole shall be restored; the Bey shall restore the property and subjects of the United States, and the latter shall make a reciprocal restoration; it being understood on both sides that the just right to what is claimed shall be proved.

Article 3.

Merchandise belonging to any nation which may be at war with one of the contracting parties, and loaded on board of the vessels of the other, shall pass without molestation and without any attempt being made to capture or detain it.

Article 4.

On both sides sufficient passports shall be given to vessels,

115605°—31—vol. 2——28

Batiments pourqu'ils soient recconus & traittés en Amis, et vû la distance des deux Païs il est accordé un terme de dix huit mois, pendant la durée duquel terme on aura egard aux dits Passeports sans qu'il soit question du Congé /qu'on appelle a tunis testa,/ mais après le susdit terme, les Congés devront etre presentés.

that they may be known and treated as friendly; and considering the distance between the two countries, a term of eighteen months is given, within which term respect shall be paid to the said passports, without requiring the congé or document (which at Tunis is called *testa*), but after the said term the congé shall be presented.

Article Cinquieme

Si les Corsaires de tunis rencontrent en mer des Batimens de guerre des Etats Unis ayant sous leur Escorte des Navires marchands de leur Nation ils ne seront point recherchés ni molestés, & en pareil Cas les Commandans seront crus sur leur parole pour exempter les Batimens de guerre Americains rendront le reciproque aux Navires Marchand escortés par les Corsaires de tunis.

Article 5.

If the corsairs of Tunis shall meet at sea with ships of war of the United States having under their escort merchant vessels of their nation, they shall not be searched or molested; and in such case the commanders shall be believed upon their word, to exempt their ships from being visited and to avoid quarantine. The American ships of war shall act in like manner towards merchant vessels escorted by the corsairs of Tunis.

Article Sixieme

Si un Corsaire tunisien rencontre un Batiment marchand Americain & qu'il le visite avec sa Chaloupe il ne pourra rien exiger sous peine d'etre severement punis, & pareillement si un Navire de Guerre des Etats Unis rencontre un Batiment marchand tunisien il en usera de même.

Dans le cas ou un Esclave se refugieroit a Bord d'un Batiment de Guerre Americain, le Consul sera requis de le faire restituer,

Article 6.

If a Tunisian corsair shall meet with an American merchant vessel and shall visit it with her boat, she shall not exact anything, under pain of being severely punished; and in like manner, if a vessel of war of the United States shall meet with a Tunisian merchant vessel, she shall observe the same rule. In case a slave shall take refuge on board of an American vessel of war, the Consul shall be required to cause

et s'il s'echappe a Bord des Batimens tunisiens quelqu'un de leur prisoniers ils seront restitués, mais si quelque Esclave se refugie sur quelque Batiment marchand Americain & qu'il soit prouvé que le Batiment ait parti avec le dit Esclave, alors on le faira revenir ou bien l'on payera sa rançon.

him to be restored; and if any of their prisoners shall escape on board of the Tunisian vessels, they shall be restored; but if any slave shall take refuge in any American merchant vessel, and it shall be proved that the vessel has departed with the said slave, then he shall be returned, or his ransom shall be paid.

Article Septieme

Un Citoyen Americain ayant achetté un Batiment de prise de notre Odgiak pourra naviguer avec notre Passeport que nous delivrerons pour le terme d'un An, moyennant lequel nos Corsaires qui le rencontreront le respecteront, le Consul de son coté le munira d'un contract d'achat & attendu la distance des deux païs, Ce terme sufira pour avoir un passeport en regle; mais passé ce terme si nos Corsaires le rencontrent sans le Passeport des Etats Unis, il serait arreté & declaré de bonne prise tant le Batiment que la Cargaison et l'Equipage.

Article 7.

An American citizen having purchased a prize-vessel from our Odgiak, may sail with our passport, which we will deliver for the term of one year, by force of which our corsairs which may meet with her shall respect her; the Consul on his part shall furnish her with a bill of sale; and considering the distance of the two countries, this term shall suffice to obtain a passport in form. But after the expiration of this term, if our corsairs shall meet with her without the passport of the United States, she shall be stopped and declared good prize, as well the vessel as the cargo and crew.

Article Huitieme

Si un batiment d'une des parties contractantes etait oblige d'entrer dans un port de l'autre et eut besoin de provision et autres objets, on les lui accordera sans aucune difficulté, aux prix courant de la place; et si un tel batiment avait souffert en mer, qu'il eut besoin de reparations, il

Article 8.

If a vessel of one of the contracting parties shall be obliged to enter into a port of the other and may have need of provisions and other articles, they shall be granted to her without any difficulty, at the price current at the place; and if such a vessel shall have suffered at sea and shall

aura la liberté de decharger et rembarquer sa cargaison sans être tenû à payer aucune droit, et le Capitaine payera seulement les journées de ceux qu'il aura employe, tant pour le debarquement des marchandises, que pour le rembarquement.

have need of repairs, she shall be at liberty to unload and reload her cargo without being obliged to pay any duty; and the captain shall only be obliged to pay the wages of those whom he shall have employed in loading and unloading the merchandise.

ARTICLE NEUVIEME.

Si par accident et par la permission de Dieu, un batiment d'une des parties contractantes venait à être jetté par la tempête sur les rochers de l'autre, et qu'il se brisa ou autrement, le Commandant du lieu donnera toute l'assistence possible pour le sauvetage sans permettre que personne puisse y mettre aucune opposition; et le proprietaire des effets payera les fraix de sauvetage à ceux qui auront été employé.

ARTICLE 9.

If, by accident and by the permission of God, a vessel of one of the contracting parties shall be cast by tempest upon the coasts of the other and shall be wrecked or otherwise damaged, the commandant of the place shall render all possible assistance for its preservation, without allowing any person to make any opposition; and the proprietor of the effects shall pay the costs of salvage to those who may have been employed.

ARTICLE DIXIEME

Dans le cas qu'un navire d'une des parties contractantes serait attaqué par un ennemi sous les canons des forts de l'autre partie, il sera defendû et protegé autant qu'il sera possible; et quand il se mettra à la voile on ne permettra à aucun ennemi de le suivre du meme port ou de tout autre voisin, que quarante huit heures après son depart.

ARTICLE 10.

In case a vessel of one of the contracting parties shall be attacked by an enemy under the cannon of the forts of the other party, she shall be defended and protected as much as possible; and when she shall set sail, no enemy shall be permitted to pursue her from the same port, or any other neighboring port, for forty-eight hours after her departure.

ARTICLE ONZIEME

Lorsqu'un batiment de guerre des Etats Unis d'Amerique vien-

ARTICLE 11.

When a vessel of war of the United States of America shall

dra dans le port de Tunis, et que le Consul demandera que le chateau le salue, il sera tiré le nombre de coups de canons qu'il demandera; et si le dit Consul ne veut point de salut, il n'en sera pas question.

Mais dans le cas ou il desirera le salut et qu'on tirera les coups de canon qu'il aura demandé, la quantité des coups de canons tirés sera comptée et rendué par le vaisseau en tant de barils de poudre à canon.

Il en sera de même pour les batimens corsaires Tunisiens, lorsqu'ils iront dans quelque port des Etats Unis.

ARTICLE DOUZIEME

Lorsqu'il viendra dans les dependences de Tunis des citoyens des Etats Unis pour y commercer, on aura pour eux les mêmes egards dont jouissent les negociants des autres nations, et s'ils veulent s'etablir dans nos ports, on ne pourra s'y opposer, et ils seront libres de se servir de tels Interpretes qu'ils jugeront necessaires, sans qu'on y puisse apporter obstacle conformement aux usages des autres nations; et si quelque sujet Tunisien allait s'etablir dans les dependences des Etats Unis, ils seront traittés sur le meme pied.

Si quelque sujet Tunisien affrete un batiment Americain, qu'il le charge de marchandises, et qu'il

enter the port of Tunis, and the Consul shall request that the castle may salute her, the number of guns shall be fired which he may request; and if the said Consul does not want a salute, there shall be no question about it.

But in case he shall desire the salute, and the number of guns shall be fired which he may have requested, they shall be counted and returned by the vessel in as many barrels of cannon powder.

The same shall be done with respect to the Tunisian corsairs when they shall enter any port of the United States.

ARTICLE 12.

When citizens of the United States shall come within the dependencies of Tunis to carry on commerce there, the same respect shall be paid to them which the merchants of other nations enjoy; and if they wish to establish themselves within our ports, no opposition shall be made thereto; and they shall be free to avail themselves of such interpreters as they may judge necessary, without any obstruction, in conformity with the usages of other nations; and if a Tunisian subject shall go to establish himself within the dependencies of the United States, he shall be treated in like manner.

If any Tunisian subject shall freight an American vessel and load her with merchandise, and

veuille ensuite les debarquer ou transborder dans un autre batiment, nous ne le permettrons qu'autant que cette affaire serait decidée par une Assemblée de Negocians, qui prononceront sur le cas, et apres la decision on se conformera à ce qu'il sera prononcé.

shall afterwards want to unlade or ship them on board of another vessel, we will not permit him until the matter is determined by a reference of merchants, who shall decide upon the case; and after the decision, the determination shall be conformed to.

Aucune Capitaine ne pourra être retenu contre sa volonté dans un port, excepté dans le cas ou nos ports seroient fermés pour les batimens de toutes les autres nations, ce qui aurait lieu pour les batiments marchands, et non pour ceux de guerre.

No captain shall be detained in port against his consent, except when our ports are shut for the vessels of all other nations, which may take place with respect to merchant vessels but not to those of war.

Les sujets des deux Puissances contractantes seront sous la protection du Prince, et sous le commandement du chef du lieu ou ils seront, sans que personne autre puisse avoir autorite sur eux.

Si le Commandant du pays ne se comporte pas selon la justice, il en sera fait des representations.

The subjects of the two contracting powers shall be under the protection of the Prince and under the jurisdiction of the chief of the place where they may be, and no other persons shall have authority over them. If the commandant of the place does not conduct himself agreeably to justice, a representation of it shall be made to us.

Dans le cas ou le gouvernement aurait besoin d'un batiment marchand Americain, il le faira affretter, et alors il sera payé un nolis convenable au capitain selon l'intention du gouvernement, et le Capitaine ne s'y refusera pas.

In case the Government shall have need of an American merchant vessel, it shall cause it to be freighted, and then a suitable freight shall be paid to the captain, agreeably to the intention of the Government, and the captain shall not refuse it.

Article Treizieme

Si parmi les equipages des batiments marchands des Etats Unis, il se trouvait des sujets nos

Article 13.

If among the crews of merchant vessels of the United States, there shall be found subjects of our

ennemis, ils ne seront pas faits esclaves, sous condition qu'ils ne passeront pas le tiers de l'equipage; et lorsqu'il y en aura audela du tiers, ils seront faits esclaves: le present article ne concerne que les Matelots, y non les passagers, qui ne pourront etre inquieté en aucune maniere

enemies, they shall not be made slaves, on condition that they do not exceed a third of the crew; and when they do exceed a third, they shall be made slaves. The present article only concerns the sailors, and not the passengers, who shall not be in any manner molested.

Article Quatorzieme

Un Marchand Tunisien qui se rendrait en Amerique avec un batiment de quelque nation que ce soit, chargé de marchandises, qui seront de productions de le Royaume de Tunis, payera la Douane (pour peu qu'elle soit) comme les negocians des autres nations, et les negocians Americains payeront egallement pour les marchandises de leur pays qu'ils apporteront à Tunis sous leur pavillon, le meme douane que les Tunisiens payeront en Amerique.

Mais si un des negocians Americains, ou de toute autre nation apportait des marchandises d'Amerique, sous tout autre pavillon, il payera dix[1] pour cent de Douane; pareillement, si un negociant etranger apportait des marchandises de son pays sous le Pavillon Americain, il payera aussi dix[1] pour cent.

Article 14.

A Tunisian merchant who may go to America with a vessel of any nation soever, loaded with merchandise which is the production of the kingdom of Tunis, shall pay duty (small as it is) like the merchants of other nations; and the American merchants shall equally pay, for the merchandise of their country which they may bring to Tunis under their flag, the same duty as the Tunisians pay in America.

But if an American merchant, or a merchant of any other nation, shall bring American merchandise under any other flag, he shall pay six[1] per cent duty. In like manner, if a foreign merchant shall bring the merchandise of his country under the American flag, he shall also pay six[1] per cent.

Article Quinzieme

Il sera libre aux Citoyens des Etats Unis de faire le Commerce qu'ils voudront dans le Royaume

Article 15.

It shall be free for the citizens of the United States to carry on what commerce they please in the

[1] See the note regarding Article 14.

de tunis sans que personne puisse s'y opposer, & seront traittés comme les Negociants des autres Nations; mais Ils ne pourront faire le Commerce du vin ni des Objets prohibés, & si quelqu'un etait trouvé en contrebande Il serait puni suivant les Loix du pays, les Commandans des ports et Chateaux veilleront a ce que les Capitaines & Matelots ne puissent embarquer des Objets prohibés mais si le Cas arrivait, ceux qui n'auroient point contribués a la Contrebande ne pourroient etre inquietés ni recherchés non plus que le Navire & la Cargaison; mais bien le Coupable qui sera demandé pour etre puni.

Aucun Cap^{ne} ne pourra etre obligé de recevoir des marchandises a son Bord ni les debarquer contre sa volonté, excepté aprés avoir été payé de son fret.

Article Seizieme

Les Batimens Marchands des Etats Unis qui mouilleront en la Rade de la Goulette ou tout autre port du Royaume de tunis, seront tenus de payer le même Ancrage d'Entrée & Sortie que payeront les Batimens français, savoir dix sept piastres & demi monoye de tunis, d'Entrée s'ils apportent des marchandises & autant de sortie s'ils prendront leur chargement, mais Ils ne seront point tenus de payer d'Ancrages s'ils arrivent, en Lest, & partent de même.

kingdom of Tunis, without any opposition, and they shall be treated like the merchants of other nations; but they shall not carry on commerce in wine, nor in prohibited articles; and if any one shall be detected in a contraband trade, he shall be punished according to the laws of the country. The commandants of ports and castles shall take care that the captains and sailors shall not load prohibited articles; but if this should happen, those who shall not have contributed to the smuggling shall not be molested nor searched, no more than shall the vessel and cargo; but only the offender, who shall be demanded to be punished. No captain shall be obliged to receive merchandise on board of his vessel, nor to unlade the same against his will, until the freight shall be paid.

Article 16.

The merchant vessels of the United States which shall cast anchor in the road of the Gouletta, or any other port of the Kingdom of Tunis, shall be obliged to pay the same anchorage for entry and departure which French vessels pay, to wit: Seventeen piasters and a half, money of Tunis, for entry, if they import merchandise; and the same for departure, if they take away a cargo; but they shall not be obliged to pay anchorage if they arrive in ballast and depart in the same manner.

Article Dixseptieme

Chaqu'une du parties contractantes sera en liberté d'etablir un Consul dans les Dependances de l'autre & si ce Consul dans les Dependances ne se conforme point aux usages du pays a l'instar des autres, le Gouvernement du lieu en informera sa puissance a fin qu'il soit changé & remplacé, mais Il jouira tant lui, que sa famille & sa suite de la Protection du Gouvernement & il pourra faire venir pour son usage toutes ses provisions & meubles sans payer aucun droit, & s'il fera venir des marchandises, comme il lui sera loisible il en payera la Douanne.

Article 17.

Each of the contracting parties shall be at liberty to establish a consul in the dependencies of the other; and if such consul does not act in conformity with the usages of the country, like others, the government of the place shall inform his Government of it, to the end that he may be changed and replaced; but he shall enjoy, as well for himself as his family and suite, the protection of the government. And he may import for his own use all his provisions and furniture without paying any duty; and if he shall import merchandise (which it shall be lawful for him to do), he shall pay duty for it.

Article Dixhuitieme

Si les Sujets ou Citoyens des parties Contractantes se trouvant dans les possessions de l'autre feroient des dettes ou Contracteroient des obligations, ni le Consul, ni sa Nation, ni aucuns Sujets ou Citoyens ne pourront en aucune maniere etre responsables, a moins que le Consul ou ses derniers se seroient precedemment obligés par Ecrit, et sans cette obligation par Ecrit, Ils ne pourront etre recherchés pour la reintegration ou Satisfaction.

Article 18.

If the subjects or citizens of either of the contracting parties, being within the possessions of the other, contract debts or enter into obligations, neither the consul nor the nation, nor any subjects or citizens thereof, shall be in any manner responsible, except they or the consul shall have previously become bound in writing; and without this obligation in writing they cannot be called upon for indemnity or satisfaction.

Article Dixneuvieme

Dans le Cas ou un Citoyen ou Sujet des parties contractantes vint a mourir dans les posses-

Article 19.

In case of a citizen or subject of either of the contracting parties dying within the possessions of

sions de l'autre, le Consul ou le Vekil s'emparera de ses Effets /s'il n'y a testament/ dont Il faira vu Inventaire & la puissance du lieu n'aura rien a y voir, & s'Il n'y a pas de Consul les Effets seroient deposés entre les mains dune personne de Confiance de l'Endroit en prennant Bonne Notte du tout, pour les remettre ensuite a qui de Droit.

the other, the consul or the vakil shall take possession of his effects (if he does not leave a will), of which he shall make an inventory; and the government of the place shall have nothing to do therewith. And if there shall be no consul, the effects shall be deposited in the hands of a confidential person of the place, taking an inventory of the whole, that they may eventually be delivered to those to whom they of right belong.

ARTICLE VINGTIEME

Le Consul sera le Juge dans toutes les disputes entre ses Citoyens ou Sujets, comme egallement entre toutes autres personnes qui seroient Immediatement sous sa protection & dans toutes les Circonstances où il requerrera l'assistance du Gouvernement ou Il residera pour autoriser ses decisions, Elle lui sera accordée.

ARTICLE 20.

The consul shall be the judge in all disputes between his fellow citizens or subjects, as also between all other persons who may be immediately under his protection; and in all cases wherein he shall require the assistance of the government where he resides to sanction his decisions, it shall be granted to him.

ARTICLE VINGTUNIEME

Si un Citoyen ou Sujet d'une des parties, tüe, Blesse, ou Bat un Citoyen ou Sujet de l'autre, la Justice sera faite suivant les Loix du pays ou sera Commis le Delit, le Consul assistera au Jugement; mais si quelque Coupable venait a s'enfuir le Consul n'en sera en aucune maniere responsable.

ARTICLE 21.

If a citizen or subject of one of the parties shall kill, wound, or strike a citizen or subject of the other, justice shall be done according to the laws of the country where the offense shall be committed. The consul shall be present at the trial; but if any offender shall escape, the consul shall be in no manner responsible for it.

ARTICLE VINGT-DEUXIEME.

S'il arrive quelques disputes ou procès sur des affaires de commerce ou autres civiles, la decision sera faite en presence du Consul, ou d'une personne de confiance de son choix et de sa volonté, qui le representera et cherchera d'accommoder le different, qui serait survenû entre les citoyens ou sujets des deux nations.

ARTICLE VINGTROISIEME

S'il arrivait quelque different ou dispute sur l'infraction de quelque article du present traitté, soit d'une part ou d'autre, la paix et la bonne harmonie ne sera point interrompue jusqu'a ce qu'une aimable aplication se soit faite pour la reintegration et on n'en viendra aux armes, que dans le cas ou une semblable aplication serait rejettée, et si alors on se declare la guerre, il sera accordé aux citoyens ou sujets des parties contractantes un an de terme pour mettre ordre à leurs affaires et se retirer avec leur proprieté.

Les Accords et conditions, convenues ci-dessus de la part des deux parties contractantes, seront exactement observés avec la volonté du tres haut, et pour le maintien et l'exacte observation des dits accords nous avons fait transcrire leur contenu ci-joint dans le courant de la Lune de Rebia Elul de L'Egire mil deux

ARTICLE 22.

If a dispute or lawsuit on commercial or other civil matters shall happen, the trial shall be had in the presence of the consul, or of a confidential person of his choice, who shall represent him and endeavor to accommodate the difference which may have happened between the citizens or subjects of the two nations.

ARTICLE 23.

If any difference or dispute shall take place concerning the infraction of any article of the present treaty on either side, peace and good harmony shall not be interrupted until a friendly application shall have been made for satisfaction; and resort shall not be had to arms therefor, except where such application shall have been rejected; and if war be then declared, the term of one year shall be allowed to the citizens or subjects of the contracting parties to arrange their affairs and to withdraw themselves with their property.

The agreements and terms above concluded by the two contracting parties shall be punctually observed with the will of the Most High. And for the maintenance and exact observance of the said agreements, we have caused their contents to be here transcribed, in the present month of Rabia Elul, of the

cens deux,[1] ce qui revient au mois d'Aout de l'année chretienne mil sept cens quatre vingt dix sept.

Hegira one thousand two hundred and twelve, corresponding with the month of August of the Christian year one thousand seven hundred and ninety-seven.

The BEY's signature
[Seal]

IBRAHIM DEY's signature
[Seal]

The AGHA SULEIMAN's signature
[Seal]

To all to whom these Presents shall come or be made known.

Whereas the Underwritten David Humphreys hath been duly appointed Commissioner Plenipotentiary by letters patent under the signature of the President and seal of the United States of America, dated the 30th day of March 1795, for negociating and concluding a Treaty of Amity and Commerce with the Most Excellent & Illustrious Lord the Bey and Supreme Commander of the State of Tunis; whereas in conformity to the necessary authority committed to him therefor, he did constitute and appoint Joel Barlow an Agent in the business aforesaid; and whereas the annexed Treaty was in consequence thereof agreed upon, in the manner and at the time therein mentioned, through the intervention of Joseph Stephen Famin invested with full Powers for the said purpose.

Now, know ye, that I David Humphreys Commissioner Plenipotentiary aforesaid, do approve and conclude the said Treaty and every article and clause therein contained, reserving the same nevertheless for the final Ratification of the President of the United States of America, by and with the advice and consent of the Senate of the said United States. In Testimony whereof I have signed the same with my name & affixed thereto my Seal, at the City of Madrid this fourteenth day of November 1797.

[Seal] DAVID HUMPHREYS.

Whereas the President of the United States of America, by his Letters patent, under his signature and the seal of State, dated [Seal] the 18th day of December 1798, vested Richard O Brien, William Eaton and James Leander Cathcart, or any two of them in the absence of the third, with full powers to confer, negotiate

[1] Error for *douze*.

and conclude with the Bey and Regency of Tunis, on certain alterations in the treaty between the United States and the government of Tunis, concluded by the intervention of Joseph Etienne Famin on behalf of the United States, in the month of August 1797; we the underwritten William Eaton and James Leander Cathcart (Richard O Brien being absent) have concluded on and entered in the foregoing treaty certain alterations in the eleventh, twelfth and fourteenth articles, and do agree to said treaty with said alterations: reserving the same nevertheless for the final ratification of the President of the United States, by and with the advice and consent of the Senate. In Testimony whereof we annex our names and the Consular seal of the United States. Done in Tunis the twenty sixth day of March in the year of the Christian Era one thousand seven hundred and ninety nine, and of American Independence the twenty third

(signed) WILLIAM EATON
JAMES LEA[r]. CATHCART

THE FRENCH TRANSLATION

The Turkish original of this treaty and the French translation thereof have been examined by Dr. J. H. Kramers, of Leiden, in collaboration with Dr. C. Snouck Hurgronje. The comment and notes of Doctor Kramers are as follows:

A comparison of the French text with the Turkish text of this treaty shows that in general the French translation is very correct and complete. It does not seem necessary, therefore, to give a new translation.

Only the cases in which the French translation is somewhat different from the Turkish have been mentioned, and the corrections have been given likewise in French. [English translations have been added in parentheses.] No reference has been made to the many instances where the translation is rather free but still renders exactly the meaning of the Turkish text.

Preamble. The Turkish text has been rendered rather freely into French, but as to the meaning the translation is quite correct.

The first words should be "C'est Lui qui aide." (He [God] is the helper.)

Further, the first clause of the Turkish text has been omitted in the French. The translation would be:

> En cherchant l'appui de la sollicitude élevée et de la grace puissante de la Majesté qui préserve l'existence de l'univers et qui a doué de beauté la terre et le ciel—qu'il soit exalté.
>
> (Seeking the support of the exalted care and the potent favor of the Majesty who preserves the existence of the universe and

who has endowed the earth and the heavens with beauty—may He be exalted.)

Article 1. Instead of "le magnifique Pacha, Bey de Tunis" (the magnificent Pasha, Bey of Tunis), the correct translation is "le Gouvernement de Tunis la bien gardée" (the Government of Tunis the well protected).

Article 5. After the words "recherchées ni molestées" (not be searched or molested) there should be added "et on n'exigera pas de passeport" (and a passport shall not be demanded).

Article 6. A literal translation of the first clause would read as follows:

> Si un de nos corsaires rencontre un navire marchand américain, le navire marchand enverra sa chaloupe, et le commandant du navire corsaire ne pourra rien prendre en dehors de ce qui est permis par l'ancien usage; s'il fait quelque chose qui est contraire à l'ancien usage, on le punira sévèrement de ce côté-ci.
>
> (If one of our corsairs shall meet an American merchant ship, the merchant ship will send her shallop, and the commander of the corsair shall take nothing beyond that which is permitted by the ancient custom. If he does anything which is contrary to the ancient custom, he will be punished severely by this Government.)

Evidently the Turkish text is wrong in speaking of the sending of a shallop by the merchant vessel.

Article 7. The word "odgiak" means originally "a hearth" and is also used for a regiment of the Janizaries. Here an adequate rendering into English would be "garrison," but the word stands for the whole place.

Instead of the last word, "équipage" (crew), the Turkish text has "chrétiens" (Christians).

Article 8. "Tant pour le débarquement des marchandises, que pour le rembarquement" (in loading and unloading the merchandise). The Turkish text here speaks only of the "rembarquement" (reloading).

Article 10. The beginning is literally:

> Si un navire appartenant à une des parties entre dans un port d'une des parties et se trouve à un lieu où les canons peuvent l'atteindre, on le protégera autant que possible contre son ennemi.
>
> (If a ship belonging to one of the parties enters a port of one of the parties and is there within cannon shot, she will be protected as far as possible against her enemy.)

Article 12. The clause in the first paragraph commencing "et s'ils veulent s'etablir" (and if they wish to establish themselves) and ending "autres nations" (other nations), would be better rendered:

> Et si un marchand américain désire se rendre à un de nos ports pour des affaires, on ne l'empêchera pas; et s'il amène une personne faisant fonction d'interprète ou un serviteur pour lui-même, il ne sera empêché non plus; mais dans le cas où le Gouvernement ferait des prohibitions à l'égard d'autres nations, ils seront frappés par les mêmes prohibitions que les autres.
>
> (And if an American merchant wishes to come to one of our ports for purposes of commerce, he shall not be prevented; and if he brings a person as interpreter or a servant for himself, he shall likewise not be prevented; but in case the Government shall make interdictions applicable to other nations, they shall be affected by the same interdictions as the others.)

The fifth paragraph is better translated, "Si le commandant du pays ne peut pas décider le cas d'après le droit, les deux parties se référeront à nous pour obtenir leur droit" (If the commandant of the place cannot decide the case according to justice, the two parties shall be referred to us to obtain their rights).

Article 13. The literal translation of the last clause, beginning "le present article" (the present article), is "mais s'il s'agit de marchands et de passagers, leur nombre ne sera pas mis en compte" (but in respect of merchants and of passengers, their number shall not be taken into account).

Article 15. The latter part of the first paragraph, beginning with "les commandants des ports" (the commandants of ports), is better rendered as follows:

> Si les commandants et matelots prendront dans leurs navires des objets de contrebande, la personne qui s'en serait rendue coupable, sera sévèrement punie, mais d'autres personnes ne seront pas mêlées dans l'affaire; et par le fait qu'un matelot se rend coupable d'actions contraires aux préscriptions de l'odgiak (la garnison), le bateau ou la cargaison ne seront pas retenus, mais seulement le coupable sera cherché et puni.
>
> (If the captains and sailors shall take into their ships prohibited articles, the person who is guilty in that regard shall be severely punished, but others shall not be involved in the matter; and by the fact that a sailor is guilty of acts contrary to the ordinances of the garrison, the ship or the cargo shall not be detained, but only the guilty one shall be sought and punished.)

Article 16. For "la Goulette" (the Gouletta) the Turkish has the name "Halk al-Wad."

For "piastre" (piaster) the Turkish text has "riyal," without adding that this is Tunisian money.

Article 18. After the words "ni le consul" (neither the consul) the Turkish text adds "ou le vekil" (or the vakil). Vekil (vakil) means representative.

At the beginning of Article 20 and (twice) in Article 21 the Turkish text is similar.

Article 19. The words "s'il n'y a testament" (if he does not leave a will) do not occur in the Turkish text.

The last words, "à qui de droit," are better translated by "au consul ou au vekil" (to the consul or to the vakil).

Article 20. The phrase "pour autoriser ses décisions" (to sanction his decisions) is better rendered by "pour faire exécuter sa décision" (in order to have his decision carried out).

Article 22. A more literal translation of this article is the following:

> Si quelques personnes d'une des deux parties auront, dans le pays de l'autre partie, des disputes à cause du commerce ou autre chose, le consul ou son vekil (représentant) sera présent, ensemble avec eux, pour que leur différend soit décidé par un homme de jugement, en sa présence; s'il désire se faire remplacer par une autre personne, il pourra faire ainsi.
>
> (If any persons of one of the two parties shall have, in the country of the other party, disputes arising from commercial or other matters, the consul or his vakil shall be present together with them, in order that their difference may be decided by a man of judgment in his presence. If he desires to substitute another person for himself, he may do so.)

Final Clause. In the Turkish text the only mentioned date is "au commencement du mois de Rabi al-awwal 1212" (at the beginning of the month of Rabia I, A. H. 1212). That month began on August 24, 1797.

The Turkish text is followed by the "name signs" of Hamuda Pasha (to the right), Ibrahim Dey (in the middle), and Suleiman ibn Mahmud (to the left). Under each sign the seal of the same person has been put.

NOTES

The exact date of the first signature of the treaty, before it was amended, is not stated therein; but a letter dated September 2, 1797, from Joseph Etienne Famin, a French merchant of Tunis who conducted the negotiations of 1797 there on behalf of the United States, to George Clark, the Chargé d'Affaires at Algiers, gives the date as August 28, 1797 (D. S., 1 Archives, Tunis, 1793–1801).

The signatures and seals then affixed were those of three officials of the Regency of Tunis. On the pages of the original treaty opposite the Turkish text (of which there are fifteen pages) is written a French translation of the respective Turkish articles. That French trans-

lation was doubtless prepared by or under the direction of Famin. However, the letter of Famin to the Secretary of State making a report of those negotiations has not been found. It was dated September 25, 1797, and is mentioned in a letter of April 6, 1798 (D. S., 3 Consular Despatches, Algiers).

While it is undoubted that the treaty text was Turkish and the French a translation, it should be added that a copy of the French text of 1797 (D. S., 1 Archives, Tunis, 1793–1801) is certified by Famin in the following words: "J'affirme la présente copie conforme a l'original."

It appears that various originals of the treaty were prepared at the time. One of them was transmitted by Col. David Humphreys, then Minister to Spain, from Madrid (D. S., 4 Despatches, Spain, No. 120, November 14, 1797), and another by Joel Barlow from Paris (D. S., 2 Consular Despatches, Algiers, January 7, 1798).

The Alterations

Alterations (here a more accurate word than amendments) were subsequently made in the treaty in March, 1799, before ratification by the United States. The changes had their beginning in the Senate resolution of March 6, 1798, which reads as follows (Executive Journal, I, 263–64):

> *Resolved,* (two-thirds of the Senators present concurring therein,) That the Senate do advise and consent to the ratification of the treaty of peace and friendship, between the United States of America and the Bey and government of Tunis, concluded in the month of August, one thousand seven hundred and ninety-seven, on condition that the fourteenth article of the said treaty, which relates to the duties on merchandise, (to be reciprocally paid by the citizens and subjects of the said parties, in their respective ports,) shall be suspended.
>
> *Resolved,* That it be recommended to the President of the United States, to enter into a friendly negotiation with the Bey and government of Tunis, on the subject of the said article, so as to accommodate the provisions thereof to the existing treaties of the United States with other nations.

While the resolution of the Senate related only to Article 14, it was considered by the Secretary of State (Pickering) that Articles 11 and 12 were also objectionable, and changes in them were proposed, an interesting and early example of the control of treaty negotiations by the President, even after Senate action. (See instructions to Richard O'Brien, William Eaton, and James Leander Cathcart, D. S., 5 Instructions, U. S. Ministers, 16–23, December 18, 1798; printed in part in American State Papers, Foreign Relations, II, 281–82.) It may be mentioned here that in connection with those instructions the cost of the treaty was estimated at $179,044.

The Negotiations of 1799

There is a full account of the negotiations carried on at Tunis by Cathcart and Eaton in March, 1799, in the journal of the latter dated April 15, 1799 (D. S., 1 Consular Despatches, Tunis). In a

despatch of June 1, 1799, in the same volume, Eaton says that the substance of the result of the negotiations was:

> The Treaty with alterations—The consent of the Bey for six months forbearance in expectation of the regalia of maritime and military stores—His *demand* for a present in jewels—and his *request* for a cruiser.

The negotiations brought about changes in the three articles mentioned—11, 12, and 14; the rest of the treaty remained unaltered. The way the alterations were made was unusual; such of the sheets of the original document as contained the original text or the translation of those three articles were removed from that document, and in place thereof were inserted other sheets on which had been written the new text of the three articles and also (but unchanged) such other articles as had appeared on the sheets removed.

It was on March 26, 1799, that the altered treaty was received from the Bey of Tunis by the representatives of the United States. The translation in French of the three altered articles was then written in, in its proper place. There was added to the document, or at least to one of its originals, the clause signed by Eaton and Cathcart on behalf of the United States, dated the day of the delivery of the altered treaty.

The Original Documents

The original which is now in the Department of State file is in the form of a pamphlet remade in the manner above indicated. Its final page (in the Turkish order) has, however, been torn off, and in lieu thereof on one of the two added sheets, as if it were on the final page, appears the French translation of the final clause of the treaty (not quite accurately copied, as "deux" is written for "douze") and a copy of the confirmation of Eaton and Cathcart.

The whole original document is embodied in a duplicate instrument of ratification, which is written in the reverse or Turkish order of pagination. Thus the opening words of the ratification are written on the reverse of the first page of the Turkish text and (in the Turkish sense) preceding it. Accordingly, the ratification begins at what would here be called the back of the paper sheets (which are together like a pamphlet, but are not bound or even stitched); and the signatures of Adams and Pickering, and formerly the wafer for the Great Seal (which has since become detached and lies loose in the file), are at the front.

The file contains also portions of four other originals; one is of the altered treaty, nearly complete, one sheet only being missing; each of the other three comprises sheets of the treaty as first written. All four have the page with the seals and signatures on behalf of Tunis.

There are also in the file various separate or single sheets or pages torn from complete instruments; one bears the original certificate signed by David Humphreys at Madrid November 14, 1797; another bears what appears to be the original certificate of Eaton and Cathcart, but the lower part of that sheet, including the signatures, is torn away; still another, with no text except the French of the final

clause, has on it the words, "approved at Paris the 12 Nov[r] 1797," and the signature of Joel Barlow. The remaking of the treaty by the substitution of new sheets for old, has made the file a strange collection of parts and pieces; indeed, some of the old (and now separate) wrappers in the file note "remnants of the Treaties" or "remnants of the detached sheets."

Note Regarding Ratification

After the amended articles had been agreed to, much remained to be done both by way of form and in matter of substance before the treaty could go into force. In transmitting "the treaty with the alterations inserted," Eaton wrote as follows regarding the ratification: "The ratified copy of the treaty which will be returned is expected to be an exact and entire copy of the entire treaty enclosed."

More important was the letter written (in French) by the Bey of Tunis to the President of the United States under date of April 30, 1799 (original letter in D. S., 1 Consular Despatches, Tunis), in which it was said very flatly that if the naval munitions promised did not arrive by the following November 1, the treaty would be void ("le terme expiré, sans que ces effets fussent parvenus, tout Traité serait nul et la bonne amitié qui existe, de nouveau rompue").

The Senate resolution of advice and consent of December 24, 1799, is in rather unusual form, as it refers to amended Articles 11, 12, and 14 only (Executive Journal, I, 329–30).

The United States instrument of ratification was forwarded to Eaton in January, 1800, and with it was a letter from the President to the Bey of Tunis. The ratification embodied "one of the originals" received from Eaton (see D. S., 5 Instructions, U. S. Ministers, 277, No. 3, January 11, 1800, and 289, No. 34, January 17, 1800); and after another wrangle about the stores to be delivered, the papers were finally put into the hands of the Bey of Tunis on March 27, 1800, as the following extracts from the letter of Eaton to the Secretary of State of March 31, 1800 (1 Consular Despatches, Tunis, No. 16), indicate:

> This day [March 26] was employed in rendering into Italian the President's letter to the Bey, his ratification of the treaty, and such of the communications of the Secretary of State as related to the regalia of naval and military stores.
>
> At the palace. Made the above communications to the Bey [March 27, 11 a. m.] He expressed great satisfaction.

At the same time it seems that an understanding was reached that the last paragraph of Article 12 of the treaty was to be carried out by Tunis only on the basis of the most favored nation. A circular letter of Eaton dated at Tunis April 10, 1800 (Prentiss, The Life of the Late Gen. William Eaton, 136), is as follows:

> Having at length amicably adjusted the affairs of the United States with the Bey and Regency of Tunis, I desire you will communicate this agreeable intelligence to the masters of American vessels, and others interested, who may come within the limits of your Consulate.
>
> The principal minister of the Bey has pledged himself that the last clause of the 12th article of our treaty with this Regency, inserted by Joseph Etienne

Famin, shall have the same effect with respect to American merchant vessels as the custom of all other nations at peace with Tunis has established with respect to their own, and no other. There is therefore now no danger to be apprehended from American vessels visiting this coast: perfect health prevails here.

Note Regarding Promulgation

There is no record of any proclamation of this treaty. No publication of the treaty has been found earlier than the text contained in The Laws of the United States, Folwell ed., V, 213–23. That volume was printed in 1801; but the first section of it, the Session Laws of the first session of the Sixth Congress and including the text of this treaty, appeared in 1800.

Announcement of the alterations of March 26, 1799, was made in the following circular letter of Cathcart, dated at Tripoli May 4, 1799 (Tripoli . . . Letter Book by James Leander Cathcart, 56):

> Being commissioned by the President of the United States of America to act in conjunction with Messrs. O'Brien and Eaton, in order to effect certain alterations in the treaty intervention of J. E. Famin, between the United States of America and the Regency of Tunis, I am happy to inform you that such alterations took place in said treaty as will meet the approbation of the President and Senate, on the 26th of March, 1799, and that for the nine next ensuing months from that date, all merchandise belonging to citizens of the United States imported into any of the ports of the Regency of Tunis pays duty only 3 per cent. advalorem, according to an old price current of the year 1753, which reduces the duty nearly one half. From Tunis I proceeded to Tripoli, where I have had the good fortune to persuade the Bashaw to receipt the sum of $18,000 in cash, in lieu of the stores and brig of war promised this regency when our peace took place. The above sum is in full of all demands from the United States forever.
>
> I therefore congratulate the seamen and merchants of the United States on their being entirely out of danger from all the Barbary States, provided they are very particular with their passports which is absolutely necessary.

Note Regarding the Texts Printed

When the treaty was first submitted to the Senate, on February 21, 1798, the message of Adams said that he laid before that body "the original treaty." This was doubtless the example transmitted by Humphreys from Madrid, for his approval (now a separate sheet in the file) is printed with the message in American State Papers, Foreign Relations, II, 123; following it is an English translation, which (aside from Articles 11, 12, and 14, subsequently altered) is that which has since been generally printed, except that its text of Article 8 is incomplete. That incompleteness is to be thus explained: The original documents show that the 1797 French translation of the treaty omitted the final phrase of Article 8 regarding the wages to be paid by the captain of a ship; the omission was noticed during the 1799 negotiations; the proper addition to the French translation written in the original was then made, the Turkish remaining without change; and the English version was corrected here accordingly. In D. S., 1 Archives, Tunis, 1793–1801, a volume of letters and papers relating mostly to Tunis, but in part to Tripoli, is a corrected draft of the French of Articles 11, 12, and 14, with a note to the effect that the final phrase of Article 8 should be added to the French translation.

The Turkish text here reproduced is from the original above described as being now in the file and embodied in a duplicate United States instrument of ratification; the Turkish is in left-to-right order of pagination and the script runs lengthways of the pages. That text is here followed by two translations in parallel columns, French and English; thereafter is copied the approval of David Humphreys of the treaty as first signed, dated at Madrid November 14, 1797, and then the approval of Eaton and Cathcart of March 26, 1799. Following those texts is a comment on the French translation of the Turkish, written in 1930 by Dr. J. H. Kramers.

The French translation here printed is a literal copy of the French written on pages of the original treaty; the English translation is from a paper in the Department of State file, the date of which appears to be not earlier than 1810; but that same English translation was printed in the Folwell edition of the laws, as noted above, in 1801. From the form of the English translation it is clear that it is a retranslation of the French and not an original translation of the Turkish; this translation is the one printed in the Statutes at Large and elsewhere generally. Doubtless the current English version of the amended Articles 11, 12, and 14, is the same as that which was laid before the Senate on December 13, 1799; but their text is not in American State Papers, Foreign Relations, II, 281–82. So far as Articles 11 and 14 are concerned, that translation of 1799 was of necessity a new one; but also in respect of Article 12 it differs from the earlier English even in those paragraphs which are the same in French.

In connection with the English text of the treaty usually printed, it is to be noted that the journal of Eaton gives the following as the English of Article 11 as agreed on during the negotiation of 1799:

> When a vessel of war of one of the parties shall enter a port of the other, and demand to be saluted, there shall be paid one barrel of powder for each gun demanded for the salute; but if the demand be not made, by the consul on the part of the United States, or by the commandant of the vessel on the part of the kingdom of Tunis, no salute shall be given, nor payment demanded for the salute.

It has not been deemed necessary to reproduce the original Turkish of the three articles which were altered—11, 12, and 14. The French translation of those three articles, as written at the time, and their English translation, appear in a note following.

Note Regarding Articles 11, 12, and 14

The French translation of the original form of Articles 11, 12, and 14, as written in 1797, is printed below, with an English translation from American State Papers, Foreign Relations, II, 124; but only the latter part of Article 12 is given here, as the first three paragraphs of the article were not changed.

Article Onzieme

Quant un Batiment de Guerre d'une des parties ira En un port de l'autre Il sera salué par les forts & rendra le Salut, Coup par Coup ni plus ni moins Il sera donné de part & d'autre un

Article 11

When a vessel of war of one of the parties shall enter a port of the other, she shall be saluted by the forts and shall return the salute gun for gun, neither more nor less. But there shall

Barril de poudre par Chaque Coup de Canon, qu'on demandera pour le Salut.

be given by the parties, respectively, a barrel of powder for every gun which shall be required for the salute.

Article Douzieme

. . . .

Les Sujets ou Citoyens des deux Nations seront protegés par le Gouvernement, ou Commandants des Lieux ou ils se trouveront & non par d'autres autorités du pays.

Dans le Cas ou le Gouvernement de tunis auroit besoin d'un Batiment Americain pour son Service alors le Capn.e affrettera son Navire & le fret lui sera payé suivant ce que le Gouvernement conviendra sans qu'il puisse s'y refuser.

Article 12

. . . .

The subjects or citizens of the two nations shall be protected by the government or commandants of the places where they may be, and not by the other authorities of the country. In case the Government of Tunis shall have need of an American vessel for its service, the captain shall freight his vessel, and the freight shall be paid to him according to the agreement of the Government, without his being allowed to refuse.

Article Quatorzieme

Les Citoyens des Etats Unis d'Amerique qui trasporteront dans le Royaume de tunis des marchandises de leur pays, sur des Navires de leur Nation payeront trois pour Cent de Douanne.

Celles chargées par les memes Citoyens sous pavillon etranger provenant des Etats Unis ou d'autre part payeront dix pour Cent de Douanne.

Celles chargées par des Etrangers sur Navires Americains provenant de tel lieu que ce soit payeront egallement dix pour Cent de Douanne.

Si quelqu'un des Negocians tunisiens vouloient porter des Marchandises de leur pays sous tel pavillon que ce soit dans les Etats Unis d'Amerique, et pour leur Compte il payera trois pour Cent de Douanne.

Article 14

The citizens of the United States of America who shall transport into the Kingdom of Tunis the merchandise of their country in the vessels of their nation, shall pay three per cent duty. Such as may be laden by such citizens under a foreign flag, coming from the United States or elsewhere, shall pay ten per cent duty. Such as may be laden by foreigners on board of American vessels coming from any place whatever, shall also pay ten per cent duty. If any Tunisian merchant wishes to carry merchandise of his country, under any flag whatever, into the United States of America, and on his own account, he shall pay three per cent duty.

The notes of Doctor Kramers regarding the Turkish of the original form of Articles 11, 12, and 14, as written in 1797, and their translation, follow:

Article 11. The text differs from the text of Article 11 in the final treaty. The French translation is not correct. It should read:

> Si un batiment de guerre américain arrive dans le port de Halk al-Wad [la Goulette; see Article 16 of the treaty], il sera salué par le fort avec le nombre de coups de canon qu'il désirera, et il donnera un baril de poudre pour chaque coup de canon qui aura été tiré.
>
> (If an American vessel of war arrives in the port of the Gouletta, she will be saluted by the fort with the number of guns that she desires, and she will give a barrel of powder for each gun.)

Article 12. The Turkish text of the first three paragraphs of this article is identical with the text of Article 12 in the treaty, except for very slight differences.

The fourth paragraph is also identical with the same paragraph in the treaty text.

The fifth paragraph in the treaty, however, is lacking in the original form.

The final paragraph of the original form has the same text as in the treaty. There is some difference in the words used, but the provisions are exactly the same.

Article 14. The French translation of this article in the original form is correct.

Note Regarding Article 14

That the rate on certain goods imported, prescribed in the second paragraph of Article 14 of the treaty, was, as the French translation shows, ten per cent, is clear from Eaton's statement: "The ten per cent on goods imported in foreign bottoms &c was forced upon us" (D. S., 1 Consular Despatches, Tunis, April 11, 1799).

The English translation usually (and here) printed gives the rate as six per cent. In the translation in the Department of State file "six" is in two places changed in pencil to "ten," with the following pencil footnote: "See the Original Treaty (verbally altered by Col: Lear)."

The explanation is probably to be found in the negotiations carried on by Col. Tobias Lear at Tunis in 1807. The "arrangement," as Lear calls it in one of his despatches, which was then made, he reported as thus stated to him by an official of Tunis on January 21, 1807:

> . . . his Master would receive the Money in preference to the Ship;—and now that all matters were settled between us; and that the Citizens of the U. States might come here and trade upon the footing of the other Nations and feel as perfect a security as they could do in their own Country. He said the Bey was satisfied, and hoped that he should always continue in harmony with the U. States. (D. S., 7 Consular Despatches, Algiers, January 25, 1807.)

Lear also wrote on February 17, 1807, to Charles D. Coxe, whom he left in charge at Tunis:

> I shall pay to His Excellency, the Bey, the sum of Ten Thousand Dollars, on behalf of the United States, as a compensation for his Cruizer and her two Prizes, which were Captured by our Squadron off Tripoli. This will settle all pecuniary matters with this Regency; and our Treaty with the Bey stands as originally agreed upon, excepting that the Citizens of the U. States, who may trade here, paying the same duties on Merchandize as are paid in the U. States, we are placed upon the footing of the most favoured Nations in Commercial Matters,—And, the Bey, will not require any Merchant Vessel of the U. States, to be Charterd to him, excepting on the same terms and Conditions as she would be Charter'd to an Individual. (*Ibid.*)

If those statements of Lear are correct, the terms of the treaty were verbally altered in various respects other than in the mere matter of the rate. Perhaps the arrangement then reached was better described by Coxe in his letter to Commodore Rogers of October 15, 1825 (D. S., 5 Consular Despatches, Tunis), where he wrote:

> It will be necessary to go back to the time of Mellimelli's return from the United States, and when Consul Genl Lear came to Tunis in 1807, in the Constitution Frigate Captain Campbell, by order of our Government, to settle all differences with the Bey, which it was found impossible to do with Mellimelli at Washington, who thought only of extorting presents. The result was, that Col. Lear and the Bey, (Hamuda Basha) came to an understanding, that we were to be placed on the same terms with the most favored nations in commercial matters; and in short, that the old Treaty should be laid on the shelf, until, our Government should think proper to take measures for a formal alteration of it. Our understanding with them, respecting Salutes was to remain the same as you had left it when you were here with the Squadron in 1805—That is, instead of paying for them, we were neither to give or receive Salutes.

Consul General Lear after this arrangement with the Bey, appointed me to take charge of our affairs here, and I soon had the satisfaction of inducing our merchants to an advantageous commerce with Tunis from 1807 to 1814—The old Treaty to the contrary notwithstanding.

The proclamation of the treaty with Tunis of 1824 (Document 45) includes the English of certain articles of this treaty; Article 14 is there written as here, that is, with the rate six per cent.

The Earlier Truce

Prior to the first signature of this treaty a "truce" with Tunis had twice been arranged; on about June 15, 1796, a "truce for six months" was concluded by Famin (American State Papers, Foreign Relations, I, 554); and Cathcart writes thus of an arrangement made in 1795 at Algiers (The Captives, 233):

. . . between those dates I had several conferences with the Dey [of Algiers] and Hadgi Ally [Ambassador of Tunis at Algiers], and this day [November 8, 1795] procured a truce for the United States with Tunis for eight months, guaranteed by the Dey of Algiers, translated it and took the original to Mr. Donaldson, who kept his bed with the gout and colic.

The Turkish original of the truce of June, 1796, is in the archives of the Department of State; it has been thus translated by Doctor Kramers:

The motive of the writing of this document is as follows: On the 11th of the month of Zu'lhijjah of this year 1210, answering to the 15th of June [June 17, 1796, according to the chronological tables] according to the Greek calendar. The glory of the princes of the Christian nation, the selected chief among the community of Jesus, Washington, the present ruler of America—may his days end with blessings—being desirous and wishing to negotiate a treaty of peace in order to lay the foundations of friendship and to strengthen the sincere amity with the frontier post of the Holy War, the victorious garrison of Tunis the well-preserved, just as our friends, the other Christian Governments, have done the same with our victorious garrison, has confided the negotiations of the said treaty to his Consul Barlow, residing in Algiers, and the said Consul again has confided the negotiations of the treaty to the French merchant, Joseph Famin, residing in Tunis the well-preserved. The said merchant has appeared in my presence and has stated and declared in general his wish and desire for a treaty between the American ruler and the Government of Tunis the well-preserved. After it has been immediately communicated and confirmed to the said merchant on what terms a treaty could be agreed to, the said merchant has communicated the stipulations of the treaty to the said Consul, and the said Consul has communicated it to his Government. Now, until the answer comes and within a limit of six months after the date of this document, security has been given. Therefore, if during the said period war vessels of our well-preserved garrison place meet at sea with ships of the said Americans, they shall not hinder them or molest them in any way, but they shall be treated as friends, and immediately order has been given to our officers to let them go their way. If American ships meet with ships belonging to our well-preserved garrison place, it has been agreed between the two Governments, that they shall treat each other in a friendly way. This convention has been written and sealed and given into the hands of the said merchant, so that he may send it to its proper place. Until the arrival of the answer this convention shall be observed between the two Governments; according to it both parties shall act, and it shall be opposed in no way. Salutations.

Written on the 11th of Zu'lhijjah and the 15th June of the year 1210.

[Tughra (name sign) of Hamuda,
commander (*mir miran*) of the
frontier post of the Holy War,
Tunis the well-preserved.]

Treaty Series, No. 107
8 Statutes at Large, 131–32

22

GREAT BRITAIN : MARCH 15, 1798

Explanatory Article to Article 5 of the Jay Treaty (Document 16), signed at London March 15, 1798. Original in English.
Submitted to the Senate May 29, 1798. Resolution of advice and consent June 5, 1798. Ratified by the United States June 7, 1798. Ratified by Great Britain March 15, 1798. Ratifications exchanged at Philadelphia June 9, 1798. Not proclaimed; but the text of the article was published at the time.

Explanatory Article.

Whereas by the Twenty Eighth Article of the Treaty of Amity, Commerce and Navigation, between His Britannick Majesty, and the United States, signed at London on the Nineteenth day of November, One Thousand Seven Hundred and Ninety Four, it was agreed, that the contracting Parties would from Time to Time, readily treat of and concerning such further Articles, as might be proposed, that they would sincerely endeavour so to form such Articles, as that they might conduce to mutual Convenience, and tend to promote mutual Satisfaction and Friendship; and that such Articles, after having been duly ratified should be added to and make a Part of that Treaty: And whereas Difficulties have arisen with respect to the Execution of so much of the Fifth Article of the said Treaty as requires that the Commissioners appointed under the same should in their Description particularize the Latitude and Longitude of the source of the River which may be found to be the one truly intended in the Treaty of Peace between His Britannick Majesty and the United States under the name of the River S[t] Croix, by reason whereof it is expedient that the said Commissioners should be released from the obligation of conforming to the Provisions of the said Article in this respect. The Undersigned being respectively named by His Britannick Majesty and the United States of America their Plenipotentiaries for the Purpose of treating of and concluding such Articles as may be proper to be added to the said Treaty in conformity to the above-mentioned Stipulation and having communicated to each other their respective full Powers have agreed

and concluded and do hereby declare in the name of His Britannick Majesty and of the United States of America—That the Commissioners appointed under the fifth Article of the above-mentioned Treaty shall not be obliged to particularize in their Description, the Latitude and Longitude of the source of the River which may be found to be the one truly intended in the aforesaid Treaty of Peace, under the name of the River St Croix, but they shall be at liberty to describe the said River in such other manner as they may judge expedient which Description shall be considered as a compleat Execution of the Duty required of the said Commissioners in this respect by the article aforesaid. And to the end that no uncertainty may hereafter exist on this subject, it is further Agreed, That as soon as may be after the decision of the said Commissioners, measures shall be concerted between the Government of the United States and His Britannick Majesty's Governors or Lieutenant Governors in America, in order to erect and keep in repair a suitable monument at the place ascertain'd and described to be the source of the said River St Croix, which measures shall immediately thereupon, and as often afterwards as may be requisite, be duly executed on both sides with punctuality and good Faith.

This Explanatory Article when the same shall have been ratified by His Majesty and by the President of the United States, by and with the advice and consent of their Senate, and the respective ratifications mutually exchanged shall be added to and make a part of the Treaty of Amity, Commerce and Navigation between His Majesty and the United States, signed at London on the nineteenth day of November One Thousand Seven Hundred and Ninety Four and shall be permanently binding upon His Majesty and the United States

In witness whereof We the said undersigned Plenipotentiaries of His Britannick Majesty and the United States of America have signed this present Article and have caused to be affixed thereto the Seal of Our Arms. Done at London this Fifteenth Day of March, One Thousand Seven Hundred and Ninety Eight.

Grenville [Seal]
Rufus King [Seal]

NOTES

The original article and the British instrument of ratification form together one document, wholly executed on March 15, 1798; that is, the document begins with the usual recitals of an instrument of ratification, then contains the treaty with the signatures and seals of

Grenville and of Rufus King, and terminates with the customary words of ratification, with the signature of George III, and with the Great Seal. The ratification by Great Britain was thus concurrent with the signature of the agreement. The procedure was suggested in the instructions to Rufus King of January 2, 1798 (D. S., 4 Instructions, U. S. Ministers, 216). While such form and practice are not usual, they made possible a prompt exchange of the ratifications; King wrote on the date of signature (D. S., 7 Despatches, Great Britain, No. 68):

> We executed four copies; two of them with their original ratifications will be sent by Lord Grenville to Mr. Liston with an Instruction to exchange them with you, when the President shall have ratified the same on our part.

The text here printed is from the document above mentioned.

The Department of State file now contains also a facsimile of the original signed treaty which is in the British archives, and a facsimile of the United States instrument of ratification, which likewise embodies as part thereof a signed original of the treaty.

A certificate of the exchange of ratifications on June 9, 1798, was signed by Pickering on June 11 under the seal of the Department of State. A facsimile thereof, from the British archives, is now in the Department of State file.

The testimonium clause of the treaty is omitted in 8 Statutes at Large, 132; but it appears in 18 Statutes at Large, pt. 2, Public Treaties, 284.

No record of a proclamation of this treaty has been found; but it was published at the time (*e. g.*, Claypoole's American Daily Advertiser, August 3, 1798; the newspaper print purports to be "by authority"). The text was printed in The Laws of the United States, Folwell ed., IV, 239–40. That volume is dated 1799; but its second part, with the acts of the second session of the Fifth Congress and including the text of this treaty, certainly appeared in pamphlet form in 1798.

23

GREAT BRITAIN : OCTOBER 25, 1798

Declaration of the Commissioners under Article 5 of the Jay Treaty (Document 16), signed at Providence October 25, 1798. Original in English.

By Thomas Barclay, David Howell and Egbert Benson—Commissioners appointed in pursuance of the fifth article of the Treaty of Amity Commerce and Navigation between His Britannic Majesty and The United States of America finally to decide the Question "What River was truly intended under the name of The River *Saint Croix* mentioned in the Treaty of Peace between His Majesty and The United States, and forming a part of the Boundary therein described.

Declaration.

We the said Commissioners having been sworn "impartially to examine and decide the said Question according to such evidence as should respectively be laid before Us on the part of the British Government, and of The United States". And having heard the evidence which hath been laid before Us by the Agent of His Majesty, and The Agent of The United States, respectively appointed and authorized to manage the business on behalf of the respective Governments—Have decided and hereby do decide the River herein after particularly described and mentioned to be the River truly intended under the name of The River *Saint Croix* in the said Treaty of Peace and forming a part of the Boundary therein described—That is to say—The Mouth of the said River is in *Passamaquaddy Bay* at a point of Land called *Joe's Point,* about one mile northward from the northern part of *Saint Andrew's Island,* and in the Latitude of forty five degrees, five minutes and five seconds north, and in the Longitude of sixty seven degrees twelve minutes and thirty seconds west from the Royal Observatory at Greenwich in Great-Britain, and three degrees, fifty four minutes and fifteen seconds east from Harvard College in the University of Cambridge, in the State of Massachusetts. And the course of the said River up from it's said Mouth is northerly to a point of Land called *The Devil's-Head,* then turning the said

point is westerly to where it divides into two Streams the one coming from the westward, and the other coming from the northward, having the Indian name of *Chiputnaticook* or *Chibnitcook*, as the same may be variously spelt, then up the said Stream so coming from the northward to it's source, which is at a Stake near a yellow-Birch Tree hooped with Iron, and marked ST and IH 1797. by Samuel Titcomb and John Harris the Surveyors employed to survey the above mentioned Stream coming from the northward. And the said River is designated on the Map hereunto annexed[1] and hereby referred to as farther descriptive of it by the Letters A. B. C. D. E. F. G. H. I. K. and L.—the Letter A being at it's said Mouth, and the Letter L being at it's said Source. And the course and distance of the said source from the Island at the Confluence of the above-mentioned two Streams is as laid down on the said Map north five degrees and about fifteen minutes west by the magnet, about forty eight miles and one quarter. In Testimony whereof We have hereunto set our Hands and Seals at Providence in the State of Rhode Island the twenty fifth day of October in the year One thousand seven hundred and ninety eight.

Witness

Ed Winslow.

Secretary to the Commissioners.

Egb[t] Benson [Seal] David Howell [Seal] Tho Barclay [Seal]

NOTES

The original declaration is in the archives of the Department of State; the original map signed by the Commissioners and the original declaration are sewn together.

The text of the declaration here printed is from the original, which is written on a single sheet of parchment about 27 inches wide by 18 inches long. While the declaration is not in the Statutes at Large and is not included in the Treaty Series, it was printed in American State Papers, Foreign Relations, VI, 921–22; but neither there nor in any other publication which has been examined, is the text of the declaration printed with entire accuracy. In particular it is to be said that the declaration begins with the words "By Thomas Barclay" and has no preceding words of description and no opening heading; the Indian name "Chibnitcook" is very clearly so spelled in the original; and the signatures of the Commissioners and their seals run across the foot of the declaration, with the signature of their secretary above. The Journal of the Commissioners is in the archives

[1] As to the original map, see the notes following the text of the declaration.

of the Department of State; and the text of the declaration is almost, but not quite, literally copied therein at pages 152–55.

It appears that the original declaration and map were in duplicate only, for the concluding entry in the Journal of the Commissioners, following the text of the declaration and preceding the certificate of the secretary, recites that only two copies of the map annexed to the declaration had been made, and orders "That the Secretary have another Copy made, and that he certify it and file it with the other proceedings of this Board." Perhaps that copy of the map was made, but it is not in the archives of the Department of State.

For a full account of the proceedings of the Commissioners which resulted in this declaration, see Moore, International Adjudications, Modern Series, I and II.

The Map

The original map measures 61⅛ by 70⅝ inches.

The map has on it this notation, referring to the Metawamkeg (now "Mattawamkeag") River: "This river runs to the South west and is said to discharge into the Penobscot—vide John Harris's letter of the 30th March 1798." The letter mentioned has not been found. John Harris was the surveyor on the part of the British Government, who, under the authority of the Commissioners, made, with Samuel Titcomb, surveyor on the part of the United States, the survey of the Chiputnaticook or Chibnitcook, the north branch of the Scoodic or Saint Croix River. The Mattawamkeag does flow into the Penobscot.

Present Official Maps

That portion of the existing boundary between the United States and Canada which is formed by the Saint Croix River, from its source to its mouth, is shown by the present maps of the International Boundary Commission entitled "International Boundary from the Source of the St. Croix River to the Atlantic Ocean," Sheets Nos. 1 to 15 (No. 13 has not yet been published); they are signed (on April 3, 1924, Nos. 1 to 6; on May 30, 1924, Nos. 7 to 9; on October 30, 1924, Nos. 10 to 12; and on July 21, 1925, Nos. 14 and 15) by the Commissioners of the United States and of His Britannic Majesty appointed pursuant to Articles 1 and 2 of the treaty of April 11, 1908.

The other three maps of the same series, Nos. 16 to 18 (signed on July 21, 1925, Nos. 16 and 17; and on January 16, 1928, No. 18), show the remaining boundary, continuing to the Atlantic Ocean.

Originals of the maps of the International Boundary Commission are in the archives of the Department of State; copies are obtainable from the office of the International Boundary Commission in Washington.

Treaty Series, No. 293
8 Statutes at Large, 162–77

24

PRUSSIA : JULY 11, 1799

Treaty of Amity and Commerce, signed at Berlin July 11, 1799. Original in French and English.

Submitted to the Senate December 6, 1799. Resolution of advice and consent February 18, 1800. Ratified by the United States February 19, 1800. Ratified by Prussia June 13, 1800. Ratifications exchanged at Berlin June 22, 1800. Proclaimed November 4, 1800.

Traité d'Amitié et de Commerce entre Sa Majesté le Roi de Prusse & les Etats-Unis de l'Amérique.

Sa Majesté le Roi de Prusse et les Etats-Unis de l'Amérique, désirant d'entretenir sur un pied stable et permanent les liaisons de bonne intelligence qui ont si heureusement subsisté jusqu'ici entre Leurs Etats respectifs, et de renouveller pour cet effet le Traité d'Amitié et de Commerce,[1] qui a été conclû entre les deux Puissances à la Haye le 10 me. Septembre 1785, pour le terme de dix années, Sa Majesté Prussienne a nommé et constitué Ses Plénipotentiaires, le Sieur Charles-Guillaume Comte de Finkenstein, Son Ministre d'Etat, de guerre et de Cabinet, Chévalier des Ordres de l'Aigle-noir & de l'Aigle-rouge, et Commandeur de celui de St: Jean de Jérusalem; le Sieur Philippe-Charles Baron d'Alvensleben, Son Minis-

Treaty of Amity and Commerce between His Majesty the King of Prussia, and the United-States of America

His Majesty the King of Prussia, and the United-States of America, desiring to maintain upon a stable and permanent footing, the connections of good understanding, which have hitherto so happily subsisted between their respective States and for this purpose to renew the Treaty of Amity and Commerce[1] concluded between the two Powers, at the Hague, the 10th: of September 1785 for the term of ten years, His Prussian Majesty has nominated and constituted as His Plenipotentiaries, the Count Charles William de Finkenstein, His Minister of State, of War, and of the Cabinet, Knight of the Orders of the black Eagle and of the red Eagle, and Commander of that of St John of Jerusalem; the Baron Philip Charles d'Alven-

[1] Document 13.

tre d'Etat, de guerre et de Cabinet, Chevalier des Ordres de l'Aigle-noir et de l'Aigle-rouge, & de celui de S$^{t.}$ Jean de Jérusalem, et le Sieur Chrétien-Henri-Curce Comte de Haugwitz, Son Ministre d'Etat de guerre et de Cabinet, Chevalier des Ordres de l'Aigle-noir et de l'Aigle-rouge; et le Président des Etats-Unis a muni de Leur plein-pouvoir Jean-Quincy Adams Citoyen des Etats-Unis et Leur Ministre Plénipotentiaire à la Cour de Sa Majesté Prussienne; Lesquels Plénipotentiaires, après avoir échangés leurs pleinpouvoirs, trouvés en bonne et düe forme, ont conclû, arrêté et signé les Articles suivans.

Article I.

Il y aura dans la suite, comme par le passé, une paix ferme, inviolable et universelle et une amitié sincère entre Sa Majesté le Roi de Prusse Ses héritiers, Successeurs et Sujets d'une part, et les Etats-Unis de l'Amérique et Leurs Citoyens d'autre part, sans exception de personnes ou de lieux.

Article II.

Les Sujets de Sa Majesté le Roi de Prusse pourront fréquenter toutes les côtes et les pays des Etats-Unis de l'Amérique, y résider et trafiquer en toutes sortes de productions, manufactures et marchandises, et n'y payeront

sleben, His Minister of State, of War, and of the Cabinet, Knight of the Orders of the black Eagle and of the red Eagle and of that of St John of Jerusalem; and the Count Christian-Henry Curt de Haugwitz, His Minister of State, of War, and of the Cabinet Knight of the Orders of the black Eagle and of the red Eagle: and the President of the United-States has furnished with their full-powers John Quincy Adams a Citizen of the United-States, and their Minister Plenipotentiary at the Court of his Prussian Majesty; which Plenipotentiaries, after having exchanged their full powers, found in good and due form, have concluded, settled and signed the following Articles.

Article I.

There shall be in future, as there has been hitherto, a firm, inviolable and universal Peace, and a sincere Friendship between his Majesty the King of Prussia, his Heirs, Successors and Subjects on the one part, and the United-States of America, and their Citizens, on the other, without exception of persons or places.

Article II.

The subjects of his Majesty the King of Prussia, may frequent all the Coasts and Countries of the United States of America, and reside and trade there, in all sorts of produce, manufactures and merchandize; and shall pay there

d'autres ni de plus forts impôts, charges ou droits, que ceux que les nations les plus favorisées sont ou seront obligées de payer. Ils jouïront aussi dans la navigation et le commerce, de tous les droits, privilèges et exemptions dont jouït ou jouira la nation la plus favorisée; se soumettant néanmoins aux lois et usages établis, auxquels sont soumis les Citoyens des Etats-Unis et les nations les plus favorisées.

ARTICLE III.

Pareillement les Citoyens des Etats Unis de l'Amérique pourront fréquenter toutes les côtes et tous les pays de Sa Majesté le Roi de Prusse, y résider et trafiquer en toutes sortes de productions, manufactures et marchandises et ne payeront d'autres, ni de plus forts impôts, charges ou droits dans les domaines de Sa dite Majesté, que ceux que la nation la plus favorisée est ou sera obligée de payer; et ils jouïront de tous les droits, privilèges et exemptions dans la navigation et le commerce, dont jouit ou jouïra la nation la plus favorisée; se soumettant néanmoins aux loix et usages établis, auxquels sont soumis les sujets de Sa Majesté le Roi de Prusse et les sujets et citoyens des nations les plus favorisées.

ARTICLE IV.

En particulier chacune des deux nations aura le droit d'importer

no other or greater duties, charges, or fees, whatsoever than the most favoured Nations are or shall be obliged to pay. They shall also enjoy in Navigation and Commerce all the rights, privileges and exemptions, which the most favoured Nation, does or shall enjoy; submitting themselves nevertheless to the established laws and usages to which are submitted the Citizens of the United States, and the most favoured Nations.

ARTICLE III.

In like manner the Citizens of the United-States of America may frequent all the Coasts and Countries of his Majesty the King of Prussia, and reside and trade there in all sorts of produce, manufactures and merchandize, and shall pay, in the dominions of his said Majesty no other or greater duties, charges or fees whatsoever than the most favoured nation is or shall be obliged to pay, and they shall enjoy all the rights, privileges and exemptions in Navigation and Commerce which the most favoured Nation does or shall enjoy; submitting themselves nevertheless to the established laws and usages to which are submitted the subjects of his Majesty the King of Prussia, and the Subjects and Citizens of the most favoured Nations.

ARTICLE IV.

More especially, each party shall have a right to carry their

ses propres productions, manufactures, et marchandises, à bord de ses propres bâtimens ou de tel autre, dans toutes les parties des domaines de l'autre, où il sera permis à tous les sujets et citoyens de l'autre nation de les acheter librement; comme aussi d'y charger les productions, manufactures et marchandises de l'autre, que tous les dits sujets ou Citoyens auront la liberté de leur vendre, en payant dans l'un et l'autre cas tels impôts, droits et charges seulement, qui sont ou seront payés par la nation la plus favorisée. Cependant Sa Majesté le Roi de Prusse et les Etats-Unis de l'Amérique se reservent le droit, au cas que quelque nation restreigne le transport des marchandises aux vaisseaux des paÿs dont elles sont la production ou la manufacture, d'établir envers cette nation des règlemens réciproques; se réservant de plus le droit de prohiber dans Leurs pays respectifs, l'importation ou l'exportation de toute marchandise quelconque, dès que la raison d'état l'éxige. En ce cas les Sujets ou Citoyens d'une des Parties Contractantes, ne pourront importer ni exporter les marchandises prohibées par l'autre. Mais si l'une des Parties Contractantes permet à quelque autre nation d'importer ou d'exporter ces mêmes marchandises, les Citoyens ou Sujets de l'autre Partie Contractante jouïront tout aussitôt d'une liberté pareille.

own produce, manufactures and merchandize in their own or any other vessels to any parts of the dominions of the other, where it shall be lawful for all the Subjects and Citizens, of that other freely to purchase them and thence to take the produce, manufactures, and merchandize of the other, which all the said citizens or subjects shall in like manner be free to sell to them, paying in both cases such duties, charges and fees only as are or shall be paid by the most favoured Nation. Nevertheless his Majesty the King of Prussia, and the United States respectively reserve to themselves the right, where any Nation restrains the transportation of merchandize to the vessells of the Country of which it is the growth or manufacture, to establish against such Nation, retaliating regulations, and also the right to prohibit in their respective countries the importation and exportation of all merchandize whatsoever when reasons of State shall require it. In this case the subjects or citizens of either of the contracting parties shall not import or export the merchandize prohibited by the other. But if one of the contracting parties permits any other nation to import or export the same merchandize the citizens or subjects of the other shall immediately enjoy the same liberty

ARTICLE V.

Les marchands, commandans de vaisseaux, et autres Sujets ou Citoyens de chacune des deux nations, ne seront pas forcés dans les ports ou dans la juridiction de l'autre, de décharger aucunes sortes de marchandises dans d'autres vaisseaux, ni de les recevoir à bord de leurs propres navires, ni d'attendre leur chargement plus longtems qu'il ne leur plaira.

ARTICLE V.

The merchants, commanders of vessels, or other subjects or citizens of either party shall not within the ports or jurisdiction of the other be forced to unload any sort of merchandize into any other vessels, nor to receive them into their own, nor to wait for their being loaded longer than they please.

ARTICLE VI.

Pour éviter que les vaisseaux de l'une des deux Parties-Contractantes ne soyent inutilement molestés, ou détenus dans les ports, ou sous la juridiction de l'autre, il a été convenu, que la visite des marchandises, ordonnée par les loix, se fera avant qu'elles ne soyent chargées sur le navire, et qu'ensuite elles ne seront plus assujetties à aucune visite. Et en général il ne se fera point de recherche à bord du vaisseau, à moins qu'on n'y ait chargé clandestinement et illégalement des marchandises prohibées. Dans ce cas, celui par l'ordre duquel, elles ont été portées à bord, ou celui qui les y a portées sans ordre, sera soumis aux lois du pays où il se trouve, sans que le reste de l'équipage soit molesté, ni les autres marchandises ou le vaisseau saisis ou déténus par cette raison.

ARTICLE VI.

That the vessels of either party loading within the ports or jurisdiction of the other, may not be uselessly harassed or detained, it is agreed, that all examinations of goods required by the laws, shall be made before they are laden on board the vessel, and that there shall be no examination after; nor shall the vessel be searched at any time, unless articles shall have been laden therein clandestinely and illegally, in which case the person by whose order they were carried on board, or who carried them without order, shall be liable to the laws of the land in which he is; but no other person shall be molested; nor shall any other goods, nor the vessel be seized, or detained for that cause.

Article VII.

Chacune des deux Parties Contractantes tâchera par tous les moyens qui seront en son pouvoir, de protéger et de défendre tous les vaisseaux et autres effets appartenant aux Citoyens ou Sujets de l'autre, et se trouvant dans l'étendue de sa juridiction par mer ou par terre et elle employera tous ses efforts pour recouvrer et faire restituer aux propriétaires légitimes, les vaisseaux et effets, qui leur auront été enlevés dans l'étendue de sa dite juridiction.

Article VII.

Each party shall endeavour, by all the means in their power to protect and defend all vessels, and other effects belonging to the Citizens or Subjects of the other, which shall be within the extent of their jurisdiction by sea, or by land, and shall use all their efforts to recover, and cause to be restored to the right owners, their vessels and effects, which shall be taken from them within the extent of their said jurisdiction.

Article VIII

Les vaisseaux des Sujets ou Citoyens d'une des deux Parties Contractantes, arrivant sur une côte appartenant à l'autre, mais n'ayant pas dessein d'entrer au port, ou qui, en y entrant, ne voudroient pas décharger leurs cargaisons, ou rompre leur charge, auront la liberté de repartir et de poursuivre leur route sans empêchement, et sans être obligés de rendre compte de leur cargaison, ni de payer aucuns impôts, charges ou droits quelconques, excepté ceux établis sur les vaisseaux une fois entrés dans le port, et destinés à l'entretien du port même, ou à d'autres établissemens, qui ont pour but la surêté et la commodité des navigateurs; lesquels droits, charges et impôts seront les mêmes et se payeront sur le même pied, qu'ils sont acquités par les Sujets ou Citoyens de l'état où ils sont établis.

Article VIII.

The vessels of the Subjects or Citizens of either party, coming on any coast belonging to the other but not willing to enter into port, or who entering into port are not willing to unload their cargoes, or break bulk, shall have liberty to depart and to pursue their voyage, without molestation, and without being obliged to render account of their cargo, or to pay any duties, charges or fees whatsoever, except those established for vessels entered into port, and appropriated to the maintenance of the port itself, or of other establishments for the safety and convenience of navigators, which duties, charges and fees shall be the same, and shall be paid on the same footing as in the case of Subjects or Citizens of the Country where they are established.

ARTICLE IX.

Au cas que quelque vaisseau appartenant à l'une des deux Parties Contractantes auroit fait naufrage, échoué ou souffert quelque autre dommage sur les côtes ou sous la domination de l'autre, les Sujets ou Citoyens respectifs, recevront tant pour eux, que pour leurs vaisseaux et effets la même assistance, qui auroit été fournie aux habitans du pays où l'accident arrive, et ils payeront seulement les mêmes charges et droits auxquels les dits habitans auroient été assujettis en cas pareil. Et si la réparation du vaisseau exigeoit que la cargaison fût déchargée en tout ou en partie, ils ne payeront aucun impôt, charge ou droit de ce qui sera rembarqué et emporté. L'ancien et barbare droit de naufrage sera entièrement aboli à l'égard des Sujets ou Citoyens des deux Parties Contractantes.

ARTICLE IX.

When any vessel of either party shall be wrecked, foundered, or otherwise damaged on the coasts or within the dominions of the other, their respective Citizens or Subjects shall receive as well for themselves as for their vessels and effects the same assistance, which would be due to the inhabitants of the country, where the damage happens, and shall pay the same charges and dues only as the said inhabitants would be subject to pay in a like case, and if the operations of repair shall require that the whole or any part of the cargo be unladed, they shall pay no duties, charges or fees on the part, which they shall relade and carry away. The ancient and barbarous right to wrecks of the sea, shall be entirely abolished with respect to the subjects or citizens of the two contracting parties.

ARTICLE X.

Les Citoyens ou Sujets de l'une des Parties Contractantes auront dans les Etats de l'autre la liberté de disposer de leurs biens personnels, soit par testament, donation ou autrement, et leurs héritiers etant Sujets ou Citoyens de l'autre Partie Contractante, succèderont à leurs biens, soit en vertu d'un testament, ou ab-intestat, et ils pourront en prendre possession, soit en personne, soit par d'autres agissant en leur place, et en dis-

ARTICLE X.

The Citizens or subject of each party shall have power to dispose of their personal goods within the jurisdiction of the other by testament, donation or otherwise; and their representatives, being subjects, or Citizens of the other party shall succeed to their said personal goods, whether by testament or *ab intestato*, and may take possession thereof, either by themselves, or by others acting for them, and dispose of the same

poser à leur volonté, en ne payant d'autres droits, que ceux auxquels les habitans du pays, où la succession est devenue vacante, sont assujettis en pareille occurence. Et en cas d'absence des héritiers, on prendra provisoirement des biens qui leur sont échus, les mêmes soins qu'on auroit pris en pareille occasion des biens des natifs du paÿs, jusqu'à ce que le propriétaire légitime ait agréé des arrangemens pour recueillir l'héritage. S'il s'éleve des contestations entre différens prétendans ayant droit à la succession, elles seront décidées en dernier ressort selon les loix et par les juges du pays, où la succession est vacante. Et si par la mort de quelque personne possédant des biens-fonds sur le territoire de l'une des Parties Contractantes, ces biens-fonds venoient à passer, selon les loix du pays, à un Citoyen ou Sujet de l'autre Partie; celui-ci, si par sa qualité d'Etranger, il est inhabile de les posséder, obtiendra un délai convenable pour les vendre, et pour en retirer le provenu sans obstacle et exempt de tout droit de retenue de la part du Gouvernement des Etats respectifs. Mais cet Article ne dérogera en aucune manière à la force des lois, qui ont déja été publiées, ou qui le seront dans la suite par Sa Majesté le Roi de Prusse pour prévenir l'émigration de Ses sujets.

at their will, paying such dues only as the inhabitants of the country wherein the said goods are, shall be subject to pay in like cases. And in case of the absence of the representative such care shall be taken of the said goods as would be taken of the goods of a native in like case, untill the lawfull owner may take measures for receiving them. And if question should arise among several claimants to which of them the said goods belong, the same shall be decided finally by the laws and judges of the land wherein the said goods are. And where on the death of any person holding real estate within the territories of the one party, such real estate would by the laws of the land descend on a citizen or subject of the other, were he not disqualified by alienage, such subject shall be allowed a reasonable time to sell the same, and to withdraw the proceeds without molestation, and exempt from all rights of detraction, on the part of the Government of the respective States. But this article shall not derogate in any manner from the force of the laws already published, or hereafter to be published by his Majesty the King of Prussia, to prevent the emigration of his subjects.

Article XI.

Il sera accordé la plus parfaite liberté de conscience et de culte aux Citoyens et Sujets de chaque Partie Contractante dans les Etats de l'autre; et personne ne sera molesté à cet égard pour quelque cause que ce soit, si ce n'est pour insulte faite à la réligion de l'autre. De plus si des Sujets et Citoyens de l'une des Parties Contractantes venoient à mourir dans la jurisdiction de l'autre, leurs corps seront enterrés dans les endroits, où l'on a la coutume de faire les enterremens, ou dans tel autre lieu décent et convenable, et ils seront protégés contre toute violence et trouble.

Article XII.

L'expérience ayant démontré que le principe adopté dans l'article douze du Traité[1] de 1785, selon lequel: *les vaisseaux libres, rendent aussi les marchandises libres,* n'a pas été suffisamment respecté dans les deux dernières guerres, et nommément dans celle qui dure encore, les deux Parties Contractantes se réservent de s'entendre après le retour de la paix générale, soit séparément entr'Elles, soit conjointement avec d'autres Puissances Cointéressées, pour concerter avec les grandes Puissances maritimes de l'Europe, tels arrangemens et tels principes permanens, qui puissent servir à consolider la

Article XI.

The most perfect freedom of conscience and of worship is granted to the Citizens or Subjects of either party, within the jurisdiction of the other, and no person shall be molested in that respect for any cause other than an insult on the religion of others. Moreover, when the subjects or Citizens of the one party, shall die within the jurisdiction of the other, their bodies shall be buried in the usual burying grounds, or other decent and suitable places, and shall be protected from violation or disturbance.

Article XII.

Experience having proved that the principle adopted in the twelfth Article of the Treaty[1] of 1785, according to which *free ships make free goods* has not been sufficiently respected during the two last Wars, and especially in that which still continues, the two Contracting Parties propose after the return of a general Peace, to agree either separately between themselves, or jointly with other Powers alike interested, to concert with the great maritime Powers of Europe, such arrangements, and such permanent principles as may serve to consolidate the liberty and the safety of the neutral Navigation

[1] Document 13.

liberté et la sûreté de la navigation et du commerce neutres dans les guerres futures.

Et si pendant cet intervalle l'une des Parties Contractantes se trouve engagée dans une guerre à laquelle l'autre reste neutre, les vaisseaux de guerre et les armateurs de la Puissance belligérante se comporteront à l'égard des bâtimens marchands de la Puissance neutre, aussi favorablement que la raison de guerre pour lors existante, pourra le permettre, en observant les principes et les règles du droit des gens généralement reconnus.

Article XIII.

Dans le cas où l'une des Parties Contractantes se trouveroit en guerre avec une autre Puissance, il a été convenu que pour prévenir les difficultés et les discussions, qui surviennent ordinairement par rapport aux marchandises de contrebande, telles que armes et munitions de toute espèce, aucun de ces articles, chargés à bord des vaisseaux des Sujets ou Citoyens de l'une des Parties, et destinés pour l'ennemi de l'autre ne sera censé contrebande, au point d'impliquer confiscation ou condemnation, et d'entrainer la perte de la propriété des individus. Néanmoins il sera permis d'arrêter ces sortes de vaisseaux et effets et de les retenir pendant tout le tems que le Preneur

and Commerce in future Wars.

And if in the interval, either of the Contracting parties should be engaged in a War to which the other should remain neutral, the ships of War, and privateers of the belligerent power, shall conduct themselves towards the merchant vessels of the neutral power, as favourably, as the course of the War, then existing may permit, observing the principles and rules of the Law of Nations generally acknowledged.

Article XIII.

And in the same case of one of the Contracting Parties being engaged in War with any other Power, to prevent all the difficulties and misunderstandings, that usually arise respecting merchandize of contraband, such as arms, ammunition, and military stores of every kind, no such articles, carried in the vessels, or by the subjects or citizens of either party to the enemies of the other, shall be deemed contraband so as to induce confiscation or condemnation and a loss of property to individuals. Nevertheless it shall be lawful to stop such vessels and articles, and to detain them for such length of time as the captors may think necessary to prevent the inconvenience or damage that might ensue from their proceed-

croira nécessaire pour prévenir les inconvéniens et les dommages qui pourroient en résulter autrement, mais dans ce cas on accordera une compensation raisonnable pour les pertes, qui auront été occasionnées par la saisie. Et il sera permis en outre aux Preneurs d'employer à leur service, en tout ou en partie les munitions militaires détenues, en payant aux Propriétaires la pleine valeur, à déterminer sur le prix qui aura cours à l'endroit de leur destination; mais si dans le cas énoncé d'un vaisseau arrêté pour des articles de contrebande, le maitre du navire consent à délivrer les marchandises suspectes, il aura la liberté de le faire et le navire ne sera plus amêné dans le port, ni détenu plus longtems, mais aura toute liberté de poursuivre sa route.

Seront censés objets de contrebande, les canons, mortiers, armes à feu, pistolets, bombes, grenades, boulets, bâles, fusils, pierres à feu, mêches, poudre, salpêtre, souffre, cuirasses, piques, épées, ceinturons, poches à cartouches, selles et brides, au délà de la quantité nécessaire pour l'usage du vaisseau, et au délà de celle que doit avoir chaque homme servant sur le vaisseau, ou passager; et en général tout ce qui est compris sous la dénomination d'armes et de munitions de guerre, de quelque espèce qu'elles puissent être.

ing, paying however a reasonable compensation for the loss such arrest shall occasion to the proprietors, and it shall further be allowed to use in the service of the captors, the whole or any part of the military stores so detained, paying the owners the full value of the same, to be ascertained by the current price at the place of its destination. But in the case supposed of a vessel stopped for articles of contraband, if the master of the vessel stopped will deliver out the goods supposed to be of contraband nature, he shall be admitted to do it, and the vessel shall not in that case be carried into any port, nor further detained, but shall be allowed to proceed on her voyage.

All cannons, mortars, fire-arms, pistols, bombs, grenades, bullets, balls, muskets, flints, matches, powder, salt-petre, sulphur, cuirasses, pikes, swords, belts, cartouch-boxes, saddles and bridles, beyond the quantity,necessary for the use of the ship, or beyond that which every man serving on board the vessel, or passenger ought to have, and in general whatever is comprized under the denomination of arms and military stores, of what description so ever, shall be deemed objects of contraband.

Article XIV.

Pour assurer aux vaisseaux des deux Parties Contractantes, l'avantage d'être promptement et sûrement reconnus en tems de guerre, on est convenu qu'ils devront être munis des lettres de mer et documens spécifiés ci-après:

1mo, d'un Passeport; exprimant le nom, le propriétaire, et le port du navire, ainsi que le nom et le domicile du maitre. Ces passeports qui seront expédiés en bonne et due forme, devront être renouvellés toutes les fois, que le vaisseau retournera dans son port, et seront exhibés à chaque réquisition, tant en pleine mer que dans le port. Mais si le navire se trouve sous le convoy d'un ou de plusieurs vaisseaux de guerre, appartenants à la partie neutre, il suffira que l'officier commandant le convoy, déclare que le navire est de son parti; moyennant quoi cette simple déclaration sera censée établir le fait et dispensera les deux Parties de toute visite ultérieure.

2do, de la Certe-partie; c'est à dire du contràt passé pour le frêt de tout le navire, ou des connoissements donnés pour la cargaison en général;

et 3^{tio}, du rôle d'équipage contenant l'indication nominale et détaillée des personnes, qui composent l'équipage du navire.

Ces documens seront toujours expédiés dans la forme établie à

Article XIV.

To ensure to the vessels of the two Contracting Parties the advantage of being readily and certainly known in time of War, it is agreed that they shall be provided with the Sea-letters and Documents hereafter specified.

1°, A Passport; expressing, the name, the property, and the burthen of the vessel, as also the name and dwelling of the master, which Passport shall be made out in good and due form, shall be renewed as often as the vessel shall return into port, and shall be exhibited whensoever required, as well in the open Sea, as in port. But if the vessel be under convoy of one or more vessels of War, belonging to the neutral party, the simple declaration of the officer commanding the convoy, that the said vessel belongs to the party of which he is, shall be considered as establishing the fact, and shall relieve both parties from the trouble of further examination.

2°, A Charter-party; that is to say, the contract passed for the freight of the whole vessel; or the bills of lading given for the cargo in detail.

3°, The list of the Ship's company, containing an indication by name and in detail of the persons composing the crew of the vessel.

These documents shall always be authenticated according to the

l'endroit, d'où le navire aura mis à la voile.

Comme leur production ne doit être exigée, que dans le cas où l'une des Parties Contractantes seroit en guerre, et que leur exhibition ne doit avoir d'autre but, que de prouver la neutralité des vaisseaux, de leurs équipages, et de leurs cargaisons, ils ne seront pas censés absolument nécessaires à bord des navires de la partie neutre, qui seront sortis de ses ports, avant ou trois mois après, que le Gouvernement aura eu connaissance de l'état de guerre où se trouve la partie belligérante. Pendant cet intervalle, le navire pourra au défaut des documens ci-dessus spécifiés, prouver sa neutralité par tel autre témoignage, que les Tribunaux, appellés à juger du cas, trouveront suffisans.

Article XV.

Pour prévenir entièrement tout désordre et toute violence en pareil cas, il a été stipulé, que lorsque les navires de la Partie neutre, navigeant sans convoi, rencontreront quelque vaisseau de guerre public ou particulier de l'autre Partie, le vaisseau de guerre n'enverra pas plus de deux ou trois hommes, dans Sa chaloupe à bord du navire neutre pour examiner les passeports et documents. Et toutes les personnes appartenantes à quelque vaisseau de guerre public ou particulier, qui molesteront ou

forms established at the place from which the vessel shall have sailed.

As their production ought to be exacted only when one of the contracting Parties shall be at war, and as their exhibition ought to have no other object than to prove the neutrality of the vessel, its cargo and company, they shall not be deemed absolutely necessary on board, such vessels belonging to the neutral party, as shall have sailed from its ports before, or within three months after the Government shall have been informed of the state of War, in which the belligerent party shall be engaged. In the interval, in default of these specific documents, the neutrality of the vessel may be established by such other evidence as the tribunals authorised to judge of the case may deem sufficient.

Article XV.

And to prevent entirely all disorder and violence in such cases, it is stipulated that when the vessels of the neutral party, sailing without convoy, shall be met by any vessel of War, public or private, of the other party, such vessel of war shall not send more than two or three men in their boat on board the said neutral vessel, to examine her Passports and documents. And all persons belonging to any vessel of War, public or private, who shall molest or insult in any manner

insulteront en quelque manière que ce soit l'équipage, les vaisseaux, ou effets de l'autre partie, seront responsables en leurs personnes, et en leurs biens de tous dommages et intérêts, pour lesquels il sera donné caution suffisante par tous les Commandans de vaisseaux armés en course avant qu'ils reçoivent leurs commissions.

whatever the people, vessels or effects of the other party shall be responsible in their persons and property for damages and interest; sufficient security for which shall be given by all commanders of private armed vessels before they are commissioned.

Article XVI.

Dans les tems de guerre et les cas de nécessité urgente, où l'une des Parties Contractantes, se verroit obligée d'établir un embargo général, soit dans tous les ports de Sa domination, soit dans certains ports particuliers, les vaisseaux de l'autre Partie resteront assujettis à cette mésure, sur le même pied, que le seront les navires des nations les plus avantagées, sans pouvoir réclamer l'exemption, qui avoit été stipulée en leur faveur dans l'Article 16 de l'ancien Traité de 1785.[1] Mais d'un autre coté les propriétaires des vaisseaux, qui auront été retenus, soit pour quelque expédition militaire, soit pour tel autre usage que ce soit, obtiendront du Gouvernement qui les aura employés une indemnité équitable, tant pour le frêt, que pour les pertes occasionnées par le retard.

De plus et dans tous les cas de saisie, de détention ou d'arrêt, soit pour dettes contractées, ou offenses commises par quelque Citoyen ou

Article XVI.

In times of War, or in cases of urgent necessity when either of the Contracting Parties, shall be obliged to lay a general embargo, either in all its ports, or in certain particular places, the vessels of the other party, shall be subject to this measure upon the same footing as those of the most favoured Nations, but without having the right to claim the exemption in their favour stipulated in the sixteenth Article of the former Treaty of 1785.[1] But on the other hand the proprietors of the vessels, which shall have been detained whether for some military expedition, or for what other use so ever, shall obtain from the Government that shall have employed them an equitable indemnity as well for the freight, as for the loss occasioned by the delay. And furthermore in all cases of seizure, detention or arrest, for debts contracted, or offences committed by any citizen or subject of the one party,

[1] Document 13.

Sujet de l'une des Parties Contractantes dans la jurisdiction de l'autre, on procédera uniquement par ordre et par autorité de la justice, et suivant les voyes ordinaires en pareil cas, usitées.

ARTICLE XVII.

S'il arrivoit que les batimens ou effets de la Puissance neutre fussent pris par l'ennemi de l'autre, ou par un pirate, et ensuite repris par la Puissance en guerre, ils seront restitués au premier propriétaire aux conditions qui seront stipulées ci-après dans l'article 21 pour les cas de reprise.

ARTICLE XVIII.

Lorsque les citoyens ou sujets de l'une des deux Parties contractantes seront forcés par des tempêtes ou par la poursuite des corsaires ou vaisseaux ennemis ou par quelqu'autre accident, à se réfugier avec leurs vaisseaux ou effets dans les havres ou dans la juridiction de l'autre, ils seront reçus protégés et traités avec humanité et honnêteté. Il leur sera permis de se pourvoir à un prix raisonnable de rafraichissements, de provisions & de toutes choses nécessaires, pour leur subsistance, santé et commodité, et pour la réparation de leurs vaisseaux.

ARTICLE XIX.

Les vaisseaux de guerre publics et particuliers des deux Parties

within the jurisdiction of the other, the same shall be made, and prosecuted by order and authority of law only, and according to the regular course of proceedings usual in such cases.

ARTICLE XVII.

If any vessel or effects of the neutral power, be taken by an enemy of the other, or by a pirate, and retaken by the Power at War, they shall be restored to the first proprietor upon the conditions hereafter stipulated, in the twenty-first Article for cases of recapture.

ARTICLE XVIII.

If the citizens or subjects of either party in danger from tempests, pirates, enemies or other accident, shall take refuge with their vessels or effects, within the harbours or jurisdiction of the other, they shall be received, protected and treated with humanity and kindness, and shall be permitted to furnish themselves at reasonable prices with all refreshments, provisions and other things necessary for their sustenance, health and accomodation, and for the repair of their vessels.

ARTICLE XIX.

The vessels of War, public and private, of both parties shall carry

Contractantes pourront conduire en toute liberté, partout où il leur plaira, les vaisseaux et effets qu'ils auront pris sur leurs ennemis, sans être obligés de payer aucuns impôts, charges ou droits aux Officiers de l'Amirauté, des Douanes ou autres. Ces prises ne pourront être non plus ni arrêtées, ni visitées, ni soumises à des procédures légales, en entrant dans le port de l'autre partie, mais elles pourront en sortir librement, et être conduites en tout temps par le vaisseau preneur aux endroits portés par les commissions, dont l'Officier Commandant le dit vaisseau sera obligé de faire montre.

Mais, conformément aux Traités[1] subsistans entre les Etats-Unis et la Grande Bretagne, tout vaisseau qui aura fait une prise sur des sujets de cette dernière Puissance, ne sauroit obtenir un droit d'asile dans les ports des Etats-Unis; et s'il est forcé d'y relâcher par des tempêtes ou quelque autre danger, ou accident de mer, il sera obligé d'en repartir le plutôt possible.

freely wheresoever they please, the vessels and effects taken from their enemies, without being obliged to pay any duties, charges or fees to officers of admiralty, of the customs, or any others: nor shall such prizes be arrested, searched or put under legal process, when they come to and enter the ports of the other party, but may freely be carried out again at any time by their captors to the places expressed in their commissions, which the commanding officer of such vessel shall be obliged to shew.

But, conformably to the Treaties[1] existing between the United States and Great Britain, no vessel that shall have made a prize upon british subjects, shall have a right to shelter in the ports of the United States, but if forced therein by tempests, or any other danger or accident of the sea, they shall be obliged to depart as soon as possible.

Article XX.

Aucun Citoyen ou Sujet de l'une des deux Parties Contractantes, n'acceptera d'une Puissance, avec laquelle l'autre pourroit être en guerre, ni commission, ni lettre de marque, pour armer en course contre cette dernière, sous peine d'être puni comme pirate; Et ni

Article XX.

No Citizen or Subject of either of the Contracting Parties shall take from any power with which the other may be at War, any commission or letter of marque for arming any vessel to act as a privateer against the other, on pain of being punished as a pirate;

[1] See the Jay Treaty, Document 16, especially Articles 24 and 25.

l'un, ni l'autre des deux Etats, ne louera, prêtera, ou donnera une partie de ses forces navales ou militaires à l'ennemi de l'autre, pour l'aider à agir offensivement ou défensivement contre l'Etat qui est en guerre.

Article XXI.

S'il arrivoit que les deux Parties Contractantes fussent en même tems en guerre contre un ennemi commun, on observera de part et d'autre les points suivans:

1mo, Lorsqu'un navire de l'une des deux nations sera repris par les vaisseaux de guerre ou armateurs de l'autre, avant d'avoir été conduit dans un port ennemi ou neutre, il sera restitué avec sa cargaison au premier propriétaire, moyennant une rétribution d'un huitième de la valeur du navire et de la cargaison, si la reprise a été faite par un vaisseau de guerre, et d'un sixième, si elle a été faite par un armateur.

2do, Dans ces cas la restitution n'aura lieu qu'après les preuves faites de la propriété, sous caution de la quote-part, qui en revient à ceux qui ont repris le navire.

3^{tio}, Les vaisseaux de guerre publics et particuliers des deux Parties Contractantes, seront admis réciproquement avec leurs prises dans les ports respectifs; cependant ces prises ne pourront y être déchargées ni vendues, qu'après que la légitimité de la prise aura été décidée suivant les lois et réglemens de l'Etat dont le

nor shall either party hire, lend, or give any part of its naval or military force, to the enemy of the other to aid them offensively or defensively against the other.

Article XXI.

If the two Contracting Parties should be engaged in a War against a common enemy, the following points shall be observed between them.

1º, If a vessel of one of the parties taken by the enemy, shall before being carried into a neutral or enemy's port, be retaken by a ship of War, or privateer of the other, it shall, with the cargo be restored to the first owners for a compensation of one-eighth part of the value of the said vessel and cargo, if the recapture be made by a public ship of War, and one sixth part, if made by a privateer.

2º, The restitution in such cases shall be after due proof of property, and surety given for the part to which the recaptors are entitled.

3º, The vessels of War, public and private of the two parties shall reciprocally be admitted with their prizes into the respective ports of each, but the said prizes shall not be discharged or sold there, untill their legality shall have been decided according to the laws and regulations of the state to which the captor

preneur est sujet, mais par la justice du lieu où la prise aura été conduite.

4to, Il sera libre à chacune des Parties Contractantes de faire tels règlemens qu'Elles jugeront nécessaires, rélativement à la conduite que devront tenir respectivement leurs vaisseaux de guerre publics et particuliers à l'égard des batimens qu'ils auront pris et aménés dans les ports des deux Puissances.

belongs, but by the judicatories of the place into which the prize shall have been conducted.

4º, It shall be free to each Party, to make such regulations as they shall judge necessary for the conduct of their respective vessels of War, public and private, relative to the vessels which they shall take and carry into the ports of the two parties.

Article XXII.

Lorsque les Parties Contractantes seront engagées en guerre contre un ennemi commun, ou qu'Elles seront neutres toutes deux, les vaisseaux de guerre de l'une prendront en toute occasion, sous leur protection les navires de l'autre, qui font avec eux la même route, et ils les défendront aussi longtems qu'ils feront voile ensemble, contre toute force et violence, et de la même manière qu'ils protégeroient et défendroient les navires de leur propre nation.

Article XXII.

When the Contracting Parties shall have a common enemy, or shall both be neutral, the vessels of War, of each shall upon all occasions take under their protection the vessels of the other going the same course, and shall defend such vessels, as long as they hold the same course against all force and violence in the same manner as they ought to protect and defend vessels belonging to the party of which they are.

Article XXIII.

S'il survient une guerre entre les Parties Contractantes, les marchands de l'un des deux Etats, qui résideront dans l'autre, auront la permission d'y rester encore neuf mois, pour récueillir leurs dettes actives et arranger leurs affaires; après quoi ils pourront partir en toute liberté et emporter tous leurs biens,

Article XXIII.

If War should arise between the two Contracting Parties, the merchants of either country then residing in the other, shall be allowed to remain nine months to collect their debts and settle their affairs, and may depart freely, carrying off all their effects, without molestation or hindrance; And all Women and children, scholars

sans être molestés ni empêchés. Les femmes et les enfans, les gens de lettres de toutes les facultés, les cultivateurs, artisans, manufacturiers et pêcheurs qui ne sont point armés, et qui habitent des villes, villages ou places non-fortifiées, et en général tous ceux dont la vocation tend à la subsistance et à l'avantage commun du genre humain, auront la liberté de continuer leurs proffessions respectives, et ne seront point molestés en leurs personnes, ni leurs maisons ou leurs biens incendiés ou autrement détruits, ni leurs champs ravagés par les armées de l'ennemi au pouvoir du quel ils pourroient tomber par les événemens de la guerre; mais si l'on se trouve dans la nécessité de prendre quelque chose de leurs propriétés pour l'usage de l'armée ennemie, la valeur en sera payée à un prix raisonnable.

of every faculty, cultivators of the Earth, artisans, manufacturers and fishermen, unarmed and inhabiting unfortified towns, villages, or places, and in general, all others, whose occupations are for the common subsistence and benefit of mankind, shall be allowed to continue their respective employments, and shall not be molested in their persons, nor shall their houses or goods be burnt, or otherwise destroyed, nor their fields wasted by the armed force of the enemy, into whose power, by the events of War, they may happen to fall; but if any thing is necessary to be taken from them, for the use of such armed force, the same shall be paid for, at a reasonable price

Article XXIV.

Afin d'adoucir le sort des prisonniers de guerre, et de ne les point exposer à être envoyés dans des climats éloignés et rigoureux, ou resserrés dans des habitations étroites et malsaines, les deux Parties Contractantes s'engagent solemnellement l'une envers l'autre et à la face de l'Univers, qu'Elles n'adopteront aucun de ces usages; que les prisonniers, qu'Elles pourroient faire l'une sur l'autre, ne seront transportés ni aux Indes Orientales, ni dans aucune contrée de l'Asie ou de l'Afrique, mais

Article XXIV.

And to prevent the destruction of prisoners of war, by sending them into distant and inclement countries, or by crowding them into close and noxious places, the two Contracting Parties solemnly pledged themselves to the world and to each other, that they will not adopt, any such practice; that neither will send the prisoners whom they may take from the other into the East-Indies, or any other parts of Asia or Africa, but that they shall be placed in some parts of their dominions in

qu'on leur assignera en Europe, ou en Amérique dans les territoires respectifs des Parties Contractantes un séjour situé dans un air sain; qu'ils ne seront point confinés dans des cachôts ni dans des prisons, ni dans des vaisseaux de prison; qu'ils ne seront pas mis aux fers, ni garotés, ni autrement privés de l'usage de leurs membres; que les officiers seront rélachés sur leur parole d'honneur dans l'enceinte de certains districts, qui leur seront fixés, et qu'on leur accordera des logemens commodes; que les simples soldats seront distribués dans des cantonnemens ouverts, assez vastes pour prendre l'air et l'exercice, et qu'ils seront logés dans des barraques aussi spatieuses et aussi commodes que le sont celles des trouppes de la Puissance au pouvoir de laquelle se trouvent les prisonniers; que cette Puissance fera pourvoir journellement les officiers, d'autant de rations, composés des mêmes articles et de la même qualité, dont jouissent en nature ou en équivalent, les officiers du même rang, qui sont à Son propre service; qu'Elle fournira également à tous les autres prisonniers, une ration pareille à celle qui est accordée au soldat de Sa propre armée. Le montant de ces dépenses sera payé par l'autre Puissance, d'après une liquidation de compte, à arrêter reciproquement pour l'entretien des prisonniers, à la fin de la

Europe or America, in wholesome situations; that they shall not be confined in dungeons, prison-ships, nor prisons, nor be put into irons nor bound, nor otherwise restrained in the use of their limbs; that the officers shall be enlarged on their paroles within convenient districts and have comfortable quarters, and the common men be disposed in cantonments open and extensive enough for air and exercize, and lodged in barracks as roomly and good as are provided by the party in whose power they are, for their own troops; that the officers shall also be daily furnished by the party in whose power they are, with as many rations, and of the same articles and quality, as are allowed by them either in kind, or by commutation to officers of equal rank in their own army; and all others shall be daily furnished by them with such ration as they shall allow to a common soldier in their own service; the value whereof shall be paid by the other party on a mutual adjustment of accounts for the subsistence of prisoners at the close of the war; and the said accounts shall not be mingled with, or set off against any others, nor the balances due on them, be withheld as a satisfaction or reprizal for any other article, or for any other cause real or pretended, whatever. That each party shall be allowed to keep a Commissary of prisoners

guerre, et ces comptes ne seront point confondus ou balancés avec d'autres comptes, ni la solde qui en est düe, retenue comme compensation ou répresailles pour tel autre article, ou telle autre prétension réelle ou supposée. Il sera permis à chacune des deux Puissances d'entretenir un Commissaire de leur choix, dans chaque cantonnement des prisonniers qui sont au pouvoir de l'autre. Ces Commissaires auront la liberté de visiter les prisonniers, aussi souvent qu'ils le désireront; ils pourront également recevoir et distribuer les douceurs que les parents ou amis des prisonniers leur feront parvenir; enfin il leur sera libre encore de faire leurs rapports par lettres ouvertes, à ceux qui les employent. Mais si un officier manquoit à sa parole d'honneur, ou qu'un autre prisonnier sortit des limites qui auront été fixées à son cantonnement, un tel officier ou autre prisonnier sera frustré individuellement des avantages stipulés dans cet Article, pour sa relaxation sur parole d'honneur, ou pour son cantonnement. Les deux Puissances Contractantes ont déclaré en outre, que ni le pretexte que la guerre rompt les Traités, ni tel autre motif quelconque ne sera censé annuller ou suspendre cet Article, et le précédent; mais qu'au contraire le tems de la guerre est précisément celui pour lequel ils ont été stipulés et durant lequel

of their own appointment, with every separate cantonment of prisoners in possession of the other, which commissary shall see the prisoners as often as he pleases; shall be allowed to receive and distribute whatever comforts may be sent to them by their friends, and shall be free to make his reports in open letters to those who employ him: but if any officer shall break his parole, or any other prisoner shall escape from the limits of his cantonment after they shall have been designated to him, such individual officer or other prisoner, shall forfeit so much of the benefit of this Article, as provides for his enlargement on parole or cantonment. And it is declared, that neither the pretence, that War dissolves all treaties, nor any other whatever, shall be considered as annulling or suspending this and the next preceding Article; but on the contrary that the state of War, is precisely that for which they are provided, and during which they are to be as sacredly observed as the most acknowledged articles in the Law of nature and nations.

ils seront observés aussi saintement que les Articles les plus universellement reconnus par le Droit de la nature et des Gens.

ARTICLE XXV.

Les deux Parties Contractantes se sont accordé mutuellement la faculté de tenir dans Leurs ports respectifs des Consuls, Vice-Consuls, Agens et Commissaires de Leurs choix, et ils y jouïront des mêmes privilèges et pouvoirs dont jouissent ceux des nations les plus favorisées. Mais dans le cas où tel ou autre de ces Consuls veuille faire le commerce, il sera soumis aux mêmes lois et usages, auxquels sont soumis les particuliers de sa nation à l'endroit où il réside.

ARTICLE XXV.

The two Contracting parties have granted to each other, the liberty of having each in the ports of the other Consuls, vice-Consuls, agents, and Commissaries of their own appointment, who shall enjoy the same privileges and powers as those of the most favoured nations. But if any such consuls shall exercise commerce, they shall be submitted to the same laws and usages to which the private individuals of their nation are submitted in the same place.

ARTICLE XXVI.

Lorsque l'une des deux Parties Contractantes accordera dans la suite quelque faveur particulière en fait de navigation ou de commerce à d'autres nations, elle deviendra aussitôt commune à l'autre Partie Contractante, et celle-ci jouïra de cette faveur gratuitement, si la concession est gratuite, ou en accordant la même compensation si la concession est conditionelle.

ARTICLE XXVI.

If either party shall hereafter grant to any other nation, any particular favour in navigation or commerce, it shall immediately become common to the other party; freely where it is freely granted, to such other nation, or on yielding the same compensation, when the grant is conditional.

ARTICLE XXVII

Sa Majesté le Roi de Prusse et les Etats-Unis de l'Amérique sont convenus que le présent Traité aura son plein effet pendant l'espace de dix Années, à compter

ARTICLE XXVII.

His Majesty the King of Prussia and the United States of America, agree that this Treaty shall be in force during the term of ten years from the exchange of

du jour de l'échange des Ratifications, et que si l'expiration de ce terme arrivoit dans le cours d'une guerre entr-Eux, les Articles ci-dessus stipulés pour règler Leur conduite en temps de guerre, conserveront toute leur force jusqu'à la conclusion du Traité, qui rétablira la paix.

Le présent Traité sera ratifié de part et d'autre, et les ratifications seront échangées dans l'espace d'une année, à compter du jour de la signature, ou plutôt si faire se peut.

En foi de quoi les Plénipotentiaires susnommés ont signé le présent Traité, et y ont apposé le cachet de leurs armes. Fait à Berlin le onze Juillet l'an mille sept-cents quatre-vingt dix-neuf.

[Seal] CHARLES GUILLAUME COMTE DE FINKENSTEIN

[Seal] PHILIPPE CHARLÈS D'ALVENSLEBEN

[Seal] CHRETIEN HENRI CURCE COMTE DE HAUGWIZ

[Seal] JOHN QUINCY ADAMS.

the ratifications; and if the expiration of that term should happen during the course of a War between them, then the Articles before provided for the regulation of their conduct during such a War, shall continue in force untill the conclusion of the Treaty which shall restore Peace.

This Treaty shall be ratified on both sides, and the ratifications exchanged within one year from the day of its signature or sooner if possible.

In testimony whereof the Plenipotentiaries before mentioned have hereto subscribed their names and affixed their Seals. Done at Berlin the eleventh of July in the year One Thousand seven hundred and ninety nine.

[Seal] CHARLES GUILLAUME COMTE DE FINKENSTEIN

[Seal] PHILIPPE CHARLES D'ALVENSLEBEN

[Seal] CHRETIEN HENRI CURCE COMTE DE HAUGWIZ

[Seal] JOHN QUINCY ADAMS.

NOTES

The original treaty in the file is a manuscript pamphlet with the French text on the left pages and the English on the right. The signatures for Prussia are at the left of the respective pages and that of John Quincy Adams at the right thereof.

The file now contains a facsimile of the first and last pages of the United States instrument of ratification and also a facsimile of the protocol of exchange of ratifications on June 22, 1800, which took place at the residence of Comte de Haugwitz. These facsimiles were obtained from the archives at Berlin.

The original proclamation is in the file, but the last page thereof, with the signatures and the Great Seal and including the date, is lacking. That the date was November 4, 1800, appears from the press of the period, *e. g.*, the Aurora General Advertiser, Philadelphia, December 2, 1800. Like the Prussian instrument of ratification, the proclamation includes the texts in each language; but the French is on the right-hand pages.

This was the second treaty of the United States with Prussia. The first treaty, that of 1785 (Document 13), had expired by limitation on August 8, 1796, ten years after the exchange of ratifications. It appears, however, that there was no record in the Department of State at the time, of the exact date of the exchange of ratifications of the earlier treaty with Prussia or of the treaty with Sweden of 1783 (Document 10). Regarding them Pickering wrote to John Quincy Adams on July 15, 1797:

> The ratifications of the Swedish treaty, it is supposed, were exchanged in the beginning of the year 1784; as, on the 9th of March of that year, Dr. Franklin wrote from Paris to the Secretary for Foreign Affairs that he had made the exchange. In like manner, Mr. Adams wrote from London, on the 27th of October, 1786, that he had been in Holland, and exchanged the ratifications of the Prussian treaty. No documents are found to show the day when the exchange took place. (American State Papers, Foreign Relations, II, 250.)

Treaty Series, No. 85
8 Statutes at Large, 178–96

25

FRANCE : SEPTEMBER 30, 1800

Convention signed at Paris September 30, 1800, with additional article and with provisos. Original in French and English.
Submitted to the Senate December 16, 1800. (Message of December 15, 1800.) Resolution of advice and consent, with proviso, February 3, 1801. Ratified by the United States February 18, 1801. Ratified by France, with proviso, July 31, 1801. Ratifications exchanged at Paris July 31, 1801. Resubmitted to the Senate December 11, 1801. Resolution of the Senate December 19, 1801, declaring the convention fully ratified. Proclaimed December 21, 1801.

Convention entre la République française et les Etats-unis d'Amérique.

Le Premier Consul de la République française, au nom du Peuple francais, et le Président des Etats-unis d'amérique, également animés du désir de mettre fin aux différens qui sont survenus entre les deux Etats, ont respectivement nommé leurs Plénipotentiaires; et leur ont donné pleins pouvoirs pour négocier sur ces différens et les terminer; c'est à dire, le premier Consul de la République française, au nom du Peuple français, a nommé pour Plénipotentiaires de la dite République les Citoyens Joseph Bonaparte ex Ambassadeur de la République française à Rome et Conseiller d'Etat; Charles-Pierre Claret Fleurieu, Membre de l'Institut national et du Bureau des Longitudes de France, et Con-

Convention between the French Republic, and the United States of America.

The Premier Consul of the French Republic in the name of the People of France, and the President of the United States of America, equally desirous to terminate the differences which have arisen between the two States, have respectively appointed their Plenipotentiaries, and given them full power to treat upon those differences and to terminate the same, that is to say, the Premier Consul of the French Republic, in the name of the People of France has appointed for the Plenipotentiaries of the said Republic, the Citizens, Joseph Bonaparte, Ex-Ambassador of the Republic at Rome, and Counsellor of State, Charles Pierre Claret Fleurieu, member of the national Institute, and of the Board of longitude of

seiller d'Etat, Président de la Section de la Marine; et Pierre Louis Roederer, Membre de l'Institut national de france et Conseiller d'Etat, Président de la Section de l'Intérieur—

Et le Président des Etats-unis d'Amérique, par et avec l'avis et le consentement du Senat desdits Etats, a nommé pour leurs plenipotentiaires, Oliver Ellsworth, chef de la justice des Etats-unis; William, Richardson, Davie, cidevant Gouverneur de l'Etat de la Caroline Septentrionale; et William Vans-Murray, Ministre résident des Etats-unis à la Haye.

Lesquels, après avoir fait l'échange de leurs pleins pouvoirs, longuement et mûrement discuté les intérêts respectifs, sont convenus des Articles Suivans.

France, and Counsellor of State—President of the section of the Marine, and Pierre Louis Roederer, member of the national institute of France; and Counsellor of State—President of the Section of the Interior: and the President of the United States of America by and with the advice, and consent of the Senate of said States, has appointed for their Plenipotentiaries, Oliver Ellsworth, Chief Justice of the United States William Richardson Davie, late Governor of the State of North Carolina, and William Vans Murray, Minister Resident of the United States at the Hague, who after having exchanged their full powers, and after full and mature discussion of the respective interests have agreed on the following articles.

Article 1er

Il y aura une Paix ferme, inviolable et universelle et une amitié vraie et Sincère entre la République française et les Etats-Unis d'Amérique, ainsi qu'entre leurs pays, territoires, villes et places et entre leurs Citoyens et habitans, sans exception de personnes ni de lieux.

Article I

There shall be a firm, inviolable, and universal peace, and a true and sincere Friendship between the French Republic, and the United States of America, and between their respective countries territories, cities, towns, and people without exception of persons, or places.

Art. 2.[1]

Les Ministres plénipotentiaires des deux parties ne pouvant, pour le présent, s'accorder relative-

Article II [1]

The Ministers Plenipotentiary of the two Parties, not being able to agree at present, respect-

[1] As to the omission of this article and as to the proviso in respect thereof, see the extracts from the instruments of ratification, following the signatures, and also the notes.

ment au Traîté d'alliance[1] du six février mil sept cent soixante dix huit, au Traité d'amitié et de commerce [2] de la même date et à la Convention [3] en date du quatorze Novembre mil sept cent quatre vingt huit, non plus que relativement aux indemnités mutuellement dues ou réclamées; les parties négocieront ultérieurement sur ces objets dans un tems convenable et jusqu'à ce qu'elles se soient accordées sur ces points, les dits Traités et Convention n'auront point d'effet et les relations des deux Nations seront règlées ainsi qu'il suit.

ART. 3.

Les Bâtiments d'Etat qui ont été pris de part et d'autre, ou qui pourraient être pris avant l'échange des ratifications, seront rendus.

ART. 4.

Les Propriétés capturées et non encore condamnées définitivement, ou qui pourront être capturées avant l'échange des ratifications, excepté les Marchandises de Contrebande destinées pour un port ennemi, seront rendues mutuellement sur les preuves suivantes de propriété, savoir:

De part et d'autre les preuves de propriété relativement aux Navires marchands, armés ou non

ing the Treaty of Alliance[1] of 6th February 1778, the Treaty of Amity and Commerce[2] of the same date, and the . . . Convention[3] of 14th November 1788, nor upon the indemnities mutually due, or claimed, the Parties will negotiate further on these subjects at a convenient time, and untill they may have agreed upon these points, the said Treaties, and . . . Convention shall have no operation, and the relations of the two Countries shall be regulated as follows.

ARTICLE III

The Public Ships, which have been taken on one part, and the other, or which may be taken before the exchange of ratifications shall be restored.

ARTICLE IV

Property captured, and not yet definitively condemned, or which may be captured before the exchange of ratifications, (contraband goods destined to an Enemy's port excepted) shall be mutually restored on the following proofs of ownership, viz, The proof on both sides, with respect to Merchant Ships, whether armed, or unarmed, shall be a Passport in the form following

[1] Document 2.
[2] Document 1.
[3] Document 15.

armés, seront un passeport dans la forme suivante:

A tous ceux qui les présentes verront soit notoire que faculté et permission a été accordée à .... Maître ou Commandant du Navire appelé........... de la ville de............ de la capacité de .... tonneaux ou environ, se trouvant présentement dans le port et havre de............ et destiné pour .... chargé de .... qu'après que son navire a été visité, et avant son départ, il prêtera serment entre les mains des officiers autorisés à cet effet, que le dit Navire appartient à un ou plusieurs sujets de............ dont l'acte sera mis à la fin des présentes, de même qu'il gardera et fera garder par son équipage les Ordonnances et règlements maritimes, et remettra une Liste signée et confirmée par témoins, contenant les noms et surnoms, les lieux de naissance et la demeure des personnes composant l'Equipage de son navire, et de tous ceux qui s'y embarqueront, lesquels il ne recevra pas à bord sans la connaissance et permission des officiers autorisés à ce; et dans chaque port ou havre où il entrera avec son navire, il montrera la présente permission aux officiers à ce autorisés, et leur fera un rapport fidèle de ce qui s'est passé durant son voyage, et il portera les Couleurs, Armes, et Enseignes de (la République française ou

To all who shall see these presents. Greeting: It is hereby made known that leave, and permission has been given to .... Master, and Commander of the Ship called .... of the town of .... burthen ...... Tons, or thereabouts, lying at present in the port, and haven of............ and bound for .... and laden with .... after that his ship has been visited, and before sailing, he shall make oath before the Officers, who have the jurisdiction of maritime affairs, that the said Ship belongs to one, or more of the subjects of .... the act whereof shall be put at the end of these presents; as likewise that he will keep, and cause to be kept by his crew on board, the marine ordinances, and regulations, and enter in the proper Office a list, signed, and witnessed, containing the names, and surnames, the places of birth, and abode of the crew of his Ship, and of all who shall embark on board her, whom he shall not take on board, without the knowledge, and permission of the Officers of the Marine; and in every port, or Haven, where he shall enter with his ship, he shall shew this present leave to the Officers, and Judges of the Marine, and shall give a faithful account to them, of what passed, and was done during his voyage, and he shall carry the

des Etats-Unis) durant son dit voyage, en témoin de quoi nous avons signé les présentes, les avons fait contresigner par .... et y avons fait apposer le Sceau de nos armes.

Donné à .... le .... de l'an de grace le .....

Et ce passeport suffira sans autre pièce, nonobstant tout règlement contraire. Il ne sera pas exigé que ce passeport ait été renouvellé ou révoqué, quelque nombre de voyages que le dit navire ait pu faire, à moins qu'il ne soit revenu chez lui dans l'espace d'une année.

Par rapport à la Cargaison, les preuves seront des Certificats contenant le détail de la Cargaison, le lieu d'où le Bâtiment est parti et celui où il va, de manière que les Marchandises deffendues et de contrebande puissent être distinguées par les certificats, lesquels certificats auront été faits par les Officiers de l'endroit d'où le Navire sera parti, dans la forme usitée dans le Pays; et si ces passeports, ou certificats, ou les uns et les autres ont été détruits par accident ou enlevés de force, leur défaut pourra être supplée par toutes les autres preuves de propriété admissibles d'après l'usage général des Nations.

Pour les Bâtiments autres que les Navires marchands, les preuves seront la Commission dont ils sont porteurs.

colours, arms, and ensigns of the (French Republic or the United States) during his voyage. In witness whereof we have signed these presents, and put the seal of our arms thereunto, and caused the same to be countersigned by .... at .... the .... day of .... A. D. ....

And this Passport will be sufficient without any other paper, any ordinance to the contrary notwithstanding: which Passport shall not be deemed requisite to have been renewed, or recalled, whatever number of voyages the said Ship may have made, unless she shall have returned home within the space of a year. Proof with respect to the cargo, shall be certificates containing the several particulars of the cargo, the place whence the Ship sailed, and whither she is bound, so that the forbidden, and contraband goods may be distinguished by the Certificates: which certificates shall have been made out by the Officers of the place, whence the ship set sail, in the accustomed form of the country. And if such passport or certificates, or both, shall have been destroyed by accident or taken away by force, their deficiency may be supplied by such other proofs of ownership as are admissible by the general usage of nations. Proof with respect to other than Merchant ships, shall be the commission they bear.

Cet article aura son effet à dater de la signature de la présente Convention, et si, à dater de la dite signature, des propriétés sont condamnées contrairement à l'esprit de la dite Convention avant qu'on ait connaissance de cette stipulation, la propriété ainsi condamnée sera, sans délai, rendue ou payée.

This article shall take effect from the date of the signature of the present Convention. And if from the date of the said signature, any property shall be condemned contrary to the intent of the said Convention before the knowledge of this stipulation shall be obtained, the property so condemned shall without delay be restored or paid for.

ART. 5.

Les Dettes contractées par l'une des deux Nations envers les particuliers de l'autre, ou par des particuliers de l'une envers des particuliers de l'autre, seront acquittées ou le payement en sera poursuivi comme s'il n'y avait eu aucune mésintelligence entre les deux Etats. Mais cette clause ne s'étendra point aux indemnités réclamées pour des Captures ou pour des Condamnations;

ARTICLE V

The debts contracted by one of the two nations, with individuals of the other, or by the individuals of one, with the individuals of the other shall be paid, or the payment may be prosecuted in the same manner, as if there had been no misunderstanding between the two States. But this clause shall not extend to indemnities claimed on account of captures, or confiscations.

ART. 6.

Le Commerce entre les deux parties sera libre: Les Vaisseaux des deux Nations et leurs Corsaires, ainsi que leurs prises, seront traités dans les Ports respectifs comme ceux de la Nation la plus favorisée; et, en général, les deux parties jouiront dans les Ports l'une de l'autre, par rapport au Commerce et à la navigation, des Priviléges de la Nation la plus favorisée

ARTICLE VI.

Commerce between the Parties shall be free. The vessels of the two nations, and their Privateers, as well as their prizes, shall be treated in the respective ports, as those of the nation the most favoured; and in general the two parties shall enjoy in the ports of each other, in regard to commerce, and navigation, the priviledges of the most favoured nation.

ART. 7.

Les Citoyens et habitans des Etats-unis pourront disposer par

ARTICLE VII

The Citizens, and inhabitants of the United States shall be at

testament, donation ou autrement de leurs biens meubles et immeubles possédés dans le territoire Européen de la République française, et les Citoyens de la République française auront la même faculté à l'égard des biens, meubles et immeubles possédés dans le territoire des Etats-Unis, en faveur de telles personnes que bon leur semblera. Les Citoyens et habitans d'un des deux Etats qui seront héritiers des biens meubles ou immeubles situés dans l'autre, pourront succéder *ab intestat,* sans qu'ils ayent besoin de Lettres de naturalité, et sans que l'effet de cette stipulation leur puisse être contesté ou empêché, sous quelque prétexte que ce soit; et seront les dits héritiers, soit à tître particulier, soit *ab intestat,* exempts de tout droit quelconque chez les deux nations. Il est convenu que cet article ne dérogera en aucune manière aux loix qui sont à présent en vigeur chez les deux Nations ou qui pourraient être promulguées à la suite contre l'émigration; et aussi que dans le cas où les loix de l'un des deux Etats limiteraient pour les Etrangers l'exercice des droits de la propriété sur les immeubles, on pourrait vendre ces immeubles ou en disposer autrement en faveur d'habitans ou de citoyens du pays où ils seraient situés, et il sera libre à l'autre nation d'établir de semblables loix.

liberty to dispose by testament, donation, or otherwise, of their goods, moveable, and immoveable, holden in the territory of the French Republic in Europe, and the Citizens of the French Republic, shall have the same liberty with regard to goods, moveable, and immoveable, holden in the territory of the United States, in favor of such persons as they shall think proper. The Citizens and inhabitants of either of the two countries, who shall be heirs of goods, moveable, or immoveable in the other shall be able to succeed *ab intestato,* without being obliged to obtain letters of naturalization, and without having the effect of this provision contested or impeded under any pretext whatever: and the said heirs, whether such by particular title, or *ab intestato,* shall be exempt from every duty whatever in both countries. It is agreed that this article, shall in no manner derogate from the laws, which either State may now have in force, or hereafter may enact to prevent emigration: and also that in case the laws of either of the two States should restrain Strangers from the exercise of the rights of Property with respect to real estate, such real estate may be sold, or otherwise disposed of, to citizens, or inhabitants of the country where it may be, and the other nation shall be at liberty to enact similar laws.

ART. 8.

Pour favoriser de part et d'autre le Commerce, il est convenu que si, ce qu'à dieu ne plaise, la guerre éclatait entre les deux Nations, on allouera de part et d'autre aux Marchands et autres Citoyens ou habitans respectifs six mois après la déclaration de guerre, pendant lequel tems ils auront la faculté de se retirer avec leurs effets et meubles qu'ils pourront emmener, envoyer ou vendre comme ils le voudront sans le moindre empêchement. Leurs effets et encore moins leurs personnes ne pourront point pendant ce temps de six-mois, être saisis. Au contraire, on leur donnera des passeports qui seront valables pour le temps nécessaire à leur retour chez eux; et ces passeports seront donnés pour eux ainsi que pour leurs bâtiments et effets qu'ils desireront emmener ou renvoyer: ces passeports serviront de sauf-conduits contre toute insulte et contre toute capture de la part des Corsaires, tant contr'eux que contre leurs effets; et si dans le terme cidessus désigné, il leur était fait par l'une des parties, ses Citoyens ou ses habitans, quelque tort dans leurs personnes ou dans leurs effets, on leur en donnera satisfaction complète.

ARTICLE VIII

To favor commerce on both sides, it is agreed that in case a war should break out between the two nations, which God forbid, the term of six months after the declaration of . . . war, shall be allowed to the Merchants and other citizens and inhabitants respectively, on one side, and the other, during which time they shall be at liberty, to with draw themselves, with their effects, and moveables, which they shall be at liberty to carry, send away, or sell, as they please, without the least obstruction; nor shall their effects, much less their persons be seized during such term of six months; on the contrary Passports which shall be valid for a time necessary for their return, shall be given to them, for their vessels, and the effects which they shall be willing to send away, or carry with them; and such Passports shall be a safe conduct against all insults, and prizes, which Privateers may attempt against their persons and effects. And if any thing be taken from them, or any injury done to them, or their effects, by one of the parties, their citizens, or Inhabitants, within the term above prescribed, full satisfaction shall be made to them on that account

ART. 9.

Les Dettes dues par des individus de l'une des deux Nations

ARTICLE IX

Neither the debts due from individuals of the one nation, to

aux individus de l'autre ne pourront, dans aucuns cas de guerre ou de démélés nationaux, être sequestrées ou confisquées, non plus que les actions ou fonds qui se trouveraient dans les fonds publics ou dans des banques publiques ou particulières.

individuals of the other, nor shares, nor monies which they may have in . . . public funds, or in the public, or private banks, shall ever, in any event of war, or national difference be sequestered, or confiscated

Art. 10.

Les deux parties contractantes pourront nommer pour protéger le Négoce, des Agens commerciaux qui résideront en france et dans les Etats-Unis; chacune des parties pourra excepter telle place qu'elle jugera à propos, des lieux où la résidence de ces Agens pourra être fixée; avant qu'aucun agent puisse exercer ses fonctions, il devra être accepté dans les formes reçues, par la partie chez laquelle il est envoyé; et quand il aura été accepté et pourvu de son *exequatur*, il jouira des droits et prérogatives dont jouiront les Agens semblables des Nations les plus favorisées.

Article X

It shall be free for the two contracting parties to appoint commercial agents for the protection of trade, to reside in France, and the United States. Either party may except such place as may be thought proper, from the residence of these agents. Before any Agent shall exercise his functions, he shall be accepted in the usual forms, by the party to whom he is sent, and when he shall have been accepted and furnished with his exequatur, he shall enjoy the rights, and prerogatives of the similar Agents of the most favored nations.

Art. 11.

Les Citoyens de la République française ne payeront dans les ports, hâvres, rades, contrées, isles, cités et lieux des Etats-unis, d'autres ni de plus grands droits, impôts de quelque nature qu'ils puissent être, quelques noms qu'ils puissent avoir, que ceux que les Nations les plus favorisées sont ou seront tenues de payer; et ils jouiront de tous les droits, libertés, priviléges, immunités et exemptions en fait de négoce, navigation

Article XI

The Citizens of the French Republic shall pay in the ports, havens, roads, countries, islands cities, and towns of the United States, no other or greater duties, or imposts, of what nature soever they may be, or by what name soever called, than those, which the nations most favored are, or shall be obliged to pay, and they shall enjoy all the rights, liberties, priviledges, immunities, and exemptions, in trade, navigation

et commerce, soit en passant d'un port des dits Etats à un autre, soit en y allant ou en revenant de quelque partie ou pour quelque partie du monde que ce soit, dont les Nations susdites jouissent ou jouiront.

Et réciproquement, les Citoyens des Etats-unis jouiront dans le territoire de la République française en Europe, des mêmes priviléges, immunités, tant pour leurs biens et leurs personnes que pour ce qui concerne le Négoce, la Navigation et le Commerce.

and commerce, whether in passing from one port in the said States, to another, or in going to, and from the same, from, and to any part of the world, which the said nations do, or shall enjoy. And the Citizens of the United States shall reciprocally enjoy in the territories of the French Republic, in Europe, the same priviledges, and immunities, as well for their property, and persons, as for what concerns trade, Navigation, and Commerce.

ART. 12.

Les Citoyens des deux Nations pourront conduire leurs vaisseaux et marchandises (en exceptant toujours la Contrebande) de tout port quelconque dans un autre port appartenant à l'ennemi de l'autre nation. Ils pourront naviguer et commercer en toute liberté et sécurité avec leurs navires et marchandises dans les pays, ports et places des ennemis des deux parties, ou de l'une ou de l'autre partie, sans obstacles et sans entraves, et non seulement passer directement des places et ports de l'ennemi sus-mentionnés, dans les ports et places neutres; mais encore de toute place appartenant à un ennemi, dans toute autre place appartenant à un ennemi, qu'elle soit ou ne soit pas soumise à la même juridiction, à moins que ces places ou ports ne soyent réellement bloqués, assiégés ou investis.

ARTICLE XII

It shall be lawful for the Citizens of either Country to sail with their ships and Merchandize (contraband goods always excepted) from any port whatever, to any port of the enemy of the other, and to sail, and trade with their ships, and Merchandize, with perfect security, and liberty, from the countries ports, and places, of those who are enemies of both, or of either party, without any opposition, or disturbance whatsoever, and to pass not only directly from the places and ports of the enemy aforementioned to neutral ports, and places, but also from one place belonging to an enemy, to another place belonging to an enemy, whether they be under the jurisdiction of the same power, or under several, unless such ports, or places shall be actually blockaded, beseiged, or invested.

Et dans le cas, comme il arrive souvent, où les vaisseaux feraient voile pour une place ou port appartenant à un ennemi, ignorant qu'ils sont bloqués, assiégés ou investis, il est convenu que tout navire qui se trouvera dans une pareille circonstance sera détourné de cette place ou port sans qu'on puisse le retenir ni confisquer aucune partie de sa Cargaison (à moins qu'elle ne soit de contrebande ou qu'il ne soit prouvé que le dit navire, après avoir été averti du blocus ou investissement, a voulu rentrer dans ce même port); mais il lui sera permis d'aller dans tout autre port ou place qu'il jugera convenable. Aucun Navire de l'une ou l'autre nation, entré dans un port ou place, avant qu'ils ayent été réellement bloqués assiégés ou investis par l'autre, ne pourra être empêché de sortir avec sa Cargaison; s'il s'y trouve lorsque la dite place sera rendue, le Navire et sa Cargaison ne pourront être confisqués mais seront remis aux propriétaires.

And whereas it frequently happens that Vessels sail for a port or place belonging to an enemy without knowing that the same is either beseiged, blockaded, or invested, it is agreed that every vessel so circumstanced may be turned away from such port, or place, but she shall not be detained, nor any part of her cargo if not contraband be confiscated, unless after notice of such blockade or investment, she shall again attempt to enter: but she shall be permitted to go to any other port or place she shall think proper. Nor shall any vessel of either, that may have entered into such port, or place, before the same was actually beseiged, blockaded, or invested by the other, be restrained from quitting such place with her cargo, nor if found therein after the reduction and surrender of such place, shall such vessel or her cargo be liable to confiscation but they shall be restored to the Owners thereof.

ART. 13.

Pour règler ce qu'on entendra par Contrebande de guerre, seront compris sous cette dénomination la poudre, le salpêtre, les pétards, mèches, balles boulets, bombes, grenades, carcasses, piques, hallebardes, épées, ceinturons, pistolets, fourreaux, selles de Cavalerie, harnois, canons, mortiers avec leurs affuts, et généralement

ARTICLE XIII

In order to regulate what shall be deemed contraband of war, there shall be comprised under that denomination, Gun-powder, salt-petre Petards, match, ball, bombs, grenades, carcasses, Pikes, Halberds, swords, belts, Pistols, holsters, cavalry saddles, and furniture, Cannon, Mortars, their carriages, and beds, and generally

115605°—31—vol. 2——32

toutes armes et munitions de guerre et ustensiles à l'usage des troupes. Tous les articles ci dessus, toutes les fois qu'ils seront destinés pour le port d'un ennemi, sont déclarés de contrebande et justement soumis à la confiscation. Mais le batiment sur lequel ils étaient chargés, ainsi que le reste de la Cargaison, seront regardés comme libres et ne pourront en aucune manière être viciés par les Marchandises de Contrebande, soit qu'ils appartiennent à un même ou à différens propriétaires.

all kinds of arms, ammunition of war, and instruments fit for the use of Troops, all the above articles whenever they are destined to the port of an enemy, are hereby declared to be contraband, and just objects of confiscation: but the vessel in which they are laden, and the residue of the cargo shall be considered free, and not in any manner infected by the prohibited goods, whether belonging to the same or a different Owner.

ART. 14.

Il est stipulé par le present traité, que les Bâtiments libres assureront également la liberté des Marchandises, et qu'on jugera libre toutes les choses qui se trouveront à bord des Navires appartenant aux Citoyens d'une des parties contractantes, quand même le chargement ou partie d'icelui, appartiendraient aux ennemis de l'une des deux; bien entendu néanmoins que la contrebande sera toujours exceptée. Il est également convenu que cette même liberté s'étendra aux personnes qui pourraient se trouver à bord du bâtiment libre, quand même elles seraient ennemies de l'une des deux parties contractantes; et elles ne pourront être enlevées des dits navires libres à moins qu'elles ne soyent militaires et actueliement au Service de l'ennemi.

ARTICLE XIV.

It is hereby stipulated that free ships shall give a freedom to goods, and that every thing shall be deemed to be free, and exempt which shall be found on board the ships belonging to the citizens of either of the contracting parties, altho' the whole lading, or any part thereof should appertain to the enemies of either, contraband goods being always excepted. It is also agreed in like manner, that the same liberty be extended to persons, who are on board a free ship, with this effect, that altho' they be enemies to either party, they are not to be taken out of that free ship, unless they are soldiers and in actual service of the enemy.

ART. 15.

On est convenu, au contraire, que tout ce qui se trouvera chargé par les Citoyens respectifs sur des Navires appartenant aux ennemis de l'autre partie, ou à leurs sujets sera confisqué sans distinction des marchandises prohibées ou non prohibées, ainsi et de même que si elles appartenaient à l'ennemi; à l'exception toutefois des effets et marchandises qui auront été mis à bord desdits navires avant la déclaration de guerre, ou même après la dite déclaration, si au moment du chargement on a pu l'ignorer; de manière que les marchandises des Citoyens des deux parties, soit qu'elles se trouvent du nombre de celles de contrebande ou autrement, lesquelles, comme il vient d'être dit, auront été mises à bord d'un vaisseau appartenant à l'ennemi avant la guerre ou même après ladite déclaration, lorsqu'on l'ignorait, ne seront en aucune manière sujettes à confiscation, mais seront fidèlement et de bonne foi rendues sans délai à leurs propriétaires qui les réclameront; bien entendu néanmoins qu'il ne soit pas permis de porter dans les ports ennemis les marchandises qui seront de contrebande. Les deux parties contractantes conviennent que le terme de deux mois passé, depuis la déclaration de guerre, leurs citoyens respectifs, de quelque partie du monde qu'ils viennent, ne pourront plus alléguer l'ignorance

ARTICLE XV.

On the contrary, it is agreed, that whatever shall be found to be laden by the citizens of either party on any ship, belonging to the enemies of the other, or their Citizens, shall be confiscated without distinction of goods, contraband, or not contraband, in the same manner, as if it belonged to the enemy, except such goods, and merchandizes as were put on board such ship before the declaration of war, or even after such declaration, if so be it were done, without knowledge of such declaration, so that the goods of the citizens of either party, whether they be of the nature of such as are prohibited, or otherwise, which as is aforesaid were put on board any ship belonging to an enemy, before the war, or after the declaration of the same, without the knowledge of it, shall no ways be liable to confiscation, but shall well, and truly be restored without delay to the Proprietors demanding the same; but so as that if the said Merchandizes be contraband it shall not be any ways lawful, to carry them afterwards to any ports belonging to the enemy. The two contracting parties agree, that the term of two months being passed after the declaration of war, their respective citizens, from whatever part of the world they come, shall not plead the ignorance mentioned in this Article.

dont il est question dans le présent article.

ART. 16.

Les Navires marchands appartenans à des Citoyens de l'une ou l'autre des deux parties contractantes, lorsqu'ils voudront passer dans le port de l'ennemi de l'une des deux parties, et que leur voyage, ainsi que les effets de leur Cargaison pourront donner de justes soupçons, les dits navires seront obligés d'exhiber, en pleine mer comme dans les ports, ou rades, non seulement leurs passeports; mais encore leurs certificats prouvant que ces effets ne sont point de la même espèce que ceux de contrebande spécifiés en l'article treize de la présente Convention.

ART. 17.

Et afin d'éviter des Captures sur des Soupçons frivoles, et de prévenir les dommages qui en résultent, il est convenu que quand une des deux parties sera en guerre et l'autre neutre, les Navires de la partie neutre seront pourvus des passeports semblables à ceux spécifiés dans l'article quatre; de manière qu'il puisse par là apparaître que les navires appartiennent véritablement à la partie neutre. Ces passeports seront valides pour un nombre quelconque de voyages, mais il seront renouvellés chaque année, si le navire retourne chez lui dans l'espace d'une année.

ARTICLE XVI.

The Merchant ships belonging to the citizens of either of the contracting parties, which shall be bound to a port of the enemy of one of the parties, and concerning whose voyage, and the articles of their cargo, there shall be just grounds of suspicion, shall be obliged to exhibit, as well upon the high seas, as in the ports or roads, not only their passports, but likewise their certificates, shewing that their goods are not of the quality of those which are specified to be contraband in the 13th Article of the present Convention.

ARTICLE XVII

And that captures on light suspicions may be avoided, and injuries thence arising be prevented, it is agreed, that when one party shall be engaged in war and the other party be neuter, the ships of the neutral party shall be furnished with passports similar to that described in the fourth Article, that it may appear thereby that the ships really belong to the citizens of the neutral party: they shall be valid for any number of Voyages, but shall be renewed every year, that is if the ship happens to return homein the space of a year. If the ships are laden they shall be provided not

Si ces Navires sont chargés, ils seront pourvus, non seulement des passeports sus-mentionnés, mais aussi de certificats semblables à ceux mentionnés au même article, de manière que l'on puisse connaître s'il y a à bord des marchandises de contrebande. Il ne sera exigé aucune autre pièce, non obstant tout usage et règlement contraires; et s'il n'apparait pas par ces certificats qu'il y ait des marchandises de contrebande à bord, les navires seront laissés à leur destination. Si au contraire il apparait, par ces certificats, que les dit navires ayent des Marchandises de contrebande à bord et que le Commandant offre de les délivrer, l'offre sera acceptée et le Navire sera rèmis en liberté de poursuivre son voyage; à moins que la quantité des marchandises de contrebande ne soit trop grande pour pouvoir être prise convenablement à bord du vaisseau de guerre ou Corsaire; dans ce cas le navire pourra être amené dans le port pour y délivrer ladite marchandise.

Si un Navire est trouvé sans avoir le passeport ou les Certificats cidessus exigés, l'affaire sera examinée par les juges ou tribunaux compétens et s'il conste par d'autres documens ou preuves admissibles par l'usage des Nations, que le Navire appartient à des Citoyens de la partie neutre, il ne sera pas condamné et il sera remis en liberté avec son charge-

only with the passports above mentioned, but also with certificates similar to those described in the same article, so that it may be known whether they carry any contraband goods. No other paper shall be required, any usage or ordinance to the contrary notwithstanding. And if it shall not appear from the said certificates that there are contraband goods on board, the ships shall be permitted to proceed on their voyage. If it shall appear from the certificates that there are contraband goods on board any such ship, and the commander of the same shall offer to deliver them up, the offer shall be accepted, and the ship shall be at liberty to pursue it's voyage; unless the quantity of the contraband goods be greater than can conveniently be received on board the ship of war, or privateer, in which case the ship may be carried into port for the delivery of the same. If any ship shall not be furnished with such passport, or certificates, as are above required for the same, such case may be examined by a proper judge, or tribunal, and if it shall appear from other documents, or proofs, admissible by the usage of nations, that the ship belongs to the citizens of the neutral party it shall not be confiscated, but shall be released with her cargo (contraband goods excepted) and be permitted to proceed on her voyage.

ment, la Contrebande exceptée, et aura la liberté de poursuivre sa route.

Si le Capitaine nommé dans le passeport du Navire venait à mourir ou a être ôté par toute autre cause et qu'un autre fût nommé à sa place, le Navire et Sa Cargaison n'en seront pas moins en Sûreté et le passeport demeurera dans toute sa force.

If the Master of a Ship named in the passport should happen to die, or be removed by any other cause, and another put in his place, the ship, and cargo shall nevertheless be equally secure, and the passport remain in full force.

Art. 18.

Si les Bâtiments des Citoyens de l'une ou l'autre nation sont rencontrés le long des Côtes ou en pleine mer, par quelque vaisseau de guerre, ou Corsaire de l'autre; pour prévenir tout désordre, lesdits vaisseaux ou Corsaires, se tiendront hors de la portée du Canon, et enverront leur canot à bord du navire marchand qu'ils auront rencontré: ils n'y pourront entrer qu'au nombre de deux ou trois hommes et demander au patron ou capitaine du dit navire, exhibition du passeport concernant la propriété dudit navire, fait d'après la formule prescrite dans l'article quatre ainsi que les certificats sus-mentionnés relatifs à la Cargaison. Il est expressement convenu que le neutre ne pourra être contraint d'aller à bord du Vaisseau visitant pour y faire l'exhibition demandée des papiers, ou pour toute autre information quelconque.

Article XVIII

If the ships of the citizens of either of the parties, shall be met with, either sailing along the coasts or on the high seas, by any ship of war, or privateer of the other; for the avoiding of any disorder, the said ships of war, or privateers shall remain out of Canon-shot, and may send their boats on board the Merchant ship, which they shall so meet with, and may enter her to the number of two, or three men only, to whom the Master or commander of such ship, shall exhibit his passport concerning the property of the ship made out according to the form prescribed in the fourth Article. And it is expressly agreed that the neutral party shall in no case be required to go on board the examining vessel for the purpose of exhibiting his papers, or for any other examination whatever.

ART. 19.

Il est expressément convenu par les parties contractantes, que les Stipulations ci dessus relatives à la conduite qui sera tenue à la mer par les Croiseurs de la partie belligérante envers les Bâtiments de la partie neutre, ne s'appliqueront qu'aux bâtiments naviguans sans convoi: et dans le cas où les dits bâtiments seraient convoyés, l'intention des parties étant d'observer tous les égards dûs à la protection du pavillon arboré sur les vaisseaux publics, on ne pourra point en faire la visite; mais la déclaration verbale du Commandant de l'escorte, que les navires de son Convoi appartiennent à la Nation dont ils porte le pavillon, et qu'ils n'ont aucune contrebande à bord, sera regardée par les Croiseurs respectifs comme pleinement Suffisante; les deux parties s'engageant réciproquement à ne point admettre sous la protection de leurs convois des bâtiments qui porteraient des marchandises prohibées à une destination ennemie.

ARTICLE XIX

It is expressly agreed by the contracting parties, that the stipulations above mentioned, relative to the conduct to be observed on the sea by the cruizers of the belligerent party, towards the ships of the neutral party, shall be applied only to ships sailing without convoy; and when the said ships shall be convoyed, it being the intention of the parties to observe all the regard due to the protection of the Flag displayed by public ships, it shall not be lawful to visit them: but the verbal declaration of the commander of the convoy, that the ships he convoys belong to the nation whose flag he carries, and that they have no contraband goods on board shall be considered by the respective cruizers as fully sufficient: the two parties reciprocally engaging not to admit under the protection of their convoys, ships which shall carry contraband goods destined to an enemy.

ART. 20.

Dans le cas où les bâtiments seront pris ou arrêtés sous prétexte de porter à l'ennemi quelqu'article de Contrebande, le *Capteur* donnera un reçu des papiers du bâtiment qu'il retiendra; lequel reçu sera joint à une liste énonciative desdits papiers. Il ne sera point permis de forcer ni d'ouvrir

ARTICLE XX.

In all cases where vessels shall be captured, or detained, under pretence of carrying to the enemy contraband goods, the Captor shall give a receipt for such of the papers of the Vessel as he shall retain, which receipt shall be annexed to a descriptive list of the said papers: and it shall be un-

les écoutilles, coffres, caisses, caissons balles ou vases trouvés à bord du dit navire, ni d'enlever la moindre chose des effets, avant que la Cargaison ait été débarquée en présence des Officiers compétens qui feront un inventaire desdits effets: ils ne pourront, en aucune manière être vendus, échangés ou aliénés, à moins qu'après une procédure légale, le juge ou les juges compétens, n'ayent porté contre les dits effets sentence de confiscation (en exceptant toujours le Navire et les autres objets qu'il contient).

lawful to break up, or open the hatches, chests, trunks, casks, bales, or vessels found on board, or remove the smallest part of the goods, unless the lading be brought on shore, in presence of the competent officers, and an inventory be made by them of the said goods. Nor shall it be lawful to sell, exchange or alienate the same, in any manner, unless there shall have been lawful process, and the competent judge or judges shall have pronounced against such goods sentence of confiscation, saving always the ship and the other goods which it contains.

Art. 21.

Pour que le bâtiment et la Cargaison soyent surveillés avec soin, et pour empêcher les dégâts, il est arrêté que le Patron, Capitaine ou Subrécargue du Navire *capturé*, ne pourront être éloignés du bord, soit pendant que le navire sera en mer après avoir été pris, soit pendant la procédure qui pourra avoir lieu[1] contre lui, sa Cargaison, ou quelque chose y relative.

Dans le Cas où le Navire appartenant à des Citoyens de l'une ou l'autre partie, serait pris saisi et retenu pour être jugé, ses officiers, passagers et équipage seront traités avec humanité.

Article XXI.

And that proper care may be taken of the vessel and cargo, and embezzlement prevented, it is agreed that it shall not be lawful to remove the master or commander or Supercargo of any captured ship, from on board thereof, either during the time the ship may be at sea, after her capture, or pending the proceedings against her, or her cargo, or any thing relative thereto. And in all cases where a vessel of the citizens of either party shall be captured, or seized, and held for adjudication, her officers, passengers, and crew shall be hospitably treated. They shall not be im-

[1] The words "qui pourra avoir lieu" are written in the margin of the original, with an asterisk indicating their position in the text; they are followed by "aprouvé—les envois" and the initials of each of the six plenipotentiaries who signed.

Ils ne pourront être emprisonnés, dépouillés de leurs vêtemens, ni de l'argent à leur usage, qui ne pourra excéder pour le Capitaine, le Subrécargue, et le Second cinq cens dollars chacun et pour les matelots et passagers cent dollars chacun.

ART. 22.

Il est de plus convenu que dans tous les cas les tribunaux établis pour les causes de prises dans les pays où les prises seront conduites pourront seuls en prendre connaissance, et quelque jugement que le tribunal de l'une ou de l'autre partie prononce contre quelque navire, ou marchandises ou propriétés réclamées par des Citoyens de l'autre partie, la sentence ou décret fera mention des raisons, ou motifs qui ont déterminé ce jugement, dont copie authentique, ainsi que de toute la procédure y relative, sera, à leur réquisition, délivrée sans délai au Capitaine ou agent du dit Navire moyennant le payement des frais.

ART. 23.

Et afin de pourvoir plus efficacement à la Sureté respective des Citoyens des deux parties contractantes, et prévenir les torts qu'ils auraient à craindre des Vaisseaux de guerre ou Corsaires de l'une ou de l'autre partie, tous Commandans des Vaisseaux de guerre et des corsaires et tous

prisoned, nor deprived of any part of their wearing apparel, nor of the possession, and use of their money, not exceeding for the captain super cargo, and mate five hundred dollars each and for the Sailors and Passengers, one hundred dollars each.

ARTICLE XXII.

It is further agreed that in all cases, the established courts for Prize Causes, in the Country to which the prizes may be conducted, shall alone take cognizance of them. And when ever such tribunal of either of the parties, shall pronounce judgement against any vessel, or goods, or property, claimed by the citizens of the other party, the sentence or decree shall mention the reasons, or motives on which the same shall have been founded, and an authenticated copy of the sentence or decree and of all the proceedings in the case shall if demanded be delivered to the commander, or agent of the said vessel without any delay, he paying the legal fees for the same.

ARTICLE XXIII

And that more abundant care may be taken for the security of the respective citizens of the contracting parties, and to prevent their suffering injuries by the men of war, or privateers of either party, all commanders of ships of war, and privateers, and all others of the said citizens shall forbear

autres citoyens de l'une des deux parties s'abstiendront de tout dommage envers les citoyens de l'autre et de toute insulte envers leurs personnes. S'ils faisaient le contraire ils seront punis et tenus à donner dans leurs personnes et propriétés satisfaction et réparation pour les dommages avec intérêts, de quelqu'espèce que soyent les dits dommages.

A cet effet, tous Capitaines de Corsaires avant de recevoir leurs Commissions, s'obligeront devant un juge compétent, à donner une garantie au moins par deux Cautions responsables, lesquelles n'auront aucun intérêt sur le dit Corsaire, et dont chacune ainsi que le Capitaine s'engagera particulièrement et solidairement pour la Somme de Sept mille Dollars ou trente six mille huit cent vingt francs et si les dits vaisseaux portent plus de Cent cinquante matelots ou Soldats, pour la Somme de quatorze mille dollars ou Soixante treize mille six cent quarante francs qui serviront à réparer les torts, ou dommages que les dits Corsaires, leurs officiers, équipages, ou quelqu'un d'eux auraient faits ou commis, pendant leur *croisière* de contraire aux dispositions de la présente Convention ou aux loix et instructions qui devront être la règle de leur conduite: En outre les dites Commissions seront révoquées et annullées dans tous les cas où il y aura en aggression.

doing any damage to those of the other party, or committing any outrage against them, and if they act to the contrary, they shall be punished, and shall also be bound in their persons, and estates, to make satisfaction and reparation for all damages and the interest thereof, of whatever nature the said damages may be.

For this cause all commanders of Privateers before they receive their commissions shall hereafter be obliged to give, before a competent judge, sufficient security, by at least two responsible sureties who have no interest in the said Privateer, each of whom together with the said commander, shall be jointly, and severally bound in the sum of seven thousand dollars or Thirty Six Thousand eight hundred and twenty Francs, or if such ships be provided with above one hundred and fifty seamen or soldiers in the sum of Fourteen thousand dollars or Seventy three Thousand six hundred and forty francs, to satisfy all damages, and injuries, which the said privateer, or her officers, or men, or any of them may do or commit, during their cruize contrary to the tenor of this convention or to the laws, and instructions for regulating their conduct; and further, that in all cases of aggressions, the said commissions shall be revoked, and annulled.

Art. 24.

Lorsque les Vaisseaux de guerre des deux parties contractantes ou ceux que leurs Citoyens auraient armés en guerre, seront admis à relâcher avec leurs prises dans les ports de l'une des deux parties, lesdits Vaisseaux publics ou particuliers, de même que leurs prises, ne seront obligés à payer aucuns droits, soit aux officiers du lieu, soit aux juges ou à tous autres; lesdites prises entrant dans les hâvres ou ports de l'une des deux parties, ne pourront être arrêtées ou saisies, et les officiers des lieux ne pourront prendre connaissance de la validité desdites prises, lesquelles pourront sortir et être conduites en toute franchise et liberté aux lieux portés par les Commissions dont les Capitaines desdits Vaisseaux seront obligés de faire apparoir. Il est toujours entendu que les Stipulations de cet article ne s'étendront pas au delà des priviléges des Nations les plus favorisées.

Article XXIV.

When the ships of war of the two contracting parties, or those belonging to their citizens, which are armed in war, shall be admitted to enter with their prizes the ports of either of the two parties, the said public or private ships, as well as their prizes, shall not be obliged to pay any duty either to the officers of the place, the judges or any others: Nor shall such prizes, when they come to, and enter the ports of either party, be arrested or seized, nor shall the Officers of the place, make examination concerning the lawfulness of such prizes; but they may hoist sail at any time, and depart, and carry their prizes, to the places expressed in their commissions, which the commanders of such ships of war shall be obliged to shew. It is always understood that the stipulations of this article shall not extend beyond the priviledges of the most favored nation.

Art. 25.

Tous Corsaires étrangers ayant des Commissions d'un Etat ou prince en guerre avec l'une ou l'autre Nation, ne pourront armer leurs Vaisseaux dans les ports de l'une ou l'autre nation, non plus qu'y vendre leurs prises, ni les échanger en aucune manière: il ne leur sera permis d'acheter de provisions que la quantité néces-

Article XXV.

It shall not be lawful for any foreign Privateers who have commissions from any Prince, or State, in enmity with either nation, to fit their ships in the ports of either nation, to sell their prizes, or in any manner to exchange them; neither shall they be allowed to purchase provisions, except such as shall be necessary

saire pour gagner le port le plus voisin de l'Etat ou prince duquel ils ont reçu leurs Commissions.

for their going to the next port of that Prince, or State, from which they have received their commissions.

Art. 26.

Il est de plus convenu qu'aucune des deux parties contractantes non seulement ne recevra point de pirates dans ses ports, rades ou villes, et ne permettra pas qu'aucun de ses habitans les reçoive, protége, accueille ou recèle en aucune manière; mais encore livrera à un juste châtiment ceux de ses habitans qui seraient coupables de pareils faits ou délits. Les Vaisseaux de ces pirates, ainsi que les effets et Marchandises par eux pris et amenés dans les ports de l'une ou l'autre nation, seront saisis partout où ils seront découverts, et restitués à leurs propriétaires ou aux agens ou facteurs duement autorisés par eux, après, toutefois, qu'ils auront prouvé, devant les juges compétens, le droit de propriété.

Que si les dits effets avaient passé, par vente, en d'autres mains, et que les acquéreurs fussent ou pussent être instruits ou soupçonnaient que les dits effets avaient été enlevés par des pirates, ils seront également restitués.

Article XXVI.

It is further agreed that both the said contracting parties, shall not only refuse to receive any pirates into any of their ports havens, or towns, or permit any of their inhabitants to receive, protect, harbour, conceal, or assist them in any manner, but will bring to condign punishment, all such inhabitants, as shall be guilty of such acts, or Offences.

And all their ships, with the goods, or merchandizes taken by them, and brought into the port of either of the said parties, shall be seized as far as they can be discovered, and shall be restored to the owners, or their Factors, or agents, duly authorised by them, (proper evidence being first given before competent judges for proving the property) even in case such effects should have passed into other hands by sale, if it be proved, that the Buyers knew, or had good reason to beleive, or suspect, that they had been piratically taken.

Art. 27.

Aucune des deux Nations ne viendra participer aux Pêcheries de l'autre, sur ses Côtes, ni la troubler dans l'exercice des droits

Article XXVII.

Neither party will intermeddle in the Fisheries of the other on it's coast nor disturb the other in the exercise of the rights, which

qu'elle a maintenant ou pourrait acquérir sur les côtes de Terre-Neuve, dans le Golfe de St Laurent ou partout ailleurs, sur les Côtes d'amérique au Nord des Etats-Unis: mais la pêche de la baleine et du Veau Marin sera libre pour les deux nations dans toutes les parties du Monde.

Cette Convention sera ratifiée de part et d'autre en bonne et due forme, et les ratifications seront échangées dans l'espace de Six mois ou plutôt s'il est possible.

En foi de quoi les Plénipotentiaires respectifs ont signé les Articles ci dessus, tant en langue française qu'en langue anglaise, et ils y ont apposé leur Sceau; déclarant néanmoins que la Signature en deux langues ne sera point citée comme exemple et ne préjudiciera à aucune des deux parties.

Fait à Paris, le huitième jour de Vendémiaire de l'an Neuf de la République française et le trentième jour de Septembre dix huit cent.

[Seal] JOSEPH BONAPARTE
[Seal] C. P. CLARET FLEURIEU
[Seal] ROEDERER
[Seal] OLIV. ELLSWORTH
[Seal] W. R. DAVIE.
[Seal] W. V. MURRAY.

it now holds or may acquire on the coast of Newfoundland, in the Gulph of Saint Lawrence or ellswhere on the American coast, northward of the United States. But the whale and seal Fisheries shall be free to both in every quarter of the world.

This Convention shall be ratified on both sides in due form, and the ratifications exchanged in the space of six months or sooner if possible.

In faith whereof the respective plenipotentiaries have signed the above articles both in the French and English languages, and they have thereto affixed their seals, declaring nevertheless that the signing in the two languages, shall not be brought into precedent nor in any way operate to the prejudice of either party.

Done at Paris the eighth day of Vendemiaire of the ninth year of the French Republic, the thirtieth day of September, Anno Domini Eighteen Hundred.

[Seal] JOSEPH BONAPARTE
[Seal] C. P. CLARET FLEURIEU
[Seal] ROEDERER
[Seal] OLIV. ELLSWORTH.
[Seal] W. R. DAVIE
[Seal] W. V. MURRAY.

[The United States Instrument of Ratification]

John Adams, President of the United States of America.
To all and singular, to whom these Presents shall come Greeting:

Whereas a certain Convention between the United States of America and the French Republic was concluded and signed be-

tween their Plenipotentiaries, The Honorable Oliver Ellsworth, William Richardson Davie and William Vans Murray Esquires, their Envoys Extraordinary and Ministers Plenipotentiary to the French Republic, and the Plenipotentiaries of the French Republic, the Citizens Joseph Bonaparte, Charles Pierre Claret Fleurieu, and Pierre Louis Roederer, at Paris, on the 30th day of September last past, which convention, is word for word, as follows to wit:

[Here follows the English text of the convention.]

And Whereas the Senate of the United States did by their resolution, on the 3d day of this present month of February (two thirds of the Senators then present concurring) consent to and advise the ratification of the said Convention; Provided the second article be expunged, and that the following article be added or inserted: "It is agreed that the present Convention shall be in force for the term of eight years from the time of the exchange of the Ratifications" Now therefore, I John Adams, President of the United States of America, having seen and considered the convention and additional Article above recited, do, in pursuance of the aforesaid advice and consent of the Senate of the said United States, by these presents accept, ratify and confirm the said Convention and additional Article and every clause and article thereof, as the same are herein before set forth, saving and excepting the second Article of the said Convention, which I hereby declare to be expunged and of no force or validity: and I do moreover hereby declare, that the said Convention (saving the second article as aforesaid) and the said additional Article form together one instrument and are a Convention between the United States of America and the French Republic, made by the President of the United States, by and with the advice and consent of the Senate thereof.

In Testimony whereof I have caused the seal of the United States of America to be hereto affixed.

(L. S.) Given under my hand at the City of Washington this 18th day of February in the year of our Lord one thousand eight hundred and one, and of the Independence of the said States the Twenty fifth.

Signed, JOHN ADAMS

By the President

Signed JOHN MARSHALL

Acting as Secretary of State

[The French Instrument of Ratification]

Bonaparte, Premier Consul, au nom du Peuple Français, les Consuls de la République ayant vu et examiné la Convention conclue, arrêtée et signée à Paris le Huit Vendémiaire an neuf de la République Française (Trente Septembre Mil huit cent), par les Citoyens Joseph Bonaparte, Fleurieu et Roederer, Conseillers d'Etat, en vertu des pleins-pouvoirs qui leur avaient été conférés à cet effet, avec Messieurs Ellsworth, Davie et Murray, Ministres Plénipotentiaires des Etats-unis, également munis de pleins-pouvoirs, de laquelle Convention la teneur suit:

[Translation]

Bonaparte, First Consul, in the name of the French people—the Consuls of the Republic having seen and examined the convention concluded, agreed to, and signed at Paris the 8th Vendémiaire, 9th year of the French Republic (30th September, 1800), by the Citizens Joseph Bonaparte, Fleurieu, and Roederer, Counsellors of State, in virtue of the full powers which have been given to them to this effect, with Messieurs Ellsworth, Davie, and Murray, Ministers Plenipotentiary of the United States, equally furnished with full powers, the tenor of which convention follows:

[Here follows the French text of the convention.]

Approuve la Convention ci-dessus en tous et chacun des articles qui y sont contenus; déclare qu'elle est acceptée, ratifiée et confirmée et promet qu'elle sera inviolablement observée.

Le Gouvernement des Etats-unis ayant ajouté dans sa Ratification que la Convention sera en vigueur l'espace de huit années, et ayant omis l'article second, le Gouvernement de la République française consent à accepter, ratifier et confirmer la Convention ci-dessus, avec l'addition portant que la Convention sera en vigueur pendant l'espace de huit années, et avec le retranchement de

Approves the above convention in all and each of the articles which are therein contained; declares that it is accepted, ratified, and confirmed; and promises that it shall be inviolably observed.

The Government of the United States having added in its ratification that the convention should be in force for the space of eight years and having omitted the second article, the Government of the French Republic consents to accept, ratify, and confirm the above convention with the addition importing that the convention shall be in force for the space of eight years and with the re-

l'article second: bien entendu que par ce retranchement les deux Etats renoncent aux prétentions respectives qui sont l'objet du dit article.

En foi de quoi sont données les présentes, signées, contresignées, et scellées du grand Sceau de la République.

A Paris le douze Thermidor an neuf de la République (trente un Juillet Mil Huit cent un).

BONAPARTE

Le Ministre des Relations Extérieures,
CH. MAU. TALLEYRAND.

Par le Premier Consul:
Le Secrétaire d'Etat
HUGUES B MARET

trenchment of the second article: *Provided*, that by this retrenchment the two states renounce the respective pretentions which are the object of the said article.

In faith whereof these presents are given, signed, countersigned, and sealed with the Great Seal of the Republic.

At Paris the 12th Thermidor, 9th year of the Republic (31st July, 1801).

BONAPARTE

The Minister of Exterior Relations
CH. MAU. TALLEYRAND.

By the First Consul
The Secretary of State
HUGUES B MARET

NOTES

The treaty document here printed consists, first, of the treaty which was signed by the respective plenipotentiaries at Paris under date of September 30, 1800, and which was submitted to the Senate on December 16, 1800.

The resolution of the Senate of February 3, 1801 (Executive Journal, I, 377), was as follows:

Resolved, by the Senate of the United States, (two-thirds of the Senators present concurring therein,) That they do consent to, and advise the ratification of the convention between the French Republic and the United States of America, made at Paris, the eighth day of Vendemaire, of the ninth year of the French Republic; the thirtieth day of September, anno Domini, eighteen hundred: *Provided*, the second article be expunged, and that the following article be added or inserted:

It is agreed, that the present Convention shall be in force for the term of eight years, from the time of the exchange of the ratifications.

The ratification of the United States by John Adams fifteen days later followed strictly the Senate resolution. Its relevant language is here printed, as being part of the agreement, immediately after the signatures to the treaty.

The negotiations which resulted in Paris from the American proposal to expunge Article 2 of the treaty and to add an article limiting the term of the treaty to eight years, lasted for some two months and had, in point of form, a somewhat unusual conclusion.

The circumstances were quite out of the ordinary. Following the action of the Senate, Adams executed the instrument of ratification, though he was opposed to the Senate proviso. When James A. Bayard refused the appointment as Minister to France, after confirmation by the Senate, Adams left the whole matter to the new administration of Jefferson, who was to take office a few days later, on March 4, 1801 (Executive Journal, I, 388). While James Madison was nominated by Jefferson and confirmed as Secretary of State on March 5, he did not take over the duties of that office until May 2; in the meantime Levi Lincoln, Attorney General, acted as Secretary of State. Instructions regarding the exchange of ratifications were sent on March 18, 1801 (American State Papers, Foreign Relations, VI, 151); the letter of credence, a purely formal document, ran to "Oliver Ellsworth and William Vans Murray [Minister at The Hague] or either of them" (D. S., 1 Credences, 115); but Ellsworth had left Paris and Murray acted alone. His instructions were silent on the points of substance that were brought forward by the French negotiators. France raised no serious objection to so much of the Senate proviso as limited the term of the treaty to eight years; and while the fact that Murray had no proper full power was mentioned, it was not pressed; but the French flatly refused to consent to the unconditional suppression of Article 2 of the treaty, as the Senate had proposed, fearing that that would mean an agreement on their part that the earlier treaties with the United States (the Treaty of Amity and Commerce of February 6, 1778, Document 1; the Treaty of Alliance of the same date, Document 2; and the Consular Convention of November 14, 1788, Document 15) were at an end (as had been contended by the United States), but at the same time leaving the American claims against France under those treaties still existing. The French insisted that the claims in question should not be advanced in the future. Accordingly, after suggestions of other procedure, a clause was written into the French instrument of ratification to the effect that the "respective pretensions which are the object" of Article 2, were renounced on each side. Murray, without instructions on the point, assumed the responsibility and agreed to the exchange; he believed, rightly, that the matter should and would go again to the Senate. The view later expressed by Jefferson that he did not "regard the declaratory clause [the French proviso] as more than a legitimate inference from the rejection by the Senate of the 2[d] article" (D. S., 6 Instructions, U. S. Ministers, 13; American State Papers, Foreign Relations, VI, 155), was one which, in the absence of further Senate action, would certainly later have been disputed; but the years of differences between the two countries which had led up to the treaty, and the bearing of the final agreement on the French spoliation claims and their long history, are not for discussion here.

The despatches of Murray regarding the negotiations which preceded the exchange of ratifications are in D. S., 4 Despatches, Netherlands, and are printed in American State Papers, Foreign Relations, VI, 137–47.

In this state of the papers the ratifications were exchanged. The French proviso had introduced a new and, as it proved, a highly important clause into the agreement, and one which it is not possible to understand except in connection with the text of the treaty as a whole, including the "omitted" Article 2 (see the reference to that article in the preambles of Documents 28 and 30). The relevant clauses of the French instrument of ratification are printed above, as being part of the agreement, following the extracts from the United States instrument of ratification.

The period for the exchange of ratifications, pursuant to Article 27, was six months from the date of signature; the date of exchange was ten months later than the signature; but no point as to the delay was raised by either party. Reference was made to it in the instructions of March 18, 1801, above mentioned.

When the French ratification was received at Washington, the advice and consent of the Senate was again asked by Jefferson; his message of December 11, 1801 (Executive Journal, I, 397), follows:

> Early in the last month, I received the ratification, by the first Consul of France, of the convention between the United States and that nation. His ratification not being pure and simple, in the ordinary form, I have thought it my duty, in order to avoid all misconception, to ask a second advice and consent of the Senate, before I give it the last sanction, by proclaiming it to be a law of the land.

The Senate on December 19 passed this resolution:

> *Resolved,* That the Senate, (two-thirds of the members present concurring therein,) consider the convention between the United States and the French Republic as fully ratified;

and then, by a separate resolution, returned the convention to the President "for the usual promulgation" (*ibid.*, 398–99).

Accordingly, the whole agreement comprises not only the signed convention, but also the modifications resulting from the respective instruments of ratification, the relevant clauses whereof are printed above; and it may be noted that, strictly speaking, all the terms of the whole agreement are not written in the two languages; the modifications of the signed convention are in part in English and in part in French. The translation of the French ratification above printed is from the original proclamation of the treaty.

Note Regarding the Signed Treaty

The convention was, in fact, signed in two slightly different forms on two dates.

Shortly before the date of signature the French plenipotentiaries raised the question of language; they proposed that the agreement should be in the French language alone, without more, or else with a separate article to the effect that the use of French should not constitute a precedent or prejudice either party; their third suggestion was that the language of the attestation clauses of the treaties of 1778 (Documents 1 and 2) be used. To this last suggestion the United States representatives "with great reluctance" agreed (American

State Papers, Foreign Relations, II, 340–42); and the agreement, then called "provisional treaty," was so signed on September 30, 1800.

The subsequent procedure is set forth in the following extracts from the journal of Ellsworth, Davie, and Murray (*ibid.*, 342):

October 2.

The French ministers called this morning with the treaties, proposing some alterations, with regard to the style of the French republic, and that the word "provisional" should be stricken out in the name or description of the treaty. The American ministers availed themselves of this opportunity to resume their opposition to the admission in favor of the French language, and consented to the proposed alterations, respecting the style of the French Government, and offered to change the term "provisional treaty" for that of "convention," on the condition that that part of the treaty which respected the French language was stricken out, agreeing, at the same time, that a clause might be inserted, saving the right of both nations; to which the French ministers acceded without any further discussion.

October 3.

Six copies being now prepared, as agreed to be amended, they were signed and sealed under the former date of the 30th of September, (9 Vendemiaire;) two copies were retained by the French commissioners, two were left with Mr. Murray, and the other two were taken in charge by Mr. Ellsworth and Mr. Davie.

So the provisional treaty became a convention, and the attestation clause was changed to its present form; and the entry of October 3 clearly indicates that there were three original sets of the treaty executed, each set being composed of two documents, one the treaty in French and one in English; one of those three sets was delivered to Murray and another to Ellsworth and Davie.

There is no doubt that the provisions of the treaty were, in general, written first in French and then put into English. The two texts, however, might have been made more precise equivalents than they are; in Article 18, the French phrase "ainsi que les certificats sus-mentionnés relatifs à la Cargaison" (and also the above-mentioned certificates regarding the cargo) is entirely absent in the English.

There are indications in the original documents of the haste with which they were written at the last moment of the negotiations. Some points of form and the question as to whether or not there would be an English text, were open as late as September 29, 1800 (American State Papers, Foreign Relations, II, 341–42). In particular the English text is poorly written in the physical sense, as instanced by the meaningless dotted spaces in Articles 2, 8, and 9; and it is poorly written in the literary sense also.

Note Regarding the File

This treaty file contains the following three papers: first, the French instrument of ratification of July 31, 1801, which has written on the page following the signatures a certificate, in French, of the exchange of ratifications on the same date, signed by the three French plenipotentiaries and by William Vans Murray; second, the original proclamation of December 21, 1801, which includes the full text of the United States instrument of ratification of February 18,

1801; and third, a copy of the French text of the signed treaty, certified by the Chief of the Division of the Archives of the French Ministry of Foreign Affairs under date of January 8, 1887.

Also in the file are facsimiles from the French archives of the treaty as signed under date of September 30, 1800, in French and English.

Thus the file contains no signed original of the treaty, either in French or in English. The absence of the documents is not to be explained. No record has been found of the French and English texts which, as above mentioned, were delivered to Murray. Those in charge of Ellsworth and Davie appear to have been duly delivered with the report of October 4, 1800 (American State Papers, Foreign Relations, II, 342), sent to the Senate and duly returned (Executive Journal, I, 359, 383); that they again went to the Senate in December, 1801, seems probable but not quite certain (*ibid.*, 397–99). The absence from the file of any signed original of the treaty was noticed in 1886, resulting in a request for and the receipt of the certified copy of the French text above mentioned (see D. S., 21 Instructions, France, No. 178, and 99 Despatches, France, No. 341).

The text of the signed treaty printed here in the two languages has been collated with that in facsimile of the originals in the French archives; the text here printed of the United States instrument of ratification is from that recited in the original proclamation; and the text here printed of the French instrument of ratification is from the original in the file. That ratification includes the French text of the convention but not the English.

Note Regarding the Alternat

It has been noted that the French and English texts of the treaty were signed as separate papers. In the testimonium clause it is declared that "the signing in the two languages, shall not be brought into precedent nor in any way operate to the prejudice of either party." The French text is here printed at the left, in view of the discussion which led up to the final form of the text and also because the *alternat* was not observed; for the signatures of the French plenipotentiaries are at the left in each paper, the French Republic is named before the United States of America, and the First Consul before the President.

Note Regarding the Proclamation

In view of the unusual procedure in respect of the ratifications of the convention and their exchange, the essential clauses of the proclamation are printed, as follows:

By the President of the United States of America.

A Proclamation.

Whereas a Convention for terminating certain differences which had arisen between the United States of America and the French Republic was concluded and signed by the Plenipotentiaries of the two nations duly and respectively authorized for that purpose, and was duly ratified and confirmed by the President

of the United States with the advice and consent of the Senate, which Convention so ratified is in the form following:

[Here follows the text of the United States instrument of ratification, including the English text of the convention.]

And Whereas the said Convention was on the other part ratified and confirmed by the first Consul of France in the form of which the following is a translation from the French language to wit:

[Here follow extracts, in translation, from the French instrument of ratification.]

Which ratifications were duly exchanged at Paris on the 31st day of July in the present year, and having been so exchanged were again submitted to the Senate of the United States, who on the 19th day of the present month resolved that they considered the said Convention as fully ratified and returned the same to the President for the usual promulgation. Now therefore to the end that the said Convention may be observed and performed with good faith on the part of the United States, I have caused the premises to be made public, and I do hereby enjoin and require all persons bearing office, civil or military within the United States and all others, citizens or inhabitants thereof, or being within the same, faithfully to observe and fulfil the said Convention and every clause and article thereof.

In Testimony whereof, I have caused the Seal of the United States to be affixed to these Presents and signed the same with my hand.

[Seal] Done at the City of Washington the twenty first day of December in the year of our Lord one thousand eight hundred and one, and of the sovereignty and independence of the United States the twenty sixth

TH: JEFFERSON

By the President
JAMES MADISON
Secretary of State

It appears that the text of the convention as signed was published at Paris and at London in October, 1800 (American State Papers, Foreign Relations, II, 343).

In The Laws of the United States, Folwell ed., VI (printed in 1803), i–xlvii (following the table of contents), the proclamation, including the ratification on the part of the United States, and the French instrument of ratification, including the certificate of exchange, are printed. The same texts are in the Bioren & Duane edition, I, 114–34 (printed in 1815); and the print in 8 Statutes at Large, 178–96, is similar, except that it omits the opening recitals of each document.

Treaty Series, No. 108
8 Statutes at Large, 196–97

26

GREAT BRITAIN : JANUARY 8, 1802

Convention Regarding Articles 6 and 7 of the Jay Treaty (Document 16) and Article 4 of the Definitive Treaty of Peace (Document 11), signed at London January 8, 1802. Original in English.
Submitted to the Senate March 29, 1802. Resolution of advice and consent April 26, 1802. Ratified by the United States April 27, 1802. Ratified by Great Britain July 10, 1802. Ratifications exchanged at London July 15, 1802. Proclaimed April 27, 1802.

Difficulties having arisen in the Execution of the Sixth Article of the Treaty of Amity, Commerce and Navigation, concluded at London, on the Fourth Day of November, One Thousand Seven Hundred and Ninety Four, between His Britannic Majesty and the United States of America, and in consequence thereof, the Proceedings of the Commissioners under the Seventh Article of the same Treaty, having been suspended, the Parties to the said Treaty being equally desirous, as far as may be, to obviate such Difficulties, have respectively named Plenipotentiaries to treat and agree respecting the same, that is to say, His Britannic Majesty has named for His Plenipotentiary, The Right Honourable Robert Banks Jenkinson, commonly called Lord Hawkesbury, One of His Majesty's Most Honourable Privy Council, and His Principal Secretary of State for Foreign Affairs; and The President of the United States, by and with the Advice and Consent of the Senate thereof, has named for their Plenipotentiary, Rufus King Esquire, Minister Plenipotentiary of the said United States to His Britannic Majesty who have agreed to and concluded the following Articles:—

ARTICLE, I^st.

In Satisfaction and Discharge of the Money which the United States might have been liable to pay in Pursuance of the Provisions of the said Sixth Article, which is hereby declared to be cancelled and annulled, except so far as the same may relate to the Execution of the said Seventh Article; the United States of America hereby engage to pay, and His Britannic Majesty consents to accept for the Use of the Persons described in the said Sixth Article, the Sum of Six Hundred

Thousand Pounds Sterling, payable at the Times and Place, and in the Manner following, that is to say, the said Sum of Six Hundred Thousand Pounds Sterling shall be paid at the City of Washington, in three annual Instalments of Two Hundred Thousand Pounds Sterling each, and to such Person or Persons as shall be authorized by His Britannic Majesty to receive the same; the first of the said Instalments to be paid at the Expiration of One Year; the second Instalment at the Expiration of two Years; and the third and last Instalment at the Expiration of three Years next following the Exchange of the Ratifications of this Convention. And to prevent any Disagreement concerning the Rate of Exchanges the said Payments shall be made in the Money of the said United States, reckoning Four Dollars and Forty-Four Cents to be equal to one Pound Sterling.

ARTICLE, II^d.

Whereas it is agreed by the Fourth Article of the Definitive Treaty of Peace, concluded at Paris, on the Third Day of September, One Thousand Seven Hundred and Eighty Three, between His Britannic Majesty and the United States, that Creditors on either Side should meet with no lawful Impediment to the Recovery of the full Value in Sterling Money, of all bonâ Fide Debts theretofore contracted, it is hereby declared that the said fourth Article, so far as respects its future Operation, is hereby recognized, confirmed and declared to be binding and obligatory on His Britannic Majesty and the said United States, and the same shall be accordingly observed with punctuality and good Faith, and so as that the said Creditors shall hereafter meet with no lawful Impediment to the Recovery of the full Value in Sterling Money of their bonâ Fide Debts.

ARTICLE, III^d.

It is furthermore agreed and concluded that the Commissioners appointed in pursuance of the Seventh Article of the said Treaty of Amity, Commerce and Navigation, and whose Proceedings have been suspended as aforesaid, shall immediately after the Signature of this Convention, re-assemble and proceed in the Execution of their Duties according to the Provisions of the said seventh Article, except only that instead of the Sums awarded by the said Commissioners being made payable at the Time or Times by them appointed, all Sums of Money by them awarded to be paid to American or British Claimants, according to the Provisions of the said Seventh Article, shall be made payable in three equal Instalments, the first whereof, to be paid at

the Expiration of one Year; the second at the Expiration of two Years; and the third and last at the Expiration of three Years next after the Exchange of the Ratifications of this Convention.

ARTICLE, IVth.

This Convention, when the same shall have been ratified by His Majesty, and by the President of the United States, by and with the advice and consent of the Senate thereof, and the respective Ratifications duly exchanged, shall be binding and obligatory upon His Majesty and the said United States.

In Faith whereof, We the Undersigned Plenipotentiaries, of His Britannic Majesty, and of the United States of America, by virtue of Our respective Full Powers, have signed the present Convention, and have caused the Seals of Our Arms to be affixed thereto.

Done at London, the Eighth Day of January, One Thousand Eight Hundred and Two.

HAWKESBURY [SEAL]

RUFUS KING [SEAL]

NOTES

It appears that the convention was executed in quadruplicate. In his letter of January 9, 1802, enclosing the convention signed the previous day (American State Papers, Foreign Relations, II, 424), Rufus King wrote:

> Two copies of the convention have been executed; one of which will be enclosed with the original of this letter; two more copies are preparing, and will, in like manner, be executed as originals, and enclosed with the duplicate and triplicate hereof.

The Department of State file of this convention is very complete. It includes two examples of a document which appears to have been intended at once as a ratification and a proclamation, as the following phrase immediately precedes the testimonium clause and follows the words of ratification: "and I do moreover hereby declare the same to be a Convention between the United States of America and his Britannic Majesty made by the President of the United States, by and with the advice and consent of the Senate thereof"; each of those examples is signed by Jefferson and attested by Madison; they are identic except that one includes a signed original of the convention and the other a copy, and the former lacks the Great Seal. Also in the file are two originals of the British instrument of ratification and two certificates of the exchange of ratifications, executed by Lord Hawkesbury.

Copies of the convention were transmitted by the President to both Houses of Congress on the date of its ratification by the United

States (Richardson, I, 341–42), and thus prior to the ratification by Great Britain and the exchange; and an act appropriating $2,664,000 for carrying the convention into effect became law on May 3, 1802 (2 Statutes at Large, 192).

The file also contains a copy of the Senate resolution of April 26, 1802, attested by Sam. A. Otis, Secretary, as follows:

> The Senate took into consideration the convention made between the United States and the British government, referred to in the message of the President of the United States of 29th March last; and
>
> Resolved, that they do consent and advise to the ratification thereof.

As printed in Executive Journal, I, 422, the resolution reads thus:

> *Resolved*, (two-thirds of the Senators present concurring therein,) That the Senate do advise and consent to the ratification of the convention between the United States of America and his Britannic Majesty, concluded on the 8th day of January, 1802, at London.

Treaty Series, No. 326
8 Statutes at Large, 198-201

27

SPAIN : AUGUST 11, 1802

Convention for Indemnification, signed at Madrid August 11, 1802. Original in Spanish and English.

Submitted to the Senate January 11, 1803. Resolution of advice and consent January 9, 1804. Ratified by the United States January 9, 1804. Ratified by Spain July 9, 1818. Ratifications exchanged at Washington December 21, 1818. Proclaimed December 22, 1818.

Convencion entre Su Magestad Catolica y los Estados Unidos de America, sobre indemnizacion de perdidas, daños y perjuicios irrogados durante la ultima guerra en conseqüencia de los excesos cometidos por individuos de ambas Naciones contra el derecho de Gentes ó Tratado existente.

Deseando Su Magestad Catolica y el Gobierno de los Estados Unidos de America, ajustar amistosamente los demandas que han ocasionado los excesos cometidos durante la ultima guerra por individuos de una y otra Nacion contra el derecho de Gentes ó el Tratado[1] existente entre los dos Paises; ha dado Su Magestad Catolica plenos poderes á este efecto á Dn Pedro Cevallos, Su Consejero de Estado, Gentilhombre de Camara con exercicio, Primer Secretario de Estado y del Despacho Universal, Superintendente General de Correos y Postas en España é Indias; y el Gobier-

A Convention between His Catholic Majesty and the United States of America for the indemnification of those who have sustain'd Losses, Damages or Injuries in consequences of the excesses of Individuals of either Nation during the late war, contrary to the existing Treaty or the Laws of Nations.

His Catholic Majesty & the Government of the United States of America, wishing amicably to adjust the Claims which have arisen from the excesses committed during the late war, by Individuals of either Nation, contrary to the Laws of Nations or the Treaty[1] existing between the two Countries; His Catholic Majesty has given for this purpose full powers to His Excellency Dn Pedro Cevallos, Councellor of State, Gentleman of the Bed Chamber in employment, first Secretary of State & Universal Dispatch, & Superintendent General of the Posts & Postoffices

[1] Document 18.

no de los Estados Unidos de America, á Dn Carlos Pinckney, Ciudadano de dichos Estados, y Su Ministro Plenipotenciario cerca de Su Magestad Catolica, quienes han convenido en lo siguiente.

1º Se formará una junta compuesta de cinco Vocales, de los quales, dos serán nombrados por Su Magestad Catolica, otros dos por el Gobierno de los Estados Unidos, y el quinto de comun consentimiento; y en el caso de no poderse convenir en el sugeto para quinto Vocal, nombrará uno cada parte dexando la eleccion entre los dos á la suerte, y se procederá en la misma forma en adelante al nombramiento ulterior de los sugetos que reemplazaren á los que actualmente lo son en los casos de muerte, enfermedad, ó precisa ausencia.

2º Hecho asi el nombramiento prestará cada uno de los Vocales el juramento de examinar, discutir, y sentenciar las demandas sobre que jurgaren con arreglo al dr̃o de Gentes y Tratado existente, y con la imparcialidad que dicta la Justicia.

3º Residirán los Vocales y celebrarán la Juntas en Madrid, en donde en el prefixo termino de diez y ocho meses, contados desde el dia en qe se junten, admitirán todas las demandas qe á conseqüencia de esta Convencion hi-

in Spain & the Indies; and the Government of the United States of America, to Charles Pinckney, a Citizen of the said States, and their Minister Plenipotentiary near His Catholic Majesty, who have agreed as follows.

1st A Board of Commissioners shall be formed, composed of five Commissioners, two of whom shall be appointed by His Catholic Majesty, two others by the Government of the United States, & the fifth by common consent—and in case they should not be able to agree on a person for the fifth Commissioner, each party shall name one & leave the decision to lot—and hereafter, in case of the death, sickness or necessary absence of any of those already appointed, they shall proceed in the same manner, to the appointment of persons to replace them.

2d The appointment of the Commissioners being thus made, each one of them shall take an oath to examine, discuss & decide on the Claims, which they are to judge, according to the Laws of Nations & the existing Treaty, & with the impartiality justice may dictate.

3rd The Commissioners shall meet & hold their sessions in Madrid, where, within the term of eighteen months (to be reckoned from the day on which they may assemble) they shall receive all Claims which in consequence

cieren tanto los Vasallos de Su Magestad Catolica como los Ciudadanos de los Estados Unidos de America, que tuvieren derecho á reclamar perdidas, daños y perjuicios, en conseqüencia de los execesos cometidos por Españoles y Ciudadanos de dichos Estados durante la ultima guerra contra el drõ de Gentes y Tratado existente.

of this Convention may be made, as well by the Subjects of His Catholic Majesty as by Citizens of the United States of America—who may have a right to demand compensation for the losses, damages or injuries sustained by them, in consequence of the excesses committed by Spanish subjects or American Citizens.

4º Se autoriza por dichas partes contratantes á los Vocales para oir y examinar baxo la Sancion del Juramento qualesquiera puntos concernientes á las referidas demandas, y á recibir como digno de fé todo testimonio de cuya autenticidad no puede dudarse con fundamento.

4th The Commissioners are authorized by the said contracting parties, to hear & examine on oath, every question relative to the said demands, & to receive as worthy of Credit all testimony, the authenticity of which cannot reasonably be doubted.

5º Bastará el acuerdo de trés Vocales paraque sus sentencias tengan fuerza de irrevocables y sin apelacion, tanto por lo que respecta á la Justicia de las demandas, como por lo q^e hace á las cantidades q^e se adjudicaren p^r indemnizacion á los demandantes; pues se obligan las partes contratantes á satisfacerlas en especie, sin rebaxa, en las epocas y parages señalados, y baxo las condiciones q^e se expresaren en las sentencias de la Junta.

5th From the decisions of the Commissioners, there shall be no appeal, & the agreement of three of them shall give full force & effect to their decisions, as well with respect to the Justice of the Claims as to the amount of the indemnification which may be adjudged to the Claimants—the said contracting parties obliging themselves to satisfy the said awards in Specie without deduction, at the times & places pointed out, & under the conditions which may be expressed by the Board of Commissioners.

6º No haviendo sido posible ahora á d̃hos Plenipotenciarios convenirse en el modo de q^e la referida junta arvitrase las recla-

6th It not having been possible for the said Plenipotentiaries to agree upon a mode by which the above-mentioned Board of Com-

maciones originadas en conseqüencia de los excesos de los Corsarios, Agentes, Consules ó Tribunales Extrangeros en los respectivos territorios, q̃e fueren imputables á los dos Gobiernos; se han convenido expresamente en que cada Gobierno se reserve, como por esta Convencion se hace, para si, sus Vasallos y Ciudadanos respectivamente todos los dr̃os q̃e ahora les asistan, y en que promuevan en adelante sus reclamaciones en el tiempo q̃e les acomodare.

7º La presente Convencion no tendrá ningun valor ni efecto hasta que se haya ratificado por las partes contratantes, y se cangearán las ratificaciones lo mas pronto que sea posible.

En fé de loqual, Nosotros los Infrascriptos Plenipotenciarios, hemos firmado esta Convencion, y hemos puesto nuestros Sellos Respectivos.

Hecho en Madrid á 11 de Agosto, de 1802.

Pedro Cevallos [Seal]
Charles Pinckney [Seal]

missioners should arbitrate the Claims originating from the excesses of foreign Cruizers, Agents, Consuls, or Tribunals in their respective Territories, which might be imputable to their two governments, they have expressly agreed that each Government shall reserve, (as it does by this Convention) to itself, its Subjects or Citizens respectively, all the rights which they now have & under which they may hereafter bring forward their Claims at such times as may be most convenient to them.

7th The present Convention shall have no force or effect, until it be ratified by the contracting parties, & the ratifications shall be exchang'd as soon as possible. In faith whereof, We the Underwritten Plenipotentiaries have signed this Convention & have affixed thereto our Respective Seals.

Done at Madrid this 11 day of August 1802.

Pedro Cevallos [Seal]
Charles Pinckney [Seal]

NOTES

The original signed convention in the Department of State file is marked as received on November 24, 1802; it bears nine other endorsements which were obviously made when the document was in the Senate. When signed, the convention had six pages of writing, three Spanish and three English, with the Spanish on the left; but when, owing to its poor condition, it was restored, one of the sheets was turned around, so that as they are now tied together there are two pages of Spanish followed by two of English, then one of Spanish followed by one of English.

There is no duplicate of the United States instrument of ratification in the file. There is, however, a rough draft or copy of the essential clauses, which is dated January 9, 1804, the date of the Senate resolution, of which there are two attested copies, one written at the time and the other in 1818.

There is also in the file, obtained from the Spanish archives, a facsimile of another document, executed by President Monroe on December 21, 1818, attested by Secretary of State John Quincy Adams, and under the Great Seal; that document is perhaps unique in character; it is not strictly an instrument of ratification but rather one of confirmation, and it was doubtless written because of the fact that nearly fifteen years had elapsed since the ratification by President Jefferson; the opening recitals of that instrument are as follows:

> Whereas a Convention between the United States and Spain was agreed upon and concluded at Madrid on the eleventh day of August, in the year one thousand, eight hundred and two, by Charles Pinckney, at that time Minister Plenipotentiary of the United States, in Spain, and Don Pedro Cevallos, Councellor of State, Gentleman of the Bed Chamber in employment, first Secretary of State and Universal Dispatch, and Superintendent General of the Posts and Post offices in Spain and the Indies, being fully authorised and empowered by their respective Governments, and was duly ratified by the then President of the United States on the ninth day of January, in the year one thousand, eight hundred and four, by and with the advice and Consent of the Senate: and whereas the said Convention was ratified by the King of Spain on the ninth day of July last past, which Convention is, word for word, as follows, to wit;—

Then, after the text of the convention in Spanish and English, are these final clauses:

> Now therefore be it known, that I James Monroe, President of the United States, do promise to fulfil and observe the said Convention and to cause the same and every clause and article thereof to be fulfilled and faithfully observed on the part of the United States.
>
> In Testimony whereof I have hereunto set my Hand, and caused the Seal of the United States to be affixed.
>
> Done at Washington this 21st day of December in the year of our Lord one thousand eight hundred and eighteen; and of the Independence of the United States, the forty third.

The certificate of exchange of ratifications at Washington on December 21, 1818, is in two papers, one Spanish and one English, and was executed in triplicate.

The Spanish instrument of ratification of July 9, 1818, includes both texts, with the Spanish on the left.

The original proclamation has not been found; but it was published at the time (*e. g.*, the Daily National Intelligencer, Washington, December 24, 1818), was transmitted to Congress on January 4, 1819, and is printed in American State Papers, Foreign Relations, IV, 407–8; it includes both texts of the convention, with the Spanish on the left.

By the act of March 16, 1804 (2 Statutes at Large, 270), an appropriation was made for carrying into effect the convention, the act to be in force from the date of the exchange of the ratifications.

The differences between Spain and the United States to which was due the long delay in the ratification of the convention by Spain, can only be mentioned here; a summary statement of the relations of the two countries during the period is in Haswell, 1384–85; some of the documents are in American State Papers, Foreign Relations, II, 596–606, 613–70, and IV, 422–626. Indeed, while the negotiations which resulted in the treaty with Spain of 1819 (Document 41) were going on in Washington in the autumn of 1818, it was at one time proposed still further to postpone the exchange of ratifications of this convention until their conclusion (*ibid.*, IV, 525, 526, 546, 615); and by Article 10 of that treaty of February 22, 1819, this convention was annulled.

There are various references in this convention to the "existing treaty" with Spain, the treaty of October 27, 1795 (Document 18); but in Article 3 the English text omits the final words in the Spanish: "during the late war, contrary to the laws of nations and the existing treaty."

Treaty Series, No. 86
8 Statutes at Large, 200–7

28

FRANCE : APRIL 30, 1803

Treaty for the Cession of Louisiana, signed at Paris April 30, 1803. Original in English and French; but "originally agreed to in the French language" (see the attestation clause).

Submitted to the Senate October 17, 1803. Resolution of advice and consent October 20, 1803. Ratified by the United States October 21, 1803. Ratified by France May 22, 1803. Ratifications exchanged at Washington October 21, 1803. Proclaimed October 21, 1803.

Treaty between the United States of America and the French Republic

The President of the United States of America and the First Consul of the French Republic in the name of the French People desiring to remove all Source of misunderstanding relative to objects of discussion mentioned in the Second and fifth articles of the Convention [1] of the 8th Vendémiaire an 9/30 September 1800 relative to the rights claimed by the United States in virtue of the Treaty [2] concluded at Madrid the 27 of October 1795, between His Catholic Majesty, & the Said United States, & willing to Strenghten the union and friendship which at the time of the Said Convention was happily reestablished between the two nations have respectively named their Plenipotentiaries to wit The

Traité Entre les Etats-unis d'Amérique et la République Française.

Le Président des Etats unis d'amérique, Et le Premier Consul de la République française, au nom du peuple françaíse, désirant prevenir tout Sujet de més intelligence, rélativement aux objets de discussion mentionnés dans les articles 2 et 5. de la Convention [1] du 8 Vendemiaire an 9 / 30 7bre 1800. et rélativement aux droits réclamés pour les Etats unis en vertu du traité [2] conclu à Madrid le 27. Octobre 1793, Entre Sa Majesté catholique et lesdits Etats unis: et voulant fortifier de plus en plus les rapports d'union et d'amitié qui, à l'époque de la ditte convention, ont été heureusement rétablis entre les deux Etats, ont respectivement nommé pour Plénipotentiaires Savoir: Le président des Etats-unis d'Amérique, par et

[1] Document 25.
[2] The treaty of October 27, 1795, is Document 18.

President of the United States, by and with the advice and consent of the Senate of the Said States; Robert R. Livingston Minister Plenipotentiary of the United States and James Monroe Minister Plenipotentiary and Envoy extraordinary of the Said States near the Government of the French Republic; And the First Consul in the name of the French people, Citizen Francis Barbé Marbois Minister of the public treasury who after having respectively exchanged their full powers have agreed to the following Articles.

avec l'avis et le consentement du Senat desdits Etats, Robert R Livingston ministre plénipotentiaire des Etats unis, & James Monroé, ministre plénipotentiaire et envoyé extraordinaire desdits Etats auprès du Gouvernement de la République francaise; Et le Premier Consul au nom du peuple français, le Citoyen françois Barbémarbois Ministre du trésor public Lesquels après avoir fait l'échange de leurs pleins pouvoirs, sont convenus des articles suivans.

ARTICLE I

Whereas by the Article the third of the Treaty[1] concluded at St Idelfonso the 9th Vendémiaire an 9/1st October 1800 between the First Consul of the French Republic and his Catholic Majesty it was agreed as follows.

"His Catholic Majesty prom-"ises and engages on his part to "cede to the French Republic six "months after the full and entire "execution of the conditions and "Stipulations herein relative to "his Royal Highness the Duke of "Parma, the Colony or Province "of Louisiana with the Same ex-"tent that it now has in the hands "of Spain, & that it had when "France possessed it; and Such as "it Should be after the Treaties[1] "subsequntly entered into be-"tween Spain and other States".

ART. 1er.

Attendu que par l'article 3 du traité[1] conclu à St Ildephonse le 9 Vendemiaire an 9/1[r] Octobre 1800. entre le Premier Consul de la République française et Sa Majesté Catholique, il a été convenu ce qui Suit:

"Sa Majesté Catholique promit "et s'engage de son côté a rétro-"céder à la République française; "six mois après l'exécution pleine "et entière des conditions et Sti-"pulations ci dessus relatives à "Son Altesse royale le duc de "Parme, la Colonie ou province de "la Louisiane, avec la même "étendue qu'elle a actuellement "entre les mains de l'Espagne, et "qu'elle avoit lorsque la france la "possédoit, et telle qu'elle doit "être, d'après les traités[1] passés "subséquemment entre l'Espagne "et d'autres Etats"

[1] See the note regarding Article 1.

And whereas in pursuance of the Treaty and particularly of the third article the French Republic has an incontestible title to the domain and to the possession of the said Territory—The First Consul of the French Republic desiring to give to the United States a strong proof of his friendship doth hereby cede to the said United States in the name of the French Republic for ever and in full Sovereignty the said territory with all its rights and appurtenances as fully and in the Same manner as they have been acquired by the French Republic in virtue of the above mentioned Treaty concluded with his Catholic Majesty.

Et comme par suite dudit traité, et spécialement dudit article 3 la République française a un titre incontestable au domaine et à la possession dudit territoire, Le premier Consul de la République désirant de donner un témoignage remarquable de son amitié aux dits Etats unis, il leur fait au nom de la République française, cession, à toujours et en pleine soveraineté, dudit territoire, avec tous ses droits et appartenances, ainsi et de la manière qu'ils ont été acquis par la République française, en vertu du traité susdit, conclu avec Sa Majesté Catholique

ART: II

In the cession made by the preceding article are included the adjacent Islands belonging to Louisiana all public lots and Squares, vacant lands and all public buildings, fortifications, barracks and other edifices which are not private property.—The Archives, papers & documents relative to the domain and Sovereignty of Louisiana and its dependances will be left in the possession of the Commissaries of the United States, and copies will be afterwards given in due form to the Magistrates and Municipal officers of Such of the said papers and documents as may be necessary to them.

ART. 2

Dans la cession faite par l'article précédent, Sont Compris les Isles adjacentes, dépendantes de la Louisiane, Les emplacemens et places publiques, les terreins vacans, tous les batimens publics, fortifications casernes et autres édifices qui ne sont la propriété d'aucun individu. Les archives, papiers et documens, directement relatifs au domaine et à la soveraineté de la Louisiane et dépendances seront laissés en la possession des Commissaires des Etats unis, et il sera ensuite remis des expeditions en bonne forme aux Magistrats et administrateurs locaux, de ceux des dits papiers & documens qui leur seront nécessaires.

Art: III

The inhabitants of the ceded territory shall be incorporated in the Union of the United States and admitted as soon as possible according to the principles of the federal Constitution to the enjoyment of all the rights, advantages and immunities of citizens of the United States, and in the mean time they shall be maintained and protected in the free enjoyment of their liberty, property and the Religion which they profess.

Article 3

Les habitans des territoires cédés, seront incorporés dans l'union des états-unis, et admis aussitôt qu'il sera possible, d'après les principes de la constitution fédérale, à la jouissance de tous les droits, avantages et immunités des Citoyens des Etats-unis, et en attendant, ils seront maintenus & protégés dans la jouissance de leurs libertés, propriétés & dans l'exercice des religions qu'ils professent.

Art: IV

There Shall be Sent by the Government of France a Commissary to Louisiana to the end that he do every act necessary as well to receive from the Officers of his Catholic Majesty the Said country and its dependances in the name of the French Republic if it has not been already done as to transmit it in the name of the French Republic to the Commissary or agent of the United States.

Article 4.

Il sera envoyé de la part du Gouvernement français, un Commissaire à la Louisiane, à l'effet de faire tous les actes nécessaires, tant pour recevoir des officiers de sa Majesté Catholique, les dits païs, contrées & dépendances, au nom de la République française, si la chose n'est pas encore faite, que pour les transmettre audit nom, aux Commissaires ou agens des Etats-unis.

Art: V

Immediately after the ratification of the present Treaty by the President of the United States and in case that of the first Consul's shall have been previously obtained, the Commissary of the French Republic shall remit all military posts of New Orleans and other parts of the ceded territory to the Commissary or Commissaries named

Article 5

Immédiatement aprés la ratification du présent traité par le Président des Etat-unis, et dans le cas où celle du Premier Consul aurait eu préalablement lieu, le Commissaire de la République française remettra tous les postes militaires de la nouvelle Orléans et autres parties du territoire cédé, au Commissaire ou aux Commissaires nommés par le

by the President to take possession—the troops whether of France or Spain who may be there shall cease to occupy any military post from the time of taking possession and shall be embarked as soon as possible in the course of three months after the ratification of this treaty.

Président, pour la prise de possession. Les troupes françaises ou espagnoles qui s'y trouveront, cesseront d'occuper les postes militaires du moment de la prise de possession et seront embarquées aussitôt que faire se pourra, dans le courant des trois mois qui suivront la ratification du traité

Art: VI

The United States promise to execute Such treaties and articles as may have been agreed between Spain and the tribes and nations of Indians until by mutual consent of the United States and the said tribes or nations other Suitable articles Shall have been agreed upon.[1]

Article 6.

Les Etats-unis promettent d'exécuter les traités et articles qui pourraient avoir été convenus entre l'Espagne et les Tribus et nations indigènes, jusqu'à ce que, du consentement mutuel des Etats-unis d'une part, & desdits indigènes de l'autre, il y ait été substitué tels autres articles qui seront jugés convenables.[1]

Art: VII

As it is reciprocally advantageous to the commerce of France and the United States to encourage the communication of both nations for a limited time in the country ceded by the present treaty until general arrangements relative to the commerce of both nations may be agreed on; it has been agreed between the contracting parties that the French Ships coming directly from France or any of her colonies loaded only with the produce and manufactures of France or her Said Colonies; and the Ships of Spain coming directly from Spain or any of her colonies loaded only

Article 7.

Comme il est réciproquement avantageux au commerce de la france et des Etats-unis, d'encourager la communication des deux peuples, pour un tems limité, dans les contrées dont il est fait cession, par le présent traité, jusqu'à ce que des arrangemens généraux relatifs au commerce des deux nations, puissent être convenus, il a été arrêté entre les parties contractantes que les navires francais venant directement de france ou d'aucune de ses Colonies, uniquement chargés des produits des manufactures de la france et de ses dites colonies, et les navires

[1] See the note regarding Article 6.

with the produce or manufactures of Spain or her Colonies Shall be admitted during the Space of twelve years in in the Port of New-Orleans and in all other legal ports-of-entry within the ceded territory in the Same manner as the Ships of the United States coming directly from France or Spain or any of their Colonies without being Subject to any other or greater duty on merchandize or other or greater tonnage than that paid by the citizens of the United States.

During the Space of time above mentioned no other nation Shall have a right to the Same privileges in the Ports of the ceded territory—the twelve years Shall commence three months after the exchange of ratifications if it Shall take place in France or three months after it Shall have been notified at Paris to the French Government if it Shall take place in the United States;[1] It is however well understood that the object of the above article is to favour the manufactures, Commerce, freight and navigation of France and of Spain So far as relates to the importations that the french and Spanish Shall make into the Said

Espagnols venant directement des ports d'espagne ou de ceux de ses colonies, uniquement chargés des produits des manufactures de l'Espagne et de ses dites colonies, seront admis pendant l'espace de douze années, dans le port de la Nouvelle Orléans et dans tous les autres ports légalement ouverts, en quelque lieu que ce soit des territoires cédés ainsi, et de la manière que les navires des Etats unis venant de france & d'espagne, ou d'aucune de leurs Colonies, sans être sujets à d'autres ou plus grands droits sur les marchandises ou d'autres ou plus grands droits de tonnage, que ceux qui sont payés par les Citoyens des Etats unis.

Pendant l'espace de tems ci dessus mentionné aucune nation n'aura droit aux mêmes privilèges, dans les ports du territoire cédé.

Les douze années commenceront trois mois après l'échange des ratifications, s'il a lieu en france, ou trois mois après qu'il aura été notifié à Paris au Gouvernement français, s'il a lieu dans les Etats unis.[1]

Il est bien entendu que le but du présent article est de favoriser les manufactures, le commerce à frêt & la navigation de la france et de l'Espagne, en ce qui regarde les importations qui seront faites par les français et par les espagnols dans les dits ports des Etats-unis,

[1] See the note regarding Article 7.

Ports of the United States without in any Sort affecting the regulations that the United States may make concerning the exportation of the produce and merchandize of the United States, or any right they may have to make Such regulations.

sans qu'il soit rien innové aux réglemens concernant l'exportation des produits et marchandises des états-unis, & aux droits qu'il ont de faire les dits réglemens.

ART: VIII

In future and for ever after the expiration of the twelve years, the Ships of France shall be treated upon the footing of the most favoured nations in the ports above mentioned.

ARTe 8.

A l'avenir, et pour toujours, après l'expiration des douze années sus dites, les navires français seront traité sur le pied de la nation la plus favorisée, dans les ports ci dessus mentionnés.

ART: IX

The particular Convention[1] Signed this day by the respective Ministers having for its object to provide for the payment of debts due to the Citizens of the United States by the French Republic prior to the 30th Septr 1800 (8th Vendémiaire an 9) is approved and to have its execution in the Same manner as if it had been inserted in this present treaty and it Shall be ratified in the Same form and in the Same time So that the one Shall not be ratified distinct from the other.

Another particular Convention[2] Signed at the Same date as the present treaty relative to a definitive rule between the contracting parties is in the like manner approved and will be ratified in the Same form, and in the Same time and jointly.

ARTe 9.

La Convention[1] particulière signée aujourd'hui, par les Ministres respectifs, ayant pour objet de pourvoir au paiement des créances dues aux Citoyens des Etats unis, par la République francaise, antérieurement au 8 Vendemiaire an 9/30 Septembre 1800. est approuvée, pour avoir son exécution de la même maniere, que si elle était insérée au présent traité, et elle sera ratifiée en la même forme et en même tems en sorte que l'une ne puisse l'être sans l'autre.

Un autre acte[2] particulier, signé à la même date que le présent traité, relatif à un réglement définitif entre les puissances contractantes, est pareillement approuvé, et sera ratifié en la même forme, en même tems & conjointement.

[1] Document 30.

[2] Document 29.

Art X

The present treaty Shall be ratified in good and due form and the ratifications Shall be exchanged in the Space of Six months after the date of the Signature by the Ministers Plenipotentiary or Sooner if possible.

In faith whereof the respective Plenipotentiaries have Signed these articles in the French and English languages; declaring neverthless that the present Treaty was originally agreed to in the French language; and have thereunto affixed their Seals.

Done at Paris the tenth day of Floreal in the eleventh year of the French Republic; and the 30th of April 1803

Robt R Livingston
[Seal]

Jas Monroe
[Seal]

Barbé Marbois
[Seal]

Arte 10.

Le présent traité sera ratifié en bonne & due forme, et les ratifications seront échangées dans l'espace de six mois, après la date de la signature des plénipotentiaires ou plutôt s'il est possible.

En foi dequoi les plénipotentiaires respectifs ont signé les articles ci-dessus, tant en langue française qu'en langue Anglaise, déclarant néamoins que le présent traité a été originairement rédigé & arrêté en langue française, & ils y ont apposé leur sceau.

Fait à Paris le dixième jour de floréal de l'an onze de la République française & le trente Avril mil huit cent trois.

Robt R Livingston
[Seal]

Jas Monroe
[Seal]

Barbé Marbois
[Seal]

NOTES

This treaty and the two conventions of the same date (Documents 29 and 30) formed together one transaction; they were concurrently signed; and by the express terms of Article 9 of the treaty their ratifications were interdependent and were concurrently exchanged.

The English and French texts of the signed originals of each of the three agreements in the Department of State file are separate papers. In the respective attestation clauses it is declared, in somewhat varying forms of wording in the English texts, that the agreements were first drafted and agreed on in French; but the *alternat* was observed throughout; in each original in the file the United States of America is named before the French Republic, the President before the First Consul, and the signatures of the American

plenipotentiaries (except in the French text of Document 30) are at the left. Accordingly, the respective English texts are here printed in the left column.

Each written page of the French text of this treaty prior to the page of signature, is initialed by Livingston and Marbois; those initials are not shown in the print here; and such of the dates mentioned in either text in two styles as are written one above the other and bracketed in the original, are here printed with a shilling mark. It may be added that the original texts of all three agreements, especially in the English, indicate haste in their preparation; as examples may be noted the year 1793 given in the preamble (French) of this treaty as the date of the treaty of 1795 with Spain (Document 18), and "présent" for "preceding" in Article 2 of Document 30.

There were three French instruments of ratification, one for each agreement. They recited the respective French texts only. The three instruments were forwarded by Livingston and Monroe to Secretary of State Madison under date of June 7, 1803, for delivery to the French Chargé d'Affaires, Louis André Pichon; and thus ratifications were agreed to be exchanged at Washington, although the texts left the point open (see Article 7 of this treaty and also American State Papers, Foreign Relations, II, 563–65).

The attested copy of the Senate resolution of October 20, 1803, which is in the Department of State file, differs slightly in wording from that printed in Executive Journal, I, 450.

One instrument of ratification on the part of the United States included the three agreements. There is a quite incomplete duplicate of it in the file, signed by Jefferson; some parts of the paper have been torn away, including the imprint of the Great Seal and the attest of Madison; and the texts of the three agreements are not now with that single sheet of paper.

The protocol of the exchange of ratifications on October 21, 1803, is affixed to the French instrument of ratification of this treaty. It is in simple form, in French and English, signed and sealed by Madison and Pichon. A French proposal and an American counter proposal to insert in the text declarations regarding the delivery of Louisiana to the United States were abandoned (D. S., 14 Domestic Letters, 213).

The message of President Jefferson to Congress of October 17, 1803 (Richardson, I, 357–62), communicated the fact of the cession of Louisiana, on the same day that the treaty and the two conventions were submitted to the Senate. The texts of the three agreements were published in the press immediately following the Senate action on October 20; thus in the Federal Gazette and Baltimore Daily Advertiser of October 22, an article dated the previous day said, "Yesterday at about 5 o'clock P. M. the senate ratified the Louisiana Treaty," and the English texts of the agreements were printed.

The original proclamation of the three agreements has not been found, but it was published at the time; its provisions (without the texts) appear in the issue of the newspaper above mentioned of November 4, 1803.

The proclamation is printed in full in The Laws of the United States, Folwell ed., VII, 167–95 (that volume is dated 1806, but its first part, including the acts of the first session of the Eighth Congress, doubtless appeared as early as 1804); it includes both texts of the treaty and of the two conventions and is dated merely "in the year of our Lord one thousand eight hundred and three, and of the sovereignty and independence of the United States, the twenty eighth"; but there is little doubt that the actual date was October 21, 1803; on that day the three agreements were communicated to both Houses of Congress (American State Papers, Foreign Relations, II, 507; Richardson, I, 362–63).

Also in the treaty file is a note of Pichon to the Secretary of State, dated January 25, 1804, enclosing the original protocol of the delivery of Louisiana by Spain to France on November 30, 1803, at New Orleans; that document is in French and Spanish, signed and sealed by the representatives of the two countries. The English text of the similar document of December 20, 1803, when Louisiana was delivered by France to the United States, is printed in American State Papers, Foreign Relations, II, 582.

In the meantime statutes for the execution of the agreements on the part of the United States had been enacted (act of October 31, and two acts of November 10, 1803, 2 Statutes at Large, 245–48), and the question of the limits of the ceded territory, which in its various phases was destined to be discussed for the next fifteen years, was kept in the background (see the letter of Madison to Livingston, March 31, 1804, American State Papers, Foreign Relations, II, 575–78; and also the letter of Jefferson to William Dunbar of September 21, 1803, The Works of Thomas Jefferson, X, 20–21).

Earlier Publication

The despatches from Paris with the treaty and the two conventions were received at Washington on July 14, 1803. On the following day Jefferson wrote to Captain Merryweather Lewis (The Works of Thomas Jefferson, IX, 430), "Last night also we received the treaty from Paris ceding Louisiana according to the bounds to which France had a right." The National Intelligencer of July 18 contained a quite complete summary of the provisions of the three agreements, which was very likely given out by the Department of State and which certainly could not have been written except from the text of the documents; and a letter of Jefferson to William Dunbar of July 17, 1803 (The Works of Thomas Jefferson, X, 19), reads in part as follows:

> Before you receive this, you will have heard, through the channel of the public papers, of the cession of Louisiana by France to the United States. The terms as stated in the *National Intelligencer*, are accurate. That the treaty may be ratified in time, I have found it necessary to convene Congress on the 17th of October; and it is very important for the happiness of the country that they should possess all the information which can be obtained respecting it, that they make the best arrangement practicable for its good government. It is the most necessary, because, they will be obliged to ask from the People an amendment of the Constitution, authorizing their receiving the province into the Union, and providing for its government; and the limitations of power which shall be given by that amendment, will be unalterable but by the same authority.

Note Regarding Article 1

The treaty of San Ildefonso of October 1, 1800, was in French; the text in that language is in the memoir of Luis de Onis (Memoria sobre las negociaciones entre España y los Estados-Unidos de America, Madrid, 1820, Appendix, 1–3); an English translation of that treaty is in the English version of the memoir of De Onis (Washington, 1821, 151–52) and is printed also in Malloy, I, 506–7. A revised translation is printed below. The vital article is of course Article 3, the original French of which is quoted in the French text of Article 1 of this treaty; the quotation in the corresponding English of Article 1 is of necessity a translation from the French. The exact meaning of the language was long debated in diplomatic correspondence because of its bearing on the limits of the province of Louisiana, and it has been much discussed by writers ever since. At least three different English words, for example, have been used to translate the French "rétrocéder"; in this treaty the word used is "cede"; in the translation first above mentioned it is "recede"; and in the translation here printed, as in Madison's long letter to Livingston of March 31, 1804 (American State Papers, Foreign Relations, II, 575–78), where the language is elaborately discussed, it is more correctly "retrocede."

[Translation]

Preliminary and Secret Treaty between the French Republic and His Catholic Majesty the King of Spain, Concerning the Aggrandizement of His Royal Highness the Infant Duke of Parma in Italy and the Retrocession of Louisiana.

His Catholic Majesty having always manifested an earnest desire to procure for His Royal Highness the Duke of Parma an aggrandizement which would place his domains on a footing more consonant with his dignity; and the French Republic on its part having long since made known to His Majesty the King of Spain its desire to be again placed in possession of the colony of Louisiana; and the two Governments having exchanged their views on these two subjects of common interest, and circumstances permitting them to assume obligations in this regard which, so far as depends on them, will assure mutual satisfaction, they have authorized for this purpose the following: the French Republic, the Citizen Alexandre Bérthier, General in Chief; and His Catholic Majesty, Don Mariano Luis de Urquijo, Knight of the Order of Charles III, and of that of St. John of Jerusalem, his Counselor of State, his Ambassador Extraordinary and Plenipotentiary appointed near the Batavian Republic, and his First Secretary of State *ad interim*, who, having exchanged their powers, have agreed upon the following articles, subject to ratification.

Article 1

The French Republic undertakes to procure for His Royal Highness the Infant Duke of Parma an aggrandizement of territory which shall increase the population of his domains to one million inhabitants, with the title of King and with all the rights which attach to the royal dignity; and the French Republic undertakes to obtain in this regard the assent of His Majesty the Emperor and King and that of the other interested states, so that His Highness the Infant Duke of Parma may be put into possession of the said territories without opposition upon the conclusion of the peace to be made between the French Republic and His Imperial Majesty.

ARTICLE 2

The aggrandizement to be given to His Royal Highness the Duke of Parma may consist of Tuscany, in case the present negotiations of the French Government with His Imperial Majesty shall permit that Government to dispose thereof; or it may consist of the three Roman legations or of any other continental provinces of Italy which form a rounded state.

ARTICLE 3

His Catholic Majesty promises and undertakes on his part to retrocede to the French Republic, six months after the full and entire execution of the above conditions and provisions regarding His Royal Highness the Duke of Parma, the colony or province of Louisiana, with the same extent that it now has in the hands of Spain and that it had when France possessed it, and such as it ought to be according to the treaties subsequently concluded between Spain and other states.

ARTICLE 4

His Catholic Majesty will give the necessary orders for the occupation of Louisiana by France as soon as the territories which are to form the aggrandizement of the Duke of Parma shall be placed in the hands of His Royal Highness. The French Republic may, according to its convenience, postpone the taking of possession; when that is to be executed, the states directly or indirectly interested will agree upon such further conditions as their common interests and the interest of the respective inhabitants require.

ARTICLE 5

His Catholic Majesty undertakes to deliver to the French Republic in Spanish ports in Europe, one month after the execution of the provision with regard to the Duke of Parma, six ships of war in good condition built for seventy-four guns, armed and equipped and ready to receive French crews and supplies.

ARTICLE 6

As the provisions of the present treaty have no prejudicial object and leave intact the rights of all, it is not to be supposed that they will give offense to any power. However, if the contrary shall happen and if the two states, because of the execution thereof, shall be attacked or threatened, the two powers agree to make common cause not only to repel the aggression but also to take conciliatory measures proper for the maintenance of peace with all their neighbors.

ARTICLE 7

The obligations contained in the present treaty derogate in no respect from those which are expressed in the Treaty of Alliance signed at San Ildefonso on the 2d Fructidor, year 4 (August 19, 1796); on the contrary they unite anew the interests of the two powers and assure the guaranties stipulated in the Treaty of Alliance for all cases in which they should be applied.

ARTICLE 8

The ratifications of these preliminary articles shall be effected and exchanged within the period of one month, or sooner if possible, counting from the day of the signature of the present treaty.

In faith whereof we, the undersigned Ministers Plenipotentiary of the French Republic and of His Catholic Majesty, in virtue of our respective powers, have signed these preliminary articles and have affixed thereto our seals.

Done at San Ildefonso the 9th Vendémiaire, 9th year of the French Republic (October 1, 1800).

[Seal] ALEXANDRE BÉRTHIER
[Seal] MARIANO LUIS DE URQUIJO

The text of the Treaty of Alliance of August 19 (not 18), 1796, mentioned in Article 7 of the above treaty of October 1, 1800, is, in French, in Von Martens, Recueil de traités, 2d ed., VI, 255–59.

In Article 1 of the Treaty of Cession there is also reference to treaties made by Spain affecting Louisiana, after the previous possession of Louisiana by France; that ownership by France had terminated in 1762; Louisiana was ceded to Spain by France on November 3, 1762, and the cession was accepted ten days later, on November 13. The treaties "subsequently entered into between Spain and other States" were the following: first, the Preliminary Treaty of Peace between Spain and Great Britain, signed at Versailles January 20, 1783, the French text of which is in Von Martens, Recueil de traités, 2d ed., III, 510–14; second, the Definitive Treaty of Peace between Spain and Great Britain, signed at Versailles September 3, 1783, the French text of which is in the same volume of Von Martens, pages 541–51; and third, the treaty of October 27, 1795, between the United States and Spain (Document 18); English translations of the Preliminary and Definitive Treaties of Peace of 1783 between Spain and Great Britain are in The Parliamentary History of England, XXIII, 351–54 and 1173–82; the provisions of those treaties of special relevancy here are Article 3 of the Preliminary Treaty and Article 5 of the Definitive Treaty, which read in translation as follows:

Art. 3. His Britannic Majesty shall cede to his Catholic Majesty East Florida, and his Catholic Majesty shall keep West Florida, provided that the term of 18 months, to be computed from the time of the ratification of the definitive Treaty, shall be granted to the subjects of his Britannic Majesty, who are settled as well in the island of Minorca as in the two Floridas, to sell their estates, recover their debts, and to transport their effects, as well as their persons, without being restrained on account of their religion, or under any other pretence whatsoever, except that of debts and criminal prosecutions. And his Britannic Majesty shall have power to cause all the effects that may belong to him in East Florida, whether artillery or others, to be carried away.

Art. 5. His Britannic Majesty likewise cedes and guarantees, in full right, to his Catholic Majesty, East Florida, as also West Florida. His Catholic Majesty agrees that the British inhabitants, or others who may have been subjects of the King of Great Britain in the said countries, may retire in full security and liberty, where they shall think proper, and may sell their estates and remove their effects, as well as their persons, without being restrained in their emigration, under any pretence whatsoever, except on account of debts, or criminal prosecutions: the term limited for this emigration being fixed to the space of eighteen months, to be computed from the day of the exchange of the ratifications of the present treaty: but if, from the value of the possessions of the English proprietors, they should not be able to dispose of them within the said term, then his Catholic Majesty shall grant them a prolongation proportioned to that end. It is further stipulated, that his Britannic Majesty shall have the power of removing from East Florida all the effects which may belong to him, whether artillery or other matters.

Note Regarding Article 6

See, in the notes to the treaty with Spain of 1795 (Document 18), the note regarding Article 5 thereof.

Note Regarding Article 7

As the exchange of ratifications took place at Washington, the period of twelve years began to run three months after the date of formal notice to the French Government that the exchange had taken place. A letter of Madison to the French Minister of Foreign Affairs of November 4, 1803, seems to have been intended as such notice (American State Papers, Foreign Relations, VI, 179); and while the date of the delivery of the communication is not stated, it appears to have been just prior to January 1, 1804 (*ibid.*, 182). The act of February 24, 1804, section 8 (2 Statutes at Large, 253), provided that the term of twelve years should "commence three months after the exchange of the ratifications of the above-mentioned treaty shall have been notified, at Paris, to the French government," but did not otherwise fix the date.

Treaty Series, No. 86a
8 Statutes at Large, 206–9

29

FRANCE : APRIL 30, 1803

Convention for the Payment of Sixty Million Francs ($11,250,000) by the United States, signed at Paris April 30, 1803. Original in English and French; but "originally agreed on and written in the French language" (see the attestation clause).

Submitted to the Senate October 17, 1803. Resolution of advice and consent October 20, 1803. Ratified by the United States October 21, 1803. Ratified by France May 22, 1803. Ratifications exchanged at Washington October 21, 1803. Proclaimed October 21, 1803.

A Convention Between the United States of America and the French Republic

The President of the United States of America and the First Consul of the French Republic in the name of the French people, in consequence of the treaty of cession of Louisiana[1] which has been Signed this day; wishing to regulate definitively every thing which has relation to the Said cession have authorized to this effect the Plenipotentiaries that is to say: the President of the United States has, by and with the advice and consent of the Senate of the Said States nominated for their Plenipotentiaries, Robert R. Livingston Minister Plenipotentiary of the United States and James Monroe Minister Plenipotentiary and Envoy-Extraordinary of the Said United States near the Government of

Convention Entre les Etats unis d'Amérique Et la République Française.

Le Président des Etats unis d'Amérique, et Le Premier Consul de la République française au nom du peuple français, par suite du traité de cession de la Louisiane,[1] qui a été signé aujourd'hui, et voulant régler définitivement tout ce qui est relatif à cette affaire, ont autorisé, à cet effet, des Plénipotentiaires; Savoir:

Le Président des Etats unis, par et avec l'avis et le consentement du Sénat des dits Etats, a nommé pour leurs plénipotentiaires Robert R. Livingston, Ministre plénipotentiaire des Etats unis et James Monroe, Ministre plénipotentiaire et envoyé extraordinaire des dits Etats-unis, auprès du Gouvernement de la République française,

[1] Document 28.

the French Republic; and the First Consul of the French Republic in the name of the French People has named as Plenipotentiary of the Said Republic the citizen Francis Barbé-Marbois: who in virtue of their full powers, which have been exchanged this day have agreed to the following articles:—

ART: 1

The Government of the United States engages to pay to the French Government in the manner Specified in the following article the Sum of Sixty millions of francs independant of the Sum which Shall be fixed by another Convention for the payment of the debts due by France to citizens of the United States.

ART: 2

For the payment of the Sum of Sixty millions of francs mentioned in the preceding article the United States Shall create a Stock of eleven millions, two hundred and fifty thousand Dollars bearing an interest of Six per cent: per annum payable half yearly in London Amsterdam or Paris amounting by the half year to three hundred and thirty Seven thousand five hundred Dollars according to the proportions which Shall be determined by the french Government to be paid at either place: The principal of

et Le Premier Consul de la République française, au nom du peuple francais, a nommé pour plénipotentiaire de la dite République le Citoyen françois Barbé-Marbois, Ministre du Trésor public; lesquels en vertu de leurs pleins pouvoirs, dont l'échange a ete fait aujourd'hui, Sont convenus des Articles suivans:

ART. 1er.

Le Gouvernement des Etats unis s'engage à payer au Gouvernem^t^ français, de la maniere qui sera spécifiée en l'article suivant, la somme de Soixante millions de francs, indépendemment de ce qui sera fixé par une autre convention, pour le paiement des sommes dues par la france à des Citoyens des Etats unis.

ART. 2.

Le paiement des Soixante millions de francs mentionnés au précédent article sera effectué par les Etats unis au moyen de la création d'un fonds de onze millions deux cent cinquante mille piatres, portant un intérêt de Six pour cent par an, payable tous les Six mois à Londres, Amsterdam ou Paris, à raison de Trois cent trente sept mille cinq cents piastres pour Six mois, dans les trois places ci dessus dites, suivant la proportion qui sera déterminée par le Gouvernement français. Le principal

the Said Stock to be reimbursed at the treasury of the United States in annual payments of not less than three millions of Dollars each; of which the first payment Shall commence fifteen years after the date of the exchange of ratifications—this Stock Shall be transferred to the Government of France or to Such person or persons as Shall be authorized to receive it in three months at most after the exchange of the ratifications of this treaty and after Louisiana Shall be taken possession of in the name of the Government of the United States.[1]

du dit fonds sera remboursé par le Trésor des Etats unis par des paiemens annuels qui ne pourront être d'une Somme moindre que Trois millions de piastres, par année, et dont le premier commencera quinze ans après la date de l'échange des ratifications. Ce fonds sera transféré au Gouvernement de france, ou à telle personne, ou tel nombre de personnes qu'il chargera de le recevoir, dans les trois mois au plus tard, après l'échange des ratifications de ce traité, et après la prise de possession de la Louisiane, au nom du Gouvernement des Etats unis.[1]

It is further agreed that if the french Government Should be desirous of disposing of the Said Stock to receive the capital in Europe at Shorter terms that its measures for that purpose Shall be taken So as to favour in the greatest degree possible the credit of the United States and to raise to the highest price the Said Stock

Il est en outre convenu que si le Gouvernement français était dans l'intention de disposer du dit fonds, et d'en toucher le capital en Europe à des époques rapprochées, les opérations qui auront lieu seront conduites de la manière la plus favorable au crédit des Etats unis, et la plus propre à maintenir le prix avantageux du fonds qui doit être créé.

ART 3

It is agreed that the Dollar of the United States Specified in the present Convention Shall be fixed at five francs $\frac{3333}{10000}$ or five livres eight Sous tournois

ART. 3.

La piastre ayant cours de monnaie dans les Etats unis, il est convenu que dans les comptes auxquels la présente convention donnera lieu, le rapport de la dite monnaie avec la france sera invariablement fixé à 5. francs $\frac{3333.}{10.000.}$ ou 5. 8^{s} Tournois.

[1] See the note regarding Article 2.

The present Convention Shall be ratified in good and due form, and the ratifications Shall be exchanged in the Space of Six months to date from this day or Sooner if possible.

In faith of which the respective Plenipotentiaries have Signed the above articles both in the french and english languages, declaring nevertheless that the present treaty has been originally agreed on and written in the french language; to which they have hereunto affixed their Seals.

Done at Paris the tenth of Floreal eleventh year of the french Republic (30th April 1803.)

Robt R Livingston
[Seal]

Jas Monroe
[Seal]

Barbé Marbois
[Seal]

La présente convention sera ratifiée en bonne et dûe forme et les ratifications seront échangées dans l'espace de Six mois, à dater de ce jour, ou plutôt s'il est possible.

En foi de quoi les Plénipotentiaires respectifs ont signé les articles ci dessus, tant en langue française qu'en langue Anglaise, déclarant néanmoins que le présent traité a été originairement rédigé et arrêté en langue française et ils y ont apposé leur Sceau.

Fait à Paris le dixième jour de floréal de l'an Onze de la République française et 30. Avril 1803./.

Robt R Livingston
[Seal]

Jas Monroe
[Seal]

Barbé Marbois
[Seal]

NOTES

This convention and the convention following (Document 30) formed, with the Treaty for the Cession of Louisiana of the same date (Document 28), one transaction. The three agreements were concurrently signed, and by the express terms of Article 9 of the Treaty of Cession their ratifications were interdependent and were concurrently exchanged.

As to the source text of this convention, its ratification, the exchange of ratifications, and the proclamation, see generally the notes to Document 28.

Note Regarding Article 2

Louisiana was delivered by France to the United States on December 20, 1803 (see American State Papers, Foreign Relations, II, 582).

Treaty Series, No. 86b
8 Statutes at Large, 208–13

30

FRANCE : APRIL 30, 1803

Convention for the Payment of Sums Due by France to Citizens of the United States, signed at Paris April 30, 1803. Original in English and French; but "originally agreed on and written in the French language" (see the attestation clause).
Submitted to the Senate October 17, 1803. Resolution of advice and consent October 20, 1803. Ratified by the United States October 21, 1803. Ratified by France May 22, 1803. Ratifications exchanged at Washington October 21, 1803. Proclaimed October 21, 1803.

Convention Between the United States of America and the French Republic

The President of the United States of America and the First Consul of the French Republic in the name of the French People having by a Treaty[1] of this date terminated all difficulties relative to Louisiana, and established on a Solid foundation the friendship which unites the two nations and being desirous in complyance with the Second and fifth Articles of the Convention[2] of the 8th Vendémiaire ninth year of the French Republic (30th September 1800) to Secure the payment of the Sums due by France to the citizens of the United States have respectively nominated as Plenipotentiaries that is to Say The President of the United States of America by and with the advice and consent of their Senate Robert R. Liv-

Convention entre les Etats-unis d'Amérique Et la République françoise.

Le Président des Etats unis d'Amérique et le Premier Consul de la République françoise, au nom du Peuple françois, ayant par un traité[1] en date de ce jour, fait cesser toutes les difficultés relatives à la Louisiane et affirmi sur des fondemens solides l'amitié qui unit les deux Nations et voulant en exécution des articles 2. et 5. de la Convention[2] du 8. Vendemiaire an 9./30. Septembre 1800. assurer le paiement des Sommes dûes par la france aux Citoyens des Etats-unis, ont respectivement nommé pour plenipotentiaires; Savoir, Le Président des Etats unis d'Amérique, par et avec l'avis et le consentement du Sénat des dits Etats, Robert R. Livingston, Ministre plénipotentiaire des Etats unis, et James

[1] Document 28.

[2] Document 25.

ingston Minister Plenipotentiary and James Monroe Minister Plenipotentiary and Envoy Extraordinary of the Said States near the Government of the French Republic: and the First Consul in the name of the French People the Citizen Francis Barbé Marbois Minister of the public treasury; who after having exchanged their full powers have agreed to the following articles.

Art 1

The debts due by France to citizens of the United States contracted before the 8th of Vendémiaire ninth year of the French Republic (30th September 1800) Shall be paid according to the following regulations with interest at Six per Cent; to commence from the period when the accounts and vouchers were presented to the French Government.

Art: 2

The debts provided for by the preceding Article are those whose result is comprised in the conjectural note[1] annexed to the present Convention and which with the interest cannot exceed the Sum of twenty millions of Francs. The claims comprised in the Said note which fall within the exceptions of the following articles Shall not be admitted to the benefit of this provision.

Monroé, Ministre plénipotentiaire et Envoyé extraordinaire des dits Etats auprès du Gouvernement de la République françoise, et Le Premier Consul au nom du Peuple françois le Citoyen francois Barbé Marbois Ministre du Trésor public: Lesquels après avoir fait l'échange de leurs pleins pouvoirs, sont convenus des articles suivans.

Arte. 1er.

Les dettes dûes par la france aux Citoyens des Etats unis, contractées avant le 8. Vendémiaire an 9./30. 7bre. 1800. seront payées conformément aux dispositions suivantes avec les intérêts à six pour cent à compter de l'époque où la réclamation et les pièces à l'appui ont été remises au Gouvernement françois.

Arte 2.

Les dettes qui font l'objet du présent article, sont celles dont le résultat par apperçu est compris dans la note[1] annéxée à la présente convention et qui ne pourront, y compris les intérêts, excéder la Somme de Vingt millions.

Les réclamations, comprises dans ladite note, ne pourront néanmoins être admises qu'autant qu'elles ne seront pas frappées des exceptions mentionnées aux articles suivants.

[1] See the note regarding Article 2.

ART: 3.

The principal and interests of the Said debts Shall be discharged by the United States, by orders drawn by their Minister Plenipotentiary on their treasury, these orders Shall be payable Sixty days after the exchange of ratifications of the Treaty and the Conventions Signed this day, and after possession Shall be given of Louisiana by the Commissaries of France to those of the United-States.[1]

ART: 4

It is expressly agreed that the preceding articles Shall comprehend no debts but Such as are due to citizens of the United States who have been and are yet creditors of France for Supplies for embargoes and prizes made at Sea in which the appeal has been properly lodged within the time mentioned in the Said Convention[2] 8th Vendémiaire ninth year, (30th Sept. 1800)

ART: 5

The preceding Articles Shall apply only, First: to captures of which the council of prizes Shall have ordered restitution it being well understood that the claimant cannot have recourse to the United States otherwise than he might have had to the Government of the French republic and only in case of insufficiency of the cap-

ARTe 3.

Le principal et les intérêts seront acquittés par les Etats unis d'Amérique, sur des mandats tirés par le Ministre plénipotentiaire desdits Etats unis sur leur Trésor. Ces mandats seront payables Soixante jours après l'échange des ratifications du traité et des Conventions Signées ce jour, et après la remise qui doit être faite de la Louisiane par le Commissaire françois aux Commissaires des Etats unis.[1]

ARTe 4.

Il est expressement convenu que les articles précédents ne comprennent que les créances des Citoyens des Etats unis ou de leur représentans, qui ont été et sont encore créanciers de la france pour fournitures, embargos et prises faites à la mer, et réclamées dans le tems nécessaire et suivant les formes prescrits par la Convention[2] du 8 Vendemiaire an 9./30. 7bre. 1800.

ARTe 5.

Les articles précédens ne seront appliqués, 1o qu'aux captures dont le Conseil des prises auroit ordonné la restitution ou main levée, bien entendu que le réclamant ne pourra avoir recours sur les Etats unis pour son payement que de la même manière qu'il l'auroit eu envers le Gouvernement francois et seulement en

[1] See the note regarding Article 3.

[2] Document 25.

tors—2[d] the debts mentioned in the Said fifth Article of the Convention contracted before the 8th Vendémiaire an 9/30th September 1800 the payment of which has been heretofore claimed of the actual Government of France and for which the creditors have a right to the protection of the United States—the Said 5th Article does not comprehend prizes whose condemnation has been or Shall be confirmed: it is the express intention of the contracting parties not to extend the benefit of the present Convention to reclamations of American citizens who Shall have established houses of Commerce in France, England or other countries than the United States in partnership with foreigners, and who by that reason and the nature of their commerce ought to be regarded as domiciliated in the places where Such houses exist.—All agrements and bargains concerning merchandize which Shall not be the property of American citizens are equally excepted from the benefit of the Said Convention Saving however to Such persons their claims in like manner as if this Treaty had not been made.

cas d'insufisance de la part des Capteurs. 2º qu'aux dettes mentionnées dans ce même article 5. de la convention, contractées avant le 8. Vendémiaire an 9./30. Septembre 1800. dont le paiement a été ci-devant réclamé auprès du Gouvernement actuel de france, et pour lesquelles le créancier a droit à la protection des Etats unis. Ledit article 5. ne comprend point les prises dont la condamnation a été ou viendroit à être confirmée; L'intention expresse des parties contractantes est pareillement de ne point étendre le bénéfice de la présente convention aux réclamations des Citoyens Américains, qui auroient établi des Maisons de Commerce en france, en Angleterre ou dans des pays autres que les Etats unis en société avec des Etrangers, et qui, par cette raison, et la nature de leur commerce, doivent être regardés comme domiciliés dans les Lieux où existent lesdites Maisons, Sont pareillement exceptés tous accords et pactes concernant des marchandises qui ne servient pas la propriété des Citoyens Américains.

Il n'est d'ailleurs rien préjugé sur le fonds des réclamations ainsi exceptées.

Art: 6

And that the different questions which may arise under the preceding article may be fairly in-

Artº 6.

Afin que les différentes questions auxqelles l'article précédent pourra donner lieu, puissent être con-

vestigated the Ministers Plenipotentiary of the United States Shall name three persons who Shall act from the present and provisionally and who shall have full power to examine without removing the documents, all the accounts of the different claims already liquidated by the Bureaus established for this purpose by the French Republic and to ascertain whether they belong to the classes designated by the present Convention and the principles established in it or if they are not in one of its exceptions and on their Certificate declaring that the debt is due to an American Citizen or his representative and that it existed before the 8th Vendémiaire 9th year/30 September 1800 the debtor shall be entitled to an order on the Treasury of the United States in the manner prescribed by the 3d Article.

Art: 7

The Same agents Shall likewise have power without removing the documents to examine the claims which are prepared for verification, and to certify those which ought to be admitted by uniting the necessary qualifications, and not being comprised in the exceptions contained in the present Convention

venablement examinées, les Ministres plénipotentiaires des Etats unis nommeront trois personnes qui dès à présent et provisoirement auront tout pouvoir d'examiner sans déplacement de pièces tous les Comptes des différentes créances déjà liquidées par les bureaux établis à cet effet par la République francoise et de reconnoître si elles appartiennent aux classes désignées dans la présente convention et aux principes qui y sont établis, ou si elles ne sont pas dans l'une des exceptions, et sur leur certificat portant que la créance est dûe à un Citoyen Américain ou à son représentant et qu'elle existoit avant le 8. Vendémiaire an 9./30. 7bre 1800. le créancier aura droit à un mandat sur le Trésor des Etats unis, expédié conformément à l'art. 3.

Art. 7.

Les mêmes Agents pourront également et dès à présent, prendre connoissance, sans déplacer, des pièces relatives aux réclamations dont le travail et la vérification sont préparés, et délivrer leurs certificats sur celles qui réuniront les caractères nécessaires pour l'admission et qui ne seront pas comprises dans les exceptions exprimées par la présente convention.

ART 8

The Same agents Shall likewise examine the claims which are not prepared for liquidation and certify in writing those which in their Judgement ought to be admitted to liquidation

ART: 9.

In proportion as the debts mentioned in these articles Shall be admitted they Shall be discharged with interest at Six per Cent: by the Treasury of the United States

ART 10

And that no debt which shall not have the qualifications above mentioned and that no unjust or exorbitant demand may be admitted, the Commercial agent of the United-States at Paris or Such other agent as the Minister Plenipotentiary of the United States Shall think proper to nominate shall assist at the operations of the Bureaus and cooperate in the examinations of the claims; and if this agent Shall be of opinion that any debt is not completely proved or if he shall judge that it is not comprised in the principles of the fifth article above mentioned, and if notwithstanding his opinion the Bureaus established by the french Government should think that it ought to be liquidated he shall transmit his observations to the board estab-

ARTᵉ 8.

À l'égard des autres réclamations dont les travaux n'ont pas encore été préparés, les mêmes Agents en prendront aussi successivement connoissance et déclareront par écrit celles qui leur paroîtront susceptibles d'être admises en liquidation.

ARTᵉ 9.

À mesure que les créances mentionnées dans lesd. articles auront été admises, elles seront acquittées avec les intérêts à 6. p %. par le Trésor des Etats unis.

ARTᵉ 10.

Et afin qu'aucune dette qui n'aura pas les caractères ci-dessus mentionnés et qu'aucunes demandes injustes, ou exhorbitantes ne puissent être admises, L'Agent Commercial des Etats unis à Paris ou tel autre Agent que le Ministre plénipotentiare des Etatsunis jugera à propos de nommer, pourra assister aux opérations des dits bureaux et concourir à l'examen de ces créances, et si cet Agent n'est pas d'avis que la dette est complettement prouvée, ou s'il juge qu'elle n'est pas comprise dans les dispositions du 5ᵉ article ci-dessus mentionné et que nonobstant son avis les bureaux établis par le Gouvernement françois estiment que la Liquidation doit avoir lieu, il transmettra ses observations au bureau établi de la part des

lished by the United States who without removing documents shall make a complete examination of the debt and vouchers which Support it, and report the result to the Minister of the United States.—The Minister of the United States Shall transmit his observations in all Such cases to the Minister of the treasury of the French Republic on whose report the French Government Shall decide definitively in every case.

The rejection of any claim Shall have no other effect than to exempt the United States from the payment of it the French Government reserving to itself, the right to decide definitively on Such claim So far as it concerns itself.

Art 11

Every necessary decision Shall be made in the course of a year to commence from the exchange of ratifications and no reclamation Shall be admitted afterwards.

Art: 12

In case of claims for debts contracted by the Government of France with citizens of the United States Since the 8th Vendemiaire 9th year/30 September 1800 not being comprised in this Convention may be pursued and the payment demanded in the Same manner as if it had not been made.

Etats unis qui fera sans déplacer l'examen complet de la créance et des pièces au soutien et fera son rapport au Ministre des Etats unis.

Ce Ministre transmettra ses observations à celui du Trésor de la République francoise et sur son rapport le Gouvernement françois prononcera définitivement.

Le rejet qui pourra avoir lieu n'ayant d'autre effet que de constater que le paiement demandé ne doit pas être fait par les Etats unis, Le Gouvernement françois se réserve de statuer définitivement sur la réclamation en ce qui pourra le concerner.

Arte 11.

Toutes les décisions nécessaires seront rendues dans le cours d'une année à dater de l'échange des ratifications, et aucune réclamation ne sera admise ultérieurement.

Arte 12.

Dans le cas où il y auroit des réclamations des Citoyens des Etats unis à la charge du Gouvernement francois pour des dettes contractées après le 1er Vendémiaire an 9./30. Septembre 1800. elles pourront être suivies et le paiement pourra être demandé comme n'étant point comprises en cette convention.

ART: 13.

The present convention Shall be ratified in good and due form and the ratifications Shall be exchanged in Six months from the date of the Signature of the Ministers Plenipotentiary or Sooner if possible.

In faith of which the respective Ministers Plenipotentiary have Signed the above Articles both in the french and english languages declaring nevertheless that the present treaty has been originally agreed on and written in the french language to which they have hereunto affixed their Seals.

Done at Paris the tenth of Floreal eleventh year of the French Republic. 30th April 1803.

ROBt R LIVINGSTON
[Seal]
JAs MONROE
[Seal]
BARBÉ MARBOIS
[Seal]

ARTe 13.

La présente convention sera ratifiée en bonne et due forme, et les ratifications seront échangées dans l'espace de six mois après la date de la signature des Ministres plénipotentiaires, ou plutôt s'il est possible.

En foi de quoi les Plénipotentiaires respectifs ont signé les articles ci dessus, tant en Langue francoise qu'en Langle Angloise, déclarant néanmoins que le présent traité a été originairement rédigé et arrêté en Langue françoise et ils y ont apposé leur Sceau.

Fait à Paris le dixième jour de Floréal de l'an onze de la République françoise et le 30. Avril 1803./.

BARBÉ MARBOIS
[Seal]
ROBt R LIVINGSTON
[Seal]
JAs MONROE
[Seal]

NOTES

This convention and the convention preceding (Document 29) formed, with the Treaty for the Cession of Louisiana of the same date (Document 28), one transaction. The three agreements were concurrently signed; and by the express terms of Article 9 of the Treaty of Cession their ratifications were interdependent and were concurrently exchanged.

As to the source text of this convention, its ratification, the exchange of ratifications, and the proclamation, see generally the notes to Document 28.

Each written page of the French text of this convention prior to the page of signature, is initialed by Marbois and Livingston; those initials are not shown in the print here; and such of the dates mentioned in either text in two styles as are written one above the other and bracketed in the original, are here printed with a shilling mark.

To the front page of the original of the English text of this convention has been affixed a small envelope marked "The Seal of the United States." The envelope contains a wafer with an imprint of the Great Seal which was formerly on some document but obviously never on this convention. Just when and why this mistaken effort at restoration was effected does not appear; but it seems probable that the wafer was originally that on the incomplete duplicate of the instrument of ratification on the part of the United States which is in the file and which is mentioned in the notes to Document 28; and it is possible that original texts of the three agreements were at one time included with that ratification.

Note Regarding Article 2

Mention is made in Article 2 of a "note" annexed to the present convention. The French and English texts differ somewhat in their form of expression. The French may be paraphrased as saying that the debts to be paid are those whose estimated (conjectured) result is comprised in the annexed note. The English says that the debts to be paid are those whose result is comprised in the annexed conjectural note. In the French it is the result of the debts which is uncertain ("par apperçu," or "aperçu" as now spelled); in the English the uncertainty qualifies the note, in a very unusual form of expression: "conjectural note." The next sentence in each text mentions "the claims comprised [French: 'comprises'] in the said note."

There was in fact no note annexed to the convention at the time of its signature. On May 13, 1803, Livingston and Monroe wrote regarding the note as follows (American State Papers, Foreign Relations, II, 560):

> The list of the debts due by France to American citizens not being yet prepared, owing to M. Marbois's absence to-day from Paris, and the previous delays of the offices in which the evidences were, cannot be sent by this conveyance. In consequence, we retain the original of the convention to which it should be annexed, and send a copy of it: we shall forward in a day or two the original.

It is clear that there was no such note or annex before the Senate No note is included in the French instrument of ratification. It is plain that none was included in the United States instrument of ratification. No annex or list of claims was printed in the press of the period or as part of the proclamation in the Folwell edition of the laws cited in the notes to Document 28.

There remains, however, the question as to just what the paper was which was prepared after the signing of the convention and which it was contemplated would be annexed to it in accordance with Article 2. That there was such a paper is certain; and it has always been supposed that the "conjectural note" was a somewhat detailed list of American claims divided into four classes, with the names of the respective claimants and the amounts of their claims and some observations thereon in respect of three of those classes. The history of that document is related below.

It now seems clear, however, that the document which was contemplated as the annex to the convention was a summary or recapitulation of the detailed list—the summary which is here printed, in French, with a translation following:

ETAT SOMMAIRE

de la dette de la France envers les Etats-Unis d'Amérique

Creances reconnues par l'ex-commission de la Comptab[té] intermédiaire	3, 459, 778	13[s]	6[d]	Les jugemens arbitraux Sur lesquels la liquidation a été faite ont déja alloué les interets de plusieurs de ces Créances
Creances dont les rapports ont été Soumis au Directeur particulier	5, 093, 679	10	2	
Creances à liquider	8, 034, 722	14	4	
Reclamations relatives à l'embargo de 1793	3, 301, 122	8	8	Susceptible d'une réduction considérable
Total	19, 889, 303	6[s]	8[d]	

[Translation]

SUMMARY STATEMENT

of the Debt of France to the United States of America

	Francs	s.	d.	
Accounts recognized by the former commission of intermediate accounting.	3, 459, 778	13	6	The arbitral decisions on which the liquidation has been based have already allowed interest on certain of these accounts.
Accounts, the reports of which have been submitted to the particular Director.	5, 093, 679	10	2	
Accounts to be liquidated	8, 034, 722	14	4	
Claims relating to the embargo of 1793.	3, 301, 122	8	8	Susceptible of considerable reduction.
Total	19, 889, 303	6	8	

In American State Papers, Foreign Relations, II, 560, is printed a letter of Livingston and Monroe dated at Paris May 16, 1803, addressed to the Secretary of State and reading as follows:

We have the honor to enclose the account which should be annexed to the convention transmitted to you. The Bordeaux embargo is in assignats and two thirds will be deducted. From many of the others, we have reason to think, from a particular account now in our hands, there will be such considerable deductions as will reduce the whole charge to less than twenty millions of livres, including the interest. The Consul has agreed to ratify immediately, and we hope to have the honor of transmitting you the ratified treaty, with an order to deliver the territory, in a few days. Such arrangements will also, we trust, be made relative to the stock as will prevent its coming on the market to any loss, or any part of it from being sold in America.

An original of the foregoing letter, headed "N° 2. Duplicate" and signed by Livingston only, is in D. S., 8 Despatches, France, 130; it is endorsed as received on September 2; at folio 141 is the enclosure to

the letter of May 16; it has this endorsement in the same handwriting as that on the letter: "Summary statement of the American claims referred to in the Convention with France of the 30 April 1803. Rec[d] 2 Sept[r] 1803."

It is that summary statement which is printed above.

It is to be observed that the above-quoted letter of May 16, 1803, speaks of two documents. First is "the account which should be annexed to the convention." This is the summary statement which was the enclosure. Thereafter reference is made to "a particular account now in our hands." Those words refer to another document not transmitted; they refer to and are quite a good description of the elaborate list which has been usually printed as the conjectural note itself. It may be added that the word "result" (French: "résultat") in the text of Article 2 rather indicates a summary of the claims than an elaborate and detailed list thereof.

The document which Livingston and Monroe called "a particular account" or detailed list of the American claims is now in the treaty file. It, like the summary, is in French only; it is headed "Tableau Général des Réclamations Américaines"; it is printed (with some editing of the names) in various treaty collections, *e. g.*, Haswell, 339–42, Malloy, I, 517–20, 18 Statutes at Large, pt. 2, Public Treaties, 239–42; in 8 Statutes at Large it is omitted for the reason, as stated in the footnote, page 210, that the document was not deposited in the Department of State until May 17, 1832. An English translation is in American State Papers, Foreign Relations, VI, 170–73.

It is to be observed that the recapitulation at the end of that detailed list is in substance the same as the summary statement here printed as the annex to the convention.

The detailed list has at the foot thereof, following the recapitulation, an unsigned certificate, in French, dated May 6, 1803, to the effect that the list conforms to the *dossiers* in the bureaus of the first section of the Fourth Division of the General Liquidation of the Public Debt. An erasure indicates the possibility that this certificate had once a signature.

The history of that detailed list, as it appears from endorsements on it or annexed to it and other sources, is as follows: It was delivered by M. Guilleau, Special Director of the Council of Liquidation, to Robert R. Livingston, then Minister at Paris; it is first mentioned in the letter of Livingston and Monroe of May 16, 1803, above quoted. Livingston endorsed the document and gave it to Fulwar Skipwith, who was then Commercial Agent at Paris and had been appointed American Agent of Claims, and who, incidentally, was one of the claimants himself. Skipwith in turn delivered it to two of the three American Commissioners appointed under Article 6 of the convention, John Mercer and Isaac Cox Barnet, some time prior to July 5, 1803, when the Commissioners first met. The third Commissioner, William McClure, was not then in Paris. The Commissioners spread the text of the document in full on their register; on July 7, 1803, they wrote a letter to Livingston and Monroe desiring "to be informed officially by you whether it [the document] is to be considered as the

one intended to be designated by the Convention." Livingston answered them on the same date saying, "The note delivered you by Mr Skipwith was, (as he informed you) received *directly* from me as the conjectural note referred to in the Treaty."

On May 17, 1832, the document was delivered to the Keeper of the Archives of the Department of State by James H. Causten, who in the course of a long endorsement describes himself as the attorney and legal representative of Skipwith; seemingly the detailed list had remained in the papers of Skipwith from 1803 to 1832; and nearly forty years later it was found in a bundle of papers regarding French spoliation claims, and was placed along with the convention on April 6, 1872.

Sharp differences of opinion arose between Livingston and the American Commissioners (see Moore, International Arbitrations, V, 4439–46). In the correspondence which ensued there was frequent reference to the detailed list, which was deemed the conjectural note; and while little light is thrown upon the precise question here discussed, two extracts from the official correspondence of the time will be quoted. The first is from Livingston's letter of February 24, 1804, to the French Minister of Exterior Relations (D. S., Manuscript; American State Papers, Foreign Relations, VI, 186):

> While the Negociations were pending, in order to form some general estimate of the amount and nature of the Debts, the Minister of the Treasury, charged with the negociation on the part of the First Consul, received from the Board of Comptability an account *apperçu* of the Debts then before them. It was declared at the time by the accounting officer to be inaccurate, and was so understood by the Plenipotentiaries on both sides, and it was even agreed, that this should be indorsed on the Note, but was in the hurry of business neglected, & for that reason has not been annexed to the Convention itself.

The following is extracted from the answering letter of Marbois, French Minister of the Public Treasury, of March 8 (translation, varying somewhat from that printed *ibid.*, 188):

> The other difficulty arose from the hypothesis that the excess [from the 20,000,000 francs or $3,750,000] would pass to the use of the United States. Such a stipulation might influence the American Commissioners to reject without sufficient cause many accounts in order to diminish to that extent the sums to be paid by their Republic. It is to provide in that regard as far as it was possible that we agreed to consider a statement (*état*) produced by the Liquidation as a rough estimate (*apperçu*) of the American account. But at the same time we were very far from considering all the articles included in that statement as liquidated, recognized, and not subject to revision. Mr. Livingston and I were in accord on this point. We thought at the same time that articles not included in that *apperçu* might be paid pursuant to the convention, and it is equally contrary to the spirit of that act and to reason, and to the principles which guided us during the whole negotiation, to suppose that legitimate debts would be rejected for the sole reason that they did not form part of that *apperçu*. The Minister of the United States and I think alike in that regard.

If the letter of Livingston of July 7, 1803, above quoted, stood alone, the conclusion would doubtless follow that the detailed list was intended as the note to be annexed to the convention. However, the earlier official letter of Livingston (and Monroe) of May 16, 1803,

also printed above, must be taken as determinative. With the two papers before them, the American plenipotentiaries stated that the summary was the annex and accordingly that the detailed list was not.

It is to be remembered, moreover, that as a practical matter there is nothing inconsistent in the apparently contradictory statements in the letters of May 16 and July 7, 1803. Of the two papers mentioned by Livingston, one was merely a summary of the other and was indeed taken from it in substance; and the summary was the more appropriate as an annex to the convention; the detailed list, on the other hand, from which the summary was made, was the paper which was needed by the American Commissioners in connection with their work of passing on the respective claims; and for their purpose it might not inappropriately be described as the conjectural note of Article 2, particularly in view of the provisions of Articles 6 and 7 of the convention regarding documents in the bureaus of the Government of France; and the following endorsement on the detailed list, written by Skipwith under date of September 24, 1827, is, at least, not inconsistent with the view expressed here.

The original of this conjectural was furnished by Mr Guilleau, Special Director of the Council of Liquidation, to the American Minister, Mr Livingston, & transmitted & indorsed by him, as above, to the American Board of Commissioners, as containing the American Claims to be first settled and paid under the Louisiana Convention.

Note Regarding Article 3

Curiously enough, December 20, 1803, was just sixty days after the exchange of ratifications; and December 20, 1803, was the date of the delivery of Louisiana by France to the United States.

Treaty Series, No. 359
8 Statutes at Large, 214–18

31

TRIPOLI : JUNE 4, 1805

Treaty of Peace and Amity, signed at Tripoli June 4, 1805 (6 Rabia I, A. H. 1220). Original in English and Arabic.
Submitted to the Senate December 11, 1805. Resolution of advice and consent April 12, 1806. Ratified by the United States April 17, 1806. As to the ratification generally, see the notes. Proclaimed April 22, 1806.
The English text of the copy of the treaty, signed by Tobias Lear, follows; to it is appended the receipt for the $60,000 ransom paid on June 19, 1805 (21 Rabia I, A. H. 1220), as written in the same document; then is reproduced the Arabic text of that paper, in the same order as the English. Following those texts is a comment, written in 1930, on the Arabic text.

Treaty Of Peace and Amity between the United States of America and the Bashaw, Bey and Subjects of Tripoli in Barbary.

Article 1st.

There shall be, from the conclusion of this Treaty, a firm, inviolable and universal peace, and a sincere friendship between the President and Citizens of the United States of America, on the one part, and the Bashaw, Bey and Subjects of the Regency of Tripoli in Barbary on the other, made by the free consent of both Parties, and on the terms of the most favoured Nation. And if either party shall hereafter grant to any other Nation, any particular favour or priviledge in Navigation or Commerce, it shall immediately become common to the other party, freely, where it is freely granted, to such other Nation, but where the grant is conditional it shall be at the option of the contracting parties to accept, alter or reject, such conditions in such manner, as shall be most conducive to their respective Interests.

Article 2nd.

The Bashaw of Tripoli shall deliver up to the American Squadron now off Tripoli, all the Americans in his possession; and all the Subjects of the Bashaw of Tripoli now in the power of the United States of America shall be delivered up to him; and as the number of Americans in possession of the Bashaw of Tripoli amounts to

Three Hundred Persons, more or less; and the number of Tripoline Subjects in the power of the Americans to about, One Hundred more or less; The Bashaw of Tripoli shall receive from the United States of America, the sum of Sixty Thousand Dollars, as a payment for the difference between the Prisoners herein mentioned.

Article 3rd.

All the forces of the United States which have been, or may be in hostility against the Bashaw of Tripoli, in the Province of Derne, or elsewhere within the Dominions of the said Bashaw shall be withdrawn therefrom, and no supplies shall be given by or in behalf of the said United States, during the continuance of this peace, to any of the Subjects of the said Bashaw, who may be in hostility against him in any part of his Dominions; And the Americans will use all means in their power to persuade the Brother of the said Bashaw, who has co-operated with them at Derne &c, to withdraw from the Territory of the said Bashaw of Tripoli; but they will not use any force or improper means to effect that object; and in case he should withdraw himself as aforesaid, the Bashaw engages to deliver up to him, his Wife and Children now in his power.[1]

Article 4th.

If any goods belonging to any Nation with which either of the parties are at war, should be loaded on board Vessels belonging to the other party they shall pass free and unmolested, and no attempt shall be made to take or detain them.

Article 5th.

If any Citizens, or Subjects with or their effects belonging to either party shall be found on board a Prize Vessel taken from an Enemy by the other party, such Citizens or Subjects shall be liberated immediately and their effects so captured shall be restored to their lawful owners or their Agents.

Article 6th.

Proper passports shall immediately be given to the vessels of both the contracting parties, on condition that the Vessels of War belonging to the Regency of Tripoli on meeting with merchant Vessels belonging to Citizens of the United States of America, shall not be permitted to visit them with more than two persons besides the rowers, these two only shall be permitted to go on board said Vessel,

[1] See the note regarding Article 3.

without first obtaining leave from the Commander of said Vessel, who shall compare the passport, and immediately permit said Vessel to proceed on her voyage; and should any of the said Subjects of Tripoli insult or molest the Commander or any other person on board a Vessel so visited; or plunder any of the property contained in her; On complaint being made by the Consul of the United States of America resident at Tripoli and on his producing sufficient proof to substantiate the fact, The Commander or Rais of said Tripoline Ship or Vessel of War, as well as the Offenders shall be punished in the most exemplary manner.

All Vessels of War belonging to the United States of America on meeting with a Cruizer belonging to the Regency of Tripoli, and having seen her passport and Certificate from the Consul of the United States of America residing in the Regency, shall permit her to proceed on her Cruize unmolested, and without detention. No passport shall be granted by either party to any Vessels, but such as are absolutely the property of Citizens or Subjects of said contracting parties, on any pretence whatever.

Article 7th.

A Citizen or Subject of either of the contracting parties having bought a Prize Vessel condemned by the other party, or by any other Nation, the Certificate of condemnation and Bill of Sale shall be a sufficient passport for such Vessel for two years, which, considering the distance between the two Countries, is no more than a reasonable time for her to procure proper passports.

Article 8th.

Vessels of either party, putting into the ports of the other, and having need of provisions or other supplies, they shall be furnished at the Market price, and if any such Vessel should so put in from a disaster at Sea, and have occasion to repair; she shall be at liberty to land and reimbark her Cargo, without paying any duties; but in no case shall she be compelled to land her Cargo.

Article 9th.

Should a Vessel of either party be cast on the shore of the other, all proper assistance shall be given to her and her Crew. No pillage shall be allowed, the property shall remain at the disposition of the owners, and the Crew protected and succoured till they can be sent to their Country.

115605°—31—vol. 2——36

ARTICLE 10th

If a Vessel of either party, shall be attacked by an Enemy within Gun shot of the Forts of the other, she shall be defended as much as possible; If she be in port, she shall not be seized or attacked when it is in the power of the other party to protect her; and when she proceeds to Sea, no Enemy shall be allowed to pursue her from the same port, within twenty four hours after her departure.

ARTICLE 11th

The Commerce between the United States of America and the Regency of Tripoli; The Protections to be given to Merchants, Masters of Vessels and Seamen; The reciprocal right of establishing Consuls in each Country; and the priviledges, immunities and jurisdictions to be enjoyed by such Consuls, are declared to be on the same footing, with those of the most favoured Nations respectively.

ARTICLE 12th

The Consul of the United States of America shall not be answerable for debts contracted by Citizens of his own Nation, unless, he previously gives a written obligation so to do.

ARTICLE 13th

On a Vessel of War, belonging to the United States of America, anchoring before the City of Tripoli, the Consul is to inform the Bashaw of her arrival, and she shall be saluted with twenty one Guns, which she is to return in the same quantity or number.

ARTICLE 14th

As the Government of the United States of America, has in itself no character of enmity against the Laws, Religion or Tranquility of Musselmen, and as the said States never have entered into any voluntary war or act of hostility against any Mahometan Nation, except in the defence of their just rights to freely navigate the High Seas: It is declared by the contracting parties that no pretext arising from Religious Opinions, shall ever produce an interruption of the Harmony existing between the two Nations; And the Consuls and Agents of both Nations respectively, shall have liberty to exercise his Religion in his own house; all slaves of the same Religion shall not be impeded in going to said Consuls house at hours of Prayer. The Consuls shall have liberty and personal security given them to travel within the Territories of each other, both by land and sea, and shall not be prevented from going on board any Vessel that they

may think proper to visit; they shall have likewise the liberty to appoint their own Drogoman and Brokers.

ARTICLE 15th

In case of any dispute arising from the violation of any of the articles of this Treaty, no appeal shall be made to Arms, nor shall War be declared on any pretext whatever; but if the Consul residing at the place, where the dispute shall happen, shall not be able to settle the same; The Government of that Country shall state their grievances in writing, and transmit it to the Government of the other, and the period of twelve Callendar months shall be allowed for answers to be returned; during which time no act of hostility shall be permitted by either party, and in case the grievances are not redressed, and War should be the event, the Consuls and Citizens or Subjects of both parties reciprocally shall be permitted to embark with their effects unmolested, on board of what vessel or Vessels they shall think proper.

ARTICLE 16th

If in the fluctuation of Human Events, a War should break out between the two Nations; The Prisoners captured by either party shall not be made Slaves; but shall be exchanged Rank for Rank; and if there should be a deficiency on either side, it shall be made up by the payment of Five Hundred Spanish Dollars for each Captain, Three Hundred Dollars for each Mate and Supercargo and One hundred Spanish Dollars for each Seaman so wanting. And it is agreed that Prisoners shall be exchanged in twelve months from the time of their capture, and that this Exchange may be effected by any private Individual legally authorized by either of the parties.

ARTICLE 17th

If any of the Barbary States, or other powers at War with the United States of America, shall capture any American Vessel, and send her into any of the ports of the Regency of Tripoli, they shall not be permitted to sell her, but shall be obliged to depart the Port on procuring the requisite supplies of Provisions; and no duties shall be exacted on the sale of Prizes captured by Vessels sailing under the Flag of the United States of America when brought into any Port in the Regency of Tripoli.

ARTICLE 18th

If any of the Citizens of the United States, or any persons under their protection, shall have any dispute with each other, the Consul shall decide between the parties; and whenever the Consul shall

require any aid or assistance from the Government of Tripoli, to enforce his decisions, it shall immediately be granted to him. And if any dispute shall arise between any Citizen of the United States and the Citizens or Subjects of any other Nation, having a Consul or Agent in Tripoli, such dispute shall be settled by the Consuls or Agents of the respective Nations.

ARTICLE 19th

If a Citizen of the United States should kill or wound a Tripoline, or, on the contrary, if a Tripoline shall kill or wound a Citizen of the United States, the law of the Country shall take place, and equal justice shall be rendered, the Consul assisting at the trial; and if any delinquent shall make his escape, the Consul shall not be answerable for him in any manner whatever.

ARTICLE 20th

Should any Citizen of the United States of America die within the limits of the Regency of Tripoli, the Bashaw and his Subjects shall not interfere with the property of the deceased; but it shall be under the immediate direction of the Consul, unless otherwise disposed of by will. Should there be no Consul, the effects shall be deposited in the hands of some person worthy of trust, until the party shall appear who has a right to demand them, when they shall render an account of the property. Neither shall the Bashaw or his Subjects give hindrance in the execution of any will that may appear.

Whereas, the undersigned, Tobias Lear, Consul General of the United States of America for the Regency of Algiers, being duly appointed Commissioner, by letters patent under the signature of the President, and Seal of the United States of America, bearing date at the City of Washington, the 18″ day of November 1803 for negociating and concluding a Treaty of Peace, between the United States of America, and the Bashaw, Bey and Subjects of the Regency of Tripoli in Barbary—

Now Know Ye, That I, Tobias Lear, Commissioner as aforesaid, do conclude the foregoing Treaty, and every article and clause therein contained; reserving the same nevertheless for the final ratification of the President of the United States of America, by and with the advice and consent of the Senate of the said United States.

Done at Tripoli in Barbary, the fourth day of June, in the year One thousand, eight hundred and five; corresponding with the sixth day of the first month of Rabbia 1220.

[Seal] TOBIAS LEAR.

Having appeared in our presence, Colonel Tobias Lear, Consul General of the United States of America, in the Regency of Algiers, and Commissioner for negociating and concluding a Treaty of Peace and Friendship between Us and the United States of America, bringing with him the present Treaty of Peace with the within Articles, they were by us minutely examined, and we do hereby accept, confirm and ratify them, Ordering all our Subjects to fulfill entirely their contents, without any violation and under no pretext.

In Witness whereof We, with the heads of our Regency, Subscribe it.

Given at Tripoli in Barbary the sixth day of the first month of Rabbia 1220, corresponding with the 4th day of June 1805.

(L. S.) JUSUF CARAMANLY *Bashaw*
(L. S.) MOHAMET CARAMANLY *Bey*
(L. S.) MOHAMET *Kahia*
(L. S.) HAMET *Rais de Marino*
(L. S.) MOHAMET DGHIES *First Minister*
(L. S.) SALAH *Aga of Divan*
(L. S.) SELIM *Hasnadar*
(L. S.) MURAT *Dulartile*
(L. S.) MURAT RAIS *Admiral*
(L. S.) SOLIMAN *Kehia*
(L. S.) ABDALLA *Basa Aga*
(L. S.) MAHOMET *Scheig al Belad*
(L. S.) ALLI BEN DIAB *First Secretary*

[Receipt]

We hereby acknowlidge to have received from the hands of Colonel Tobias Lear the full sum of sixty thousand dollars, mentioned as Ransum for two hundred americans, in the Treaty of Peace concluded between Us and the United States of America on the Sixth day of the first Month of Rabbia 1220—and of all demands against the said United States.

Done this twenty first day of the first month of Rabbia 1220.[1]

(L. S.) Signd (JOSEPH CARMANALY) *Bashaw*

[1] June 19, 1805.

الحمد لمستحقه

هذه صورة الاتفاق على الصلح والمحبة بين الامريكان
وبين المعظم السيد الباشا والسيد الباي واهل ايالة طرابلس غرب

الشرط الاول

يكون بعقد هذا الاتفاق صلحا ثابتا عاما من غير خلاف ومحبة صافية بين المقدمين البلديين
من الامريكان وهم وبين رعيتهم وبين المعظم السيد الباشا والسيد الباي واهل ايالة طرابلس وهم وبين
وقع ذلك بتسبيب نفس من الجانبين وعلى قواعد الكثيرة من الخواص المصالحين
وان احد من الجانبين يفعل في المستقبل لجنس اخر جميلا او تخصيصا في السفر في البحر او
في الاسباب يكون حينئذ يفعل مثله مع الجانب الاخر ان وقع ذلك بتسبيب نفسه واما اذا
كان الجميل او التخصيص متوقفا على شروط بقي الامر على اختيار الجانبين ان شاء و يفعلوه
او يبيعوه او يتحكموا على الوجه الذي يكون فيه صلاح الجانبين

الشرط الثاني

السيد الباشا والي ايالة طرابلس يعطي للعمارة الامريكان التي الآن على وجه ايالة طرابلس جميع الامريكان
الذين تحت يده كما ان جميع من هو من اهل ايالة طرابلس تحت يد الامريكان يعطوه له وحيث ان عدد
الامريكان الذين عند السيد الباشا والي ايالة طرابلس يتحكموا نحو ثلاثماية نفر زايدا وعدد اهل ايالة طرابلس
الذين تحت يد الامريكان يتحكموا نحو ماية نفر زايدا لاجل ذلك ياخذ السيد الباشا والي ايالة طرابلس من
الامريكان ستون الف ريال دورو عوضا عن الزايد من العدديين

الشرط الثالث

جميع الفوة متاع الميركان الذي كانت او يمكن ان تكون في المحاربة مع السيد الباشا واهل طرابلس
في ناحية درنة او مواضع اخرى من عمالات السيد الباشا المذكور يستخفوا ويرتفعوا وان الميركان
لم يعاونوا بشي الا بانفسهم ولا باحد اخر في مقاومتهم ما دام هذا الصلح مدة او يعاونوا احدا من رعايا
السيد الباشا الذين يكونون معه في المحاربة في اي موضع يكون من جميع اوطانه والميركان
يبذلوا جهدهم لاجل ان يغلبوا اخو السيد الباشا الذي كان وافقهم على درنة وغيرها لاجل
ان يخرجوا من اوطان السيد الباشا والاكي ايضا يقوى ولا يفعلوا الشي الذي ينفعهم بسبب ذلك
واذا كان هو خرج بما ذكر فالسيد الباشا نتحمل بان يعطيه عياله وذريته الذين تحت يده

الشرط الرابع

اذا كان ارتاف احد مراكب الاجناس التي يكون واحد من الاجانب على ملكهم الفيم يوسفوا من مراكب
احد من الاجانب ينتعون بسبيله من غير تغيير ولا يوخذ منهم اخذ او مسلم

الشرط الخامس

اذا يكون احد من البلديين الميركان او الناس الطرابلسية يلتقي بزوفه راكبا في بعض الغنايم
الذين يوخذوا من عدو الجانب الاخر وليعط البلديين او الناس الطرابلسية يكونوا مسجونين
في الحين ورزقهم يرجعوا اليهم او لمن يوكلوه عليه

الشرط ـــــــــ السادس

كل واحد من الجانبين يعطى من غير مهلة باصبورتوات صحاح لمراكبه على شرط انهم مراكب
القوم متاع وحاق اهل البلد اذا تلاقوا بمراكب كبير ولاتة المركان ما يركبوا اليهم الا في تشيبو نهم
مركان الا اثنين من الناس من غير الذين يجدفون المجاذف وهاذين الاثنين الغير يركبوا الى المركب
الا ان ياذن الرايس لغيرهما بطيب نفس يركبوا ويحققوا الباصبورتوا ويتركوا المركب بعد الحين
تسافر على سبيل حالها وان احد من اهل البلد يمسه ويجبر على الرايس او واحد اخر من الذين
في المركب المركان او ياخذ بعض الحوايج من المركب الكوماندانت او الرايس متاع مراكب القوم او القرصان
سواء كانوا ريسا او غيرهم ممن يظلم يعاقب شديد العقوبة ليكون عبرة لغيرهم ويكون ذلك
حين يشتكى بهم قنصل المركان المقيم في اهل البلد ويقيم البينة على ثبوت فعلهم وجميع
مراكب القوم المركان الذين يتلاقوا بقرابين وحاق اهل البلد حين يطلعوا على الباصبورتوا
وشهادة القنصل المركان المقيم في اهل البلد يتركوهم يسافروا على سبيل حالهم
ولا يعطلوهم ولا يجبروا عليهم وليس لاحد من الجانبين ان يعطى باصبورتو لمركب ليست
تلبسه لاحد من البلديين او لاناس اهل البلد بوجه من الوجوه

الشرط ـــــــــ السابع

اذا احد من البلديين او اناس اهل البلد اشترى غنيمة طايبة من الجانب الاخر او من جنس اخر شهادة
ثبوت طياب الغنيمة والكنتراتو متاع البيوع يقيموا مقام الباصبورتو لهذه المركب على سنتين
لاجل البعد الكاين من العمالتين يكون السنتين بحفظها احياء لان يمكنه ان ياخذ الباصبورتو
الصحيح

الشرط الثامن

المراكب الذي يكونوا الاحد من الجانبين اذا دخلوا المراسي الجانب الاخر ويلزمهم عوين او معاونة
يعطوا لهم ذلك بالسوم الذي هو كاين في البلاد واذا واحد من المراكب تدخل من غير فصد
بسبب النو ويلزمه يصلح مركبه فله ان ينزل ويسو مركبه ويركبه من غير ان يعطي شيا
من اللوازم ولا يتمسك بان ينزل بوجه من الوجوه

الشرط التاسع

اذا مركب احد من الجانبين تغرق على شط الجانب الاخر يعطو لرايسها وبحريتها
جميع ما يلزمهم من امر المعاونة ولا يضيعوا لهم شيا والرزق يكون به الامان على ذمة اصحابه
والبحرية يكونوا تحت النظر ويعاونوهم حتى يجد والقدرة على الرجوع الى بلادهم

الشرط العاشر

اذا بعض المراكب من الجانبين يطارده عدوه تحت رمية مدفع ابراج الجانب الاخر يصيروا احجرهم
للامان يعطوه واذا كانت المركب في المرسى لم تنخذ ولم يطارده عدوه بعد الوقت الذي يمكن الجانب
الاخر ان يمسكه ولما ان يسافر لا ينبغي ان يكون عدوه يسافر على اثره الا بعد اربعة وعشرين ساعة من سفره

الشرط الحادي عشر

امر الاسباب ما بين الميركان واهل اطرابلس والحرمة التي تلزم ان تعطى للتسبيبير والرياس والبحريه وسبيل العاده في سكنى القنا صل في اوطان الجانبين والاكرام والتفضيل والتخصيص الذي يكون عند هولاء القنا صل يكون كذلك موافق لقواعد الاجناس الاكثر محبة وحرمة عند الجانبين

الشرط الثاني عشر

القنصل الميركاني ليس يكون ضامنا في الديون الذين ينتموا على البلد يون الميركان الا اذا كان تحمل قبل ذلك بالكتب على نفسه بانه ضامن

الشرط الثالث عشر

المراكب الفيم نتاع الميركان اذا رموا المخطاف على وجه بلاد اطرابلس والقنصل يستحق ان يعلم المعظم السيد الباشا بوصولهم ويسلم عليهم بواحد وعشرين مدفعا ويردوا عليه مثل هذا العدد

الشرط الرابع عشر

ان المتصرفين بامور الميركان ليس عندهم في انفسهم عداوة مخالفة للشرع والمذهب والهنا
لسلاسلام وانهم يعني الميركان ما وقعت منهم قط ابدا بطيب نفس منهم الى محاربة مع احد
من الاعمال المحمدية عدى في حمايتهم في سفر البحر وقع الاتفاق بين الجانبين
بانه بوجه من وجوه امور الدين ما يكون بينهم فساد المحبة الواقعة بين الجانبين والقناصل
والوكلا من الجانبين يفعلوا ما واجب عليهم من امور دينهم في حياتهم وجميع
الاساري الذين عندهم من ذلك المذهب لم يمنعوا من المشي لحيا ش القناصل المذكورين
في وقت العبادة ويعطي الحرية والاذن للقناصل على انفسهم لاجل يسافروا ويروا كما
عملات الجانبين ووابي البر وفي البحر لا يمنعوا من المشي للمراكب الذين يريدوا ان ينظروهم
وياخذوا من يختارونه حرية من الترجمان والسمسار

الشرط الخامس عشر

اذا وقعت خصومة من سبب مخالفة واحد من هذه الشروط التي في هذا الاتفاق لم تكن
لاجلها المحاربة في الحين ولا توقع القيم بوجه من الوجوه واذا كان القنصل المقيم في البلاد
التي تقع هذه الخصومة لم يمكنه ان يصلح امرها يجيبوا المتصرفون بالوطن يكتبوا سبب
الموجعة التي عندهم الى ان ترسل للمتصرف من الجانب الاخر ويكون الاجل بينهما اثنى عشر شهرا
لكي الاجل يأتي الجواب وفي ذلك الاجل لم تقع محاربة من احد من الجانبين واذا هذه
الموجعة لم تنقضي ووقعت من سببها القيم فالقناصل والبلديون واهل الجانبين
يتركوا بعضهم بعضا يكون عندهم الاذن يركبوا هم وارزاقهم من غير تعطيل المركب والمراكب
التي يبيعوا لهم صالحا

الشرط السادس عشر

اذا في حال الفتنة امور الدهر تكون فيما بين الجانبين والناس الذي ياخذوهم واحد من الجانبين
لم يكونوا اسارى ويستخلفوا ان يبدلوا صنفا بصنف واذا تكون زيادة عند واحد من الجانبين
تتكمل بدفع خمسماية ريال دورو على كل رايس وثلاثماية ريال دورو على كل بلوط او صوبر
كارغو وماية ريال دورو واحدة على كل بحري الذي يزاد وان وقع الاتفاق بانهم المستخدمين
يبدلوا في اجلة اثني عشر شهرا بعد اخذهم وذلك التبدال يكون على يد كل من هو بيده الاذن
من واحد من الجانبين في ملكه

الشرط السابع عشر

اذا واحد منهم من اعمال بر العرب او جنس اخر الذين هم يكونوا في القيام مع الميركان يا اخذوا
غنيمة من مراكب الميركان ويرسلوها الواحدة من مراسي وجالي اهل بلدنا لم يعطي لهم الاذن في
بيوعها هنا الا ويستحقوا ان يسافروا من المرسى بعدما يقضوا مصالحهم من العوين ولم يطالب
الميركان بدفع عوايد على نوع بيوع الغنايم الذي ياخذوا مراكب الميركان اذا اتوا بها الى مراسي
اهل بلدنا

الشرط الثامن عشر

ان احد من البلديون الامريكان او واحد من الذين تحت حمايتهم تكون عندهم دعوى فيما بينهم فالقنصل يفصل بينهم ولا القنصل طلب معاونة من عند حكم اهل ايالة لاجراء حكمه يعطوها له في الحين واما اذا كانت الدعوى بين احد من البلديون الامريكان وبين احد من البلديون من اجناس الاخرين فالقناصل من الجانبين يفصلوا دعواهم فيما بينهم

الشرط التاسع عشر

ان احد من البلديون الامريكان يقتل او يجرح واحد من اهل ايالة طرابلس او بالعكس فمثل ذلك في البلاد تجري عليهم والحكم يكون مثل بعضه بعضا ويكون القنصل حاضرا واذا كان احد منهما هرب فليس يتمسك القنصل فيه بوجه من الوجوه

الشرط العشرون

ان احد من البلديون الامريكان يهلك في حدود عمالة وجاق اهل طرابلس ليس للسيد الباشا او لاحد من رعيته ان يدخلوا في رزق الهالك وجميع متاعه يكون تحت نظر القنصل الا اذا كان الهالك جعل شي لهذا الزلط في وصيته وان لم يكن هناك قنصل يكون رزقه في يد امين حتى يأتي من له فيه حق يطالبه وحينئذ يعطيه حساب جميع متاعه وليس للسيد الباشا ولا لاحد اخر من رعيته ان يمنع اجراء الوصية التي ياتوا بها

وعلى انه اتفاق تم اسفله طوبياس ليرفنط جنرال الميركان متاع الجزاير
جعلوه كومصاري ثابت صحيح ببرهان مختوم من المفدع وطابع الميركان بتاريخ ثمانية
عشر من شهر نونبر من عام الف وثمانماية وثلاثة في بلاد واشنطون لاجل يتكلم
ويعقد اتفاق الصلح بين الميركان وبين المعظم السيد الباشا والسيد الباي اهل الطرابلس غرب
يكون مشهور انه انا طوبياس ليركومصاري كما ذكر اعلاه بطيب نفسي
عقدت وثبت هذا الاتفاق وجميع الشروط والفصول الذي فيه ويبقى على كل
حال موافقة ختمه البينة المفدع متاع الميركان بحضرة المدبرين ومشورة الديوان
متاع الميركان توقع خلاطرابلس غرب يوم اربعة ايام في يونيه عام ثمانية عشر ماية وخمسة
الموافق لحساب الاسلام لستة ايام في ربيع عام اثنين عشر ماية وعشرين .

الحمد لمستحقه

لما عهد امنا الكونسل طوبياس ليرفنط جنرال الميركان متاع الجزاير
كومصاري للصلح بعقد بيننا وبين الميركان الصلح والمهادنة وبين صورة هذا الاتفاق
وما فيه من الشروط واطلعنا على جميع ما فيه بفصوله وحققناه وصححناه واوجبنا
على جميع اناسنا ان يثبتوا ويكملوا على جميع ما فيه من غير مخالفة لذلك بوجه
من الوجوه ولاجل ذلك ختمنا فيه نحن وارباب دولتنا وقعت لمحة في طرابلس
غرب بتاريخ سنة من اشهر ربيع عام الف ومايتين وعشرين

صح منه

شرط الثاني في المذكورين دورو ريال الف الستين مقابض بانتمام مقبوض ... قبيـ
معنى الاتفاق على الصلح والمحبة الذي وقعت بيننا وبين الامريكان المورخ في ستة من ربيع
الاول عام اثنى عشر مائة وعشرين جرى ذلك في تاريخ احد وعشرين من الثاني الربيعين
عام التاريخ

THE ARABIC TEXT

The Arabic of this treaty was probably in the legal sense an original text; but in fact it was a translation of the previously written English. The texts have been examined by Dr. C. Snouck Hurgronje, of Leiden, who, after remarking generally that the Arabic is "in the usual bad and ungrammatical style," makes the following detailed comments:

Article 1. This article is exactly rendered in the Arabic, the only addition being the superscription, "Praise be to Him to whom praise is due."

Article 2. "Dollar" is rendered by "reyal duro."

Article 3. The Arabic is in many parts rather inept; sometimes it would be almost unintelligible without the English original.

Article 5. The Arabic has "with their effects," not "or their effects."

Article 6. The words "insult or molest" in the English are rendered by words meaning "beat or do violence"; the word meaning "do violence" is also used to translate "detention" in the next to the last sentence.

It deserves mention that in this article the word *ojak* (*odgiak*) has been used by the Arabic translator to render "Regency"; so evidently the Tripolitans took the word in the sense of "province."

Article 7. The Arabic words used for "condemned" (*ta'ibah*) and "condemnation" (*tayâb*) are not known in common Arabic in this sense.

Article 8. The word rendering the English "disaster" is unknown in common Arabic.

Article 9. "To her and her crew" is in the Arabic "to her captain and her crew." The last eight words are, in the Arabic, "until they shall be able to return to their country."

Article 11. The three words used to translate "privileges, immunities, and jurisdictions" all mean something like "honor" or "favor," but the idea of jurisdiction is not expressed.

Article 13. Instead of "the Bashaw" the Arabic has "the exalted Lord the Pasha," and instead of "quantity or number" it has only "number."

Article 15. After the words "no appeal shall be made to arms" the Arabic inserts "immediately."

Article 16. Instead of the words, "The prisoners captured by either party shall not be made slaves," the Arabic has, "The men captured by either party shall not be made prisoners of war"; but the inten-

tion seems to have been to express the same idea. For "deficiency" and "wanting" the Arabic has "excess" and "exceeding" (the number of the other party), which gives no different meaning. For "mate" there is the Arabicized European word "pilot."

Article 17. Here and elsewhere the Arabic renders "shall be obliged" by a word meaning rather "shall be entitled to." In this article again "Regency" is rendered by *ojak* (*odgiak*).

Article 18. The words "having a consul or agent in Tripoli" and "or agents," have been left untranslated in the Arabic.

Article 19. This article, although not so badly drawn up as the corresponding article (21) in the treaty with Morocco of 1786 (Document 14), is still ambiguous. The beginning of the Arabic reads, "If any American citizen should kill or wound a Tripolitan, or the contrary, then the law [the Arabic word used here is generally used to denote the sacred law of Islam] of that [which?] country shall be applied to them, and justice shall be equal, and the consul shall be present, and if a delinquent shall escape, the consul shall not in any way be detained for that reason."

Article 20. Here again *ojak* (*odgiak*) is used to render "Regency."

The next page of Arabic text (nine lines), corresponds to the final clauses on the part of the United States; it is translated awkwardly, although not inaccurately. There are slight differences: "the Americans" instead of "the United States of America"; omission of "Regency" before "Algiers"; "signature" and "seal" are both translated by different Arabic words meaning "seal"; the closing words of the first paragraph read, "the exalted Lord the Pasha, the Lord the Bey, and the people of Tripoli of the West"; "Now know ye" is rendered "Be it testified"; instead of "conclude" the Arabic has "conclude and confirm by my free will"; instead of "by and with the advice and consent of the Senate of the said United States," the Arabic has "in the presence of the administrators [rulers] and after consultation of the Divan of the Americans"; the last words read, "corresponding with the sixth of the noblest of the two Rabias (which is indeed Rabia I) of the year twelve hundred and twenty of the era of Islam."

The page of Arabic text following does not call for any important remark; it corresponds to the final clauses on the part of Tripoli but has no seals or signatures. It bears the superscription, "Praise be to Him to whom praise is due"; here again is "the Americans" instead of "the United States of America"; "Regency" before "Algiers" is omitted; at the end, for "our Regency," the Arabic is "*daulah*," which usually means "dynasty" or "government"; the words "negotiating and" are omitted in the Arabic. The wording of the date is here the same as on the preceding page of the Arabic.

The last page, the receipt, contains four lines of Arabic text with the superscription, "Praise be to Him to whom praise is due"; after

"mentioned" the Arabic has "in the second article of the treaty of peace and friendship concluded between us and the Americans"; the words, "as ransom for two hundred Americans," are not translated; in reciting the date of the treaty the Arabic has simply "the first Rabia," whereas the final date of the document has again "the noblest of the two Rabias."

NOTES

This treaty concluded the Tripolitan War, which commenced in 1801. The treaty was negotiated by Col. Tobias Lear, Consul General at Algiers, whose account of the negotiations, dated on board the U. S. frigate *Constitution* July 5, 1805, is in the archives of the Department of State (7 Consular Despatches, Algiers) and is printed in American State Papers, Foreign Relations, II, 716–18.

The Original Documents

It appears from that report of Lear to Secretary of State Madison that the original treaty was in English and Arabic, though first drawn up in English in the form of preliminary articles; but there is no original in the Department of State file; there is a copy, in the two languages, with the signature of Lear; it is in the nature of a pamphlet, but the sheets are not now bound or tied together. The document has the twenty articles of English text, one on a page, running in the usual order on the left pages, with corresponding Arabic on the opposite right pages. Then comes a left page with the English of the final clauses on the part of the United States, signed and sealed by Lear. On the opposite right page is Arabic text. Then comes a left page with the English of the final clauses on the part of Tripoli and English translations of the thirteen signatures for Tripoli, twelve of which are indicated to have been sealed. The opposite right page is of Arabic text, but with no signatures or seals; and finally, there is the receipt for $60,000 ransom, in English and Arabic.

Thus (including the receipt) there are twenty-three pages of English and twenty-three opposite pages of Arabic.

The report of Lear of July 5, 1805, above mentioned, includes the following:

> In the forenoon of the 2d of June, Mr Nissen, His Danish Majesty's Consul at Tripoli, came off to the Constitution bringing a Commission from the Bashaw to negotiate with me on the Articles of the Treaty. As I had a sketch prepared I communicated it to Mr Nissen, who observed that there were some articles more favourable to the U. S. than were to be found in any treaty which the Bashaw had with any other nation; yet he would take them on shore, and submit them to the Bashaw. He did so, and returned on board again about 4 P. M. saying that the Bashaw had acceded to the Articles; but was very desireous of having an article expressive of our determination to withdraw our Forces, &c from Derne, and that we should endeavour to persuade his brother to leave his dominions. To the first I could have no objection, as it would be a natural consequence of the peace; but I insisted that if his brother should leave his territory, he should have his wife and family restored to him. Mr Nissen thought this latter clause would meet objections. However, he took it on shore.

In the morning of the 3d of June Mr Nissen came on board again, and declared that the Bashaw would not agree to deliver up the wife and children of his brother. I adhered to that part of the Article, and after a little time he went on shore, saying that if the Bashaw still persisted in refusing that part of the Article the white flag would be hauled down on shore. . . .

At 4 P. M. Mr Nissen came off again with the seal of the Bashaw to the Preliminary Articles; but with a condition that time should be allowed for the delivery of the wife and family of his brother: I consented to it. . . .

So according to that report, the "Preliminary Articles" (which must have been in English) were sealed and were delivered on board the *Constitution* on June 3, 1805. Lear says that this was "the only instance where a peace has been concluded by any of the Barbary States on board a Ship of War"; but there is no record of what became of the document called the preliminary articles; and it is not even certain that it contained all of the provisions of the definitive treaty. Lear reports a part of his interview with the Pasha of Tripoli on June 4, the textual date of the treaty, thus:

We spoke but little on the subject of the Treaty &c He observed that he had given stronger evidences of his confidence in us than he had ever before given to any nation. he had delivered our people before he had received his own, and as to the money he was to receive, it was merely nominal—the sum was nothing; but it was impossible to deliver our people without something—The other Articles of the Treaty I might form as I pleased; being convinced I should not insert anything which was not just. I returned his compliments, and assured him he would find our Nation as just, as he had found them brave and persevering.

Indeed the actual date of the execution of the treaty was not June 4, 1805, as stated in its text, but June 10, for Lear's report says:

On the 10th [June] I sent the Bashaw two Copies of the Treaty, with translations in the Arabic language, to be signed by him and his Divan. He requested me to attend the Divan, and see the form of doing business there; and as this was a favour never before granted to a Christian he gave it as an evidence of his respect &c I accordingly attended, and was placed on the same seat with the Bashaw, on his right hand. Great order and solemnity were observed. I presented the Treaty to the Bashaw, who delivered it to his first Secretary to read, article by article. Some observations, and short debates took place on several of the articles; but the Bashaw appeared to explain them satisfactorily. After the whole was read, the form of its presentation and acceptance was written by the Secretary, and the Seals of the Bashaw and members of the Divan affixed to the two Copies; one of which the Bashaw delivered to me in a solemn manner, and with many expressions of friendship. He speaks good Italian.

Thus there were two originals of the treaty; one was retained by the Pasha of Tripoli; the other was delivered to Lear, who turned it over to Dr. John Ridgely, of Maryland, formerly surgeon of the frigate *Philadelphia*, whom Lear left in charge at Tripoli when he sailed on June 21. The receipt for the $60,000 ransom paid on June 19, 1805, was, Lear says, "given on the Treaty left with Dr Ridgely"; but there is no record of the subsequent history of the document.

That Lear regarded the original treaty as being in English and Arabic and its date June 4, 1805, as recited in its text, appears from the following extract from his letter to Ridgely, dated June 6, 1805

(American State Papers, Foreign Relations, II, 713–14; D. S., 7 Consular Despatches, Algiers):

> You will receive herewith the Treaty of Peace and Amity between the United States of America and the Bashaw of Tripoli, in English & Arabic, and executed in due form on the fourth day of the present month.

The File Papers

The only papers in the Department of State file of this treaty, aside from the copy which has been described, are the attested Senate resolution of April 12, 1806, and a draft in seventeen articles prepared by James Leander Cathcart in 1802 or 1803, in English and Italian (see D. S., 2 Consular Despatches, Tripoli, letter of Cathcart to the Secretary of State of May 5, 1803). All of thirteen of those seventeen articles and parts of two others appear in similar language in the treaty negotiated by Lear; except for Articles 2, 3, 18, 19, and 20, the text of the treaty is in substance that of the earlier draft; and various articles of that draft were taken from the treaty of 1796–1797 (Document 20). Articles 18 (in part), 19, and 20 of the treaty are similar, respectively, to clauses of other Barbary treaties (Document 14, Articles 20 and 21, and Document 17, Article 13).

Accordingly the texts printed here are the English from the copy above described, including the "receipt" of June 19, 1805, for the $60,000 paid as ransom, and then the Arabic from the same document and in the same order as the English. Following those texts is a comment on the Arabic, which was written in 1930 by Dr. C. Snouck Hurgronje, of Leiden.

The Ratification

The instructions of June 24, 1806, to Dr. George Davis, who had then just been appointed Consul to Tripoli, do not mention the ratification (D. S., 1 Instructions to Consuls, 269–72); but from the report of Davis of June 2, 1807 (American State Papers, Foreign Relations, II, 724–25), from Tripoli, it may perhaps be inferred that the ratification was in his possession; and it is possible that it was delivered to the Tripolitan Government, for it is there said:

> He [the Pasha] asked [on May 12, at a meeting of the Divan] if I would certify that the treaty had been ratified: to which I consented, provided he would execute the third article. He replied . . . that the wishes of our Government should be complied with.

As to the procedure generally in the Barbary States in respect of the ratification and exchange of ratifications of treaties, see the notes to the treaty of 1786 with Morocco (Document 14), to the treaty of 1795 with Algiers (Document 17), and to the treaty with Tripoli of 1796–1797 (Document 20). In this case the final clauses of the treaty, on the part of Tripoli, have express words of ratification: "we do hereby accept, confirm and ratify them."

The Proclamation

The original proclamation has not been found; but it is printed in the Session Laws of the first session of the Ninth Congress, published in 1806, and in The Laws of the United States, Folwell ed., VIII, 167–77, published in 1807; the date of the ratification by the United States is given therein as April 17, 1806; the proclamation does not include the receipt for ransom, but that receipt is printed with the treaty text in American State Papers, Foreign Relations, II, 698.

Note Regarding Article 3

Article 3 of the treaty provides for the withdrawal of the United States forces from the province of Derne (or Derna, as now spelled, in Cyrenaica, one of the two colonies of Italian Libia; its port of the same name on the Mediterranean is roughly 500 miles west of Alexandria); that the United States "will use all means in their power to persuade the Brother of the said Bashaw, who has co-operated with them at Derne," to withdraw from Tripoli; and further that if he, the brother, should so withdraw, "the Bashaw engages to deliver up to him, his Wife and Children now in his power."

"The Bashaw" was Yussuf, who signed the treaty; "the brother," who was older, was Hamet Caramalli (this is one of the various spellings; see the comment of Doctor Snouck Hurgronje on the clan name "Karamanli," following his translation of the "receipt" in Document 20, the earlier treaty with Tripoli). Yussuf had become the Pasha in 1796 (Allen, Our Navy and the Barbary Corsairs, 88).

The relations between Hamet Caramalli and the United States have a direct bearing on the documental history of this treaty. Only a summary of them can be given here. A collection of documents in the matter is printed in American State Papers, Foreign Relations, II, 695–725. The page references in the following paragraphs are to that volume.

The message of Jefferson to Congress of January 13, 1806 (696), transmitting an application of Hamet for relief, included the following statement of facts "according to the views and information of the Executive":

> During the war with Tripoli, it was suggested that Hamet Caramalli, elder brother of the reigning Bashaw, and driven by him from his throne, meditated the recovery of his inheritance, and that a concert in action with us was desirable to him. We considered that concerted operations by those who have a common enemy were entirely justifiable, and might produce effects favorable to both, without binding either to guaranty the objects of the other. But the distance of the scene, the difficulties of communication, and the uncertainty of our information inducing the less confidence in the measure, it was committed to our agents as one which might be resorted to, if it promised to promote our success.
>
> Mr. Eaton, however, our late consul, on his return from the Mediterranean, possessing personal knowledge of the scene, and having confidence in the effect of a joint operation, we authorized Commodore Barron, then proceeding with his squadron, to enter into an understanding with Hamet, if he should deem it useful; and, as it was represented that he would need some aid of arms and ammunition, and even of money, he was authorized to furnish them to a moderate extent, according to the prospect of utility to be expected from it. In order

to avail him of the advantages of Mr. Eaton's knowledge of circumstances, an occasional employment was provided for the latter as an agent for the navy in that sea. Our expectation was that an intercourse should be kept up between the ex-Bashaw and the Commodore; that, while the former moved on by land, our squadron should proceed with equal pace, so as to arrive at their destination together, and to attack the common enemy by land and sea at the same time. The instructions of June 6 to Commodore Barron show that a co-operation only was intended, and by no means an union of our object with the fortune of the ex-Bashaw; and the commodore's letters, of March 22 and May 19, prove that he had the most correct idea of our intentions. His verbal instructions, indeed, to Mr. Eaton and Captain Hull, if the expressions are accurately committed to writing by those gentlemen, do not limit the extent of his co-operation as rigorously as he probably intended, but it is certain, from the ex-Bashaw's letter of January 3, written when he was proceeding to join Mr. Eaton, and in which he says, "your operations should be carried on by sea, mine by land," that he left the position in which he was, with a proper idea of the nature of the co-operation. If Mr. Eaton's subsequent convention should appear to bring forward other objects, his letter of April 29 and May 1 views this convention but as provisional, the second article, as he expressly states, guarding it against any ill effect, and his letter of June 30 confirms this construction. In the event it was found, that, after placing the ex-Bashaw in possession of Derne, one of the most important cities and provinces of the country, where he had resided himself as Governor, he was totally unable to command any resources, or to bear any part in co-operation with us. This hope was then at an end, and we certainly had never contemplated, nor were we prepared to land an army of our own, or to raise, pay, or subsist an army of Arabs, to march from Derne to Tripoli, and to carry on a land war at such a distance from our resources. Our means and our authority were merely naval; and, that such were the expectations of Hamet, his letter of June 29 is an unequivocal acknowledgment. Whilst, therefore, an impression from the capture of Derne might still operate at Tripoli, and an attack on that place from our squadron was daily expected, Colonel Lear thought it the best moment to listen to overtures of peace, then made by the Bashaw; he did so; and, while urging provisions for the United States, he paid attention also to the interests of Hamet, but was able to effect nothing more than to engage the restitution of his family; and even the persevering in this demand suspended for some time the conclusion of the treaty.

That "cooperation" between the United States forces in the Tripolitan War and those of Hamet was formally authorized, is beyond doubt (the Secretary of State to Cathcart, August 22, 1802, page 701; the Secretary of the Navy to Commodore Barron, June 6, 1804, page 702; verbal orders of Commodore Barron to Captain Hull, September 15, 1804, page 703).

William Eaton, who had been appointed "navy agent for the several Barbary regencies" by the Secretary of the Navy on May 30, 1804, under Commodore Barron (702), was in command of such Americans as were at Derne with Hamet in the spring of 1805. In his letter to the Secretary of the Navy of December 5, 1805 (719), Eaton says that the above-mentioned verbal instructions of Commodore Barron to Captain Hull of September 15, 1804, "and my convention with Hamet Bashaw, of February 23, 1805, comprise all the obligations entered into with Hamet." The convention itself (706) is near enough to being an international act to be printed here in full:

God Is Infinite.

ARTICLE 1. There shall be a firm and perpetual peace and free intercourse between the Government of the United States of America and His Highness Hamet Caramanly Bashaw, the legitimate sovereign of the kingdom of Tripoli, and between the citizens of the one and the subjects of the other.

ART. 2. The Government of the United States shall use their utmost exertions, so far as comports with their own honor and interest, their subsisting treaties, and the acknowledged laws of nations, to re-establish the said Hamet Bashaw in the possession of his sovereignty of Tripoli, against the pretensions of Joseph Bashaw, who obtained said sovereignty by treason, and who now holds it by usurpation, and who is engaged in actual war against the United States.

ART. 3. The United States shall, as circumstances may require, in addition to the operations they are carrying on by sea, furnish the said Hamet Bashaw, on loan, supplies of cash, ammunition, and provisions, and if necessity require, debarkations of troops; also to aid and give effect to the operations of the said Hamet Bashaw, by land, against the common enemy.

ART. 4. In consideration of which friendly offices, once rendered effectual, His Highness Hamet Caramanly Bashaw engages, on his part, to release to the commander-in-chief of the forces of the United States, in the Mediterranean, without ransom, all American prisoners who are, or may hereafter be, in the hands of the usurper, said Joseph Bashaw.

ART. 5. In order to indemnify the United States against all expense they have or shall incur, in carrying into execution their engagements, expressed in the second and third articles of this convention, the said Hamet Bashaw transfers and consigns to the United States the tribute stipulated by the last treaties of His Majesty the King of Denmark, His Majesty the King of Sweden, and the Batavian republic, as the condition of peace with the regency of Tripoli, until such time as said expense shall be reimbursed.

ART. 6. In order to carry into full effect the stipulation expressed in the preceding article, said Hamet Bashaw pledges his faith and honor faithfully to observe and fulfil the treaties now subsisting between the regency of Tripoli and their Majesties the Kings of Denmark and Sweden, and with the Batavian republic.

ART. 7. In consideration of the friendly disposition of His Majesty the King of the Two Sicilies towards the American squadron, His Highness Hamet Bashaw invites His said Sicilian Majesty to renew their ancient friendship, and proffers him a peace on the footing of that to be definitively concluded with the United States of America, in the fullest extent of its privileges, according to the tenor of this convention.

ART. 8. The better to give effect to the operations to be carried on by land in the prosecution of the plan, and the attainment of the object pointed out by this convention, William Eaton, a citizen of the United States, now in Egypt, shall be recognised as general and commander-in-chief of the land forces which are or may be called into service against the common enemy; and His said Highness Hamet Bashaw engages that his own subjects shall respect and obey him as such.

ART. 9. His Highness, said Hamet Bashaw, grants full amnesty and perpetual oblivion towards the conduct of all such of his subjects as may have been seduced by the usurper to abandon his cause, and who are disposed to return to their proper allegiance.

ART. 10. In case of future war between the contracting parties, captives on each side shall be treated as prisoners of war, and not as slaves, and shall be entitled to reciprocal and equal exchange, man for man, and grade for grade; and in no case shall a ransom be demanded for prisoners of war, nor a tribute required, as the condition of peace, neither on the one part nor on the other. All prisoners on both sides shall be given up at the conclusion of peace.

ART. 11. The American consular flag in Tripoli shall for ever be a sacred asylum to all persons who shall desire to take refuge under it, except for the crimes of treason and murder.

Art. 12. In case of the faithful observance and fulfilment on the part of His Highness, said Hamet Bashaw, of the agreements and obligations herein stipulated, the said commander-in-chief of the American forces in the Mediterranean engages to leave said Hamet Bashaw in the peaceable possession of the city and regency of Tripoli, without dismantling its batteries.

Art. 13. Any article suitable to be introduced in a definitive treaty of peace between the contracting parties, which may not be comprised in this convention, shall be reciprocally on the footing of the treaties subsisting with the most favored nations.

Art. 14. This convention shall be submitted to the President of the United States for his ratification. In the mean time there shall be no suspense in its operations.

Done at Alexandria, in Egypt, February 23, 1805, and signed by said Hamet Bashaw, for himself and successors, and by William Eaton, on the part of the United States.

Additional article, secret.

His Highness Hamet Bashaw will use his utmost exertions to cause to surrender to the commander-in-chief of the American forces in the Mediterranean the usurper Joseph Bashaw, together with his family, and chief admiral called Maurad Rais, alias Peter Lisle, to be held by the Government of the United States as hostages, and as a guaranty of the faithful observance of the stipulations entered into by convention of the 23d February, 1805, with the United States, provided they do not escape by flight.

The text of that convention is also printed in Prentiss, The Life of the Late Gen. William Eaton, 297–301. For some account of the military operations of Eaton and the march from Alexandria to Derne, see *ibid.*, 295–392, and also Allen, Our Navy and the Barbary Corsairs, Chapter XIV.

A Senate committee report of March 17, 1806, which is severely critical of the course of Colonel Lear, is in Compilation of Reports of the Senate Committee on Foreign Relations, VIII, 17–20.

The Lear Declaration

The relations between the United States and Hamet were thus the reason for Article 3 of the treaty; but the remarkable part of the documental history is that Lear concealed from his own Government an essential part of his action at the time in respect of Hamet.

In Lear's report of July 5, 1805, to the Secretary of State, cited above, he says that the seal of the Pasha of Tripoli to the preliminary articles of June 3, 1805, was on "condition that time should be allowed for the delivery of the wife and family of his brother"; and he adds, "I consented to it."

But Lear said nothing of the fact that on June 5, 1805, one day after the textual date of the treaty, he signed, as Commissioner of the United States, a formal declaration which expressly modified the third article of the treaty by giving four years for the delivery of the family of Hamet Caramalli; that declaration remained wholly unknown to the Government of the United States until some time in 1807.

Furthermore, in view of the situation of General Eaton and the Americans with him at Derne at the time of the treaty, the substance

of its terms was of necessity to be communicated to him. Lear's letter to Eaton on the subject was written on June 6, 1805, one day after the date of his secret declaration, and was sent by the U. S. frigate *Constellation*, Captain Campbell. In that letter Lear gives an account of the treaty which in this respect is as incomplete as, and even more misleading than, his report to the Secretary of State of July 5, 1805. One paragraph of the letter, which is printed in part in American State Papers, Foreign Relations, II, 714–15, and in full in Prentiss, The Life of the Late Gen. William Eaton, 364–66 (the original is in the library of the Historical Society of Pennsylvania), is as follows:

I found that the heroic bravery of our few countrymen at Derne, and the idea that we had a large force and immense supplies at that place, had made a deep impression on the Bashaw. I kept up that idea, and endeavored from thence to make an arrangement favorable to his brother, who, although not found to be the man whom many had supposed, was yet entitled to some consideration from us. But I found that this was impracticable; and that if persisted in would drive him to measures which might prove fatal to our countrymen in his power. I, therefore, engaged, of course, that, on the conclusion of peace, we should withdraw all our forces and supplies from Derne, and other parts of his dominions; and the Bashaw engages, that if his brother withdraws himself quietly from his dominions, his wife and family should be restored to him. This is all that could be done; and, I have no doubt, the United States will, if deserving, place him in a situation as eligible as that in which he was found.

It seems, however, that Eaton knew that there was some secret engagement made by Lear at the time of the treaty. Referring to Lear, Eaton wrote in his letter of August 9, 1805, to the Secretary of the Navy (Prentiss, The Life of the Late Gen. William Eaton, 389–90) as follows:

He goes further. He not only negociates Hamet Bashaw out of his own territories, but pledges the faith of the United States to carry the stipulation into execution; and, at the same time, secretly convenes with Joseph Bashaw that the fulfilment of his engagement in this article shall never be made a subject matter of consideration. Was Mr. Lear sent out to cooperate with Joseph Bashaw! Or is this a crisis in the circumstances of the United States which renders darkness and duplicity necessary to our political safety or existence? Is it possible that anything can render it so, in favor of a piratical chieftain of a Barbary garrison whom one frigate and a few tenders had so often driven from his strong holds? If so, it ought to appear to justify our conduct to the world.

When George Davis arrived as Consul at Tripoli on May 7, 1807, and demanded the execution of Article 3 of the treaty, he was handed the declaration which was signed by Lear in the following terms:

Whereas his Excellency the Bashaw of Tripoli has well grounded reasons to believe, if the wife and children of his brother should be delivered up to him immediately on his leaving his (the Bashaw's) dominions, as expressed in the third article of the treaty of peace and amity concluded between the United States of America and the Bashaw of Tripoli on the fourth day of the present month, that he, the said brother, would engage in new operations of hostility against him, to the disturbance of the internal tranquility of his dominions; And the said United States being willing to evince their good disposition to preserve the said treaty with sincerity, and that tranquility should be secured in the dominions of the said Bashaw—do hereby agree to a modification of the said article of the treaty aforesaid, so that the term of four years, from the conclusion of said treaty, shall be fixed for the execution of the engagement of the Bashaw to deliver to his

brother, his wife and children; during which time the said brother is to give evident proofs of his peaceful disposition towards the Bashaw, and of his determination not to disturb the internal tranquility of his dominions.

Given under my hand and seal, at Tripoli in Barbary this fifth day of June in the year one thousand eight hundred & five.

(Seal.) Tobias Lear
Commissioner of the U. States of America for concluding a peace with the Bashaw of Tripoli.

A copy of this "secret article," as Ridgely calls it, certified by him as "a true and faithful copy of the original," is in the archives of the Department of State (3 Consular Despatches, Tripoli).

Davis stood firm in his demand for the execution of the third article of the treaty, notwithstanding the declaration of Lear; the effect of the "secret article" he brushed aside; and he told the Pasha that "our treaty was known to all the world, and our public faith pledged in their [the family of Hamet] behalf: that his brother had co-operated with us, and to deceive him in such a tender point was to disgrace us as a nation"; and the Pasha of Tripoli yielded. The report of Davis, dated at Tripoli June 2, 1807, which has been quoted, is in D. S., 3 Consular Despatches, Tripoli; it is printed with the text of the declaration of Lear of June 5, 1805, in American State Papers, Foreign Relations, II, 724–25.

The message of Jefferson to the Senate of November 11, 1807 (*ibid.*, 696–97; Executive Journal, II, 58), explains the ignorance of the Government regarding the Lear declaration of June 5, 1805. It concludes as follows:

How it has happened that the declaration of June 5, has never before come to our knowledge, cannot with certainty be said; but whether there has been a miscarriage of it, or a failure of the ordinary attention and correctness of that officer in making his communications, I have thought it due to the Senate, as well as to myself, to explain to them the circumstances which have withheld from their knowledge, as they did from my own, a modification, which, had it been placed in the public treaty, would have been relieved from the objections which candor and good faith cannot but feel in its present form.

As the restoration of the family has probably been effected, a just regard to the character of the United States will require that I make to the Bashaw a candid statement of facts; and that the sacrifices of his right to the peace and friendship of the two countries, by yielding finally to the demand of Mr. Davis, be met by proper acknowledgments and reparation on our part.

32

GREAT BRITAIN : MAY 12, 1813

Cartel for the Exchange of Prisoners of War, signed at Washington May 12, 1813. Original in English.

Ratified by the United States May 14, 1813. As to ratification by Great Britain, and as to promulgation, see the notes.

Cartel for the exchange of prisoners of war
between Great Britain and the United States of America.

The Provisional agreement[1] for the exchange of naval prisoners of war, made and concluded at Halifax in the province of Nova Scotia on the 28th day of November 1812 between the Honourable Richard John Uniacke His Britannic Majestys attorney and advocate General for the province of Nova Scotia and William Miller Esquire Lieutenant in the Royal navy and agent for Prisoners of War at Halifax; and John Mitchell Esquire late consul of the united states at St Jago de Cuba, american agent for Prisoners of war at Halifax, having been transmitted to the Department of state of the United States for approval and John Mason Esquire Commissary General for Prisoners for the United States having been duely authorised to meet Thomas Barclay Esquire his Britanic Majestys agent for Prisoners of war and for carrying on an exchange of Prisoners for the purpose of considering and revising the said provisional agreement and the articles of the said agreement having been by them considered and discussed—it has been agreed by the said Thomas Barclay and John Mason subject to the ratification of both their governments that the said provisional agreement shall be so altered and revised as to stand expressed in the following words.

Article first—The Prisoners taken at sea or on land on both sides shall be treated with humanity conformable to the usage and practise of the most civilized nations during war; and such prisoners shall without delay, and as speedily as circumstances will admit, be exchanged on the following terms and conditions. That is to say—An admiral or a General commanding in cheif shall be exchanged for

[1] For the text of this agreement, see the notes following the text of the cartel.

officers of equal rank or for sixty men each: a vice admiral or a Lieutenant General for officers of equal rank or for forty men each, a Rear Admiral or a Major General, for officers of equal rank, or for thirty men each; a Commodore with a broad pendant and a Captain under him or a Brigadier General for officers of equal rank or for twenty men each; a Captain of a line of Battle ship or a Colonel for officers of equal rank or for fifteen men each; a Captain of a frigate, or Lieutenant Colonel for officers of equal rank or for ten men each; Commanders of sloops of war, Bomb Catches, fire ships, and Packets or a Major for officers of equal rank, or for eight men each; Lieutenants or masters in the navy, or Captains in the army, for officers of equal rank, or for six men each; Masters-Mates, or Lieutenants in the army for officers of equal rank, or for four men each; Midshipmen, warrant officers, Masters of merchant vessels, and Captains of private armed vessels, or sub Lieutenants and Ensigns for officers of equal rank, or for three Men each: Lieutenants and mates of private armed vessels Mates of merchant vessels and all petty officers of ships of war, or all non commissioned officers of the army, for officers of equal rank, or for two men each—seamen and private soldiers one for the other.

Second—All non combatants that is to say, surgeons and surgeons mates, Pursers, secretaries Chaplains and Schoolmasters, belonging to the army or men of war; surgeons and surgeons mates of merchant vessels, or Privateers; passengers, and all other men who are not engaged in the naval or Military service of the enemy, not being sea faring persons; all women and girls, and all Boys under twelve years of age; every person of the foregoing description, or of whatever description exempt from capture by the usage and practise of the most civilized nations when at war—if taken shall be immediately released without exchange and shall take their departure at their own charge, agreeably to passports to be granted them, or otherwise shall be put on board the next cartel which sails; persons found on board recaptured ships, whatever situation they may have held in the Capturing ship, shall not be considered as non combatants—non combatants are not to be imprisoned except for improper conduct, and if poor or unprovided with means to support themselves, the government of each nation will allow them a reasonable subsistence, having respect to their rank and situation in life.

Third—American prisoners taken and brought within any of the dominions of his Brittanick majesty shall be stationed for exchange at Halifax in Nova Scotia-- Quebec, Bridgetown in Barbadoes, Kings-

town in Jamaica—Falmouth and Liverpool in England and at no other posts or places.—and British prisoners taken and brought into the United States shall be stationed at Salem in Massachusets—Schnecteday in the state of New York—Providence in Rhode Island—Wilmington in Deleware, Annapolis in Maryland—Savannah in Georgia—New Orleans in Louisiana and at no other ports or places in the United States.—The Government of Great Brittain will receive and protect an agent to be appointed by the Government of the United States, to reside at or near each of the before mentioned places in the British Dominions for the purpose of inspecting the management and care which is taken of the american prisoners of war at each station: and the Government of the United States will in like manner receive and protect an agent, to be appointed by the British Government to reside at or near each of the stations before mentioned within the dominions of the United States for the like purpose of inspecting the management and care taken of the British prisoners of war at each of the stations—and each Government shall be at liberty to appoint an agent to reside at or near any Depot established for prisoners by the other nation, for the purpose of taking care and inspecting the state and situation of such prisoners—and such agents shall be protected respectively in the same manner as the agents at the stations for exchange.

Fourth Whenever a Prisoner is admitted to parole the form of such parole shall be as follows—

Whereas the agent appointed for the care and custody of prisoners of war at   in   has been pleased to grant leave to the undersigned   Prisoner of war as described on the back hereof to reside in   upon condition that   give parole of honor not to withdraw from the bounds prescribed   there without leave for that purpose from the said agent. That   will behave decently and with due respect to the laws of this country and also that   will not during   continuance in either directly or indirectly carry on a correspondence with any of the enemies of   or receive or write any letter or letters whatever, but through the hands of said agent, in order that they may be read and approved by him   do hereby declare   have given   parole of honor accordingly, and that   will keep it inviolably, dated at

Signature.	Quality	Ships or Corps	Men of War Privateer or Merch[ts] in which taken

And the agent who shall take such parole shall grant a certificate to each prisoner so paroled, certyfying the limits to which his parole extends, the hours and other rules, to be observed, and granting permission to such person to remain unmolested within such limits and every commissioned officer in the navy or army, when so paroled, if in health shall be paid by the agent that has granted such parole to him during the continuance thereof the sum of three shillings sterling per day each, for subsistence; and all other prisoners so paroled shall be paid each person at the rate of one shilling and six pence per day sterling, at the rate of four shillings and six pence sterling per American milled dollar; which pay in case of actual sickness shall be doubled to each so long as the surgeon shall certify the continuance of such sickness; and each sick prisoner shall also be allowed the attendance of a nurse, in case the surgeon shall certify the person to be so ill as to require such help; all which subsistence and pay is to be paid in advance twice in every week. and prisoners who shall wilfully disobey the rules and regulations established for Prisoners on parole, may be sent to Prison. and all rules and regulations to be observed by prisoners on parole, are to be published and made known to each prisoner—and when any prisoner shall be allowed to depart at his own expence if he has not a sufficiency of money for that purpose he shall be allowed necessary money not to exceed the parole subsistence, to which he would have been entitled for one month, if he had remained.

Fifth—And in case any prisoner be permitted to return to his own country on parole, on condition of not serving untill duly exchanged such prisoner shall sign an engagement in the following form—

Whereas Agent for the care and custody of Prisoners of War at has granted me the undersigned prisoner, described on the back hereof, permission to return to upon condition that I give my parole of honor that I will not enter into any naval military or other service whatever against the or any of the dominions thereunto belonging; or against any powers at peace with untill I shall have been regularly exchanged, and that I will surrender myself, if required by the agent of the government at such place and at such time as may be appointed, in case my exchange, shall not be effected; and I will untill exchanged, give notice from time to time of my place of residence. Now in consideration of my enlargement I do hereby declare, that I have given my parole of honour accordingly and that I will keep it inviolably—given under my hand at
this day in the year of our Lord

and to the Prisoner so granted his enlargement on parole, shall be given a certificate and passport specifying the terms and conditions of

his–enlargement, and a description of his person, & notice of such parole agreement shall be sent to the agent for prisoners of war at the nearest station to the place where such parole shall be granted.

Sixth—In case any prisoner of war shall become unmindfull of the honourable obligation he lies under, to the nation which shall have granted him his parole, and shall violate the same, he shall be liable to be dealt with according to the usages and customs observed in such cases, by the most civilized nations, when at war; and either nation shall have a right to demand from the other, the surrender and restoration of any prisoner of war who shall violate his parole, and every just & reasonable satisfaction shall be given to the nation demanding the same, to shew that if such prisoner be not returned, it is by reason of its not being in the power of the nation to which he originally belonged.

Seventh—No prisoner shall be struck with the hand, whip, stick or any other weapon whatever, the complaints of the prisoners shall be attended to, and real grievances redressed; and if they behave disorderly, they may be closely confined, and Kept on two thirds allowance for a reasonable time not exceeding ten days. They are to be furnished by the government in whose possession they may be, with a subsistence of sound and wholesome provisions, consisting of, one pound of Beef, or twelve ounces of pork; one pound of wheaten bread, and a a quarter of a pint of pease, or six ounces of rice, or a pound of potatoes, per day to each man; and of salt and vinegar in the proportion of two quarts of salt and four quarts of vinegar to every hundred days subsistence. Or the ration shall consist of such other meats and vegetables (not changeing the proportion of meat to the vegetables, and the quantity of bread salt and vinegar always remaining the same) as may from time to time be agreed on, at the several stations, by the respective agents of the two goverments, as of equal nutriment with the ration first described—Both Goverments shall be at liberty, by means of their respective agents to supply their prisoners with clothing, and such other small allowances, as may be deemed reasonable, and to inspect at all times the quality and quantity of subsistence provided for the prisoners of their nations respectively, as stipulated in this article.

Eighth—Every facility shall be given, as far as circumstances will permit, to the exchange of prisoners; and they shall be selected for exchange according to the scale hereby established on both sides, by the respective agents of the country to which they may belong,

without any interference whatever of the government in whose possession they may be—and if any prisoner is kept back, when his exchange shall be applied for, good and sufficient cause shall be assigned for such detention.

Ninth—To carry on a regular exchange of prisoners between the two countries, four vessels shall be employed, two of which shall be provided by the British government and two by the government of the United States; and the two vessels of each government shall be as near as possible, of the burthen of five hundred tons together and neither of them less than two hundred tons; and shall be manned, victualled and provided with every necessary and convenience for the safe transportation of prisoners, The expence of the two british vessels is to be defrayed by the British government and of the two american vessels, by the government of the United States; when these vessels are provided, surveyed and approved of, by the proper officers of both governments, they shall be furnished with passports from each government, as flags of truce, and shall carry arms and ammunition sufficient with a guard not exceeding a non commissioned officer and six men, to guard the Prisoners, and keep them in subjection; and shall each carry one signal gun with a few charges of powder, and shall carry a white flag constantly at the fore top-mast head; the British Cartel ships shall carry a British ensign at the gaff end, or ensign staff, and the american ensign at the main top-mast head and the american cartel ships shall carry the american ensign at the gaff end or ensign staff, and the British ensign at the main top-mast head. no cartel shall be suffered to proceed to sea with less than 30 days full allowance of water and provisions for the ships company, and the number of Prisoners embarked on board; and when such cartels shall be established, they shall be kept at all times, constantly well provided with sails rigging and every thing proper and necessary to make them staunch, safe and sea worthy; and shall be constantly employed in carrying prisoners to and from the different stations herein before named and appointed for the exchange of prisoners; and when carrying american prisoners from a British port to an american port the american agent at the port of embarkation shall direct the station at which such prisoners shall be delivered: and when carrying British prisoners from an american port the British agent shall direct at which of the british stations such prisoners shall be delivered—and the agents for prisoners of war on both sides, shall by agreement settle and fix the several species of provisions which shall constitute the daily ration to be served out to prisoners

while on board cartels, with the value thereof: and a regular account shall be kept of the number of days each prisoner shall have been victualled on board each cartel, and the British government shall pay at that rate the expence and cost of victualling the British prisoners delivered at a British station; and so the american government shall in like manner pay at the same rate the daily charge for victualling the american Prisoners, delivered at an american station; but no charge is to be introduced for the transportation or carriage of Prisoners as each nation is to furnish for that service an equal number of tons of shipping—no cartel shall be permitted to remain in port more than ten days after her arrival, unless delayed by winds or weather, or the order of the Commanding officer of the station at which she may be, whether british or american. and in future cartels shall on no account unless driven by stress of weather or some other unavoidable necessity, put into any british or american port—save the ports herein before appointed for the exchange of Prisoners, unless specially agreed upon by the principal agents of the two governments—and in case the number of vessels now agreed on, to be provided as cartels, shall be found insufficient the number may be encreased, and so in like manner diminished, by agreement, as the occasion may require–each nation alwas furnishing an equal share of the tonnage necessary.

TENTH—Untill regular Cartels shall be provided as stipulated in the foregoing article, the transportation of prisoners is to be conducted and paid for by each nation, according to the method hitherto observed in the present war; and after regular cartels are established in case a number of prisoners, not less than one hundred may be collected at any British or american port, different from the ports before named a temporary cartel may be fitted out by order of the Commanding officer at such post or Ports, for the purpose of carrying such prisoners, if British to one of the British stations before named, and if american to one of the american stations before named–and to no other port or place, provided always that such cartel shall bring at least one hundred prisoners, and shall receive an equal number in exchange with liberty to return with them to any port of the nation to which she belongs; and the prisoners so delivered in exchange on board such temporary cartel, shall be certified to one of the regular stations of exchange, where they shall be credited to the nation so delivering them in exchange, whether they arrive at the port of destination or not–But should there not be an equal number at such station to exchange for the number brought, the transportation in such temporary Cartel, must be paid for so many prisoners as shall not be exchanged.

115605°—31—vol. 2——38

ELEVENTH—Commanders of all public ships of war of either of the two nations shall be permitted to send flags of truce into any of the established stations for exchange of prisoners of the other nation, with prisoners to be delivered to the agent for prisoners of war of the nation to which such port belongs, and the agent receiving them, shall give a receipt for them, specifying their names, quality, when and in what ship taken, and the prisoners so delivered shall be placed to the credit of the nation sending them.

TWELFTH Commanders of ships of war Captains of Privateers and letters of marque of either of the two nations shall be permitted to send prisoners belonging to the other nation, in neutral vessels to any of the stations for exchange aforementioned of the nation to which the prisoners belong: and they shall be delivered to the agent and receipted for in the same manner as is directed and expressed in the eleventh article; and the prisoners when delivered shall be placed to the credit of the nation sending them in the neutral vessel—The expences incurred under this and the eleventh article are to be paid by the nation sending the prisoners–and the prisoners so embarked in neutral vessels shall be permitted to proceed to the port of destination without molestation or other interruption by the subjects or citizens of either of the nations.

THIRTEENTH—Lists shall be exchanged by the agents on both sides, of the prisoners hitherto delivered and after such lists are adjusted and signed agreeably to the rule of exchange hereby established, the persons named therein shall be considered as liberated and free to serve again, as well as those heretofore exchanged, notwithstanding any parole or engagement they may have previously entered into; and in future prisoners embarked in a cartel–belonging to the nation sending such prisoners, shall not be credited to the nation so sending them untill they are delivered at one of the stations of the nation to which such prisoners belong, and a receipt is obtained from the proper agent of such delivery–But where the Prisoners and Cartel both belong to the same nation the delivery shall take place and receipts be given at the port of embarkation; provided that the delivery shall not be considered compleat, untill the cartel is in the act of departing the port, and the nation delivering the prisoners, shall retain the custody of them by mantaining a sufficient guard on board the Cartel untill she is actually under way–when the receipt shall be duely executed and delivered. and when special exchanges are negotiated in discharge of special paroles, a certificate of such exchange must be forwarded to the station where the parole was granted.

Fourteenth—If either nation shall at any time have delivered more prisoners than it has received, it is optional with such nation to stop sending any more prisoners on credit, untill a return shall be made equal in number to the balance so in advance.

Fifteenth—This cartel is to be submitted for ratification to the secretary of State for and in behalf of the government of the United States and to the Right Honourable the Lords Commissioners of the Admiralty for and in behalf of the Government of Great Brittain, and if approved by the Secretary of state of the United States–shall be provisionally executed untill the assent or dissent of the Lords Commissioners of the admiralty of Great Britain be known—and it is further agreed that after the mutual ratification of this cartel, either of the parties on six months notice to the other may declare and render the same null and no longer binding.

In witness whereof, we the undersigned, have hereunto set our hands and Seals, at Washington this twelfth day of May in the Year of our Lord one thousand eight hundred and thirteen.

[Seal] J. Mason
[Seal] Tho Barclay

NOTES

The original of this cartel is in the archives of the Navy Department (Naval Records and Library); the text here printed has been collated with that document.

Note Regarding Ratification

The ratification of the cartel by Secretary of State Monroe does not appear on the original. It forms part, however, of the broadside of the cartel printed at the time as follows:

Having seen and considered the foregoing Cartel for the Exchange of Prisoners, in all and every one of its Articles, and approved the same, I do hereby declare that the said Cartel is accepted, ratified and confirmed on the part of the United States.

IN FAITH WHEREOF, I have caused the Seal of the Department of State for the said United States, to be hereunto affixed. Done at Washington, this 14th day of May, in the year of our Lord 1813, and of the Independence of these States the thirty seventh.

James Monroe, *Sec'ry of State.*

From the British archives now in the Public Record Office in London, it appears that this cartel of Washington, after its ratification by Secretary of State Monroe, was sent in original to the Admiralty by the Commissioners of Transport on July 14, 1813, accompanied by a memorandum in which objection was taken to several of its clauses. As the Admiralty was not the competent authority to

settle questions, the papers were put into circulation for the Cabinet and were referred to Lord Bathurst, then Secretary of State for War.

From a memorandum of the Commissioners of Transport of July 14, 1813, and a letter written on behalf of Lord Bathurst dated August 19, 1813, it appears that the objections to the cartel made by the British Government went to the following points:

Article 2. No person whatever taken in a privateer should be considered as a non-combatant except the surgeon.

Article 3. The naming of Falmouth and Liverpool as the only places for American prisoners to be stationed in England.

Article 4. The allowances in case of sickness "may lead to much imposition."

Article 6. The second sentence, as not being sufficiently explicit.

Article 7. Regarded as "highly objectionable."

Article 8. The final clause, "and if any prisoner is kept back, when his exchange shall be applied for, good and sufficient cause shall be assigned for such detention."

Article 9. Water and provisions for thirty days would not be sufficient.

Articles 11 and 12. Inadmissible because they "militate against the decision of the Admiralty not to ratify exchanges made at sea, and as they give great encouragement to privateering on the shores of the British Dominions."

The last paragraph of the above-mentioned letter of August 19, 1813, reads thus:

Lord Bathurst directs me to state that he sees no objection to the Cartel Agreement being ratified when amended upon the several points before noticed.

In February, 1814, the objections of the British Government were communicated to the Government of the United States; there was then transmitted from Barclay to Mason a new draft of a cartel proposed by the Admiralty as a substitute for that of May 12, 1813, with an explanation of the objections raised; and Mason replied on February 10, 1814, that the papers had been received on February 8 and had been submitted to the President for his consideration.

No copy of that new draft or of the explanation of the objections raised, has been found, either in London or in Washington.

There is no doubt whatever that this Washington cartel was treated by both sides, pursuant to Article 15 thereof, as being provisionally in full force from May 14, 1813, the date of its ratification by the United States, until February 8, 1814, the date when the objections of the British Government to certain of its clauses were made known.

There has been nothing found in the archives of either Government to support the view that the formal assent of the Governments was ever given to any amendments to the Washington cartel or to any substituted agreement.

The correspondence of the period indicates that there was an understanding (though not a formal agreement) that the Washington cartel should continue from February, 1814, to be acted on by both sides, so far as it was not objected to by the British Government;

and from the correspondence it seems highly probable that the Washington cartel continued to be regarded as an operative agreement (subject to the objections of the British Government) throughout the War of 1812.

Various letters confirm the view expressed, and nothing looking the other way has been found; and indeed the correspondence in the archives of the Navy Department shows that arrangements were being made in December, 1814, for the return of the last of the prisoners of war then at Halifax.

During the period in question, various particular agreements were made for the exchange of prisoners; the most important was the convention of April 15, 1814, signed at Montreal, modified by an agreement signed at Champlain Town on July 16, 1814, for a general exchange of the American prisoners theretofore taken by, and the British prisoners theretofore taken from, the forces under the command of Sir George Prevost; but none of those particular agreements seems to have been regarded as militating against the Washington cartel. (See Niles' Weekly Register, VII, 145–48, and IX, supplement, 65–70.)

The conclusion, accordingly, is that during none of the period from May, 1813, on, was the action of the parties under the Washington cartel at any time more than temporarily suspended, and that this was so notwithstanding the very grave controversies that arose between the two Governments regarding certain prisoners and their treatment, and the measures of retaliation that were not only threatened but to some extent carried out on both sides (see American State Papers, Foreign Relations, III, 630–92, and also the Pictorial Field Book of the War of 1812, 788–89).

In this connection it is to be noted that the Treaty of Ghent (Document 33) was signed on December 24, 1814, and went into force on February 17, 1815, the day that it was ratified by the United States.

Note Regarding Promulgation

There are various examples of the broadside of the cartel now extant, indicating its wide promulgation at the time. Several of them are in the archives of the Navy Department, one is in the Library of Congress, and one in the archives of the Department of State.

Furthermore, in the archives of the Navy Department is a press release in the handwriting of John Mason, dated May 17, 1813, endorsed "Draft of a Paragraph for the National Intelligencer." That notice appeared generally in the press of the period, *e. g.*, Niles' Weekly Register, IV, 195, as follows:

> We have the pleasure to state, that effectual measures are in progress for the relief of our unfortunate countrymen, in captivity with the enemy. A cartel, by which all the system for the proper treatment, release and exchange of prisoners has been fixed, was agreed on and signed some days since, between general Mason, commissary general of prisoners, on the part of the United States, and col. Barclay, general agent for prisoners on the part of Great Britain.—By this, among other things, it is stipulated that two cartel vessels of the burthen of five hundred tons together, shall be constantly kept by each government in the service of removing prisoners of the two nations, to be released on account or exchanged.

On our part, the two vessels have been already purchased, fitted and dispatched, to bring home our prisoners suffering in the West-Indies. The U. S. cartel Analostan, capt. Smith, left this place for Jamaica on the 2nd inst. to touch in Hampton Roads, and take off British prisoners, and on the 13th inst. the U. S. cartel ship Perseverance, capt. Dill, sailed from Philadelphia for Barbadoes, to touch at New-York to take in British prisoners in like manner. Both vessels are to return with American prisoners to Providence in Rhode Island—one of the stations agreed on for the exchange of prisoners of war.

The Agreement of November 28, 1812

The provisional agreement of November 28, 1812, mentioned in the opening clause of the cartel, did not go into force, as it met with objections on the part of the United States. The original of that provisional agreement has not been found; but there is a broadside of it in the archives of the Navy Department (Naval Records and Library) and a facsimile thereof in the archives of the Department of State, from which the text following is taken:

A PROVISIONAL AGREEMENT, for the Exchange of Naval Prisoners of War, made and concluded at HALIFAX, in the Province of NOVA-SCOTIA, on the 28th day of November, in the Year of Our Lord One Thousand Eight Hundred and Twelve, between the Government of GREAT-BRITAIN and the Government of the UNITED STATES of AMERICA.

The Government of the United States of America having sent to Halifax, JOHN MITCHELL, Esquire, late Consul of the United States of America at St. Jago de Cuba, to act as Agent on the Part of the United States of America, for the purpose of adjusting with the Admiral Commanding at Halifax and the West-Indies the Exchange of Prisoners taken at sea; And His Excellency the Right Honourable Sir JOHN BORLASE WARREN, a Privy Counsellor in the United Kingdom of Great-Britain and Ireland, Knight of the Most Honourable Order of the Bath, Knight of the Crescent, Admiral of the Blue, and Commander in Chief of all His Majesty's Ships of War stationed on the coasts of North America and the West-Indies, having appointed Richard John Uniacke, Esquire, a Member of the Honourable His Majesty's Council, and the Attorney and Advocate General of His Majesty for the Province of Nova-Scotia, and William Miller, Esquire, Lieutenant in the Royal Navy and Agent for Prisoners of War at Halifax, as Agents to treat with the said John Mitchell on the part of His Majesty's Government for the Exchange of such of His Majesty's Subjects as have been or may hereafter be captured at sea, by the public or private Ships of War belonging to the United States of America, for the American Prisoners which have been or hereafter may be taken at sea by His Majesty's Ships of War and Privateers; and the said Agents having met and discussed the Matters to them referred, have agreed upon the following Articles:—

First—The Prisoners taken at Sea on both sides shall be treated by the Government of each Nation with humanity, conformable to the usage and practice of the most Civilized Nations during War; and such Prisoners shall without delay, and as speedily as circumstances will permit, be Exchanged upon the following Terms and Conditions—*That is to say*—An Admiral or a General Commanding in Chief shall be exchanged for Officers of equal rank, or for sixty Prisoners each; a Vice-Admiral, or a General of Division, shall be exchanged for Officers of equal rank, or forty Prisoners; a Rear-Admiral, or a General of Brigade, for Officers of equal rank, or thirty Prisoners; a Commodore carrying a Broad Pendant, with a Captain under him, or a Chief of Division, shall be exchanged for Officers of equal rank, or twenty Prisoners; the Captain of a Line-of-Battle Ship, or a Chief of Brigade, shall be exchanged for Officers of equal rank, or fifteen Prisoners; a Captain of a Frigate or Sloop of War, or a Chief of Battalion, shall be exchanged for Officers of equal rank, or eight Prisoners; a Lieutenant, or Mas-

ter in the Navy, or a Captain in the Army, shall be exchanged for Officers of equal rank, or six Prisoners; Ensigns, or Masters Mates in the Navy, or Lieutenants in the Army, shall be exchanged for Officers of equal rank, or four Prisoners; Midshipmen, Warrant Officers in the Navy, Masters of Merchant Vessels, Commanders of Privateers, or Sub-Lieutenants or Ensigns in the Army, shall be exchanged for Officers of equal rank, or three Prisoners; Second Captains, Lieutenants, or Mates of Merchant Vessels, or Privateers, and all Petty Officers in the Navy, and all Non-Commissioned Officers in the Army, shall severally be exchanged for persons of equal rank, or for two Seamen; and common Seamen, or Soldiers, shall be exchanged the one for the other.

SECOND.—All Non-combatants, that is to say, Surgeons and Surgeon's Mates, Pursers, Secretaries, Chaplains and Schoolmasters, belonging to the Army or to Men of War; Surgeons and Surgeon's Mates, belonging to Merchant Vessels or Privateers; Passengers, and all other Men who are not engaged in the Naval or Military Service of the Enemy, not being sea-faring persons; all Women and Girls, and all Boys under twelve years of age; every Person of the foregoing description, if taken, shall be immediately released without Exchange; provided there is no particular reason, or objection made, by the Commanding Officer on the station where detained; in which case they shall be admitted to their Parole, and when ordered to leave the Country, shall take their departure at their own charge, agreeably to Passports to be granted them, or otherwise shall be put on board of the next Cartel which sails; persons found on board recaptured ships, whatever situation they may have held in the capturing ship, shall not be considered as Non-combatants. Non-combatants are not to be imprisoned, except for improper Conduct, and if poor, or unprovided with means to support themselves, the Government of each Nation will allow them a reasonable Subsistence, having respect to their rank and situation in life.

THIRD.—American Prisoners taken and brought within the Command of His Excellency the Admiral, shall be stationed for exchange at HALIFAX, QUEBEC, BRIDGETOWN in the Island of Barbadoes, and KINGSTON in the Island of Jamaica, and at no other ports. And British Prisoners taken and brought into the United States of America, shall be stationed at BOSTON, NEW-YORK, PHILADELPHIA, and CHARLESTOWN, and at no other ports in the United States. The Government of Great Britain will receive and protect an Agent, to be appointed by the Government of the United States, to reside at each of the before-mentioned places, in the British Dominions, for the purpose of inspecting the management and care which is taken of the American Prisoners of War at each Station; And the Government of the United States will in like manner receive and protect an Agent to be appointed by the British Government, to reside at each of the four Stations mentioned within the Dominions of the United States, for the like purpose of inspecting the management and care taken of the British Prisoners of War at each Station; and Naval Prisoners of War shall not be sent for Exchange to any other port or place within the Command of His Excellency the Admiral, save the four ports before mentioned, nor into any other port or place in the United States, save the four ports before mentioned.

FOURTH.—Admirals, Generals, Commodores, Field-Officers and Staff-Officers, in the Army; Captains in the Navy or Army, Lieutenants and Ensigns in the Navy or Army, Masters and Master's Mates, Midshipmen and Warrant Officers of Men of War, Masters and Chief Mates of Merchant Vessels, being of fifty tons and upwards, Captains and First and Second Lieutenants of Privateers being of fourteen carriage guns mounted, of four pound shot or more, and all Non-combatants, as before described, if captured on the sea, shall be admitted to Parole, the form of which shall be as follows—That is to say,—

Whereas, the Agent appointed for the Care and Custody of Prisoners of War at in has been pleased to grant leave to the Undersigned Prisoner of War, as described on the back hereof, to reside in upon Condition that give Parole of Honour not to withdraw from the bounds prescribed there, without leave for that purpose from the said Agent. That will behave decently and with due regard to the laws of this Country. And also that will not during continuance in either directly or indirectly carry on a Correspondence with any of the enemies of or receive or write any letter or letters whatever but through the hands of the said Agent, in order that they may be read and approved by him do hereby declare have given Parole of Honour accordingly; and that will keep it inviolably. Dated at

Signature.	*Quality.*	*Ships Name, or Corps.*	*Man of War, Privateer, or Merchant Vessel in which taken.*

And the Agent who shall take such Parole, shall grant a Certificate to each Prisoner so paroled, Certifying the limits to which his Parole extends, the hours and other rules, to be observed, and granting permission to such person to remain unmolested within such limits; and every Commissioned Officer in Navy or Army when so paroled, if in health, shall be paid by the Agent of the Government that has granted such parole to him, during the continuance thereof, the sum of Three Shillings sterling each per day, for subsistence; and all other prisoners, so paroled, shall be paid each person at the rate of One Shilling and Six Pence sterling per day; which pay, in case of actual sickness, shall be doubled to each, so long as the Surgeon shall certify the continuance of such sickness; and each sick Prisoner shall also be allowed the attendance of a Nurse, in case the Surgeon shall certify the person to be so ill as to require such help; all which subsistence and pay is to be paid in advance, twice in every week; and Prisoners who shall wilfully disobey the rules and regulations established for prisoners on parole, may be sent to prison. And all Rules and Regulations to be observed by Prisoners on Parole, are to be published and made known to each Prisoner; and when any Prisoner shall be allowed to depart at his own expence, if he has not a sufficiency of money for that purpose, he shall be allowed necessary money, not to exceed the Parole Subsistence, to which he would have been entitled for one month, if he remained.

Fifth,—And in case any Prisoner be permitted to return to his own Country on Parole, on condition of not serving until duly exchanged, such Prisoner shall sign an engagement in the following form:—

Whereas, Agent for the Care and Custody of Prisoners of War at has granted me the Undersigned Prisoner, described on the back hereof, permission to return to upon condition that I give my Parole of Honour, that I will not enter into any Naval, Military, or other Service whatever, against the or any of the Dominions thereunto belonging; or against any Powers in Alliance with until I shall have been regularly Exchanged, and that I will surrender myself, if required by the Agent of the Government, at such place and at such time as may be appointed, in case my Exchange shall not be effected; and I will until exchanged, give notice from time to time of my place of residence—Now, in Consideration of my Enlargement, I do hereby declare, that I have given my Parole of Honour accordingly, and that I will keep it inviolably.—Given under my hand at This day of in the Year of our Lord

And the Prisoner so granted his Enlargement on Parole, shall be given a Certificate and Passport, specifying the terms and conditions of his Enlargement, and a description of his person. And Notice of such Parole Agreement shall be sent to the Agent for Prisoners of War at the nearest Station to the place where such Parole shall be granted.

Sixth.—In Case any Prisoner of War, the Subject of either Nation, shall become unmindful of the honourable obligation he lies under to the Nation that shall have granted him his Parole, and shall violate the same, he shall be liable to be dealt with according to the usages and customs observed in such cases, by

the most civilized Nations, when at war; and either Nation shall have a right to demand from the other, the surrender and restoration of any Prisoner of War, who shall violate his Parole; and every just and reasonable satisfaction shall be given to the Nation demanding the same, to shew that if such Prisoner be not returned, it is by reason of his not being within the power or dominion of the Nation to which he originally belonged.

Seventh.—No person shall be struck with the hand, stick, whip, or any other weapon whatever; their Complaints shall be attended to, and real grievances redressed; they are to be allowed a sufficient subsistence, and if they behave disorderly, they may be close confined, and kept on two thirds allowance, for a reasonable time, not exceeding ten days.

Eighth.—Every Facility shall be given, as far as circumstances will permit, to the Exchange of Prisoners, giving a preference to exchange those longest in confinement, beginning first with the Officers and Men in the Naval or Military Service of each Government; next with the Officers and Men belonging to Merchant Vessels; and last, with the Officers and Men belonging to Privateers; and if any Prisoner is kept back, when his turn for Exchange shall arrive, good and sufficient cause shall be assigned for such detention; and if the Government of either Country shall express a desire that any particular Prisoner or Prisoners should be exchanged before their regular turn shall arrive, due attention will be paid to such request; and if refused, the reasons and causes of such refusal shall be assigned.

Ninth.—To carry on a regular Exchange of Prisoners between the two Countries, four Vessels shall be employed, which shall be as near as possible of the burthen of One Hundred and Fifty Tons each; two of which vessels shall be provided by the British Government, and two by the Government of the United States, and are to be manned, victualled, and provided with every necessary and convenience, for the safe transportation of Prisoners: The expence of the two British vessels is to be defrayed by the British Government; and of the two American vessels, by the Government of the United States; when those vessels are provided, surveyed and approved of by the proper Officers of both Governments, they shall be furnished with passports from both Governments as Flags of Truce, and shall carry arms and ammunition sufficient to guard the Prisoners and keep them in subjection, and shall each carry one signal gun, with a few charges of powder, and shall carry a White Flag constantly at the Foremast Head; the British Cartels shall carry a British Ensign at the Gaff-end, or Ensign-staff, and the American Ensign at the Main Topmast Head; and the American Cartels shall carry the American Ensign at the Gaff-end, or Ensign staff, and the British Ensign at the Main Topmast Head.—No Cartel shall be suffered to proceed to sea with less than thirty days full allowance of Water and Provisions for the ships Company and the number of Prisoners embarked on board; and when such Cartels shall be established, they shall be kept at all times constantly well provided with sails, rigging, and every thing proper and necessary to make them staunch, safe and sea-worthy; and shall be constantly employed in carrying Prisoners to and from the different stations herein before named and appointed for the Exchange of Prisoners; and when carrying American Prisoners from a British port to an American port, the American Agent at the port of embarkation, shall direct the station at which such Prisoners shall be delivered; and when carrying British Prisoners from an American port, the British Agent shall direct at what British station such Prisoners shall be delivered. And the Agents for Prisoners of War on both sides, shall, by agreement, settle and fix the several species of Provisions which shall constitute the daily ration to be served out to Prisoners, while on board Cartels, with the value thereof; and a regular account shall be kept of the number of days each Prisoner shall have been victualled on board of each Cartel; and the British Government shall pay at that rate the expence and cost of victualling the British Prisoners delivered at a British station; and so the American Government shall, in like manner, pay at the same rate the daily charge of Victualling the American Prisoners delivered at an American Station; but no charge is to be introduced for the transportation or carriage of

Prisoners, as each Nation is to furnish for that service an equal number of Tons of Shipping. No Cartel shall be permitted to remain in Port more than five days after her arrival, unless delayed by winds or weather, or the order of the Commanding Officer of the Station at which she may be, whether British or American. And in future, Cartels shall on no account, unless driven by stress of weather, or some other unavoidable necessity, put into any British or American port, save the ports herein before appointed for the Exchange of Prisoners. And in case the number of vessels now agreed on, to be provided as Cartels, shall be found insufficient, the number may be increased; and so, in like manner, diminished by agreement, as the occasion may require—each Nation furnishing always an equal share of the Tonnage necessary.

Tenth.—Until regular Cartels shall be provided, as stipulated in the foregoing Article, the transportation of Prisoners is to be conducted and paid for by each Nation, according to the Method hitherto observed in the present war; and after regular Cartels are established, in case a number of Prisoners, not less than One Hundred, may be collected at any other British or American Port, different from the ports before-named a temporary Cartel may be fitted out by order of the Commanding Officer at such port or ports, for the purpose of carrying such Prisoners, if British, to one of the British Stations before-named, and if American, to one of the American Stations before-named, and to no other port or place. Provided always, that such Cartel shall bring at least One hundred Prisoners, and shall receive an equal number in Exchange, with liberty to return with them to any port of the Nation to which she belongs; and the Prisoners, so delivered in Exchange, on board of such temporary Cartel, shall be Certified to one of the regular Stations of Exchange, where they shall be credited to the Nation so delivering them in Exchange, whether they arrive at the port of destination or not; but should there not be an equal number at such Station to exchange for the number brought, the transportation and victualling, in such temporary Cartel, must be paid for so many Prisoners as shall not be exchanged.

Eleventh.—Lists shall be exchanged by the Agents on both sides, of the Prisoners hitherto delivered, and after such Lists are adjusted and signed, agreeably to the Rule of Exchange hereby established, the Persons named therein shall be considered as liberated and free to serve again, notwithstanding any Parole or Engagement they may have previously entered into; and in future, no Prisoner embarked in regular Cartels, shall be credited to either Nation as exchanged, until delivered at one of the Stations of the Nation to which such Prisoner belongs, and a Receipt obtained from the proper Agent, Certifying such delivery; and when special Exchanges are negotiated in discharge of special Paroles, a Certificate of such Exchange must be forwarded to the Station where such Parole was granted.

Twelfth.—If either Nation shall, at any time, have delivered more Prisoners than it has received, it is optional with such Nation to stop sending any more Prisoners on Credit, until a return shall be made of Prisoners, equal to the balance so in advance.

Thirteenth.—His Excellency the Admiral, will execute these Articles provisionally, subject however to be discontinued, if hereafter His Majesty's Government should disapprove of the same, or any part thereof; And the Admiral will transmit a Copy of these Articles to His Excellency Lieutenant-General Sir George Prevost, Baronet, His Majesty's Governor General and Commander in Chief of His Majesty's Armies in North America, and will recommend to him to agree to the same, so that the Exchange of Prisoners taken on the Land, may be made agreeably thereto, and the Admiral will request the Lieutenant General to make known to the Government of the United States his Assent or Dissent thereto, through Anthony St. John Baker, Esquire, His Britannic Majesty's Agent for the Care and Exchange of British Prisoners in the United States of America.—And it is moreover further agreed, That if any difference of opinion should hereafter arise in carrying these several Articles into execution according to the true intent and meaning thereof, the Exchange of Prisoners shall not be delayed or retarded, in consequence of such misunderstanding, but the particular

points in difference shall be discussed and arranged by Agents to be appointed for that special purpose by both Governments, who shall govern themselves in such arrangements by what is the known and established Law of civilized Nations, when at war, relative to the subject in difference.

IN WITNESS whereof, We the Undersigned, have hereunto set our Hands and Seals, the Day and Year Beforewritten.

RICH. J. UNIACKE.
WM. MILLER.
JOHN MITCHELL,
To be approved by the President of the United States.

Approved.
JOHN BORLASE WARREN,
Admiral of the Blue and Commander in Chief.

Treaty Series, No. 109
8 Statutes at Large, 218–23

33

GREAT BRITAIN : DECEMBER 24, 1814

The Treaty of Ghent. Treaty of Peace and Amity, signed at Ghent December 24, 1814. Original in English.
Submitted to the Senate February 15, 1815. Resolution of advice and consent February 16, 1815. Ratified by the United States February 17, 1815. Ratified by Great Britain December 31, 1814. Ratifications exchanged at Washington February 17, 1815. Proclaimed February 18, 1815.

Treaty of Peace and Amity between His Britannic Majesty and the United States of America.

His Britannic Majesty and the United States of America desirous of terminating the war which has unhappily subsisted between the two Countries, and of restoring upon principles of perfect reciprocity, Peace, Friendship, and good Understanding between them, have for that purpose appointed their respective Plenipotentiaries, that is to say, His Britannic Majesty on His part has appointed the Right Honourable James Lord Gambier, late Admiral of the White now Admiral of the Red Squadron of His Majesty's Fleet; Henry Goulburn Esquire, a Member of the Imperial Parliament and Under Secretary of State; and William Adams Esquire, Doctor of Civil Laws: And the President of the United States, by and with the advice and consent of the Senate thereof, has appointed John Quincy Adams, James A. Bayard, Henry Clay, Jonathan Russell, and Albert Gallatin, Citizens of the United States; who, after a reciprocal communication of their respective Full Powers, have agreed upon the following Articles.

ARTICLE THE FIRST.

There shall be a firm and universal Peace between His Britannic Majesty and the United States, and between their respective Countries, Territories, Cities, Towns, and People of every degree without exception of places or persons. All hostilities both by sea and land shall cease as soon as this Treaty shall have been ratified by both parties as hereinafter mentioned. All territory, places, and possessions whatsoever taken by either party from the other during the war,

or which may be taken after the signing of this Treaty, excepting only the Islands hereinafter mentioned, shall be restored without delay and without causing any destruction or carrying away any of the Artillery or other public property originally captured in the said forts or places, and which shall remain therein upon the Exchange of the Ratifications of this Treaty, or any Slaves or other private property; And all Archives, Records, Deeds, and Papers, either of a public nature or belonging to private persons, which in the course of the war may have fallen into the hands of the Officers of either party, shall be, as far as may be practicable, forthwith restored and delivered to the proper authorities and persons to whom they respectively belong. Such of the Islands in the Bay of Passamaquoddy as are claimed by both parties shall remain in the possession of the party in whose occupation they may be at the time of the Exchange of the Ratifications of this Treaty until the decision respecting the title to the said Islands shall have been made in conformity with the fourth Article of this Treaty. No disposition made by this Treaty as to such possession of the Islands and territories claimed by both parties shall in any manner whatever be construed to affect the right of either.

Article the second.

Immediately after the ratifications of this Treaty by both parties as hereinafter mentioned, orders shall be sent to the Armies, Squadrons, Officers, Subjects, and Citizens of the two Powers to cease from all hostilities: and to prevent all causes of complaint which might arise on account of the prizes which may be taken at sea after the said Ratifications of this Treaty, it is reciprocally agreed that all vessels and effects which may be taken after the space of twelve days from the said Ratifications upon all parts of the Coast of North America from the Latitude of twenty three degrees North to the Latitude of fifty degrees North, and as far Eastward in the Atlantic Ocean as the thirty sixth degree of West Longitude from the Meridian of Greenwich, shall be restored on each side:—that the time shall be thirty days in all other parts of the Atlantic Ocean North of the Equinoctial Line or Equator:—and the same time for the British and Irish Channels, for the Gulf of Mexico, and all parts of the West Indies:—forty days for the North Seas for the Baltic, and for all parts of the Mediterranean:—sixty days for the Atlantic Ocean South of the Equator as far as the Latitude of the Cape of Good Hope:—ninety days for every other part of the world South of the Equator, and one hundred and twenty days for all other parts of the world without exception.

ARTICLE THE THIRD.

All Prisoners of war taken on either side as well by land as by sea shall be restored as soon as practicable after the Ratifications of this Treaty as hereinafter mentioned on their paying the debts which they may have contracted during their captivity. The two Contracting Parties respectively engage to discharge in specie the advances which may have been made by the other for the sustenance and maintenance of such prisoners.

ARTICLE THE FOURTH.

Whereas it was stipulated by the second Article in the Treaty of Peace[1] of one thousand seven hundred and eighty three between His Britannic Majesty and the United States of America that the boundary of the United States should comprehend "all Islands within twenty leagues of any part of the shores of the United States and lying between lines to be drawn due East from the points where the aforesaid boundaries between Nova Scotia on the one part and East Florida on the other shall respectively touch the Bay of Fundy and the Atlantic Ocean, excepting such Islands as now are or heretofore have been within the limits of Nova Scotia," and whereas the several Islands in the Bay of Passamaquoddy, which is part of the Bay of Fundy, and the Island of Grand Menan in the said Bay of Fundy, are claimed by the United States as being comprehended within their aforesaid boundaries, which said Islands are claimed as belonging to His Britannic Majesty as having been at the time of and previous to the aforesaid Treaty of one thousand seven hundred and eighty three within the limits of the Province of Nova Scotia: In order therefore finally to decide upon these claims it is agreed that they shall be referred to two Commissioners to be appointed in the following manner: viz: One Commissioner shall be appointed by His Britannic Majesty and one by the President of the United States, by and with the advice and consent of the Senate thereof, and the said two Commissioners so appointed shall be sworn impartially to examine and decide upon the said claims according to such evidence as shall be laid before them on the part of His Britannic Majesty and of the United States respectively. The said Commissioners shall meet at St Andrews in the Province of New Brunswick, and shall have power to adjourn to such other place or places as they shall think fit. The said Commissioners shall by a declaration or report under their hands and seals decide to which of the two Contracting parties the several

[1] Document 11.

Islands aforesaid do respectively belong in conformity with the true intent of the said Treaty of Peace of one thousand seven hundred and eighty three. And if the said Commissioners shall agree in their decision both parties shall consider such decision as final and conclusive. It is further agreed that in the event of the two Commissioners differing upon all or any of the matters so referred to them, or in the event of both or either of the said Commissioners refusing or declining or wilfully omitting to act as such, they shall make jointly or separately a report or reports as well to the Government of His Britannic Majesty as to that of the United States, stating in detail the points on which they differ, and the grounds upon which their respective opinions have been formed, or the grounds upon which they or either of them have so refused declined or omitted to act. And His Britannic Majesty and the Government of the United States hereby agree to refer the report or reports of the said Commissioners to some friendly Sovereign or State to be then named for that purpose, and who shall be requested to decide on the differences which may be stated in the said report or reports, or upon the report of one Commissioner together with the grounds upon which the other Commissioner shall have refused, declined or omitted to act as the case may be. And if the Commissioner so refusing, declining, or omitting to act, shall also wilfully omit to state the grounds upon which he has so done in such manner that the said statement may be referred to such friendly Sovereign or State together with the report of such other Commissioner, then such Sovereign or State shall decide ex parte upon the said report alone. And His Britannic Majesty and the Government of the United States engage to consider the decision of such friendly Sovereign or State to be final and conclusive on all the matters so referred.

Article the fifth.

Whereas neither that point of the Highlands lying due North from the source of the River St Croix, and designated in the former Treaty of Peace[1] between the two Powers as the North West Angle of Nova Scotia, nor the North Westernmost head of Connecticut River has yet been ascertained; and whereas that part of the boundary line between the Dominions of the two Powers which extends from the source of the River St Croix directly North to the abovementioned North West Angle of Nova Scotia, thence along the said Highlands which divide those Rivers that empty themselves into the River St Lawrence from those which fall into the Atlantic Ocean to the

[1] Document 11.

North Westernmost head of Connecticut River, thence down along the middle of that River to the forty fifth degree of North Latitude, thence by a line due West on said latitude until it strikes the River Iroquois or Cataraquy, has not yet been surveyed: it is agreed that for these several purposes two Commissioners shall be appointed, sworn, and authorized to act exactly in the manner directed with respect to those mentioned in the next preceding Article unless otherwise specified in the present Article. The said Commissioners shall meet at St Andrews in the Province of New Brunswick, and shall have power to adjourn to such other place or places as they shall think fit. The said Commissioners shall have power to ascertain and determine the points above mentioned in conformity with the provisions of the said Treaty of Peace of one thousand seven hundred and eighty three, and shall cause the boundary aforesaid from the source of the River St Croix to the River Iroquois or Cataraquy to be surveyed and marked according to the said provisions. The said Commissioners shall make a map of the said boundary, and annex to it a declaration under their hands and seals certifying it to be the true Map of the said boundary, and particularizing the latitude and longitude of the North West Angle of Nova Scotia, of the North Westernmost head of Connecticut River, and of such other points of the said boundary as they may deem proper. And both parties agree to consider such map and declaration as finally and conclusively fixing the said boundary. And in the event of the said two Commissioners differing, or both, or either of them refusing, declining, or wilfully omitting to act, such reports, declarations, or statements shall be made by them or either of them, and such reference to a friendly Sovereign or State shall be made in all respects as in the latter part of the fourth Article is contained, and in as full a manner as if the same was herein repeated.

Article the sixth.

Whereas by the former Treaty of Peace[1] that portion of the boundary of the United States from the point where the forty fifth degree of North Latitude strikes the River Iroquois or Cataraquy to the Lake Superior was declared to be "along the middle of said River into Lake Ontario, through the middle of said Lake until it strikes the communication by water between that Lake and Lake Erie, thence along the middle of said communication into Lake Erie, through the middle of said Lake until it arrives at the water communication into the Lake Huron; thence through the middle of said Lake to the water communication between

[1] Document 11.

that Lake and Lake Superior:" and whereas doubts have arisen what was the middle of the said River, Lakes, and water communications, and whether certain Islands lying in the same were within the Dominions of His Britannic Majesty or of the United States: In order therefore finally to decide these doubts, they shall be referred to two Commissioners to be appointed, sworn, and authorized to act exactly in the manner directed with respect to those mentioned in the next preceding Article unless otherwise specified in this present Article. The said Commissioners shall meet in the first instance at Albany in the State of New York, and shall have power to adjourn to such other place or places as they shall think fit. The said Commissioners shall by a Report or Declaration under their hands and seals, designate the boundary through the said River, Lakes, and water communications, and decide to which of the two Contracting parties the several Islands lying within the said Rivers, Lakes, and water communications, do respectively belong in conformity with the true intent of the said Treaty of one thousand seven hundred and eighty three. And both parties agree to consider such designation and decision as final and conclusive. And in the event of the said two Commissioners differing or both or either of them refusing, declining, or wilfully omitting to act, such reports, declarations, or statements shall be made by them or either of them, and such reference to a friendly Sovereign or State shall be made in all respects as in the latter part of the fourth Article is contained, and in as full a manner as if the same was herein repeated.

Article the Seventh.

It is further agreed that the said two last mentioned Commissioners after they shall have executed the duties assigned to them in the preceding Article, shall be, and they are hereby, authorized upon their oaths impartially to fix and determine according to the true intent of the said Treaty of Peace[1] of one thousand seven hundred and eighty three, that part of the boundary between the dominions of the two Powers, which extends from the water communication between Lake Huron and Lake Superior to the most North Western point of the Lake of the Woods;—to decide to which of the two Parties the several Islands lying in the Lakes, water communications, and Rivers forming the said boundary do respectively belong in conformity with the true intent of the said Treaty of Peace of one thousand seven hundred and eighty three, and to cause such parts of the said boundary as require it to be surveyed and marked. The said Commissioners

[1] Document 11.

shall by a Report or declaration under their hands and seals, designate the boundary aforesaid, state their decision on the points thus referred to them, and particularize the Latitude and Longitude of the most North Western point of the Lake of the Woods, and of such other parts of the said boundary as they may deem proper. And both parties agree to consider such designation and decision as final and conclusive. And in the event of the said two Commissioners differing, or both or either of them refusing, declining, or wilfully omitting to act, such reports, declarations or statements shall be made by them or either of them, and such reference to a friendly Sovereign or State shall be made in all respects as in the latter part of the fourth Article is contained, and in as full a manner as if the same was herein repeated.

Article the Eighth.

The several Boards of two Commissioners mentioned in the four preceding Articles shall respectively have power to appoint a Secretary, and to employ such Surveyors or other persons as they shall judge necessary. Duplicates of all their respective reports, declarations, statements, and decisions, and of their accounts, and of the Journal of their proceedings shall be delivered by them to the Agents of His Britannic Majesty and to the Agents of the United States, who may be respectively appointed and authorized to manage the business on behalf of their respective Governments. The said Commissioners shall be respectively paid in such manner as shall be agreed between the two contracting parties, such agreement being to be settled at the time of the Exchange of the Ratifications of this Treaty.[1] And all other expenses attending the said Commissions shall be defrayed equally by the two parties. And in the case of death, sickness, resignation, or necessary absence, the place of every such Commissioner respectively shall be supplied in the same manner as such Commissioner was first appointed; and the new Commissioner shall take the same oath or affirmation and do the same duties. It is further agreed between the two contracting parties that in case any of the Islands mentioned in any of the preceding Articles, which were in the possession of one of the parties prior to the commencement of the present war between the two Countries, should by the decision of any of the Boards of Commissioners aforesaid, or of the Sovereign or State so referred to, as in the four next preceding Articles contained, fall within the dominions of the other

[1] See the note regarding Article 8.

party, all grants of land made previous to the commencement of the war by the party having had such possession, shall be as valid as if such Island or Islands had by such decision or decisions been adjudged to be within the dominions of the party having had such possession.

Article the Ninth.

The United States of America engage to put an end immediately after the Ratification of the present Treaty to hostilities with all the Tribes or Nations of Indians with whom they may be at war at the time of such Ratification, and forthwith to restore to such Tribes or Nations respectively all the possessions, rights, and privileges which they may have enjoyed or been entitled to in one thousand eight hundred and eleven previous to such hostilities. Provided always that such Tribes or Nations shall agree to desist from all hostilities against the United States of America, their Citizens, and Subjects upon the Ratification of the present Treaty being notified to such Tribes or Nations, and shall so desist accordingly. And His Britannic Majesty engages on his part to put an end immediately after the Ratification of the present Treaty to hostilities with all the Tribes or Nations of Indians with whom He may be at war at the time of such Ratification, and forthwith to restore to such Tribes or Nations respectively all the possessions, rights, and privileges, which they may have enjoyed or been entitled to in one thousand eight hundred and eleven previous to such hostilities. Provided always that such Tribes or Nations shall agree to desist from all hostilities against His Britannic Majesty and His Subjects upon the Ratification of the present Treaty being notified to such Tribes or Nations, and shall so desist accordingly.

Article the Tenth.

Whereas the Traffic in Slaves is irreconcilable with the principles of humanity and Justice, and whereas both His Majesty and the United States are desirous of continuing their efforts to promote its entire abolition, it is hereby agreed that both the contracting parties shall use their best endeavours to accomplish so desirable an object.

Article the Eleventh.

This Treaty when the same shall have been ratified on both sides without alteration by either of the contracting parties, and the Ratifications mutually exchanged, shall be binding on both parties, and the Ratifications shall be exchanged at Washington in the space of four months from this day or sooner if practicable.

In faith whereof, We the respective Plenipotentiaries have signed this Treaty, and have thereunto affixed our Seals.

Done in triplicate at Ghent the twenty fourth day of December one thousand eight hundred and fourteen.

GAMBIER.	[Seal]
HENRY GOULBURN	[Seal]
WILLIAM ADAMS	[Seal]
JOHN QUINCY ADAMS	[Seal]
J. A. BAYARD	[Seal]
H. CLAY.	[Seal]
JON[a] RUSSELL	[Seal]
ALBERT GALLATIN	[Seal]

NOTES

It is stated in the final clause that this treaty was executed in triplicate. However, there are two signed originals in the treaty file and a third is bound in a volume of papers relating to the negotiations (D. S., Ghent, etc.). The following explanatory paragraph is from the letter of the American plenipotentiaries of December 25, 1814, to the Secretary of State (American State Papers, Foreign Relations, III, 733):

> To guard against any accident which might happen in the transmission of a single copy of the treaty to the United States, the British plenipotentiaries have consented to execute it in triplicate; and, as the treaty with the British ratification may be exposed to the same danger, the times for the cessation of hostilities, the restoration of captures at sea, and the release of prisoners, have been fixed, not from the exchange of ratifications, but from the ratification on both sides, without alteration by either of the contracting parties. We consented to the introduction of this latter provision at the desire of the British plenipotentiaries, who were willing to take a full, but were unwilling to incur the risk of a partial, ratification, as the period from which the peace should be considered as concluded.

It was on February 11, 1815, that the Treaty of Ghent reached this country, according to the following statement from Niles' Weekly Register, VII, 393:

> The British sloop of war Favorite arrived at New-York on Saturday evening last [February 11, 1815]—passengers Mr. *Carrol*, one of the secretaries to our ministers at *Ghent*, and Mr. *Baker*, secretary to the British legation to the United States. The former with a copy of the TREATY OF PEACE concluded and signed by the British commissioners at Ghent on the 24th December, and the latter with the same ratified by the prince regent, and which being approved by the president and senate, is *immediately* to be communicated by him to tne British fleets and armies in this quarter of the globe.

On the evening of February 13 the Secretary of the Mission at Ghent, Christopher Hughes, jr., arrived at Annapolis with another original of the treaty; it appears that Carroll (and doubtless Hughes also) reached Washington on February 14 (the Daily National Intelligencer, February 15 and 16, 1815).

On the back cover page of one of the two originals in the file there is written a duplicate of the United States instrument of ratification signed by Madison and under the Great Seal, but lacking the usual attest.

The file of this treaty includes the British instrument of ratification of December 31, 1814, the attested Senate resolution of February 16, 1815, and also the certificate of the exchange of ratifications mentioned below in the note regarding Article 8.

The original proclamation has not been found; but it was published at the time, *e. g.*, Niles' Weekly Register, VII, 397–400; and see also Richardson, I, 560.

Note Regarding Article 8

An agreement regarding the payment of the Commissioners was made when the ratifications were exchanged; it was to the effect that such payment should be made on the same principles as those observed in respect of the Jay Treaty (Document 16). The terms of the agreement were embodied in the certificate of the exchange of ratifications as follows:

> This is to certify that on the seventeenth day of February one thousand eight hundred and fifteen, at eleven o'Clock P. M. the Honourable James Monroe, Acting Secretary of State of the United States, delivered and exchanged a ratified Copy of a Treaty, signed at Ghent on the twenty fourth day of December last between His Britannic Majesty and the United States of America for a like copy on the part of His said Britannic Majesty.
>
> At the same time Mr Monroe expressed the willingness of the Government of the United States to arrange the payment of the Commissioners to be appointed in pursuance of the Treaty on the same principles as were observed in carrying into Execution the Treaty of one thousand seven hundred and ninety four between the same Powers, that is, the expense to be equally borne by the two Governments, to which arrangement the Undersigned consented.
>
> In witness whereof the Undersigned has hereunto set his hand and seal of arms at Washington this seventeenth day of February, one thousand eight hundred and fifteen.
>
> [Seal] Anthony St Jno Baker.

Note Regarding the Alternat

In this treaty the *alternat* was not observed as it has since been; His Britannic Majesty was named before the United States of America, and the British plenipotentiaries signed above those of the United States.

It appears that verbal representations on the point were made by Monroe at the time of the exchange of ratifications; the following is extracted from his letter to John Quincy Adams of March 13, 1815 (D. S., 7 Instructions, U. S. Ministers, 390–91):

> In the treaty lately concluded at Ghent, Great Britain takes a priority over the United-States, as is presumed, in both instruments; she does so, in that received here, and it is inferred that she does it in that received by her government, from the circumstance that she holds that rank in the ratification of the Prince Regent. Great-Britain takes the first rank as a power, and our Ministers likewise sign under those of Great-Britain. This though comparatively an inferior object, is not unimportant. It was, there is no doubt, lost sight of in the very important object

of peace. In all other treaties between the United-States and other powers, the Ministers of each party sign in the same line. This was done in the Treaty of peace with Great-Britain, and in the subsequent Treaties with her government. In the Treaty with France in 1803., the United-States took rank in the instrument delivered to this government, which was reciprocated in that delivered to the government of France. In the Treaty with Spain in 1795., M[r] Pinckney signed before the Prince of the Peace; the United-States had rank likewise, over Spain, in the instrument delivered to them. It is understood, that in treaties between all powers, this principle of equality is generally, if not invariably recognized and observed. In the exchange of ratifications it was thought proper to advert to these circumstances, that neither this Treaty or those which preceded it, might become a precedent, establishing a relation between the United-States and Great-Britain, differing from that which exists between them and other powers. As the governments of Europe attach much importance to this circumstance, it is one to which we ought not to continue, to be altogether inattentive. It is a mortifying truth that concessions, however generous the motive, seldom produce the desired effect. They more frequently inspire improper pretensions in the opposite party. It may be presumed that M[r] Baker will communicate the substance of my remarks to him on this subject to his government. They were made with that calculation. Should a suitable opportunity present itself, it may have a good effect, that you should explain to the British government, the sentiments of The President on it.

Treaty Series, No. 1½
8 Statutes at Large, 224–27

34

ALGIERS : JUNE 30 AND JULY 3, 1815

Treaty of Peace, signed at Algiers June 30 and July 3, 1815. Original in English.

Submitted to the Senate December 6, 1815. Resolution of advice and consent December 21, 1815. Ratified by the United States December 26, 1815. As to the ratification generally, see the notes. Proclaimed December 26, 1815.

Treaty of peace concluded between His United States of America and his Highness Omar Bashaw Dey of Algiers.

Article 1st

There shall be from the Conclusion of this treaty, a firm inviolable and universal peace and friendship between the President and Citizens of the United States of America on the one part, and the Dey and Subjects of the Regency of Algiers in Barbary, on the other, made by the free consent of both parties and upon the terms of the most favored nations; and if either party shall hereafter grant to any other nation, any particular favor or privilege in navigation or Commerce it shall immediately become common to the other party, freely when freely it is granted to such other nation; but when the grant is conditional, it shall be at the option of the contracting parties to accept, alter, or reject such conditions, in such manner as shall be most conducive to their respective interests.

Article 2d

It is distinctly understood between the Contracting parties, that no tribute either as biennial presents, or under any other form or name whatever, shall ever be required by the Dey and Regency of Algiers from the United States of America on any pretext whatever.

Article 3d

The Dey of Algiers shall cause to be immediately delivered up to the American Squadron now off Algiers all the American Citizens now in his possession, amounting to ten more or less, and all the Subjects of the Dey of Algiers now in the power of the United States

amounting to five hundred more or less, shall be delivered up to him, the United States according to the usages of civilized nations requiring no ransom for the excess of prisoners in their favor.

Article 4th.

A just and full compensation shall be made by the Dey of Algiers to such citizens of the United States, as have been Captured, and detained by Algerine Cruizers, or who have been forced to abandon their property in Algiers in violation of the 22d article of the treaty of peace and amity[1] concluded between the United States and the Dey of Algiers on the 5 September 1795.

And it is agreed between the contracting parties, that in lieu of the above, the Dey of Algiers shall cause to be delivered forthwith into the hands of the American Consul residing in Algiers the whole of a quantity of Bales of Cotton left by the late Consul General of the United States in the public magazines in Algiers; and that he shall pay into the hands of the said Consul the sum of ten thousand Spanish dollers.

Article 5th.

If any goods belonging to any nation with which either of the parties are at war should be loaded on board of vessels belonging to the other party, they shall pass free and unmolested, and no attempt shall be made to take or detain them.

Article 6th.

If any Citizens or subjects belonging to either party shall be found on board a prize vessel taken from an Ennemy by the other party, such Citizens or subjects shall be liberated immediately, and in no case or on any pretence whatever whatever shall any American Citizen be kept in Captivity or Confinement, or the property of any American Citizen found on board of any vessel belonging to any nation with which Algiers may be at War, be detained from its lawful owners after the exhibition of sufficient proofs of american Citizenship, and American property, by the Consul of the United States residing at Algiers.

Article 7th.

Proper passports shall immediately be given to the vessels of both the Contracting parties, on condition that the vessels of war belonging to the Regency of Algiers on meeting with Merchant Vessels be-

[1] Document 17.

longing to Citizens of the United States of America, shall not be permitted to visit them with more than two persons besides the rowers; these only shall be permitted to go on board without first obtaining leave from the Commander of said vessel, who shall compare the passports and immediately permit said vessel to proceed on her voyage; and should any of the subjects of Algiers insult or molest the Commander or any other person on board a vessel so visited, or plunder any of the property contained in her, on complaint being made to the Consul of the United States residing in Algiers, and on his producing sufficient proofs to substantiate the fact, the Commander or Rais of said Algerine ship or vessel of war, as well as the offenders shall be punished in the most exemplary manner.

All vessels of war belonging to the United States of America, on meeting with a Cruizer belonging to the Regency of Algiers, on having seen her passports, and Certificates from the Consul of the United States residing in Algiers shall permit her to proceed on her Cruize unmolested, and without detention. No passport shall be granted by either party to any vessels but such as are absolutely the property of Citizens or subjects of the said contracting parties, on any pretence whatever.

Article 8th.

A Citizen or subject of either of the contracting parties having bought a prize Vessel condemned by the other party, or by any other nation, the Certificates of Condemnation and bill of sale shall be a sufficient passport for such vessel for six months, which, considering the distance between the two countries is no more than a reasonable time for her to procure passports.

Article 9th.

Vessels of either of the contracting parties putting into the ports of the other and having need of provisions, or other supplies shall be furnished at the market price, and if any such Vessel should so put in from a disaster at sea and have occasion to repair, she shall be at liberty to land, and reembark her Cargo, without paying any customs, or duties whatever; but in no case shall she be compelled to land her Cargo

Article 10th.

Should a vessel of either of the contracting parties be cast on shore within the Territories of the other all proper assistance shall be given to her, and to her crew; no pillage shall be allowed. The property shall remain at the disposal of the owners, and if reshipped

on board of any vessel for exportation, no customs or duties whatever shall be required to be paid thereon, and the crew shall be protected and succoured until they can be sent to their own Country.

Article 11th.

If a vessel of either of the contracting parties shall be attacked by an ennemy within Cannon shot of the forts of the other, she shall be protected as much as is possible. If she be in port she shall not be seized, or attacked when it is in the power of the other party to protect her; and when she proceeds to sea, no Ennemy shall be permitted to pursue her from the same port within twenty four hours after her departure.

Article 12th.

The Commerce between the United States of America and the Regency of Algiers, the protections to be given to Merchants, masters of vessels, and seamen, the reciprocal right of establishing Consuls in each country, the privileges, immunities and jurisdictions to be enjoyed by such Consuls, are declared to be upon the same footing in every respect with the most favored nations respectively.

Article 13th.[1]

On a vessel or vessels of war belonging to the United States of America anchoring before the City of Algiers, the Consul is to inform the Dey of her arrival when she shall receive the Salutes, which are by treaty or Custom given to the ships of war of the most favored nations on similar occasions, and which shall be returned gun for gun: and if after such arrival so announced, any christians whatever, Captives in Algiers make their escape and take refuge on board of the said ships of war, they shall not be required back again, nor shall the Consul of the United States, or commander of the said Ship be required to pay anything for the said Christians.

Article 14th[1]

The Consul of the United States of America shall not be responsable for the debts Contracted by the Citizens of his own Country unless he gives previously written obligations so to do.

Article 15th.

As the Government of the United States of America has in itself no character of enmity against the laws, religion, or tranquility of

[1] As to the order of Articles 13 and 14, see the notes following the treaty text and also the notes to Document 37.

any nation, and as the said States have never entered into any voluntary war, or act of hostility, except in defence of their just rights on the high seas, it is declared by the Contracting parties that no pretext arising from religious opinions shall ever produce an interruption of Harmony between the two nations; and the Consuls and agents of both nations, shall have liberty to Celebrate the rights of their respective religions in their own houses.

The Consuls respectively shall have liberty and personal security given them to travel within the territories of each other, both by land, and by sea, and shall not be prevented from going on board of any vessel they may think proper to visit; they shall likewise have the liberty of apointing their own Dragoman, and Broker.

Article 16th.

In Case of any dispute arrising from the violation of any of the articles of this Treaty no appeal shall be made to arms, nor shall war be declared, on any pretext whatever; but if the Consul residing at the place where the dispute shall happen, shall not be able to settle the same, the Government of that country shall state their grievance in writing, and transmit the same to the government of the other, and the period of three months shall be allowed for answers to be returned, during which time no act of hostility shall be permitted by either party; and in case the grievances are not redressed, and war should be the event, the Consuls, and Citizens, and subjects of both parties respectively shall be permitted to embark with their families and effects unmolested, on board of what vessel or vessels they shall think proper. Reasonable time being allowed for that purpose.

Article 17th.

If in the Course of events a war should break out between the two nations, the prisoners Captured by either party shall not be made slaves, they shall not be forced to hard labor, or other confinement than such as may be necessary to secure their safe keeping, and they shall be exchanged rank for rank; and it is agreed that prisoners shall be exchanged in twelve months after their Capture, and the exchange may be effected by any private individual, legally authorized by either of the parties.

Article 18th.

If any of the Barbary powers, or other states at war with the United States shall Capture any american Vessel, and send her into any port of the Regency of Algiers, they shall not be permitted to sell her, but shall be forced to depart the port on procuring the requisite supplies

of provisions; but the vessels of war of the United States with any prizes they may capture from their Ennemies shall have liberty to frequent the ports of Algiers for refreshment of any kinds, and to sell such prizes in the said ports, without paying any other customs or duties than such as are customary on ordinary Commercial importations.

ARTICLE 19TH.

If any Citizens of the United States, or any persons under their protection, shall have any disputes with each other, the Consul shall decide between the parties, and whenever the Consul shall require any aid or assistance from the Government of Algiers to enforce his decisions it shall be immediately granted to him. And if any dispute shall arise between any citizens of the United States, and the citizens or subjects of any other nation having a Consul or agent in Algiers, such disputes shall be settled by the Consuls or agents of the respective nations; and any dispute or suits at law that may take place between any citizens of the United States, and the subjects of the Regency of Algiers shall be decided by the Dey in person and no other.

ARTICLE 20TH.

If a Citizen of the United States should kill wound or strike a subject of Algiers, or on the Contrary, a subject of Algiers should kill wound or strike a Citizen of the United States, the law of the country shall take place, and equal justice shall be rendered, the consul assisting at the tryal; but the sentence of punishment against an american Citizen, shall not be greater or more severe, than it would be against a Turk in the same predicament, and if any delinquent should make his escape, the Consul shall not be responsable for him in any manner whatever.

ARTICLE 21st

The Consul of the United States of America shall not be required to pay any customs or duties whatever on any thing he imports from a foreign Country for the use of his house & family.

ARTICLE 22d

Should any of the citizens of the United States die within the Regency of Algiers, the Dey and his subjects shall not interfere with the property of the deceased, but it shall be under the immediate direction of the Consul, unless otherwise disposed of by will; should there be no Consul the effects shall be deposited in the hands of some person worthy of trust until the party shall appear who has a right to demand them, when they shall render an account of the property;

neither shall the Dey or his subjects give hindrance in the execution of any will that may appear.

Done at Algiers on the 30th day of June A. D. 1815.

(Signed) Omar Bashaw (L. S.)

Whereas the undersigned William Shaler a Citizen of the United States, and Stephen Decatur Commander in chief of the U. S. naval forces now in the medeterrenean, being duly appointed Commissioners by letters patent under the signature of the President, and Seal of the U. S. of America, bearing date at the City of Washington the 9th day of April 1815 for negotiating and concluding a treaty of peace between the U. S. of America, and the Dey of Algiers.

Now Know Ye that we William Shaler and Stephen Decatur commissioners as aforesaid, do conclude the foregoing treaty, and every article, and clause therein contained, reserving the same, nevertheless for the final ratification of the President of the United States of America, by and with the advice and consent of the Senate

Done on board of the United States Ship Guerriere in the bay of Algiers on the 3[d] day of July in the year 1815 and of the independence of the U. S. 40th.

(Signed) W[m] Shaler
Stephen Decatur.

NOTES

No original of this treaty has been found in the archives of the Department of State. It is believed that the original treaty was written in the English language only.

The report of the American Commissioners, Commodore Stephen Decatur and William Shaler, Consul General at Algiers, dated on the U. S. S. *Guerriere*, Bay of Algiers, July 4, 1815 (American State Papers, Foreign Relations, IV, 6), gives the circumstances of the negotiations. The act of March 3, 1815 (3 Statutes at Large, 230), had authorized naval operations against the Dey of Algiers, whose predecessor had commenced hostilities in 1812; the United States naval forces had been successful; the treaty was dictated as a result; and such negotiations as there were, took place on board the *Guerriere*. On that vessel "the model of a treaty" was brought forward by the American representatives on June 30, 1815; to that vessel the boat came back from the shore "within three hours, with the treaty signed as we had concluded it, and the prisoners." That signed treaty was surely written in English; but was perhaps in preliminary form only, for the report of July 4, 1815, says: "The treaty has since been drawn out anew, translated by them, and duly executed by the Dey; which we have the honor to transmit herewith." Two originals of

that report, one signed by Decatur and for Shaler and the other signed by Shaler and for Decatur, are in D. S., Negotiations Mediterranean.

It appears that there were at least three originals of the treaty. A despatch of Shaler to the Secretary of State, dated July 5, 1815 (D. S., 9 Consular Despatches, Algiers), says: "A copy [meaning an original] of the treaty remains with the Regency, a second is in my hands, and a third is dispatched by Captain Lewis [U. S. S. *Epervier*] for ratification."

Thus there were duplicate originals in the possession of the American representatives; this appears also from a statement over the signature of Shaler, dated November 3, 1815, and copied below. The original transmitted to Washington by Captain Lewis in the U. S. S. *Epervier* did not arrive, as that vessel was lost at sea; but there is nothing in any of the available documents or papers to indicate that the original language of the treaty was anything other than English. In the letter of Shaler of April 15, 1816, cited below, he writes that at an interview with the Dey of Algiers, the Consul of Sweden compared the United States instrument of ratification with "the copy in the Bashaw's possession"; and later on he mentions "the Treaty as signed by himself [the Dey of Algiers] in our language."

The intrinsic evidence alone would be sufficient to prove that the treaty was written first in English; Articles 2, 3, and 4, for example, were certainly not written as a translation. Obviously the treaty was in great part adapted from the treaty with Tripoli of 1805 (Document 31), the text of which was certainly first written in English. As Commodore Decatur wrote on July 7, 1815, to the Secretary of State (D. S., Negotiations Mediterranean): "With the exception of a few of the Articles, candour requires, that we should acknowledge our plagiary from Mr Lear's treaty with Tripoli."

There was, indeed, a Turkish translation of the treaty in the hands of the Dey of Algiers; and there were stipulations in that version which had no equivalent in the English; these were disclosed at an interview between Shaler and the Dey of Algiers on April 3, 1816 (letter of Shaler of April 15, 1816, D. S., 9 Consular Despatches, Algiers), as to which Shaler reported:

> He [the Swedish Consul] then had the Turkish translation read to him, and I was much surprized to find the promise to return his ships, and to give a consular present introduced into his instrument as a treaty stipulation. . . . I declared to him [the Dey of Algiers] that the United States would regard the Treaty as executed in our language, which had been so fully explained to him, thro' his interpreters by the Consul of Sweden previous to his affixing his signature to it, as the only rule for our relations with Algiers, for he well knew that it was impossible for me to obtain any positive assurance of the fidelity of its translation into the Turkish language, which he acquiesced in and again assured me that he intended to preserve the peace inviolate.

The Source Text

The text of the treaty here printed is from an authenticated copy in the archives of the Department of State (9 Consular Despatches, Algiers), which may be called the existing authenticated copy. The text in 8 Statutes at Large, 224–27, and in other treaty collections,

is from another authenticated copy which is not now available. That other authenticated copy is almost certainly the one which was transmitted to the Senate by President Madison, who first sent to the Senate "an office copy" and then a copy "certified by one of the Commissioners . . . , the original of the treaty not having been received" (Executive Journal, III, 3, 4; also American State Papers, Foreign Relations, IV, 4–6). There are a few variances between the texts of the articles in the two copies, none of which is very material; and, for some quite unexplained reason, Articles 13 and 14 in the one come in reverse order in the other; but the existing authenticated copy seems to be the one more carefully prepared; the other was drawn up on the U. S. S. *Guerriere* on July 6, 1815; the existing authenticated copy was compared at the consulate at Algiers with the original there. As will be seen from 8 Statutes at Large, 224–27, the authenticated copy there printed omits the two final clauses here printed; namely, that of June 30, 1815, with the signature of the Dey of Algiers, and that of July 3, 1815, with the signatures of William Shaler and Stephen Decatur; and the date of July 6, 1815, given in the Statutes at Large, is merely the date of the authentication by Shaler, not any date of the treaty.

There are two authentications signed by Shaler in the copy of the treaty from which the text here is printed; the first is dated at Algiers August 30, 1815, and reads as follows: "A true Copy from the original in the Consulate General of the U. S. in Algiers."

Then follows this much more elaborate certificate, under the seal of the consulate and bearing also the individual seal of Shaler:

> I William Shaler Consul General of the United States of America for the city and Kingdom of Algiers do hereby certify the foregoing to be a true copy of the original treaty of peace and amity concluded at Algiers on the thirtieth day of June last between the Commissioners of the United States, and Omar Bashaw Dey of Algiers as therein expressed. The said original being deposited in the Chancery of this Consulate, and a duplicate of the same duly executed, was forwarded to the Secretary of State by Captain William Lewis of the United States navy in the U. S. Brig Epervier, which sailed from this port of Algiers on the 7 July 1815.
>
> In testimony whereof I have hereunto set my hand and seal of office, in the Chancery of the Consulate General of the U. S. in the City of Algiers, this 3 of November 1815 and of the independence of the U. S. the 40th.
>
> Wm Shaler

Note Regarding Ratification

There is no duplicate or written copy of the United States instrument of ratification in the Department of State file; but there is little doubt that the date of the ratification was December 26, 1815, as stated in Laws of the United States, Bioren & Duane ed., VI, 656; the document was forwarded to Shaler on January 9, 1816, to be delivered to the Dey of Algiers; from the covering letter (D. S., 8 Instructions, U. S. Ministers, 29–30) the following is extracted:

> I have the satisfaction to inform you that the President has, with the advice and consent of the Senate, ratified the Treaty, negotiated by Commodore Decatur and yourself with the Dey of Algiers, and I have now the honor to transmit you the ratified Copy signed by the President, to be delivered to the Dey. . . .
>
> You will have been informed that the Original of the Treaty, which was put on board the Epervier, never reached this country. We have of course been obliged

to rely on a Copy brought over by Commodore Decatur, to which the Signatures were not annexed. This fact will enable you to explain to the Dey the reason why they are not inserted in the ratified Copy now sent. You will judge of the expediency of applying to the Dey for a Copy of the Treaty signed and ratified by himself, to be transmitted to this Department.

Accordingly, the ratification was duly delivered on April 3, 1816, but it was returned three days later. Shaler wrote in his above-mentioned letter of April 15, 1816:

On the evening of the 6th instant the Bashaw sent back the ratification of the treaty, by the Drogoman saying that such a thing was unknown here; that he had consulted the oldest men in the Regency, who informed him that it was without any precedent, and he did not wish to introduce any new customs into his government.

Despite that statement, it is at least possible that the practice in Algiers had varied from time to time; some observations on the point will be found in the notes to the treaty of 1795 with Algiers (Document 17), and the notes to the treaty of 1786 with Morocco (Document 14) should also be consulted.

Moreover, in April, 1816, the question of ratification was hardly a separate one; for a dispute had then arisen which went to the very existence of the treaty; the Dey of Algiers alleged that the non-delivery of a captured Algerine brig, the return of which had been promised by Commodore Decatur during the negotiations of 1815, had avoided the whole agreement; he finally consented to write to President Madison, the treaty remaining more or less provisionally in force until the receipt of an answer; still, the letter was a quite blunt repudiation of the treaty, saying, "a new treaty must be made." A translation of the letter of the Dey of Algiers, dated April 24, 1816, is in Sketches of Algiers, by William Shaler, pages 276–78 (date there misprinted 1815). The same volume, at pages 295–97, contains the text of the answer of President Madison. Both letters are also printed as Appendix VII in Our Navy and the Barbary Corsairs, by Gardner W. Allen; and in that volume, at pages 294–98, is an account of the April, 1816, negotiations. The result was the renewal of the treaty by a new agreement, the treaty with Algiers of December 22 and 23, 1816 (Document 37), the notes to which should be consulted.

Note Regarding the Proclamation

The original proclamation has not been found; but it was published at the time (*e. g.*, Niles' Weekly Register, IX, 312–14, December 30, 1815); it says that the treaty "was concluded at Algiers on the 30th day of June last" and that it "is in the words following, to wit," and then recites the text in English as in the authenticated copy now missing, but without the certificate of Shaler of July 6, 1815, which follows Article 22 in 8 Statutes at Large, 227. The proclamation also omits the two final clauses of the treaty which are here printed, dated respectively June 30 and July 3, 1815; in similar form the proclamation was also printed in the Session Laws of the first session of the Fourteenth Congress, 162–66, published in 1816.

Treaty Series, No. 110
8 Statutes at Large, 228-31

35

GREAT BRITAIN : JULY 3, 1815

Convention to Regulate Commerce, signed at London July 3, 1815, with British declaration of November 24, 1815. Original in English. Submitted to the Senate December 6, 1815. Resolution of advice and consent, subject to the exception contained in the British declaration, December 19, 1815. Ratified by the United States December 21, 1815. Ratified by Great Britain July 31, 1815. Ratifications exchanged at Washington December 22, 1815. Proclaimed December 22, 1815.

A Convention To regulate the Commerce between the Territories of The United States and of His Britannick Majesty.

The United States of America and His Britannick Majesty being desirous, by a Convention, to regulate the Commerce and Navigation, between their respective Countries Territories, and people, in such a manner as to render the same reciprocally beneficial and satisfactory, Have respectively named Plenipotentiaries and given them full powers to treat of and conclude such Convention that is to say The President of the United States by and with the advice and consent of the Senate thereof hath appointed for their Plenipotentiaries John Quincy Adams, Henry Clay, and Albert Gallatin Citizens of the United States, And His Royal Highness The Prince Regent acting in the name & on the behalf of His Majesty has named for His Plenipotentiaries The Right Honourable Frederick John Robinson Vice president of the Committee of Privy Council for Trade and Plantations, Joint Paymaster of His Majesty's Forces, and a Member of the Imperial Parliament, Henry Goulburn Esquire a Member of the Imperial Parliament and Under Secretary of State, and William Adams Esquire, Doctor of Civil Laws, and the said Plenipotentiaries having mutually produced and shewn their said full powers, and exchanged copies of the same, have agreed on and concluded the following articles, vide licet.

Article the first

There shall be between the Territories of the United States of America and all the Territories of His Britannick Majesty in Europe

a reciprocal liberty of Commerce. The Inhabitants of the two Countries respectively shall have liberty freely and securely to come with their ships and cargoes to all such places Ports and Rivers in the Territories aforesaid to which other Foreigners are permitted to come, to enter into the same, and to remain and reside in any parts of the said Territories respectively, also to hire and occupy Houses and warehouses for the purposes of their commerce, and generally the Merchants and Traders of each Nation respectively shall enjoy the most complete protection and security for their Commerce but subject always to the Laws and Statutes of the two countries respectively

Article the Second

No higher or other Duties shall be imposed on the importation into the United States of any articles the growth, produce or Manufacture of His Britannick Majesty's Territories in Europe and no higher or other duties shall be imposed on the importation into the Territories of His Britannick Majesty in Europe of any articles the growth produce or manufacture of the United States than are or shall be payable on the like articles being the growth produce or manufacture of any other foreign country nor shall any higher or other duties or charges be imposed in either of the two Countries, on the Exportation of any articles to the United States, or to His Britannick Majesty's Territories in Europe respectively than such as are payable on the Exportation of the like articles to any other foreign Country nor shall any prohibition be imposed on the exportation or importation of any articles the growth produce or manufacture of the United States or of His Britannick Majesty's territories in Europe to or from the said Territories of His Britannick Majesty in Europe, or to or from the said United States, which shall not equally extend to all other Nations.

No higher or other duties or charges shall be imposed in any of the Ports of the United States on British Vessels, than those payable in the same ports by Vessels of the United States; nor in the ports of any of His Britannick Majesty Territories in Europe on the Vessels of the United States than shall be payable in the same ports on British Vessels.

The same duties shall be paid on the importation into the United States of any articles the growth produce, or manufacture of His Britannick Majestys territories in Europe, whether such importation shall be in Vessels of the United States or in British Vessels, and the same duties shall be paid on the importation into the ports of any of His Britannick Majesty's Territories in Europe of any article the growth produce or manufacture of the United States whether

such importation shall be in British vessels, or in vessels of the United States.

The same Duties shall be paid and the same Bounties allowed on the exportation of any articles the growth produce or manufacture of His Britannick Majesty's Territories in Europe to the United States whether such exportation shall be in vessels of the United States or in British Vessels, and the same duties shall be paid and the same Bounties allowed on the exportation of any articles the growth, produce or manufacture of the United States to His Britannick Majesty's Territories in Europe whether such exportation shall be in British Vessels, or in Vessels of the United States.

It is further agreed that in all cases where Drawbacks are or may be allowed upon the reexportation of any Goods the growth, produce or manufacture of either Country respectively the amount of the said drawbacks shall be the same whether the said goods shall have been originally imported in a British or an American vessel—But when such reexportation shall take place from the United States in a British Vessel or from the Territories of His Britannick Majesty in Europe in an American Vessel to any other foreign Nation the two Contracting Parties reserve to themselves respectively the Right of regulating or diminishing in such case the amount of the said drawback.

The intercourse between the United States and His Britannick Majesty's possessions in the West indies and on the Continent of North America shall not be affected by any of the provisions of this article, but each party shall remain in the complete possession of its rights with respect to such an Intercourse.

Article the Third

His Britannick Majesty agrees that the vessels of the United States of America shall be admitted and hospitably received at the principal settlements of the British Dominions in the East Indies vide licit, Calcutta, Madras Bombay and Prince of Wales' Island, and that the Citizens of the said United States may freely carry on Trade between the said principal settlements and the said United States in all articles of which the importation & Exportation respectively to and from the said Territories shall not be entirely prohibited—provided only that it shall not be lawful for them in any time of War between the British Government and any State or Power whatever to export from the said Territories without the special permission of the British Government any military stores or Naval stores or Rice. The Citizens of the United States shall

pay for their vessels when admitted no higher or other duty or charge than shall be payable on the vessels of the most favord European Nations and they shall pay no higher or other duties or charges on the importation or exportation of the Cargoes of the said Vessels than shall be payable on the same articles when imported or exported in the vessels of the most favored European Nations. But it is expressly agreed that the vessels of the United States shall not carry any articles from the said principal settlements to any Port or place Except to some Port or Place in the United States of America where the same shall be unladen.

It is also understood that the permission granted by this article is not to extend to allow the vessels of the United States to carry on any part of the Coasting Trade of the said British Territories, but the vessels of the United States having in the first instance proceeded to one of the said principal settlements of the British Dominions in the East Indies and then going with their Original Cargoes or part thereof from one of the said principal settlements to another shall not be considered as carrying on the Coasting Trade.

The Vessels of the United States may also touch for refreshment but not for commerce in the course of their Voyage to or from the British Territories in India, or to or from the Dominions of the Emperor of China, at the Cape of Good Hope the Island of St Helena or such other places as may be in the possession of Great Britain in the African or Indian Seas, it being well understood that in all that regards this article The Citizens of the United States shall be subject in all respects to the Laws and regulations of the British Government from time to time Established.

Article the fourth

It shall be free for each of the two Contracting Parties respectively to appoint Consuls for the protection of Trade to reside in the dominions and Territories of the other party, but before any Consul shall act as such He shall in the usual form be approved and admitted by the Government to which He is sent, and it is hereby declared that in case of illegal or improper conduct towards the Laws or Government of the Country to which He is sent such Consul may either be punished according to Law if the Laws will reach the case or be sent back the offended Government assigning to the other the reasons for the same.

It is hereby declared that that either of the contracting parties may except from the residence of Consuls such particular places as such Party shall judge fit to be so excepted

Article the fifth

This Convention, when the same shall have been duly ratified by The President of the United States by and with the advice and consent of their Senate and by His Britannick Majesty and the respective ratifications mutually Exchanged shall be binding and obligatory on the said United States and His Majesty for four Years from the date of its Signature and the Ratifications shall be exchanged in six months from this time or sooner if possible.

Done at London this third day of July in the year of our Lord one Thousand eight Hundred and Fifteen.

[Seal]	John Quincy Adams	[Seal]	Frederick John Robinson
[Seal]	H. Clay	[Seal]	Henry Goulburn
[Seal]	Albert Gallatin	[Seal]	William Adams

Declaration.

The Undersigned, His Britannick Majesty's Chargé d'Affaires in the United States of America, is commanded by His Royal Highness the Prince Regent, acting in the name and on the behalf of His Majesty, to explain and declare upon the Exchange of the Ratifications of the Convention concluded at London on the third of July of the present year, for regulating the Commerce and Navigation between the two Countries, That in consequence of events which have happened in Europe subsequent to the signature of the Convention aforesaid, it has been deemed expedient and determined in conjunction with the Allied Sovereigns, that St Helena shall be the place allotted for the future residence of General Napoleon Buonaparte, under such regulations as may be necessary for the perfect security of his person; and it has been resolved, for that purpose, that all Ships and vessels whatever, as well British Ships and vessels as others, excepting only Ships belonging to the East India Company, shall be excluded from all Communication with or approach to that Island.

It has therefore, become impossible to comply with so much of the third Article of the Treaty as relates to the liberty of touching for refreshment at the Island of St Helena, and the Ratifications of the said Treaty will be exchanged under the explicit Declaration and Understanding that the vessels of the United States cannot be allowed to touch at, or hold any communication whatever with the said Island, so long as the said Island shall continue to be the place of residence of the said Napoleon Buonaparte.

Anthony St Jno Baker.

Washington
November 24. 1815.

NOTES

It is to be noted that the *alternat* was observed in this convention; the United States is named before His Britannic Majesty, and the American plenipotentiaries signed at the left.

Besides the signed original, the file of this treaty includes the attested resolution of the Senate of December 19, 1815, the British instrument of ratification, a certificate of the exchange of ratifications of December 22, 1815, signed and sealed by James Monroe and Anthony St. John Baker, and a facsimile of the United States instrument of ratification, obtained from the British archives.

There is also in the file, in a mutilated form, the original proclamation. The sheets are loose and four of the pages have been cut away so that the document does not now contain the text of the convention, though it appears otherwise to be complete. The language of the proclamation is very similar to that of the United States instrument of ratification; but in the final clause of the latter the words of acceptance, ratification, and confirmation are in the present tense, and in the proclamation, in the past. A broadside of the proclamation, printed at the time, is in the Library of Congress; a facsimile thereof is now in the treaty file.

The British declaration of November 24, 1815, excepting the island of Saint Helena from the third article of the convention so long as that island should be the residence of Napoleon Bonaparte, was transmitted to the Senate with a copy of the convention on December 6, 1815 (it was not until December 11 that the original convention was transmitted). The declaration is not noticed in the British instrument of ratification, which was of earlier date; and there is no mention of the declaration in the certificate of the exchange of ratifications; but it is referred to in the Senate resolution of December 19 (Executive Journal, III, 6), and its text appears in the United States instrument of ratification following the signatures to that document, and similarly in the proclamation. The original declaration, with which its text here has been collated, is in D. S., 8 Notes from the British Legation.

The death of Napoleon on the island of Saint Helena took place on May 5, 1821; and under date of July 30, Lord Londonderry wrote to Richard Rush, American Minister at London, as follows (D. S., 26 Despatches, Great Britain, No. 204, enclosure):

> The Undersigned His Majesty's principal Secretary of State for Foreign Affairs has the honor to acquaint Mr Rush, that the death of Napoleon Buonaparte renders it no longer necessary to restrict the communication of foreign vessels with the Island of St Helena, and that they are accordingly now at liberty to communicate with that Island, in the same manner and under the same regulations as applied to their intercourse with the Island previous to the detention there of Napoleon Buonaparte.

Treaty Series, No. 347
8 Statutes at Large, 232–43

36

SWEDEN AND NORWAY : SEPTEMBER 4, 1816

Treaty of Friendship and Commerce, signed at Stockholm September 4, 1816. Original in French.
Submitted to the Senate December 13, 1816. Resolution of advice and consent, with the exception of Articles 3, 4, and 6, February 19, 1817. Ratified by the United States May 27, 1818. Ratified by Sweden and Norway July 24, 1818. Ratifications exchanged at Stockholm September 25, 1818. Proclaimed December 31, 1818.
The text of the omitted Articles 3, 4, and 6 appears in the notes following the treaty text.

Au nom de la très sainte et indivisible Trinité.

Les Etats Unis d'Amérique et Sa Majesté le Roi de Suède et de Norvège, également animés du désir sincère de maintenir et consolider les rélations d'amitié et de commerce qui ont subsisté jusqu'ici entre les deux Etats et étant convaincus, q'on ne saurait mieux remplir cet objet qu'en établissant réciproquement le commerce entre les deux Etats, sur la base solide de principes libéraux et équitables également avantageux aux deux Pays, ont nommé pour cet effet des Plénipotentiaires et les ont munis des pouvoirs nécessaires pour traiter et conclure en leur nom, savoir: le Président des Etats Unis, Monsieur Jonathan Russel, Citoyen des dits Etats Unis et actuellement Leur Ministre Plénipo-

[Translation]

In the name of the most holy and indivisible Trinity.

The United States of America and His Majesty the King of Sweden and Norway, equally animated with a sincere desire to maintain and confirm the relations of friendship and commerce which have hitherto subsisted between the two states, and being convinced that this object can not be more effectually accomplished than by establishing, reciprocally, the commerce between the two states upon the firm basis of liberal and equitable principles equally advantageous to both countries, have named to this end plenipotentiaries, and have furnished them with the necessary full powers to treat and in their name to conclude a treaty; to wit: the President of the United States, Jonathan Russell, a citizen

tentiaire à la Cour de Stockholm, et Sa Majesté le Roi de Suède et de Norvège Son Excellence Monsieur le Comte Laurent d'Engeström, Son Ministre d'Etat pour les affaires Etrangères, Chancélier de l'Université de Lund Chevalier Commandeur des Ordres du Roi, Chevalier de l'Ordre du Roi Charles XIII, Grand Croix des Ordres de St. Etienne de Hongrie, de la Legion d'Honneur de France, de l'Aigle Noir et de l'Aigle Rouge de Prusse, et Monsieur le Comte Adolphe George de Mörner, Son Conseiller d'Etat et Commandeur de l'Ordre de l'Etoile Polaire, lesquels Plénipotentiaires, après avoir produit et échangés leurs plein-pouvoirs trouvés en bonne et dûe forme, sont convenus des Articles suivans:

Article Premier.

Il y aura liberté réciproque de commerce entre tous les pays de la domination des Etats Unis d'Amérique et de Sa Majesté le Roi de Suède et de Norvège. Les habitans de l'un des deux pays pourront avec toute sûreté, pour leurs personnes, vaisseaux et cargaisons aborder librement dans les ports, places et rivières du territoire de l'autre, partout où l'entrée est permise aux vaisseaux des nations les plus favorisées. Ils pourront s'y arrêter et résider dans quelque partie que ce soit des dits territoires; ils pourront

of the said United States and now their Minister Plenipotentiary at the Court of Stockholm; and His Majesty the King of Sweden and Norway, His Excellency the Count Laurent d'Engeström, his Minister of State for Foreign Affairs, Chancellor of the University of Lund, Knight Commander of the Orders of the King, Knight of the Order of Charles XIII, Grand Cross of the Orders of St. Etienne of Hungary, of the Legion of Honor of France, of the Black Eagle and of the Red Eagle of Prussia, and the Count Adolphe George de Mörner, his Counselor of State and Commander of the Order of the Polar Star; and the said plenipotentiaries, after having produced and exchanged their full powers, found in good and due form, have agreed on the following articles:

Article 1.

There shall be between all the territories under the dominion of the United States of America and of His Majesty the King of Sweden and Norway, a reciprocal liberty of commerce. The inhabitants of either of the two countries shall have liberty, with all security for their persons, vessels, and cargoes, to come freely to all ports, places, and rivers within the territories of the other into which the vessels of the most favored nations are permitted to enter. They can there remain and reside in any part whatsoever

y louer et occuper des maisons et des Magazins pour leur commerce et généralement les négocians ou trafiquans de chacune des deux nations jouiront chez l'autre de la plus entière sécurité et protection pour les affaires de leur négoce, étant seulement tenus à se conformer aux loix et ordonnances des deux pays respectifs.

Article Second.

Il ne sera point imposé de plus forts ou autres droits, impôts ou charges quelconques sur l'importation dans les Etats Unis des productions du sol ou des manufactures des Etats de Sa Majesté le Roi de Suède et de Norvège, ni sur l'importation dans les Etats de Sa Majesté le Roi de Suède et de Norvège des productions du sol ou des manufactures des Etats Unis, que ceux auquels seraient assujettis les mêmes Articles dans chacun des deux pays respectifs, si ces denrées étaient le produit du sol ou des manufactures de tout autre pays. Le même principe sera aussi observé pour l'exportation, en sorte que dans chacun des deux pays respectifs les articles qui seront exportés pour l'autre ne pourront être chargés d'aucun droit, impôt ou charge quelconque plus fort ou autre que ceux auxquels seraient assujettis les mêmes articles, s'ils étaient exportés pour tout autre pays quelconque.

of the said territories; they can there hire and occupy houses and warehouses for their commerce; and, generally, the merchants and traders of each of the two nations shall enjoy in the other the most complete security and protection for the transaction of their business, being bound, alone, to conform to the laws and statutes of the two countries respectively.

Article 2.

No other or higher duties, imposts, or charges whatsoever, shall be imposed on the importation into the territories of His Majesty the King of Sweden and Norway of the produce or manufactures of the United States, nor on the importation into the United States of the produce or manufactures of the territories of His Majesty the King of Sweden and Norway, than those to which the same articles would be subjected in each of the two countries respectively, if these articles were the growth, produce, or manufacture of any other country. The same principle shall likewise be observed in respect to exportation, in such manner that in each of the two countries respectively, the articles which shall be exported for the other cannot be charged with any duty, impost, or charge whatsoever, higher or other than those to which the same articles would be subjected if they were exported to any other country whatever.

Il ne sera non plus imposé aucune prohibition, ni sur l'exportation ni sur l'importation d'aucun Article provenant du sol ou des manufactures des Etats Unis ou des pays de Sa Majesté le Roi de Suède et de Norvège, dans ou hors les dits Etats Unis, et dans ou hors les dits pays de Sa Majesté le Roi de Suède et de Norvège, qui ne s'étende également à toutes les autres nations.

Nor shall any prohibition be imposed on the exportation or importation of any article, the growth, produce, or manufacture of the territories of His Majesty the King of Sweden and Norway or of the United States, to or from the said territories of His Majesty the King of Sweden and Norway or to or from the said United States, which shall not equally extend to all other nations.

Les vaisseaux des Etats Unis d'Amérique arrivant sur leur lest ou important dans les Etats de Sa Majesté le Roi de Suède et de Norvège, des produits du sol ou de l'industrie de leur pays, ou exportant des Etats de Sa Majesté Suédoise et Norvegienne les produits du sol ou de l'industrie nationale des dits Etats, ne seront tenus à payer, ni pour les vaisseaux ni pour les cargaisons aucuns droits, impôts ou charges quelconques, plus forts ou autres que ceux que payeraient dans le même cas les vaisseaux des Etats de Sa Majesté le Roi de Suède et de Norvège, et vice versa; les vaisseaux des Etats de Sa Majesté le Roi de Suède et de Norvège qui arrivent sur leur lest ou qui importent dans les Etats Unis de l'Amérique des productions du sol ou de l'industrie nationale de la Suède et de la Norvège, ou qui exportent des Etats Unis des produits du sol ou de l'industrie de ces pays, ne payeront ni pour les vaisseaux ni pour les cargai-

Swedish or Norwegian vessels arriving in ballast, or importing into the United States the produce or manufactures of their countries, or exporting from the United States the produce or manufactures of said States, shall not be obliged to pay, either for the vessels or the cargoes, any other or higher duties, imposts, or charges whatsoever, than those which the vessels of the United States would pay in the same circumstances; and, vice versa, the vessels of the United States arriving in ballast, or importing into the territories under the dominion of His Majesty the King of Sweden and Norway the produce or manufactures of the United States, or exporting from the territories under the dominion of His Majesty the King of Sweden and Norway the produce or manufactures of these territories, shall not pay, either for the vessels or the cargoes, any other or higher duties, imposts, or charges whatsoever, than those

sons aucuns droits, impôts ou charges quelconques, autres ou plus forts que ceux qui seraient payés si ces mêmes denrées étaient transportées par des vaisseaux des Etats Unis respectivement.

Ce qui est statué ci-dessus s'étendra aussi à la Colonie Suédoise de St. Barthelemy, tant par rapport aux droits et avantages dont les vaisseaux des Etats Unis jouiront dans ses ports, que par rapport à ceux dont les vaisseaux de la Colonie jouiront dans les ports des Etats Unis; bien entendu que les propriétaires soyent Colons établis et naturalisés à St. Barthelemy et qu'ils y ayent fait naturaliser leurs vaisseaux.

which would be paid if these articles were transported by Swedish or Norwegian vessels respectively.

That which is here above stipulated shall also extend to the Swedish colony of Saint-Barthélemy, as well in what relates to the rights and advantages which the vessels of the United States shall enjoy in its ports as in relation to those which the vessels of the colony shall enjoy in the ports of the United States, provided the owners are inhabitants of Saint-Barthélemy and there established and naturalized and shall have there caused their vessels to be naturalized.

Article Cinquième.

Les Hautes Parties Contractantes S'accordent mutuellement la faculté d'entretenir dans les ports et places de Commerce de l'autre, des Consuls, Vice-Consuls ou Agentes de Commerce, qui jouiront de toute la protection et assistance nécessaire pour remplir dûement leurs fonctions, mais il est ici expressement declaré, que dans le cas d'une conduite illégale ou impropre envers les lois ou le Gouvernement du pays auquel il est envoyé, le dit Consul, Vice Consul ou Agent pourra, ou être puni conformément aux loix, ou être mis hors de fonction ou renvoyé par le Gouvernement offensé, celui-ci en donnant les

Article 5.

The high contracting parties grant mutually the liberty of having in the places of commerce and ports of the other, consuls, vice consuls, or commercial agents, who shall enjoy all the protection and assistance necessary for the due discharge of their functions. But it is here expressly declared that in case of illegal or improper conduct in respect to the laws or Government of the country to which they are sent, the said consul, vice consul, or agent may be either punished according to law, dismissed, or sent away by the offended Government, that Government assigning to the other the reasons therefor. It is,

raisons à l'autre, bien entendu cependant que les Archives et documens rélatifs aux affaires du Consulat, seront à l'abri de toute recherche et devront être soigneusement conservés, étant mis sous le scellé du dit Consul et de l'autorité de l'endroit où il aura résidé.

Les Consuls ou leurs suppléans auront le droit comme tels de servir de juges et d'arbitres dans les différends qui pourraient s'élever entre les Capitaines et les équipages des vaisseaux de la nation dont les affaires sont confiées à leurs soins. Les Gouvernemens respectifs n'auront le droit de se mêler de ces sortes d'affaires qu'en tant que la conduite des equipages ou du Capitaine troublerait l'ordre et la tranquillité dans le pays où le vaisseau se trouve, ou que le Consul du lieu se verrait obligé d'appeller l'intervention du pouvoir exécutif pour faire respecter ou maintenir sa décision. Bien entendu que cette espèce de jugement ou d'arbitrage ne saurait pourtant priver les Parties Contendantes du droit qu'elles ont à leur retour de recourir aux autorités judiciaires de leur patrie.

Article Septième.

Les Citoyens ou sujets de l'une des Parties Contractantes, arrivant avec leurs vaisseaux à l'une des côtes appartenantes à l'autre, mais ne voulant pas entrer dans

nevertheless, understood that the archives and documents relative to the affairs of the consulate shall be protected from all examination and shall be carefully preserved, being placed under the seal of the consul and of the authority of the place where he shall have resided.

The consuls and their deputies shall have the right, as such, to act as judges and arbitrators in the differences which may arise between the captains and crews of the vessels of the nation whose affairs are entrusted to their care. The respective Governments shall have no right to interfere in matters of this kind, except the conduct of the captain and crew shall disturb the peace and tranquility of the country in which the vessel may be, or that the consul of the place shall feel himself obliged to resort to the interposition and support of the executive authority to cause his decision to be respected and maintained. It being, nevertheless, understood that this kind of judgment or award shall not deprive the contending parties of the right which they shall have, on their return, to recur to the judicial authorities of their own country.

Article 7.

The citizens or subjects of one of the contracting parties, arriving with their vessels on any coast belonging to the other but not willing to enter into port, or being

le port, ou après y être entrés ne voulant pas décharger quelque partie de la cargaison ou déranger quelque chose du chargement, auront la liberté de partir et de poursuivre leur voyage sans être en quelque sorte molestés ou obligés de rendre compte du contenu de la cargaison et sans payer d'autres droits, impots ou charges quelconques pour les vaisseaux ou la cargaison que les droits de pilotage quand on s'est servi d'un pilote, et ceux pour le quayage ou pour l'entretien des fanaux, là où ces mêmes droits sont perçus sur les nationaux dans le même cas. Bien entendu cependant que lorsque des vaisseaux appartenans aux citoyens ou sujets de l'une des parties contractantes se trouveraient dans l'enceinte de la jurisdiction de l'autre, ils se conformeront aux reglemens et ordonnances concernant la navigation et les places ou ports dans lesquels on peut aborder, qui sont en vigueur à l'égard des nations les plus favorisées, et il sera permis aux officiers de douane dans les districts desquels les dits vaisseaux se trouvent, de les visiter, de rester à bord et de prendre telles précautions qui peuvent être nécessaires pour prévenir tout commerce illiçite pendant que les mêmes vaisseaux restent dans l'enceinte de cette même jurisdiction.

entered into port and not willing to unload or break bulk, shall have liberty to depart and to pursue their voyage without molestation and without being obliged to render account of their cargo or to pay any duties, imposts, or charges whatsoever on the vessels or cargo, excepting only the dues of pilotage, when a pilot shall have been employed, or those of quayage or light money whenever these dues are paid in the same circumstances by the citizens or subjects of the country. It being, nevertheless, understood that whenever the vessels belonging to the citizens or subjects of one of the contracting parties shall be within the jurisdiction of the other, they shall conform to the laws and regulations concerning navigation and the places and ports into which it may be permitted to enter, which are in force with regard to the citizens or subjects of the country;[1] and it shall be lawful for the officers of the customs in the district where the said vessels may be, to visit them, to remain on board, and to take such precautions as may be necessary to prevent all illicit commerce while such vessels remain within the said jurisdiction.

[1] The words "with regard to the citizens or subjects of the country" are a mistranslation; "with regard to the most favored nations" would be a correct equivalent of the French; the difference in the sense is important.

Article Huitième.

Il est aussi convenu, que les vaisseaux de l'une des parties contractantes, étant entrés dans les ports de l'autre, ils pourront se borner à ne decharger qu'une partie de leur cargaison selon que le Capitaine ou propriétaire le désire, et qu'ils pourront s'en aller librement avec le reste de la cargaison sans payer de droits, impots ou charges quelconques que pour la partie qui aura été mise à terre et qui sera marquée et biffée sur la liste ou le manifeste contenant l'énumération des éffets que le vaisseau aura dû apporter laquelle liste devra toujours être présentée en entier à la Douane du lieu où le vaisseau aura abordé. Il ne sera rien payé pour la partie de la cargaison que le vaisseau aura emporté et avec laquelle il pourra continuer sa route pour un ou plusieurs autres ports du même pays dans lesquels l'entrée est permise aux vaisseaux des Nations les plus favorisées, et y disposer du reste de sa cargaison en payant les droits qui y sont attachés, ou bien il pourra s'en aller avec la cargaison qui lui reste pour les ports de quelque autre pays.

Il est cependant entendu que les droits, impôts ou charges quelconques qui sont payables pour le vaisseau même, doivent être acquittés dans le premier port où il rompt le chargement et en déscharge une partie et

Article 8.

It is also agreed that the vessels of one of the contracting parties, entering the ports of the other, shall be permitted to discharge a part only of their cargoes whenever the captain or owner shall desire so to do, and they shall be allowed to depart freely with the remainder without paying any duties, imposts, or charges whatsoever, except on that part which shall have been landed, and which shall be marked and noted on the list or manifest containing the enumeration of the merchandise which the vessel ought to have on board, and which list ought always to be presented, without reservation, to the officers of the customs at the place where the vessel shall have arrived; and nothing shall be paid on the part of the cargo which the vessel takes away; and the said vessel may proceed therewith to any other port or ports in the same country into which vessels of the most favored nations are permitted to enter, and there dispose of the same; or the said vessel may depart therewith to the ports of any other country. It is, however, understood that the duties, imposts, or charges which are payable on the vessel itself, ought to be paid at the first port where it breaks bulk and discharges a part of the cargo, and that no such duties or impositions shall be again demanded in the

qu'aucuns droits ou impositions pareils ne seront demandés de nouveau dans les ports du même pays, où le dit vaisseau pourrait vouloir entrer après, à moins que les nationaux ne soyent sujets à quelques droits ultérieurs pour le même cas.

ports of the same country where the said vessel may thereafter enter, except the inhabitants of the country be subjected to further duties in the same circumstances.

Article Neuvième.

Les citoyens et sujets de l'une des parties Contractantes jouiront dans les ports de l'autre tant pour leur vaisseaux que pour leurs marchandises de tous les droits et facilités d'entrepôt dont jouissent les nations les plus favorisées dans les mêmes ports.

Article 9.

The citizens or subjects of one of the contracting parties shall enjoy in the ports of the other, as well for their vessels as for their merchandise, all the rights and privileges of entrepôt which are enjoyed by the most favored nations in the same ports.

Article Dixième.

Au cas que quelque vaisseau appartenant à l'un des deux Etats ou à leurs citoyens et sujets aura échoué, fait naufrage ou souffert quelque autre dommage sur les côtes de la domination de l'une des deux Parties Contractantes, il sera donné toute aide et assistance aux personnes naufragés ou qui se trouvent en danger et il leur sera accordé des passeports pour assurer leur retour dans leur patrie. Les navires et marchandises naufragés ou leur provenu, si les effêts eussent été vendûs, étant reclamés dans l'an et jour par les propriétaires ou leurs ayant cause, seront réstitués, en payant les mêmes frais du sauvement conformement aux loix et coutumes des deux nations, que payéraient les nationaux dans le même cas.

Article 10.

In case any vessel belonging to either of the two states or to their citizens or subjects, shall be stranded, shipwrecked, or have suffered any other damage on the coasts under the dominion of either of the parties, all aid and assistance shall be given to the persons shipwrecked, or who may be in danger thereof, and passports shall be granted them to return to their own country. The ships and merchandise wrecked, or the proceeds thereof if the effects be sold, being claimed in a year and a day by the owners or their attorney, shall be restored on paying the same costs of salvage, conformably to the laws and usages of the two nations, which the citizens or subjects of the country would

Les Gouvernemens respectifs veilleront à ce que les Compagnies qui sont ou pourront être instituées pour sauver les personnes et effêts naufragés, ne se permettent point de vexations ou actes arbitraires.

ARTICLE ONZIÊME.

Il est convenu que les vaisseaux qui arrivent directement des Etats Unis à un port de la domination de Sa Majesté le Roi de Suède et de Norvège, ou des Pays de Sa dite Majesté en Europe à un port des Etats Unis et qui sont pourvûs d'un certificat de santé donné par l'officier compétent à cet égard du port d'où le vaisseau est sorti et assurant qu'aucune maladie maligne ou contagieuse n'éxistait dans ce port, ne seront soumis à aucune autre Quarantaine que celle qui sera nécessaire pour la visite de l'officier de santé du port où le vaisseau est arrivé, après laquelle il sera permis au vaisseau d'entrer immédiatement et de decharger sa cargaison, bien entendu toujours qu'il n'y ait eu personne à bord du vaisseau qui s'est trouvé attaqué pendant le voyage d'une maladie maligne ou contagieuse et que la contrée d'où vient le vaisseau ne soit pas à cette époque si généralement regardée comme infectée ou suspecte, qu'on ait été obligé de donner auparavant une ordonnance par laquelle tous les vaisseaux qui viendraient de ce pays, seraient

pay in the same circumstances. The respective Governments shall watch over the companies which are or may be instituted for saving shipwrecked persons and property, that vexations and abuses may not take place.

ARTICLE 11.

It is agreed that vessels arriving direct from the United States at a port under the dominion of His Majesty the King of Sweden and Norway, or from the ports of His said Majesty in Europe at a port of the United States, furnished with a certificate of health from the competent health officer of the port whence they took their departure, certifying that no malignant or contagious disease existed at that port, shall not be subjected to any other quarantine than such as shall be necessary for the visit of the health officer of the port at which they may have arrived, but shall, after such visit, be permitted immediately to enter and discharge their cargoes; provided always, that there may not be found any person on board who has been, during the voyage, afflicted with a malignant or contagious disease, and that the country from which the vessel comes may not be so generally regarded at the time as infected or suspected, that it has been previously necessary to issue a regulation by which all vessels

regardés comme suspects et soumis à la Quarantaine.

ARTICLE DOUZIÈME.

Le traité d'Amitié et de Commerce,[1] conclû à Paris, en 1783. par les Plénipotentiaires des Etats Unis et de Sa Majesté le Roi de Suède, est renouvellé et mis en vigueur par le present Traité pour tout ce qui est contenu dans les Articles Deux, Cinq, Six, Sept, Huit, Neuf, Dix, Onze, Douze Treize, Quatorze, Quinze, Seize, Dissept, Dixhuit, Dixneuf, Vingtun, Vingt Deux, Vingt trois et Vingt Cinq du dit Traité, ainsi que les Articles Separés, Un, Deux, Quatre et Cinq, qui furent signés le même jour par les mêmes Plénipotentiaires, et les Articles designés designés seront regardés comme ayant force et vigueur tout comme s'ils étaient ici insérés mot à mot. Bien entendu que les stipulations contenues dans les Articles précités, seront toujours censées ne rien changer aux conventions précedemment conclués avec d'autres Nations Amies et Alliées.

ARTICLE TREIZIÈME.

Vû l'éloignement des pays respectifs des deux Hautes Parties Contractantes et l'incertitude qui en résulte sur les divers événémens

coming from that country are regarded as suspected and subjected to quarantine.

ARTICLE 12.

The Treaty of Amity and Commerce [1] concluded at Paris in 1783 by the plenipotentiaries of the United States and of His Majesty the King of Sweden, is renewed and put in force by the present treaty in respect to all which is contained in the second, fifth, sixth, seventh, eighth, ninth, tenth, eleventh, twelfth, thirteenth, fourteenth, fifteenth, sixteenth, seventeenth, eighteenth, nineteenth, twenty-first, twenty-second, twenty-third, and twenty-fifth articles of the said treaty, as well as the separate articles one, two, four, and five, which were signed the same day by the same plenipotentiaries; and the articles specified shall be considered to have as full force and vigor as if they were inserted word for word; provided, nevertheless, that the stipulations contained in the articles above mentioned shall always be considered as making no change in the conventions previously concluded with other friendly and allied nations.

ARTICLE 13.

Considering the distance of the respective countries of the two high contracting parties and the uncertainty that results therefrom

[1] Document 10.

qui peuvent avoir lieu, il est convenu qu'un batiment marchand appartenant à l'une des Parties Contractantes et se trouvant destiné pour un port qui serait supposé bloqué au moment du depart de ce batiment, ne sera cependant pas capturé ou condamné pour avoir essayé une prémière fois d'entrer dans le dit port, à moins qu'il ne puisse être prouvé, que le dit batiment ait pû et dû apprendre en route, que l'état de blocus de la place en question continuait; mais les batimens qui après avoir été renvoyés une fois essayéraient pendant le même voyage d'entrer une seconde fois dans le même port ennemi, durant la continuation du blocus, se trouveront alòrs sujets à être detenûs et condamnés.

Article Quatorzième.

Le présent Traité dès qu'il aura été ratifié par le Président des Etats Unis par et avec l'avis et le consentement du Sénat, et par Sa Majesté le Roi de Suède et de Norvège, restera en vigueur et sera obligatoire pour les Etats Unis et Sa Majesté le Roi de Suède et de Norvège pendant l'espace de huit ans, à compter de l'échange des ratifications et celles-ci seront échangées dans huit mois après la signature de ce Traité, et plutôt si faire se peut.

in relation to the various events which may take place, it is agreed that a merchant vessel belonging to one of the contracting parties and destined to a port supposed to be blockaded at the time of her departure, shall not, however, be captured or condemned for having a first time attempted to enter the said port, unless it may be proved that the said vessel could and ought to have learned on her passage, that the place in question continued to be in a state of blockade. But vessels which, after having been once turned away, shall attempt a second time during the same voyage to enter the same port of the enemy while the blockade continues, shall be liable to detention and condemnation.

Article 14.

The present treaty, when the same shall have been ratified by the President of the United States by and with the advice and consent of the Senate, and by His Majesty the King of Sweden and Norway, shall continue in force and be obligatory on the United States and His Majesty the King of Sweden and Norway for the term of eight years from the exchange of the ratifications; and the ratifications shall be exchanged in eight months from the signature of this treaty, or sooner if possible.

En foi de quoi les Plénipotentiaires respectifs ont signé le présent Traité et y ont apposé le cachet de leurs armes. Fait à Stockholm le Quatre Septembre l'an de Grace, mil huit Cent Seize.

JON[a] RUSSELL
[Seal]
LE COMTE D'ENGESTRÖM
[Seal]
LE COMTE A. G. DE MÖRNER
[Seal]

In faith whereof the respective plenipotentiaries have signed the present treaty and have thereunto set the seal of their arms. Done at Stockholm the fourth day of September in the year of grace one thousand eight hundred and sixteen.

JON[a] RUSSELL
[Seal]
LE COMTE D'ENGESTRÖM
[Seal]
LE COMTE A. G. DE MÖRNER
[Seal]

NOTES

The file of this treaty now contains a facsimile of the United States instrument of ratification, obtained from the Swedish archives. That instrument includes the French text of the entire treaty as in the signed original and also, in the right column, the translation. The clause of ratification concludes with these words: "saving and excepting the Third, Fourth and Sixth Articles of the said Treaty, which I hereby declare to be expunged and of no force and validity."

The corresponding clause in the instrument of ratification of Sweden and Norway, a French translation of which accompanies the original, may be thus rendered from the Swedish:

> Accordingly, and as the United States, through their Minister Plenipotentiary near our Court, have declared that, for reasons which have arisen, they are prevented from ratifying the third, fourth, and sixth articles of the above treaty, and we have found the tenor of these articles such that they can be excluded from the treaty without prejudice to the interests of our faithful subjects; we have therefore decided to ratify, approve, and accept the Treaty of Commerce inserted above, with the exception of the third, fourth, and sixth articles thereof, as we also hereby accept, approve, and ratify the same with respect to all the other articles, points, and clauses thereof, promising and undertaking in the most emphatic manner possible, sincerely, faithfully, and honestly, to fulfil and perform the said Treaty of Commerce in all its parts.

The file contains no protocol or other record of the exchange of ratifications. The date is from two letters of Jonathan Russell (D. S., 2 Despatches, Sweden and Norway, No. 7, September 26, and No. 11, September 30, 1818).

In Article 14 of the treaty, provision is made for the exchange of the ratifications within eight months from the date of signature; but more than two years elapsed. No reference to the point has been noticed in the diplomatic correspondence; so there appears to have been a tacit assent to the extension of time.

The original proclamation is in the form of a pamphlet; but the sheets are now loose. Like the ratification, it includes the original French of the entire treaty in the left column, and the translation in the right, mentioning the exception of Articles 3, 4, and 6 both in the opening and in the final clauses.

The translation in the proclamation of the preamble and of Articles 1 to 11, inclusive, is on strips of paper which have been pasted on the document over what appears to be another English version; such of the phrases of that other version as it is now possible to read indicate that it is a draft of the treaty, written prior to signature.

Note Regarding the Translation

The translation of the treaty which appears above is that which has been heretofore generally printed in the Statutes at Large and elsewhere. It is the same as that which was transmitted to the Senate (American State Papers, Foreign Relations, IV, 98–103) and was included in the United States instrument of ratification and in the proclamation. This translation came originally from Jonathan Russell and was an enclosure to his despatch of September 5, 1816 (D. S., Manuscript). In that letter Russell said that upon the signature of the treaty he had given to the Swedish plenipotentiaries a copy of that English translation, they giving him at the same time a Swedish translation of the French text.

It is to be noted that the English translation is imperfect; thus in Article 2 the order of statement of the provisions in their application to the respective countries is reversed; in the omitted Article 6, printed below, the French phrase, "d'où l'exportation aura été faite" (from which the exportation shall have been made), has no equivalent in the English; similarly in Article 8, the French "en payant les droits qui y sont attachés" (upon payment of the duties thereon) is omitted in the English; and a footnote above calls attention to the mistranslation of the wording of Article 7.

Note Regarding the Omitted Articles

The Senate resolution of advice and consent of February 19, 1817, excepted Articles 3, 4, and 6. As the Government of Sweden and Norway assented, the three articles were, as described above, similarly excepted in the ratifications and do not form part of the final agreement. Their text, in the original and in translation, follows, the English being that of the translation of Jonathan Russell above mentioned:

Article Troisiéme.

Sa Majesté le Roi de Suède et de Norvège consent que tous les articles qui sont le produit du sol ou des manufactures des Indes Occidentales et dont l'entrée est permise dans des vaisseaux Suédois ou Norvégiens, soit

Article 3.

His Majesty the King of Sweden and Norway agrees that all articles, the growth, produce, or manufacture of the West Indies, which are permitted to be imported in Swedish or Norwegian vessels, whether these articles be im-

que ces marchandises viennent directement ou indirectement des dites Indes, puissent aussi être importés dans Ses Etats par des vaisseaux des Etats Unis, et qu'alors il ne sera payé ni pour les dits vaisseaux, ni pour les cargaisons de droits, impôts ou charges quelconques, plus forts ou autres que ceux qui seraient payés par des vaisseaux Suédois ou Norvégiens dans le même cas, avec une addition seulement de dix pour Cent sur les dits droits, impots ou charges, et pas davantage.

Pour éviter tout mésentendu à cet égard il est ici expressement declaré, que la dénomination d'Indes Occidentales doit être prise dans le sens le plus étendu en y comprenant toute cette partie du monde soit îles ou terre ferme qui de tout tems a été appellée Indes Occidentales, en opposition avec cette autre partie du monde appellée Indes Orientales.

ported directly or indirectly from said Indies, may likewise be imported into its territories in vessels of the United States, and there shall not be paid, either for the said vessels or the cargoes, any higher or other duties, imposts, or charges whatsoever, than those which would be paid by Swedish or Norwegian vessels in the same circumstances, with an addition only of ten per centum on the said duties, imposts, and charges, and no more.

In order to avoid misapprehension in this respect, it is expressly declared that the term "West Indies" ought to be taken in its most extensive sense, comprising all that portion of the earth, whether mainland or islands, which at any time has been denominated the West Indies, in contradistinction to that other portion of the earth denominated the East Indies.

Article Quatrième.

De leur coté les Etats Unis d'Amérique consentent à ce que tous les articles qui sont les produits du sol ou des manufactures des pays qui bordent ou environnent la Mer Baltique et dont l'entrée est permise dans les vaisseaux des Etats Unis, soit que ces denrées viennent directement ou indirectement de la Baltique, puissent aussi être importés de même dans les Etats Unis, par des vaisseaux Suédois ou Norvégiens, et qu'alors il ne sera payé ni pour les dits vaisseaux ni pour les cargaisons de droits, impots ou charges quelconques plus forts ou outres que ceux qui seraient payés par des vaisseaux des Etats Unis dans le même cas, avec une addition de dix pour Cent sur les dits droits, impots ou charges et pas davantage.

Afin de prévenir toute incertitude à l'égard des droits, impots ou charges quelconques que devrait payer un vaisseau appartenant aux Citoyens ou sujets de l'une des Parties Contractantes, et arrivant dans les ports de l'autre avec une cargaison qui consistérait en partie des produits du sol ou des manufactures du pays, auquel le vaisseau appartiendrait, et en partie de quelques autres marchandises, dont l'importation est permise au dit vaisseau par les Articles précédens, il est convenu, qu'en cas d'une cargaison ainsi melée, le dit vaisseau payera toujours les droits, impots ou charges

Article 4.

The United States of America on their part agree that all articles, the growth, produce, or manufacture of the countries surrounding the Baltic Sea or bordering thereon, which are permitted to be imported in vessels of the United States, whether these articles be imported directly or indirectly from the Baltic, may likewise be imported into the United States in Swedish or Norwegian vessels; and there shall not then be paid for the said vessels or for the cargoes any higher or other duties, imposts, or charges whatsoever, than those which would be paid by vessels of the United States in the same circumstances, with an addition only of ten per centum on the said duties, imposts, and charges, and no more.

In order to avoid all uncertainty in respect to the duties, imposts, or charges whatsoever, which a vessel belonging to the citizens or subjects of one of the contracting parties ought to pay on arriving in the ports of the other with a cargo consisting partly of articles, the growth, produce, or manufacture of the country to which the vessel belongs, and partly of any other merchandise, which the said vessel is permitted to import by the preceding articles, it is agreed that in case a cargo should be thus mixed, the vessel shall always pay the duties, imposts, and charges, according to the nature of that part of the cargo which is subjected to the

suivant la nature de cette partie de la cargaison qui est sujette aux plus gros droits, tout comme si le vaisseau n'eut apporté que cette seule espèce de marchandises.

highest duties, in the same manner as if the vessel imported this sort of merchandise only.

ARTICLE SIXIÈME.

Afin de prévenir toute dispute ou incertitude à l'égard de ce qui devra être réputé comme étant le produit du sol ou des manufactures des parties Contractantes respectivement, il est convenu que ce qui aura été désigné ou spécifié comme tel dans l'expedition que le chef ou l'intendant de la douane aura donnée aux vaisseaux qui sortiront des ports Européens des Etats de Sa Majesté le Roi de Suède et de Norvège sera reconnu et admis comme tel dans les Etats Unis et que de même ce que le chef ou Collecteur de la Douane dans les ports des Etats Unis aura designé et specifié comme étant le produit du sol ou des manufactures des Etats Unis, sera admis et reconnu comme tel dans les Etats de Sa Majesté le Roi de Suède et de Norvège. La spécification ou désignation donnée par le Chef de la douane dans les Colonies de Sa Majesté le Roi de Suède et de Norvège et certifiée par le Gouverneur de la Colonie d'où l'exportation aura été faite, sera regardée comme preuve suffisante de l'origine des Articles ainsi désignés ou specifiés, pour qu'ils soyent admis à ce titre dans les ports des Etats Unis.

ARTICLE 6.

In order to prevent all dispute and uncertainty in respect to what may be considered as being the growth, produce, or manufacture of the contracting parties respectively, it is agreed that whatever the chief or intendant of the customs shall have designated and specified as such in the clearance delivered to the vessels which depart from the European ports of His Majesty the King of Sweden and Norway, shall be acknowledged and admitted as such in the United States; and that, in the same manner, whatever the chief or collector of the customs in the ports of the United States shall have designated and specified as the growth, produce, or manufacture of the United States, shall be acknowledged and admitted as such in the territories of His Majesty the King of Sweden and Norway. The specification or designation given by the chief of the customs in the colonies of His Majesty the King of Sweden and Norway and confirmed by the governor of the colony, shall be considered as sufficient proof of the origin of the articles thus specified or designated to obtain for them admission into the ports of the United States accordingly.

Treaty Series, No. 2
8 Statutes at Large, 244-48

37

ALGIERS : DECEMBER 22 AND 23, 1816

Treaty of Peace and Amity, with Article Additional and Explanatory, signed at Algiers December 22 and 23, 1816. Original in English. Submitted to the Senate January 7, 1822. (Message of December 30, 1821.) Resolution of advice and consent February 1, 1822. Ratified by the United States February 11, 1822. As to the ratification generally, see the notes. Proclaimed February 11, 1822.

Following the English text is a reproduction of the Turkish translation or summary, and thereafter is an English translation of the Turkish, made in 1930.

Treaty of Peace and Amity, concluded between the United States of America and the Dey and Regency of Algiers.

The President of the United States and the Dey of Algiers being desirous to restore and maintain upon a stable and permanent footing, the relations of peace and good understanding between the two powers; and for this purpose to renew the Treaty of Peace and Amity [1] which was concluded between the two States by William Shaler, and Commodore Stephen Decatur, as Commissioners Plenipotentiary, on the part of the United States and His Highness Omar Pashaw Dey of Algiers on the 30th of June 1815.

The President of the United States having subsequently nominated and appointed by Commission, the above named William Shaler, and Isaac Chauncey, Commodore and Commander in chief of all the Naval Forces of the United States in the Mediterranean, Commissioners Plenipotentiary, to treat with His Highness the Dey of Algiers for the renewal of the Treaty aforesaid; and they have concluded, settled, and signed the following articles:

Article 1st

There shall be from the conclusion of this Treaty, a firm, perpetual, inviolable and universal peace and friendship between the President and Citizens of the United States of America on the one part, and the Dey and subjects of the Regency of Algiers in Barbary on the other, made by the free consent of both parties, and on the terms of

[1] Document 34.

the most favoured Nations; and if either party shall hereafter grant to any other Nation, any particular favor or privilege in Navigation, or Commerce, it shall immediately become common to the other party, freely, when freely it is granted to such other Nations, but when the grant is conditional, it shall be at the option of the contracting parties, to accept, alter, or reject such conditions in such manner as shall be most conducive to their respective interests.

Article 2^{d}

It is distinctly understood between the contracting parties, that no tribute, either as biennial presents or under any other form, or name whatever, shall be required by the Dey and Regency of Algiers from the United States of America on any pretext whatever.

Article 3^{d}

Relates to the mutual restitution of prisoners & subjects and has been duly executed.

Article 4th

Relates to the delivery into the hands of the Consul General of a quantity of Bales of Cotton &c and has been duly executed.

Article 5th

If any goods belonging to any Nation with which either of the parties are at War, should be loaded on board vessels belonging to the other party, they shall pass free and unmolested and no attempt shall be made to take or detain them.

Article 6th

If any citizens or subjects belonging to either party shall be found on board a prize-vessel taken from an enemy by the other party, such citizens or subjects shall be liberated immediately and in no case, or on any pretence whatever shall any American citizen be kept in captivity or confinement, or the property of any American citizen found on board of any vessel belonging to any Nation with which Algiers may be at War, be detained from its lawful owners after the exhibition of sufficient proofs of American citizenship and American property by the Consul of the United States, residing at Algiers.

Article 7th

Proper passports shall immediately be given to the vessels of both the contracting parties on condition that the vessels of War belonging to the Regency of Algiers on meeting with Merchant vessels belong-

ing to the Citizens of the United States of America shall not be permitted to visit them with more than two persons besides the rowers; these only shall be permitted to go on board, without first obtaining leave from the Commander of said vessel, who shall compare the passports and immediately permit said vessel to proceed on her voyage; and should any of the subjects of Algiers insult or molest the Commander or any other person on board a vessel so visited, or plunder any of the property contained in her, on complaint being made to the Consul of the United States residing in Algiers, and on his producing sufficient proofs to substantiate the fact, the Commander or Rais, of said Algerine ship or vessel of War, as well as the offenders, shall be punished in the most exemplary manner.

All vessels of War belonging to the United States of America on meeting a cruizer belonging to the Regency of Algiers, on having seen her passports, and certificates from the Consul of the United States residing in Algiers; shall permit her to proceed on her cruize unmolested and without detention.

No passport shall be granted by either party to any vessels but such as are absolutely the property of citizens or subjects of the said contracting parties, on any pretence whatever.

ARTICLE 8th

A citizen or subject of either of the contracting parties, having bought a prize vessel condemned by the other party or by any other Nation, the Certificates of condemnation, and bill of sale, shall be a sufficient passport for such vessel for six months, which considering the distance between the two Countries, is no more than a reasonable time for her to procure passports.

ARTICLE 9th

Vessels of either of the contracting parties, putting into the ports of the other, and having need of provisions or other supplies shall be furnished at the Market price, and if any such vessel should so put in from a disaster at sea, and have occasion to repair, she shall be at liberty to land and reembark her cargo, without paying any customs or duties whatever; but in no case shall be compelled to land her cargo.

ARTICLE 10th

Should a vessel of either of the contracting parties be cast on shore within the territories of the other, all proper assistance shall be given to her and her crew; no pillage shall be allowed. The property

shall remain at the disposal of the owners, and if re-shipped on board of any vessel for exportation, no customs or duties whatever shall be required to be paid thereon, and the crew shall be protected and succoured until they can be sent to their own country.

ARTICLE 11th.

If a vessel of either of the contracting parties shall be attacked by an enemy within cannon-shot of the forts of the other, she shall be protected as much as is possible. If she be in port she shall not be seized or attacked when it is in the power of the other party to protect her; and when she proceeds to sea, no enemy shall be permitted to pursue her from the same port within twenty four hours after her departure.

ARTICLE 12th.

The commerce between the United States of America and the Regency of Algiers, the protections to be given to Merchants, Masters of vessels, and seamen, the reciprocal rights of establishing consuls in each country, the privileges, immunities, and jurisdictions to be enjoyed by such consuls, are declared to be on the same footing in every respect with the most favoured nations respectively.

ARTICLE 13th.

The Consul of the United States of America shall not be responsible for the debts contracted by the citizens of his own country, unless he gives previously, written obligations so to do.

ARTICLE 14th.

On a vessel or vessels of War belonging to the United States, anchoring before the city of Algiers the consul is to inform the Dey of her arrival when she shall receive the salutes which are by Treaty, or custom given to the Ships of War of the most favoured nations on similar occasions and which shall be returned gun for gun; and if after such arrival so announced, any Christians whatever, captives in Algiers, make their escape and take refuge on board any of the said ships of war, they shall not be required back again, nor shall the Consul of the United States or Commander of the said ship be required to pay any thing for the said Christians.

ARTICLE 15th.

As the Government of the United States has in itself no character of enmity against the laws, religion, or tranquillity of any Nation,

and as the said states have never entered into any voluntary War or act of hostility, except in defence of their just rights on the high seas, it is declared by the contracting parties, that no pretext arising from Religious Opinions shall ever produce an interruption of the Harmony between the two Nations; and the Consuls and Agents of both Nations shall have liberty to celebrate the rites of their respective religions in their Own houses.

The Consuls respectively shall have liberty and personal security given them to travel within the territories of each other by land and sea and shall not be prevented from going on board any vessel they may think proper to visit; they shall likewise have the liberty to appoint their own Drogoman and Broker.

Article 16th

In case of any dispute arising from the violation of any of the articles of this Treaty, no appeal shall be made to arms, nor shall War be declared on any pretext whatever. But if the Consul residing at the place where the dispute shall happen, shall not be able to settle the same, the Government of that country, shall state their grievance in writing and transmit the same to the Government of the other, and the period of three months shall be allowed for answers to be returned, during which time, no act of hostility shall be permitted by either party; and in case the grievances are not redressed and a War should be the event, the Consuls and Citizens and Subjects of both parties, respectively shall be permitted to embark with their effects unmolested, on board of what vessel or vessels they shall think proper, reasonable time being allowed for that purpose.

Article 17th

If in the course of events a War should break out between the two Nations the prisoners captured by either party, shall not be made slaves; they shall not be forced to hard labour or other confinement than such as may be necessary to secure their safe-keeping, and shall be exchanged rank for rank; and it is agreed that prisoners shall be exchanged in twelve months after their capture and the exchange may be effected by any private individual, legally authorized by either of the parties.

Article 18th

If any of the Barbary powers or other States at war with the United States shall capture any American vessel and send her into any port of the Regency of Algiers, they shall not be permitted to sell her;

but shall be forced to depart the Port on procuring the requisite supplies of provisions; but the vessels of War of the United States with any prizes they may capture from their enemies shall have liberty to frequent the Ports of Algiers for refreshment of any kind, and to sell such prizes in the said Ports, without paying any other Customs or duties than such as are customary on ordinary commercial importations.

ARTICLE 19th.

If any of the Citizens of the United States or any persons under their protection, shall have any disputes with each other, the Consul shall decide between the parties, and whenever the Consul shall require any aid or assistance from the Government of Algiers to enforce his decisions it shall be immediately granted to him: and if any disputes shall arise between any citizens of the United States and the citizens or subjects of any other Nations having a Consul, or Agent in Algiers, such disputes shall be settled by the Consuls or Agents of the respective nations; and any disputes or suits at law, that may take place between any Citizens of the United States and the subjects of the Regency of Algiers, shall be decided by the Dey in person and no other.

ARTICLE 20th.

If a citizen of the United States should Kill, wound or strike a subject of Algiers, or on the contrary, a subject of Algiers, should kill, wound or strike a citizen of the United States, the law of the country shall take place and equal justice shall be rendered, the consul assisting at the trial; but the sentence of punishment against an American citizen shall not be greater, or more severe, than it would be against a Turk, in the same predicament, and if any delinquent should make his escape, the Consul shall not be responsible for him in any manner whatever.

ARTICLE 21st.

The Consul of the United States of America, shall not be required to pay any customs or duties whatever on any thing he imports from a foreign country for the use of his house and family.

ARTICLE 22d

Should any of the Citizens of the United States of America die within the Regency of Algiers, the Dey and his subjects shall not interfere with the property of the deceased, but it shall be under the immediate direction of the Consul, unless otherwise disposed of by

Will; Should there be no Consul, the effects shall be deposited in the hands of some person worthy of trust, until the party shall appear who has a right to demand them, when they shall render an account of the property; neither shall the Dey, or his subjects give hindrance in the execution of any will that may appear.

Article additional & Explanatory

The United States of America in order to give to the Dey of Algiers a proof of their desire to maintain the relations of peace and amity between the two powers upon a footing the most liberal; and in order to withdraw any obstacle which might embarrass him in his relations with other States, agree to annul so much of the Eighteenth Article of the foregoing Treaty, as gives to the United States any advantage in the ports of Algiers over the most favoured Nations having Treaties with the Regency.

Done at the Palace of the Government in Algiers on the 22^d^ day of December 1816. which corresponds to the 3^d^ of the Moon Safar Year of the Hegira 1232.

Whereas the undersigned William Shaler a Citizen of the State of New York and Isaac Chauncey, Commander in chief of the Naval Forces of the United States, Stationed in the Mediterranean, being duly appointed Commissioners by letters patent under the signature of the President and Seal of the United States of America, bearing date at the City of Washington the twenty fourth day of August A. D. 1816. for negociating and concluding the renewal of a Treaty of Peace between the United States of America, and the Dey and subjects of the Regency of Algiers.

We therefore William Shaler and Isaac Chauncey, Commissioners as aforesaid, do conclude the foregoing Treaty, and every article and clause therein contained, reserving the Same nevertheless for the final ratification of the President of the United States of America, by and with the advice, and consent, of the Senate of the United States.

Done in the Chancery of the Consulate General of the United States in the City of Algiers on the 23^d^ day of December in the Year 1816 and of the Independence of the United States the Forty First

[Seal] Wm Shaler
[Seal] I. Chauncey

سبب تحریر عهدامانی باعث ترقیم کتاب مبینت عنوانی اولدرکه ابتو بیک
ایکیوز اوتوز ایکی سنه‌سی ماه صفر الخیرک ابتداسنده وشهر عجمیه‌نک
یکرمی ایکنجی کوننده جزایر بحر محیطده واقع مریکان نام جزیره‌لر متمکنه
طائفه‌ء مریکان حاکمی وضابطلری طرفندن حالا دار الجهاد جزایر غرب
اوجاغی ایله مجدداً عقد وصلح ایتکده مکالمه وسیله واسطه
اتخاذ ایدوب تقییده اولنان قومانداننک عایده جانبی معاً
قونسلوس ویلیم شالر قونسلوس وکیل اولوب قونسلوس مرسوم
قومانداننک وکالتلکی ایله شرط وشروط اولنوب دولتلو
دستور مکرم مشیر مفخم صدرنشینه اوجاق عمر پاشا یسر الله ما یشاء
حضور عالیلرنده وجمله ارباب دیوان محضرلرنده تقویه
ومودت ومحبت ایتمکه مکالمه اولنوب مقدم مسفورلرده
اخذ اولنان سنویه دخی بطال اولوب فرانسز وانکلیز
منوال اوزره صلح وصلاح میانه‌ده اولنمش ایکن بو مریکان
مسفورلرینه دخی اول منوال اوزره شرط وشروط اولمشدر

شهر عجمیه‌نک دجنبر ۲۲ سی سنه ۱۸۱٦

شرط اول

اشبو قول وقراری بودرکه مریکان متصرف اولدقی دوستلر ایله میانمزده
مجددا دوستلق ومهر محبت وصفوت قلوب اولمغله ایکی طرفدن
بو مرتبه دوستلغه متراضی اولنوب واقع اولدقی شرط وشروطمز
انکلیز ویاخود فرانسزلر منوالی اوزره معامله اولندی سائر جنسه
نیجه حرمت اولنور ایسه مریکانلره دخی اولنه تحریرا فی صوکی

شرط ثانی

مذکور مریکانلر ایله بیزده معاهده اولنان شرط موجبنجه
اوتکی کبی سنویه وعوائد ومهمات کندولردن مطلوب ومطالبه
اولنمیه جق دکلدر ا[illegible] محرر

شرط ثالث

مذكورلردن مقدم قول قرارمز برزم يسيرلرى وفرقته‌ىٔ وبوندىره‌يى عسكرلريله كتيره‌جكلر كمنولرى دخى جزايرده بولنان يسيرلرينى وماللرينى الەجقلرى قول اولنمش ايدى شمدى بو قولى ابطال اولنمش شمدى يكنه طلبندن فراغت كلندى

شرط رابع

مذكورلرك جزايرده بولنان يابانەلرينى ويدملرينى واقدارەيه بهالرينى جملەسنى پادشاه حضرتلرينك وآلتى جزاير حفتلرى مسقوفلرە تماما ويردى

شرط خامس

مثلو جزایر قورسانلری بر سائر دشمن تکنه‌سی پیرازه
الدقلرنده ده ودن سفینه‌ده بر مریکان جاوزکاری بولنوب
یدنده بصه پورطی بولنورایسه پیرازه اولمیه بزم جزایر
ادملرکه دخی مریکانلک الدیغی دشمان تکنه‌سنده
بولنورایسه انلر دخی جزایر آدمنی پیرازه ایتمیه‌لر
مالیله وجانیله

شرط سادس

مثلو جزایرک دشمنلرندن بر دشمن تکنه‌سنی مریکانلو
کرالیوب مالی تحمیل ایدوب دومی ودریاده جزایر قورصانلری
اول تکنه‌یی پیرازه ایدوب جزایره کتیردکلرنده مریکانلک
ماللرینی کندولره ویروب تکنه مذکوری غنیمه ایده‌لر
کمسنه مانع اولمیه

115605°—31—vol. 2——42

شرط سابع

مثلو روی دریاده جزایر قورصانلری برمریکان تکنه‌سی یوقلامق اقتضا ایدرکن صندال کوندردکده صندال ایله ایکی آدمدن زیاده کوندرمیه‌لر و مسفورلره ظلم و رنجیده اولنمیه شرطه اعتماد اولنه

شرط ثامن

مثلو مریکان سائرکمنه‌لردن بر تکنه اشترا ایلدکده محلنه کیدرکن جزایر قورصانلرینه راست کلدکده یاصه یورطک یوقدر دیه‌رک مسفورلرک اشترا ایلدکلری تکنه‌یه ال اوزاتمیه‌لر قونسلوسلرینک ویاخود تکنه الدقدری تمسک التی ماهه قدر یصه‌یورتلق ایدر

شرط تاسع

مثلا بر مریکان سکنه سی کرکن مرقندی وکرک قورصان
دریاده صقلیه جزایر لیمانلرنده برلیمانه وارد قده
یوکنی طشره اخراج ایدوب سکنه سنی تعمیر ایدوب الله جهتنه
الماده و صاتمه ده کمسنه طرفندن مسفورلره مانع اولمیلر
جزایر سکنه لری دخی انلرک عندنده بو منوال اوزره
اوله هیچ کلام

شروط عشره

مثلا بر مریقان سکنه سی جزایرک حکمی کجدیکی محلده
قضایه اوغراسه مالنی یغما ایتدیرمیه مالدینی مسفورلره
ارجاع اوله هیچ بزم جزایرک دخی بونلر کبی احوالی

شرط عشر حادی

مثلو جزایر لیمانلرنده مریکانک دشمانی بولنوب
مریکالو تکنه سنه ال اوزاتدرمیه لر طوب اتلنده
جزایرلو دخی بو منوال اوزره دوشمانلری اولدقی
تکنه بربرلرندن یکرمی دورت ساعت صوکره
سفر ایتدیره لر

شرط ١٢

اکرکه جزایرده ساکن اولان مریکان قونسلوسی جزایرک
سائر لیمانلرنه قونسلوس وکیلی نصب ایتمک دیلرایسه
سائرلری کبی اول دخی وکیل نصب ایدر

شرط
۱۳

مثلو بر مریکان آدمی جزایره کلوب سائرلردن اقچه
سلف الورلیسه قونسلونك اذنیله الورایسه نه کوزل
قونسلونك اذنی اولمزدن الورلیسه قونسلوس اول
اقچه یه ضامن اولمز

شرط
۱۴

مثلو بر مریکان قورصانی لیمانمزه کلدکده طوبنه طوب
اطمه‌لی مریکان قورصاننه بر یسیر فرار ایدرلیسه
ویرمزلر خلاص بولور

شرط
١٥

شو مریکاده قونسلوسی کندی ساکن اولدیغی خانه سنده
علم فاسقنجه کیف ایدر قونسلوس هر نه زمان کندی کمیلرینه
کیتمک دیله سه کیتمسنه مانع اولمیه کیده کرک برّاً وکرک بحراً
قونسلوس اکرکی ترجمانی ویاخود سمساری استدکده
استدیکنی یاپه

شرط
١٦

شو بوندن صوکره مریکانلر ایله کره اوطلق اقتضا ایدرلر
سفودلره اوج ماه وعده ویریلور اوج ماهدن
صوکره کره دن غنیمه اولورلر

شرط
١٧

مثلو مریکانلر ایله کره اولنوب یسیر النودلیم
وار دیانلر جوق جوق طیاق اودمیه لر وهم یسیرالدیلر
اکرکی جزایرده انلره یسیر دوشرایسه اسقابنجه اولنور
برسینه قدر میدان ویریلیور

شرط
١٨

مثلو مریکان دشمانلری جزایره مریکان اقزادمه‌کی
کتیروب جزایرده صاتمق دیلرلرایسه صاتلمیه اکرکی
مریکان کفره اقدامه کتیررایسه فروخت ایده

شرط

١٩

مثلو برجزايرلى ايله برمريكانك دعواسى اولورايسه
قونسلوس ياننده واروب دعوالرينى كورسون واكركى
برمريكالو ايله برجزايرلى زياده جه غوغا ايدوب قباحته
باعث اولدقلرنده دعوالرى پاشا افندمز حضورنده
كورلميه

شرط

٢٠

مثلو برمريكالو ايله برجزايرلى محاربه ايدوب قتال
وياخود مجروح واقع اولسه شريعت اولنوب قباحت
هركمده ايسه انك حقنده كلسه اكركى قباحت صاحبى
فرار ايدرسه قونسلوس قارشماز

شرط
٢١

شو مريكان قونسلوسنك دونيادن مأكولاتى
ومشروباتى كلدكده يانندن اولورسه كمركى
ويا خود سائر عوائد النميه جق

شرط
٢٢

شو جزايرده بر مريكاده كفره مرد اولورسه
هر شيئيسنى قونسلوس الور بيت المالدى قونسلوسدر

شرط جدید
۲۳

مشلو مریکاده دشمنلری بر مریکاده غنیه الوب
جزیره کتیروب صاتمق دیلرایسه صاتمسونلر
مریکاده دخی غنیه کتیریر ایسه صاتمه مانع اولنمیه

ENGLISH TRANSLATION OF THE TURKISH

The Turkish translation or summary which is written in the original treaty and which is reproduced above, has been examined by Dr. J. H. Kramers, of Leiden, in collaboration with Dr. C. Snouck Hurgronje. The English translation of the Turkish made by Doctor Kramers, with his notes thereon, is printed below, following this general comment of Doctor Kramers on the Turkish:

The Turkish text accompanying this treaty is written in a very barbaric Turkish, full of orthographical and grammatical faults.

The contents are in most instances a mere compendium of the English text, but contain some clauses that are not found in the English. Therefore it has seemed necessary to give a new English translation of the Turkish text.

[Translation]

The reason for the drawing up of this beneficent treaty and the motive for the writing of this convention of good omen, is that in the beginning of the month of Safar of this year 1232, and on the 22d of the Christian month, the President and ruler of the American people, living in the island called America, belonging to the islands of the ocean, has now taken steps and opened negotiations for the conclusion of a new treaty of peace with the garrison of Algiers, the frontier post of the Holy War. For this purpose have been designated Commander Isaac Chauncey and Consul William Shaler. By the Consul, acting as delegate of the said Commander,[1] the following articles and stipulations have been drawn up in the exalted presence of His Excellency, the strong Vizier and the noble Marshal, Omar Pasha—may God grant to him what he desires—as President of the Divan, and with the assistance of all its members, and it has been agreed that the mutual friendship shall be strengthened; the yearly tribute, which was formerly taken from the said people, has been abolished, and, in the same way as peace has been concluded with the French and the English, the treaty has been established with the said Americans.

The 22d of the Christian month of December, 1816.

The 3d Safar, 1232.

[Tughra[2] of OMAR PASHA, Dey and Governor of Algiers]

[Seal of OMAR PASHA]

ARTICLE 1.

This article states that there shall be, between our friend the American ruler and ourselves, a renewal of friendship and cordial and sincere relations, and that a treaty has been concluded, according to the present articles, in the same way as with the English and the

[1] Here the Turkish is not clear.

[2] Name sign.

French. All honors that are granted to other nations shall also be granted to the Americans.

Written 3 Safar, 1232.

ARTICLE 2.

It has been agreed between the said Americans and ourselves that there shall not be required from them, as formerly, a yearly tribute, revenues, and necessaries.

ARTICLE 3.

It has been agreed before with the said people that they shall bring back our prisoners, ships, bilander, and soldiers, and that they shall receive back their prisoners and properties that are in Algiers. This agreement has now come to an end and accordingly been canceled, and the claim to ships has been abandoned.

ARTICLE 4.

The cotton, the men, and the equivalent of the prizes belonging to the said people, have been completely delivered by His Excellency the Pasha, the Governor of Algiers, to the said people.

ARTICLE 5.

If the war vessels of Algiers take an enemy ship as a prize, and they find in the ship an American merchant in possession of a passport, he shall not be a prize.[1] Equally, if Algerians are found on an enemy ship taken by the Americans, the latter shall not take them as prize with their goods and lives.

ARTICLE 6.

If the Americans charter an enemy ship, belonging to the enemies of Algiers, for the transport of goods, and if the Algerian war vessels take this ship as a prize and bring it to Algiers, they shall restore the American properties to the Americans and take the ship as a prize, and nobody shall object to this.

ARTICLE 7.

If it is necessary for Algerian vessels of war to visit on the open sea an American ship, they shall send a boat with no more than two persons; they shall not molest the said people, and this article shall be obeyed.

ARTICLE 8.

If the Americans have bought from other persons a ship, and they meet with Algerian war ships on their way home, the latter shall not seize the ship bought by the said people, under pretext that there is no passport. The statement of their Consul or the bill of sale of the vessel shall be as valuable as a passport during a period of six months.

[1] This is the literal translation.

ARTICLE 9.

It is understood that if an American ship, either a merchant vessel or a vessel of war, meets with a disaster at sea and arrives at one of the Algerian ports, where her cargo is discharged and she is repaired, nobody shall oppose the said people in the buying or selling of what they want, and that the Algerian vessels shall be treated in the same way in their country.

ARTICLE 10.

If an American vessel meets with an accident at a place under the rule of Algiers, their goods shall not be plundered and shall be restored to the said people. It shall be the same way with our Algerian ships.

ARTICLE 11.

If there are enemies of the Americans in the Algerian ports, those shall not be allowed to lay hands on the American ships within cannon shot. The Algerians shall allow the departure of ships which are enemies of each other only within twenty-four hours after each other.

ARTICLE 12.

If the American Consul residing at Algiers wishes to appoint vice consuls in the other ports of Algiers, he may appoint them in the same way as other nations.

ARTICLE 13.

If an American comes to Algiers and takes a loan of money from other persons with permission of the Consul, it is right. If this takes place without the Consul's permission, the Consul shall not be responsible for that money.

ARTICLE 14.

If an American war vessel enters our port, her salute must be returned. If a prisoner takes refuge in an American vessel of war, they are not bound to deliver him and he is free.

ARTICLE 15.

The American Consul can exercise, within the house where he lives, his unbelief, according to its abominable precepts. Whenever the Consul wishes to go on board his ships, nobody may oppose him, either by land or by sea. If the Consul wishes to have his own dragoman or his own broker, he may do so.

ARTICLE 16.

If hereafter there should arise trouble with the Americans, a delay of three months shall be given to the said people. Three months afterwards there shall be war and they will be prisoners.

ARTICLE 17.

If, in case of war with the Americans, they are taken prisoners, the guards may not treat them with heavy blows and keep them as slaves.[1] If Algerian prisoners should arrive in their country, they shall be exchanged; a delay of a year shall be given.

ARTICLE 18.

If enemies of the Americans bring to Algiers American prizes and they wish to sell them, this shall not be allowed; if, however, the American unbelievers bring prizes, they may sell them.

ARTICLE 19.

If there is a suit at law between an Algerian and an American, they shall go to the Consul, who shall settle their dispute. And if a very serious dispute arises between an American and an Algerian, so that it causes criminal acts, it shall be judged in the presence of our lord the Pasha.

ARTICLE 20.

If there occurs, between an American and an Algerian, a fight in which someone is killed or wounded, the law [2] shall be applied and the guilty person shall be punished. If the guilty person escapes, the Consul shall not be involved in the matter.

ARTICLE 21.

If there arrive by sea, for the American Consul, eatables or drinkables, and these come into the port, customs or other duties shall not be taken.

ARTICLE 22.

If an American unbeliever dies at Algiers, the Consul shall take all his properties, the Consul being their public treasury.[3]

NEW ARTICLE 23.

If the enemies of the Americans take an American prize and bring it to Algiers in order to sell it, they may do so. Equally, if the Americans bring a prize, nobody shall oppose its sale.

The 3d Safar, 1232.

[Seal of OMAR PASHA]

---

[1] Here the Turkish has the same word for "slaves" as previously for "prisoners."

[2] Here the Turkish has the word "Shari'at," which means the sacred Mohammedan law.

[3] For "public treasury" the Turkish has "bait al-mal," which is a term proper to Mohammedan law.

NOTES

It is believed that the official text of this treaty is in the English language only.

This treaty was a renewal, with a modification, of the treaty with Algiers of 1815 (Document 34, the notes to which should be consulted). The provisions of that treaty were in general copied almost literally into this, including even errors of grammar; Articles 3 and 4 of this treaty are merely statements that the articles previously so numbered had been executed. The order of Articles 13 and 14 in this treaty is the same as that in the missing authenticated copy of the treaty of 1815, but it is the reverse of the order in the text of that treaty which is printed as Document 34. The desired modification of the former agreement was made by means of the additional article.

The Government of the United States considered that the earlier treaty was in English; this treaty, like the prior one, was dictated to Algiers; in August, 1816, the Algerine naval forces had been almost wholly destroyed by a British fleet, and when Commodore Chauncey and William Shaler, Consul General, reached Algiers in December, 1816, the Dey of Algiers was in no position to refuse to sign any treaty presented to him. The frankly stated alternative was war.

A full account of the negotiations is in the "Journal of the Mission to Algiers" (D. S., 9 Consular Despatches, Algiers) written by Charles O. Handy, Secretary to the Mission.

The language question was then one of much difficulty. Writing some years later, Shaler says (Sketches of Algiers, 13):

> The Turkish is the language of the government, though the Arabic is the predominant tongue; French is in general use in the society of the foreign agents residing here, and the *Lingua Franca*, which is a barbarous compound of Spanish, French, Italian, and Arabic, is the ordinary medium of communication between foreigners and natives.

And in a note to the Dey of Algiers, the text of which is set forth in the above-mentioned journal, the American Commissioners wrote:

> In order to facilitate to the Government of Algiers the understanding of this note, the under-signed herewith transmit to H. H. an informal translation of it into the Arabic language—and they expect that H. H. will cause a reply to be made to this Communication in writing, in either the English, French, Spanish or Italian languages, or by a Foreign Consul authorized by him to vouch for the same.

The original treaty in the Department of State file is in the form of a pamphlet of forty-eight pages; the English text as here printed is written on twenty-two of the left pages, with the signatures and seals of Shaler and Chauncey at the end. On each of various opposite right pages (sixteen in all) appear some lines of Turkish script; on the last of those pages is the seal of the Dey of Algiers, and on the first of them the same seal and the signature as well; and from the position of the Turkish script on the various pages of the original document, it is obvious and beyond question that the English was

first written and the Turkish later added. As to this, the comment in the journal above mentioned is as follows:

The Translation of the Treaty was effected through the agency of Mr Bensammon a Jew, who was employed in this affair by the Dey & under the personal inspection of Mr Shaler. It may be considered as having more of the character of Marginal notes than of a literal and exact Copy of the original articles in English. This, from the necessity of despatch to frustrate the earnest wish & endeavour of the Dey to obtain delay, we were compelled to submit to. No intention was manifested to pervert the meaning of any part of it; and Mr Shaler has the fullest conviction, from the known integrity and intelligence of Mr Bensammon that the substance of each article is correctly stated.

In view of the insistence of the Government of the United States regarding the language of the earlier treaty, the fact that this treaty was a renewal thereof, and the circumstances of the signature, there can hardly be any doubt that the official text of this treaty is the English only. However, as the Turkish is on the pages of the original document, it is here reproduced, following the English text and in the same order, which is the order of the original.

There are some notable differences between the Turkish translation or summary and the English text, *e. g.*, Article 12. Accordingly, an English translation of the Turkish, made in 1930, is printed above, following the reproduction of the Turkish.

The dates given for the signatures to the treaty are those recited in its text—December 22, 1816, for the Dey of Algiers, and the next day for the American Commissioners; the Mohammedan date given in the treaty for its execution on the part of Algiers is 3 Safar, A. H. 1232, the equivalent of which, according to the usual calculation, is December 23, 1816; but strictly speaking, December 22 is also correct, as the Mohammedan day begins at sunset. But the following extract from the above-mentioned journal of the mission for December 25 leaves no doubt that the treaty was executed by the Dey of Algiers on that day:

Repaired with Mr Shaler to the Palace. The Dey sent for Mr Bensammon the interpreter and on his arrival observed that he was now ready to sign the Treaty. Mr S. requested that his Seal might be put both to the Preamble & concluding Article. The Dey answ^d that it had been usual for him to affix his Seal only to the Concluding part—but to oblige Mr S. he would comply with his request. After the Treaty was executed, he observed, that he hoped Mr Shaler was Perfectly satisfied, as he had attained his wishes & brought the negotiation to a close on his own terms.

It is probable that Shaler put his signature to the document on Monday, December 23, 1816, the textual date of its execution by the American Commissioners; but Commodore Chauncey was not then in Algiers and was not even informed of the signature of the treaty until December 29 at Port Mahon (Minorca); so his signature must have been added at some later date.

NOTE REGARDING RATIFICATION

The delay of nearly five years in the submission of this treaty to the Senate was due to an oversight, explained by President Monroe in his message (Executive Journal, III, 260).

Ratification by the United States is declared in the proclamation; the date is not quite certain, but it may be assumed to be February 11, 1822, the date of the proclamation.

There is no reason to suppose that notice of the belated ratification was given to the Dey of Algiers; as to this, the Government had been advised in 1816 (letter of Handy to Commodore Chauncey, December 30, 1816, part of the journal of Handy above mentioned):

> The Treaties which Algiers has heretofore had with the Maratime Powers of Europe, appear more in the light of capitulations made with their respective Consuls, acting with plenary Powers, than with their Governments of whose sentiments they are only the authorized organs. Consequently the rejection, or ratification, of such Treaties, is never with the Regency a Subject of interest, or importance. From the long and unvaried Custom, arbitrarily adopted, and resolutely pursued, by this Barbary State, they never have, & probably never will, recognize, the approbation of a Government, as essential to the completion and execution of a Treaty. Our Treaty in June 1815 they refused to receive after it had been approved of by the President & Senate, alledging as a reason therefor, that the Algerine Regency never had acknowledged the necessity of such a measure & would never be governed by it in any manner whatever. For these reasons Mr Shaler is of opinion that it will be unnecessary to return to him the Treaty after it has received the Sanction of the President & Senate. He has with him an executed Copy of it, with the promise of the Dey that in the event of accident to the one to be transmitted to our Government, he will sign a third.

NOTE REGARDING THE PROCLAMATION

The original proclamation is in the file; it includes within its two pages the original treaty; in form it is similar to the proclamation mentioned in the notes to Document 35. The proclamation was printed in the press of the period (*e.g.*, the Daily National Intelligencer, Washington, February 14, 1822); a facsimile of the newspaper print is now in the treaty file.

NOTE REGARDING ANOTHER ORIGINAL

There was at least one other original of the treaty executed, which was in the hands of Shaler, as stated in the letter of Handy of December 30, 1816, quoted above, and which was retained in the files of the consulate at Algiers. The journal of William Buell, who was Agent at Algiers in the absence of Shaler, records under date of March 16, 1818, that "the treaty was this day sent for and ratified by the new Sovereign" (D. S., 10 Consular Despatches, Algiers). The predecessor of that Dey had died on March 1, 1818 (Shaler to the Secretary of State, April 15, 1818, *ibid.*), and had himself, during his brief term of power, which began on September 8, 1817, also confirmed or ratified the treaty (Buell to Shaler, September 20 and November 2, 1817, D. S., 9 Consular Despatches, Algiers).

115605°—31—vol. 2——43

In June, 1929, there was sold at auction in London an original of this treaty; perhaps that document, which is to be placed in the archives of the Department of State, is the one mentioned in the preceding paragraph and perhaps it is still another. On one of the pages of that original is written the ratification or confirmation recorded, as mentioned above, in the journal of William Buell under date of March 16, 1818. The page in question has been examined by Dr. J. H. Kramers, of Leiden, who observes that it is written in another hand than the articles of the treaty itself and that its Turkish style and language are much better and nearly correct. The ratification is that of Husein Pasha, who succeeded on the death of his predecessor Ali on March 1, 1818. The page has the tughra or "name sign" of Husein and his seal, which reads, "The confident in the Compassionate [God], His [God's] servant, Husein, son of Hassan, 1233." The writing is dated 23 Rabia II, A. H. 1233, or March 2, 1818, and is thus translated by Doctor Kramers:

The motive of the writing and the reason for the drawing up of the present document are as follows: On the 23d day of the month Rebi el-Akhir of this year 1233 Ali Pasha has moved to the abode of eternity and in his place His Excellency the illustrious and august Husein Pasha—may God make easy for him what he wishes—has taken the regency under auspicious signs, our peace and good understanding with the ruler and commander of the American people has remained firm and our friendship has remained stable according to the previously established treaty-articles. This has been stated and put down in the present document.

Written in the last days of the month of Rebi el-Akhir, on the 23d day, of the year 1233.

Treaty Series, No. 110½
8 Statutes at Large, 231

38

GREAT BRITAIN : APRIL 28 AND 29, 1817

Exchange of Notes Relative to Naval Forces on the American Lakes, signed at Washington April 28 and 29, 1817. Originals in English. Submitted to the Senate April 6, 1818. Resolution of approval and consent April 16, 1818. Proclaimed April 28, 1818.

WASHINGTON
April 28. 1817

The Undersigned, His Britannick Majesty's Envoy Extraordinary and Minister Plenipotentiary, has the honour to acquaint Mr Rush, that having laid before His Majesty's Government the correspondence[1] which passed last year between the Secretary of the Department of State and the Undersigned upon the subject of a proposal to reduce the Naval Force of the respective Countries upon the American Lakes, he has received the Commands of His Royal Highness The Prince Regent to acquaint the Government of the United States, that His Royal Highness is willing to accede to the proposition made to the Undersigned by the Secretary of the Department of State in his note[1] of the 2^d^ of August last.

His Royal Highness, acting in the name and on the behalf of His Majesty, agrees, that the Naval Force to be maintained upon the American Lakes by His Majesty and the Government of the United States shall henceforth be confined to the following Vessels on each side—that is

On Lake Ontario to one Vessel not exceeding one hundred Tons burthen and armed with one eighteen pound cannon.

On the Upper Lakes to two Vessels not exceeding like burthen each and armed with like force.

On the Waters of Lake Champlain to one Vessel not exceeding like burthen and armed with like force.

And His Royal Highness agrees, that all other armed Vessels on these Lakes shall be forthwith dismantled, and that no other Vessels of War shall be there built or armed.

---

[1] See the note regarding the correspondence.

His Royal Highness further agrees, that if either Party should hereafter be desirous of annulling this Stipulation, and should give notice to that effect to the other Party, it shall cease to be binding after the expiration of six months from the date of such notice.

The Undersigned has it in command from His Royal Highness the Prince Regent to acquaint the American Government, that His Royal Highness has issued Orders to His Majestys Officers on the Lakes directing, that the Naval Force so to be limited shall be restricted to such Services as will in no respect interfere with the proper duties of the armed Vessels of the other Party.

The Undersigned has the honour to renew to Mr Rush the assurances of his highest consideration.

Charles Bagot

Department of State,
April 29. 1817.

The Undersigned, Acting Secretary of State, has the honor to acknowledge the receipt of Mr Bagot's note of the 28th of this month, informing him that, having laid before the Government of His Britannick Majesty, the correspondence[1] which passed last year between the Secretary of State and himself upon the subject of a proposal to reduce the naval force of the two countries upon the American Lakes, he had received the commands of His Royal Highness The Prince Regent to inform this Government that His Royal Highness was willing to accede to the proposition made by the Secretary of State in his note of the second of August last.

The Undersigned has the honor to express to Mr Bagot the satisfaction which The President feels at His Royal Highness The Prince Regent's having acceded to the proposition of this Government as contained in the note alluded to. And in further answer to Mr Bagot's note, the Undersigned, by direction of The President, has the honor to state, that this Government, cherishing the same sentiments expressed in the note of the second of August, agrees, that the naval force to be maintained upon the Lakes by the United-States and Great Britain shall, henceforth, be confined to the following vessels on each side,—that is:

On Lake Ontario to one vessel not exceeding One Hundred Tons burden, and armed with one eighteen-pound cannon. On the Upper Lakes to two vessels not exceeding the like burden each, and armed with like force, and on the waters of Lake Champlain to one vessel not exceeding like burden and armed with like force.

[1] See the note regarding the correspondence.

And it agrees, that all other armed vessels on these Lakes shall be forthwith dismantled, and that no other vessels of war shall be there built or armed. And it further agrees, that if either party should hereafter be desirous of annulling this stipulation and should give notice to that effect to the other party, it shall cease to be binding after the expiration of six months from the date of such notice.

The Undersigned is also directed by The President to state, that proper orders will be forthwith issued by this Government to restrict the naval force thus limited to such services as will in no respect interfere with the proper duties of the armed vessels of the other party.

The Undersigned eagerly avails himself of this opportunity to tender to M[r] Bagot the assurances of his distinguished consideration and respect.

RICHARD RUSH.

NOTES

The original British note of April 28, 1817, is in D. S., 9 Notes from the British Legation; the text of the note of April 29 is from D. S., 2 Notes to Foreign Legations.

The agreement embodied in the notes exchanged was immediately put into operation on both sides. The necessary orders of the Secretary of the Navy were dated May 2, 1817 (American State Papers, Foreign Relations, IV, 206–7). Nearly a year elapsed, however, before the arrangement was submitted to the Senate by President Monroe on April 6, 1818, with this message (Executive Journal, III, 132):

> An arrangement having been made and concluded between this government and that of Great Britain, with respect to the naval armament of the two governments respectively, on the Lakes, I lay before the Senate a copy of the correspondence upon that subject, including the stipulations mutually agreed upon by the two parties. I submit it to the consideration of the Senate, whether this is such an arrangement as the Executive is competent to enter into, by the powers vested in it by the Constitution, or is such an one as requires the advice and consent of the Senate; and, in the latter case, for their advice and consent, should it be approved.

In the Memoirs of John Quincy Adams, IV, 41–42, under date of January 14, 1818, appears this interesting and relevant statement:

> Met and spoke to Mr. Bagot this morning on my way to the President's. He asked me if it was the intention of the President to communicate to Congress the letters which had passed between the Secretary of State and him (Bagot) containing the arrangement concerning armaments on the Lakes, which he said was a sort of treaty. I spoke of it to the President, who did not think it necessary that they should be communicated. It has been usual heretofore with the message at the opening of the session of Congress to send a collection of documents with it relating to the principal subjects mentioned in it. This was not done at the present session, and some inconvenience has resulted from the omission.

Reference is also to be made to the act of February 27, 1815 (3 Statutes at Large, 217), which authorized the President "to cause all the armed vessels thereof on the lakes, except such as he may deem necessary to enforce the proper execution of the revenue laws, to be sold or laid up, as he may judge most conducive to the public interest; such vessels being first divested of their armament, tackle and furniture, which are to be carefully preserved."

The following resolution of the Senate of April 16, 1818 (*ibid.*, 134), an attested copy of which is in the treaty file, was voted unanimously:

Resolved, two thirds of the Senators present concurring therein, that the Senate do approve of, and consent to the arrangement made in April 1817, and contained in the President's message of the 6th of April 1818, between the United States, and his Britannic Majesty, relative to the Naval force of the respective nations, to be maintained on the Lakes; and recommend that the same be carried into effect by the President of the United States.

The original proclamation has not been found; the text below is from that printed in Laws of the United States, Bioren & Duane ed., VI, 597–98, a volume which is dated 1822. The proclamation, in part, is in 8 Statutes at Large, 231, and in 18 Statutes at Large, pt. 2, Public Treaties, 296, and is in full in 11 Statutes at Large, 766–67; it appears also, with the notes and various other papers in the matter, in American State Papers, Foreign Relations, IV, 202–7. It may be added that the proclamation was published in the press of the period. It appeared in the Daily National Intelligencer of April 30, 1818, two days after its date; and it was printed in the pamphlet edition of the Session Laws for the first session of the Fifteenth Congress, published in 1818. The proclamation is printed here because of its unusual form; and it is to be observed that, like some other proclamations of about the same period, it does not purport to have passed under the Great Seal. The bracketing of its text in Treaty Series, No. 110½ was intended, as a note in the file shows, to indicate that the original was not available; but the use of a bracket in such case gives, in itself, no such indication; and while various original proclamations of early date are not to be found, in no other case is a bracket used for the purpose stated.

Whereas an Arrangement was entered into at the City of Washington, in the month of April, in the year of our Lord one thousand eight hundred and seventeen, between Richard Rush, Esquire, at that time acting as Secretary for the Department of State of the United States, for and in behalf of the government of the United States, and the right honorable Charles Bagot, his Britannic majesty's envoy extraordinary and minister plenipotentiary, for and in behalf of his Britannic majesty; which Arrangement is in the words following, to wit:

"The naval force to be maintained upon the American lakes, by his majesty and the government of the United States, shall henceforth be confined to the following vessels on each side; that is—

"On lake Ontario, to one vessel not exceeding one hundred tons burden, and armed with one eighteen pound cannon.

"On the upper lakes, to two vessels, not exceeding like burden each, and armed with like force.

"On the waters of lake Champlain, to one vessel not exceeding like burden, and armed with like force.

"All other armed vessels on these lakes shall be forthwith dismantled, and no other vessels of war shall be there built or armed.

"If either party should hereafter be desirous of annulling this stipulation, and should give notice to that effect to the other party, it shall cease to be binding after the expiration of six months from the date of such notice.

"The naval force so to be limited shall be restricted to such services as will, in no respect, interfere with the proper duties of the armed vessels of the other party."

And whereas the Senate of the United States have approved of the said Arrangement, and recommended that it should be carried into effect; the same having also received the sanction of his royal highness the Prince Regent, acting in the name and on behalf of his Britannic majesty:

Now, therefore, I, James Monroe, President of the United States, do, by this my proclamation, make known and declare that the Arrangement aforesaid, and every stipulation thereof, has been duly entered into, concluded, and confirmed, and is of full force and effect.

Given under my hand, at the City of Washington, this twenty-eighth day of April, in the year of our Lord one thousand eight hundred and eighteen, and of the independence of the United States the forty-second.

James Monroe.

By the President.
John Quincy Adams,
Secretary of State.

Note Regarding the Correspondence

The notes exchanged on April 28 and 29, 1817, refer to the correspondence which passed between the British Minister and the Secretary of State in 1816; that correspondence (from the same volumes as the final notes) follows; but the "account of the actual state of the naval force of the United-States on the Lakes," which was enclosed in the letter of Monroe of November 7, 1816, is from The Neutrality of the American Lakes, 82, by James Morton Callahan.

Washington *July 26: 1816.*

Sir, Mr Adams having intimated to His Majesty's Government, that it was the wish of the Government of the United States, that some understanding should be had, or agreement entered into between the two Countries, in regard to their Naval armaments upon the Lakes, which while it tended to diminish the expenses of each country, might diminish also the chances of collision, and prevent any feelings of jeaslousy; I have the honour to acquaint you, that I have received Lord Castlereagh's instructions to assure you, that His Royal Highness the Prince Regent will cheerfully adopt, in the spirit of Mr Adams's suggestion, any reasonable system which may contribute to the attainment of objects so desirable to both States.

Mr Adams not having entered into any detailed explanation of the precise views of his Government for giving effect to the principle which he had offered for consideration, the British Government is unacquainted with the particular arrangements which the Government of the United States would propose to make for this purpose. but I have been instructed to assure you of the general disposition of His Royal Highness the Prince Regent to listen with satisfaction to any proposal which may secure such ends, and of His readiness to act in a spirit of the most entire confidence upon the principle which has been suggested by Mr Adams.

I have the honour to be with the highest consideration Sir, Your most obedient humble Servant.

Charles Bagot

The Honble James Monroe
&c. &c. &c

DEPARTMENT OF STATE, *August 2. 1816.*

The Right Honorable CHARLES BAGOT

SIR I have had the honor to receive your letter of the 26th of July, by which you inform me, that Mr Adams had intimated to your government, the desire of The President to arrange by compact, the naval force which should be retained on the Lakes by both Nations, with a view to lessen equally the expence of each, and likewise to guard against collision, but that he had not explained in sufficient detail, the proposal, which he had been authorized to make, to lead, at that time, to any practical result. You assure me that H. R. H. the Prince Regent is well disposed, to the object, and that, in concert with this government, he is willing to adopt, such measures, as may be deemed expedient, to give it effect.

The President, being satisfied, that if each nation should maintain on the Lakes, a large naval force, it would expose both, to considerable and useless expence, while it would multiply the risks of collision, between them, instructed Mr Adams, shortly after the peace, to make the proposal which you mention, in the hope, from the amicable spirit in which it was conceived, and the advantage, which it was believed, both parties would derive from it, that it might be carried into immediate effect. It is very satisfactory, to The President, to find, that your government, approves the principle, on which the proposal is founded, and that H. R. H. the Prince Regent is willing to act on it.

I infer from your letter that you are desirous of obtaining a precise project, either for the purpose of acting on it here, immediately, in conformity with the powers already given you, or of transmitting it to your government for its consideration. Whether it be for the one or the other purpose, I am instructed to afford all the facility that I may be able; though it would undoubtedly be more agreeable to The President, that the arrangement should be made, and executed, with the least delay possible.

I have the honor now to State that The President is willing, in the spirit of the peace which so happily exists between the two nations, and until the proposed arrangement shall be cancelled, in the manner herein after suggested, to confine the naval force to be maintained on the Lakes on each side, to the following vessels, that is, on Lake Ontario, to One Vessel not exceeding One Hundred Tons burthen and One Eighteen Pound Cannon, and on the Upper Lakes to Two Vessels of like burthen and force, and on the Waters of Lake Champlain to One Vessel not exceeding the like burthen and force; and that all other armed vessels on those Lakes, shall be forthwith dismantled, and likewise that neither party shall build or arm any other vessel on the Shores of those Lakes.

That the Naval Force thus retained by each party on the Lakes, shall be restricted in its duty, to the protection of its Revenue Laws, the transportation of troops, and goods, and to such other Services, as will in no respect interfere with the armed vessels of the other party.

That should either of the parties be of opinion hereafter that this arrangement did not accomplish the object intended by it, and be desirous of annulling it, and give notice thereof, it shall be void and of no effect, after the expiration of months from the date of such notice.

If this project corresponds with the views of your government, and you are authorized to accede to it, under any modifications which you may propose, and in which we can agree, I am instructed to give it immediate effect, either by Convention, the interchange of Notes, or in any form, which may be thought, best adapted, to the ends proposed. If, on the other hand, you consider it your duty, to submit this project to your government, for consideration, and to wait its sanction, before you can adopt it, and have power to make, ad interim, any provisional reciprocal arrangement, having the same objects in view, I shall be happy to digest with you such provisional arrangement, and to carry it, reciprocally, into effect, for such time, and in such manner, as may be agreed on: or, should your powers be adequate, I am ready to concur in an immediate Suspension of any further construction or equipments of armed vessels for any of the waters above named.

I have the honor to be &c.

JAMES MONROE.

WASHINGTON *August 6: 1816.*

SIR. I have had the honour to receive your letter of the 2d instant, containing the project of an arrangement into which it is proposed that, our respective Governments should enter, for the purpose of giving effect to the principle, upon which I had the honour to acquaint you, in my letter of the 26th ulto, that His Royal Highness The Prince Regent was willing to act in respect to the Naval Armaments upon the Lakes.

The general coincidence of sentiment which exists between our Governments in regard to entering into some arrangement upon this subject, gives reason to hope that, the several parts of it will become matter of easy adjustment; but as, in the consideration of any precise proposition to this effect, reference must necessarily be had to various points connected with the internal administration of His Majesty's Provinces, and to the naval assistance which the ordinary business of a Peace establishment may require, I am not authorized to conclude definitively any agreement as to details, without previously submitting it to my Government.

I shall therefore immediately forward for consideration the proposal contained in your letter: But I shall, in the mean time, willingly take upon myself to give effect to any arrangement upon which we may mutually agree, for the purpose of suspending the further construction and equipment of armed Vessels upon the Lakes, and of generally abstaining from exertion in those quarters.

I have the honour to be with the highest consideration, Sir, Your most obedient humble Servant

CHARLES BAGOT

The Honble JAMES MONROE
&c. &c. &c.

DEPARTMENT OF STATE, *August 12. 1816.*

The Right Honble Mr BAGOT

SIR I have had the honor to receive your letter of the 6th of this month, by which, you inform me, that altho' you have full confidence, that an agreement will finally be entered into by our governments, to limit in a satisfactory manner, the naval force to be maintained by them on the Lakes, you consider it your duty to submit to your government, the project which I lately communicated to you to that effect, and to wait its orders before you can proceed to make a definitive arrangement on the subject. You intimate however that you are willing to give effect to any arrangement, on which we may agree, for suspending in the mean time, the farther construction and equipment of armed vessels on the Lakes, and for abstaining from farther exertion there.

To this delay no objection is entertained, provided such a provisional arrangement is made, as may accomplish the just objects which our governments have in view. This arrangement however, like the other, should be equal. In the same spirit, therefore, I now propose the regulations stated in my former Note, to be adopted as a provisional arrangement. If your powers authorize, and you approve those regulations, on being assured that you will adopt a similar measure, an order will be immediately issued by this government, for carrying them fully into effect.

If your powers do not extend to this object, but are confined exclusively to the suspension of the further augmentation of the naval force on the Lakes, I have then to observe, that on receiving from you a statement, of the force which your government now has, on the Lakes, with an assurance that its further augmentation shall be suspended, an order will be immediately issued by this government, for confining the naval force of the United States there, strictly within the same limit.

I have the honor to be &c.

JAMES MONROE.

WASHINGTON *August 13th 1816.*

SIR, I have had the honour to receive your letter of yesterday's date.

For the same reasons which I have assigned in the letter which I had the honour to address to you on the 6th instant, I conceive, that I am not authorized to make, even provisionally, any precise agreement as to the exact manner in

which the respective Naval Forces upon the Lakes shall be limited; as in any such agreement, whether permanent or provisional, reference must equally be had to the arrangements of a peace establishment, and the ordinary administration of His Majesty's Provinces.

I am not in possession of a correct statement of His Majesty's Naval Force now in commission upon the Lakes, but I will take the earliest means of procuring, and communicating to you the most accurate information upon this point; and I can in the mean time give you the assurance, that all further augmentation of it will be immediately suspended.

I have the honour to be with the highest consideration—Sir, Your most obedient humble Servant.

CHARLES BAGOT

The Hon[ble] JAMES MONROE
&c. &c. &c.

WASHINGTON, *Nov[r] 4th 1816.*

SIR, In conformity with the arrangement made between us in our correspondence of the 12th and 13th of August last, I have now the honour to enclose to you an account of the actual state of His Majesty's Naval Force upon the Lakes; and to acquaint you, that its further augmentation is suspended, until the sentiments of His Majesty's Government, upon the project contained in your note of the 5th of August, and which I have transmitted to Lord Castlereagh, are known.

I have the honour to be with the highest consideration, Sir, Your most obedient humble servant.

CHARLES BAGOT

The Hon[ble] JAMES MONROE
&c. &c. &c.

[Enclosure]

Statement of His Majesty's Naval Force on the Lakes of Canada 1st September 1816.

Lake Ontario.

St Lawrence	can carry	110 guns—	laid up in ordinary.
Psyche	do.	50.	do.
Princess Charlotte	do.	40.	do.
Niagara	do.	20.	Condemned as unfit for service.
Charwell	do.	14	Hauled up in the mud condemned likewise.
Prince Regent	do.	60.	In Commission but unequipped being merely used as a Barrack or receiving Ship, and the Commander in Chief's Head Quarters.

Montreal, in Commission carrying 6 guns used merely as a Transport for the service of His Majesty.
Star. Carrying 4 guns used for current duties only, and unfit for actual service.
Netley Schooner. Carrying no guns attached for the most part to the Surveyors, and conveying His Majesty's servants from Port to Port.

There are besides the above some Row Boats capable of carrying long guns—2 seventy four gun Ships on the Stocks, and one Transport of 400 Tons, used for conveying His Majesty's Stores from Port to Port.

On Lake Erie.

Tecumseth and Newash carrying 4 guns each, and Huron and Sauk which can carry 1 gun each. these Vessels are used principally to convey His Majesty's Servants and Stores from Port to Port.

On Lake Huron.

The Confiance and Surprize Schooners which may carry one gun each, and are used for purposes of Transport only.

On Lake Champlain.

12 gun Boats, 10 of which are laid up in ordinary, and the other two (one of which mounts 4 guns and the other 3 guns) used as guard boats, besides the above there are some small row Boats which are laid up as unfit for service.

Keel, Stem, and Stern Port of a Frigate laid down at the Isle Aux Noix.

(signed) J BEAUMGARDT
Capt[tn] of H. M. Ship Prince Regent *and Senior Officer.*

DEPARTMENT OF STATE *November 7. 1816.*

The Right Hon[ble] CHARLES BAGOT

SIR, I have received and laid before The President your letter of the 4th instant, in which you do me the honor to give me an account of the actual state of His Britannic Majesty's naval force on the Lakes; with an assurance that its further augmentation is suspended, until the sentiments of your Government upon the project contained in my Note of the 5 Aug[st], are known.

As this proceeding is in conformity to one of the propositions heretofore made by me, I have now the honor to enclose to you an account of the actual state of the naval force of the United-States on the Lakes, and to assure you, that orders will be immediately given by this government to prevent any augmentation of it, beyond the limit of the British naval force on those waters.

I have the honor to be &c.

JAMES MONROE.

[Enclosure]

On Lake Ontario

Brig *Jones* (18 guns). Retained for occasional service.
Schooner *Lady of the Lake* (1 gun). Employed in aid of the revenue laws.
Ship *New Orleans* (74 guns). On the stocks, building suspended.
Ship *Chippewa* (74 guns). On the stocks, building suspended.
Ships *Superior* (44 guns), *Mohawk* (32 guns), *General Pike* (24 guns), *Madison* (18 guns); and the brigs *Jefferson* (18 guns), *Sylph* (16 guns), and *Oneida* (18 guns). Dismantled.
Schooner *Raven*. Receiving vessel.
15 barges (each, 1 gun). Laid up for preservation.

On Lake Erie

Schooners *Porcupine* and *Ghent* (each, 1 gun). Employed in transporting stores.
Ship *Detroit* (18 guns), and brigs *Lawrence* (20 guns), and *Queen Charlotte* (14 guns). Sunk at Erie.
Brig *Niagara* (18 guns). Dismantled at Erie.

On Lake Champlain

Ships *Confiance* (32 guns), and *Saratoga* (22 guns); brigs *Eagle* (12 guns), and *Sinnet* (16 guns); the schooner *Ticonderoga* (14 guns); and 6 galleys (each, 1 gun). All laid up at White Hall.

DEPARTMENT OF STATE, *November 8. 1816.*

The Right Hon[ble] CHA[s] BAGOT

SIR, I have the honor to inform you that the orders alluded to in my letter of yesterday's date, in relation to the naval force on the Lakes, have been given by this Department.

I have the honor to be &c.

JAMES MONROE.

WASHINGTON *Novr 8: 1816.*

SIR, In the statement of the American Naval Force upon the Lakes which I yesterday morning received from you at your Office in exchange for a similar statement at the same time delivered to you of the Naval Force of His Majesty, I observe that no return is made of any Force upon the Upper Lakes.

I shall be much obliged to you if you will have the goodness to acquaint me, whether the Force upon those Lakes is comprehended in the return of that upon Lake Erie.

I have the honour to be with the highest consideration—Sir, Your most obedient humble servant

CHARLES BAGOT

The Honble JAMES MONROE
&c. &c. &c.

DEPARTMENT OF STATE *November 8. 1816.*

The Right Honble CHA^s BAGOT

SIR, I hasten to inform you in reply to your letter of this date, that the naval force of the United States upon the Upper Lakes is comprehended in the return of that, upon Lake Erie, which I gave to you yesterday.

I have the honor to be &c.

JAMES MONROE.

An elaborate report on the agreement, transmitted by President Harrison to the Senate on December 7, 1892, with earlier and later correspondence, is in Senate Executive Document No. 9, 52d Congress, 2d session; that document was reprinted with certain subsequent material in House Document No. 471, 56th Congress, 1st session.

Treaty Series, No. 111
8 Statutes at Large, 250–51

39

GREAT BRITAIN : NOVEMBER 24, 1817

Decision of the Commissioners under Article 4 of the Treaty of Ghent (Document 33), signed at New York November 24, 1817, with covering letter of the same date. Originals in English.

By Thomas Barclay and John Holmes Esquires.

Commissioners, appointed by virtue of the fourth Article of the Treaty of Peace and Amity between His Britannic Majesty and The United States of America concluded at Ghent on the twenty fourth day of december One Thousand eight hundred and fourteen to decide to which of the two Contracting parties to the said Treaty the several Islands in the Bay of Passamaquoddy which is part of the Bay of Fundy and the Island of Grand Menan in the said Bay of Fundy do respectively belong in conformity with the true intent of the second Article of the Treaty of Peace[1] of One Thousand seven hundred and eighty three between His said Britannic Majesty and the aforesaid United States of America.

We the said Thomas Barclay and John Holmes Commissioners as aforesaid having been duly sworn impartially to examine and decide upon the said claims according to such evidence as should be laid before us on the part of His Britannic Majesty and The United States respectively Have decided and do decide that Moose Island, Dudley Island, and Frederick Island, in the Bay of Passamaquoddy which is part of the Bay of Fundy do and each of them does belong to The United States of America and we have also decided and do decide that all the other Islands and each and every of them in the said Bay of Passamaquoddy which is part of the Bay of Fundy and the Island of Grand Menan in the said Bay of Fundy do belong to His said Britannic Majesty in conformity with the true intent of the said second Article of said Treaty of One Thousand seven hundred and eighty three.

In faith and Testimony whereof we have set our hands and affixed our Seals at the City of New York, in the State of New York in The

[1] Document 11.

United States of America This twenty fourth day of November, in the Year of Our Lord One thousand eight hundred and Seventeen.

Witness

JAMES T. AUSTIN. *Ag^t USA*

ANTH: BARCLAY *Sec^y*

JOHN HOLMES [Seal]

THO BARCLAY [Seal]

[Covering Letter]

NEW YORK *24th November 1817.*

SIR The undersigned Commissioners appointed by virtue of the fourth Article of the Treaty of Ghent have attended to the Duties assigned them; and have decided that Moose Island, Dudley Island, and Frederick Island in the Bay of Passamaquoddy, which is part of the Bay of Fundy do each of them belong to the United States of America, and that all the other Islands in the Bay of Passamaquoddy and the Island of Grand Menan in the Bay of Fundy do each of them belong to His Britannic Majesty, in conformity with the true intent of the Second Article of the Treaty of Peace[1] of One Thousand, Seven hundred and eighty three. The Commissioners have the Honor to enclose herewith their Decision.

In making this decision it became necessary, that each of the Commissioners should yield a part of his individual opinion; several reasons induced them to adopt this measure, one of which was the impression and belief that the navigable Waters of the Bay of Passamaquoddy, which by the Treaty of Ghent is said to be part of the Bay of Fundy are common to both Parties for the purpose of all lawful and direct communication with their own Territories and Foreign Ports. The undersigned have the Honor to be with perfect respect Sir Your obedient and humble Servants

J HOLMES

THO BARCLAY

The Honble JOHN QUINCY ADAMS

&c &c &c

NOTES

Two originals of the decision, engrossed on parchment, are with the covering letter in the treaty file.

Communication of the fact of the decision was made by President Monroe in his annual message to Congress of December 2, 1817; and copies of the papers were transmitted on February 25, 1818 (Richardson, II, 12, 28).

---

[1] Document 11.

For an account of the proceedings of the Commissioners under Article 4 of the Treaty of Ghent (Document 33), see Moore, International Arbitrations, I, 45–64.

The Islands

A comparison of the present maps of the International Boundary Commission with the map dated September, 1817, which accompanied the Memorial of the Agent of the United States before the Commissioners under Article 4 of the Treaty of Ghent, shows that the islands which in 1817 were known as Moose, Dudley, and Frederick Islands, are now respectively known as Moose, Treat, and Dudley Islands. In other words, the Dudley Island of the award is now known as Treat Island, and the Frederick Island of the award is now known as Dudley Island.

Treat Island is mentioned in the treaties with Great Britain signed at Washington on April 11, 1908 (Article 1), and on May 21, 1910 (Article 1).

The maps compared (originals whereof are in the archives of the Department of State) are the following:

"A Map to accompany and elucidate the Memorial of the Agent of the United States in support of their claim to the Islands in the Bay of Passamaquoddy and the grand Manan in the Bay of Fundy. September 1817 Copied from a Map compiled from Actual Surveys by George Sproule Esqr Surveyor Gen^{rl} of the Province of New Brunswick. By Wm Taylor for James T. Austin Agent of U. S. under the 4th Art^{le} Treaty of Ghent." "International Boundary from the Source of the St. Croix River to the Atlantic Ocean," sheets Nos. 16 and 17, signed on July 21, 1925, by the Commissioners of the United States and of His Britannic Majesty appointed pursuant to Article 1 of the treaty of April 11, 1908, and to Articles 1 and 2 of the treaty of May 21, 1910.

The two maps of the International Boundary Commission above mentioned are part of a series of eighteen maps which are described in the notes to Document 23.

Treaty Series, No. 112
8 Statutes at Large, 248–50

40

GREAT BRITAIN : OCTOBER 20, 1818

Convention signed at London October 20, 1818. Original in English. Submitted to the Senate December 30, 1818. (Message of December 29, 1818.) Resolution of advice and consent January 25, 1819. Ratified by the United States January 28, 1819. Ratified by Great Britain November 2, 1818. Ratifications exchanged at Washington January 30, 1819. Proclaimed January 30, 1819.

The United States of America, and His Majesty The King of the United Kingdom of Great Britain and Ireland, desirous to cement the good Understanding which happily subsists between them, have, for that purpose, named their respective Plenipotentiaries, that is to say: The President of the United States, on his part, has appointed, Albert Gallatin, Their Envoy Extraordinary and Minister Plenipotentiary to the Court of France; and Richard Rush, Their Envoy Extraordinary and Minister Plenipotentiary to the Court of His Britannic Majesty: And His Majesty has appointed The Right Honorable Frederick John Robinson, Treasurer of His Majesty's Navy, and President of the Committee of Privy Council for Trade and Plantations; and Henry Goulburn Esquire, One of His Majesty's Under Secretaries of State: Who, after having exchanged their respective Full Powers, found to be in due and proper Form, have agreed to and concluded the following Articles.

Article I.

Whereas differences have arisen respecting the Liberty claimed by the United States for the Inhabitants thereof, to take, dry, and cure Fish on certain Coasts, Bays, Harbours, and Creeks of His Britannic Majesty's Dominions in America, it is agreed between The High Contracting Parties, that the Inhabitants of the said United States shall have for ever, in common with the Subjects of His Britannic Majesty, the Liberty to take Fish of every kind on that part of the Southern Coast of Newfoundland which extends from Cape Ray to the Rameau Islands, on the Western and Northern Coast of Newfoundland, from the said Cape Ray to the Quirpon Islands on the Shores of the

Magdalen Islands, and also on the Coasts, Bays, Harbours, and Creeks from Mount Joly on the Southern Coast of Labrador, to and through the Streights of Belleisle and thence Northwardly indefinitely along the Coast, without prejudice however, to any of the exclusive Rights of the Hudson Bay Company: and that the American Fishermen shall also have liberty for ever, to dry and cure Fish in any of the unsettled Bays, Harbours, and Creeks of the Southern part of the Coast of Newfoundland hereabove described, and of the Coast of Labrador; but so soon as the same, or any Portion thereof, shall be settled, it shall not be lawful for the said Fishermen to dry or cure Fish at such Portion so settled, without previous Agreement for such purpose with the Inhabitants, Proprietors, or Possessors of the Ground. And the United States hereby renounce for ever, any Liberty heretofore enjoyed or claimed by the Inhabitants thereof, to take, dry, or cure Fish on, or within three marine Miles of any of the Coasts, Bays, Creeks, or Harbours of His Britannic Majesty's Dominions in America not included within the above mentioned Limits; provided however, that the American Fishermen shall be admitted to enter such Bays or Harbours for the purpose of Shelter and of repairing Damages therein, of purchasing Wood, and of obtaining Water, and for no other purpose whatever. But they shall be under such Restrictions as may be necessary to prevent their taking, drying or curing Fish therein, or in any other manner whatever abusing the Privileges hereby reserved to them.

Article II.

It is agreed that a Line drawn from the most North Western Point of the Lake of the Woods, along the forty Ninth Parallel of North Latitude, or, if the said Point shall not be in the Forty Ninth Parallel of North Latitude, then that a Line drawn from the said Point due North or South as the Case may be, until the said Line shall intersect the said Parallel of North Latitude, and from the Point of such Intersection due West along and with the said Parallel shall be the Line of Demarcation between the Territories of the United States, and those of His Britannic Majesty, and that the said Line shall form the Northern Boundary of the said Territories of the United States, and the Southern Boundary of the Territories of His Britannic Majesty, from the Lake of the Woods to the Stony Mountains.[1]

[1] See the note regarding Article 2.

Article III.

It is agreed, that any Country that may be claimed by either Party on the North West Coast of America, Westward of the Stony Mountains, shall, together with it's Harbours, Bays, and Creeks, and the Navigation of all Rivers within the same, be free and open, for the term of ten Years from the date of the Signature of the present Convention, to the Vessels, Citizens, and Subjects of the Two Powers: it being well understood, that this Agreement is not to be construed to the Prejudice of any Claim, which either of the Two High Contracting Parties may have to any part of the said Country, nor shall it be taken to affect the Claims of any other Power or State to any part of the said Country; the only Object of The High Contracting Parties, in that respect, being to prevent disputes and differences amongst Themselves.

Article IV.

All the Provisions of the Convention[1] "to regulate the Commerce between the Territories of the United States and of His Britannic Majesty" concluded at London on the third day of July in the Year of Our Lord One Thousand Eight Hundred and Fifteen, with the exception of the Clause which limited it's duration to Four Years, & excepting also so far as the same was affected by the Declaration of His Majesty respecting the Island of St Helena, are hereby extended and continued in force for the term of ten Years from the date of the Signature of the present Convention, in the same manner, as if all the Provisions of the said Convention were herein specially recited.

Article V.

Whereas it was agreed by the first Article of the Treaty of Ghent,[2] that "All Territory, Places, and Possessions whatsoever taken by either Party from the other during the War, or which may be taken after the signing of this Treaty, excepting only the Islands hereinafter mentioned, shall be restored without delay; and without causing any destruction, or carrying away any of the Artillery or other public Property originally captured in the said Forts or Places which shall remain therein upon the Exchange of the Ratifications of this Treaty, or any Slaves or other private Property"; and whereas under the aforesaid Article, the United States claim for their Citizens, and as their private Property, the Restitution of, or full Compensation for all Slaves who, at the date of the Exchange of the Ratifications of the

[1] Document 35.

[2] Document 33.

said Treaty, were in any Territory, Places, or Possessions whatsoever directed by the said Treaty to be restored to the United States, but then still occupied by the British Forces, whether such Slaves were, at the date aforesaid, on Shore, or on board any British Vessel lying in Waters within the Territory or Jurisdiction of the United States; and whereas differences have arisen, whether, by the true intent and meaning of the aforesaid Article of the Treaty of Ghent the United States are entitled to the Restitution of, or full Compensation for all or any Slaves as above described, the High Contracting Parties hereby agree to refer the said differences to some Friendly Sovereign or State to be named for that purpose; and The High Contracting Parties further engage to consider the decision of such Friendly Sovereign or State, to be final and conclusive on all the Matters referred.

ARTICLE VI.

This Convention, when the same shall have been duly ratified by The President of the United States, by and with the Advice and Consent of their Senate, and by His Britannic Majesty, and the respective Ratifications mutually exchanged, shall be binding and obligatory on the said United States and on His Majesty; and the Ratifications shall be exchanged in Six Months from this date, or sooner, if possible.

In witness whereof the respective Plenipotentiaries have signed the same, and have thereunto affixed the Seal of their Arms.

Done at London this Twentieth day of October, in the Year of Our Lord One Thousand Eight Hundred and Eighteen.

ALBERT GALLATIN [Seal]
RICHARD RUSH. [Seal]
FREDERICK JOHN ROBINSON [Seal]
HENRY GOULBURN [Seal]

NOTES

The "documents showing the course and progress of the negotiation" of this convention, which were transmitted to the Senate, are printed in American State Papers, Foreign Relations, IV, 348–407.

There are two signed originals of this convention in the Department of State file; no variances between them have been noticed. Also in the file is a facsimile of the United States instrument of ratification, obtained from the British archives; and with the British instrument of ratification is a certificate of the exchange of ratifications on January 30, 1819, signed and sealed by John Quincy Adams and Charles Bagot.

The original proclamation has not been found; but it was published at the time (*e. g.*, Niles' Weekly Register, XV, 434–36); it states the dates of the respective ratifications and also that they had been exchanged on the day of proclamation.

Note Regarding Article 2

The northwesternmost point of the Lake of the Woods is in fact about 27½ miles north of the 49th parallel of north latitude. Accordingly, the effect of Article 2 was to provide "that a Line drawn from the said Point due . . . South . . . until the said Line shall intersect the said Parallel of North Latitude, and from the Point of such Intersection due West along . . . the said Parallel . . . shall form the Northern Boundary of the . . . United States . . . from the Lake of the Woods to the Stony [Rocky] Mountains."

That portion of the existing boundary between the United States and Canada which runs from the Lake of the Woods to the Rocky Mountains is shown by the present maps of the International Boundary Commission entitled "International Boundary from the Gulf of Georgia to the Northwesternmost Point of the Lake of the Woods"; the series comprises fifty-nine charts (Sheets Nos. 1 to 59, inclusive), and there is also an Index Sheet and a Profile Sheet. The line showing the summit of the Rocky Mountains appears on Sheet No. 19; the boundary eastwards from the Rocky Mountains to the Lake of the Woods is shown on Sheets Nos. 19 to 59, inclusive; Sheet No. 59 shows the northwesternmost point of the Lake of the Woods and also the turning point adopted in lieu thereof by the treaty of February 24, 1925. The charts are signed by the Commissioners of the United States and of His Britannic Majesty as adopted under Articles 6 and 7 of the treaty signed at Washington April 11, 1908. Sheets Nos. 1 to 19 were published in 1913; Sheets Nos. 20 to 41 were published in 1921; Sheets Nos. 42 to 44 and Nos. 53 to 58 are dated November 17, 1921; Sheets Nos. 45 to 52 are dated April 7, 1922; Sheet No. 59 is dated December 7, 1927.

Originals of the maps of the International Boundary Commission are in the archives of the Department of State; copies are obtainable from the office of the International Boundary Commission in Washington.

O